Joining Europe's Monetary Club

This book is to be returned on
or before the date stamped below

UNIVERSITY OF PLYMOUTH

PLYMOUTH LIBRARY

Tel: (01752) 232323
This book is subject to recall if required by another reader
Books may be renewed by phone
CHARGES WILL BE MADE FOR OVERDUE BOOKS

Joining Europe's Monetary Club

The Challenges for Smaller Member States

Edited by

Erik Jones, Jeffry Frieden, and Francisco Torres

MACMILLAN

First published 1998 by

MACMILLAN PRESS LTD
Houndmills, Basingstoke, Hampshire RG21 6XS
and London
Companies and representatives
throughout the world

ISBN 0-333-74638-4
A catalogue record for this book is available
from the British Library.

10 9 8 7 6 5 4 3 2 1
07 06 05 04 03 02 01 00 99 98

Internal design and typesetting by Letra Libre

Printed in the United States of America by
Haddon Craftsmen
Bloomsburg, PA

For Alexander Azevedo . . .

Contents

Tables and Figures

Figures

Contributors

John Considine, Department of Economics, University College Cork

Eleanor Doyle, Department of Economics, University College Cork

Jeffry Frieden, Department of Government, Harvard University

Liam Gallagher, Department of Economics, University College Cork

Heinz Handler, Austrian Ministry of Economic Affairs

Eduard Hochreiter, Oesterreichische Nationalbank

Torben Iversen, Center for European Studies, Harvard University

Erik Jones, Department of Politics, University of Nottingham

Catherine Kavanagh, Department of Economics, University College Cork

Ella Kavanagh, Department of Economics, University College Cork

Jonathon W. Moses, Department of Sociology and Political Science, University of Trondheim

Eoin O'Leary, Department of Economics, University College Cork

Niels Thygesen, Department of Economics, University of Copenhagen

Francisco Torres, Centro de Estudos Europeus, Universidade Católica Portuguesa

Miranda Xafa, Salomon Brothers, London

Preface

We would like to take the opportunity to thank the members of the Center for European Policy Studies (CEPS) Economic Policy Group for their generous comments on the different chapters in this volume. The first drafts of these case studies were commissioned in 1994 and have been the subject of the several of the Economic Policy Group's meetings. We also would like to extend a particular thanks to Daniel Gros, chairman of the Economic Policy Group, and to Peter Ludlow, director of CEPS, without whose support we would not have been able to complete our work. In thanking the Economic Policy Group, we would like to acknowledge the initial financial support of the Deutsche Bundesbank, the Sveriges Riksbank, the Banco de España, and the German Marshall Fund, all of whom underwrote the group's activities.

Two years is a long time in European monetary affairs, and so we were very fortunate to be able to present and review these case studies in their near-final form at a workshop held at the Universidade Católica in Lisbon, at the occasion of the 1996 annual spring meeting organized by the Centro de Estudos Europeus within the framework of the Portuguese Inter-University Group on European Integration. We would like the thank the organizers and participants of that workshop as well as the European Commission and European Parliament, whose financial support made it possible to see this project through to the end. We also are grateful to the Association for the Monetary Union of Europe and the Luso-Americano Foundation for financial support.

Erik Jones, Nottingham
Jeffry Frieden, Cambridge
Francisco Torres, Lisbon
November 1997

INTRODUCTION

EMU and the Smaller Member States

Erik Jones, Jeffry Frieden, and Francisco Torres

Preparation for economic and monetary union (EMU) has become a central function of economic policy making in Europe, and the Maastricht convergence criteria now are regarded as litmus tests for sound economic governance. Even member states that obviously are uneager to join a monetary union in the near future have shown a remarkable unwillingness to renounce the goal of monetary integration or to fail to meet the convergence criteria. In a sense, the Maastricht plan for EMU has become both a litany and a rite of passage, words to say and things to do in joining Europe's monetary club.

The purpose of these chapters is to illustrate that membership does not mean the same thing to all participants. More specifically, our objective is to focus on the particular challenges for smaller member states. Therefore, we have asked our contributors to focus on who wins and who loses from the process of monetary integration, what institutions are created or modified, what practices are suppressed or adopted, and how it is sold to different electorates.

The Small-Country Case

The starting point for our analysis is that there is no single "small-country case." Taken as a group, the smaller countries are not somehow structurally predestined to benefit from monetary integration—even within the restricted sample of smaller member states. Consider, for example, the claim that smaller countries tend to be more open to international trade than larger countries, particularly in the European context. The argument here is that the more these countries rely on trade with France and Germany—the two member states at the core of EMU—the more they will benefit from the reduction in transaction costs associated with trading in multiple currencies (McKinnon, 1963). And given that smaller countries have presumably lost any domestic monetary sovereignty to Germany and to market speculators within Europe's liberalized capital markets, the conclusion drawn is that the smaller countries have little to lose and much to gain from participation in EMU.

Certainly there is much truth to this structural argument about smaller countries. However, even a cursory survey of trade patterns in Europe suggests that the advantages of monetary union vary substantially from case to case. Moreover, there is no fundamental difference between smaller country trading patterns and those for larger countries. The smaller countries may be more open to international trade on average, but their trade is not excessively directed toward France and Germany. Evidence on this point is assembled in Table I.1, which provides an overview of bilateral trade between the member states of the European Union (EU) and the Franco-German core. Smaller countries such as Finland and Ireland conduct substantially less of their trade with France and Germany than do larger countries such as Italy or Spain.

The same point can be made in more complicated fashion by examining how the small-country economies interact with core Europe. Here the argument is not that the smaller countries are structurally predetermined to participate in EMU, but rather the opposite. Given the tendency toward specialized production witnessed in smaller countries (Katzenstein, 1985), it is more likely that they would suffer in the event of an asymmetric shock from the imposition of a common monetary policy. Larger countries, by contrast, have more diversified industrial structures and therefore are less likely to suffer from an asymmetric shock under a common monetary regime. The conclusion drawn from this line of argument is that the smaller countries might be better advised to weigh the costs and benefits of membership carefully. Even if they have little trouble qualifying for EMU, there may be strong reasons for remaining outside.

Here again, however, the generalization does not stand up to the data. If we rank order indicators for symmetrical economic performance (that is, for possessing economic structures capable of supporting a common monetary regime with core Europe in the presence of asymmetric shocks), there is some reason to believe that the smaller countries will fare less well, as a rule, than the larger countries. However, the negative relationship between size and suitability breaks down altogether once we consider the small countries as a single group. This can be seen in Figure I.1, which provides a scatter plot of population (y-axis) and average ranking across a number of indicators for structural similarity (x-axis). From the structural standpoint, the answer to

Table I.1: European Trade Dependence on France and Germany, 1994

Country	Share of Total Trade Flows (percent)		Share of Domestic GDP (percent)	
	Exports	Imports	Exports	Imports
Austria	42.6	51.0	16.2	19.2
Belgium (Lux.)	35.4	37.8	25.3	25.0
Denmark	27.9	9.7	9.7	8.5
Finland	18.5	19.3	6.6	5.6
Greece	26.6	24.1	4.7	6.5
Ireland	22.6	13.1	15.9	7.3
Netherlands	38.6	28.6	19.9	13.2
Portugal	33.4	26.9	8.7	9.2
Sweden	18.4	25.5	6.8	8.3
Average	29.3	28.4	12.6	11.4
Larger Countries				
France	16.8	22.9	3.8	4.7
Germany	12.0	11.1	2.6	2.4
Italy	32.1	35.6	8.1	7.6
Spain	34.3	35.1	7.7	7.8
United Kingdom	21.4	25.6	5.6	6.9
Average	23.3	26.1	5.6	5.9

Note: Averages are not weighted.
Data sources: IMF; European Commission.

the question "Should the smaller countries strive for membership in EMU?" is ambiguous.

A parallel question might be "Do the smaller countries want to join EMU?" Here the argument is not idiosyncratic but—again—structural. The globalization of financial markets has meant that daily capital flows dwarf even the largest economies. For the smaller countries, then, any attempt to hold on to national currencies is anachronistic and futile: Not only are they unlikely to preserve domestic monetary sovereignty in any meaningful fashion, they also leave themselves vulnerable to adverse and even arbitrary speculation. Joining into a European monetary union, along this line of argument, offers at least a small voice in global monetary affairs.

Figure I.1

Size versus Suitability

Population and Optimum Currency Areas

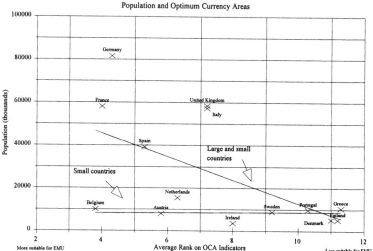

Source: European Commission; and Gros (1996b: 15).

This question should be answered on two levels—the governmental and the popular. At the governmental level, most ruling elites seem committed to monetary integration. All of the smaller countries have announced plans to participate in EMU at some point with the partial exceptions of Denmark and Sweden. And even in those countries there are strong indications that the governments would join if allowed. The trouble lies in building popular support. Voters in Denmark have insisted on the right to opt out of any future EMU, and voters in Sweden are similarly reticent.

However, there is nothing to suggest that opposition to EMU is either strong or weak depending on the size of the country. An attempt to correlate popular attitudes toward EMU with population size fails. Although elites may be generally in favor of monetary integration, popular opinion perhaps is best described as idiosyncratic: By their own admission in a recent Eurobarometer survey, well more than half of the respondents from each country do not feel well informed on the issue of monetary integration. (See Table I.2.) Indeed, if there is a correlation to be found in the polling data, it is that in countries where people feel less well informed they tend to be more supportive of monetary integration (the coefficient of correlation is 0.12), and where people feel better informed they tend to be more opposed to EMU (the coefficient of correlation is 0.32).

Table I.2: Attitudes and Information on EMU

Attitudes Toward EMU			Information About EMU		
Country	For	Against	Country	Well-informed	Not well-informed
Italy	68	10	Denmark	41	58
Netherlands	64	28	Netherlands	31	69
Ireland	60	17	Luxembourg	30	68
Luxembourg	59	22	Germany	27	71
France	58	23	Austria	25	70
Spain	58	18	Belgium	24	74
Greece	52	20	Finland	23	76
Belgium	51	25	UK	22	76
EU 15	47	33	EU 15	20	79
Portugal	46	21	Ireland	19	79
Germany	34	45	Sweden	19	80
Finland	33	53	France	18	81
UK	32	56	Spain	13	85
Denmark	32	60	Italy	12	86
Sweden	29	54	Greece	11	88
Austria	23	43	Portugal	7	92

Note: Figures are in percentages of respondents. Respondents answering without preference are counted but not recorded in the table.
Source: Eurobarometer (1996), pp. 49, 52.

Such correlations probably are spurious. Nevertheless, they raise concern about how well elites have succeeded in communicating their own enthusiasm for monetary union to the electorate as well as about how debates over EMU are presented. If popular attitudes toward monetary integration are idiosyncratic, varying from country to country and context to context, then national approaches to EMU membership are likely to be idiosyncratic as well.

Expectations, Convergence, and Divergence

National attitudes toward Europe are also highly volatile. Since these case studies were drafted, the political climate surrounding EMU has changed dramatically. The surprise election of French Socialist Lionel Jospin's left-wing cabinet inaugurated a tense period of cohabitation in France and in the Franco-German relationship. Almost immediately, the prospects for a monetary union starting by the end of the century diminished. Hence it is hard to say with any certainty what the future will bring in terms of monetary integration.

What we can say is that current concern over monetary union derives in large measure from a perceived contrast between "convergence" as defined by the Maastricht treaty and popular notions of "strong" economic performance. On the one hand, it is clear that considerable "Maastricht-style" convergence has taken place whether in terms of inflation, interest rates, or government accounts. On the other hand, it is also clear that some economies have maintained consistently lower rates of unemployment, higher rates of real growth, and stronger balances on current accounts than others have. Evidence for this proposition can be found in Tables I.3 and I.4, which provide the Maastricht convergence data and three other macroeconomic indicators (real growth in gross domestic product [GDP], unemployment rates, and current account balances) for 1992 and 1997.

The comparison across time provides a useful check on Europe's progress toward monetary union. Although it is not clear whether Europe's political leaders will muster the effort to complete EMU, it is striking how far they have come toward meeting their convergence objectives. In 1992, for example, barely half of the (then twelve) member states met the inflation criterion and only four met the deficit criterion. For 1997, the Organization for Economic Cooperation and Development (OECD) estimates that only one of the (now 15) member states will miss the inflation criterion and only four will miss the deficit criterion. The hitch, of course, is that two of the four laggards in deficit convergence are France and Germany. It is also a problem that while GDP growth and current account balances have improved over the five-year period, unemployment has worsened.

Nevertheless, the data do not lend obvious support to the contention that the Maastricht plan for EMU is somehow inherently flawed. If convergence exacts a price from the "real" economy, clearly this differs from one country to the next without relation to the extent of convergence undertaken. Put another way, Maastricht convergence does not seem to necessitate real economic divergence. In order to illustrate this point, Table I.5 gives a measure of the variation in performance across countries using the standard deviation of the different indicators. When the variation across countries diminishes—and the countries "converge" on one another—the standard deviation decreases, and when variation across countries increases, the standard deviation increases as well. The standard deviations of the Maastricht indicators clearly

Table I.3: Actual Convergence in 1992

Country	Maastricht Convergence Indicators (percent)				Other Indicators (percent)		
	Consumer Price Inflation[a]	Long-term Interest Rates	Deficit-to-GDP Ratio	Debt-to-GDP ratio	Real GDP Growth	Unemploy-ment Rate	Current Account Balance[b]
Austria	3.9	8.3	1.9	58.3	2.0	5.3	-0.1
Belgium	2.1	8.7	7.2	130.6	1.7	10.4	3.0
Denmark	2.0	8.9	2.9	73.2	0.2	11.3	3.4
Finland	4.1	12.1	5.8	46.2	-3.6	13.1	-4.6
France	2.4	9.0	3.8	45.8	1.2	10.4	0.4
Germany	4.7	7.9	2.8	45.8	2.2	7.7	-1.0
Greece	15.0	n/a	12.3	99.2	0.4	8.7	-2.2
Ireland	2.5	9.1	2.5	94.0	4.0	15.3	1.1
Italy	5.6	13.3	12.1	117.3	0.6	8.8	-2.3
Luxembourg	3.4	n/a	n/a	n/a	4.5	1.6	0.0
Netherlands	3.1	8.1	3.9	79.6	2.0	5.4	2.3
Portugal	9.1	20.6	3.6	64.3	1.8	4.2	-0.2
Spain	6.4	11.7	3.6	54.2	0.7	18.4	-3.2
Sweden	2.2	10.0	7.8	71.1	-1.4	5.3	-3.5
United Kingdom	5.0	9.1	6.3	47.6	-0.5	9.9	-1.7
Criteria	*3.6*	*10.7*	*3*	*60*			

Notes: [a]Consumer price inflation is private consumption deflator; [b]Current account balance is percentage GDP.
Source: OECD.

have diminished over time. Meanwhile, real GDP growth has converged somewhat even as the variation in unemployment rates and current account balances has remained stable.

The simple conclusion to draw from this survey of the economic data is that the numbers by themselves do not tell us that EMU is good or bad, likely or unlikely. Of course we do not suggest that the macroeconomic data are uninteresting or irrelevant. Most of our contributors rely on macroeconomic indicators to enlighten one part of the EMU story or another, and many refer back to those statistics just provided. Our point that the macroeconomic picture is only meaningful (albeit more complicated) when viewed from up close. The broader discussions of EMU should be

Table I.4: Estimated Convergence in 1997

Country	Maastricht Convergence Indicators (percent)				Other Indicators (percent)		
	Consumer Price Inflation[a]	Long-term Interest Rates	Deficit-to-GDP Ratio	Debt-to-GDP ratio	Real GDP Growth	Unemployment Rate	Current Account Balance[b]
Austria	2.0	5.0	3.0	71.3	1.5	6.4	-1.7
Belgium	1.6	5.9	2.8	127.2	2.2	12.7	6.0
Denmark	2.2	6.3	-0.0	71.5	2.5	8.1	1.0
Finland	1.5	4.8	2.0	60.7	4.6	14.7	2.9
France	1.6	5.8	3.2	64.3	2.5	12.6	1.7
Germany	1.7	5.8	3.2	65.9	2.2	11.1	0.1
Greece	6.0	n/a	5.2	106.9	3.0	10.4	-3.5
Ireland	2.0	6.5	1.2	72.0	6.7	10.8	0.9
Italy	2.0	7.5	3.2	124.1	1.0	12.1	4.3
Luxembourg	1.5	n/a	n/a	n/a	4.1	3.3	0.0
Netherlands	1.8	5.7	2.3	74.5	3.0	6.2	4.4
Portugal	2.4	6.8	2.9	66.3	3.3	7.1	-0.2
Spain	2.3	6.9	3.0	74.1	2.8	22.1	0.3
Sweden	2.0	6.9	2.1	79.4	2.0	8.1	3.0
United Kingdom	2.4	7.2	2.8	60.8	3.0	6.1	0.2
Criteria	3.1	7.0	3	60			

Notes: [a]Consumer price inflation is private consumption deflator; [b]Current account balance is percentage GDP.
Source: OECD.

considered within appropriate national contexts. And for Europe's smaller countries, this is what we do.

A Common Template

Idiosyncrasy is awkward as an organizing principle. Therefore, we have asked our contributors to pay particular attention to five specific sets of issues: optimum currency areas, labor market institutions, fiscal policy, variable geometry, and political union. Not all of the issues have the same importance from country to country, yet we believe the aggregate of the five concerns

Table I.5: Statistical Convergence Across Macroeconomic Indicators

Standard Deviations	1992	1993	1994	1995	1996	1997
Consumer price inflation[a]	3.3	3.0	2.2	2.2	1.8	1.1
Long-term interest rates	3.3	2.2	1.3	1.8	1.2	0.8
Deficit-to-GDP ratio	3.2	3.3	2.9	1.9	1.7	1.1
Debt-to-GDP ratio	26.7	25.7	25.4	23.3	22.5	21.6
Real GDP growth	1.9	2.6	1.4	2.0	1.6	1.3
Unemployment rate	4.3	5.0	5.1	4.7	4.5	4.4
Current account balance[b]	2.3	2.3	2.1	2.4	2.4	2.4

Notes: [a]Consumer price inflation is private consumption deflator. [b]Current account balance is percentage GDP.
Source: OECD.

encompasses the process of monetary integration both in terms of the motives for joining EMU and in terms of the consequences of membership.

The discussion of optimum currency areas turns primarily on the structural or economic reasons for joining a monetary union. In other words, it includes the gains or losses resulting from particular trade or industrial patterns as well as the institutional benefits from membership. Therefore, it is necessary to examine how much the country trades with Europe, whether its economic structures are symmetrical, and whether it has experienced asymmetric shocks. For most of our contributors, this part of the inquiry was among the most important. However, it was not restricted solely to EMU per se but rather to the selection of *any* exchange rate regime and the adjustments made in reaction to that policy choice.

Focusing attention on labor market institutions was a natural extension of the inquiry into optimum currency area issues. Wage bargaining is a necessary counterpoint to monetary and exchange rate policy, either in a complementary or a competitive manner. For example, participation in a fixed-exchange rate regime is facilitated by wage moderation and complicated by wage inflation. And participation in a monetary union depends on wage flexibility as a means of economic adjustment. Therefore, it is important to assess whether a country will be able to provide both the discipline for joining a monetary union and the flexibility required inside one. In practical terms, that means that the degree of centralization in wage bargaining, the structure and generosity of labor market support programs, and the size and composition of unemployment must be examined.

A similar point can be made with reference to fiscal policy. However, given the convergence requirements laid out in the Maastricht plan for monetary union, it is necessary also to consider the politics of fiscal adjustment. Although attitudes toward EMU may be idiosyncratic, attitudes toward austerity are not (Frieden, 1991). Therefore, we have asked our contributors to assess whether and/or when their countries will meet the fiscal criteria for convergence, which groups will be affected, and if opposition to fiscal consolidation has extended into opposition to monetary union.

The prospect that some countries will not join, or might not be allowed to join, EMU is a complicating factor. While it may be attractive to participate in monetary union with a large number of countries, it may be less attractive in a smaller group and with significant trade competitors on the outside. Moreover, being part of a core EMU is only one side of the coin. The other side of the coin is exclusion, whether by choice or not. Being part of Europe's periphery is likely to be one of the thornier issues over the next several years, so it is useful to know how that prospect may influence domestic political choices.

Finally, the question of political union refers to the larger project of European integration, of which monetary union is only a part. Here too there are two sides to the issue. On the one hand, some may call for the creation of EMU in order to ensure progress in other areas. On the other hand, others may try to slow down the progress of monetary integration in order to preserve their rights or privileges in other contexts. This question of policy linkage is perhaps the most difficult issue to address systematically. Public opinion polling data is often difficult to interpret or to compare across countries. Popular debates about the relationship between monetary integration and other issues are also hard to disentangle. Nevertheless, the linkage between EMU and other policies is an essential part of the story.

Chapter Summaries

The results of the inquiry confirm both the assumption of idiosyncrasy and the importance of having a common frame of reference. Each of the contributors covers the necessary material, yet each also concentrates on a specific theme or themes of particular importance to a given country.

For Heinz Handler and Eduard Hochreiter, the authors of Chapter 1, that theme is credibility. Austria has operated in a de facto monetary union with Germany arguably since the mid-1970s. Nevertheless, that should not suggest either that Austria is somehow structurally predisposed to monetary integration in core Europe or that the country has undergone a massive real convergence on German-style economic structures. To the contrary, Handler and Hochreiter suggest that credible determination is the principal ingredient to the success of Austrian exchange rate policy. And, in turn, the consistent application of the "hard-currency" principle is necessary to earn "credibility" in ever more integrated financial markets. Their argument is based not on tautology but on consensus. If Austria has succeeded in its currency relations with the Deutschemark, it is because the Austrians themselves were willing to share the burdens associated with that exchange rate policy. Through a system of centralized wage bargaining and peak cooperation between representatives of business and labor, the Austrians were able to generate the economic flexibility necessary to prosper under a hard-currency regime as well as the economic solidarity essential to smooth out the distributional consequences of adverse shocks.

However, Handler and Hochreiter are careful to note that the consensus in support of a hard-currency regime has not translated directly into a consensus in favor of monetary union. Indeed, as the data presented indicate, EMU is less popular in Austria than anywhere else in Europe. Handler and Hochreiter suggest that the explanation for this unpopularity lies in the failings of economists and other professionals to communicate their arguments about the advantages of European integration more carefully in the run-up to accession. As a result, short-term adjustment costs have been widely misinterpreted as evidence of the long-term disadvantages of EU membership. And as the European Union has become more unpopular, EMU also has become more unpopular. In this sense, the linkage between other aspects of integration and EMU works to the disadvantage of monetary union. Handler and Hochreiter conclude by suggesting that once the period of adjustment has ended, the Austrian consensus on hard-currency policy will reassert itself, and Austria will be prepared to join EMU.

The question of policy linkages holds a more central position in Erik Jones's analysis of Belgium, presented in Chapter 2. He argues that while Europe is integrating, Belgium appears to be disintegrating. Any display of ineffectiveness on the part of the federal government in participating in Europe is likely to reinforce arguments in favor of the decentralization of Belgium. This suggests the paradox that for the Belgian state to assert its legitimacy, it must be qualified to relinquish its sovereignty. To survive, Belgium must demonstrate its ability to keep up with the pack.

Qualifying for monetary union according to the Maastricht convergence criteria will be difficult for Belgium. Not only does the government have to contend with an enormous mountain of outstanding public debt, it also must work to reform the social welfare system responsible for creating that debt. Finally, the government must accomplish all this within the agreement forged by the ruling center-left coalition and without upsetting the tenuous balance between regions and linguistic groups.

In essence, however, Jones argues that the debate over EMU is not really a debate about monetary integration at all. Contrary to popular assumptions,

Belgian monetary authorities have long managed a relatively close short-term relationship with the Deutschemark. Moreover, there is a deep consensus among economic elites about the virtues of a hard currency in general and of monetary union in particular. Finally, the ruling center-left government seems to have an economic policy agenda sufficient to bring the Belgian economy to within the Maastricht norms—an agenda backed by extraordinary enabling legislation allowing the government to plan for budgetary adjustment along the Maastricht line without consulting parliament. Jones concludes, however, that while it is likely that Belgium will make it into EMU, it is less likely that participation will resolve the underlying tensions within the Belgian state.

Torben Iversen and Niels Thygesen's analysis of Denmark, in Chapter 3, provides a useful complement to the discussion of consensus and policy linkages. In Denmark, the major transition in monetary policy arguably took place in 1982 and 1983, when Danish economic authorities adopted fiscal austerity measures and a hard-currency policy at approximately the same time. Iversen and Thygesen argue that this policy shift resulted not from consensus or from policy linkage but rather from a change in the distributional coalition controlling monetary affairs.

Iversen and Thygesen argue that the collapse of social partnership between business and labor in the 1970s paved the way for the economic reforms of the 1980s. The breakdown of the Danish social partnership during a period of low growth and high inflation created a new cleavage in the country's politics. On one side of the cleavage, unskilled and public sector workers looked to fast nominal wage inflation to sustain real incomes. On the other side of the cleavage, business leaders and workers in export manufacturing looked to a strong currency and wage restraint in order to bolster competitiveness and therefore profits. Denmark's economic transformation started when the exposed and industrial sectors came to power, bringing with them a decisively different outlook on the relationship between exchange-rate policy and the welfare state.

As with Austria, the success of Denmark's exchange rate policy lies in its credibility and not in the similarity between Danish economic structures and those found elsewhere in Europe. Iversen and Thygesen conclude, therefore, that the success of Danish participation in EMU will rely more on the commitment of Danish policy makers than on the convergence of Danish economic structures. Evidence for this commitment is to be found in Denmark's achievement of the convergence criteria, if not in the results of public opinion polling. What remains to be seen is whether elite commitment can be translated into a sustainable coalition in support of membership.

The dissimilarity of economic structures is even more pronounced in Finland than in Denmark. As Jonathon Moses points out in Chapter 4, Finland's specialization in timber, pulp, and paper products makes it a very unlikely candidate for participation in EMU. Because wood products are quoted in dollar terms, Finland might suffer disproportionately from movements between the common European currency and the dollar. Nevertheless, the Finnish government appears committed to the cause of monetary integration and joined the exchange rate mechanism (ERM) of the European monetary system (EMS) in November 1996.

In order to explain the contrast between government policy and economic interest, Moses argues that monetary integration with Europe will help the Finnish economy to wean itself from excessive dependence on exports of wood and paper. Moreover, closer monetary links with Europe will aid in reorienting Finnish trade from the former Soviet Union (once its largest trading partner) to the West. In other words, participation in EMU is part of Finland's economic adjustment to the end of the Cold War. Therefore, the prospect for Finnish participation in EMU should be gauged in terms of the strength of the coalition in favor of adjustment vis-à-vis the coalition in favor of maintaining the status quo. Given the political strength of the wood, pulp, and paper lobby, the outcome of Finland's bid to join EMU remains undecided.

Miranda Xafa's analysis of Greece in Chapter 5 parallels the Finnish case in many respects. The Greek economy is dissimilar in structure to those economies in Europe's core, and the motivation for monetary integration derives from deeper ambitions to liberalize and modernize the country. She concludes that while there is support for a "hard drachma" policy, much remains to be accomplished on the larger agendas of convergence and modernization. For example, the Greek government must continue its efforts to consolidate its fiscal position and to privatize the large, publicly owned sectors of the Greek economy.

As with Denmark and Finland, the success of government efforts will hinge on the development of a stable and powerful coalition in support of monetary integration and all that monetary integration entails. This will require overcoming significant vested interests—not least among workers in the public and parapublic sectors, suppliers to government industry, politicians used to relying on patronage for support, and farmers dependent on subsidies. Each of these groups is capable of complicating Greece's bid to join EMU, and so, as with Finland, prospects for the future remain ambiguous.

The Irish case, related in Chapter 6 by Ella Kavanagh and her colleagues from the Economics Department of University College Cork, bears many similarities with Finland and Greece, but with a different outcome. Of the smaller countries, Ireland has performed exceptionally well in terms of the Maastricht convergence criteria, and is almost certain to join EMU from the outset.

Nevertheless, Ireland's economy is not ideal for participation in a monetary union with France and Germany—a fact made evident by the currency crisis of 1992–93, when the Irish pound was forced out of the ERM. Still, Kavanagh and her co-authors argue that Ireland's dissimilarities are part of the motivation behind the country's participation in the EMS as well as its desire to participate in EMU. The decision taken to join the European Community in the early 1970s, and the EMS later that decade, was bound up with the ambition to transform the Irish economy from its agricultural roots as well as from its excessive dependence on United Kingdom (UK) markets. And the combined result of EC membership and EMS participation has been a substantial, although still only partial, adjustment. The Irish economy now trades considerably more with mainland Europe, and the composition of Irish trade includes a large share of sophisticated manufacturing output.

The problem for Ireland is that the links between the Irish and UK markets remain strong, particularly in the context of employment: Trade with the UK has a much greater employment content than trade with mainland Europe; Irish labor markets rely on emigration to the UK to relieve domestic unemployment; and Irish trade unions have strong institutional links with their counterparts in Britain. Thus while it is clear that Ireland could participate in EMU on the basis of the Maastricht convergence criteria, it is less clear that Ireland would benefit from EMU membership in the event that the UK remained on the outside. The Irish case is one where the prospect of variable geometry holds a special importance. To at least a certain extent, therefore, the prospects for Irish membership in EMU lie outside national control.

The Dutch case reveals no such ambivalence. As Erik Jones argues in Chapter 7, the Dutch are clearly among the best performers in European monetary affairs and therefore among the most likely to participate in EMU from the start. Jones suggests, however, that climbing to the top of Europe's monetary class was not an easy achievement. Therefore, while Dutch membership in EMU is very likely, it also may prove difficult.

Jones's claims about the Dutch case rely on two supporting contentions. First, the Dutch have been able to sustain their currency relationship with the Deutschemark through a combination of concerted wage restraint and unemployment support measures—such as expanding higher education, placing workers on disability or early retirement, and promoting part-time rather than full-time employment. Second, the financial arrangements necessary to support this combination of wage restraint and labor market supports are incompatible with the fiscal requirements of the Maastricht Treaty. Therefore, Jones argues, either the Dutch must learn to live in a hard-currency regime without concerted wage restraint and labor market support measures, or they must find an alternative means to finance such flanking policies.

On the surface, the difficulty of resolving this conundrum is perhaps no greater for the Netherlands than it is for any other small welfare state. However, Jones suggests that matters are complicated by the juxtaposition of a national political culture over distinct regional economies—with financial and public services to the West, energy to the North, manufacturing to the South and Southeast, and agriculture to the Northeast and Southwest. Any national government hoping to reform Dutch economic policy making must satisfy each of these regional constituencies or risk increasing support for the opposition. Indeed, the political difficulties involved in such a task explain perhaps why the formula for Dutch adjustment to pegging on the Deutschemark was so complex in terms of public expenditure programs. What formula the Dutch will adopt in preparation for EMU remains to be seen.

In the Portuguese case, Francisco Torres contends in Chapter 8 that participation in EMU promises to yield larger economic benefits than potential costs. For example, the high degree of Portuguese trade integration with the EU points to high benefits and low costs of participation in EMU. Moreover, while differences in industrial structures will persist—and with them the possibility of asymmetric shocks—Portuguese wages are highly elastic with respect to both inflation and unemployment. Therefore, forgoing exchange rate autonomy seems not to be very costly.

Torres focuses much of his analysis on the importance of EMU to institutional reform in Portugal. He argues that the EMU challenge has worked as a mechanism for economic stabilization and as a precondition for structural reform and longer-term development. It has helped create the necessary consensus to overcome specific interests in the pursuit of social and economic reform. The political consensus took long to build—much longer than in countries such as Ireland or Spain—and it still faces a loud opposition—a time-lagged mimic of France's—but seems to be maturing with respect not only to EMU but also to the wider goals of European integration and economic policy making.

Considering the political implications for European monetary integration, Torres points out that even the sectors more favorable to Portugal's participation in EMU caution against the negative effects of monetary union on unemployment and growth. He finds no economic justification for that presumption. Nevertheless, although people cannot explain why and how EMU may be a problem for Portugal and do understand that exchange-rate autonomy does not serve to resolve the structural problems that affect Portugal and Europe, there is a generalized concern that the Portuguese economy cannot compete at any level within the Internal Market, especially with the forthcoming enlargement of the European Union to Central European countries and with the increasing liberalization of world trade. Pessimists warn that social and political unrest will spread across Europe, focusing on the "real versus nominal convergence" issue as a means of expressing their "ideological reservations" with respect to the process of European integration. This attitude contradicts the other widespread concern that Portugal's position in the EU as a whole will weaken if it were to be left out of EMU. To begin with, the first group of countries to be represented on the executive board of the European Central Bank will move forward in all other domains of political cooperation, leaving the others effectively out of the political core. Moreover, it is argued that convergence will be more difficult for the outsiders. Torres contends that these two facts, together with the possibility of Portugal's satisfying all the convergence criteria by 1997, have generated a strong consensus between the government and the main opposition party on the objective of participating in EMU from the outset. That consensus applies now irrespective of any automatic transfers and of what happens to other southern countries (such as neighboring Spain), the two most commonly cited arguments against Portugal's participation in EMU.

Jonathon Moses's presentation of the Swedish case in Chapter 9 illustrates the importance of institutions as well as economic structures. In Sweden, the urgency of monetary integration derives from the need to reassure large corporations of the viability of making investments. The dilemma derives from an overblown public sector and a long-standing social welfare tradition among the most generous in Western Europe. For Swedish politicians to participate in EMU, they will have to convince their electorates of the necessity for institutional convergence and for placing restrictions on the functioning of the welfare state.

The political debate in Sweden is marked by a deep cleavage between genders: Women tend to perceive EMU as a threat to the maternity, day care, and other public sector programs that help to guarantee their equal status, while men tend to associate EMU with a brighter economic future. This cleavage comes on top of an economic cleavage much like that found in Denmark—pitting unskilled and public sector workers, on the one hand, against traded-goods sector managers and employees on the other hand. And given the crosscutting nature of these cleavages, the outcome is even more uncertain than in the Danish case. Swedish politicians continue to plan for EMU, but whether they will be able to generate popular support is another matter altogether.

Conclusion

The national case studies are arranged alphabetically from Austria to Sweden. This arrangement is arbitrary but in many ways more useful than a more systematic organization. We argue from the outset that generalizations

about small countries tend to fail more than they succeed. This argume
also could be extended to subsets of small countries. In particular, we ha
found that ranging countries on a spectrum from core to periphery to be
more a hindrance than an aid to analysis: Not only do such generalizations
rely on hidden assumptions about the structural attributes of countries, they
also obscure the interrelationships between politics, economics, and diverse
policy issues that we have found to be so important.

Yet this is not to imply that there are no useful generalizations to be
drawn from the study of smaller countries. These generalizations are reserved for the concluding chapter.

CHAPTER ONE

Austria

Heinz Handler and Eduard Hochreiter[1]

Following membership in the European Union (EU), the big challenge for Austrian policy makers and the public alike is to prepare for full participation in economic and monetary union (EMU). On an economic-political level, Austria always has been integration-minded and trade relations have been centered on the EU. In the monetary field, Austria has long been integrated—via a de facto monetary union with Germany—into the likely core of EMU. Therefore, support to join EMU has been widespread and solid. In contrast to other small countries, the collective bargaining process embedded in the Austrian system of social partnership not only has survived up to now but, so far, has nourished hope that it can adjust to the new challenges ahead.

This chapter has five sections. The first assesses the economic and political developments in Austria prior to the country's accession to the EU in January 1995 and during the following 18 months. One focus of this section is on the issue of whether Austria forms an optimum currency area with Germany or, more broadly, with the European hard-core countries. The second section discusses the unique role of the social partners in Austria. The third covers the thorny fiscal issues. The burning areas of unemployment and structural adjustment are discussed in the fourth section. The final section offers some concluding remarks and gives an outlook on the future.

General Economic and Political Features

Economic Background

When Austria applied for EU membership in mid-1989, the country was on a strong, Maastricht-convergent real growth path of around 4 percent per annum (and cumulatively of some 15 percent in the period from 1988 to 1991) without signs of bottlenecks or other strains. This was made possible by:

1. A well-balanced tax reform (effective January 1989) entailing a substantial lowering of personal and corporate taxation
2. The liberalization of foreign transactions in a number of steps (completed in November 1991), while the rather slow pace of deregulation of the domestic economy apparently did not retard economic growth measurably
3. Structural adjustment in the nationalized industries (redimensioning, spin-off and closing of plants, resulting in a reduction of the workforce by one-third, or 33,000 employees)
4. Moderate wage settlements with high productivity gains in industry
5. Credible medium-term fiscal consolidation measures, also designed to raise the incentives to work and to improve the supply side of the economy
6. A favorable international economic environment

In short, economic policy attempted to raise potential growth and thereby lift sustainable actual growth.[2] Moreover, Austria substantially benefited from the opening of Eastern Europe with cumulative net exports of roughly 65 billion Austrian schillings (1990 to 1994), which, despite sizable structural adjustments, are estimated to have increased (net) overall employment by 10,000 to 15,000 persons. (See, for example, Schebesch and Wörgötter, 1995.)[3]

In contrast to most other European countries, Austria's 1993 recession was rather shallow. Its mildness can be explained by the introduction of fiscal support measures by the government (including the second phase of a tax reform), by the working of automatic stabilizers and by buoyant demand from reunified Germany. The downswing did, however, highlight and accentuate the weak structural position of the budget, which deteriorated sharply. (See Genser and Holzmann, 1995.)[4] By 1993, Austria was for the first time unable to fulfill the fiscal convergence criteria contained in Protocol Number 5 to the Maastricht Treaty. By 1994, it was clear that the Austrian fiscal position was becoming unsustainable. Both the deficit and the public debt soared and made retrenchment measures urgent regardless of Austria's desire to be part of the core of EMU. Yet it took until 1996 before decisive fiscal consolidation measures could be implemented.

Austria's inflation performance in the past two decades by and large has mirrored that of Germany—an outcome of the fixed peg. However, the rate of consumer price inflation was on average (with the notable exception of 1991 to 1993, when Germany was coping with the unification shock) about one percentage point higher than in Germany, reflecting competition deficiencies in the sheltered sector (Hochreiter and Winckler, 1995a: 172). Moreover, inflation has responded only with substantial delay to increasing competition in the wake of European Economic Area (EEA) and EU memberships.

More recently, the structural weaknesses of the Austrian economy in certain important and highly visible industries, for example, tourism (foreign tourism accounts for about 8 percent of gross domestic product [GDP]), the paper industry (competing, among others, with Finland and Sweden), and textile and clothing (outsourcing of low value-added production to Eastern Europe) became highly visible. This has been due to fundamental changes in the economic environment, such as the opening of the East, and Austria's membership in the EEA as of 1993 and in the EU as of 1995. Judging from previous performance, however, Austrian industry all in all appears to be flexible enough to cope with such shocks. Such flexibility will be decisive for smooth economic adjustment in stage 3 of EMU.

Political Background

Austria always has been integration-minded and thus over time has furthered European integration. As a small country at the edge of the Western industrialized world, Austria in 1955 chose to remain neutral between the Eastern and Western blocs and fulfilled some bridging functions (Hochreiter, 1994). Austria, in contrast to Switzerland, has seen its position in world politics as an active partner, becoming a member of UN organizations, including the Bretton Woods institutions, at a rather early stage.

Bound by the State Treaty of 1955, Austria was not in a position to join the European Economic Community (EEC) from its beginning in 1958. In particular, Austria was prohibited from entering any formal integration arrangement with Germany, and therefore opted for the foundation of the European Free Trade Association (EFTA). This course was favored by the Socialist Party (SPÖ), which, at the time, viewed the European Communities as a bloc of conservative governments. Attempts in the 1960s to reinterpret the State Treaty so as to allow Austrian membership in the EEC were frustrated by the Soviet Union. It was not until 1972 that Austria (together with other EFTA countries) was able to sign an association agreement with the EEC, providing for the gradual abolition of tariffs on trade and for rules to secure fair competition between the trading partners. Although Austria's membership in EFTA induced substantial trade diversion at the expense of trade with the EEC, the Community member states remained by far Austria's most important trading partners. It was always clear that Austria, from an economic point of view, would prefer EEC to EFTA membership. At the same time, the increasing EEC links with Western political and defense organizations made it ever more unlikely that Austria would join the Common Market.

A fundamental change in attitude both in Austria and in the other EFTA countries became apparent in the mid-1980s, when the European Commission published the White Paper on the completion of the Single Market. For Austria in particular, the fortunate events in Central and Eastern Europe since 1989 opened the political window to negotiate EC membership. As early as 1987, the federal government—newly formed as a grand coalition between the renamed Social Democrats (SPÖ) and the conservative People's Party (ÖVP)—had started to evaluate the legal and economic adjustment needs vis-à-vis the EC. A Working Group on European Integration, comprising experts from federal and regional authorities as well as from the social partners, was set up under the auspices of the Federal Ministry of Foreign Affairs. The early involvement of the social partners, in particular the chambers of labor, commerce, and agriculture, in this process was one of the major characteristics in the preparation of future EU membership. This attitude of cooperation proved to be instrumental in the June 1989 parliamentary decision to support the government's move to apply for EU membership, which was carried out a month later. The broad consensus of the Austrian population in favor of joining the EU was strengthened by myriad discussions organized within the memberships of the individual social partner groupings.[5] The consensus rested on economic arguments but was augmented by political considerations (participation in the EU decision-making process) and by security reasons provoked by the breakdown of the former East bloc.

With some delay the antagonists organized themselves, formulating their arguments around the topics of neutrality; the loss of Austrian sovereignty; the watering-down of social, health and environmental standards; excessive transit traffic; and the evils of Euro-bureaucracy. The opposition flag was carried by the right-wing Freedom Party and the Greens. The Freedom Party, initially in favor of EU membership, changed its position under the populist leadership of Jörg Haider, who emphasized the nationalistic party wing at the expense of the liberal wing. The latter split off in 1994 to form the new Liberal Forum party, which has strongly advocated EU membership. On a European level, the Maastricht referenda in Denmark (June 1992 and May 1993) and France (September 1992), as well as the rejection by the Swiss population of EEA membership (December 1992), fueled opposition to further integration steps. Indecisive EU policies in the wake of Yugoslavia's dissolution and the recession in Europe added to the mounting critique. According to Austrian opinion polls, opponents of EU membership equaled its supporters by the end of 1993 (Plasser and Ulram, 1994).

In early 1994, when the accession negotiations with the European Commission were communicated over the media, the supporters began to gain ground. Although opposition to EU membership stiffened as the date of the referendum approached, the EU referendum brought a decisive majority of 66.4 percent in favor of EU membership, the highest affirmative vote among all the (potential) accession countries. Although opinion polls pointed toward a positive outcome, the large majority was by no means clear, given the rising appeal to the general public of demagogic arguments against membership, particularly from Freedom Party representatives, as the referendum was coming due. Opinion polls in Austria revealed that 32 percent of assenting voters took their decision during the "last few weeks before" the referendum while only 22 percent of dissenting voters decided that late. According to exit polls, all major population groups had, on average, voted in favor of EU membership. The younger population (less than 30 years of age) was much more skeptical (55 percent in favor) than the generation of 60 years and more (70 percent in favor). People with higher education were more in favor of membership than those with basic education only. Uncertainties about the consequences of participation in the EU were particularly widespread among farmers, who voted 70 to 30 percent against accession. Sympathizers with political parties were quite diverse in their voting behavior: 75 percent of Liberal Forum followers voted in favor of membership, as did 73 percent of SPÖ voters and 66 percent of ÖVP voters. In contrast, only 41 percent of the Freedom Party and 38 percent of the Green Party voted in favor of EU membership, dampening the overall result (Plasser and Ulram, 1994).

In the parliamentary elections of October 1994, the grand coalition of the SPÖ and the ÖVP was thought to gain from the euphoria in the wake of the EU referendum. However, the election campaign of the two parties failed and they lost heavily, particularly to the Freedom Party of Jörg Haider. Through his radically populist approach, Haider has been able to appeal to the discontented followers of other political parties over the years. Although the SPÖ and the ÖVP were able to form a new government, quarrels concerning budget consolidation (required regardless of the provisions contained in the Maastricht Treaty) dominated joint efforts to help businesses and consumers to adjust smoothly to the new situation. In the media, most of the blame for the projected budget deficit was put on the EU. During the election campaign, the SPÖ and the ÖVP had promised to refrain from tax increases and to reduce the budget deficit by cutting expenditures only. However, as the social partners had not been consulted for the elaboration of the consolidation program, they felt free to oppose the government's plans of cutting social transfers and investment support. In the early months of 1995, public disappointment rose over the disputes within the government and the lack of immediately visible economic gains from EU membership. If opinion polls can be trusted, a new referendum in mid-1995 would have turned down EU membership.[6] This corresponds with Plavsak's (1995) conclusions that the outcome of the referendum was a conditional public consensus reached at a specific point in time and sensitive to various changing factors.

Such disappointment is to a large extent related to overdrawn short-term economic expectations and to the political polarization associated with the referendum and the parliamentary elections. In hindsight, politicians were at times not careful enough in their wording when explaining the long-term advantages of EU membership (as were opposition parties in demonstrating the evils). In addition, economists, generally in favor of membership, were not able to properly get the caveats associated with the results of their research across to the public. Above all, the federalism provided for in the Austrian constitution has led to an ongoing struggle over the financial consequences of EU membership. Disenchantment with the EU continued to be high throughout 1996, as evident in the strong showing of parties critical of the Union in the October 1996 elections to the European Parliament.[7]

Optimum Currency Area (OCA) Issues

Austria, unlike many other countries, has favored a pegging strategy ever since the unification of the exchange rate in 1953. Under the Bretton Woods system, the Austrian schilling was pegged to the U.S. dollar with an unchanged fixed parity. In August 1971, when the United States closed the gold window, Austria opted for a trade-weighted basket peg (the so-called indicator peg) and thereby pioneered the nominal effective exchange rate concept.[8] Over time, more and more currencies were removed from the basket, either because they devalued against the Deutschemark or because they were too volatile (Swiss Franc). Since late 1981 the Austrian schilling has remained practically fixed vis-à-vis the Deutschemark.

Considerations of optimum currency areas concern the sustainability of a fixed peg or, indeed, the viability of a monetary union. Of particular concern is the ability of a country or region to deal with asymmetric shocks (Pauer, 1996). So long as shocks within a monetary union are symmetric, there is no need to change relative prices among regions, and hence there is no need to change the exchange rate between regions. If, however, asymmetric shocks dominate, labor and capital have to be mobile in order to maintain the exchange rate. If factors of production are immobile, wages and prices have to be flexible enough to allow the necessary adjustment of relative prices. In fact, the evolution of Austria's exchange rate policy and its growing support by the social partners over time reflected the policy makers' conviction that the domestic economy (for example, wages) would indeed be flexible and productive enough to adjust and, hence that Austria could forgo the exchange rate as an adjustment instrument.

There are, however, a few exceptions. In May 1974, when inflation surged worldwide, Austrian policy makers urgently sought measures to bring inflation down. Aware of the fast pass-through and the close link between domestic inflation and wages because of the social partnership system, policy makers explicitly employed the exchange rate as an instrument to bring down inflation; that is, the exchange rate was revalued both in nominal (against the Deutschemark) and in real terms. Note also that this occurred in a situation of quite unfavorable fundamentals with respect to Germany.

Policy makers were aware of the negative effects of this policy on profits, but at the same time they were confident that the profit squeeze in the exposed sector due to the real revaluation was temporary. Yet overall domestic adjustment during the 1970s turned out to be insufficient, resulting in an unsustainable current account deficit of about 4.5 percent of gross domestic product in 1977. In its wake, macroeconomic policies (especially fiscal and wage policies) were tightened and the Austrian schilling was devalued slightly against the Deutschemark. These measures were successful, and, by the time of the second oil crisis, Austrian policy makers were confident enough that they could yet again revalue against the Deutschemark to rein in inflation. This revaluation happened in September 1979, when the schilling was revalued against the Deutschemark by 1.5 percent, followed by a gradual appreciation between September 1979 and late 1981 amounting to some 4.5 percent. Since then the schilling/Deutschemark exchange rate has been practically fixed.

By the late 1970s and early 1980s, policy makers and the social partners saw more clearly the requirements and the depth of measures necessary to make a fixed peg sustainable, and arguments stressing the need for credibility of policy, in particular exchange rate policy, surfaced for the first time. These statements reflected the view that for a small open economy, a simple, straightforward and transparent rule that is understood by the public would be the best way to earn credibility fast and to achieve and maintain price stability. (See Handler, 1989; Hochreiter and Winckler, 1995a and 1995b; Gnan, 1995.) The strategy has been underpinned by a credible commitment by the Oesterreichische Nationalbank to maintain price stability in difficult times and by a broad consensus within society (both employers and employees) that price stability is a necessary condition for growth and employment in the medium term. Moreover, it was understood that the sustainability of the peg (with low economic cost) hinges on fiscal soundness and wage moderation. As a consequence, Austria also could cope with sizable asymmetric shocks.

Hochreiter and Winckler (1995a) deal empirically with the issue of shocks for Austria and find that when the current exchange rate policy was shaped in the early 1970s, asymmetric shocks with regard to Germany dominated. The authors identify the following asymmetric shocks relative to Germany between 1975 and 1985 using cross-section analysis over 20 industrial branches in Austria and Germany:

1975:   Wage shock (unit labor costs: predominantly asymmetric, permanent, negative supply and positive demand shock)

1978:   Restrictive policy measures in Austria to overcome the current account crisis (predominantly asymmetric, temporary, negative demand shock)

1980–82:   Fiscal shock (slightly asymmetric, temporary, positive demand shock)

1980–81:   Wage shock (unit labor costs: asymmetric, permanent, positive supply and negative demand shock)

1982–83:   Debt crisis (predominantly asymmetric, permanent, negative demand shock)

1983–85:   Crisis of nationalized industries (asymmetric, permanent, negative supply shock)

Moreover, the authors' empirical evidence indicates that there is no strong evidence for a significant weakening of this asymmetry since the 1970s. Hence, the criterion of symmetric shocks in an optimum currency area has, with some exceptions, especially 1987 to 1989, not been satisfied for Austria. All tests to determine whether there is a trend toward more symmetry or whether there was a structural change around 1980 produced only negative results. Hence the sustainability of the fixed Deutschemark peg requires real wage flexibility. The authors argue that the Austrian economy exhibits a high degree of such flexibility, due mainly to the Austrian system of social partnership, which is seen as being conducive for a longer term, rule-oriented economic policy.

Knöbl (1990) estimates an augmented Phillips curve for the period 1967 to 1988 for Austria, Denmark, the Netherlands, and Sweden and calculates a ratio of real wage rigidity, which he defines as the relation between the wage elasticity of inflation and the wage elasticity of unemployment. The ratio comes to 0.3 for Sweden, 0.6 for Austria, 1.21 for Denmark, and 1.75 for the Netherlands. These findings support the notion that in Austria, real wages are quite flexible, at least compared to Denmark and the Netherlands.

Hochreiter and Winckler (1995a) employ an indirect test of real wage flexibility. Suppose that shocks are asymmetric and factor mobility as well as real wage flexibility is insufficient. If so, one would expect that the real exchange rate or other economic fundamentals, such as the unemployment rate or the current account of the balance of payments, would fluctuate widely. If, however, these variables, in particular the real exchange rate, are relatively stable in spite of asymmetric shocks and factor immobility, it is an indication that a sufficient degree of real wage flexibility is provided. Indeed, fundamentals in Austria have been rather stable (Handler and Hochreiter, 1996). The same is true for the real exchange rate against the Deutschemark, as is documented in Table 1.1.

Of course, data problems may exist. (In Austria, industrial branches exhibit diverse fluctuations thereby limiting the statistical significance of the correlation coefficients.) Hence in contrast to the reported results, one can still argue that the rising share of intraindustry trade in total trade of Austria with Germany, in particular, the Austrian subcontracting industry for German automotive production, leads to more symmetric shocks (De Grauwe,

Table 1.1: Standard Deviation of Bilateral Real Exchange Rates

Country	January 1980 - March 1987	April 1987 - August 1992	September 1992 - March 1997
Austria	2.96	0.66	0.55
Belgium	5.35	1.14	1.11
Denmark	2.55	1.48	1.88
Finland	5.53	5.78	2.87
France	3.41	0.97	1.37
Great Britain	7.85	5.06	3.08
Ireland	6.04	0.95	3.54
Italy	4.73	3.78	n/a
Netherlands	1.15	1.08	0.96
Portugal	5.07	8.96	n/a
Switzerland	4.68	3.36	n/a
Sweden	7.18	5.42	3.20
Spain	5.31	7.09	2.67

Note: The real exchange rate is defined as an index (Jan. 1980 = 100). Therefore, the results are similar to those obtained using a coefficient of variation.
Source: Hochreiter and Winckler (1995), and authors' calculations.

1992: 31–32).[9] In addition, the degree of openness (see McKinnon, 1963) between Austria and Germany, as measured by foreign trade flows, increased: Between 1973 and 1992, the ratio of exports (imports) of goods to GDP rose from 19.0 percent (25.7 percent) to 24.0 percent (29.3 percent).[10] Germany's share in Austrian exports (imports) increased from 23.1 percent (42.4 percent) to 39.8 percent (42.9 percent). Taking into account that the Deutschemark-zone today also comprises the Netherlands, Belgium, and France, the foreign trade linkage for exports comes to 49.1 percent, while for imports it reaches 53.0 percent.[11]

Exchange Rate Policy since the EU Referendum in 1994

After the positive outcome of the June 1994 referendum, the Oesterreichische Nationalbank was quick to reiterate that there would be no change in the fixed peg. There has also been broad consensus among interest groups and politicians to enter into the core of EMU. Hence Austria—in contrast to Finland and Sweden—joined the exchange rate mechanism (ERM) of the European Monetary System (EMS) as early as 9 January 1995.[12] The Oesterreichische Nationalbank abstained from concluding a special narrow margin agreement with the Bundesbank along Dutch lines because it wanted to signal continuity, that is, that there had been and would be no change in the fixed peg to the Deutschemark.

One of the lessons emanating from the Austrian experience is that credibility has to be earned. As a reward of credibility, the schilling has not been affected by the currency turmoil since 1992, with two minor exceptions. The speculative attack of 1993 quickly burned out as it was based on false premises (wrong information). (For analysis, see Arpa, 1995.)[13] There was another mild attack in the autumn of 1995 surrounding the collapse of the government and the ensuing uncertainties regarding the chances for fiscal consolidation. Again, however, it dissipated quickly.

In the wake of the sharp deprecations of various European currencies—in particular the Italian lire, the Swedish kroner and the Finnish markka—following speculative attacks on these currencies, the broad consensus in Austria regarding the fixed peg temporarily weakened somewhat when some industrialists from most affected manufacturing sectors (paper, forestry) and representatives of the tourist industry called for a weakening of the schilling. While the criticism of the Deutschemark peg in the paper, forestry and most recently the textile industry died down because of the turnaround in profitability due to sizable and painful cost cutting and (in some cases) to re-dimensioning, part of the tourist industry, which faces severe structural problems, continues to call for a weakening of the schilling against the Deutschemark.[14] In our opinion, these arguments are based on the false premise that the problems in the tourist industry are due predominantly to exchange rate-induced relative price changes rather than a shift in preferences away from Austrian tourist exports.[15]

The response by the National Bank and the social partners to such calls for a softer exchange rate policy, echoing the arguments already used in the late 1970s and early 1980s, is as follows: An Austrian schilling devaluation would affect all sectors while the exchange rate movements of other currencies affect only some sectors, and this to a strongly varying degree. In any event, devaluation would give only very short-term respite while having significant long-term costs for the economy as a whole (especially the budget) in form of increased risk premiums on interest rates. In addition, such a move would run counter to the need for structural adjustment, which has become necessary in view of the changed international environment and Austria's EU accession.

At the same time, however, the size and speed of the exchange rate changes (for example, the Italian lire depreciated by nearly 20 percent during the first half of 1995 but appreciated by about 20 percent during the first half of 1996), the slow pass-through of exchange rate changes to domestic inflation in these countries, and the opening of the frontiers to direct personal imports as a consequence of EU membership cause considerable short-term adjustment costs. Most affected are the forestry and paper industries, as well as the tourist industry, which also suffers from a change in preferences of both the populations in the countries that traditionally furnish a large part of the clientele (Germans) and of Austrians who increasingly go abroad. Direct personal imports have affected especially shops in those areas near the frontier—Carinthia, Salzburg, the Tyrol, and Vorarlberg—where people have reacted strongly not only to changes in relative prices but also to wider varieties of goods offered in Italy or Germany. Interestingly, it appears that the demands voiced by parts of industry in response to the sharp depreciation of the Italian lire and other currencies are no longer to call for a weakening of the Austrian schilling but rather to speed up the move to stage 3 of EMU, which would prevent such currency swings in a large part of the market, at least.[16]

In the EMU context, the following lessons seem to emanate from the Austrian experience:

1. Successful stabilization policy (at low cost) requires a broad political consensus about the desirability of price stability and the policy mix to achieve it.
2. For a small, open economy, a fixed peg provides a clear, transparent, and simple strategy that is understood and supported by policy makers, interest groups, and the public.

3. In order to peg, optimum currency area arguments are perhaps less important than "Maastricht-type" economic policies including real wage flexibility to be able to cope with asymmetric shocks.
4. Credibility has to be earned.

The Role of the Social Partners

As has been noted already, the social partners were involved in the assessment of the economic adjustment needs of an eventual EU membership right from the beginning, and they have maintained their pro-EU position ever since. Their support is, to a large extent, based on the expected long-term economic benefits of EU membership and the desire of the social partners to smooth the quite painful, but unavoidable, short-term adjustment measures. Two particular examples are the support measures for agriculture and for parts of industry.

Against this background it appears worthwhile to review the unique features of the Austrian social partnership system. It is based on two pillars: On substance, the system is based on consensus in matters of economic and social policy; and on form, it is based on dialogue aimed at consensus.

The social partnership encompasses the major social groups and constitutes an informal and voluntary institutional forum not regulated by law. It relies on producer group coordination, highly centralized wage bargaining, and consensus policies as well as compulsory membership in various chambers.[17] Its main function is to elaborate solutions to economic and social questions. Its success is based on its ability to internalize the macroeconomic benefits of stabilization policies successfully by neutralizing the opposition of losing interest groups (Froats, 1995). Social partnership therefore covers much more than "incomes policy" (in the Anglo-Saxon sense).

The social partnership is embodied in the Joint Commission for wages and prices (the "Parity Commission") and its three subcommittees (prices, wages, and the Economic and Social Advisory Board), of which the subcommittee on prices has been reduced in scope to some prices in the sheltered sector. In each body the social partners are represented, guaranteeing parity between employers and employees as well as between the Social Democratic Party and the People's Party. Participation is strictly voluntary. Decisions are taken unanimously, with the government representative being excluded from voting.

Despite its political foundations, its economic success is due to sound underlying economics. In fact, "social partnership economics" is nothing more than basic economics reduced to its first principles:

1. The highly centralized wage negotiations are based on the assumption that real wage increases depend on productivity advances and not so much on nominal wage claims.

2. There is an understanding that without reasonable price stability, economic growth may not be sustainable. A lower rate of inflation also is assumed to reduce the risk of volatility and hence to lengthen the time horizon for investors. In this context, trade unions can support an independent central bank (with price stability as its prime objective) because in the longer term this is seen to bolster employment.[18]

3. There is no free lunch in the longer term, and therefore the scope for running fiscal deficits is limited. At the same time, it is recognized that "excessive" fiscal deficits may endanger macroeconomic stability, which is—as has been pointed out—not in the trade unions' interest.

With these principles in mind, it comes as no surprise that the social partners have consistently supported EU membership and are in favor of Austria joining the hard core of European Monetary Union, provided that the single currency is at least as stable as the Austrian schilling.[19]

Since the inception of the social partnership in 1957, its tasks have changed continuously. By now, for example, price controls have been virtually abolished. Interestingly, and in contrast to other countries such as Sweden, the centralized collective wage bargaining process has not broken down although the 14 specialized unions are, in principle, free to set their wage claims independently. In practice, the president of the Trade Union Federation has the decisive voice in making wage claims because he has to allow the individual unions to open wage negotiations. If he deems the wage demands of the union in question to be "too high" (based on the productivity advances of the sector and the overall consumer price inflation rate), he simply refuses to open wage negotiations. This, in fact, did happen from time to time. More recently, the emphasis has shifted somewhat. In the mid-1990s, the union that first opens wage negotiations after the summer pause—usually the metal workers' union—in effect sets the "wage guideline." Its wage agreement, in practice, sets the pattern for other negotiations.

The centralized wage bargaining process has been based on the notion of solidarity, implying forgone contracted wage increases of sectors with above-average productivity increases to the benefit of sectors with below-average productivity advances. As a consequence, one could expect (apart from wage distortions in the longer term) that sectoral wage differentials would not move much over time. However, this has not been the case in Austria. The reason is that contracted wage increases have been supplemented/offset by substantial positive/negative wage drift, as can be seen from Figure 1.1.

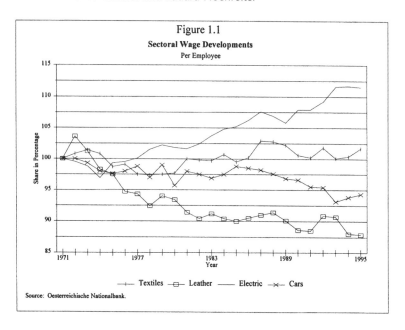

Figure 1.1

Sectoral Wage Developments
Per Employee

Textiles —+—   Leather —□—   Electric ——   Cars —×—

Source: Oesterreichische Nationalbank.

As society has become more fragmented and the political landscape has changed tremendously, the influence of the social partners has declined over time. The general drive for deregulation and liberalization, for European integration, and toward a more heterogeneous society not only have made many of the traditional tasks of the social partnership obsolete (for example, price control) but also have led to political demands for abandoning compulsory membership, among other things. Such a move could—according to conventional Austrian thinking—seriously affect the smooth working of consensus politics.

If the social partnership broke down, a new set of rules would have to be designed to solve economic and social questions—for example, the wage bargaining process, structural policies, and so forth. In our view, such a development could cause significant social strife in the transition period, as has been demonstrated in Sweden.

In response to the severe criticism of social partners from some quarters (among others, the Freedom Party and the Greens), including demands to abolish compulsory membership, the various chambers have initiated a substantial reform program. Between November 1995 and mid-1996, the various chambers asked their constituents if membership should remain compulsory or become voluntary. Perhaps surprisingly, the membership approved the status quo (compulsory membership) with impressive margins.[20]

In addition, the social partners showed strong signs of life in the 1996 budget negotiations, when they were called upon by the government to propose measures to cut the expected 1996 budget deficit by nearly 1.5 percent of GDP. The social partners were not only able to deliver their proposals on time, but, more important, they did not shy away from painful measures affecting their own clientele.[21]

Finally, Schuberth and Wehinger (1997) argue that the wage formation process in Austria could fundamentally change with the changeover to EMU, because the social partners, in particular the trade unions, will have to adjust to the new monetary policy rule of the European Central Bank (ECB). Although no decision will be taken before the establishment of the ECB in 1998, it is already clear that the new monetary policy rule will be different from the exchange rate rule that has been followed by the Oesterreichische Nationalbank. Up to now the wage formation process has been anchored on the fixed peg of the schilling to the Deutschemark and on the incorporation of the trade unions and other social partnership organizations into the monetary policy decision making process through their position as shareholders of the Oesterreichische Nationalbank (Hochreiter, 1994a). The changeover to EMU will pose a big challenge for the social partners.

Yet, all in all, in our assessment, there appears to be a good chance that the social partners will be able to adapt to the new economic and political environments and thereby gain a new lease of life. We are therefore of the opinion that there is a future for a revamped social partnership in Austria.

In an Austrian context, we can foresee the following tasks for social partnership:

1. Satisfying the demand for an institutional design that allows consensus solutions to economic and social problems as opposed to solutions forced top-down. We believe that economically sound compromises are, in general, less costly than forced solutions.
2. Contributing to the institutional framework in which competition can flourish—a liberalized economy also needs a set of rules to work efficiently.
3. Policing adherence to that framework.
4. Devising and supporting the implementation of (supply-side) measures to enhance productivity—this point appears to be especially important in an EU context. As the Maastricht convergence criteria put a lid on macroeconomic policies, microeconomic measures are the only policy freedom left at a national level. It has been the Austrian experience (with some exceptions, such as the nationalized industries in the 1970s) that the social partners have been able to agree on policies that strengthen the supply side and hence growth.

An important aspect in this context concerns commensurate wage developments.

5. Contributing to the "targeting" of social expenditure.

Fiscal Issues

The stagnation of economic activity in 1993, the measures taken to counterbalance the cyclical downswing, and the 1994 tax reform pushed central government net borrowing up from 3.3 percent of GDP in 1992 to 4.6 percent in 1993 and 4.4 percent in 1994. About half of this development can be attributed to automatic stabilizers (Genser and Holzmann, 1995). Government officials justified the size of the deficit as the unavoidable cost of keeping the economy from sliding into a full-fledged recession. To stimulate investment demand, tax allowances were raised temporarily for investments undertaken between February 1993 and March 1994. From mid-1993, a new system of federal nursing care assistance was introduced, partly paid for by an increase in social security contributions. The second phase of the tax reform, which became effective in 1994, brought the permanent abrogation of certain taxes (among others the property tax) and some relief in personal income taxation.

General government net borrowing mirrored the developments in the federal budget: As a percentage of nominal GDP, it jumped from 2 percent in 1992 to more than 6 percent in 1995. After a restrictive course in 1992, when the consolidation of the structural balance dominated over expansionary automatic stabilizers, structural consolidation efforts weakened in 1993 and ceased in 1994. (See Table 1.2.)

Additional strain has been put on public finances by Austria's accession to the EU. Austria was a net contributor to the EU budget, to the amount of some 13.6 billion schillings (or 0.57 percent of Austrian GDP) in 1995. This amount is likely to rise to about 18 billion schillings in 1998.

Table 1.2: General Government Fiscal Policy Stance (percent GDP)

	1992	1993	1994
Annual change in general government net borrowing (percent)	-0.4	0.9	0.9
of which			
• due to automatic stabilizers	0.8	1.5	0.7
• due to change in structural balance	-1.2	-0.6	0.2
Source: OECD (1994a).			

Gross contributions from public Austrian budgets are estimated at 23.6 billion schillings for 1995 (33 billion schillings for 1998), while refunds from the EU budget amounted to some 10 billion schillings in 1995 (an estimated 17 billion schillings in 1998). The federal budget carried an exceptional burden in 1995, by providing partial relief from temporary adjustment costs for the agricultural and manufacturing sectors. Combined with the direct contributions to Brussels, the overall net effect of EU membership on the federal budget in 1995 amounted to more than 30 billion schillings. Because of rapidly diminishing adjustment aid, this burden was expected to decline to some 16 billion schillings in 1996 and 1997. (See Breuss, Guger, and Lehner, 1995; Lehner, 1995; WIFO, 1994; and Wirtschaftskammer, 1996.)

The first attempt to consolidate the budget in 1995 was inadequate for regaining fiscal stability. Austria quickly found itself in the group of countries subject to the excessive deficit procedure according to Article 104c of the Maastricht Treaty. Austria thus is obliged to stick to a convergence program that is closely monitored by the European Commission.

To conform with Article 104c, the government established a medium-term budget program for the period from 1995 to 1998 that showed that achieving the deficit target and the debt criterion would be rather intricate. Although the government was firm in its goal to slash expenditures and not to raise taxes to any significant extent, affected interest groups were partially successful in opposing crucial elements of the budgetary consolidation proposal. As the political debate progressed, the government seemed more and more unlikely to arrive at the deficit target without also relying on revenue-raising measures.

Learning from the quarrels over the 1995 budget, the federal government elected in late 1995 agreed to a two-year fiscal consolidation program. According to this program, which was passed by parliament, the central government deficit of more than 5 percent of GDP in 1995 was to be slashed to 2.7 percent of GDP by 1997. Considering the deficits of other public households in Austria, this would be sufficient, if implemented successfully, to fulfill the Maastricht deficit reference value. However, the ratio of public debt to GDP of more than 69 percent in 1995 would rise further if not contained by the sale of public assets. (See Table 1.3).

Based on the voted budget, the government proposed a new convergence program to the European Community (Bundesministerium für Finanzen, 1996), which was approved by the Economic and Finance Ministers' Council of July 1996. According to this program, major items of the budget consolidation are (with supposed effect on the budget deficit 1997 in parentheses):

Table 1.3: Budget Projections (percent GDP, on accrual basis)

	1994	1995	1996	1997	1998	1999
	Central Government					
Net borrowing	4.4	5.3	4.1	2.7	2.6	2.3
Debt outstanding	58.7	62.0	64.4	65.5	n/a	n/a
	General Government					
Net borrowing	4.5	6.2	4.5	3.0	2.9	2.6
Debt outstanding	65.2	69.2	71.3	72.8	74.7	74.4

Note: Debt outstanding includes ASFINAG and Bundesfonds, but disregards possible debt reductions in the wake of privatization.
Sources: Schebeck (1996); Federal Ministry of Finance; WIFO forecasting exercise; authors' calculations.

Expenditure-Reducing Measures:
• Cuts in public consumption through virtually freezing nominal salaries and reducing the staff by 11,000 persons (16 billion schillings)
• Reducing family allowances for long-term students (6.3 billion schillings)
• Freezing contributions to the nursing care system (1.9 billion schillings)
• Stiffening the conditions for obtaining unemployment benefits (4.2 billion schillings)
• Increasing the self-financing capacity of the pension systems for entrepreneurs and farmers (18.4 billion schillings)
• Freezing government subsidies (2.8 billion schillings)
• Changes in government contributions to public utilities and the subsidized mortgage loan system (13.0 bn schillings)
• Changes in earmarked government contributions to various funds (4.0 billion schillings)

Revenue-Raising Measures (part of the revenues raised will
accrue to regional and local governments):
• Abandoning exemptions from wage and personal income taxation (22.9 billion schillings)
• Raising the minimum level of corporate income taxation but maintaining the marginal tax rate at 34 percent (8.1 billion schillings)
• Introducing an energy tax on electricity and natural gas (7 billion schillings)

- Raising the flat tax rate on interest income from 22 to 25 percent (3 billion schillings)
- Changes in the value-added taxation system (2 billion schillings)
- Other revenue raising measures (3.8 billion schillings)

Unemployment and Structural Adjustment

The employment situation in Austria has for many years been markedly more favorable than in other industrial countries. Although unemployment in Austria has increased over a number of years, it has remained much below that of most West European countries. For some time until the late 1980s, this could be attributed to the social consensus, which favored labor hoarding over a hire-and-fire system.[22] In addition, foreign labor served as a buffer against cyclical changes of demand; following more restrictive legislation in 1993 against the influx of foreign workers, in the future this situation will not continue to the same extent. Due to the recent trough, the unemployment rate climbed from 3.6 percent in 1992 to 4.4 percent in 1994 and further to 4.6 percent in 1995.

As employment has been on the rise for most of the time, higher unemployment resulted from an expansion of the labor supply. Some of this increase stems from the inflow of foreign workers following the opening of the Eastern borders, but much is to be attributed to the rise in participation rates (from 68.2 percent in 1991 to 69.8 percent in 1994) as a reaction to cyclically depressed income growth.[23] Further increases in participation rates are likely when the government succeeds in lifting the currently rather low average retirement age of some 58 years (in order to consolidate the financing of the pension system), and more part-time jobs are provided for, and accepted by, the working population. Concurrently, policy measures such as early retirement plans, generous provisions for invalid pensions, and ceilings to foreign employment have been adopted to reduce the labor force.

One of the often-cited reasons for comparatively low and stable unemployment rates in Austria is the flexibility of real wages. As has been mentioned, this is also an effect of social partnership and the macroeconomic orientation of the centralized trade union system. However, there seems to be a lack of sufficient flexibility on the microlevel to cope with the sudden supply of low-wage labor from Eastern countries. Free movement of labor within the EU will in the medium-term create pressure to reshape the wage-formation process in such a way as to provide for more microflexibility while preserving the undisputed virtues of macroflexibility. In the short term, no significant migration of cheap labor would endanger the precarious stability of the Austrian labor market.

To combat unemployment, but also to achieve other policy goals, such as cost reductions for enterprises, structural adjustment policies have become increasingly important as compared with stabilization policies, and thus will be encompassed more and more in the decision-making process on a European level. With national borders losing their function as a shelter, it has become obvious to all EU member countries that competitiveness of their industrial base will in future rest on cost-efficient companies and the location quality of a country. In Austria too, improving such quality is one of the policy goals that will necessitate policy action in the following areas:

1. Speeding up technological innovations through more target-oriented public aid
2. Supporting facilities for job-oriented postschool education and adult training, including a restructuring of the university system to provide for more specialized courses of the "Fachhochschule" type
3. Providing a modern and cost-efficient infrastructure by deregulating natural and legal monopolies in the transport and telecommunications sector (the railway system, the postal system) as well as in the energy sector (including liberalization of administered electricity prices)
4. Realizing cost-saving simplifications of the legal and administrative system, particularly by deregulating opening hours of shops and increasing working-time flexibility
5. Enhancing competition by harmonizing Austrian with EU competition law and policy
6. Continuing privatization of state-owned companies, particularly in the nationalized industries and in the banking sector
7. Cutting back on the number of, and the incentive system for, civil servants while improving the quality and scope of government services

The result of policy measures in these areas should be a visible modernization of business life in Austria. Of course, some of the fields just mentioned touch vital interests of the social partners, and the government almost certainly will have to fight an uphill battle to achieve this goal.

Some help is being provided from the EU, which presses for legal harmonization but also directs structural funds to ailing industries and regions. Austria has put particular emphasis on the preparation of structural programs for EU cofinancing of investment and labor market projects. National subsidization schemes have been adjusted as to conform to the EU regulations concerning cofinancing.

Concluding Remarks and Outlook

Austria, a country in the center of Europe and at the crossroads of European culture, has experienced a relatively smooth transition into the EU. The step-by-step approach via the European Economic Area has helped, particularly in political terms, to overcome the antagonism toward adjustment, toward opening up to "European" thinking, and toward increased access to, but also competition from, international markets. In this context, Austria's social partners have played a decisive role in formulating the principles for EU access and in preparing the groundwork for a positive outcome of the 1994 accession referendum. After having joined the EU, uncertainties over the current and future legal and administrative systems remain latent, particularly for those who are not traditionally involved in international business, such as consumers and small and medium-size enterprises. This uncertainty concerns, among other things, the relative importance and the future application of harmonization versus mutual recognition, and, in case of harmonization, of directives versus regulations. But there is also a rising awareness of Austria's possibilities to influence the decision processes in Brussels, including lobbying by interest groups.

So far as European economic policy is concerned, there is agreement in Austria that the Maastricht Treaty should not be opened again. Nonetheless, as in some other countries, there is a discussion relating to a possible extension of the current monetary and fiscal criteria to some indicator of real convergence, such as the unemployment rate. This aspect has, as was to be expected, particularly been emphasized by the Austrian trade unions.

Austria's experience with the fixed peg of the schilling to the Deutschemark might prove to be a useful case study about feasible policy responses to make such a peg sustainable in adverse circumstances. Sound fiscal policies, real wage flexibility, and sustained measures to improve the supply side and raise productivity have proven to be the keys to success. The Austrian system of social partnership, which is based on centralized wage bargaining and continuous involvement in policy formulation and the decision making process, is, in many instances, conducive to structural change and has facilitated the maintenance of sound economic policies. In order to survive, however, the social partnership has to adapt to the new deregulated, liberalized environment of a much more heterogeneous society and will have to learn to think in European dimensions. It also will have to adapt to the new monetary policy rule of the ECB, which—for the Austrian social partners—will involve a new anchoring of the wage formation process. If it succeeds, and there are good indications that it can, there also might be useful lessons to be learned for Europe as a whole.

In the EU, Austria has joined the group of hard-core countries, and there is widespread political consensus to keep this position and to meet the Maastricht (fiscal) criteria in time. The collapse of the government in October 1995 because of disagreements about the measures to be taken to consolidate the federal budget shows that this task is taken seriously. Therefore, the current government and the social partners have arrived at a credible fiscal consolidation package—also in the judgement of financial markets—which makes Austria a candidate again for immediate EMU membership.

Austria is striving to become an active member of the EU by participating in the Intergovernmental Conference and through early preparation for the Austrian presidency of the EU to take place in the second half of 1998. In accordance with the policy priorities of the Council of Ministers (formulated in particular at the Essen European Council in December 1994) and the public opinion in this country, Austria will contribute to the search for measures to fight unemployment, to enforce transnational environmental protection, and to solve regional problems of transit traffic.

Notes

1. The views expressed in this chapter are the personal opinions of the authors and not the official positions either of the Ministry of Economic Affairs or of the Oesterreichische Nationalbank. The chapter draws heavily on Handler and Hochreiter (1996).
2. This is in sharp contrast to the 1970s, when raising public and private demand through expansionary policies increased actual growth. These expansionary policies had to be aborted in the late 1970s, when the current account deficit of the balance of payments became unsustainable.
3. Cumulative surpluses during the period from 1985 to 1989 were only about 10 billion schillings. Eastern Europe includes both Yugoslavia and the former Soviet Union. Kramer (1993) calculates a gain of 60,000 to 65,000 and at the same time a loss of 50,000 jobs in the three to five years starting in 1992.
4. About half of the increase of the (federal) budget deficit in 1993 and 1994 can be attributed to structural factors.
5. Based on poll data provided by Plasser and Ulram (1994), Plavsak (1995) argues that, in contrast to the "national elites," the population at large was left uninformed and thus had no opportunity to participate in the decision-making process on equal grounds. This is true only to the extent that the "elites" also had difficulty gathering relevant information. The piecemeal dissemination of information via the social partner organizations and the media may at times have created disturbances and uncertainties, but cannot be interpreted as a deliberate withholding of information.
6. According to Fessel+GFK (1995), poll results of May 1995 reveal that in a new referendum, some 50 percent of voters would have declined EU membership while only 42 percent would have supported it.

7. The Freedom Party gained nearly 7 percentage points, making it equal in support to the SPÖ (with 29.2 percent) and the ÖVP (with 29.6 percent).

8. The indicator basket initially contained six currencies representing the currencies of nine countries; the Deutschemark, Swiss franc, Dutch guilder (also representing the Belgian franc), Swedish kronor (also representing the Danish kroner), Italian lire and British pound.

9. At the beginning of the 1970s there was practically no Austrian subcontracting industry. By contrast, in 1992, some 85 percent of the value of Austria's car imports were offset by exports of the automotive sub-contracting industry.

10. Foreign trade flows typically are employed to proxy the degree of openness, which is a simple but theoretically unsatisfactory method. To be theoretically correct, the share of tradeable goods and services would have to be calculated; very likely, this share also increased considerably during the last 20 years.

11. Accordingly, Brandner and Jäger (1992: 40) report that Austria's real GDP growth rate has become more symmetric with that of Germany, in particular after 1979.

12. Finland joined the ERM on 14 October 1996.

13. Note also that there were some capital outflows after the collapse of the government in October 1995. This evidently reflects increased uncertainty regarding the fiscal course of the future government to be formed after the elections on 17 December 1995.

14. The textile industry, which was heavily discriminated against by the EU Association Agreements with reform countries of Eastern Europe, benefited a great deal from Austria's entry in the EU. In addition, this branch of industry undertook strenuous efforts to cut costs and raise productivity.

15. In a very interesting study on the effects of the Swiss franc's appreciation on economic activity, Tatom (1996) reports that he did not find a negative relationship between the franc's exchange rate and output of traded goods or nominal exports, *especially tourism* (emphasis added).

16. An opinion survey of Austrian industry regarding EU membership after the first six months showed that three-quarters of the export-oriented firms covered in the survey are in favor or strongly in favor of a common currency (*Salzburger Nachrichten*, 18 August 1995).

17. Participants in the social partnership include the Federal Economic Chamber, the Federal Chamber of Labor, the Standing Committee of the Presidents of the Austrian Chambers of Agriculture, and the Austrian Federation of Trade Unions. There is also a social partner that relies on voluntary membership— the trade unions. (The Austrian Federation of Industrialists is not formally a social partner but is represented on a Federal Economic Chamber ticket).

18. There is also a political reason for the unions' support of price stability: It is generally accepted that the hyperinflation after the end of World War I destroyed the middle class and thereby laid the groundwork for the rise of fascism in Austria.

19. It must be pointed out, however, that if the social partners do not arrive at a consensus, social partnership can be detrimental to structural adjustment. Alternatively, it must be recognized that social partnership solutions also may be "structure-conserving."

20. Referenda by the Economic Chambers in the Länder were held between November 1995 and January 1996 and yielded heavy majorities, ranging from 74 percent in Styria to 89 percent in the Burgenland; between 30 percent (Vienna) and 53 percent (Burgenland) of the members cast their vote in favor of maintaining the status quo, that is, compulsory membership (cf. *Die Presse,* 2 February 1992: 8). Referenda in the Chamber of Labor will be held during 1996. The first ballots took place in March and April 1996 and, as had been the case for the Chambers of Commerce, also resulted in members' voting in favor of maintaining compulsory membership by a very high margin (Burgenland: 93.2 percent; Carinthia: 92.3 percent; participation 75 percent and 60 percent respectively; *Die Presse,* 7 May 1996).

21. There is some disagreement about how substantial the spending cuts the social partners agreed upon really are.

22. Up to now, early retirement and "sliding pension" schemes have helped conceal the unemployment problem.

23. In contrast to immigration from the East, no measurable influx from other EU countries has been observed. Data on participation rates according to OECD (1994a) estimates.

CHAPTER TWO

Belgium: Keeping Up with the Pack?

Erik Jones

In the run-up to the May 1995 parliamentary elections, Prime Minister Jean-Luc Dehaene contended that the choice before voters was about whom was best prepared to lead Belgium into the first group of countries to form an economic and monetary union (EMU). And while much of the pre-electoral debate centered on reforming welfare state institutions and gaining control over the country's mountain of public debt, virtually all sides of the political spectrum agreed on membership in EMU as a major objective (Goosens, 1995). Of course, Belgian public finances are long overdue for an overhaul, which will cause pain for virtually every class of voters. The consolidation of Belgian public financing would have to take place whether Europe was headed for EMU or not. The point is that membership in Europe's select monetary club is the biggest carrot Belgian politicians have to offer voters in exchange for continuing austerity. The threat of exclusion from EMU is the stick.

Early participation in EMU has become a litmus test for the effectiveness of the Belgian federal government. Belgium is a founding member of the European Union as well as its antecedents, the European Economic Community, Euratom, and the European Coal and Steel Community. Just under two-thirds of all Belgians support membership in the EU:[1] Belgian national politicians are, on the whole, staunch advocates of a federal Europe (Eurobarometer, 1994: 11),[2] and Belgian industry—which exports almost 40 percent of its total production to European markets—is more integrated with the other member states of the Union than the industry of any other country. Many fear that a failure to join in the first round of

EMU will signal the end of Belgium's central role in Europe, politically and economically.

The danger is that achieving the Maastricht criteria will be an uphill struggle and Belgium cannot rely on being given exceptional treatment. When German finance minister Theo Waigel suggested a strengthening of the convergence criteria in autumn 1995, Belgium had little choice but to go along in spite of the difficulties more stringent convergence criteria threaten to impose. While Belgium seems to have little difficulty conforming to the monetary requirements for convergence—those relating to consumer price inflation and long-term interest rates—its problems paying off the mountain of outstanding public debt are considerable. (See Table I.3.) Indeed, this dichotomy holds even if we relax the mechanical interpretation of the 60 percent ratio of debt to gross domestic product (GDP) and adopt a numerical standard for "sufficient downward convergence" like that proposed by Gros (1996b).

This chapter examines the relationship between Belgium and EMU from the Belgian point of view. It has five sections. The first looks at the exchange rate preferences of political parties, both historical and contemporary. The second examines how Belgium has managed its external price competitiveness within the context of a hard-currency regime. The third describes the implications of social welfare reform for regional solidarity. The fourth looks at the restructuring of the Belgian welfare state. The final section returns to the larger question of the role of European integration in the domestic politics of Belgium.

Consensus on "Hard" Currency

Historically, Belgian political elites from all points on the spectrum have preferred a strong currency to a weak one and have resisted devaluations. In economic terms, this preference is logical given the extensive import penetration in Belgian consumer goods and manufacturing input markets.[3] Currency depreciation or devaluation leads to a rise in consumer price inflation and production costs, cutting into real wages and corporate profits. Thus while there is a relatively high price elasticity of demand for Belgian exports, Belgian labor and industry leaders have little confidence in the effects of depreciation/devaluation on export competitiveness and great concern about the effects on domestic costs and prices. (See Ullmo, 1989: 60.)

Faith in the strong franc, however, often has exceeded clear economic justification, whether among its proponents on the left or on the right. For example, in a memorable exchange about the virtues of devaluation in 1949, Belgian Socialist leader Achille van Acker argued that any reduction of the external value of the franc would accelerate inflation, lower exports, increase unemployment, raise the cost of imports, and lower tax receipts (Eyskens, 1993: 269). Since that time, the symbolic importance of the strong franc as an indicator of underlying economic health has only increased—sometimes leading to bizarre rhetoric on the part of embarrassed Belgian finance ministers. In response to the appreciation of the Deutschemark in the latter 1970s, for example, Liberal finance minister Willy De Clercq argued that the Belgian currency was the "hardest" in Europe because it had moved neither up nor down (De Clercq, 1978).

Throughout the turbulent 1970s and 1980s, Belgian policy makers strove to consolidate the relationship between the franc and the Deutschemark first in the "snake"—a system for coordinating European exchange rates in the 1970s—and then in the European Monetary System (EMS). During the maiden realignment of the exchange rate mechanism (ERM) in September 1979, Germany had to insist that Belgium accept depreciation that neither the Belgian National Bank or Wilfried Martens's center-left cabinet desired (Gros and Thygesen, 1992: 73). Later, during the crisis leading up the February 1982 devaluation, the domestic debate was between National Bank president Cecil de Strycker, who advocated a deep devaluation "once and for all," and Christian trade union economists, who wanted to make the minimum necessary readjustment. Neither side could be accused of seeking a competitive devaluation with any real enthusiasm. (De Strycker resisted any change in the currency until only days before the devaluation took place.) Rather, they recognized the adjustment as a necessary, albeit humiliating, corrective (Jones, 1995: 176).

The general consensus on maintaining exchange rate stability can be seen in the Belgian National Bank's impressive management of month-to-month exchange rate fluctuations. The bank assumed responsibility for exchange rate policy in 1973, when the final collapse of the Bretton Woods system made it impossible for every change in the parity of the franc to be ratified in parliament. And despite Belgium's widespread reputation for currency weakness in the late 1970s and early 1980s, the National Bank supported the franc-Deutschemark exchange rate more consistently than currencies with stronger reputations, such as the Dutch guilder. This can be seen in Table 2.1, which shows the short-term variability for Deutschemark exchange rates of a number of European countries. The different columns in the table reflect periods in the history of European monetary cooperation, including the run-up to the EMS, the months prior to François Mitterrand's famous decision to choose for Europe and against the "Albanian option," and the relative stability that ended with the exchange rate crises of 1992 and 1993.

National Bank efforts to stabilize the franc-Deutschemark exchange rate culminated in the June 1990 decision to make the currency peg "official."

Table 2.1: Short-term Deutschemark Exchange Rate Variability

Country	February 1975 - August 1979	September 1979 - March 1983	April 1983 - January 1987	February 1987 - December 1993
Belgium	0.52	1.34	0.39	0.55
Netherlands	0.66	0.72	0.40	0.47
Denmark	1.03	1.00	0.59	0.89
France	1.71	1.57	0.91	0.63
Ireland	2.68	1.09	1.25	1.03
Italy	2.97	1.27	0.99	1.93

Note: Variability is the standard deviation of month-to-month log changes [t - (t-1)].
Source: IMF.

For more than three years, Belgium was able to shadow closely on the mark; at times politicians even alluded to currencies stronger than the German.[4] Belgian pride ended abruptly, however, when the speculative attack on the franc in the August 1993 EMS crisis forced the currency off its peg. From the end of the July until the end of November, the Belgian franc lost 3.6 percent of its value against the German currency. Nevertheless, the consensus on the strong franc remained, and by December the franc was fluctuating within its "narrow band" of 2.25 percent despite the less strict requirements of the reformed EMS.[5]

The job of the National Bank is complicated by the dependence of the Belgian economy on developments in the economies of its three largest trading partners: Germany, France, and the Netherlands. In 1990, for example, these three countries combined accounted for 55 percent of Belgian exports, with 21 percent going to Germany, 20 percent to France, and 14 percent to the Netherlands. Thus, whenever there is currency realignment between the Belgian franc and one of these countries, the external value of the franc comes under pressure.

From 1972 to 1983, the Belgian and Dutch currencies floated jointly between the French franc and the Deutschemark. While the bilateral franc-guilder exchange rate was stable on a month-to-month basis, Belgium's three-way dependence ensured that the franc would show the influence of both France and Germany over the longer term. Whenever there was severe instability in the relationship between the French franc and the Deutschemark, the pressure on the Belgian franc to realign was greater than on the guilder. In this way, the Belgian franc tended to follow the longer-term development of the French franc and the Dutch guilder tended to remain more closely aligned with the Deutschemark. However, the fact that the Dutch gave priority to stabilizing exchange rates in the Benelux rather than the guilder-Deutschemark parity often served to lessen the speculative pressure on Belgium. (See chapter 7 for the history of Dutch exchange rate policy.) After 1983, the Dutch central bank tightened the relationship between the guilder and the Deutschemark. This change in Dutch exchange rate policy effectively increased the pull of the Deutschemark on the Belgian franc as well. As a consequence, Belgium began to gravitate more toward the German currency while still remaining vulnerable to the fluctuations of the French franc. The "hard" EMS after 1987 promised to eliminate the vulnerability of the Belgian franc altogether. Nevertheless, the 1993 speculative attack on the French franc spread quickly to Belgium and, in doing so, demonstrated that Belgium's dual dependence on French and Deutschemark zone markets remains an important consideration even in spite of an impressive current account surplus (equal to 5 percent of GDP in 1993).

Competitiveness and International Trade

The obvious question to ask is how Belgium has been able to survive with such a large export sector, a high price elasticity of demand for exports, and a strong currency. Often, as during the 1970s, the answer has been "not very well." Because Belgium has not traditionally enjoyed fast productivity growth relative to other European countries, it has faced a constant battle to hold down its real effective exchange rate measured in terms of unit labor costs. When the real effective exchange rate appreciated—as during the 1950s and again during the 1970s—Belgian growth rates slowed relative to other European countries. Reciprocally, when the real effective exchange rate depreciated—as during the 1960s and 1980s—Belgian growth tended to accelerate. Thus the challenge for growth-minded Belgian politicians has been to manipulate the real effective exchange rate without depreciating the nominal exchange rate.

For students of small-country (political) economics, the Belgian answer is a familiar one—negotiated price-incomes policies implemented by representatives of industry, labor, and government. (See, for example, Katzenstein, 1985.) The Belgian government has sought to control the growth of real labor costs by negotiating wage ceilings with labor representatives in exchange for investment commitments on the part of industry and the extension of social welfare benefits. This practice may sound surprising to some. Belgian trade unions belong to national or "peak" organizations but are divided both sectorally and regionally. And while it is true that the peak organizations have considerable influence in government, it is less obvious that the state would be able to control sectoral wage negotiations in the interests of price-incomes policy. (See, for example, Calmfors and Driffil, 1988.)

The Belgian government has been able to effect price income policies through a careful combination of corporatist intermediation and legislated wage ceilings that spread sectoral agreements to cover national labor markets. Such "interprofessional" agreements almost invariably result in the suppression of nominal wage growth. And by inducing trade unions to moderate real wage claims, the government was able to control the real effective exchange rate.

The difficulty in relying on corporatist institutions to enforce wage moderation lies in generating a willingness to cooperate on both sides of the social partnership. In the 1960s, the economic situation and particularly the tight labor market conditions gave strong incentives for industry to participate but weaker incentives for labor. The government compensated for this by offering to broaden the welfare state in return for trade union cooperation. During the 1980s, the situation was reversed as loose labor markets already had begun to exert downward pressure on wages. The government encouraged industry participation with the promise of greater social harmony and lower non-wage labor costs. In both instances, however, the linchpin for success was the existence of well-disciplined peak organizations capable of enforcing the agreement across diverse industrial and labor groups.

In the 1990s, the Belgian government faces three fundamental difficulties in maintaining the price competitiveness of manufacturing exports while adhering to a strong currency policy. First, the Belgian trade unions are beginning to act more like "small" rather than "large" interest groups, according to the categories described by Olson (1971). Thus while labor representatives continue to adhere to the strong currency preference described earlier, they have adopted a more narrow position on income redistribution in the face of wide-scale structural unemployment. Where in the 1960s and 1980s labor leaders retained some confidence that wage moderation would increase levels of employment and—in the longer run—productivity, in the 1990s their outlook is less sanguine. Labor leaders express little faith that industry will translate lower wages into more jobs, and constituent trade unions have begun to struggle for the preservation of real wages in spite of rising levels of unemployment. By implication, the government has had to take more direct control over the questions of "competitiveness" within a hard-currency regime rather than relying on more indirect corporate intermediation, and it is paying a high price in terms of social harmony.

Because neither the trade unions (for collective action reasons) nor industrial associations (for financial reasons) can shoulder the burdens of managing a price-incomes policy, the Belgian state has had to intervene directly in price and wage setting and to focus almost exclusively on the question on manufacturing competitiveness. In January 1989, the parliament passed a "competitiveness" law empowering the state to manipulate wage and non-wage labor costs in order to maintain Belgium's export competitiveness at 1987 levels relative to other European countries. The 1989 Belgian National Bank Report describes the law as follows:

> Each year, competitiveness is the subject of assessment by the Central Council of the Economy, followed by consultation between the Government and both sides of industry. If, after these examinations, it is found that competitiveness may be threatened in the light of the criteria defined above [namely, labor cost per employee in the private sector, financial costs, energy costs and certain structural determinants of the competitive position] the Government may make a statement on the subject, supported by reasons, to the Legislative Chambers, which may in turn confirm this observation by a vote. The Government is then authorized to take, by a Royal Decree enacted in the Council of Ministers, corrective measures, including with regard to the formation of labor costs and corporate taxation (Belgian National Bank, 1989: 36).

Although adopted by a center-left cabinet (Martens VIII), this law ignited large-scale trade union opposition on its first application in the autumn of 1993—largely as a result of (Maastricht-encouraged) constraints on government room for fiscal maneuver. The Dehaene center-left government announced a two-year wage freeze coupled with social welfare reforms and changes in the price index used for wage and benefits increases. The government's objective was to help industry recover from the Europe-wide recession while at the same time reining in public deficits. The centrist Christian Social Movement—the largest (and predominantly Flemish) labor organization—responded by announcing a staggered series of regional strikes together with the more syndicalist, left-wing (and principally Walloon) General Federation of Belgian Labor.

In the end, the government prevailed and implemented both its competitiveness measures and an updated fiscal convergence program at the same time. Victory, however, carried a high price in terms of the popularity of the Christian Democrats and in terms of relations between political elites and the leadership of the Christian labor movement. The combined effects of the 1993 peseta, lire and sterling devaluations, which worked to offset the competitive gains made through wage moderation, compounded this political cost. By autumn 1995, employers in Flanders suggested that a change in the external value of the franc was necessary to supplement other efforts to promote competitiveness. Their argument was that while they supported the idea of a hard currency in principle, they could not maintain competitiveness given the prevailing value of the franc in international currency markets. The National Bank responded that any weakening of the franc would impose unacceptable costs on the economy (Bohets, 1995). This means that for the ruling coalition to address industry concerns, likely it will have to place further constraints on wage growth even as trade union discipline wears thin.

A second problem is that price-incomes policies contradict the free-market ethos underlying the drive for economic and monetary integration. As many of the early proponents of the 1989 report on EMU by European Commission President Jacques Delors realized, price-incomes policies within a member state are inimical to the functioning of the monetary union because they segment the European labor market (Italianer, 1993). Those countries able to implement price-incomes policies can maintain relatively low labor costs and thereby export unemployment to other countries. In a worst-case scenario, all members of the Union try for price-wage restraint and thereby reduce aggregate European consumption. This worst-case scenario was noted by the Belgians themselves in their national contribution to the 1993 Delors White Paper on growth, competitiveness, and employment (Commission of the European Communities, 1993: 72).

Nevertheless, Belgium is dependent on the exercise of price-wage restraint as a means to ensure the price competitiveness of its manufacturing exports. In order to square the circle, the Belgians face two alternatives. Either they have to find some other means to ensure price competitiveness through the manipulation of non-wage labor costs, or at least they must ensure that the rest of Europe does not object to (or worse, emulate) Belgian exercise of coordinated price-wage restraint. Of the two alternatives, the manipulation of non-wage labor costs is preferable. Nevertheless, it is also more difficult because it relies on the Belgian government's being able to overcome its third major dilemma—the refinancing of social welfare.

The Belgian welfare state is being forced to abandon—at least in part—nineteenth century notions of social insurance. Traditionally the state has managed the finances for social welfare almost from a distance, serving as a clearinghouse for payroll tax revenues that were to be disbursed by privately managed unemployment, pension, health, and social welfare services.[6] During the wage moderation program of the early to mid-1980s, the government began to rely on general coffers in order to lessen the pressure of non-wage labor costs on corporate profits. Now the government carries direct responsibility for the financing of social welfare benefits out of general coffers, more in the sense of a pay-as-you-go-style welfare state than a nineteenth century insurance provider. By 1995, for example, fully 20 percent of the financing for Belgian social insurance derived from general government revenues (Despiegelaere, 1995: 18). The implications of this are important not only for efforts to consolidate public finances but also for efforts to consolidate Belgium *tout court*.

The Regional Political Economies of Belgium

The solution to Belgium's problem of maintaining export competitiveness in the future lies in an extensive social insurance reform rather than (or, perhaps, in addition to) price-incomes policy. As Prime Minister Jean-Luc Dehaene argued in his election manifesto, "Keys for Tomorrow," the only viable means to continue to cut Belgian labor costs without sacrificing nominal wages is to find alternate financing for the country's social welfare (1995: 62–64). At present, employer contributions add more than 40 percent to unit labor costs and account for just over one-half of the financial resources for the social welfare system.

In order to lower non-wage labor costs, the state must cut its payroll tax revenues even further. However, this raises potentially explosive considerations about who pays and who benefits from the social welfare system. Putting it bluntly, any drive to enhance competitiveness through social insurance reform risks upsetting the tenuous regional balance in Belgium. During the 1980s, Belgium's three regional economies diverged sharply in terms of unemployment. Table 2.2 shows the evolution of regional (and national) unemployment as a percentage of total population. The recession at the start of the 1980s hit all parts of the country equally, driving up unemployment rates across the three regions. However, the export-led recovery of the 1980s tended to favor Flanders more than either Wallonia or Brussels. By the early 1990s, the unemployment rate in Wallonia and Brussels—measured as a ratio to total population—was almost twice that in Flanders. Over the same period, the dependency ratio—the ratio of those under the age of 15 and over the age of 65 to total population—improved in Flanders vis-à-vis the other regions.

As unemployment rates and dependency ratios have diverged across regions, Flemish—and particularly Flemish nationalist—politicians have begun to complain that Flanders is unfairly disadvantaged by the nationwide system of transfers. Flemings work more and therefore pay more, and regionalist firebrands have taken to claiming that the fruits of Flemish labors are being abused to support Walloon indigence.

As a problem of interregional solidarity, the disparate fortunes of north and south Belgium are serious enough. The situation is even more complicated, however, by the distinctly different political cultures of the country's three major regions—political cultures that derive from their differing linguistic and historical backgrounds. Evidence for this can be found in Tables 2.3 and 2.4. Table 2.3 gives results from the May 1995 elections at the national and regional levels. Because Belgian political movements have different parties in the different regions of the country, these are listed in terms of broadly comparable political groups—Christian Democrat, Socialist, Liberal,

Table 2.2: Regional Unemployment and Dependency in Belgium

	Unemployment Rates (percent)			Dependency Ratios (percent)	
	April 1983	April 1988	April 1993	1981	1991
Belgium	11.8	10.1	8.7	34.1	33.2
Flanders	11.2	8.1	6.6	33.7	32.4
Wallonia	12.5	13.1	11.9	34.8	34.0
Brussels	13.1	12.1	11.2	34.5	34.8

Source: Eurostat.

Table 2.3: Regional Vote Distribution in May 1995 Parliamentary Elections (Lower House, percent)

Political Group	Flanders	Wallonia	Brussels	Belgium
Christian Democrat (PSC/CVP)	27.6	22.5	18.5	24.9
Socialist (PS/SP)	20.7	33.7	18.2	24.4
Liberal (PRL-FDF/VVD)*	20.9	23.9	33.5	23.4
Regional (VU)	7.3	0.0	4.3	4.7
Environmental (Ecolo/Agalev)	7.2	10.3	9.4	8.4
Extreme Right (Agir, FN/VB)	12.3	6.3	12.0	10.4

Note: *The Liberal vote is exaggerated in francophone areas by the electoral federation between the Liberal PRL and the regionalist FDF.
Source: Belgian National Institute for Statistics.

Regional Separatist, Environmentalist, and Extreme Right. Meanwhile, Table 2.4 reviews 1985 figures for sectoral employment in terms of both total regional employment and national employment.

The data in these tables reveal the extent of political and economic division in the country. Flanders tends to vote on the confessional center-right, Wallonia on the socialist left, and Brussels on the regional and liberal right. Flanders is the industrial stronghold of the country, Brussels is the capital for services, and Wallonia—one of the first industrialized regions on the European continent—suffers under high unemployment, relatively low percapita incomes, and a declining industrial base.

This pattern of cleavages is not a new one, although it is more extreme than during times past. The north and south of the country have always spoken different languages and—with the rise of Flemish "nationalism" after World War I—have claimed different ethnic cultures. The economic cleavage is long-standing as well; however the relative prosperity of different regions has changed. Until the early 1960s, Flanders was per capita the poorest

Table 2.4: Regional Industrial Structures in Belgium, 1985

Country or Region	Agriculture	Industry	Services
	Share of Regional Employment (percent)		
Belgium	2.9	28.9	68.1
Flanders	3.4	34.6	62.0
Wallonia	3.9	28.0	68.1
Brussels	0.1	13.6	86.3
	Share of National Employment (percent)		
Flanders	62.8	64.3	48.9
Wallonia	37.0	27.0	27.8
Brussels	0.4	8.6	23.3
Memoranda	GDP share (percent)	Population share (percent)	Unemployment (percent)
Flanders	57.8	57.5	10.1
Wallonia	26.7	32.5	13.1
Brussels	15.5	9.9	12.5

Source: Eurostat.

region in the country. By 1981, however, Walloon real per-capita income was only 86 percent of that in Flanders, and by 1991 it had fallen to just less than 80 percent.

The most important transformation of the post–World War II period is the extent to which ideological and economic cleavages have come to coincide with the linguistic divisions between Flemish speakers and francophones. Traditionally, the ideological cleavages cut across linguistic and regional lines. Thus, in spite of the obvious regional differences, the primary conflict in Belgian society was between Christian Democrats, Socialists, and Liberals. And when elites from these groups agreed to cooperate with each other, Belgium benefited from a remarkable degree of political stability despite its many divisions (Lijphart, 1969).

The national character of the ideological cleavages was essential to the success of Belgian consociationalism—a system of democratic governance where ideological elites made bargains over public policy matters with the implicit support of their followers. So long as national ideological "families" transcended the politics of region or language, elites could foster the discipline necessary to translate peak bargains into mass political behavior. Once the national character of ideological cleavages diminished, however, so too did the internal stability of the ideological families as well as the bargaining authority of traditional elites. Since the 1960s, the national co-herence of political families has declined in line with the decreasing im-portance of ideology in everyday life. The political parties representing the three central groups—the Christian Democrats, Socialists, and Liberals—have divided across regional and linguistic lines. Moreover, a host of new political groups representing nonideological concerns related to the el-derly, the environment, or regional autonomy have garnered an increasing vote share from the electorate. Thus, while Belgium continues to be ruled by ideological elites, these elites can no longer rely on the disciplined com-mitment of their followers. This inability to exert discipline within politi-cal groups has placed ever more rigid constraints on elite bargaining because, in order to mobilize electoral support, elites have had to address ever more diverse and regional perceptions of political self-interest.

Moreover, this regionalization of Belgian politics has coincided with a de-centralization of the state, giving ever more power to regional administra-tions. The most recent culmination of this dual process of political and constitutional reform came in the early 1990s, with the complete restruc-turing of the Flemish Liberals and Democrats and the adoption of a "fed-eral" constitution. By 1995, the French-speaking Liberal Party (PRL) also adopted a more regionalist attitude and formed an electoral federation with the anti-Flemish group Front for French Democracy (FDF) in Brussels and Wallonia. Therefore, if the stability of Belgian society could once be ex-plained by the national character of its politics, there is strong reason to be-lieve that such stability is ebbing.

In such an environment, any effort at major social welfare reform risks opening up a Pandora's box that could lead to the "federalization" of Belgian social welfare—a step many believe would result in the breakup of the coun-try. Not surprisingly, the francophone Socialist Party is strongly against a federalization of Belgian social welfare while the Flemish Liberals and Democrats (VLD) are strongly in favor of it. Dehaene's Flemish Christian People's Party (CVP) holds a centrist position between the Liberal right and the Socialist left, arguing in favor of social welfare reform and against a fur-ther round of federalization. Given his narrow victory in the May 1995 elec-tions—where victory should be understood to mean that the CVP governs on the center-left, without the participation of the newly reformed Flemish Liberals and Democrats—Dehaene's chances of implementing such a com-promise position were viewed to be fairly good. Indeed, many regarded the strong showing for the scandal-ridden Flemish Socialist Party as a mandate for moderation in social welfare reform. During the early months of 1996, however, government reforms began to run into opposition. For example, Dehaene's May 1996 pact for employment was rejected by the trade unions—revealing deep regional cleavages in both the Socialist and Christian Democratic labor movements. As of this writing, it is still too early to tell whether the center-left cabinet can succeed in refashioning the Belgian welfare state. Nevertheless, it is still possible to be optimistic. Besides the Christian Democrats, both of the other major political families also have an interest in finding alternate means to finance social welfare—the Socialists to create jobs in their predominantly service-sector regional economy, and the Liberals to protect the competitiveness of Flanders' large manufacturing base. Indeed, of the two political groups, the Liberals arguably have the most to gain from preserving export competitiveness, given that most economists are doubtful that even a large drop in labor costs will spark a dramatic increase in employment.

Prime Minister Dehaene's difficulties lie in the attitudes of the trade unions—including particularly the Flemish Christian Social Movement from which he (and many other top Christian Democrats) emerged. The Belgian trade unions have a strong institutional stake in maintaining the present financing structure for Belgian social "insurance," because their ideologically affiliated health mutuals and employment agencies have wide latitude in controlling disbursements. Thus, apart from pure ideological reasons, the trade unions see any reform of the financial structure of the welfare state as a threat to their own institutional power base. The prime minister's declared intention to pursue welfare reform has further strained relations between his Christian People's Party and the Christian Social Movement, leading to speculation that the Christian Democratic and Socialist trade unions will try to form a "progressive front"—ostensibly to preserve the welfare state, but more cynically perhaps, to preserve their privileged position in the management of welfare state institutions.

Fiscal Reform versus Fiscal Convergence?

Although given top billing in the run-up to the 1995 parliamentary elections, convergence on the Maastricht criteria for fiscal performance is only an underlying theme in the broader debate about export competitiveness and social welfare reform that surrounds efforts to consolidate government accounts. All political parties, interest groups, and social classes are in agreement that something must be done about the disastrous state of Belgian public finances. Where there is disagreement is about the pace of activity. Politicians on the (moderate) right—particularly the Flemish Liberals and Democrats—have seized on the need for radical fiscal reform as a means to drive a wedge between the Christian Democrats and the Christian Social Movement. Politicians on the left, such as Walloon and Flemish Socialists, have responded by trying to rally the working class in defense of the welfare state.

If this were the principal political choice to be faced, the centrist Christian Democrats would have an easy time governing on the center-left through the end of the century. However, a tenuous alliance between the extreme-right-wing Flemish Bloc, the francophone National Front, and a group of smaller protest parties representing the elderly has complicated the debate by promising to solve the problems of the welfare state by withholding benefits from families of immigrants and guest workers. Coming on the heels of numerous scandals within the ranks of the main political families (Christian Democrats, Socialists, and Liberals), such anti-immigrant rhetoric has had a persuasive impact on the electorate—particularly in Flanders, but in Wallonia as well.

In the October 1994 regional elections, 28 percent of Antwerp voters lent support to the right-wing Flemish Bloc. Prior to that, in the June 1994 European elections, the right-wing francophone National Front gained almost 8 percent of the vote in Wallonia. The electoral support for the Flemish Bloc was alarmingly high in the 1995 elections—garnering them some 7.8 percent of the national vote, as compared to 6.6 percent in 1991. The success of this group—with its strong program for fiscal federalization—complicates Dehaene's efforts to consolidate government accounts, let alone his plan to reform social insurance.

Nevertheless, so long as Dehaene can continue to govern from the center-left, it is likely that Belgium will meet the deficit criteria by the end of the decade and that it will be judged to show "satisfactory downward convergence" toward the debt criteria as well. The danger for Belgium lies in two directions: On the one hand, if the Flemish Liberals and Democrats succeed in forcing the government to push for radical fiscal convergence in line with the Maastricht norms, there is the possibility that the government will be paralyzed by an aggressive trade union response. Certainly the centrist Christian Democrats and the left-wing Socialists will work hard not to antagonize their ideologically affiliated labor movements. As Dehaene has pointed out in numerous interviews, fiscal convergence is important, but it should be considered in the context of political reality.

On the other hand, Belgium faces the danger that failure to meet the Maastricht norms will result in its exclusion from Europe's monetary hard core. Such exclusion would be a disaster for Belgium in that, by casting doubts on the credibility of the hard franc, it would reintroduce large premiums in long- and short-term interest rates, further complicating the process of fiscal convergence. Moreover, failure to remain in Europe's core would send a strong signal of the ineffectiveness of the Belgian state at a time when regional politicians are claiming greater legitimacy.

Federal Belgium in a Federal Europe[7]

In either event, Belgium's central place in Europe faces a threat. In turn, a loss of national status in Europe could further exacerbate regional tensions and thereby threaten the viability of the Belgian state. To understand this point, it is necessary to consider that participation in Europe has long smoothed relations between the political economies of Flanders and Wallonia. During the early 1950s, for example, financial support from the European Coal and Steel Community helped predominantly Flemish Catholic governments to pacify Walloon Socialists who sought to avoid a painful restructuring of Belgian coal mining (Milward, 1992). Later, during the early 1960s, access to foreign direct investment encouraged by the Treaty of Rome enabled the center-left Lefèvre-Spaak government to continue subsidizing mature industries in Wallonia while promoting the modernization of Flanders. Even in the early 1980s, the success of the EMS in stabilizing European exchange rates was an essential ingredient to the center-right Martens government's efforts to implement price-incomes policy and austerity measures while at the same time attempting to bail out the Walloon steel industry (Jones, 1995).

In each of these three historical cases, European integration gave international support for the Belgian government's domestic political agenda. Moreover, in each case, this political agenda was intimately linked with the changing relations between the regions and between the regions and the federal government. The early 1950s saw the rise of Flemish politicians, the early 1960s saw the rise of the Flemish economy, and the 1980s witnessed the consolidation of linguistic and regional identities. Finally, the support afforded by European integration went beyond simple economics. Participation in Europe provided strong symbolic reinforcement of the legitimacy of the Belgian state—often in times of profound national crisis, as during the Walloon Socialist uprisings of 1950 and 1960 or during the constitutional upheaval of the early 1980s.

The onset of the 1990s brought with it another change in the structure of the Belgian constitution as well as the imminent danger of a crisis in Belgian public finances. It is a problem, therefore, that EMU offers little other than the promise of continued price and exchange rate stability. Monetary integration will not promote the rejuvenation of Wallonia or the further growth of Flanders, and it cannot solve the problem of unemployment. Moreover, the advantages of EMU will be limited by the number of countries participating; a smaller EMU means that there is more likelihood of competitive devaluation from countries outside Europe's monetary club.[8]

For Belgium, participation in EMU possibly cuts two ways. On the one hand, the Belgian federal government stands to benefit from the legitimacy that membership confers. Having proven that it can manage is fiscal accounts on a par with the strongest economies of Europe, the Belgian federal state may be able to present a strong case that decentralization will only make matters worse. This argument draws strength from the special position of Brussels and from the complexity of "decentralizing" the federal debt. Not only must Wallonia and Flanders compete for the large tax revenues from the capital city (one of Europe's richest in per-capita terms), they also must find some formula for allocating responsibility for paying down the mountain of debt. Even the most aggressive regionalists in Belgium acknowledge that these two issues are likely to bind Flanders and Wallonia together well into the future.

Nevertheless, the legitimacy afforded by participation in EMU and the complications of Brussels and the federal debt might not prove to be enough to hold the country together. There is a pessimistic scenario for Belgium's future post-EMU, in which "keeping up with the pack" is the last service of the federal government. Regional politicians such as Minister President Luc van den Brande in Flanders and José Happart in Wallonia are calling for a new round of constitutional discussions to start in 1999. At issue will be a further devolution of the economic authority of the Belgian state including—according to *The Economist* (16 March 1996: 30)—foreign trade, fiscal policy, and social security. Should such reforms take place while Belgium is a member of EMU, "there may not be a lot left for Mr. Dehaene, or his successors, to do." The issue will no longer be Belgium and EMU but the Belgian regions and EMU. The prospects for such a future are decidedly unclear.

Notes

1. Note that support for membership has declined from a peak of close to 75 percent in 1991, to a low of 56 percent in 1994. However, much of this fluctuation is due probably to economic performance and the controversy surrounding the ratification of the Maastricht Treaty elsewhere, and not due to fundamental changes in Belgian attitudes regarding European integration. Thus, in spite of the decline in Belgian popular support for membership, the positive gap between Belgian support and average European support remains roughly constant through the first four years of the 1990s.

2. Former King Boudouin, the present King Albert, and the last four prime ministers (Leo Tindemans, Marc Eyskens, Wilfried Martens, Jean-Luc Dehaene) all have gone on record in favor of a federal Europe. What is interesting to note, however, is that the Belgian understanding of "federalism" is more closely tied to decentralization than to centralization—a point that British Prime Minister John Major (and his advisors) seems to have overlooked in the run-up to the June 1994 Corfu summit.

3. Almost 28 percent of Belgian imports in 1992 fell within the SITC categories for crude materials excluding mineral fuels (2) and basic manufactures (6), compared to the European average of only about 21 percent imports in those categories. Data source: Eurostat.

4. It is not uncommon for the headline of a local newspaper to declare "Franc stronger than Mark!" However, the possibility that the franc could move upward against the mark also in ingrained in the decision to peg the franc—in the words of central bank governor Alfons Verplaetse—"firmly to the EMS currencies which are regarded as stability anchors, in present circumstances the German mark." (Belgian National Bank, 1990: xx).

5. The exchange rate data are from the International Monetary Fund. After the 1993 ERM crisis, the European leaders decided to widen the banks for "normal" fluctuations within the ERM to 15 percent instead of 2.25 percent.

6. The insurance basis for Belgian social welfare is something of a historical anomaly. During the early postwar period, government representatives met with trade union leaders and employers to set down the principals for the welfare state. Overwhelmingly, both sides of the social partnership favored an insurance-based system, financed by payroll taxes, over a national welfare system financed through general taxation. The advantage of an insurance-based system for both employers and workers was that it would be controlled by ideologically affiliated trade unions and health mutuals rather than directly by the state (Vanthemsche, 1994).

7. The argument in this section has benefited greatly from my conversations with Paulette Kurzer, whose recent work also examines the changing role of Europe in Belgian domestic politics.

8. The Belgians are clearly aware that a small EMU will pose a large danger of competitive devaluation among those countries outside. Given the price dependence of Belgian exports and the recent complaints of Belgian industrialists, national leaders have a strong desire to ensure that EMU is as large and encompasses as many countries as possible.

CHAPTER THREE

Denmark: From External to Internal Adjustment

Torben Iversen and Niels Thygesen

When the Danes voted no to the Maastricht Treaty in the summer of 1992 and shortly thereafter won the European soccer championship by beating Germany, the expression of national pride and joy reached levels unparalleled since the Allied liberation of the country in 1945. Even the foreign minister, for whom the referendum was a major political defeat, could not help but to join in this expression of national hubris and joked to the international press: "As we say in Denmark: if you can't join them, beat them!"

Alas, since then Denmark has joined the European Union and Germany has won back the European soccer championship. However, the surprising Danish no vote was not simply an emotional outburst of old-fashioned nationalism. Rather, it was an expression of the deep divisions within the Danish electorate over continued integration into the political-institutional framework of the Community. While low-paid, sheltered, and predominantly female public sector employees perceived the EU as a serious threat to the Danish welfare state, better-paid, exposed, and predominantly male private sector employers saw the Maastricht Treaty as an opportunity for further modernizing the Danish economy and for bringing Danish institutions into line with the new realities of a fiercely competitive global economy.

The battle over European integration is more than two decades old in Denmark and so is the conflict over one important aspect of this integration: exchange rate policies. Since the breakdown of the Bretton Woods system, Danish governments have pursued different strategies of exchange rate management—with clear implications for monetary policy and domestic economic conditions—and participation in European monetary institutions has been an important element in this management. Compared to its Scandinavian neighbors, Denmark always has been more concerned with keeping its currency aligned with the other European currencies, but the policy was notably "hardened" after the coming to power of a center-right government in 1982. Since then, and despite the opt-out of the final stage of the EMU, governments of all hues have strictly observed this hard-currency policy.

A standard economic explanation for a country's willingness to participate in international currency arrangements like the European Monetary System (EMS) or economic and monetary union (EMU) is the so-called optimum currency area approach (McKinnon, 1963; Mundell, 1961). According to this theory, governments face a trade-off between monetary policy autonomy, which permits flexible responses to real shocks to the national economy, and the fixing of exchange rates, which reduces the transaction costs of trade. If the shocks to two or more economies are very similar, then there is little to be gained from policy autonomy, and the concern for exchange rate stability takes prominence. Such countries form part of an optimum currency area. Conversely, when shocks are asymmetric, the need for policy autonomy and exchange rate flexibility becomes more pressing. Such countries are not part of the same optimum currency area.

While perhaps compelling as a normative theory of welfare maximization, Denmark presents something of a puzzle for optimum currency area theory when it comes to *explaining* variance in exchange rate policies. Historically, the Danish economy has responded differently from other European countries to international economic shocks due to a greater reliance on agricultural exports. With the waning importance of agriculture and the growing internationalization of manufacturing, business cycles have become more synchronized with those of its main trading partners in Europe. Nevertheless, a comparison of all 14 EU member states (excluding Luxembourg) in terms of the most commonly used indicators in the optimum currency approach shows that Denmark is ranked close to bottom on virtually all indicators. In particular, Denmark appears to have been cyclically out of phase with other European economies during the 1980s. Even such countries as Britain, Ireland, and Sweden, which have pursued much more flexible exchange rate policies than Denmark, rank higher (Gros, 1996a: 13–14). The correlation between exchange rate policies and "distance" to the center of an optimum currency area thus would appear to be rather weak.

The theory of optimum currency areas is even less helpful in explaining why Danish exchange rate policies changed over time. Policies during the 1970s and early 1980s required numerous exchange rate devaluations within the "snake"—a system for coordinating European exchange rates in the

1970s—and the EMS, while the policy that has been adhered to since 1982 has aimed at maintaining a strong and highly stable currency. This policy reversal hardly corresponds to any fundamental changes in the structure of the Danish economy or in the cyclical movements that it has experienced. In order to understand Danish exchange rate policies, therefore, we have to pay attention to the distributive effects of such policies and how they interact with changing political coalitions and economic institutions. More specifically, we argue that Danish exchange rate policies during the 1970s reflected a particular sectoral and parliamentary balance of power that was upset by a political-sectoral realignment in the early 1980s. Danish exchange rate policies, and government policies toward the EMU, have reflected the stability of this new alignment at the elite level, while the no vote to the Maastricht Treaty and the subsequent opt-out of the final stage of the EMU reflect the continued salience of sectoral divisions in the electorate.

This chapter is organized into five sections. The first focuses on Danish exchange rate policies up until the early 1980s, emphasizing their linkages to political conflicts over macroeconomic management and incomes policies. The second section discusses the economic policy turnaround after 1982 and specifically the adoption of a "hard" currency policy. The third suggests how we may explain this policy reversal by focusing on sectoral alignments and realignments. The fourth extends the analysis to the conflict over the Maastricht Treaty and EMU, emphasizing the stability both in exchange rate policies and in underlying electoral cleavages. The final section concludes by briefly discussing some of the unresolved issues in adapting the Danish political economy to continued European integration.

A "Hard" Currency with Domestic Overcommitments

Since the end of Bretton Woods, the issue of choosing a monetary regime in Denmark (as in most small European countries) has been tightly related to the issue of choosing an exchange rate regime. If the value of the national currency is credibly pegged to another noninflationary currency (or basket of currencies), this exchange rate regime is similar to following a monetarist policy rule: Any growth in domestic costs or inflation that threatens the government's ability to maintain the current exchange rate in the medium term must be met by restrictive monetary and fiscal policy responses. And just as with any "domestic" monetary policy rule that is not believed to be fully credible, any doubts about the capacity and determination of the government to defend the value of the currency will manifest themselves in a higher level of interest rates (the "risk premium"), higher unemployment (as a result of higher interest rates), and a higher external debt burden (if the central bank seeks to deter speculative runs against the currency through the build up of large foreign currency holdings).

In practical terms, for Danish governments the hard-currency option was associated with a linking of the value of the national currency to the value of the Deutschemark through the Exchange Rate Mechanism (ERM) in the EMS. By doing so—to put it a bit crudely—domestic monetary policies would be dictated, or at least severely constrained, by the policies of the German Bundesbank. In lieu of strict controls on capital flows, pegging a currency to the Deutschemark makes it practically impossible to maintain interest rates below those prevailing in Germany.[1] However, if the hard-currency policy is *credible,* interest rates can be kept very close to the German level. With pegging it is difficult to sustain inflation rates at levels above those in Germany since such a differential will cause a real appreciation of the currency and thereby undermine competitiveness, creating a current account deficit and causing international confidence in the currency to slip. A truly committed hard-currency policy, therefore, will lead to a convergence of both inflation and interest rates to the German level.

The Danish experience from the early 1970s reflects many of these economic dynamics, but it also shows that political commitments are not necessarily well calibrated to satisfy economic ones. Danish participation in first the European "snake" and then the EMS was favored by the central bank, by the financial community, and, crucially, by the Radical Left Party on whose support consecutive social democratic governments depended for legislative majorities. Representing farming interests, the Radicals were eager to maintain an alignment between the value of the "Green krone"—which was used by the European Community to compensate Danish agricultural producers for goods sold under the auspices of the Common Agricultural Policy—and the main exchange rate. If the value of the krone devalued more rapidly than the Green krone, Danish farmers would in effect be selling their goods in an overvalued currency and lose purchasing power in terms of the price on foreign goods "denominated" in the core currency.[2]

The restrictions on Danish monetary policies resulting from membership in the European currency arrangements had important, and partly unintended, consequences for the functioning of the domestic economy and especially for the relationship between the Social Democratic Party and the unions. The problem for the Danish government was twofold. On the one hand, because Danish inflation was above the German level, there was a persistent expectation that the krone could not, over time, retain its value against the Deutschemark. Consequently, Danish interest rates incorporated a substantial "risk premium" that compensated foreign investors for the loss they would face in the event of a devaluation, and the central bank had to accumulate large (and expensive) foreign currency holdings as a hedge against speculation (Johansen, 1987: 194). Real long-term interest rates in Denmark in the period from 1973 to 1982 were an average of 2.7 percent above those in Germany, while in a committed hard-currency country like Austria (where there was virtually no uncertainty about the value of the schilling), interest rates were held at (nearly) the same level as in Germany. (See Table 3.1.) Nominal long-term interest rates hit a peak of 22 percent in 1982 (when inflation was 10 percent), and the construction industry came to a near standstill while public budgets were strained by a rapidly rising debt burden (one that still prevents Denmark from meeting the Maastricht convergence criteria on debt). High interest rates—transmitted through the exchange rate policy—thus became symptomatic for the adverse effect that German monetary policies had on the Danish economy.

Of course, the Danish government could have solved this problem by convincing labor representatives to contain wage increases at a level that would have kept inflation in line with those in Germany, but consecutive Social Democratic governments failed to do so. To the recurrent frustration and embarrassment of the government, Landesorganisation i Danmark (LO—the main union confederation) defiantly refused to accept the limits for wage increases that the government—trying to heed the advice of its own economists—tried to impose on the social partners, meaning representatives of labor and industry. Although there were extensive consultations between the government and LO over wage policies, they could not come to any consensus and clashed again and again, sometimes in very public ways. More than any other political problem during the 1970s, this growing gulf between the "restrained" impulse in the government's macroeconomic policies

Table 3.1: Economic Indicators for the Danish Economy, 1973-94

	1973-77	1978-82	1983-88	1989-94
Average Annual Growth Rates (percent)				
Nominal effective exchange rate	0.5	-3.5	1.1	1.6
Unit labor costs	10.9	8.1	4.4	0.9
CPI inflation	11.4	10.7	5.0	2.5
Average Annual Levels (percent)				
Trade balance (percent GDP)	-2.8	-1.9	0.2	6.1
Long-term interest rate differential with Germany	4.6	9.3	5.3	1.2

Sources: OECD; IMF.

and the escalating wage demands of LO became symptomatic for the structural imbalances in the Danish economy.

From the perspective of LO, the core dilemma was that the government could no longer credibly promise full employment as a quid pro quo for "responsible" wage policies by the unions. This became particularly clear to the LO during the 1975 and 1977 bargaining rounds when the Social Democratic government, hard pressed by a negotiation deadlock and a deteriorating economy, felt compelled to resort to statutory incomes policy. In the first case, the existing agreement was extended for another two years, while in the second the compromise proposal by the public conciliator was put into law (Nannestad, 1991: 197–181). Both settlements placed limits on wage increases that the LO was not willing to adopt voluntarily, and both were combined with tripartite negotiations over their implementation as well as the determination of future targets for the macroeconomic policy. Nevertheless, they failed to achieve any improvement in either the current account or in unemployment.

It is important to note that the income policies were not unqualified failures, at least not when measured against some reasonable standards. Real wage increases declined from the middle of 1975 and turned negative in 1977, and unit labor cost performance was similar to the rest of the Organization for Cooperation and Development (OECD) countries and significantly better than in Sweden (an average of 1 percent lower rate of increase in Denmark compared to Sweden during the period from 1973 to 1980). Even in terms of employment, Denmark did not fare as poorly as overall unemployment figures would suggest. Thus the number of gainfully employed people in Denmark actually increased by 3.1 percent in the years between 1974 and 1979, while in Germany it decreased by 2 percent (OECD, 1992a). This improvement, however, was achieved primarily through a rapid expansion of public employment (a nearly 70 percent increase between 1970 and 1980), and it did not suggest any improvement of in the international competitiveness of Danish industry.

On the other hand, measured against the Swedish employment record—and against the professed full employment goal of the Social Democratic government—the policy clearly failed. The main problem was that despite downward real wage flexibility, *nominal* wage increases in Denmark were too high for the negotiated devaluations within the "snake" to give any scope for competitive improvements. The central bank exerted a strong influence over exchange rate policies, and like the center-right majority in the parliament, it was opposed to devaluations. Instead, it defended the krone by accumulating large foreign currency reserves to deter speculation and by raising interest rates. This combination of high wage increases and an inflexible exchange rate caused the Danish real effective exchange rate to appreciate by

18 percent in the first three years of membership in the "snake," and even when exchange rate adjustment policies became more permissive during the period between 1976 and 1978, Danish price competitiveness failed to improve (Gros and Thygesen, 1992: 19).

It is instructive here briefly to compare this situation to Sweden, where labor market institutions were similar but exchange rate policies differed. Sweden is one of the small European countries that have most persistently defended its autonomy in monetary policies. The value of the currency has been determined by a "basket" of the currencies of major trading partners. Not only was this exchange rate policy in itself "softer" than using the Deutschemark or the ECU as the reference currency (because the basket currencies were generally more inflationary than the Deutschemark), it also allowed for occasional "technical" adjustments of the exchange rate, and during the 1970s and early 1980s the Swedish full employment strategy was premised on occasional and large devaluation. Sweden had joined the European currency "snake" in 1973, but when the rise in cost levels came into conflict with the aim of maintaining exchange rate stability in the system, Sweden resolutely withdrew (in 1977). Subsequent to this withdrawal, the Swedish krona was devalued by 10 percent, even though it had been granted a 6 percent devaluation within the "snake" less than one year earlier (Gylfason, 1990: 186).[3] The result was an immediate improvement in the international competitiveness of Swedish industry, as expected in standard economic theory. Yet the key to the medium-term success of the policy was the fact that the wage agreement in 1978 (following the devaluation) was characterized by across-the-board wage restraint (Mjøset, 1986: 258–259). In fact, real wages *fell* between 1977 and 79 (Scharpf, 1991), thereby contributing to a substantial improvement in the current account.[4] By most accounts the devaluation policy was, therefore, a success and LO's open commitment to accept wage restraint in response to full employment policies seemed to have been an important factor in this success (Mjøset, 1986: 206).

The Danish government tried to achieve a similar employment effect through expansionary fiscal policies, but it repeatedly ran up against the currency constraint and the anti-inflationary policies of the central bank (Nationalbanken). For its part, the central bank felt frustrated in its pursuit of stable prices and exchange rates, and openly criticized the government's policies in its annual reports.[5] Notwithstanding the political objectives and ideological commitment of the government, Danish economic institutions were not well suited to maintain full employment in a severe and prolonged international economic crisis. Ironically, while a bourgeois government in Sweden championed a full employment policy that had been introduced by the Social Democrats, in Denmark a Socialist government committed to full employment presided over policies resulting in rising unemployment and a souring of relations with the social partners.

Yet the social democratic government *could* claim that it had been successful in two areas. First, the solidarity element of LO's wage strategy had been strengthened by the introduction of a flat-rate cost-of-living compensation mechanism in 1975 and a minimum-wage guarantee in 1977. Second, by replacing the percentage-based cost-of-living regulation of public sector wages with a new private-public sector compensation mechanism, wages for public employees did not keep pace automatically with those of private employees (Nannestad, 1991: 162). Although public sector employees were provided with some wage guarantees, the policy began to create a wedge between the evolution of wages in the private and public sectors. In this way, the government made an accommodating step toward those in the private sector that were increasingly critical of public sector unions and wage policies (Due and Madsen, 1988: 41–42).

Against the background of rising unemployment and a chronic current account deficit, the government's policies did little to shore up support for either its macroeconomic cure or the centrally coordinated income policy. Thus high-wage groups resented the fact that their relative wages were falling as a result of the solidarity wage policies, while their sacrifices had no discernible positive effects on the economy. Employers, especially in the export-oriented engineering sector, complained loudly that the centralized bargaining system had led to an inflexible wage system that undermined work motivation and inhibited adjustment to new technology while hardly contributing to price competitiveness (Iversen, 1996). Even low-wage unions expressed discontent because the government failed to honor what was perceived to be its historical responsibility to secure full employment. By the late 1970s, therefore, the centralized collective bargaining system and the economic policy program of the government were in a deep crisis. In the words of Due, Madsen, Jensen, and Petersen (1994: 188), "[t]he Danish collective bargaining model had reached its peak level of centralization, which at the same time led to a crisis in which the collapse of the system seemed imminent."

Resolving the Tension: Domestic Institutional Adaptation to the External Constraint

After yet another government-mandated income policy settlement in 1979, the Liberal-Social Democratic coalition government, coming to power in August 1978, enacted an anti-inflationary economic package in response to the second oil shock. Having ignored its previous pledges to coordinate its policies with the social partners, the government defended its unilateral measures by referring to the unanticipated deterioration of the economy. But the government earned no sympathy from LO, whose chairman, Thomas Nielsen, engaged in spiteful attacks and increasingly public confrontations with Prime Minister Anker Jørgensen. The unions argued that it was precisely during times of economic hardship that close consultations and policy coordination between the two segments of the labor movement was most needed, and they felt betrayed by the decision of the Social Democrats to enter into a government "over the middle," with the much more pro-market-oriented Liberal Party.

By this time Denmark had entered the European Monetary System, and it received some initial relief within this new system as the krone was devalued twice in 1979. Additional relief came when the effects of the German locomotive strategy caused the Deutschemark to depreciate in 1980. Even when the Bundesbank put on the monetary brakes in early 1981, system flexibility was maintained by permitting Italian and French devaluation and by revaluing the Deutschemark against all the other currencies. Clearly, the participation of large European countries in the EMS initially had the effect of making exchange rate policies, and hence monetary policies, less dependent on Germany than was the case during the "snake" (Gros and Thygesen, 1992). In any case, the Deutschemark was fairly weak in 1979 and 1980 as inflation rose and the current account swung into deficit under the joint impact of higher oil prices and lax budgetary policies. This environment allowed a substantial depreciation of the Danish currency and led to a considerable (while temporary) improvement in Danish competitiveness.[6]

The greater scope for exchange rate maneuvering in the early turbulent phase of the EMS opened the prospect that a new Social Democratic minority government could embark on a Swedish-type strategy of devaluation's followed by negotiated wage restraint. However, the institutional conditions for such a strategy had begun to erode in 1981, when wage bargaining was decentralized to the industry level. The employers' association (Dansk Arbejsgiverforening, or DA) was squarely opposed to a resumption of centralized bargaining, and stronger employee groups such as those represented by the Metalworker's Union (in strong opposition to the unskilled worker's union) were in no hurry to resume the solidarity wage policies of the 1960s and 1970s.

In the absence of any institutional mechanisms to link devaluation to wage restraint, the government's incomes policy was insufficient to cause a substantial improvement of the current account balance. Besides, with the steep rise in international interest rates following the reversal of US monetary policies in 1979, domestic real interest rates were now so high that housing construction had come to an almost complete halt and the public debt (domestic and foreign) was rising exponentially. Against this bleak economic background the government started to search for fundamental policy alternatives that would have a more drastic and lasting effect on the problems of inflation, current account deficits, and super-high interest rates. In a dramatic television appearance the finance minister, Knud Heinesen, argued that Denmark was standing on the edge of an economic abyss and that the only way to prevent the Danish economy from free-falling was through an all-out assault on the problems of rising wage costs, inflation, and the public debt. The opposition parties and the main employers' organizations could not have agreed more.

A decisive policy reversal, however, did not occur until a center-right coalition government took office in 1982, after a tired Social Democratic Party suddenly dropped the reins of power. The new government quickly initiated four fundamental economic reforms: (1) a firm pegging of the krone in the EMS, (2) a sweeping liberalization of capital markets, (3) a complete elimination of the fiscal budget deficit, and (4) suspension of all cost-of-living indexation.[7] After a relatively short transition period, the lifting of capital controls and the initiation of dramatically restrictive fiscal policies (an 8 percent deficit was converted into a 4.5 percent surplus in the course of five years!) convinced markets that the government meant business and that the new hard currency policy was credible. In addition, by suspending the automatic cost-of-living indexation and by repealing the mechanism compensating public employees for private sector wage increases, the government reduced the inflationary contagion from wage drift.

The new economic policies lowered the inflationary costs of decentralized wage increases, and simultaneously deterred unions from pursuing militant strategies. By abandoning full employment as a policy goal and by pegging the currency to the Deutschemark, the government had created an unambiguous bottom line for the economic policy: Any wage-price behavior that was incompatible with the fixed exchange rate policy would be met by a tightening of monetary policies, and hence with a rise in unemployment. Once this commitment was made, all domestic economic policy instruments had only one objective: to maintain confidence in the currency. Essentially, this meant that the government had to toe the policy line of the German Bundesbank.

As illustrated in Figure 3.1—which shows the difference in Danish and German consumer price inflation—the center-right government completed a process of almost perfect convergence to German inflation rates, starting after the initial Danish EMS devaluations in 1979. Moreover, because the hard-currency policy was perceived to be credible, and because of improvements in the trade balance and current account, Danish real interest rates gradually fell close to the German level. (See Table 3.1.) With it, investment and employment started to rise dramatically. Between 1983 and 1988, Denmark experienced a nearly 10 percent increase in the level of employment, an improvement that was unparalleled in other European countries and took even the government by surprise. "The Danish economy is doing unbelievably well" ("det går ufatteligt godt for dansk økonomi") became the motto of the Conservative Prime Minister, Poul Schlüter. And despite intense protests from representatives of unskilled labor and especially public sector unions, a decisive portion of the electorate agreed by returning the government to power in 1984 and 1988.

The change in the exchange rate policy is clearly captured in the evolution of the trade-weighted exchange rate (see Table 3.1), which went from a *negative* annual growth rate of 3.5 percent before the new government took power, to a *positive* growth rate slightly over 1 percent thereafter. At the same time, unit labor costs and inflation decelerated considerably and the interest differential with Germany started to dwindle. It was this ability of the government to contain inflation and wage costs simultaneously that made the hard-currency policy credible and produced the reduction in long-term interest rates. Nominal rates were more than halved between 1982 and 1986 (from 21.4 to 10.1 percent), and real rates fell by nearly as much (from 10.9 to 5.5 percent).[8] The expansionary effect of this decline, leading to massive wealth gains in securities and one-family houses, was stronger than the contractionary effects of the government's freeze on public consumption and

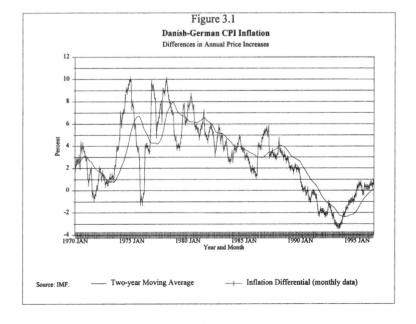

Figure 3.1

Danish-German CPI Inflation

Differences in Annual Price Increases

Source: IMF. — Two-year Moving Average —+— Inflation Differential (monthly data)

simultaneous tax increases. Consequently, consumer demand rebounded while competitiveness improved, leading to a remarkable recovery of the Danish economy.

In light of this experience, criticism of the exchange rate policy gradually vanished and the political opposition, industry, and labor unions have not called into question the policy of a stable krone. Although the opt-out of the third stage of the EMU (discussed later) can be seen as a deviation from a logical trajectory of the Danish fixed exchange rate policy, the turnaround in 1982–83 stands out as the most important innovation in Danish currency policies because it forged a new political consensus among elites over the course of macroeconomic policies. In the next section we suggest an interpretation of this policy reversal in light of existing political-economic theories of open economies as well as the specific circumstances surrounding the Danish policy shift.

Explaining the Policy Turnaround: A Sectoral Realignment Argument

In the introduction it was noted that a simple optimum currency area argument could not readily account for the Danish policy turnaround in 1982 and 1983. Instead, we argue that a better understanding can be gained by examining the underlying political-economic cleavages and (re-)alignments that shaped the policy responses to the economic crisis of the early 1980s. We offer this interpretation from the perspective of an amended Mundell-Fleming model where credible monetary policy commitments and the organization of wage setting enter as important conditioning variables.

The basic Mundell-Fleming model implies that, at most, two of the following three conditions can be satisfied simultaneously: 1) (financial) capital mobility, 2) a fixed exchange rate, and 3) monetary policy autonomy. For example, if capital is perfectly mobile, a credibly fixed exchange rate will cause an in- or outflow of money in response to incipient interest rate differentials that arbitrage away these differentials, and hence eliminate monetary policy autonomy. On the other hand, if the exchange rate is flexible, it is possible to pursue an independent monetary policy, even in the presence of capital mobility. The reason is that active monetary policies will tend to be reinforced, rather than canceled out, by movements in the exchange rate.

Jeffry Frieden (1991) has argued that the Mundell-Fleming model implies a specific set of sectoral conflicts over the level and fixity of the exchange rate. Thus, nontraded (or "sheltered") sectors tend to favor high and flexible exchange rates because they benefit from cheap imports (which increases the wealth of consumers) as well as from flexible monetary policies that can secure high levels of domestic demand. Exporters, by contrast, prefer a low and fixed real exchange rate because this maximizes competitiveness and minimize transaction costs, while monetary policy flexibility is much less of a concern since internal demand conditions are relatively less important than external conditions.

As a first approximation, the evolution of Danish exchange rate policies since the end of Bretton Woods now can be hypothesized to have drifted from a policy of favoring a coalition of sheltered interests (the situation until 1982), to a policy of favoring a coalition of export-dominated interests (the situation after 1982). Yet while this interpretation captures important aspects of the political circumstances that precipitated the adoption of a hard-currency policy in 1982 to 1983, it does *not* explain why the policy shift occurred in the first place, and it papers over important details in the *evolution* of Danish exchange rate policies. For example, it obscures the fact that governments in the 1970s were trying to placate several different sectoral interests simultaneously, and it conceals a politically important cross-cutting cleavage like the one over solidarity wage policies that is tied to, but not defined by, exchange rate movements. Finally, it fails to address the issue of monetary policy credibility, which has played a crucial role in the Danish case. Paying attention to these additional issues provides a more convincing causal explanation of (changing) sectoral coalition patterns and exchange rate policies.

During the 1970s, the government accepted the need for *some* constraint on the movement on the exchange rate. Yet while this was presumably desirable from the perspective of traders and exporters, the real exchange rate actually went through a period of considerable appreciation. The main reason was that the government was pursuing policies that generated inflation as a by-product. In addition to an expansionary fiscal policy stand (prompted primarily by rising unemployment), the government's support for LO's solidarity wage policy—enshrined in the mandated wage settlements of the 1970s and directly promoted through the cost-of-living and public sector wage compensation mechanisms—spurred local wage drift and added to inflationary pressures. More specifically, wage compression encouraged attempts by workers and firms in strong market positions to "undo" the solidarity wage norms through local wage agreements, which in turn triggered new cost-of-living increases and demands from low-wage workers to be "compensated" for anticipated wage drift in the centralized bargaining process. This logic resembled the situation in Sweden, even though the mechanisms were somewhat different (see Hibbs and Locking, 1991; Pontusson and Swenson, 1996). What distinguished the Danish situation from the Swedish was that the exchange rate policy was considerably tighter and therefore precluded "externalization" of these costs through devaluation.

The government was, in fact, trying to please multiple constituencies at the same time, and ended up satisfying none. Thus the implicit support to farm interests via a semifixed exchange rate created a substantial *real* appreciation of the currency because of the government's bow to the solidarity wage demands of its core blue-collar constituencies. This undermined competitiveness and alienated export-oriented manufacturing interests. But the successful pursuit of solidarity (a main campaign slogan for the Social Democrats) actually bought the government few friends among the unions, which were increasingly concerned with the problem of rising unemployment. Unemployment, in turn, could at least partly be blamed on the government's exchange rate policy.[9] To make matters worse, although the high real exchange rate was potentially beneficial to the nontradable sectors, private consumption and public spending were so severely undermined by high interest rates that many in these sectors (especially in construction and real estate) felt betrayed. High interest rates, in turn, reflected the lack of credibility of the government's fixed-but-adjustable exchange rate policy.

The problem for the government's macroeconomic policy in general, and its exchange rate policy in particular, was that it rested on an alliance of interests that was too broad to address the imbalances in the economy effectively. Farmers, public employees, and low-wage unions were all essential elements in the government's parliamentary alliance, while export industries were indispensable for the success of its economic policy. The attempt to bridge these diverse interests reached its peak in the unlikely coalition government between Social Democrats and the Liberal Party (1978–79). From the beginning, the alliance was wrought with tension, and it soon became clear that it could not be sustained.

The breakup of the coalition occurred along several dimensions, at the level of both group and electoral politics. Thus employers in the exposed metalworking industries grew weary of the centralized bargaining system, which failed to deliver wage restraint while at the same time blocking more flexible wage structures that could help companies encourage workers to develop their skills further and facilitate a delegation of responsibilities to the shop floor. Within LO, skilled workers lost interest in solidarity wage policies as their market positions improved relative to those of unskilled workers. These conflicts were overlaid by divisions between private and public sector employees, where stronger private sector unions tended to view public unions as both free riders on productivity increases in private industry and as inflationary wage leaders for low-wage unions (due to a very high compression of public sector wages). Reflecting these cross-class divisions, the main political force behind the continuous process of decentralization during the 1980s came from export-oriented engineering employers and from unions dominated by highly skilled and relatively well-paid workers (Iversen, 1996).[10]

With the disintegration of the coalition behind peak-level bargaining, the economic rationale for a soft currency policy disappeared. Without any institutionalized vehicle for coordinating monetary and income policies, the government could not even hope that unions would hold back wages following devaluation. Rather, the only way the government could expect to induce wage restraint was through firm adherence to a nonaccommodating policy that would "punish" unions and employers for inflationary wage agreements. For the center-right government taking office in 1982, the vehicle for this strategy became the hard-currency policy, and unlike the situation in the 1970s, domestic economic policies were designed explicitly to defend the value of the krone by keeping wage costs down. This prevented a rising real exchange rate to the benefit of exporters.

What made the new policy politically feasible was an emerging electoral realignment that increasingly pitted low-wage and sheltered public sector employees against better-paid and internationally exposed private sector employees. Figure 3.2 shows this emerging electoral configuration in terms of the proportion of public sector employees voting for different party "families" minus the proportion of private sector employees voting for these parties.

Figure 3.2

Differences in Political Support

Public versus Private Sector

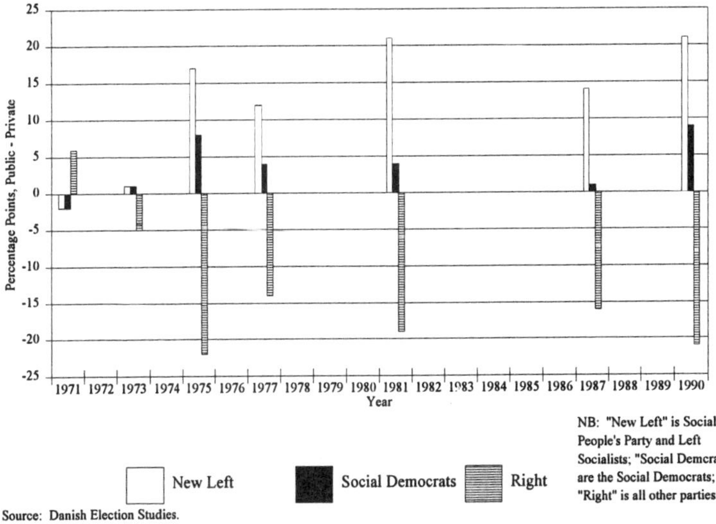

NB: "New Left" is Socialist People's Party and Left Socialists; "Social Demcrats" are the Social Democrats; "Right" is all other parties.

New Left   Social Democrats   Right

Source: Danish Election Studies.

Note that in the early 1970s, private sector employees were as prone as public sector employees to vote for left parties. Over time, however, public employees became much more likely to vote for New Left parties (especially), while private sector employees were far more likely to vote for right parties. This pattern persisted over the 1980s and has been documented extensively by Goul-Andersen (1989; 1992). The Social Democrats remained comparatively "neutral" in this transition, drawing support from both constituencies (although most of the private sector support came from unskilled, blue-collar workers).[11]

Although the division between private and public is a very rough measure of the sheltered-exposed cleavage, it captures a central dimension of this division and helps us understand why the shift in government power was accompanied by such a clear-cut reversal of economic policies. Because the center parties—especially the Radical Left Party, which had backed Social Democratic governments in the past—threw their support behind the new policy, the transition became a reality. It is also noteworthy that although the government sought to strengthen the export sector, it was able to broaden its electoral base to sheltered branches in the private sector (especially construction), which benefited greatly from the reduction in interest rates.

The Danish Opt Out of EMU: Policy Reversal or Bump on the Road?

The policy turnaround of 1982 and 1983, and associated sectoral realignment, created the basis for a sustainable and coherent monetary policy that has not been seriously contested since. The economy responded favorably to the new policy regime with growth rates and employment performance that marked a clear departure from the late 1970s and early 1980s. Although economic growth slowed after 1987, partly as a result of more accommodating policies toward public sector unions, which necessitated a subsequent tightening of budgetary policies, the current account deficit was turned into a healthy surplus of approximately 3 percent of gross domestic product (GDP), a fact that is generally viewed as an indication of good international competitiveness. (See Table 3.1.)

The turmoil in the EMS in 1992–93 received much negative coverage in the Danish press, but the strong krone policy was pursued steadfastly even when two important trading partners, Sweden and the United Kingdom, allowed their currencies to fall by 20 percent or more in the context of the weak dollar. Moreover, the German policies that triggered the crisis in the EMS did not cause the uproar in Denmark they did in, say, France, and none of the main parties (including the Social Democrats) advocated a change in policy course. The depreciation of the krone following the widening of EMS margins in August 1993 was regarded as a necessary evil by both the government and most employer organizations and unions, and markets returned the currency to the previous narrow band relatively quickly. Recently the krone has been within 1 percent of its former threshold, and the monetary policy required to sustain it has not been criticized by markets. To the contrary, the policy has been applauded, and the central bank has been encouraged to continue its cautious stance by the Social-Democrat-led government that replaced the center-right coalition government in 1993.

Against this background it may appear odd that Danish voters rejected the Maastrict treaty in a referendum on 2 June 1992. Although it is virtually impossible to disentangle attitudes toward monetary union cleanly from the larger issues of macroeconomic management and European economic and political integration—especially the emotionally charged symbolic aspects of these issues—opinion polls indicate that opposition to the common currency influenced many voters' decisions (Siune, 1993: 100). It is significant to note, however, that the pattern of opposition to Maastricht is broadly consistent with what we would expect from a sectoral cleavage model of the type explained in the last section. Thus opposition to the treaty was far greater among white-collar workers in the sheltered public sector (58 percent opposed) than among white-collar workers in the exposed private sector (37 percent opposed), unskilled blue-collar workers were similarly more prone to vote against the treaty (65 percent against) than skilled workers (46 percent against) (authors' calculations from data presented in Siune, Svensson, and Tonsgaard, 1994: 111). Since low-paid public sector workers are much more prone to vote for parties of the left than of the right, this division in opinions created a rift in the Social Democratic electorate, concentrating opposition to the Maastricht Treaty in the Socialist People's Party and in smaller groupings even farther to the left. The divisions and alignments thus resemble those discussed earlier. In this sense there clearly exists a potential electoral constituency for reform in Danish exchange rate policies.

However, it is highly unlikely that this reform would happen. Opposition to Maastricht among elites is weak, partly because Danish voters rejected Social Democratic opposition to the Single European Act in a referendum in 1986. Reflecting this elite consensus, 82 percent in the parliament voted for the Maastricht Treaty immediately prior to its submission for the June 1992 referendum. Another, and perhaps more fundamental, barrier to a radical policy reversal is the experience of the 1970s, which taught most politicians that uncertainty about the value of the currency could have substantial negative effects on the performance of the economy. Consequently, to the extent that voters are sociotropic, only parties whose constituencies stand to gain very substantially from the distributive effects of a flexible exchange rate policy would be likely to favor it. This may apply to the Socialist People's Party, it probably does not apply to the Social Democrats, and it almost certainly does not hold for the small center parties whose votes would be required for a parliamentary majority.

Consistent with this interpretation, only the Socialists People's Party put up a serious fight against the Maastricht Treaty. The party also played a pivotal role in the national compromise between seven of the eight parties represented in parliament, which resulted in the Danish demand for exemptions to the treaty in the areas of defense, European citizenship, police and justice, and (most important for our purposes) the third and final stage of the EMU. The compromise subsequently was accepted by the other EU countries in a meeting in Edinburgh in December of 1992, and this paved the way for ratification of the treaty as modified or interpreted in the Edinburgh Agreement in a second referendum in May the following year.

Yet for all the drama and international media attention that accompanied the surprising Danish no vote, it hardly signaled a departure from the hard-currency policy instituted more than a decade earlier. The political and economic elite stands behind the policy, and leaders from the main parties on the left and right joined union and business leaders in expressing dismay over the outcome of the first referendum. More important, the continuation of the old exchange rate policy was explicitly confirmed in the document outlining the national compromise: "Denmark attaches great importance to participation in exchange rate cooperation as formulated in the EMS and in the form which is to be carried forward in the second stage" (authors' translation from the text of the national compromise document of October 1992). Perhaps the supporters of the Socialist People's Party sensed the limited significance of the opt-outs and voted overwhelmingly against the compromise, and their own party's recommendation, in the second referendum (Siune, Svensson, and Tonsgaard, 1994: 110).

The opt-out of the common currency thus bears the marks of political pragmatism in the face of a delicate political situation. Moreover, at the time of the compromise, the prospect of completing the final stage of EMU after the European exchange market crisis looked rather dim, and political party elites did not want to risk another rejection in a second referendum. Instead, the hard-currency policy was confirmed while the government continued to pursue a fiscal and monetary policy that complied with the Maastricht convergence criteria. Inflation is near 2 percent, long-term interest rates are less than 100 basis points above German rates, and in 1995 the deficit-to-GDP ratio moved below the 3 percent target. The only criteria that currently is not satisfied is the debt-to-GDP target of 60 percent (it was 72 percent in early 1996), but it is being reduced at a satisfactory rate. Denmark was exempted from the excessive-deficit procedure of the Council of Economics and Finance Ministers in June 1996. Market reactions have indicated some costs may be associated with the opt-out. In particular, some important institutional investors appear to lump the Danish and Swedish currencies together, although the underlying fundamentals of the two economies are very different. Sweden, unlike Denmark, runs a large budget deficit, and although action has been taken to reduce it, the imbalance will justify for some time a considerable risk premium on assets denominated in Swedish kronor. Neither Sweden nor Denmark is regarded by market participants as a likely candidate for EMU; Sweden may not qualify under the Maastricht criteria, while Denmark could but is politically unwilling. In these circumstances, investors do not find it worthwhile to distinguish between the two currencies, and this hurts the confidence in the krone and raises the interest premium.

The government and most of the right opposition parties are clearly eager to reverse the opt-out decision, but opinion polls keep indicating a clear majority against the common currency. The Danes are pragmatic people, however, and it is not inconceivable that clearly visible costs of the opt-out would prompt a policy reversal. But regardless of whether Denmark remains outside the common currency, the broad sectoral coalition supporting a continuation of the hard-currency policy instituted in 1982–83 is clearly not about to break up. With a firmly entrenched decentralized bargaining system and a reformed social democratic party possessing little nostalgia for the political-economic impasse of the 1970s, a clear commitment to a strong currency policy has turned into a unifying issue among political elites. Currency markets may have some doubts about the ability of Danish governments to maintain a steady course—a problem that can be addressed fully only by participation in the final stage of the EMU—but the period from 1982 to 83 on has been one of stability.

Conclusions

Based on a standard optimum currency area analysis, Denmark is not an obvious candidate for membership in a common European currency area. This, however, is not the reason for the Danish opt-out—an opt-out opposed by an overwhelming majority of the economic and political elite—and it does not explain the pattern of change and stability in Danish exchange rate policies. Instead, we should understand the Danish hard-currency policy as a convenient framework for coping with domestic economic problems that emerge among domestic political-economic institutions, the international economy, and political alliance formation.

Future difficulties for Denmark in the continued economic integration process lie not so much in the prospect of a reversal of current monetary and exchange rate commitments—despite the drama produced by the rejection of the Maastricht Treaty—but in a continued and even growing maladaptation of domestic economic institutions to the realities of the new European political economy. In particular, the large Danish welfare state and the associated high levels of taxation pose some difficult dilemmas for Danish economic policies. For example, the unemployment benefit system, which guarantees much higher replacement rates for low-paid workers (despite a considerable reduction over the 1980s in average replacement rates), can hardly be exempted from carrying some of responsibility for the high unemployment rate among unskilled laborers. Without a bargaining system that facilitates the subsidization of low-end wages by better-paid workers, stronger incentives are required in order to make unions of unskilled workers consent to lower wages and a more dispersed wage structure.

There is also a general recognition that the size of the public economy has reached its zenith and that future employment growth will have to come in the private sector, primarily in services. Such private-sector growth requires a more rational tax structure in addition to greater labor market flexibility, and the government has used the completion of the Internal Market as pretext for initiating a massive tax reform that will be phased in over a number of years. Marginal income tax rates and value-added taxes are to be reduced, while more emphasis will be placed on employer contributions and environmental taxes. While these reforms probably would have been on the agenda without participation in the EU, they have become part of the politics of European integration that undoubtedly will continue to spark controversy. For example, while the reforms will help to reassure financial markets that the government's commitment to a generous welfare state is compatible with a continuation of the hard-currency policy, some groups will continue to see EMU as a potential threat to the Danish government's ongoing commitment to such a welfare state.

Notes

1. A useful illustration comes from Austria, where the currency has long been pegged to the Deutschemark. Thus, when Austrian interest rates in 1979 were lowered to a level below those in Germany, it caused large capital outflows, and interest rates had to be raised immediately to defend the currency (Scharpf, 1991: 66).

2. The actual operation of the "green money rates" and the so-called monetary compensation amounts is a great deal more complicated than we have implied, but the basic tendency for the system to disadvantage weak-currency countries is relatively straightforward and well documented, and this deter-

mined the position of farm interests on the exchange rate issue. See McNamara (1993) for a discussion of the operation of the Common Agricultural Policy.

3. After Sweden left the "snake" in 1976, the value of the Swedish krone was again pegged to a basket of foreign currencies weighted by relative trade shares. The Swedish government sovereignly decided de- or revaluations.

4. Theoretically, current account improvements from devaluations occur whenever the sum of the price elasticity of exports and imports exceeds 1 (the so-called Marshall-Lerner condition). According to most studies, elasticities on *both* imports and exports in Scandinavia vary between 0.8 and 2.2, thus easily satisfying this condition (Gylfason, 1990: 187).

5. In its 1980 report, for example, the bank charged that fiscal policies had been persistently too expansionary from the mid-1960s to the late 1970s and that the only solution would be "several years of severe restraint on increases in nominal incomes and public sector activities" combined with a monetary policy aimed at "holding the rate of inflation low and the foreign exchange conditions stable" (quoted in Johansen, 1987: 168).

6. However, when Belgium and Denmark asked for another devaluation in early 1982, they met strong opposition from the other members.

7. The hard-currency policy was singled out as the centerpiece in the new government's economic strategy: "The new government is firmly determined to re-create the balance in the Danish economy. The government has no intentions of devaluing the krone. Confidence in the value of the Danish krone at home and abroad is a good start for a new economic policy" (Inauguration speech, 10 September 1982; quoted in Kristensen, Larsen, and Ulveman, 1992: 167—author's translation).

8. Using rates on ten-year government bonds and the GDP deflator.

9. Besides, unions were increasingly divided over the issue of solidarity. (See Iversen, 1996.)

10. Correspondingly, the decentralization of the system during the 1980s was associated with disintegration and loss of influence for the peak associations and for low-wage unions, but with a strengthening of the role played by unions and employers at the sectoral level, especially in the internationally oriented engineering sector.

11. During the 1980s, the proportion of public employees voting for New Left parties in Denmark (especially the Socialist People's Party) was about three times that of private employees.

CHAPTER FOUR

Finland and EMU

Jonathon W. Moses[1]

This chapter aims to explain Finnish attitudes and ambitions with regard to joining an eventual economic and monetary union (EMU). To do so, it examines the Finnish body politic from several disparate angles; the intent is to provide an economic and a political analysis of the current movement toward EMU. As one of the youngest members of the European Union (EU), the character of the debate in Finland on EU issues is somewhat less developed than it is in some of the older member states. In some ways, Finnish support for the EU is vocal, endearing, and almost naive. In other ways, the discussion is more muted and nuanced. On matters regarding EMU, there is support and concern in both the public and private debates. This chapter tries to map these conflicting concerns.

The chapter is divided into six sections. The first section provides a historical backdrop: Finland relied heavily on exchange rate changes as an active policy instrument throughout the postwar period. This history, along with that of the successful EU referendum campaign, is important for understanding the radical nature of the changes currently being considered. The second section looks at the potential economic costs and criteria for Finland's participation in EMU. The third section examines Finland's institutional arrangements, in particular its labor market institutions, for signs of costly constraints on effective EMU participation. The fourth section speculates on the distributional divides that can be expected on the road to EMU and after; the fifth section—on issue linkages—returns us full circle, describing how EMU is linked to other significant Finnish policy issues in an attempt to make EMU membership more attractive. The sixth section forms a conclusion.

In general, the picture painted is one of cautious support. Whereas Finland's economic structure is not very well suited for participation in EMU and its history with past exchange rate adjustments makes a currency union of questionable utility, the country is in the mood for change. Finns want and need an economic transformation of some sort and apparently they are willing to pay the costs. In terms of meeting the convergence criteria and providing enthusiastic support more generally, Finns are strong candidates for participating in EMU. These ambitions, however, will require rather large social costs.

The Finnish Context

Over the postwar period, Finland, probably more than any other European country, relied on devaluations as a regular and systematic part of its economic policy arsenal. It is important to understand this history in order to evaluate the difficulties that lie ahead for Finland in a future EMU.

Exchange Rate History

Finnish economists introduced the world to the phrase and concept of a "devaluation cycle" (Korkman, 1978, 1980). Throughout the century, Finns have effectively wielded an offensive exchange rate policy to protect their domestic price level and/or secure its competitiveness in a world economy. In the postwar period, devaluations were used in roughly ten-year intervals (1949, 1957, 1968, and 1977–78) to rescue the Finnish economy from self-induced recessions. The devaluation cycle now is perceived to have been a vicious cycle. Since 1973, the value of the markka has been adjusted nearly a dozen times (see Table 4.1); devaluations were, until quite recently, an explicit part of the Finnish competitiveness policy. It would be costly to forget this history in the rush to establish EMU. (See Moses, 1995b.)

Finland's flexible exchange rate history is a long one. The Bank of Finland withdrew from the gold standard in the fall of 1914, allowing the markka to decline to about one-eighth its previous value by 1923. Accepting inflation, Finland was one of the very few countries that avoided the international depression of 1921 and learned a valuable lesson in the use of flexible exchange rates (Haavisto and Jonung, 1993; Lester, 1939/1970). This lesson was not quickly lost on following generations. During the 1930s, Finland avoided the deepest depths of the international depression by using an undervalued currency to protect its domestic price level and afterward rebuild its economy on the back of an export-led recovery.

This tradition was maintained even under the relatively rigid Bretton Woods regime. As a signatory since 1948, Finland was granted adjustments

Table 4.1: Postwar Exchange Rate Adjustments of the Finnish Markka

Date	Movement	Notes
31 May 1945	42.9 percent devaluation	
27 July 1945	28.5 percent devaluation	
16 October 1945	11.2 percent devaluation	
4 July 1949	15.0 percent devaluation	
19 September 1949	30.8 percent devaluation	
16 September 1957	28.1 percent devaluation	Bretton Woods period
12 October 1967	23.8 percent devaluation	
21 December 1970	2.4 percent revaluation	
15 February 1973	5.1 percent revaluation	
4 June 1973		Markka floats
5 April 1977	5.7 percent devaluation	
1 September 1977	3.0 percent devaluation	
17 February 1978	8.0 percent devaluation	
21 September 1979	1.3 percent revaluation	
25 March 1980	2.0 percent revaluation	Trade-weighted basket peg
6 October 1982	4.3 percent devaluation	
11 October 1982	6.0 percent devaluation	
16 May 1986	1.6 percent devaluation	
17 March 1989	4.0 percent revaluation	
7 June 1991	(no adjustment)	
15 November 1991	12.3 percent devaluation	ECU-peg
8 September 1992		Markka floats

Source: Moses (1995a).

to its exchange rate several times: Each adjustment was submitted to, and accepted by, the International Monetary Fund (IMF) on its own criteria of "fundamental disequilibrium." In the wake of Bretton Woods, in 1973, Finland was one of the first countries (following Austria) to set an autonomous exchange rate course on the basis of a trade-weighted basket. This basket facilitated frequent adjustments; an aspect of the regime used with great enthusiasm throughout most of the 1970s.

In 1982—following in the wake of the Swedish "Big Bang" devaluation and the new Swedish commitment to fixed rates of exchange—Finland's government announced its intent to establish a more fixed exchange rate regime. Unlike the Swedish attempt, however, the Finnish regime was tested frequently, and adjustments continued throughout the 1980s. The most recent promise of fixed rates came with Finland's unilateral fixing of the markka to an ECU basket in June of 1991. This commitment lasted five months before the 12.3 percent devaluation in November.

As was the case in Sweden (see Chapter 9), the 1992 market-forced devaluation has been instrumental in orchestrating Finland's most recent economic recovery: Finland's international competitiveness has been boosted significantly. Although it remains to be seen how long it will take before this competitive edge is worn away by increased wage demands, the current slack in the Finnish economy—with unemployment approaching 20 percent— has lessened the expected inflationary legacy.

As we shall see, Finland hopes to overcome its past reliance on the devaluation cycle; participation in a common currency area is seen as an important link in an effort to restructure the Finnish economy on a broader footing. But the structure of the Finnish economy and its (not unrelated) reliance on adjustable exchange rates act as a strong counterbalance to these reformist ambitions. Movement toward the convergence criteria and participation in a future EMU will cause significant economic and social discomfort for a country that has been so reliant on flexible exchange rates in the past.

European Union Membership

In the 16 October 1994 referendum, 56.9 percent of the Finnish voting public supported EU-membership; but the outcome was even more divided than the aggregate figures suggest: Support was strongly divided along regional lines. Indeed, over 70 percent of the 445 municipalities opposed membership, with the southern urban centers providing the strongest support. (See Moses and Jensen, 1998.) All of Finland's northern rural districts were opposed to membership; they were simply outnumbered by the urban vote. It is along these regional lines that we also can expect to find divided support for Finnish participation in EMU. The reasons for this will become more evident after a short description of the Finnish EU campaign.

Finland's enthusiasm for EU membership was driven (by and large) by the same factors found in the other Nordic countries, only the stakes in Finland were much higher. The collapse of the former Soviet Union has meant a radical reorientation of Finland's security as well as economic policies. Throughout most of the postwar era, Finland relied heavily on Soviet bilateral trade arrangements; its precarious neutrality made EC-membership a nonissue in the years prior to 1988.

The reasons for Finland's European policy turnaround are fairly obvious, and we need touch upon them only briefly. The security issue is probably paramount, although Finns deny that they are searching for extra security; but changes in the international political order undoubtedly have made Finnish EU membership less controversial. A second argument for membership also relates to the fall of the Soviet Union. No other Western industrialized country was more dependent on trade with the Soviet Union. Whereas the Soviet share of Finnish exports was at 27 percent in 1982, it fell precipitously to 11 percent in 1990. The repercussions on the Finnish economy were enormous. EU membership, generally, is seen as a means of reinvigorating the Finnish economy and reorienting it toward Western markets: Both the type of exports and the markets they are sold in required immediate attention.

In the first round of Finland's 1995 presidential campaign, party (and particularly party leader) positions with respect to EU membership were established. Of the six candidates, all four of the major-party candidates originally supported EU membership.[2] Only Claes Andersson from the Left Party and the independent Keijo Korhonen—each representing fairly small groups—opposed membership. After the election, the Center Party's Paavo Väyrynen actively opposed Finnish membership (a change that reflects the underlying tensions within the Center Party on the issue of EU membership).[3]

While security and economic issues appear to play a significant role in influencing Finland's positive attitudes toward EU membership, pessimism has grown with the more recent extension of Community powers. Support for membership (at its peak in Finland in 1992) took a beating after the Danish no vote to the Maastricht Treaty—in every party setting. (See Table 4.2.) The opposition, however, did not seem to reap the full benefit of this fall in support, as the difference was split between the opposition and those with no opinion. Still, indecision in Europe (particularly in Denmark) about the benefits of greater integration can be seen as one of the primary causes of the pre-referendum increase in Euro-skepticism among Finns.

This interpretation was reflected in a survey taken in November 1993. Finns were weary of a European Union with too much power: 82 percent of those asked believed security and defense should remain primarily the responsibility of the Finnish government; 90 percent thought that health and social welfare policies should be decided by national governments (and not jointly with the European Community); 65 percent thought that industrial policy, 64 percent thought that value-added tax (VAT) rates, and 53 percent of those polled thought that the currency should remain in the hands of national, not EC governments (Ludlow, 1994). The Finnish general public, like many in Europe, is apparently leery of too much power centered in Brussels.

Table 4.2: Party Support for EC/EU Membership Before and After the Danish Veto

	Left	Social Democrats	Green	Agricultural	Conservative	Total
Before the Danish Veto (May 1992, percent)						
For	42	65	69	46	85	61
Against	50	22	24	43	7	27
Other	9	12	7	11	8	12
After the Danish Veto (June 1992, percent)						
For	51	59	51	34	74	50
Against	30	26	27	50	14	31
Other	19	16	22	16	12	18

Source: Lindström, (1992) 24-25.

During the referendum campaign, there was little explicit reference to monetary issues. Finns expect great economic gains from EU membership, but this optimism is attached more to the opportunities offered by the single market than to any dynamic potential of an EMU. On EMU, Finnish attitudes seem to be influenced more by the fears of capital flight, the extra incentive it provides for fiscal rectitude, and the hopes of restructuring the Finnish economy on a broader, more productive footing.

EMU support in Finland is complicated. Finland's exchange rate history does not speak well for its ability to embrace a common currency area. In the postwar period, Finland has relied heavily on exchange rate adjustments, and they have—by and large—been successful. Still, since the early 1980s, there has been a concentrated effort to try and move in the direction of more fixed rates of exchange; it may be that EMU membership will provide the extra confidence and support necessary to facilitate that move. Whereas the exchange rate picture is not clear-cut, the nature and strength of Finnish support for the EU suggests that voters will be willing to bear what adjustment costs are necessary to achieve EMU. Not only do they see great economic benefit from being associated with the other aspects of EU membership, but they are also willing to pay a large security deposit for protection against potential Eastern aggressors.

Economic Criteria

The economic prospects of participating in EMU can be evaluated in two ways. First, one can ask whether Finland will be able to satisfy the Maastricht criteria, and if so, when. The second issue concerns the structural characteristics of the Finnish economy. If Finland's economy is not well integrated with the rest of Europe's, and/or if the Finnish economy is particularly susceptible to asymmetric shocks, the costs of participating in EMU can be quite large.

Convergence Criteria

The Finnish economy is in a shambles: Unemployment hovers around 20 percent. Still, Finland can be considered an honorary member of Europe's elite convergence club. In 1993, Finland was one of a handful of countries that actually met three of the four convergence criteria.[4] Finland's record in terms of the Maastricht criteria is impressive, especially when one considers the severity of the current crisis (and ignores the exchange rate clause, as is vogue). The debt figure in 1994 was within a whisper of the criterion, and two of the remaining three criteria were satisfied. Although the deficit remains a problem, there is broad consensus that this indicator also will fall within the criterion in the very near future. Indeed, the European Commission expects Finland's deficit to fall to 1.1 percent in 1996 and its debt level to hold steady at around 64 percent (Barber, 1995).

Nor is this record a single-shot performance: Finland has a history of fiscal conservatism. It is only with the enormity of the current crisis that Finland's debt burden has come even close to approaching the 60 percent (of gross domestic product, or GDP) level. Throughout most of the 1980s, Finnish government debt hovered around 20 percent.[5] The same could be said for Finnish budget deficits, which stayed within the 3 percent of GDP margins throughout the entire postwar period—up to 1990. On the other two criteria, inflation and interest rates, the Finnish postwar period is less impressive. Still, over the past four years, the Finnish inflation rate has been held under the Maastricht criterion, and the same can be said for Finnish long-term interest rates after January 1993.

Thus there is little doubt that Finland can and will fulfill the convergence criteria in the very near future. The Organization for Economic Cooperation and Development (OECD, 1993a) calculated that more than 90 percent of the Finnish budget deficit was cyclical, mostly a reflection of the current economic crisis. The surge in public spending (from 40 to 55 percent of GDP from 1989 to 1992) is also a result of the crisis, as is the decline in public revenues (Söderström, 1993: 188–192). The government has accepted strict spending guidelines for the next few years, and to fulfill these it has made explicit and concrete decisions on how to reduce the deficit. Once the current, deep depression is over, Finland should be able to adapt fairly easily to meeting the demands of the Maastricht criteria. Indeed, Finland's economy may have turned the corner: Industrial output in 1995 grew by 7.5 percent, and trade with the former Soviet Union (particularly Russia) is reviving.

Economic Structure

While Finland's record with respect to the convergence criteria is positive, the structure of its economy lends itself to rather severe asymmetric demand shocks. This section looks at Finland's economic structure from two vantage points: trade and production.

Like the other Nordic countries on the periphery of Europe, Finland relies on Europe as both a market for its exports and a producer of its imports.[6] Forty percent of Finland's exports and 40 percent of its imports are with EU member states. Indeed, four out of Finland's top five export markets are within the EU: Germany (13 percent of all exports), Sweden (11 percent), the United Kingdom (10 percent), and France (5 percent). Still, the Finnish economy is less open than that of other small European countries, and its openness is decreasing. During the 1980s, Finland's ratio of exports (to GDP) fell from about one third to less than one-quarter (Currie, 1993: 106). In the share of both value added and employment, the Finnish tradables' sector shrunk over the 1990s.

What may be more relevant is the type of export goods upon which the Finnish economy is most dependent. Table 4.3 suggests that the country is heavily reliant on the forest industry—in particular paper and paper products, but also cork and wood exports. Paper and paper products make up a quarter of Finland's total exports, significantly more than the percentiles for any of the other export goods. Studies of European trade structures and their interaction find Finland's trade structure, like Greece's, to be clearly different from the EU average.

Another way to measure export dependence is in terms of the proportion of total manufacturing that goes to export. Although production and export figures are not completely complementary, Table 4.4 attempts to gauge the share of manufactures that is exported in some of Finland's most significant industries.[7] Table 4.4 begins like the previous table by listing the five most important export industries for 1992 (at the two-digit SITC level). It then gives the nearest production equivalent, measured in ISIC terms. Comparing these two gives us a rough estimate of how much of an industry's production goes to export. For Finland's most significant export industry (paper and paper products), nearly 60 percent of production is exported. This industry also represents a substantial percentage (18.5 percent) of industrial employees in Finland (*Yearbook of Nordic Statistics,* 1994). Indeed, this sector represents the largest industrial employer at the two-digit ISIC level in 1992. In short, the nation's

Table 4.3: Five Most Important Finnish Export Items, 1993

SITC Product Group	Description	Export Share (percent)
64	Paper and paper products	25
67	Iron and steel	6
72	Specialized industrial machinery	6
76	Telecommunications equipment	5
24	Cork and wood	5
Total export share of all five products		47

Source: Yearbook of Nordic Statistics, (1995).

Table 4.4: Top Five Export Industries and Export Composition of Manufacturing, 1992

Export Industry		Share in Total Exports (percent)	Nearest Product Equivalent		Export Share in Production (percent)
SITC Code	Description		ISIC Code	Description	
64	Paper, paper products	26.7	34	Paper, paper products	57.4
67	Iron and steel	6.3	371	Iron-steel, basic industry	58.5
72	Specialized machinery	5.1	n/a		
24	Cork and wood	4.7	n/a		
78	Road vehicles	4.6	384	Transport manufacturing	43.8

Note: The ranking of export industries differs from that in Table 4.3 because in 1992 "road vehicles" was a more important export industry than "telecommunications equipment."
Source: Yearbook of Nordic Statistics, (1994, 1995).

employment and economic dependence on these export sectors is quite large, especially in the paper and paper products industries.

Another way to capture the degree of economic integration is to try to measure a nation's reliance on intraindustrial and interindustrial trade. The study by Assarsson and Olsson (1993) used in the Swedish case also included Finland, so its results are directly comparable. Using a Grubel-Lloyds (GL) index for measuring the degree of intraindustrial trade (see chapter 9 for details), they found Finland to be modestly placed among its European brethren: below Sweden, Denmark, and Britain, but above others such as Greece. Like Sweden, only more so, Finland's large export of forest industry products handicaps its ability to score highly in either the GL or the interindustry indices. Like the other Nordic countries, the Finnish economy is not particularly well integrated or diversified compared to other West European economies.

Finland's economy is highly susceptible to negative external demand shocks because of its overreliance on forest industry exports. On this point there is fairly broad consensus. The price of timber products fluctuates widely in world markets and is affected significantly by the dollar's value. Price slumps can be exacerbated by a low dollar level because a low dollar will increase the supply of timber and paper products from North American producers, depressing world timber and paper prices in European currency terms. Maintaining fixed exchange rates to a basket that does not include the dollar will exacerbate booms and slumps in the Finnish economy.

However, studies that have looked at the symmetry of shocks between Finland and specific EU member states have found their relationship to be more nuanced than the export figures might suggest. In particular, Finland's shocks with respect to Europe's core economies (Germany, France and the United Kingdom) appear to be predominantly symmetric. Haaparanta and Heinonen (1991) found this to be the case, although they found that asymmetries increased during the 1980s.[8] These conclusions were supported (at least with respect to the core economies) by Tarkka and Åkerholm's (1992) study, although they found significant asymmetric disturbances between Finland's economy and some of Europe's more marginal economies (for example, Denmark, Portugal, Ireland, and Greece).

Thus the structure of the Finnish economy, as it now stands, would not appear to support an argument for participation in a future EMU. Finland's reliance on forest industry exports—an industry that experiences volatile price movements, and is influenced by the value of the dollar—suggests that Finland will pay in terms of exaggerated business cycles without recourse to exchange rate adjustments.

The lessons here are mixed. On the one hand, Finland's ability to quickly reach the Maastricht criteria suggests that the cost of adapting during the transition period to a single currency will be relatively small. The costs are small, because these are decisions that would be made regardless of the convergence criteria: Finland's fiscal history is a conservative one. The social and employment costs can be considerable. On the other hand, should Finland enjoy the rewards of meeting the criteria and become a member of EMU, the costs may be quite large. If the Finnish economy does not go through a radical, structural transition at the same time, its overreliance on forest industry products is likely to exacerbate the Finnish boom-bust cycle.

Institutional Setting

My primary concern here is to investigate the degree to which specific institutional cleavages in Finland can be expected to facilitate or handicap the move to EMU and its performance afterward. While the focus of my investigation is on labor market institutions, the end of the section investigates the potential for both bureaucratic and political party cleavages.

The Finnish labor market—like the Swedish, and in contrast to those in much of the rest of the world—is characterized by high levels of unionization and centralization under peak bargaining organizations. Finland's bargaining coverage rate is 95 percent, second only to Austria (at 98 percent), while 72 percent of its labor force is unionized (Traxler, 1994: 173). More than in Sweden, economy-wide bargaining is entrenched in Finland: Peak associations of employers and employees negotiate package deals on wages and prices as well as economic and social policy. The degree of coverage and coordination is such that Traxler describes Finland's capacity for implementation as "high" (Traxler, 1994: 175).

The Finnish labor market, however, is unique in that its peak labor organizations are split along ideological lines—which happen to correspond with different sectors of the economy. This division has not only made the obtainment of centralized agreements more difficult (and tardy; in the Nordic context, Finland's move to centralized bargaining was quite late), but it also has led to some lack of discipline among collective bargaining partners. Thus some of the benefits of collective, centralized bargaining have been lost because of the internecine struggles among unions.[9]

Workers in Finland's private sector are mainly organized under four umbrella organizations: the Central Organization of Finnish Trade Unions (SAK; about 60 percent of unionized employees), the Confederation of Salaried Employees (TVK; about 21 percent), the Finnish Central Organization of Professional Workers (Akava; about 12 percent) and the Confederation of Technical Employees' Organizations in Finland (STTK; about 7 percent). Both ideologically and organizationally, the labor movement is divided broadly into a Social Democratic majority and a strong Communist minority. Trade union leadership, both in the central unions and in most branch unions, is in the hands of the Social Democrats. The principal Communist-led unions are those organizing the construction and foodstuffs industries; however, the Communists are active also in a number of other industries. On the employer side of the Finnish equation, there are two major organizations: the Finnish Employers' Federation (STK) and the Employers' Confederation of Service Industries (LTK). Together these two organizations cover over 60 percent of private sector employees.

Since 1977, these institutions have been formally linked to, and informed about, exchange rate policy decisions. In that year, the SAK would accept the terms of a comprehensive wage agreement only if it contained a devaluation clause. The Bank of Finland was strongly opposed to this clause, but its resistance was in vain. The eventual agreement called for the initiation of negotiations between labor market representatives on the possible compensation of wage earners in the event of a substantive devaluation (Waris, 1979). As a result, wage-earner organizations are both aware of and instrumentally involved in decisions regarding exchange rate adjustments.

What is the effect of this institutional framework? For present purposes, the most important consequence of this would be whether it can facilitate the adjustments that will be required in EMU—given Finland's rather unique economic structure. In particular, does the high degree of coverage facilitate greater or less wage flexibility?

Characterizing the flexibility of national labor markets is not easy, and I have applied some of the same measures used in Chapter 9 to try to find a comparable measure of wage rigidity in the Finnish economy. As Table 4.5 suggests, Finnish real wage growth greatly outstripped productivity increases throughout most of the past two decades. Compared to the other Nordic countries, Finland scored exceptionally low in terms of the discrepancy remainder. Although the difference between product real wage and productivity growth rates appears to be diminishing, by 1987 the Finnish record was still disturbing. Yet the picture may be changing. During the mid-1990s, because of the depression, there have been no negotiated collective pay rises. Because of the carry-over effects and a small wage drift, wages and salaries did rise by one percent over this period, but real wages in Finland actually declined. (See *Nordic Economic Outlook,* 14 February 1994, p. 9.) Neither did the 1991–92 depreciations lead to immediate compensatory wage claims, as might have been expected.

Christian Bordes (1993) has investigated the degree of wage flexibility in Finland. He found that the country has a particularly high value of elasticity for its nominal wage rate with respect to inflation, and a relatively high value with respect to unemployment. Compared to other OECD economies, Finland has the highest value for its elasticity of nominal wage rates with respect to inflation. These conditions facilitated the devaluation cycle: The economy adjusted to negative shocks with a deterioration in employment. This, in turn, slowed nominal pay increases. The adjustment itself was facilitated by the high elasticity of nominal wages to unemployment (Bordes, 1993: 83).

This is not to suggest that the centralized bargaining structure in Finland can be held responsible for the current economic difficulties. Throughout the 1980s, this system delivered rather moderate wage increases, even during the boom conditions that followed the liberalization of

Table 4.5: Finnish Labor Productivity and Real Wage Development in Manufacturing

	1967-72	1973-77	1978-83	1984-87
Product real wage growth	6.4	5.0	3.8	5.0
Productivity Growth	4.8	-0.4	4.8	5.0
Discrepancy	1.6	5.4	-1.0	0.0

Note: Data are average annual percentage change.
Source: Calmfors (1990b), p. 24.

Finland's financial markets. Indeed, Finland's share of total wage costs to national income actually fell throughout the 1970s and 1980s, boosting the Finnish profit levels. Wage shares increased only after the Finnish output fell off, suggesting that the country's high wage share is a consequence, rather than a cause, of the current slump (Currie, 1993: 123).

The relevant question is: How will wages be affected by EMU? The lessons here are more encouraging. If we assume that the EMU will be inflation adverse, Finland's high nominal wage elasticities with respect to inflation will be less problematic. More important, should Finland be hit hard by an asymmetric demand shock, such that unemployment levels begin to rise, we can expect fairly strong nominal wage drops (due to the strong negative elasticity of nominal wages with respect to unemployment). This is significant, as the burden of adjustment costs within EMU most likely will be borne on the backs of workers. Under these unique conditions, one might suggest that Finnish labor benefits from lower wages.

Two other institutional legacies in Finland are significant with respect to movement toward EMU. First, divisions between the Finnish central bank and government over the necessity of fixed exchange rates have been developing for some time. This difference came to light in 1991, when the markka was linked to an ECU basket. The then central bank governor, Rolf Kullberg, forced the hands of the government on the issue: He unexpectedly announced in a press conference that Finland would benefit by following the Swedish example (in linking to the ECU). Eventually—in the beginning of 1992—Kullberg was forced to resign, taking with him much of the credibility of Finland's hard-currency policy.

Whereas the government may have won its 1992 skirmish with the central bank, its victory was almost certainly pyrrhic. In order to participate in the third stage of EMU, legislation governing Finland's bank will have to be reformed significantly—granting it more independence. In the short to medium term, then, the central bank and its long-standing preference for fixed rates will benefit. Eventually, however, this hard-won independence might be lost in the halls of the European Monetary Institute (EMI). In this way, the recent division between the central bank and the government will be of historical interest only. For the time being, both the government and its central bank have their sights set on EMU.

The final arena in which we might expect institutional division is the political one. But, as in Sweden, this does not appear to be so. During the February 1995 general election campaign, for example, all of the main parties appeared to compete with one another in terms of fiscal virtuousness: Each promised its own ambitious cuts to public expenditures. The result, Paavo Liponen's "rainbow" government, found broad ideological support for deep cuts in public expenditures and its balanced budget ambitions.[10] The depth of the current crisis seems to have numbed Finland's ideological senses. Indeed, recent history suggests that ideological divisions may be less than relevant for understanding fixed or floating preferences. On the decision to link to ECU, for example, another government itself was split along sectoral lines (within the parties): While the finance minister was in favor of linking, his colleagues from the same Conservative Party were opposed (Moses, 1997).

Despite the fact that Finnish labor market conditions were not particularly well suited for utilizing frequent devaluations, devaluations were the hallmark of Finnish postwar adjustment strategy. Apparently, however, these labor market institutions will not hamper the move to EMU, and they may even thrive under those conditions. Other institutional divisions appear to be less significant, and are more likely ephemeral in nature.

Distributional Consequences

Here I ask what the move to an EMU might entail in terms of distributional consequences. In particular, there are two overlapping distributional concerns: one sectoral, the other more wide-ranging. At an even more general level, however, the anti-inflationary discipline imposed by EMU membership will act as a serious constraint on labor in those industries where the bargaining power of trade unions is strong. EMU, combined with free trade and factor mobility, will tend to equalize the prices of input factors between participating countries. As labor is less mobile than other production factors, relative production costs within EMU will be determined largely by unit labor costs. So, while the institutional framework of the Finnish labor market will not hamper moves to EMU, participation in a monetary union will limit the bargaining power of labor (vis-à-vis capital) within those institutions. In addition to this general tendency, however, we can expect sectoral and social cleavages to develop.

Providing an overview or survey of partisan and societal interests in Finland on monetary issues is not an easy task. Not only are such issues kept out of the light of public debate; the institutional arrangement in Finland (among Finland's central bank, the Parliamentary Supervisory Board, and the government) allows these decisions to be made by a small group of relatively autonomous actors. Interest rates, exchange rate policy, and monetary policy in general have been described traditionally in technical, apolitical terms.

Having said that, two important sectoral interests predominate in the battle for Finnish monetary policy (and hence in the fight for support of EMU): those more traditional interests that benefited and actively encouraged a Finnish adjustment policy based on frequent exchange rate adjustments, and those more nascent interests that want to pursue a fixed rate policy in order to discipline wage earners and encourage investments in high-tech industries.

The forest industry sector in Finland has enormous political and economic resources at its disposal.[11] With these resources it has been able to influence monetary policy and has benefited tremendously by Finland's active devaluation policy. This reliance on devaluations has, however, undermined the price competitiveness of labor-dependent productive firms in the nascent Finnish high-tech sectors. These industries argue that frequent devaluations encourage continued investment in the forest industry sector at the expense of other sectors. The original hope of the fixed exchange rate strategy (since 1982) was that it would aid in diversifying the Finnish economy: to force a move out of the forest and into more high-tech industries.[12] These industries benefit less from a devaluation strategy and are more dependent on domestic wage competitiveness. Although the original strategy failed, the new push for EMU in Finland can be seen as a second attempt to employ this sort of diversification strategy. Should this strategy prove successful, distributional consequences along sectoral, and hence regional (that is, rural-urban), lines can be expected.

The organization of Finland's peak union affiliations also provides some interesting insights into sectoral interests with respect to support for a potential EMU. As mentioned earlier, unions are divided along sectoral and ideological lines. This division provides us with an opportunity to see how different sectors react to a given monetary policy (at least among organized workers in that sector). These divisions can be seen in the 1991 "Sorsa proposal," which called for a 7 percent wage cut instead of a devaluation. While the closed sector unions preferred this proposal, exposed unions were vehemently opposed, preferring instead an equivalent devaluation. In the end, the exposed unions were strong-armed into conceding, but there was a great deal of uncertainty during the industry-level bargaining round. The threat of exit haunted the whole process. Eventually, because of a run on the reserves, the central bank devalued, and the markka fell by 15 percent.

As a result, the Sorsa proposal collapsed. However, the proposal—and the divided response to it by closed and exposed sectors—shows how salient these sectoral divisions can be, given institutional fortification and an appropriate venue.

The second main distributional concern is the potential effect on unemployment. Traditionally, Finns have been less willing than their Nordic neighbors to employ counter-cyclical solutions to economic woes; the result is an acceptance in Finland of a higher rate of unemployment than in either Norway or Sweden. It was not peculiar to run the Finnish economy at the 5 percent unemployment level throughout most of the 1980s. However, in recent years there has obviously been a very large shock to the economy: Adjustment will require some time and resources.

As many of the economic costs to fulfilling the convergence criteria are being paid already, the additional costs of bringing the budget deficit into line will be minimal (at least in political terms). There is a fairly broad and historical consensus in Finland over the need to maintain fiscal conservatism and pursue classical/neoclassical solutions to the country's economic problems. The Ministry of Finance's medium-term survey from February 1993 predicted that unemployment would remain at 12.5 percent in 1997 (Currie, 1993: 141). This is a phenomenal social cost to be paid, but one that cannot be mitigated given the overriding ambition to meet the demands of a balanced budget.

The Finnish policy model always has emphasized supply, cost, and competitiveness factors; it might even be described as anti-Keynesian. Until recently, the state was nearly always a net saver; it fostered savings and generally avoided loan financing. Throughout most of the postwar era, Finnish fiscal policy has been strongly pro-cyclical. Although the picture began to change in the 1980s, the tradition of fiscal conservatism is long-lived in Finland. Fiscal adjustment is perceived as necessary, regardless of the Maastricht criteria, and the political costs of budget cutting (although high in a period with overwhelming unemployment levels) are affordable.

Linkage Issues

Because of the historical and economic arguments against Finnish participation in EMU, support for EMU is generated by linking it to issues that are more important to Finnish voters. In particular, participation is seen as part in parcel of three larger policy issues: political participation, economic restructuring, and as an incentive to attract increasingly mobile finance capital.

Politically, support for EMU is linked to participation, more generally, in the European Union. As mentioned earlier, Finns support EU membership for a variety of reasons, and full membership—in all EU projects—is seen as a necessary and important element in convincing others of their new geopolitical position. But political support need not be read only in security terms. For the time being, there is great hope that participating in the EU will bring about the investment and employment sparks currently lacking in the Finnish economy. While the 1992–93 depreciation has helped to increase competitiveness in Finland, there remains a great deal of uncertainty. Because of this, the fortunes of Finland's economic and political future have been tied to the hope of an economic recovery in the rest of Europe. The sagacity of this decision remains to be seen. Politically, however, there is great support for European solutions. In contrast to Swedes, Finns have maintained optimism about the EU. Polls taken in June of 1995 showed stable support for EU membership, with 55 percent of the people polled being "fairly satisfied" with membership and 40 percent being dissatisfied (Carnegy, 1995b). These results were close to those of the referendum outcome in October 1994, where 56.9 percent supported membership.

In addition, as is the case in many other countries, there is a hope that Finland may have some say about the nature of European monetary policy in the European Central Bank. Under contemporary economic conditions, Finns have effectively lost control of their monetary policy. Because of the increased mobility of finance capital, it has been difficult for them to maintain confidence in, and support for, their basket-pegged exchange rates. Popular opinion has it that Finnish monetary policy is now being made in Germany. The hope is that participating in EMU will return some element of Finnish control over the interest rate policies that affect the domestic economy.

The second main linkage issue has to do with restructuring the Finnish economy. As previous sections have alluded to, participation in EMU is seen as bitter but necessary medicine for improving the health of the Finnish economy. In Finland there is broad consensus about the importance of further integrating with the rest of Europe. Economic integration is seen as the only hope for escaping from the threat of economic volatility. With the collapse of its near-monopolistic trade relationship with the Soviet Union, Finland is facing a world economy that demands higher product standards than did the Soviet Union and it remains an export economy in search of a market. Almost overnight, Finland lost its principal supplier of cheap energy. Membership in the EU, with its generous transition funds, is seen as a means of restructuring the Finnish economy to meet the needs of a new, more demanding marketplace. Participation in EMU is seen as a significant element in this restructuring process.

Over the past decade, there has been a general recognition of the need for the Finnish economy to move away from its heavy dependence on the forest industry sector and into a more diversified, more production-based economy. Forsman, Haaparanta, and Heinonen (1993) argue that an active exchange rate policy, like the one Finland pursued throughout most of the postwar period, accommodates negative demand shocks for key export industries; but in so doing, it also may prevent an economy from achieving a higher degree of diversification by blocking structural change. As we saw earlier, devotion to a new fixed-exchange-rate regime is one important aspect of a policy designed to spur diversification.

In order to meet the requirements of the European Common Market and maintain competitiveness, Finland has had to streamline its trade and subsidy policies, liberalize large segments of its economy, and reorient its export outlook. As Finland has the most liberal (that is, noninterventionist) of the Nordic economies, this transition might have been less painful for it than for the others—had it not been for the severe depression. Preparing for European integration, although painful, is seen as part of the necessary costs of re-orienting the Finnish economy in a more westerly direction. One main element of this restructuring plan has to do with the final linkage item: attracting European investment capital.

Although the most recent depreciation has not prompted inflation, fears of previous devaluation cycles still haunt the Finnish investment environment—at least that part of it which is potentially mobile. In the middle of the 1980s, Finnish companies rapidly began expanding their foreign direct investments in Europe both in reaction to the Single European Act and out of concern that the government would return to its devaluation cycle. By the late 1980s, every third markka was invested abroad by a handful of major Finnish international firms. In the 1990s, the outflow has decreased, but it is still substantially higher than the inflow (Väyrynen, 1993: 70).[13] It is hoped that participation in EMU will stop the outflow of Finnish capital. (See Figure 4.1.)

Curiously, the devaluation cycle may have contributed to Finland's relatively high level of general investment; its removal as an instrument could have drastic consequences on domestic investment. The earlier environment was described by Korkman (1992: 289): "A common interpretation is that there used to be an 'implicit understanding' between industry, the forest industry in particular, and the central bank, that investment activity should be strong, and that, as part of such a policy, the exchange rate would be devalued if this was necessary to ensure some minimum return on investment. Arguably, this is one explanation for the high investment ratio which has been characteristic of the Finnish economy. . . ."

Thus more mobile investment capital—fearing future devaluations—has begun to flee. The remaining investment capital can no longer expect to benefit from future devaluations. Arguably, the Finnish investment climate

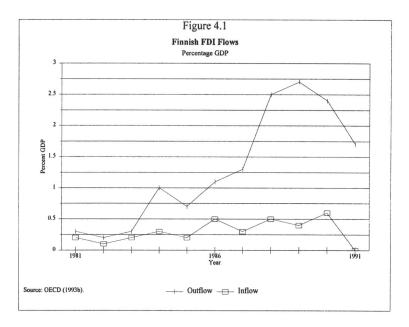

Figure 4.1

Finnish FDI Flows
Percentage GDP

Source: OECD (1993b).   —+— Outflow —□— Inflow

is in transition. During this transitionary period, until more mobile capital pools can be encouraged to return to the country, the domestic investment environment looks dour. The difference, unfortunately, has not been made up for with stocks of inward foreign direct investment (FDI). In this regard, the Finnish case is strikingly deviant: Finland has a very small stock of FDI. (See Figure 4.2.) Thus EMU participation could be seen as part of a larger strategy to minimize the potential risks for foreign capital in an attempt to attract more of it.

As a result of the overlapping (as opposed to crosscutting) nature of Finnish political, regional, and ideological cleavages, there remain strong sectoral and societal pressures for future devaluations. How these will be placated along the road to EMU remains to be seen. As in the rest of the Nordic region, financial markets in Finland are small, young, and relatively uninfluential. The strongest advocate for EMU membership is (and will remain) the Finnish central bank. For the Bank of Finland, EMU membership will finally provide a firm nominal constraint on Finnish wage earners and eager governments—a policy for which it has been arguing over several decades. It also will relieve the bank from (traditionally strong) governmental and industrial pressure to devalue. In this policy, the central bank has converted most of Finland: Finns are willing and confident that they will be among the first group of countries to constitute the EMU.

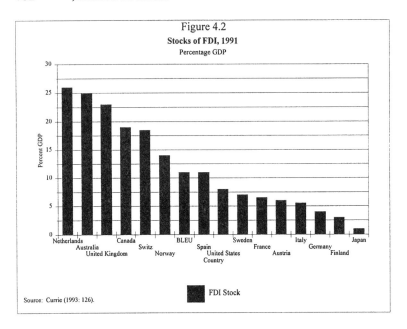

Figure 4.2
Stocks of FDI, 1991
Percentage GDP

Source: Currie (1993: 126).

Conclusion

In conclusion we might ask: What are the costs of Finnish membership in EMU, and what is the likelihood of Finland achieving membership, given those costs? As is the case with many of the other countries discussed in this volume, answers to these questions are difficult and subtle. Economically, there are strong arguments against Finland's joining EMU. Politically, there appears to be strong support for participation. How can these differences be reconciled?

From a historical perspective, the conclusion is quite clear: Finns always have relied on flexible exchange rates. Unless there is a radical transformation of the Finnish economy, participation in EMU will be very costly. Finns have developed other adjustment mechanisms in the past and have become heavily reliant on them. The reason for this reliance on exchange rate adjustments is clearly demonstrated in the unique production and export structure of the Finnish economy. Overdependence on a specific export sector, forest products, makes the Finnish economy terribly susceptible to asymmetric demand shocks. Without recourse to adjustable exchange rates, the Finnish economy—should it not undergo a radical restructuring—will have to rely even more heavily on unemployment and wage flexibility as mechanisms for adjusting to these shocks.

The key element of the economic analysis is locked in the phrase "unless there is a radical restructuring or transformation." This is where the political argument enters and takes center stage. In Finland there are strong political pressures for just that sort of economic restructuring. Using the collapse of the Soviet market as an excuse and an engine for change, Finland hopes to begin rebuilding its economy on a broader, more Western-oriented export foundation. Participation in the European Union and its EMU are seen as important elements in that restructuring drive.

Because of these ambitions, there is an apparent willingness to pay what could amount to be very significant social costs of transformation. To be fair, the alternative—maintaining an overdependence on the forest industry—could be equally costly as the fortunes of this industry are notoriously cyclical. Still, Finland's economic past does not bode well for membership in a European currency union. Restructuring will mean that adjustments to international demand shocks will be taken from the macropolicy arena and forced down to the microlevel: onto the pay slips of wage earners. Thus, in the long run, participation in EMU is linked to a strategy for restructuring the Finnish economy. This strategy, in turn, will depend on the ability of Finland's elites to maintain political support for a transformation that will be both enduring and costly.

Notes

1. I would like to thank Jeffry Frieden and Erik Jones, along with all of the other members of the EPG, for their comments and suggestions over the many drafts of this chapter. Of course, I alone remain responsible.
2. Specifically, they were: Martti Ahtisaari (Social Democrats), Paavo Väyrynen (Center Party); Raimo Ilaskivi (Samlingspartiet: the Conservative Party); and Elisabeth Rehn (Swedish People's Party).
3. Politically, agrarian interests have been more powerful in Finland than in the other Nordic countries. See Andersson, Kosonen, and Vartiainen (1993).
4. The members that met three of the four criteria (none met all four) in 1993 were; France, Ireland (exempted debt), Luxembourg, the Netherlands, and the United Kingdom.
5. According to Bank of Finland figures, about half of the central government's debt is denominated in foreign currencies.
6. Unless otherwise noted, the figures in this paragraph are from *Yearbook of Nordic Statistics* (1995).
7. In 1992, the most recent year for which we have comparable statistics, Finland's export structure changed from the year after (1993). In 1992, Road

Vehicles were more important than Telecommunications Equipment in Finnish export terms. Contrast Table 4.3 with Table 4.4.

8. These asymmetries, the authors argue, are probably the result of the relatively late deregulation of the Finnish financial sector; the radical change in Finland's eastward trade; and, of course, dependence on the forest industry.

9. Industrial negotiations did not really become centralized until the 1960s, since which time they have taken on several of the characteristics of the Swedish and Norwegian models. See Golden and Wallerstein (1995).

10. Though Liponen, the prime minister, is a Social Democrat, his crisis government included Conservatives, Greens, and former Communists.

11. In 1992, the manufacturing of paper and paper products alone (ISIC 34) accounted for 20 percent of all Finnish industrial production and 12 percent of Finnish GDP (*Yearbook of Nordic Statistics,* 1995).

12. Two examples are almost universally presented as the sort of firms that the adjustment policy was supposed to encourage: Nokia (a high-tech, electronics firm) and Kone (a forklift producer).

13. Väyrynen notes that in 1992, Finnish companies invested about 8.9 billion markkas (net) abroad, while a total of 1.7 billion was invested in Finland.

CHAPTER FIVE

Greece and EMU

Miranda Xafa[1]

This chapter addresses a number of issues in assessing Greece's prospects for convergence with the European Union and its integration in EMU:

- Is Greece a good candidate for monetary union with the rest of the EU based on the criteria set out in the optimum currency area literature?
- What drives positive sentiment toward EMU and support for the "hard drachma" policy?
- How far is Greece from fulfilling the convergence criteria laid out in the Treaty as a prerequisite for joining EMU?
- What are the prospects for, and obstacles to, convergence?
- Does compliance with the fiscal convergence criteria ensure convergence?

Political Economy Considerations

Support for membership in the European Community (EC) in public opinion and across political parties has increased significantly since full membership in January 1981. (See Figure 5.1.) Public opinion turned mildly negative with the election of a Socialist government in October 1981, which denounced the European Community (and the North Atlantic Treaty Organization [NATO]) on grounds of conspiring to reduce Greece's sovereignty. Nonetheless, growing transfers to Greece from the EC structural funds and agricultural support funds subsequently helped increase public support for membership.

The deepening of European integration with the Single Market program and the Maastricht Treaty, the collapse of the Soviet Union, and the end of

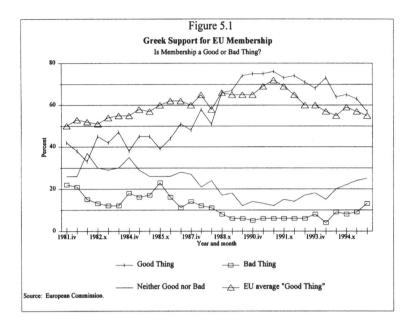

Figure 5.1
Greek Support for EU Membership
Is Membership a Good or Bad Thing?

the postwar world order all had a profound impact on Greece's attitudes toward the EU. The Union was viewed as a pole of stability and prosperity in an otherwise turbulent region, particularly in view of Greece's geographical proximity to the armed conflict in Bosnia and the perceived threat of a change in Balkan borders. Greece's membership in the Western EU, agreed in principle in November 1992 and in effect since April 1995, was viewed as a guarantee of solidarity and as an improvement in Greece's ability to respond to perceived external threats to its security.

On the economic side, worldwide competition for export markets became more intense with the integration of the former planned economies and a growing number of developing countries in the world economy. The doubling of the EU structural funds in 1993 was considered as Greece's last chance to restructure its economy and acquire badly needed infrastructure so as to enable it to compete in a world that suddenly had become far more competitive. From a macroeconomic perspective, the EU structural funds were viewed as the only viable way of increasing public investment, catalyzing private direct investment, and pulling Greece out of stagflation without putting fiscal convergence at risk.

Time was running short. It was clear that the widening of the EU to include the former European Free Trade Associations (EFTA) countries and, eventually, the Central and Eastern European countries (CEECs) was a matter of time. Official statements by the government often warned that the CEECs were making faster progress in restructuring and privatizing their economies than Greece was. Unless Greece speeded up its convergence process, it was clear that it would become marginalized within an expanding EU, with core countries eventually moving to monetary union.

The Maastricht Treaty was ratified by parliament in 1992 with the overwhelming support of nearly all parties, including the Socialist Party, which had expressed concern over loss of sovereignty with EC membership while in government in the 1980s. The exception was the Communist Party, whose support for the former Soviet Union remained unabated despite its collapse, which voted against the treaty. In the 1996 national election, in which the Socialist Party won a fresh popular mandate, both major parties campaigned on a pro-European platform and pledged to continue ongoing efforts at convergence within the EU. Opinion polls taken at election time similarly confirm the widely held view that EU membership presupposes, and contributes to, stability and prosperity.

Costs and Benefits from EMU

The prospective EMU in Europe has revived recent interest in the optimum currency area literature pioneered by Mundell (1961) and rooted in the long-standing controversial discussion of the optimal exchange rate regime. In a region such as the EU, the function of money as a medium of exchange is enhanced, and the cost of currency conversion is reduced, the smaller the number of independently floating currencies. From the viewpoint of an individual economy, the benefits of lower transaction costs increase if: (1) the economy is open, (2) exchange risk is high, and (3) the external use of its currency is low. The more open the country's economy, the more it saves on transaction costs and the more it stands to gain by eliminating exchange risk through the adoption of a single currency. The savings on transaction costs is higher the lower the use of its currency in external transactions.

However, the benefits of larger size in terms of reduced transaction costs must be set against the costs arising from giving up the exchange rate as an instrument of adjustment in a single currency area. The costs arising from difficulties in correcting payment imbalances increase if: (1) shocks are asymmetric across countries, (2) intraregional factor mobility is low, and (3) wages and prices are inflexible. The more asymmetric the demand/supply shocks across countries, the greater the difficulties of adjustment with a single currency if factor mobility and wage/price flexibility is low. Inadequate labor mobility in response to price/wage signals implies rising unemployment in countries adversely affected by external shocks. Similarly, price/wage stickiness with a fixed exchange rate implies that the real exchange rate will not move sufficiently to prevent unemployment in response to an external shock.

Greece stands to gain relatively little from EMU in terms of savings on transaction costs since the openness of its economy to intra-EU trade is low relative to the rest of the Union. However, this small gain must be set against the low exchange rate uncertainty since Greece adopted the hard drachma policy in 1990 and by the low use of the drachma in external transactions.

Turning to the costs, available evidence suggests that Greece is not a strong candidate for EMU. Greece's economic and trade structure deviates substantially from that of other EU countries and from the EU average. (See Gros and Thygesen, 1992; Gros and Vandille, 1995.) This deviation suggests that shocks tend to be asymmetric. Evidence from econometric estimates suggests, moreover, that nominal wages are not highly responsive to unemployment, indicating that external shocks would raise unemployment in the absence of exchange rate movements. At the same time, however, the pass-through from prices to wages is moderate to high, limiting the usefulness of exchange rate movements as a tool of adjustment (Alogoskoufis, 1992; Alogoskoufis and Philippopoulos, 1992; Layard, Nickell, and Jackman, 1991). Structural reforms aimed at increasing the downward flexibility of wages in the face of unemployment (such as the possibility of firms with losses to offer zero or negative wage increases) would improve Greece's potential to gain from EMU.

Background on Economic and Financial Policies

Greece has never joined the European exchange rate mechanism (ERM). During the 1980s, it pursued a crawling peg policy vis-à-vis a basket of currencies, including the dollar and the yen. Growing external and internal imbalances in the first half of the 1980s led to two successive devaluations, in 1983 and in 1985. Following the EC-supported 1986–87 stabilization program, during which the drachma depreciated significantly in real terms as a result of the temporary suspension of wage indexation and imposition of a strict economy-wide incomes policy, the real effective exchange rate appreciated somewhat.

The Socialist government elected in 1981 faced strong demands for redistribution, as it was the first left-wing government since the defeat of Communist insurgencies in 1946 to 1949. Minimum wages were raised significantly, entitlements were granted to various groups, and the size and scope of public sector activities were increased. These policies failed to elicit a sustained output response. Throughout the 1980s, economic performance was characterized by sluggish growth, double-digit inflation, and high external and fiscal deficits. (See Table 5.1.) The exchange rate depreciated by

Table 5.1: Greek Macroeconomic Performance, 1971-94

	1971-80	1981-90	1991	1992	1993	1994	1995
GDP growth (percent)	4.7	1.5	3.2	0.8	-0.5	1.1	1.6
Inflation (percent)	13.2	18.3	18.8	15.1	13.6	10.9	9.6
Fiscal balance (percent GDP)	-2.8[a]	-12.3	-11.6	-12.3	-13.2	-12.5	-11.3
Current account balance (percent GDP)	-1.9	-4.4	-6.1	-4.0	-3.2	-2.4	-2.3
Unemployment rate (percent)	2.2	6.4	7.0	7.9	8.6	8.9	8.8
Adjusted wage share (percent)	70.4	77.0	72.0	70.6	69.1	70.6	71.3
Gross fixed capital formation (percent GDP)	30.1	23.6	21.2	20.4	19.5	18.9	19.2

Note: [a]1979-80 average--figures not available on same basis for earlier years.
Source: European Commission.

more than necessary to offset differences in wage costs between Greece and its trading partners during that decade. Reliance on the exchange rate as an instrument of adjustment not only failed to improve export performance but also may have delayed needed modernization of production and products. There was thus growing awareness that competitiveness depends on the removal of structural rigidities and macroeconomic imbalances that impede investment, and on the containment of real wage increases below productivity growth, rather than on the level of the exchange rate. This experience gave the impetus for the hard drachma policy in the 1990s, pursued both because of European policy choices and on economic policy grounds independently of EMU.

Financial policies were tightened considerably in 1991–92 under a new EC-supported adjustment program undertaken by the Conservative government, which took office in May 1990. The program aimed to bring the deficit into a sustainable path so as to stabilize the public debt, reduce inflationary pressures, and release resources for investment. Expenditure reduction largely relied on a tight income policy in the public sector and on social security reform, while indirect tax increases and privatization provided additional revenue. In parallel with financial discipline, structural reforms were pursued to increase the responsiveness of the economy to market signals by curtailing state intervention in economic activity and lifting regulatory barriers to competition. These policies were expected to contribute to a leaner, more competitive economy and to a sustained rise in private investment and growth. The role of exchange rate policy in this strategy was to help contain inflationary pressures rather than to attempt to gain a temporary competitive advantage that soon would be eroded by inflation. The ultimate objective was to join the ERM after the inflation rate had dropped to single digits so as to enable Greece to meet the timetable for EMU set out in the Maastricht Treaty.

These efforts contributed to nominal and fiscal convergence. The general government deficit declined to 12 percent of gross domestic product (GDP) in 1991–92 from 15 percent in 1989, inflation fell, and the balance on external accounts improved. But disinflation and the end of financial repression served to highlight the size of the debt problem. The debt burden continued to rise as deficits remained high and the government took over previously unrecorded debts of the broader public sector. Moreover, progress toward fiscal consolidation was partly reversed in the 1993 electoral cycle, when the Socialist Party returned to power. With public debt already in excess of 100 percent of GDP, the new government recognized that the room for maneuver was very limited. Thus it favored substantial continuity in economic policies, except in the scope and pace of the privatization program.

The Hard Drachma Policy and EMU

Since 1990, monetary policy and exchange rate management has been targeted at the disinflation effort. Under the hard drachma policy, authorities aim to keep the depreciation of the drachma relative to the ECU below the inflation differential, leading to a small real appreciation of the currency. ERM membership was targeted for mid-1996 under Greece's convergence program, with a view to facilitating participation in EMU by 1999, but was postponed as inflation remained well above the 5 percent target for end–1996.

The hard drachma policy was pursued against the background of important structural reforms in labor and financial markets and in the foreign exchange market, reforms that served to increase the credibility of the policy. The suspension of wage indexation and its replacement by free collective bargaining in 1991 was accompanied by government warnings that competitive devaluations were ruled out and that the exchange rate targets would be observed irrespective of the outcome of wage negotiations. The dampening effect on wages of the hard drachma policy in turn reinforced the sustainability of the policy. From 1991 to 1993, real wage restraint and productivity gains improved cost competitiveness despite a real appreciation based on relative prices. (See Figure 5.2.) However, excessive real wage increases from 1994 to 1996 eroded cost competitiveness, raising relative unit labor costs above their 1990 level. As financial liberalization accelerated, interest rates became the main policy instrument targeted at the exchange rate objective. In parallel, exchange controls were dismantled rapidly, in line with EC directives. Greece lifted remaining current account restrictions and accepted the obligations of Article VIII of the International Monetary Fund in

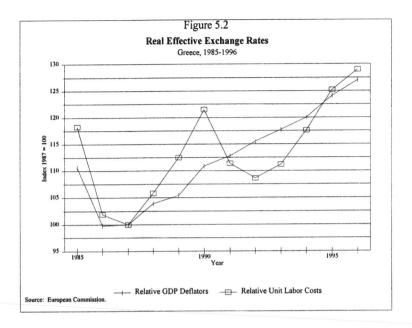

Figure 5.2
Real Effective Exchange Rates
Greece, 1985-1996

Source: European Commission.

July 1992; restrictions on long-term capital movements and most restrictions on short-term movements vis-à-vis EC countries were lifted in March 1993; the liberalization was extended to third countries in June 1993, and all remaining restrictions on short-term capital were lifted in May 1994.

Despite concerns about deflationary policies in a country with low growth and rising unemployment, the hard drachma policy has not been strongly challenged by interest groups or policy makers (although the markets have challenged it). The Federation of Greek Industries (SEV) occasionally has linked the hard drachma policy to Greece's loss of competitiveness but has not opposed it outright, recognizing that wage moderation since 1991 ruled out a significant additional real wage compression following devaluation. The only solution, therefore, was to pursue fiscal consolidation efforts so as to reduce borrowing costs and release resources for investment.

Increased recourse of the business community to foreign borrowing to avoid high domestic borrowing costs has created yet another constituency against devaluation. The General Confederation of Labor similarly has not opposed the hard drachma policy nor Greece's objective to participate in EMU as early as possible because the suspension of wage indexation probably has reinforced wage earners' preference for low inflation and also because participation in EMU is seen to favor labor demands through the implementation of the treaty's "social chapter." Moreover, investment and product upgrading are viewed as more important than short-term gains in price competitiveness achieved through exchange rate action.

The Bank of Greece, for its part, points to the inefficiency of monetary policy compared with structural policies as an instrument targeted at growth. (The "assignment problem" literature is sometimes evoked in this regard.) Policy makers also recognize that the structure of the public debt is such that it closes the escape route of devaluation and inflation sometimes used to reduce the real value of the debt. With 36 percent of the debt denominated in, or linked to, foreign currencies and with the domestic debt consisting of short-term government paper and floating-rate notes, the devaluation and inflation needed to achieve a given reduction in the debt burden becomes very high. There is thus broad consensus on the need to maintain the hard drachma policy.

Markets have challenged the exchange rate policy on two occasions. The currency came under pressure during the September 1992 ERM crisis and again in May 1994, a month ahead of the scheduled removal of all controls on short-term capital. In 1992, the drachma was defended by imposing controls on short-term capital and by accelerating the rate of crawl relative to the ECU. By contrast, in 1994 interest rates were raised to three-digit levels, exchange controls were lifted ahead of schedule, and the exchange rate target was fully observed. State-controlled banks played an important role in preventing the high interest rates from damaging the economy by continuing to lend at precrisis rates and getting compensated for their losses by the government and the Bank of Greece after the crisis was over.

The authorities' successful defense of the hard drachma in May 1994 demonstrated the primacy of monetary stability as a policy objective. Mild pressures on the drachma triggered by the impact of the depreciation of the dollar on the EMS in early 1995 receded quickly as local investors were convinced of the authorities' resolve to stick to the hard drachma policy almost at any cost. However, the policy mix of high interest rates and still-high fiscal deficits may prove difficult to sustain without damaging growth prospects and adding to an already high debt burden. Doubts about how this dilemma will be resolved add to the premium embedded in interest rates.

Financial Sector Reforms

Financial liberalization in Greece started in the mid-1980s and accelerated in the 1990s. EU membership played an important role in promoting financial sector reform, initially by expanding the role of market forces as trade was liberalized and later through the Single Market program and EMU requirements. Today the liberalization process is virtually complete. However, new reforms are needed to develop the domestic financial market, not all of which are mandated by the Maastricht Treaty. These reforms include central bank independence; the privatization of state-controlled banks; the development of a bond market, a yield curve, and a domestic institutional investor base by lifting restrictions on pension fund investments.

Reforms since the mid-1980s focused on lifting restrictions on bank lending and interest rates intended to channel credit to preferred sectors, facilitate the financing of budget deficits, and reduce borrowing costs. These reforms have been largely completed. Interest rate controls have been lifted and government paper bears market-related returns. Obligatory purchases of treasury bills by commercial banks were phased out and were completely eliminated for new deposits in mid-1993. Direct financing of budget deficits by the Bank of Greece also was phased out and eliminated in January 1994 under a 1992 law that implemented the EU Second Banking Directive. Now the budget deficit is financed mainly through sales of government paper to the non-bank public. To encourage the development of capital markets, drachma denominated bonds issued by international organizations were given tax-free status in 1993. A number of organizations issued three- to five-year bonds since early 1994, including the European Investment Bank, the World Bank, and the European Bank for Reconstruction and Development. These fixed-rate bonds issues were the first on the Greek market and thus marked the beginning of a long-term interest rate and a yield curve as a benchmark for financial and policy decisions. But the amounts issued were small and were followed, with a long lag, by government bond issues in November 1996.

Despite substantial reforms already implemented, additional reforms are needed to develop the domestic financial market, improve its ability to assess creditworthiness, and increase the effectiveness of monetary policy. First, as of July 1997, formal independence has not yet been granted to the central bank. Second, obligatory investment of pension fund assets in Treasury bills prevents the development of an institutional investor base that would increase market efficiency and liquidity. It is also unclear whether restrictions on pension fund investments are compatible with the spirit of the Maastricht Treaty's ban on privileged access (Karamouzis, 1995). Third, the presence of large state-controlled banks implies that, despite the phase-out of compulsory purchases of T-bills by banks, the ban on privileged access cannot be enforced effectively. Moreover, lending to uncreditworthy public or private entities by state-controlled banks adds to the creation of public debt. Fourth, the bond market will not be fully developed until the government—by far the largest borrower—taps that market with large and regular issues. Until that happens, no long-term interest rate will be needed as a benchmark to guide financial and policy decisions and eventually to assess compliance with the interest rate criterion of convergence.

Competition Policy

The stricter enforcement of EC provisions on competition policy under the Single Market program has also had a strong, if somewhat delayed, impact on Greek economic policies. In certain areas, the implementation of EU rules on state aids has increased competition and contributed to a leaner, more efficient economy. However, the impact came too late to avoid large subsidies, which significantly increased the public debt. The direct cost of these subsidies was not transparent because they were largely extrabudgetary, taking the form either of loan guarantees granted directly to state-controlled companies or capitalization of their debts due to state-controlled banks. Moreover, pressures from special interest groups often resulted in policy reversals.

The two sectors where the impact has been most controversial is shipbuilding and air transport. Two state-owned shipyards were privatized between 1992 and 1995, and the management of a third one (the largest) was transferred to the private sector as a result of EU directives on state aids to shipbuilding. However, one privatized shipyard was returned to state management in 1995 under the pressure of continued losses. The national airline, Olympic Airways, started implementing a restructuring program agreed with the European Commission in 1994 as a condition for debt write-offs. The program involved large reductions in personnel, suspension of unprofitable routes and other cost-cutting measures, and abolition of Olympic Airway's monopoly on ground handling. Again, program implementation was interrupted in 1995 under pressure from the unions. Similarly, the 1991 privatization of Olympic Catering, a subsidiary of Olympic Airways, was partially reversed in 1994.

In view of the large amount of subsidies granted to both sectors since the late 1970s, it could be argued that privatization and restructuring were inevitable at a time of fiscal consolidation. While pressures from the European Commission enabled the government to argue with the labor unions that its hands were tied by obligations undertaken in the context of EU membership, pressures from the public sector labor unions were equally effective in aborting the reforms.

Labor Market and Unemployment

Labor negotiations in Greece are highly centralized. Since 1991, the General Confederation of Labor—the umbrella organization representing both private and public sector unions—negotiates annual or biannual wage contracts with the Federation of Greek Industries. Wage bargaining occurs at national, sectoral, and firm levels, with national wage settlements imposing minimum remuneration levels. About one-third of the labor force is unionized, but this conceals large differences between the public sector—where union membership is compulsory—and the private sector. Restrictive practices impeding labor market flexibility include seniority built into collective wage agreements and the inability of firms with low or negative profits to grant wage increases below the national level.

Unemployment has increased in the 1990s but remains below the EU average. As mentioned, the wage indexation system introduced in 1981 was abolished in 1991 and replaced by free collective bargaining. The government is no longer directly involved in wage negotiations but influences their outcome through its announced exchange rate target and through wage policy in the public sector. Under the hard drachma policy, wage increases incompatible with the exchange rate target lead to a loss of competitiveness.

Real wage growth remained well above productivity growth in the 1980s, thus raising the share of wages in value added and contributing to unemployment. Although this trend was reversed in the 1990s, unemployment continued to rise. These data do not support the thesis that unemployment in the 1990s is neoclassical—that is, that labor is unemployed because it is overpriced. Rather, the rise in unemployment is linked to sluggish investment. With private investment crowded out by high real interest rates and public investment constrained by budgetary austerity, the share of investment in GDP declined from 20 percent in 1990 to 17 percent in 1994. Compounding the sharp fall in the investment ratio during the 1980s, this further decline in turn constrained economic growth and job creation.

Labor market rigidities are likely to have contributed to unemployment. For example, wage rigidities may explain why redundancies in connection with privatization permanently raise the unemployment rate. The exceptionally high unemployment rate among the young also suggests labor market rigidities. On the other hand, relatively low unemployment benefits for a maximum duration of 12 months do not suggest that overgenerous benefits have contributed to unemployment. An important rigidity remains in the broader public sector, where powerful unions have often pushed for, and received, higher wage increases than civil servants and even private sector employees. Demekas and Kontolemis (1996) find empirical evidence that public sector wage and employment decisions have had an adverse effect on employment in Greece.

The unemployment problem is central to the domestic policy debate but has not been linked directly to Maastricht requirements, perhaps because all governments in power during the 1990s have emphasized that Greece's fiscal imbalance required tight policies independent of EU commitments. Both the center-right and Socialist governments ruled out countercyclical policies as a cure for unemployment, so as to avoid compounding the debt problem. At the same time, however, no major labor market reforms have been undertaken, except for the suspension of wage indexation and the introduction of free collective bargaining in 1991. Regional disparities in unemployment exist, with the highest rates of unemployment recorded in the northeast region of Thrace, but the regional dimension is not evoked frequently in public debate.

Convergence Targets

Greece submitted a convergence program to the EU in March 1993. The main target of the program was rapid fiscal adjustment so as to enable Greece to participate fully in EMU from the outset in 1997. Fiscal convergence was to be facilitated by broad-based privatization, expected to increase the efficiency of resource use, remove structural impediments to growth, and generate fiscal revenue. However, the program's fiscal targets were exceeded by a wide margin as a result of the government's loss of majority in parliament, which triggered national elections in October 1993, and the new government's subsequent cancellation of major privatization efforts then under way. An increase in public spending and a relaxation of tax collection efforts ahead of the elections, typical in Greece's electoral cycle (see Figure 5.3), contributed to the overruns.

A revised convergence program was submitted to the EU in June 1994. The revised program envisaged a somewhat slower convergence, both as a result of the slippage that had occurred in 1993 and because growth was revised downward compared with the previous program. Thus it was no longer envisioned that Greece would meet the convergence criteria by 1997 but only in 1999. Under the program, there was an initial "adjustment" period from 1994 to 1996, during which time the debt would be stabilized, followed by a "growth" period from 1997 to 1999. Summaries of the main targets follow.

The fiscal target for 1994 was broadly met, but the gross public debt exceeded the targeted amount both because the privatization revenue envisioned in the program did not materialize and because the program did not sufficiently take into account the government's takeover of bad debts of the broader public sector. Despite the progress achieved, Greece is still far from meeting any of the convergence criteria. (See Table I.4.) Prospects for convergence depend on the government's sustained resolve to go against special interest groups that oppose spending cuts, additional taxation, and privatization.

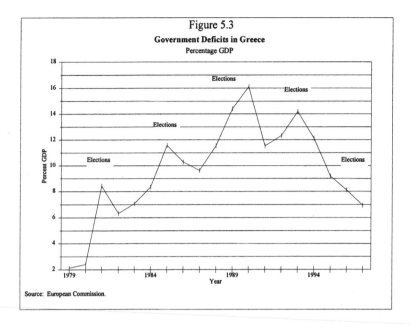

Figure 5.3
Government Deficits in Greece
Percentage GDP

Source: European Commission.

Table 5.2: Greek Convergence Targets

	1994	1995	1996	1997	1998	1999
Percent GDP						
Fiscal deficit	-13.2	-10.7	-7.6	-4.2	-2.4	-0.9
Primary surplus	1.3	3.5	4.9	5.1	5.4	6.1
Public debt	112.1	115.2	115.3	113.4	109.3	103.4
Percent						
GDP growth	1.1	1.2	1.7	2.6	3.0	3.5
Inflation (private consumption)	10.8	7.9	6.1	3.9	3.5	3.3
Short-term interest rate	18.5	14.1	10.6	7.9	6.8	6.2

Note: First three rows are general government figures. These figures include privatization revenue of 0.6 percent of GDP per year between 1994 and 1996.
Source: Ministry of National Economy, Convergence Program, June 1994.

Obstacles to Convergence

Elections in Greece are dominated by interest group politics to a greater extent than in other EU member countries because the legacy of state intervention of the 1970s and 1980s fuels political patronage. Parties win elections largely because they are viewed by the organized recipients of state largesse as most likely to maintain or increase their entitlements (Kollyntzas, 1995). This fact may explain why political parties behave very differently in government than in opposition, with the party in power often not keeping pre-election promises and with the opposition party often engaging in populist rhetoric. Beyond the rhetoric, sometimes reforms initiated by one party are reversed by the other because they are not seen to favor their constituents. An institutional feature that promotes political patronage is the existence of state entitlement programs that are highly politicized and abused (for example, disability and veterans' pensions cover an implausibly large share of the population). More generally, the dominance of interest group politics, reinforced by their control over the media and by the lack of transparency in political parties' financing, adversely affects the country's ability to carry out macroeconomic adjustment and structural reforms.

The list of interest groups is long. Examples include: public sector labor unions opposing privatization on the grounds that the required restructuring would lead to job cuts and loss of benefits; suppliers selling goods and services to the state sector at perhaps twice the world market price; politicians offering public sector jobs and other entitlements to win votes; and farmers opposing a reduction in the subsidies and pensions they were handed in the 1980s and refusing to be taxed.

Privatization, the key element of the needed economic restructuring and budgetary consolidation, has been impeded by interest group politics. The first attempt to privatize telecommunications ended with the government's loss of parliamentary majority in 1993, the second was canceled in 1995 despite lifetime job tenure granted to existing employees, and the third was limited to an initial public offering of 8 percent of the shares in 1996. With the change of government in 1993, the privatization of the Athens Bus Company was reversed and a law abolishing the state monopoly in power generation was rescinded less than year after they took effect.

Additional impediments to the implementation of adjustment programs are poor public administration, soft budget constraints on public enterprises and entities, and limited consensus for privatization based on the belief—often cultivated by special interest groups—that a sell-off of state assets is not in the national interest. Prospects for convergence would improve with administrative reforms linking public sector pay more closely with performance, greater independence, and accountability of the management of state enterprises; more transparent accounting practices and audits based on international standards; improved public understanding of the trade-off between present and future consumption; and equitable burden sharing of the short-term costs of adjustment.

Issues in Assessing Fiscal Sustainability

Does compliance with the fiscal convergence targets ensure convergence? Two issues are of importance here: the stock-flow adjustment and the behavior of public enterprises that are outside the definition of general government. Public debt in Greece has increased substantially, more than one would expect from the officially reported deficits. Over the past 15 years, the increase in the debt has been almost twice as high as the integral of the deficits. Contingent liabilities of the central government fully account for this stock-flow discrepancy. Since 1990, the government has issued bonds and credits to assume bad debts of the broader public sector ("consolidation bonds"), explicitly recognize liabilities due to the Bank of Greece arising from exchange rate guarantees, and inject capital to state-owned banks. A portion of the interest due was capitalized or postponed, adding further to the debt burden. At end–1995 the explicit takeover of bad debts and other contingent liabilities accounted for 23.4 percent of GDP, or nearly one-fourth of central government debt (see Table 5.3), while outstanding guaranteed debt amounted to a further 9 percent of GDP.

The large amount of outstanding guaranteed debt and other contingent liabilities of the central government, and the continued issuance of such guarantees, cast doubt on the prospects for debt convergence even if the deficit targets are achieved, since part of the existing contingent liabilities are likely to be taken over by the government in future years, while new liabilities continue to be issued. Considerable moral hazard is involved in debt consolidation operations as borrowers and lenders expect that the government will bail them out in the future, as it has in the past.

Table 5.3: Contingent Liabilities in Greek Public Debt, 1995

	Percent GDP
Central government debt	120.8
of which	
Contingent liabilities	23.4
• Consolidation bonds	10.1
• Bank of Greece	11.7
• Capital increase of state-owned banks	1.6
Interest capitalization	4.8

Source: Greek budget, 1996.

In 1996, the government imposed a legal limit on the issuance of new guarantees, equal to 3 percent of budgeted public expenditures. Moreover, Eurostat methodology was adopted, under which debt consolidation is considered a capital transfer and is included in expenditure. Based on the new methodology, the 1993 deficit was revised upward by 2.1 percent of GDP to include the debt consolidated in that year. (See Table 5.4.) However, a part of the guarantees called in subsequent years had not been consolidated as of November 1996 and therefore were excluded from both debt and the deficit, thereby exaggerating their decline in 1994–95. Moreover, the authorities have started making use of Eurostat rules that permit budget transfers to public enterprises to be excluded from expenditures provided they are matched by increased equity participation by the state. In addition, the legal limit on the issuance of new guarantees does not appear binding since it was revised upward within a few months of its imposition through the exclusion from the limit of guaranteed credits extended by the European Investment Bank and the EU Social Fund.

What rules or practices at national or EU level would help assess fiscal sustainability in light of the stock-flow adjustment problem? At the national level, a share of contingent liabilities issued in any given year could be included in budgetary expenditure (as the Commission already does for capitalized interest). The current practice, under which contingent liabilities are included in expenditures only when consolidated, provides perverse incentives for governments to delay consolidations, and thus generates arrears to the state-controlled banks that adversely affect the liquidity of the banking system. Also, the exclusion of debt consolidations matched by increased equity participation by the state maintains the stock-flow adjustment problem intact. Greater transparency—and probably control—in the issuance of contingent liabilities would result if they were taken into account in assessing compliance with the fiscal convergence targets. It is nevertheless clear that accounting rules cannot be a substitute for structural reforms, including privatization or closure of unprofitable public enterprises and entities, needed to prevent the issuance of further contingent liabilities.

Public enterprise operations were excluded from the Maastricht Treaty's definition of the fiscal deficit on the basis of the argument that they are of a commercial nature even if publicly owned. This is not necessarily the case. In countries where the government appoints the management and has strict control over the pricing, employment, and investment policies of public enterprises, their deficits include quasi-fiscal operations. The temptation to "park the deficit in the next parking lot" is significant. In 1994, the deficit of public enterprises in Greece increased from 0.3 percent of GDP to 0.8 percent, reflecting tariff increases below cost increases and increased transfers to the central government in the form of dividends or

Table 5.4: Successive Revisions of the 1993 Greek Deficit

	Deficit	Revision	Justification
	Percent GDP		
Revised convergence program, June 1994	12.5		
September 1994 revision	13.3	+0.9	Inclusion of capitalized interest
March 1995 revision	13.2	-0.1	Correction on military debt service
September 1995 revision	12.1	-1.2	Inclusion of revenue collected by hospitals
March 1996 revision	14.2	+2.1	Inclusion of consolidated debt

Note: Under Eurostat methodology, debt consolidation is considered a capital transfer and is included in expenditure.
Source: Ministry of National Economy.

loan repayments, which are recorded as revenue of the general government. Although the amounts involved are comparatively small, they should in principle be taken into account, if only qualitatively, in assessing fiscal sustainability.

 ## Conclusions

Greece meets the economic requirements for monetary union with the EU set out in the optimum currency area literature to a lesser extent than other EU members. Structural reforms aimed at greater price and wage flexibility would increase Greece's compatibility with EMU. Much progress toward convergence has been secured in the 1990s, but much remains to be achieved, given the initial conditions. Fiscal consolidation efforts have not yet secured a primary surplus sufficient to reverse the dynamics of rising debt. Greater deregulation and competition in goods, services, and factor markets would reduce costs and make price formation more sensitive to market conditions. The scope for privatization and deregulation to increase competition and efficiency in sectors dominated by the public sector (transport, telecommunications, energy, education, and health) remains large.

Note

1. The views presented in this chapter are strictly personal. The author wishes to thank George Alogoskoufis, Haralambos Christophides, Dimitri

Demekas, Michael Massourakis, and Paul Mylonas for helpful comments and suggestions. She has benefited from discussions with Jason Stratos and Nicos Analytis of the Federation of Greek Industries and Christos Protopappas of the General Confederation of Greek Labor.

CHAPTER SIX

The Political Economy of EMU in Ireland

Ella Kavanagh, John Considine, Eleanor Doyle, Liam Gallagher, Catherine Kavanagh, and Eoin O'Leary

In 1992, Ireland voted by referendum for the Maastricht Treaty. Following a government campaign emphasizing the benefits of financial transfers from the European Union (EU), 67 percent of the voters supported the treaty. During the debate, dissent focused not on economic concerns but on issues such as neutrality and sovereignty.[1] Since then support for a single currency in Ireland has remained consistently over 60 percent with opinion polls indicating that 66 percent of the population are in favor (Eurobarometer, 1996). Aside from the neutrality issue, there has always been widespread political support for economic and monetary union (EMU). All the main political parties back the movement toward EMU. The general political opinion is that Ireland, as a small economy with a high financial, economic, and trade dependence on the EU is "best served by an external environment conducive to economic growth based on price stability" (Ireland, 1992: 23). Economic and monetary union is expected to provide such an environment through a single currency, a fully integrated market, and coordinated national macroeconomic policies. Successive governments have believed that increased growth and employment can be generated in this environment—aided by the European Community's financial support for economic and social cohesion.

Irish fiscal and monetary policies are directed toward meeting the Maastricht criteria, which has become an explicit aim of the government since 1992. This is in line with government policy that Ireland will be among the member states eligible to participate in EMU from the outset. The Irish Central Bank is a strong supporter of monetary union.[2] Since 1990, the explicit aim of Irish monetary policy has been to maintain price stability. For a small, highly open economy like Ireland, exchange rate stability is the key intermediate target to achieve this goal. In Ireland, the central bank is responsible for the conduct of monetary policy and the day-to-day management of the exchange rate, whereas the minister for finance determines exchange rate arrangements. During the "Currency Crisis" of 1992–93, the central bank consistently supported the government's antidevaluation stance. The devaluation of the Irish pound in January 1993 did not affect either the government's or the central bank's commitment to EMU. As then central bank governor Maurice Doyle (1994: 47) pointed out with reference to Ireland's membership of a future EMU: "it remains our objective to implement sound financial policies both because they are correct in their own right and because we want to be in a position to go forward with other Community countries when the time comes to do so."

Although there are benefits from joining EMU, Ireland also faces costs, especially if the United Kingdom (UK) does not join. Despite a large decline in its bilateral trade dependence, Ireland still sends 28 percent of its exports to—and obtains 36 percent of its imports from—the UK. A sterling depreciation reduces the competitiveness of Irish goods in the United Kingdom and in third-country markets and increases competition from UK imports in the domestic market. The "Currency Crisis" highlighted the link between the trade pattern and the exchange rate regime by focusing attention on the costs Irish industry would face with the United Kingdom as a nonmember of EMU and on the effect that this would have on Irish employment. The crisis also highlighted the interaction between the wage determination process and the costs of exchange rate fluctuations. Finally, the "Currency Crisis" damaged the consensus on monetary union, particularly among sections of Irish business.

The purpose of this chapter is to explore the political economy of EMU in Ireland. The first of the chapter's five sections discusses the exchange rate policy debate in Ireland, with particular attention to EMU. The second section examines the consequences of Irish industrial policy and trade patterns for the costs and benefits of Irish membership in EMU. The third section focuses on the problem of high unemployment and how this will be affected by EMU membership. This section also explores the wage bargaining process and the consequences this has for Irish employment in EMU in the face of asymmetric shocks. The fourth section highlights the economic and political reasons for the fiscal adjustment, which has made Irish entry to EMU possible, and the implications that meeting the fiscal criteria has for

Irish economic performance in the run-up to EMU. The fifth section is the conclusion.

The Exchange Rate Policy Debate

Ireland's exchange rate history is one of managed fixed exchange rates. In March 1979, the decision to join the European Monetary System (EMS) effectively ended the exchange rate parity with sterling that had existed since 1922. The appropriateness of the sterling link had been discussed on a number of occasions between 1922 and 1972, but the debate started in earnest when Britain experienced rapid inflation during the 1970s. As a small open economy with a high import dependence on the United Kingdom, Ireland effectively imported the higher UK inflation (Bradley, 1977; Geary, 1976). Consequently adherence to the sterling exchange standard was no longer perceived to be in Ireland's interest. The proposals to form the EMS therefore were seen as timely because they emerged when the fixed rate with sterling was being questioned. The perceived advantages at the time of joining the EMS included: lower price inflation as a result of adherence to a harder currency regime (that is, the Deutschemark);[3] commitment to a major European initiative; European Community support in the form of a significant transfer of resources; and diversification of the economy away from the slow growing UK economy.

In addition, some political circles believed that the break with sterling would represent the completion of the process of national independence, while the forging of new links with continental Europe would help to diversify the economy away from that of the United Kingdom, which had not been a model of sustainable growth (Doyle, 1992). Upon Ireland's entry into the EMS, exchange controls were extended to the UK. From the outset it was recognized that, given Ireland's high inflation rate, "joining . . . [the EMS] . . . [would] not in itself reduce inflation *unless membership [was] backed by appropriate domestic policies. . . .* In joining the EMS we have committed ourselves to actions which will require fundamental adjustments in national policies and attitudes. These adjustments . . . will undoubtedly cause problems and difficulties in the short term. . . . *[G]iven sensible domestic policies,* the adjustment problems will be manageable and of relatively short duration" (Murray, 1979a: 106).

At the time of EMS membership, monetary, fiscal, and incomes policy were in need of corrective action (Murray, 1979b). In the first quarter of 1979, bank lending increased by 11.9 percent relative to an annual guideline of 18 percent (Leddin and Walsh, 1995). Expansionary fiscal policy in the late 1970s increased the exchequer borrowing requirement to 13.2 percent of gross national product (GNP) in 1979, which laid the foundation for the fiscal contractions of the 1980s. Centralized bargaining also had resulted in unsustainable pay awards. The adoption of sensible monetary and fiscal policies would lend credibility to the government's commitment to the exchange rate target and reduce the adjustment costs of lowering wage and price inflation. Otherwise wage and price disinflation would take time if firms or workers lacked confidence in the exchange rate commitment, and EMS membership would prove costly in terms of lost output and employment. During the early 1980s, Irish unemployment rose. Some economists have argued that the loss of competitiveness resulting from EMS membership was the reason for this increase (Dornbusch, 1989; Leddin, 1991). The alternative view is that worsening world economic conditions, combined with contractionary fiscal policy, reduced the demand for and the competitiveness of Irish goods (Bradley and Whelan, 1992).

The government's intention to maintain a stable exchange rate within the ERM was not achieved. Over the period 1979 to 1987, the Irish pound was devalued explicitly on two occasions, March 1983 and August 1986. (See Figure 6.1.) The driving force behind these devaluations was the loss of competitiveness vis-à-vis the United Kingdom, induced by the depreciation of the Deutschemark/sterling exchange rate. The weakness of the dollar relative to the Irish pound is another reason for the 1986 devaluation (Central Bank of Ireland, 1986). These devaluations suggest that during this period of EMS membership, the Irish government targeted an effective exchange rate index with weights given to sterling, the dollar, and the Deutschemark.

As hoped, Irish price inflation did fall toward the lower German level, although not until 1982, three years after EMS entry. (See Figure 6.2.)[4] It is difficult to determine how much of this fall was due to Ireland's membership in the EMS, the decline in UK inflation (and world inflation in general), and the Irish fiscal contraction in the early 1980s, which depressed domestic demand (Honohan, 1989 and 1993). Although the timing of the fiscal contraction suggests a link with EMS entry, the need to consolidate Irish public finances at the time meant that this policy shift had to occur anyway. Honohan (1993) has argued that the EMS undoubtedly provided a brake on any tendency that might have emerged for aggressively devaluationist policies, although the same also would have been true of the sterling link. Certainly the importance of the United Kingdom as a determinant of Irish wholesale prices has declined over time as Germany's importance increased although UK prices still remain an important determinant of Irish consumer prices (Callan and Fitzgerald, 1989; Duggan, Fitzgerald, Johnson, and Kelly, 1996).

Membership in the EMS also increased the impact of policies of other European countries—particularly Germany—on Irish interest rates. When Ireland adhered to the sterling exchange standard, Irish and UK financial

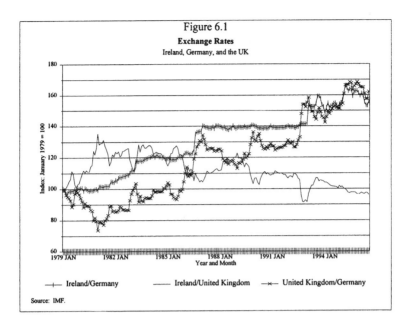

Figure 6.1
Exchange Rates
Ireland, Germany, and the UK

Source: IMF.

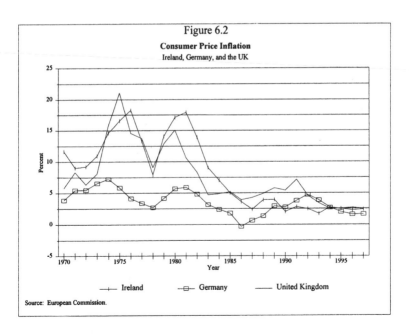

Figure 6.2
Consumer Price Inflation
Ireland, Germany, and the UK

Source: European Commission.

markets were very closely integrated and Irish interest rates were determined totally by UK interest rates. (See Figure 6.3.) Between 1979 and 1987, Irish interest rates fell toward the lower German level, and movements in German interest rates began to exert a stronger influence on Irish interest rates.

Between 1987 and 1992, the Irish pound was stable against the Deutschemark and Irish interest rates and price inflation converged on German levels. On the surface, this may appear to result from the determination of Irish policy makers and the hard-won credibility of Irish policies. However, on closer examination, at least part of the cause may have been the nominal appreciation of sterling coupled with relatively high rates of UK inflation that undermined the competitiveness of British industry.

One feature of adjustable peg systems such as the EMS is the built-in devaluation risk resulting in an interest rate premium (Honohan, 1993). In the Irish case, movements in the value of sterling determine an additional devaluation risk. Sterling depreciations have caused Irish interest rates to systematically increase because of investors' efforts to hedge their positions against the risk of devaluation. For example, every ten-pence fall in the value of sterling against the Deutschemark has tended to be associated with a 2.5 to 3.0 percentage point increase in short-term interbank market interest rates (Honohan and Conroy, 1994). Any depreciation of sterling relative to the Irish pound reduces the competitiveness of those goods exported to the

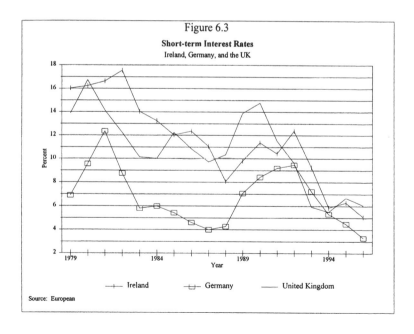

Figure 6.3

Short-term Interest Rates
Ireland, Germany, and the UK

Source: European

United Kingdom and those in competition with UK goods in third country markets and in Ireland. Therefore sustained sterling depreciation would be expected to increase Irish unemployment. This relationship suggests that it is *expected increases* in unemployment, caused by the reduction in competitiveness relative to the United Kingdom, rather than the *actual level* of unemployment that affects the credibility of Irish exchange rate policy. Consequently, the ability to sustain the Deutschemark peg is conditional on the absence of exogenous shocks, especially those resulting from a fall in the value of sterling.

Therefore, one feature of Ireland's membership in the EMS is high and peculiarly volatile interest rates, making Ireland's interest rate movements unique among EMS countries. These movements are damaging for economic performance, especially in their effect on small businesses, the majority of which are indigenous. The "Currency Crisis" of 1992–93 highlighted the negative effects of high and volatile interest rates on Irish business.

The "Currency Crisis" of 1992–93

The "Currency Crisis" from September 1992 to early 1993 proved a stumbling block to Ireland's participation in the European exchange rate mechanism (ERM). It also highlighted the costs that Ireland might face as a member of EMU with the United Kingdom as a nonmember, and it damaged somewhat the previously held consensus toward monetary union. A combination of factors, many of which were linked to the United Kingdom, led to the devaluation of the Irish pound. Between 11 September 1992—five days before sterling left the ERM—and 29 January 1993, the Irish pound appreciated against sterling by 15 percent. This made the Irish economy vulnerable to contagion from sterling. The perception in the financial markets was that this value for the sterling/Irish pound exchange rate was politically unsustainable given the high proportion of exports to the United Kingdom, the already high level of unemployment, and the labor-intensive nature of exports to the United Kingdom. This perception was dictated largely by foreign commentators who possibly overestimated the linkage between the two economies (Honohan, 1994) and sparked heavy selling of the Irish pound and unprecedentedly high short-term interest rates.

Despite efforts by the central bank to insulate retail markets from these developments, the cost of borrowing to business and mortgage holders increased sharply (Central Bank of Ireland, 1992).[5] Most of the debt of smaller corporate and household borrowers in Ireland is at short term or variable interest rates. It is widely agreed that during the "Currency Crisis," the high levels of nominal interest rates had a more severe effect on the economy than the loss of competitiveness against sterling (Honohan, 1993). The removal of the risk premium on Irish interest rates associated with movements in sterling is perceived as one of the primary advantages of EMU membership for Ireland.

Initially there appeared to be a consensus among the government, the central bank, the Irish Business and Employers Confederation (IBEC), the Trade Union movement, and most economic commentators that devaluation should not take place. The government initially resisted devaluation because of the effect that it was expected to have on the credibility of Irish exchange rate policy, because of the possibility of a future risk premium on Irish interest rates, and because a devaluation would reduce the possibility of Ireland being part of the first group in EMU. The IBEC (or the Confederation of Irish Industry, as it was then called) was opposed to devaluation. Its view was that maintaining a strong currency was advantageous for the Irish economy and that the depreciation of sterling was possibly a temporary phenomenon. Employers successfully lobbied the government for assistance (in the form of the Market Development Fund) for small and medium-size producers supplying to the Irish, UK, and Italian markets.

Over time the consensus was eroded. Honohan (1994) argues that even by November 1992, the balance had swung in favor of devaluation because the weakness of sterling looked unlikely to be reversed and the severity of foreign exchange market pressures had become evident in the form of high interest rates. These had begun to threaten employment seriously. A number of the firms that did close down at this time blamed their decision on the "Currency Crisis," although to what degree this was true is open to debate. An important factor too was the changing attitude of economic commentators as the crisis progressed, which in turn affected both public and business opinion. Although several trade union spokesmen supported the strong currency stance and pointed to the "unpatriotic behavior of speculators" (Leddin and O'Leary, 1995: 186), they were unwilling to accept any flexibility in wage agreements.

There was also political instability. The government (a coalition between Fianna Fail and the Progressive Democrats) was dissolved on 5 November 1992, and the new coalition government (Fianna Fail and Labor) was not formed until 12 January 1993. Even the political commitment to nondevaluation was at times equivocal with hints that the Irish pound might be devalued should an opportunity present itself. Finally, the new government, although stating that it was committed to resisting devaluation, also insisted its first priority was to tackle the problem of unemployment by creating growth. These aims were inconsistent. The official external reserves were also severely depleted. Leddin and O'Leary (1995) estimated that the Irish Central Bank spent IR£5 billion (the equivalent of

17 percent of GDP in 1993) in foreign currency, intervening in the foreign exchange market.

The remaining exchange controls were eliminated at the end of December 1992. The United Kingdom's decision to reduce interest rates further in late January led to repeated speculative attacks and the possibility of further interest rate increases for business and mortgage holders. At this stage the government had little alternative. The combination of further interest rate increases, an appreciating currency, and the fall in the official external reserves affected the decision to devalue on 30 January 1993.

Generally, Irish devaluation has been associated with depreciation of sterling. The difficulty in this case was the actual size of the depreciation of sterling and the very high real interest rates that ensued. Also, the change occurred very quickly; by mid-November, the Irish pound had reached £1.09 sterling. Given the government's antidevaluation stance, the effect on the Irish economy was protracted. This episode contrasts with the 1986 devaluation, when the appreciation of sterling was followed quickly by devaluation.

It could be argued that the government's commitment to the Deutschemark peg is now more credible because it held out for so long during the 1992–93 crisis. Irish companies exporting to the United Kingdom also would be expected to have learned from this experience and now would work within wider margins. Hence there may be a ratchet effect in terms of the sterling/Irish pound exchange rate that can be sustained. Both of these factors would give increased credibility to the exchange rate commitment.

Such increased credibility would in turn reduce speculative attacks and the need to increase interest rates to sustain the exchange rate target. It also has been suggested that the wider bands of 15 percent have greater credibility in themselves and thus have enabled the central bank to target a composite peg comprising sterling and the Deutschemark that also has greater credibility in financial markets relative to a solely Deutschemark peg (Thom, 1995). Even if speculative attacks were to occur, a quick devaluation would be unlikely given the government's present commitment to monetary union. Nevertheless, the difficulty of holding out against a sustained speculative attack would mean that devaluation would occur eventually.

Membership of the Hard Core?

Ireland currently satisfies the nominal criteria for entry into EMU. The advantages of EMU membership for Ireland are the continuation of a stable low inflation rate and lower and less volatile interest rates. In particular, EMU will eliminate the premium on Irish interest rates associated with sudden depreciation of sterling. This will be true regardless of whether the

United Kingdom joins. In our discussion of exchange rate policies, we noted that one of the reasons for membership of the ERM was to reduce dependence on the slow-growing UK market and increase exports to mainland Europe. One of the primary concerns in Ireland about EMU entry is continued trade with the United Kingdom. For Ireland, exchange rate policy and trade policy are inextricably linked.

Irish Trade Patterns

In 1979, at the time of EMS entry, 47 percent of Irish exports were destined for the United Kingdom which represented a dramatic decline from 1922 (the year of independence), when the UK accounted for 98 percent of Irish exports. Over the same 57-year period, Irish imports from the United Kingdom remained relatively unchanged. The reduced dependence on UK export markets made it possible for Ireland to consider an alternative exchange rate policy during the mid- to late 1970s. Since then the destination of Irish exports has continued to change. By 1994, the "EU Core" accounted for 35 percent of Irish exports, the United Kingdom for 28 percent, and the United States for 8 percent. (See Table 6.1.)[6] Import dependence on the United Kingdom also declined to 36 percent in 1994.[7] Such developments suggest that the difficulty in determining the appropriate exchange rate policy has increased since 1979 simply because Ireland now has a more diversified trading structure. With the main trading partners grouped in different currency blocs (Deutschemark, Sterling and the U.S. dollar), no single peg gives a truly fixed exchange rate for Ireland.

The diversification of exports away from the United Kingdom to mainland Europe and other countries began in the 1960s. It was the outcome of three factors: the Irish government's policy of encouraging industrialization, the resulting changes in the composition of Irish exports, and the slower economic growth of the UK market relative to the United States and mainland Europe. During the 1950s and 1960s, a sequence of measures was introduced to improve export performance. An export tax relief scheme was introduced in 1956 and expanded in 1957–58. Nonrepayable cash grants were offered to new enterprises, and the government actively sought foreign direct investment. The policy was aided by the worldwide increase in direct investment abroad by multinational companies. As exports to the United Kingdom traditionally have been food and textiles, the growth in exports of manufactures (particularly chemicals and electronics) to non-UK markets, which was an outcome of Irish industrial policy, further reduced the share of exports destined for the UK market. By the time of Ireland's entry to the EMS, the share of exports to the United Kingdom had halved relative to the 1922 figure. In the first four years of EMS membership, there was a further

Table 6.1: The Market Structure of Irish Exports (percent)

	1979	1986	1994[a]
EU Core[b]	29	33	35
United Kingdom	47	34	28
Rest of EU[c]	5	8	10
Japan	1	2	3
United States	5	9	8
Others	13	14	16
Memorandum Items			
Export/GDP ratio	49	53	72
Export Volume Index	40	68	153

Notes: [a]A new system for collecting Intra-EU trade statistics was introduced on 1 January 1993. Between 1992 and 1993 there was a decline in the UK share of Irish exports from 32 percent to 28 percent. This appears to be the result of a once-off statistical change, rather than any real alteration in trade patterns. [b]EU Core is Germany, France, Benelux, Denmark, Austria. [c]Rest of EU is Italy Greece, Spain, Finland, Sweden.
Source: Irish Central Statistics Office.

sharp decline in the export share of the United Kingdom. In addition to the continuing importance and growth of the multinational sector, the closing down of a significant number of British subsidiaries in Ireland over that period also contributed to the decline.

There are two different categories of industry in Ireland. The first of these is the high-tech sector (pharmaceuticals, office and data processing industries, instrument and electrical engineering) in which multinational enterprises predominate.[8] Irish industrial policy has been largely responsible for its development and growth. This sector is characterized by relatively high levels of productivity. (In the late 1980s, the level of output per head in the foreign-owned sector was two and a half times that of the indigenous sector.)[9] In 1994, the overseas sector accounted for 47 percent of Irish manufacturing employment with 87 percent of their output exported (Central Statistics Office, 1994a). The strong growth in the Irish economy in the late 1980s and early 1990s can be traced primarily to this rapidly expanding export sector, which is evident in the rising export-to-GDP ratio shown in Table 6.1.

Since Ireland joined the European Community in 1973, American multinationals have replaced the UK multinationals as the dominant group of foreign direct investors in the Irish industrial sector. In addition to the financial incentives,[10] the advantage of locating in Ireland is unrestricted

access to the large EU market. It would be expected that EMU membership would reinforce the attractiveness of Ireland for foreign direct investment. As shown in Table 6.2, exports from these high-tech industries
(chemicals, office and data equipment and electrical machinery) account
for a very high share of the value of total Irish exports. They also are oriented toward the EU market and are largely traded in dollars or other international currencies. In fact, over 50 percent of the export value of large
companies producing electronic and chemical products are quoted in dollars (Bannon, 1996).[11]

The second sector comprises Irish-owned industries, which tend to have
lower productivity, are usually price takers, and are more price sensitive than
multinational enterprises.[12] In 1994, indigenous Irish companies accounted
for 53 percent of manufacturing employment. In contrast to the multinational sector, 65 percent of the output of indigenous Irish companies is destined for the domestic market (Central Statistics Office, 1994a). Whether

Table 6.2: The Product Structure of Irish Exports, 1994 (percent)

SITC Classification	To UK	To EU	To Other	Share of Total Exports
Food	35.3	40.8	23.9	18.6
Beverages	31.9	35.1	33.0	2.0
High Dependence on the UK				
Animal Oils	74.7	20.8	4.5	0.1
Cork	65.4	24.5	10.1	0.2
Paper	80.9	9.9	9.2	0.3
Road Vehicles	54.1	38.0	7.9	0.5
Prefabricated Goods	66.8	24.3	8.9	0.1
Furniture	65.7	21.0	13.2	0.3
Clothing	63.3	21.8	14.9	1.4
Footwear	75.0	23.1	1.9	0.3
Low Dependence on the UK				
Chemicals	14.5	46.1	39.4	20.8
Office/Data Equipment	26.7	39.9	33.4	17.8
Electrical	20.9	41.2	37.9	6.1
Scientific Equipment	14.7	43.6	41.7	2.1

Source: Irish Central Statistics Office (1994).

this group will suffer as a result of UK nonmembership in EMU will depend on how open the domestic market is to competition from UK producers (Baker, Duffy, and Duggan, 1996). In terms of export markets for indigenous products, the United Kingdom is the most significant destination, with some sectors exporting a very high proportion there—for example, 81 percent of exports of paper and paper products, 63 percent of clothing, and 75 percent of footwear. (See Table 6.2.) According to Baker, Duffy, and Duggan (1996), the clothing sector faces the highest exchange rate risk given its high export share to the United Kingdom and a virtually unprotected domestic market.

High dependence on a traditionally slower-growing economy, such as the United Kingdom, has important implications for these indigenous industries and for the economy as a whole. Consequently, some initiatives directed at domestic industry have been taken in recent years to diversify export markets (Gallagher and McAleese, 1994). The Irish Trade Board has been encouraging exporters to orient themselves toward the markets of continental Europe. So long as the UK performance is poor, incentives exist for Irish companies to forge links with more dynamic trade partners. An additional reason for orienting companies toward mainland European markets would be UK nonmembership in EMU. However, for many small Irish companies, the cost of entering into the mainland European market rather than the UK market is substantially higher.[13] Since 1986, the share of Irish exports to the United Kingdom has remained relatively unchanged.

One of the questions highlighted by the "Currency Crisis" was the proportion of employment exposed to sterling fluctuations. Work done by Baker, Duffy, and Duggan (1996) on the Irish manufacturing sector for 1993 estimated that the clothing sector is highly exposed to sterling fluctuations and another three sectors—processed meat products; sugar, cocoa and confectionery; and textiles other than knitted garments—are fairly highly exposed. These four sectors account for 13 percent of total manufacturing employment. A further 23.9 percent of manufacturing employment can be considered to be moderately affected. The remaining 63.1 percent appears to have a sterling exposure ranging from fairly to very low, because they either serve mainly non-UK export markets or have a large and reasonably protected domestic market. Therefore, a substantial and sustained depreciation of sterling relative to the Euro—as the future European currency will be called—will have a significant affect on 37 percent of manufacturing employment. However, recent employment trends suggest that the proportion of manufacturing employment in sectors particularly exposed to sterling fluctuations has tended to decline since 1993 (Baker, Duffy, and Duggan, 1996). Moreover, small indigenous firms would be expected to benefit from interest rate gains accruing from EMU membership.

The currencies in which Irish exports are quoted reinforce the importance of sterling and the dollar to Irish trade. In terms of export values, 85 percent of Irish exports are quoted in foreign currencies (Bannon, 1996). The dollar emerges as the principal export currency, with a share of just over 31 percent, while sterling is next in line at almost 26 percent. The Deutschemark is used for only 12 percent. Small and medium-size enterprises are most dependent on sterling; 35 percent of the value of their exports is quoted in sterling, 17 percent in Irish pounds, and 13 percent in Deutschemarks.[14] In over 40 percent of firms in the consumer products and food and drink sectors, the proportion of exports quoted in sterling is greater than 60 percent. Consequently, an appreciation of the Irish pound would significantly lower the profitability of these companies. In fact, the proportion of small and medium-size enterprises classified as having low profitability increases from just over 30 percent to 85 percent as a result of a 1 percent depreciation of sterling relative to the Irish pound for one year (Bannon, 1996). The current usage of non-ERM currencies in trade suggests that the savings in transaction costs for companies in Ireland through using a single currency will be small, and that many Irish companies either will have to introduce or continue management of currency risk.

In addition to exchange rate movements, wage costs also affect the competitiveness of Irish goods. Curtis and Fitzgerald (1994) have shown that UK labor costs play a major role in determining labor costs in Ireland, with the timing of the transmission affected by movements in the exchange rate. A number of factors are identified to explain this: migration to the United Kingdom, changing expectations of employees who do not choose to migrate, and close trade union links between the two countries. If this labor market connection were not to alter over the short to medium term, high nominal wages in the United Kingdom could translate into high nominal wages in Ireland, which would reduce the competitiveness of Irish goods in European markets. Membership in EMU is expected, however, to result in a much more cautious approach to wage bargaining (Honohan, 1996).

Attitudes of Irish Business toward EMU

The IBEC, and Irish business in general, supports membership in a European Monetary Union. In a survey of large Irish companies, 90 percent said Ireland should be either one of the first group of countries to move toward EMU or should at least keep that option open by continuing to pursue the Maastricht convergence criteria (Chambers of Commerce of Ireland, 1995).[15] A stable exchange rate is viewed as the primary benefit of EMU, were the United Kingdom to join, for 78 percent of the respondents, with 10 percent considering lower interest rates to be the principal attraction.

Sixty-five percent of the companies reviewed believe that Ireland should join EMU even without the United Kingdom.

However, given the direction of Irish trade, it is not surprising that particular groups within Irish business have expressed concern about possible UK nonmembership and the nature of the relationship that would exist between sterling and the proposed Euro currency. In telephone conversations with the authors, spokespersons for the Small Firms Association, which represents companies with less than 50 employees expressed anxiety about UK non-membership, as have representatives of the Irish Small and Medium-Sized Enterprise Association (ISME). Small Irish companies conduct 40 percent of their trade with the United Kingdom, in contrast to small foreign-owned companies, which conduct less than 25 percent with the UK (Central Statistics Office, 1994a). The ISME also has expressed reservations about membership in EMU. Irish companies, whatever their size, are generally biased toward the domestic and UK markets. (See Table 6.3.) The views of Irish business contrast with that of the multinational sector. The latter favors EMU membership, believing that their firms would become more competitive with a single European currency (Irish Business and Employers Confederation, 1995).

Among companies that export primarily to the United Kingdom, there is a stronger bias against Ireland's membership in EMU if the UK does not join. In a survey conducted by the Irish Business and Employers Confederation (IBEC) of its members, only 52 percent of companies exporting 50 percent or more to the UK market said that Ireland should join EMU.[16] This contrasts with companies selling over 50 percent of their product to the

Table 6.3: Domestic and Export Shares of Gross Output, 1994 (percent)

	For Domestic Use	For Export to			
		UK	Other EU	USA	ROW
Irish-owned firms (*of which*)	65	16	10	3	6
• less than 50 employees	77	9	7	2	6
• more than 50 employees	58	16	10	3	6
Foreign-owned firms (*of which*)	12	20	43	9	15
• less than 50 employees	17	20	40	13	9
• more than 50 employees	12	20	43	9	15
Total Manufacturing	33	19	31	7	12

Note: ROW is the "rest of the world" outside the European Union and the United States.
Source: Irish Central Statistics Office (1994).

EU; 91 percent of them believed that Ireland should join a single currency. Particular sectoral groups also have expressed reservations. Chief among these are the food sector and the clothing and textile sector, which face competition not only within the United Kingdom but also in the domestic market and in third-country markets from UK competition. The farming sector also has stated, given its close links with the agrifood sector, that Ireland's interest would be best served outside the system if initially only a very narrow single currency of four or five countries is created.

Implications

The trade pattern and the Irish industrial structure suggest that the effects of EMU membership are ambiguous. On the one hand, industries that are dependent on domestic demand and small indigenous companies dependent on indigenous finance will benefit from the lower interest costs associated with EMU membership. On the other hand, Irish industries dependent on the UK market will suffer because of sudden sterling depreciations if the United Kingdom remains outside EMU. This difference highlights the importance of the variable geometry question to Ireland and the nature of the relationship that will exist between the currencies of the outsiders and the proposed single currency.

Even if the United Kingdom does join EMU, evidence suggests that Ireland does not comply very well with the indicators used to assess whether EU members form an optimum currency area. The very high degree of trade with EU members suggests that Ireland will benefit from savings on transaction costs from EMU (Gros, 1996b). However, the currencies used in Irish trade suggest that these savings will be small. Out of the total of 14 EU countries, Gros (1996b) ranks Ireland tenth in terms of the similarity of trade structure and eleventh in terms of the degree of intraindustry trade. The very high growth rates experienced in Ireland also make Irish real GDP and industrial growth relatively uncorrelated with other EU countries. Thus Ireland may be more susceptible to asymmetric shocks within EMU. The current high rate of unemployment in the country makes the potential cost of asymmetric disturbances, particularly sterling fluctuations, of even greater concern.

The Unemployment Problem

The unemployment rate in Ireland is one of the highest in the EU (OECD, 1996a; Viñals and Jimeno, 1997). Long-term unemployment is also high, with more than 60 percent of those unemployed out of work for over a year. It is expected that lower price inflation, lower interest rates, and the introduction of a single currency in EMU will improve competitiveness and economic growth, thereby increasing the demand for labor. However, the labor supply in Ireland will continue to rise over the medium term for two reasons: the high rate of natural increase in the recent past and an expected rise in the participation of women in the workforce. This rapid growth in the labor force makes Ireland unique by European standards. The openness of the labor market also means that the Irish labor supply increases in response to improved domestic economic conditions. Duggan, Fitzgerald, Johnson, and Kelly (1996) have predicted that, if the United Kingdom remains out, Irish membership in EMU will, on average, reduce the country's unemployment rate by 1.1 percentage points per annum in the three years after EMU entry.

The sectoral composition of Irish employment is shown in Table 6.4. Employment in the agricultural sector is expected to continue to decline independent of EMU entry. In contrast, employment is expected to expand in both the manufacturing and building sectors. In market services, because employment growth is still significantly lower than for the EMU as a whole, there is also scope for employment expansion. Moreover, higher economic

Table 6.4: Sectoral Composition of Employment -- 1979, 1986, and 1993 (percentage share)

Sector	1979	1986	1993
Agriculture	19.3	15.5	12.6
Industry (*of which*)	31.9	28.4	27.2
• Manufacturing[a]	23.1	21.7	21.1
• Building	8.8	6.7	6.1
Services	48.8	56.1	60.2
Total Employment (thousands)	1145.3	1080.9	1145.0

Memorandum: Composition of Employment in Manufacturing[b]

Sector	1979	1986	1991
Food	18.9	17.5	15.5
High Tech[c]	28.4	32.8	34.8
Traditional[d]	52.5	49.7	49.6
Total Manufacturing Employment (thousands)	256.0	223.5	232.0

Note: [a]Manufacturing includes food, high-tech, traditional, and utilities. [b]Manufacturing excludes utilities. [c]High Tech includes metals, machinery, vehicles and chemicals. [d]Traditional includes drink, clothing, textiles, wood and paper, printing.
Source: O'Connell and Sexton (1994), pp. 37, 38.

growth should favor increased employment in this sector. The exception is the financial sector. Hutchinson (1996) has estimated that as EMU becomes operational, up to 7 percent of employment in the financial sector could be in the balance.

Table 6.4 also shows the composition of total manufacturing employment. In the high-tech sector, employment is relatively volatile because it is subject to changing international conditions. Most firms in this group are foreign-owned multinational companies. EMU membership should ensure that Ireland will remain an attractive location for these companies, provided that cost competitiveness is sustained. Improved competitiveness also should ensure expansion in the traditional and food sectors (Duggan, Fitzgerald, Johnson, and Kelly, 1996). However, the structure of industry and trade in Ireland suggests that the economy will be exposed to asymmetric shocks, particularly if the United Kingdom does not join EMU. A depreciation of sterling relative to the Euro will have implications for the clothing, textiles, and food processing sectors in particular.

The wage bargaining process is important in determining how a country will respond to these types of shocks in a monetary union. Since 1987, there have been a series of national wage agreements in Ireland among the government, trade unions, employers, and farmers.[17] These agreements set ceilings on wage increases over a three-year period, with the objective of strengthening the economy's potential for sustainable employment and economic growth.[18] The Irish Congress of Trade Unions (ICTU) represents the majority of trade unions (both public and private sector unions) at the bargaining table, whereas IBEC is responsible for negotiating on behalf of employers. In Ireland, the average unionization rate is 56 percent, one of the highest in the EU apart from the Scandinavian countries. These agreements are adhered to in the public sector, where up to 76 percent of the workforce is unionized, and are generally adhered to in the private sector, although there are clauses for opt-out if companies are financially unable to award the pay increases. In the production sector, the unionization rate is lower, at 54 percent.

These agreements can be criticized on the grounds that they are tailored to the needs of stronger unionized sectors (especially the public sector) rather than those of small and medium-size firms facing international competition where a competitive cost structure is essential for success. These agreements also have not altered the emphasis of Irish wage bargaining on protecting the after-tax income of those who are employed, with little evidence of practical concern for the unemployed, who are not represented at the bargaining table. Therefore, the benefits of these long-term agreements in the run-up to EMU and indeed within EMU must be questioned. The "Currency Crisis" illustrated how damaging the combination of a fixed exchange rate and rigid wages can be for an economy. At that time, although trade union leaders strongly supported the government's policy on the exchange rate, there was no prospect of the unions renegotiating the Program for Economic and Social Progress (PESP) in order to make the exchange rate sustainable (Walsh, 1993).

The ICTU declares itself to be strongly supportive of the move toward EMU. However, when the exchange rate is fixed, nominal wages must be flexible so as to accommodate external shocks. The recent national wage agreements in Ireland are inconsistent with this requirement. One suggestion that has been put forward to reduce the problems of companies with high levels of sterling exposure is to introduce exchange rate-linked wage contracts (Geary and Honohan, 1995). Inability to pay clauses such as that incorporated into recent national agreements represent an imperfect and one-sided response to the problem. The introduction of a hedging strategy such as this may reduce the unemployment costs associated with sudden sterling depreciation.

Emigration is another way in which the Irish economy traditionally has responded to shocks. In Ireland, emigration is viewed as an acceptable alternative to unemployment and has acted as a safety valve.[19] More than 250,000 people have emigrated from the country since 1980, amounting to 7 percent of the current population. Approximately 46,000 people emigrated in 1988 alone. However, in contrast to the predictions of the Optimum Currency Area literature, emigration during the EMS period has been primarily to the United Kingdom and not to the anchor country, Germany.

The Irish labor market also shares many of the problems of the European labor market, such as wage rigidity and hysteresis effects. Although it is difficult to gauge the degree of labor market flexibility, evidence indicates that the market is characterized by significant rigidities. The relatively generous social welfare system tends to support high reservation wages—wages below which unemployment is more financially attractive than work—and unemployment assistance can be drawn indefinitely, provided the claimant meets certain conditions. High marginal tax rates at low incomes and combined with the social welfare system result in relatively high replacement ratios. The disincentive effects of the social welfare and tax systems have led to unemployment and poverty traps, and have exacerbated the problem of long-term unemployment. During the 1980s, there was an increase in the propensity for the short-term unemployed (unemployed for less than a year) to become long-term unemployed (unemployed for more than a year).

Since the 1980s, as the labor market became accustomed to ever-higher levels of unemployment, there may have been a reduction in its sensitivity to the pressure of excess supply. Evidence also suggests that the insider-outsider relation is a feature of the Irish labor market. Apart from reversals during the recessions of 1973–74 and the early 1980s, there was a strong upward trend in real take-home pay despite the high level of unemployment. Moreover, Irish labor laws contain serious obstacles to the termination of employment contracts, thereby increasing the bargaining power of the employed (Browne and McGettigan, 1993). This bargaining power is reinforced by the presence of strong trade unions. Meeting the Maastricht fiscal criteria has implications for the extent to which the Irish government can introduce fiscal reforms (such as taxation changes) to improve the functioning of the labor market.[20]

Fiscal Adjustment

Given the state of the Irish public finances in the late 1970s and early 1980s, it is extraordinary that Ireland satisfies the fiscal convergence criteria for progression to EMU. This remarkable fiscal situation means that Ireland will not suffer increased unemployment from this source in the run-up to EMU. Since 1988, the general government deficit has been below 3 percent of GDP and the gross debt-to-GDP ratio, although greater than the guideline of 60 percent, is "sufficiently diminishing and approaching the reference value at a satisfactory rate" to fulfill this requirement for entry to EMU (Buiter, Corsetti, and Roubini, 1993: 61). According to the OECD (1995), if the Irish government's stated fiscal policy were adhered to for five years from 1994, and if there were no reductions in the tax ratio, then the debt ratio would fall to 60 percent by 1999. Although reductions in government borrowing were initiated in 1981, meeting the Maastricht criteria has become an explicit aim of Irish fiscal policy since 1992.[21] Dowling (1989) points out that the existence of such a target is vital if support for fiscal adjustment should begin to wane. The presence of a target set externally also can be used to remove political pressure from domestic policy makers over austere fiscal policies. This target, with its perceived benefits of future EMU membership, may be the reason why support for fiscal adjustment has remained strong despite high unemployment; although in Ireland such support has been aided by access to other labor markets (particularly the United Kingdom), a generous social welfare system, and a lack of organization among the unemployed.

For all but the first two years since Ireland joined the EMS in 1979, successive governments have made efforts at fiscal retrenchment. The initial efforts in the early 1980s, based on higher taxation and put forward by a Fine Gael and Labor coalition, were opposed by the parties in opposition and did not receive widespread public support. This changed in 1987 with a new minority Fianna Fail government and coincided with electoral support for the Single European Act in a referendum in that year. Fiscal adjustment then took the form of expenditure cuts and was supported by all the major political parties.[22] The debt-to-GDP ratio fell from 115 percent in 1987 to approximately 90 percent in 1995. The conventional deficit-to-GDP ratio declined from its highest point in 1981 of 15 percent to below 3 percent since 1988. If debt service payments are excluded from the deficit, the adjustment is more marked. The primary deficit declined after 1981 and became a surplus from 1985 onward.

The unique feature of the Irish experience is that fiscal adjustment coincided with exceptional economic growth. (See Bertola and Drazen, 1993; Giavazzi and Pagano, 1990.) The initial adjustment between 1982 and 1986, although decreasing interest rate differentials between Ireland and other EU countries, did not translate into increased private sector investment or consumption. Over the period 1980 to 1985, average annual GDP growth was 1.6 percent. In contrast, the adjustment from 1987 coincided with increases in private consumption and private investment that outweighed the decline in public consumption and public investment expenditures so that annual GDP growth averaged 4.7 percent over the period 1980 to 1990.

Various views on the exact cause of the turnaround in economic performance, which coincided with the fiscal contraction of the late 1980s, are advanced in studies of the Irish experience. A common theme concerns the role of expectations in producing what has become known as "expansionary fiscal contraction." Bertola and Drazen (1993), Blanchard (1990), and Giavazzi and Pagano (1990) agree that private individuals perceived the expenditure cuts in 1987 as permanent, thereby inducing a positive wealth effect on consumption. Blanchard (1990) and Giavazzi and Pagano (1990) acknowledge a possible role for political consensus in generating these expectations.[23] Bertola and Drazen (1993) argue that fiscal policy had become unsustainable by 1987 and that fiscal adjustment would have occurred anyway; it was the size of the fiscal adjustment that made expectations credible. On the other hand, Barry and Devereux (1995: 216–217) have argued that factors other than fiscal policy were at work that "more than outweighed the short-run contractionary effects of fiscal contraction." These factors included increased world demand resulting in increased export growth, improvements in cost competitiveness, and an inflow of foreign investment in the lead-up to EMU.

Both domestic and external factors were responsible for the fiscal correction. In terms of domestic fiscal policy, the government concentrated real expenditure cuts in the three years between 1987 and 1989 only. In 1988, the government introduced a tax amnesty, which resulted in a sharp fall in the current budget deficit (CBD)-to-GDP ratio in that year (see Figure 6.4) and reduced the Exchequer borrowing requirement (EBR) from 5.9 percent of

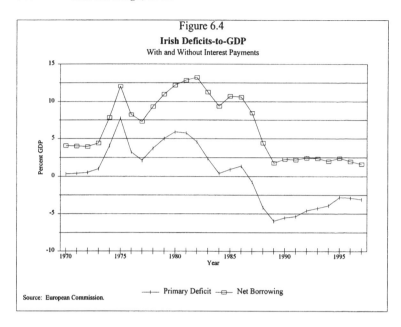

Figure 6.4

Irish Deficits-to-GDP

With and Without Interest Payments

Source: European Commission.

—+— Primary Deficit   —□— Net Borrowing

GNP to 3.3 percent. Despite this, the CBD net of the tax amnesty fell as a percentage of GNP in 1988 to a greater extent than in any other year except 1976 (Honohan, 1992).

External factors were at least as important. Export growth, aided by the devaluation in 1986, contributed largely to high GDP growth rates. Meanwhile, falling world interest rates reduced the sizable interest payments included in the deficit. With a large stock of debt denominated in foreign currency, large changes in Ireland's debt repayments can occur through exchange rate movements. By the end of 1990, based on the end–1986 portfolio, the Exchequer would have made a capital gain equivalent to 3 percent of GNP on exchange rate movements alone (Honohan, 1992). It is also estimated that, based on the end–1992 portfolio, the devaluation in January 1993 added 10.1 percent to the government debt (Considine, 1996).

Transfers from the EU also aided the fiscal adjustment. As one of four countries with the lowest GDP per capita in the Union, Ireland receives substantial Structural Funds. Between 1989 to 1993, 6.4 percent of the total allocation went to Ireland despite its population share of only 1.1 percent.[24] Table 6.5 shows the principal sources of EU grants and subsidies included in the calculation of the deficit. EU grants and subsidies enabled the Exchequer's contribution to the public capital expenditure program to remain below its 1985 level. This issue may assume greater importance for Ireland

Table 6.5: Exchequer Capital Expenditure Program and EU Financing, 1985-93

Year	Public capital program, Exchequer		European Regional Development Fund		European Social Fund		European Cohesion Fund	
	IR£ millions	Percent GDP	IR£ millions	Percent GDP	IR£ millions	Percent GDP	IR£ millions	Percent GDP
1985	976	6	76	0.4	n/a	n/a	n/a	n/a
1986	967	5	77	0.4	n/a	n/a	n/a	n/a
1987	924	4	83	0.4	n/a	n/a	n/a	n/a
1988	713	3	94	0.4	n/a	n/a	n/a	n/a
1989	696	3	76	0.3	n/a	n/a	n/a	n/a
1990	787	3	225	0.8	5	0.02	n/a	n/a
1991	816	3	342	1.2	10	0.04	n/a	n/a
1992	845	3	289	1.0	104	0.35	9	0.03
1993	1018	3	464	1.4	8	0.02	42	0.13

Note: 1992 figures are estimates.
Source: Budget books (various issues).

in the future rounds of Structural and Cohesion Fund allocations because if EU transfers fall, the Exchequer will have to make bigger contributions to capital expenditure.

Despite the success of the policy to gain control of the public finances in the last decade, the fiscal position remains susceptible to political and economic shocks during both the run-up to and membership in EMU. The large stock of outstanding debt is susceptible to exchange and interest rate shocks because approximately half is denominated in currencies other than the Irish pound. This cost would be expected to be reduced within EMU because the proportion of Irish debt in "outside" currencies would decrease. Increases in Irish unemployment or reduced employment opportunities in the United Kingdom would increase current expenditure. The already high unemployment rate hinders further fiscal adjustment because of the size of transfer payments involved and the disincentive effects resulting from increased income tax. Ireland's narrow tax base provides another potential problem because raising extra revenue, should it be required, would be difficult. Tax revenue is sensitive to employment changes due to the larger share of total taxes made up by income tax relative to the EU as a whole (Ruane and O'Toole, 1995). In Ireland, the "feasibility gap" is small because of the high marginal tax rates and the narrow tax base.[25] At the same time, the openness of the labor market places restrictions on Irish fiscal policy as increased taxes in Ireland relative to the

United Kingdom reduce the competitiveness of the traded sector (Curtis and Fitzgerald, 1994).

It is also likely that if Ireland was excluded from the first group of countries in EMU, the widespread support for fiscal adjustment will weaken. In this event, the literature suggests that the proportional representation electoral laws might make it more difficult to exclude the views of diverse interest groups from the decision-making process. (See Alesina and Perotti, 1995; Grilli, Maciandaro, and Tabellini, 1991.) The result would be a bias toward increased public expenditure, with resulting chaos for the public finances, and would cast doubt over the future possibility of Irish participation in a monetary union.

Conclusion

The perceived economic advantages of EMU for Ireland are lower interest rates, low inflation, a continuation of EU transfer payments, higher growth, and lower unemployment. Membership in EMU also represents the continuation of Ireland's integration into mainland Europe and reduced dependence on the United Kingdom. In Ireland, the costs of EMU are focused on possible UK nonentry and the implications that this will have for the sterling-Euro exchange rate. Given the high proportion of trade and the labor market linkages with the United Kingdom, Ireland will continue to be affected by policy shifts there, particularly if they cause unanticipated depreciations of sterling relative to the Euro. Indeed, the "Currency Crisis" of 1992–93 highlighted the costs that Ireland might face as an EMU member if the United Kingdom does not join. Consequently, certain sectors of Irish industry and some Irish economists have questioned whether it is in Ireland's interest to join.

Nevertheless, there has been little consideration of alternative exchange rate arrangements in Ireland. Where discussion has taken place, the belief is that alternatives such as targeting a composite peg or returning to a sterling standard would result in other kinds of costs such as higher inflation and higher interest rates due to reduced policy credibility (Baker, Fitzgerald, and Honohan, 1996). There is also the fear that nonmembership in EMU would weaken Ireland's position within the European Union as a whole. However, if Ireland were to join EMU, then this change in regime would be expected to reduce further the industrial, trade, and labor market linkages between Ireland and the United Kingdom over the medium term, thereby reducing potential costs in the short run. It is also expected that if EMU progresses, it would be unlikely that the United Kingdom would remain outside indefinitely.

Notes

1. The exception here is Raymond Crotty (1987), whose espousal of self-sufficiency attracted relatively little support.

2. Given the function of the Irish Central Bank and the fact that there is no provision for the issue of a ministerial or government directive that would require the bank to discharge any of its functions and duties in accordance with government wishes, the governor of the Irish Central Bank has stated that the bank already matches, in general, the main conditions enshrined in the Treaty on EU on central bank independence (O'Connell, 1995).

3. The appreciation of sterling after Ireland's membership the EMS meant that the exchange rate regime that Ireland joined turned out to be significantly weaker than the sterling link.

4. The large appreciation of sterling, the sharp rise in the tax wedge, and the large pay awards all helped to increase inflation in the early years of EMS membership (Bradley and Whelan, 1992; Walsh, 1993).

5. Most households were insulated from cash-flow difficulties associated with high interest rates on mortgages by the decision of mortgage lenders to capitalize the additional interest charges for six months (Honohan, 1994).

6. The "EU Core" consists of Germany, France, Belgium, Netherlands, Luxembourg, Denmark, and Austria. The importance of the United Kingdom and EU countries is supported by gravity models of Irish trade.

7. Import data are compiled on a country of consignment basis up to 1935 and therefore overstate the amount originating in the United Kingdom. McAleese (1977) has stated that imports of UK origin probably amounted to between 50 percent and 60 percent of the total in the immediate postin-dependence years.

8. In 1973, the Industrial Development Authority (IDA) set out a plan to concentrate on attracting foreign direct investment in the electronics, chemicals and other high-tech sectors (O'Sullivan, 1995).

9. Some economists have argued that these figures reflect the transfer pricing of multinational companies rather than improvements in the real productive capabilities of Irish-based industry (O'Leary, 1997; O'Sullivan, 1995).

10. The EU Commission has allowed state incentives to industrialization to continue in the less developed countries.

11. These figures are obtained from a series of surveys conducted by the Irish Trade Board. Large companies refer to those with over 250 employees.

12. The low-tech sector now includes a substantial and growing overseas presence so that the dichotomy between overseas-owned, high-tech industry and Irish-owned, low-tech industry may need to be qualified in the future (National Economic and Social Council, 1993).

13. Some studies, such as that of Gallagher and McAleese (1994), argue that Irish trade dependence with the Unite Kingdom is unlikely to decline any further. Factors such as language, proximity, tradition, and culture all support the view that the United Kingdom will remain, for the foreseeable future, the single most important market for Irish exports and a strong competitor for Irish industry on both domestic and foreign markets (McArdle, 1994).

14. In the surveys conducted by the Irish Trade Board and used by Bannon (1996), small and medium-size enterprises are those with less than 250 employees.

15. This survey was conducted in association with Allied Irish Bank Corporate and Commercial Treasury. Of the 350 companies contacted for the survey, 93 percent had more than 200 employees, and 81 percent (283 companies) conducted some share of their trade in sterling.

16. Early in 1995, IBEC carried out a random sample of its members to ascertain their views on EMU. See IBEC (1995).

17. Centralized bargaining also existed from 1979 to 1981. In 1981, employers refused to participate in centralized bargaining and decentralized bargaining was resorted to until 1987.

18. These were the Program for National Recovery 1987–1990 (PNR), which coincided with the introduction of fiscal retrenchment. The other programs were the Program for Economic and Social Progress 1991–1994 (PESP) and the Program for Competitiveness and Work 1994–1997 (PCW).

19. The estimated elasticity of the net migration rate with respect to relative wages is about 3 and with respect to unemployment about 2 (National Economic and Social Council, 1991). These elasticities are high, indicating the sensitivity of Irish migration to cyclical economic factors in Ireland relative to the United Kingdom.

20. "To qualify for EMU, our national fiscal policy is being driven by objectives set at EU levels" (Quinn, 1996: 7).

21. In the 1994 budget, Minister for Finance Ruairi Quinn also referred to the problem of unemployment. "It would not be sensible in our situation to pursue debt reduction to the exclusion of all other objectives. It is a means to an end, the aim being faster sustainable economic and employment growth" (Ireland, 1994).

22. A minority Fianna Fail government was supported by Fine Gael, the second largest party in parliament, on the condition that it continued the fiscal retrenchment of the previous government.

23. For the early 1980s, Dornbusch (1989) also noted the importance of political consensus for the adjustment.

24. Although Ireland as a whole may not get funds in the next round, Irish national income accounts are in the process of being prepared on a subregion basis so that all of the country except Dublin would continue to get funding.

25. The "feasibility gap" is the difference between the current (average or marginal) tax rate and the potential (maximum) tax rate (Chouraqui, Hagermann, and Sartor, 1990).

CHAPTER SEVEN

The Netherlands: Top of the Class

Erik Jones

The Netherlands will be at the top of the list of countries ready to join in a European economic and monetary union (EMU), whether at the end of this decade or early in the next. The guilder-Deutschemark link is the only couple in the European Monetary System (EMS) to have survived the exchange rate crises of 1992, 1993, and 1995 unfazed. The Dutch business cycle tracks closely on the German (Fase and de Bondt, 1994), and Dutch inflation and interest rates do so as well (Berk and Winder, 1994). For all intents and purposes, the Netherlands is already in an economic and monetary union with Germany. All that remains is for the procedures outlined in the Maastricht Treaty to consummate the marriage.

The purpose of this chapter is to place the close relationship between the guilder and the Deutschemark in the larger context of Dutch economic adjustment and fiscal consolidation during the 1980s and 1990s. The analysis is based on two prior assumptions. The first is that the decision to peg the guilder to the Deutschemark was a political one. Although there was substantial economic analysis in support of a hard currency peg, that should not be misconstrued to mean that de facto monetary integration with Germany was economically predetermined. Put another way, Dutch attitudes toward monetary integration derive from the national interest and cannot be taken for granted.

The second assumption is that pegging on the Deutschemark was not an isolated decision. Rather, the choice for de facto monetary integration was made within a particular macroeconomic policy framework—constraining some policies while supporting others. In a sense, this assumption is less polemical than the first: If the Netherlands can be considered the best student of European monetary integration, it was not always easy to be at the top of the class, and it will not necessarily be easy to stay there.

This chapter has four sections. The first examines the history of Dutch exchange rate policy in order to explain how the Dutch came to rely almost exclusively on the Deutschemark peg. The second explores the larger challenges faced by Dutch economic authorities during the 1980s. The third highlights the political compromises at the heart of the Dutch macroeconomic policy mix. Finally, the concluding section provides an estimation of the challenges that the Netherlands has yet to face.

The Politics of De Facto Monetary Integration

Exchange rate stability has long been a concern of Dutch economic policy makers. As in the case of Belgium, this preference derives from the high import penetration of Dutch consumer and supplier markets corresponding to an immediate pass-through of exchange rate depreciation into domestic consumer and producer prices. Trade unions are loath to accept the inevitable impact of currency devaluation on real wages, and employers recognize that any competitive advantage obtained by altering the currency would soon disappear in production costs. Consequently, while the Dutch government was able to generate support for a deep depreciation of the guilder in 1949, that was the last time a ruling coalition has made a major change in the parity of the currency.

Nevertheless, the Dutch decision to align the guilder with the Deutschemark was incremental rather than automatic, and evolved over five periods: During the first period (1960–1971), Dutch authorities focused their attention on the dollar exchange rate within the context of the Bretton Woods system. During the second period (1972–1978), the Dutch placed a strong emphasis on currency stability within the Benelux—and between the Benelux and Germany—as a means to compensate for the collapse of the Bretton Woods system. During the third period (1979–1983), the Dutch began to balance the guilder between the Belgian franc and the Deutschemark, sometimes revaluing with Germany and sometimes "staying behind" with Belgium. During the fourth period (1984–1992), the Dutch—and also the Belgians—began to focus more exclusively on relations with the Deutschemark than on those within the Benelux. Finally, during the fifth period (1993-present), the Dutch and Belgian currencies were pegged independently to the Deutschemark. Evidence in support of this chronology can be found in Table 7.1, which gives the percentage variability (standard deviations) of changes in the

Table 7.1: Variability and Periodization in Dutch Exchange Rate Targets

	1960-71	1972-78	1979-83	1984-92	1993-95
Belgian franc/Deutschemark	0.69	0.89	1.16	0.37	0.74
Dutch guilder/Belgian franc	0.53	0.91	1.16	0.51	0.72
Dutch guilder/Deutschemark	0.57	1.17	0.65	0.47	0.23

Note: Variability is standard deviation of month-to-month log changes.
Source: IMF.

month-to-month exchange rates between the Netherlands, Belgium, and Germany.

The close relationship between the guilder and the Deutschemark during the two periods after 1983 is characteristically different from the guilder-Deutschemark relationship during any period prior to 1984. In this context, it is necessary to reconsider the domestic consensus in favor of stable exchange rates. Put another way, the long-term stability of the Dutch guilder should not be taken to mean that exchange rate policy was uncontroversial.

Although there was firm agreement within the Netherlands, and across Dutch political interests, that international prices should be held stable, there was often disagreement about the reference point for stability. During the Bretton Woods period, for example, there were important political debates about whether the guilder should follow the Deutschemark revaluations of 1961 and 1969. In the first of these instances, Dutch monetary authorities chose to revalue against the dollar in order to slow down domestic economic activity. The economy had moved into a period of full employment, and central bankers were concerned that a failure to match the Deutschemark's revaluation would result in an increase in demand for Dutch exports that would further fuel domestic inflation. In the second instance, 1969, the Dutch were already beginning to experience the first symptoms of stagflation—simultaneous rising unemployment and accelerating inflation—and so Dutch monetary authorities were willing to accept an appreciation of the Deutschemark against the guilder in order to retain export competitiveness and preserve domestic employment.[1]

The contrast between these two experiences highlights an important aspect of Dutch attitudes toward the relative importance of domestic and international price stability. While there was a general commitment in the Netherlands in favor of stabilizing exchange rate movements, this did not translate into a firm commitment to dedicate monetary instruments to the maintenance of domestic price stability as a singular objective.[2] Throughout most of the postwar period, the Dutch central bank was not statutorily independent, and the Ministry of Finance retained the right to overrule central bank actions that ran contrary to the broader objectives of government economic policy (Eizinga, 1983). The reasoning behind this legal dependency was simply that while most Dutch politicians agreed that exchange rate realignments served "speculative" rather than "real" interests (Abert, 1969: 27), there was no consensus on the distributional consequences of domestic inflation. Instead, Dutch government officials believed they faced broad trade-offs in their attempts to satisfy five primary objectives—full employment, price stability, current account equilibrium, production growth, and a "reasonable" distribution of income (de Wolff and Driehuis, 1980: 37). Dutch central bankers strove to balance the assignment of monetary instruments to these objectives by working to stabilize the liquidity ratio, which can be defined loosely as the ratio of available liquidity to nominal gross domestic product (GDP) (Fase, 1992).[3]

Central bankers preferred targeting on the domestic liquidity ratio, although an explicit inflation or exchange rate target would have been more transparent. Their reasoning was that an objective—albeit complicated—standard better enabled them to justify their actions in terms of the broad range of economic objectives held important by the government (Den Dunnen, 1973: 294). The alternative—or so central bankers feared—was that changing government coalitions would change the assignment of monetary instruments to economic objectives. And while the central objective of exchange rate stability would remain, this politicization of monetary policy would destabilize economic performance.

The collapse of the Bretton Woods system diminished the central bank's ability to target the domestic liquidity ratio while stabilizing international trade prices. At the same time, the acceleration of domestic inflation and the volatility in international currency markets increased the importance of having a transparent target as an anchor for monetary policy (Fase, 1979; Zijlstra, 1979). Wage bargaining conflicts began to accelerate inflation, and wage explosions following the breakdown of collective bargaining set in motion a large-scale process of job destruction through labor-saving investment (Den Hartog and Tjan, 1976).[4] Nevertheless, Dutch central bank officials were reluctant to adopt a firm Deutschemark exchange rate target out of a commitment that price stability should be considered in the context of other economic objectives and for fear that a failure to do so would lead to conflict with the government.[5]

In this context, the Bundesbank's 1974 switch to monetary targeting around a strict price stability objective made an informal Deutschemark exchange rate target even more difficult to manage for the Dutch central bank. Attempts to stabilize the exchange rate required a tightening of domestic monetary conditions during an important slowdown in economic activity.

Although the central bank made a halfhearted attempt to follow the Deutschemark in its 1975 revaluation within the "snake" mechanism, the determination to sacrifice domestic employment in order to stabilize the Deutschemark exchange rate rapidly diminished (Wellinck, 1987). After 1976, the guilder tended to depreciate against the Deutschemark in line with the Belgian franc. Meanwhile, officials in the Dutch government began to argue for more symmetrical intervention rules within the "snake" mechanism in order to maximize domestic monetary autonomy while still remaining true to the objective of stable exchange rates (Ludlow, 1982). When more and more countries dropped out of the "snake," the Dutch again were left to focus their efforts at stabilizing international trade prices on the relationship within the Benelux and with Germany (Thygesen, 1979). As in 1972, the Benelux link remained the most important.

The creation of the European monetary system in 1979 promised to provide a more symmetrical arrangement for the maintenance of exchange rate stability and therefore also for the preservation of some limited domestic monetary autonomy. Here the contrast with Belgium sheds important light on Dutch attitudes and objectives. During the maiden realignment of the exchange rate mechanism (ERM), the Belgian government asked to be allowed to revalue with the Deutschemark and was refused. At the same time, Dutch central bankers would have been able to revalue but chose to stay back with the Belgian franc (Gros and Thygesen, 1992: 73–77).

During the period from 1979 to 1983, however, Dutch central bank officials became aware that the symmetry provided by the EMS was less than expected. Although there was more extensive exchange rate stability in Europe, the ERM was prone to frequent (and sometimes substantial) realignments. And although there were mechanisms to increase the symmetry of exchange rate interventions, these were ineffective in use and the asymmetry again favored the Deutschemark (Gros and Thygesen, 1992: chapter 3). A final observation was to prove decisive. Central bank officials noticed that the increasing integration of international capital markets made it imperative that they find a more transparent standard for the conduct of monetary policy. Failure to do so would result in the introduction of a "risk" premium on Dutch borrowing rates, which would have an adverse effect on prospects for investment and employment. This change in the international environment was less obvious to government officials. As a result, the first administration under Minister President Ruud Lubbers expected the Dutch central bank to be as flexible in its assignment of monetary instruments in the 1980s as it had been in the 1970s and before (Bosman, 1984: 11). The government's failure to appreciate the heightened limitations on monetary policy ultimately sparked a fundamental change in the priority of economic targets, with the Deutschemark exchange rate gaining ascendence over the liquidity ratio.

The visible signs of conflict between the Ministry of Finance and the central bank centered on the exchange rate realignment of March 1983. Officials in the central bank argued that a failure to revalue with Germany would have an adverse effect on Dutch domestic interest rates through the widening of the risk premium in the Dutch-German interest rate differential (Voormeulen, 1994: 69). Officials in the government, and particularly Finance Minister Onno Rudding, believed that it would be possible to accept a modest relative devaluation against the Deutschemark in order to loosen domestic monetary conditions. The finance minister overruled the central bank's decision to revalue with the Deutschemark. His action had immediate consequences for the Dutch-German nominal long-term interest rate differential, which almost doubled from 63 basis points in March 1983 to 125 basis points in May (Brakman, de Haan, and Jepman, 1991).

The experience of the 1983 realignment had a twofold effect in the Netherlands. To begin with, it was an important victory for advocates of central bank independence, who were able to argue that political intervention in exchange rate policy had negative effects on the economy. Second, the failure to revalue with the Deutschemark served a stark lesson regarding the importance of having a transparent target for monetary policy (Voormeulen, 1994). Any benefits derived from changing the level of the exchange rate had to be set against the cost imposed by the market in the form of a premium on long-term Dutch interest rates. From 1984 onward, Dutch central bankers remained committed to the need to consider monetary policy in the context of the broader range of governmental economic objectives (Kurzer, 1988: 29). Nevertheless, they recognized that such broader considerations could not be allowed to undermine the market's faith in its ability to read the direction of monetary policy in movements of the exchange rate. Put another way, the broader context of monetary policy could not be allowed to undermine the credibility of the Deutschemark exchange rate target (Szász, 1993; Wellinck, 1989).

This new confidence in exchange rate targeting effectively eliminated relations between the Dutch guilder and the Belgian franc as a possible reference point for trade-price stability and created a strong presumption in favor of maintaining the level of the guilder-Deutschemark exchange rate. Given the poor state of the Dutch economy, however, the guilder was not always in a position to follow the Deutschemark in its revaluations within the ERM. In the period to 1989, the Dutch were forced to prove the credibility of their commitment to peg on the Deutschemark, often by driving domestic inflation rates even lower than those in Germany. Nevertheless, by the early 1990s, the link between the Deutschemark and the guilder was widely accepted, as evidenced by the eventual elimination of the risk premium in Dutch-German interest rate differentials. The final test came with the exchange rate crises of 1992, 1993, and 1995. While the Belgian franc was forced off its narrow peg on the Deutschemark, the Dutch central bank was rewarded with a unique bilateral agreement indicating the Bundesbank's support for the guilder-Deutschemark peg.

Convergence and Adjustment

Building on the version of Dutch exchange rate history just provided, this discussion of Dutch adaptation to de facto monetary union begins during the period surrounding the devaluation of March 1983. From mid-1982 through 1984, Dutch economic policy making experienced a more general changeover that combined price-wage restraint with fiscal austerity measures. This new policy mix promised to shift value added from labor to industry and national income from the public to the private sector. By comparing data for 1983 with that from 1973, it is easy to see the motivation behind such a redistribution of resources. During the first 11 years after the 1973 oil price shock, the labor share of value added increased from 68.9 percent to 78.1 percent, having peaked in 1981 at 80.1 percent. Meanwhile, the government revenue share of GDP grew from 46.7 percent to 56.2 percent.

The catalyst behind the overhaul of Dutch economic policy making was the simultaneous explosion of unemployment rates and fiscal deficits. From 1979 to 1982, the unemployment rate more than doubled, from 5.7 percent of the labor force to 11.9 percent. At the same time, government net borrowing increased from 3.7 percent of GDP to 7.1 percent. Policy makers from all points of the political spectrum recognized the need for drastic action. What they lacked was a precise notion of what exactly should be done.

Wage Restraint and Unemployment

The break in terms of wage restraint came shortly before the victory of the center-right in the September 1982 elections. To understand the significance of this development, it is useful to consider that the Netherlands has a long tradition of using price-incomes policy to adjust for balance-of-payments disequilibrium. Price-incomes policy was first adopted by the center-left during the 1950s through the development of corporatist institutions such as the Foundation of Labor (established in 1945) and the Social and Economic Council (SER; established in 1950). However, corporatist price-incomes policy broke down in the early 1960s, and neither the Foundation of Labor nor the SER was able to control the growth of real wages. The 1970s witnessed a rapid growth of structural unemployment and of the labor share of value added. Meanwhile real wage rigidity hardened as a result of aggressive trade union behavior and extensive nominal indexation. Government attempts to foster price-wage negotiations between business and labor failed dramatically in 1972 and subsequently were abandoned.

During the summer of 1982, leaders of the national employers federation (VNO) and the Socialist/Catholic trade unions (NVV) met to discuss the prospects for negotiated price-wage moderation in exchange for the promise of job creation (Nypels and Tamboer, 1985: 113–122). As a result, soon after the formation of the center-right Lubbers cabinet, the trade unions and employers federation agreed on the first nationwide wage settlement in more than a decade. And although official membership in the Dutch labor movement only accounted for some 39 percent of the workforce in the early 1980s, the government extended the wage agreement to cover the whole of the country.

Throughout the decade, Dutch unit labor costs continued to decline against those in Germany as well as against other EMS countries—increasing the competitiveness of Dutch exports while at the same time shifting the distribution of value added from labor back to industry. (See Figures 7.1, 7.2, and 7.3.) In this way, the exchange rate target and the policy of wage restraint complemented each other explicitly, with the Deutschemark peg holding down the cost of imported inputs to production and reining in the

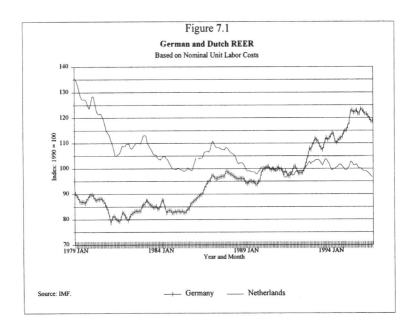

Figure 7.1

German and Dutch REER

Based on Nominal Unit Labor Costs

Source: IMF.   —+— Germany   —— Netherlands

157

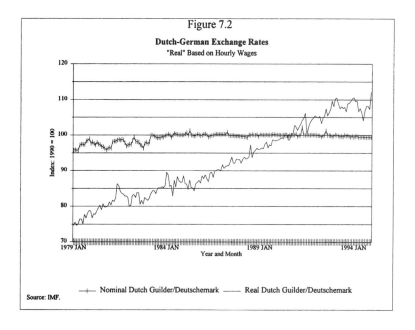

Figure 7.2

Dutch-German Exchange Rates

"Real" Based on Hourly Wages

Source: IMF.

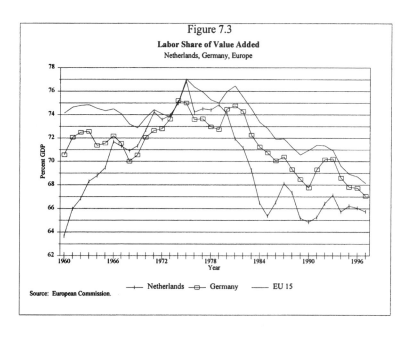

Figure 7.3

Labor Share of Value Added

Netherlands, Germany, Europe

Source: European Commission.

inflation rate while the policy of wage restraint ensured a cost advantage for Dutch exports.

Nevertheless, the effects of the redistribution of value added on employment prospects were less than might have been hoped for. Unemployment declined from a peak of 11.9 percent in 1982 to a low of only 5.6 percent in 1992. However, much of this apparent decline was exaggerated by the growth of part-time work in the Dutch economy as well as by the tremendous rise of workers listed as "disabled" rather than unemployed. From 1983 to 1989, the percentage of men holding part-time employment more than doubled, from 6.8 percent to 15 percent, and part-time employment among women increased from 49.5 percent to 60.1 percent. Thus, although the activity rate measured in terms of persons remained relatively stable at 59 percent, the activity rate in terms of person-years declined to 47 percent (Commission of the European Communities [CEC], 1992: 34–36).

The figures for worker disability are, if anything, even more startling. By 1989, almost 900,000 people were listed as disabled workers in the Netherlands, representing almost 13 percent of the total labor force (CEC, 1992: 37–38). Adding these figures together with data for early retirement and other non-unemployment subsidies, the Organization for Economic Cooperation and Development (OECD) has estimated a broad unemployment rate of 26.8 percent for 1985, which declined to only 25.1 percent in 1991 (OECD, 1994c: 63). The explanation for at least part of this figure can be found in labor market rigidities and in the growth of the labor force. During the 1980s, for example, the labor force grew by more than 10 percent, from under 6 million to over 6.6 million. Thus, while the Dutch government spent considerable resources on labor market policies—equal to more than 1 percent of GDP (OECD, 1990: 34)—these efforts were insufficient to the task at hand. Moreover, government social welfare programs greatly complicated the process of hiring and firing, introducing new rigidities into a sluggish and overburdened labor market.

The major failing of the Dutch labor market derived from the pattern of industrial restructuring during the 1980s (OECD, 1994c: 75–79). Dutch employers took advantage of the redistribution in value added primarily to strengthen corporate balance sheets and to make capital-intensive investments. Both of these effects can be traced—at least in part—to the macroeconomic policy mix supporting the hard-currency regime. The strengthening of corporate balance sheets served to shield the "real" economy from fluctuations in short-term interest rates necessary to support the exchange rate peg and in order to take advantage of the convergence of long-term interest rates on German norms (Mallekoote and Moonen, 1994). And the capital deepening of the Dutch manufacturing sector served to strengthen the international competitiveness of Dutch exports both in terms of traditional product markets and in terms of emerging markets (Söderström, 1986).[6] The result was a general reduction of Dutch dependence on German export markets simultaneous to a chronic shortage in productive capacity.[7] In terms of market diversification, this combination of factors might be labeled a success. In terms of job creation, however, it was at least a partial failure.

For the trade unions, the inability to translate wage restraint into employment growth carried a high price. Soon after the Lubbers cabinet extended the 1982 price-incomes agreement across the private sector, the trade unions were compelled by their followers to withdraw from public participation in trilateral negotiations with industry and government (Compston, 1994: 133). The institutions for consensus building on economic policy issues ceased to fulfill their appointed functions, and left-wing academics began to turn away from the social partnership (Akkermans and Nobelen, 1983). In the political arena as in the workplace, the labor movement continued to suffer from defections through the disappointing elections of 1985—which resulted in a second center-right Lubbers coalition—and up until the economic upturn at the end of the 1980s. By the early 1990s, the percentage of the workforce participating in the trade unions had fallen from 39 to 25 percent, in what some have regarded as among the most dramatic declines in Europe (Mielke, Rütters, and Tudyka, 1994: 213). Nevertheless, trade union leaders remained committed to the program of wage moderation, and there is substantial evidence to suggest that this commitment was a key to the program's success. (See, for example, Graafland, 1992.)

Fiscal Austerity

Renewed efforts to gain control over government spending were both less remarkable and less fruitful. Successive Dutch cabinets struggled to control the growth of outlays since the mid-1970s. Center-right and center-left Dries Van Agt cabinets attempted to enforce fiscal reform measures and failed—by some accounts due to the opposition within the ruling Christian Democratic party (Wellink, 1989) and by others as a result of the weakness of the coalition agreement (Toirkins, 1989). With the continuation of fiscal problems during the successive Lubbers coalitions, however, it became apparent that the roots of the crisis were more structural than political—deriving from the composition of government outlays rather than the discipline of the ruling coalition. From 1976 to 1987, total government spending grew from 52.1 percent of GDP to 59.5 percent. Meanwhile the deficit on government accounts deteriorated from 2.6 percent of GDP to 5.9 percent, having peaked in 1982 at 7.1 percent.

The government's inability to control public spending was endemic, and derived primarily from the failure of the center-right cabinets to rationalize the public sector, both as an administrative organization and as an aggregate of social welfare programs. Anecdotal evidence drawn from interviews of senior officials close to the Lubbers cabinets relates this failing to the prime minister's disinterest in the mechanics of bureaucratic government. Thus, while the cabinet was able to take a strong public stand on the need for fiscal control, it was unable to manipulate the machinery necessary to establish such control in practice (Joustra and van Venetië, 1991).

The statistical evidence for the Dutch failure to control the public sector is even more convincing. One example of the government's inability to reform the structure of the public sector can be seen in the contrast between the development of outlays for public sector employment and expenditures for the broader categories of debt service and social welfare. The government was able to make headway in terms of compensation for public employees—which by 1987 had declined by more than 2 percent of GDP from its peak of 13.1 percent in 1980. Nevertheless, such gains came as a result of public test of wills between the governing coalition and the trade unions. In 1984, the public sector trade unions walked out on talks with the government, forcing the center-right coalition to enforce restraint on public sector wage increases directly rather than through less obtrusive corporatist mechanisms (Wolinetz, 1989). Meanwhile, the public administration was unable to control the growth of debt service and social welfare payments. Taken together, current transfers and debt service grew from 30.1 percent of GDP in 1976 to 38.6 percent in 1987, meaning that the increase in these two categories more than accounted for the total increase in government outlays during the same period and erased almost one-half of the "progress" made on public sector payroll outlays. This confluence of factors explains why the Lubbers cabinets were able to develop a strong reputation for fiscal control without actually having a decisive impact on the balance in government finances. It also explains why the Netherlands came into the 1990s still requiring a considerable fiscal reform (Kuipers and Kuper, 1990: 437).

Building Solidarity both Socially and Geographically

It would be a mistake, however, to judge the fiscal consolidation measures of the Lubbers cabinets too hastily. Generating support for wage moderation and fiscal austerity is politically complicated in a country making the transition from ideologically motivated mass political parties to less ideological catchall parties. This is true in general terms, but particularly in the Netherlands, where the pattern of elite-directed and ideologically based politics was a cornerstone for the country's remarkable stability and effectiveness (Lijphart, 1975).

To begin with, the weakening of ideology in Dutch politics has not softened support for the principles underlying the Dutch welfare state while it has increased competition between political parties. This increase in competition has had the perverse effect of rallying elites around the preservation of social welfare programs. Where under the old ideological system of mass parties it was possible for ruling elites to call for a sharing of the burdens of adjustment in the interests of the community (be it Catholic, Protestant, or Socialist), once ideology lost force as a mobilizing factor, elites had to appease their residual ideologically motivated supporters as well as a pivotal electoral group motivated more by self-interest than ideology. Under such conditions, elites must first regenerate the sense of communal solidarity in the pursuit of adjustment and then work to appease the concerns of the marginal voters. The Lubbers center-right cabinets were only partially successful in this regard, and their attempts to enforce fiscal austerity were regarded more often as authoritarian than communitarian (Scholten, 1987).

The second explanation for the complexity of generating support for adjustment is that while Dutch politics is almost wholly national, the Dutch economy contains important regional divisions. The national basis for Dutch political competition has been suggested by Ken Gladdish (1991: 92–93), who argues that once it may have been possible to talk about the nonconfessional West, the Protestant North and East, and the Catholic South, but the geographic breakdown of electoral support no longer supported such assertions in the 1980s. Nevertheless, as the data in Table 7.2 illustrate, the geographic divisions still hold with respect to the economy. The West contains the largest population group in the country as well as the largest service sector, the highest participation rate, and the highest average income per capita. The North and East are considerably less populous, less wealthy (with the exception of gas-rich Groningen), have lower participation rates and slightly larger agricultural sectors. Finally, the South has the largest share of manufacturing employment, and otherwise falls somewhere between the West and the North and East.

The problem for the government lay in the fact that the primary instrument for adjustment, price-wage restraint, had decidedly asymmetric effects across economic sectors and therefore across regions. For capital-intensive export industries such as those in the South, strict wage moderation raises profits, facilitates investments, and enhances price competitiveness. For sheltered service sectors such as those in the West, wage moderation primarily lowers worker morale and therefore work-time productivity. Even worse, wage moderation lays the foundations for real wage gains in manufacturing through higher productivity growth. In the service sector—where fostering

Table 7.2: Overview of the Dutch Economy by Region, 1991

	Population / Activity (percent)		Employment Shares (percent)			ECU per capita NL=100
	Thousands	Participation Rate	Agriculture	Industry	Services	
Netherlands	15008	56.9	4.3	25.4	69.6	100
North						
Groningen	555	52.7	3.9	25.7	69.8	135
Friesland	600	53.7	6.8	26.8	65.7	82
Flevoland	222	58.9	8.0	22.9	68.9	78
East						
Drenthe	444	54.8	3.9	28.3	67.4	87
Overijsel	1026	53.5	6.3	30.8	62.4	89
Gelderland	1817	56.9	5.8	26.9	66.7	88
West						
Utrecht	1027	61.5	2.1	17.1	79.8	105
North-Holland	2397	59.5	2.6	20.0	76.9	111
South-Holland	3245	56.7	3.9	21.2	74.1	104
Zeeland	358	55.8	7.1	28.0	64.6	105
South						
North-Brabant	2209	57.6	4.8	33.5	61.2	98
Limburg	1110	54.5	4.5	33.3	61.8	93

Source: Eurostat.

productivity growth is perhaps less important than sustaining productivity levels—wage moderation prepares the ground for a relative decline in wages as compared to manufacturing workers.[8]

The asymmetry inherent to price-wage restraint faced the government with an impossible political trade-off. On the one hand, a failure to maintain export competitiveness would increase unemployment—and therefore alienate voters—in those regions centered on manufacturing, such as the southern provinces of North Brabant and Limburg and the eastern province of Overijsel. On the other hand, a successful implementation of price-wage restraint would aggravate voters in the service-sector provinces of the West. To illustrate this prospect, it is useful to note that the regional diversity of the Netherlands is also important in the context of unemployment and underemployment, or part-time work. (See Table 7.3.)

Table 7.3: Dutch Unemployment by Region and Duration, 1991 (percent)

	Unemployment	Share > 1 year	Part-time/ Full-time Work
Netherlands	7.0	41.4	32.6
North			
Groningen	10.2	44.1	38.3
Friesland	9.0	33.3	34.8
Flevoland	7.1	32.4	27.0
East			
Drenthe	7.4	40.5	31.8
Overijssel	7.1	36.6	33.7
Gelderland	7.1	39.4	33.5
West			
Utrecht	6.2	29.0	36.3
North-Holland	7.1	47.9	34.2
South-Holland	6.7	44.8	30.6
Zeeland	5.3	28.3	27.5
South			
North-Brabant	6.6	36.4	31.3
Limburg	6.8	48.5	30.6

Source: Eurostat.

The solution for the government lay in a relaxation of fiscal austerity, and particularly in the development of three categories of social outlays: investment subsidies, worker disability, and early retirement. Investment subsidies were to encourage manufacturing industries to broaden capacity. Worker disability removed from the unemployment roles younger workers who would otherwise have been made redundant, and early retirement removed the near elderly. In each case, the government effectively made a transfer to industry—either directly, as a subsidy, or indirectly, by removing redundant workers as a burden on payroll taxes and placing them on the public coffers. To this might be added the promotion of higher education, which "occupied" almost 200,000 more people during the middle of the 1980s than it had at the start of the decade (CEC, 1992: 26–31; OECD, 1990: 20–21, 32; OECD, 1994c: 54–99).

In a sense, the government's solution for maintaining solidarity in the face of economic adjustment became the problem in terms of fiscal adjustment.

The growth of structural outlays alluded to previously is the direct result of these government programs. And eliminating these programs risks unwinding support for wage moderation in the context of a hard-currency regime. The government declared an end to the investment subsidy program in the late 1980s and has made some efforts to reform worker disability, early retirement and old-age pensions, and higher education. Nevertheless, these issues are so deeply ingrained in popular perceptions of the Dutch welfare state that they are likely to remain contentious well into the future.

The Challenges that Remain

In spite of their impressive adaptation to de facto monetary union with Germany, the Dutch face many of the same challenges to be confronted by other would-be participants of EMU. Namely, the Dutch must generate popular support for further integration, they must continue to make progress toward fiscal convergence, and they must find some means to maintain export competitiveness. The ongoing struggle to lower unemployment levels forms a backdrop to these challenges, for as we argue repeatedly in this volume, there is little reason to believe that unemployment is strongly related to monetary integration.

Of the three challenges, the generation of popular support for EMU is likely to be the easiest for Dutch governmental officials. The Dutch have consistently polled higher-than-average levels of support for European integration—usually in the range between 70 and 80 percent—whether the question concerns the goal of unification or the benefits of Europe for the Netherlands. More specifically, some 55 percent of the Dutch favor European control over monetary policy, 59 percent favor a single European currency, and 73 percent favor a European central bank.[9] On this basis, it should be safe to assume that almost two-thirds of the Dutch already support monetary integration and, given the strong consensus on exchange rate stability, there is little reason to suspect that this level of support will deteriorate dramatically.[10]

Having said that, it is important to note that the Maastricht Treaty is not an ideal document from the Dutch perspective—for reasons in many ways divorced from the subject of monetary integration. The perceived transfer of power from the European Commission to the European Council revives concern about "large power hegemony" in intergovernmental negotiations and the three pillar organization is all too reminiscent of Charles de Gaulle's Fouchet Plan (Wester, 1992). However, the Dutch attempt to tailor the Maastricht negotiations more to their own liking—the "Dankert" draft—was soundly rejected by France and Germany, and so the Dutch resigned themselves to accept the Maastricht Treaty. The 1992 Danish veto of the treaty came as a shock in the Netherlands (as everywhere else) and the difficult French referendum sparked some Dutch to call for a plebiscite of their own. All this suggests that the Dutch are unlikely to remain silent partners in the European Union.

Moreover, the Dutch are not without their idiosyncrasies regarding European integration. The 1994 European elections reveal that the Dutch are not as ardent in their support of the EU—or at least the European Parliament— as the numbers suggest. Only 35.6 percent of the electorate voted in the June polling, which is more than a third lower than the record 57.8 percent turnout in 1979. And while this decline may be exaggerated by acute electoral fatigue, the 1994 turnout also reflects a broader decline in participation rates from each Euro-parliamentary election to the next. Even more disturbing is the fact that the electoral results at the European level were very different from those at the national level. This can be seen in Table 7.4, which compares the results of national and European elections in 1994 with those from national and European elections in 1989. While party preference was quite stable across the two types of elections in the late 1980s, there were dramatic differences in the early 1990s.

The explanation for this difference across European and national elections in 1994 reveals much about Dutch attitudes toward European integration. The Christian Democratic Party (CDA) campaigned in European elections on the platform that if it gained back support relative to the May national elections, then Ruud Lubbers stood a better chance of becoming president of the European Commission. Voters responded—particularly in the Dutch "Bible Belt"—with a strong vote of confidence in Lubbers. And, perversely, they were encouraged by the unanimous support of the other political parties for the Lubbers candidacy. Dutch elites from across the political spectrum were willing to sacrifice potential *party* gains in the European parliament in order to have a stronger *national* representation in the Commission. Such evidence underscores what observers of the Netherlands have

Table 7.4: Dutch Electoral Results in 1989 and 1994

Political Party (percentages)	1989 Elections		1994 Elections	
	National	European	National	European
Christian Democrats (CDA)	35.3	34.6	22.2	30.8
Labor (PvdA)	31.9	30.7	24.0	22.9
Right Liberals (VVD)	14.6	13.6	20.0	17.9
Left Liberals (D'66)	12.0	5.9	15.5	11.7

Source: European Parliament.

known since the Fouchet debates of the early 1960s: Dutch national interest remains a stronger force for political mobilization than any nascent European identity.

The challenge of convergence on the Maastricht criteria is both more straightforward and more difficult to meet. The Dutch accept the need for macroeconomic convergence in preparation for EMU—a position they have held since the "economist-monetarist" debates of the early 1970s. Moreover, they seem well on their way to meeting the convergence criteria outlined in the Maastricht Treaty. (See Table I.4.) Political debates have not been about the necessity of convergence but rather about the speed. (See, for example, Hilbers and Wolswijk, 1994.) When the Council of Ministers suggested that the Netherlands raise taxes to bring down the budget deficit in October 1994, the Liberal finance minister squared off against his Labor colleague in the Ministry of Social Welfare in a debate over whether, in order to meet the Maastricht criteria, the 1995 deficit had to be reduced to 1.5 percent of GDP or "only" 2.5 percent. In the end, both targets appeared overly optimistic.

Popular debate about fiscal convergence is limited by the difficulties of welfare reform. Although there is general agreement that "something" should be done, there is little agreement as to what. The Liberal VVD campaigned successfully in the 1994 election for greater liberalization of the labor market but was not granted any of the labor-related ministerial portfolios—which were reserved for the Labor Party (PvdA). The Labor prime minister has been accused of breaking links with his trade union constituency, but even if this is true, it is unlikely to result in radical labor market reforms.

In this sense, the link between efforts to generate social solidarity and the failure of fiscal reform measures is explicit. As argued earlier, much of the structural weakness of Dutch government accounts can be attributed to generous social outlays for worker disability (WAO), postsecondary education, and old-age insurance (AOW). Moreover, present demographic trends indicate that the Netherlands will experience a 19 percent rise in social security disbursements during the course of the present and following decades (1990 to 2010) if the social security system is not reformed.

Reforming either the worker disability program or the old-age pension support scheme threatens to unravel huge domestic political bargains: The WAO has been used to remove jobless workers from the unemployment rolls without overburdening payroll taxes and thereby increasing non-wage labor costs. The AOW pension program had a similar function but also served to consolidate social benefits in the hands of the state, rather than disbursing benefits through ideologically affiliated organizations such as churches or trade unions. Thus, the disability payments smooth over the social partnership, and old-age pensions soften ideological cleavages (Gladdish, 1991: 142). Dismantling these programs promises to renew conflicts along ideological and class lines. Nevertheless, it is clear that further budgetary consolidation is necessary for the Netherlands to participate in EMU. In April 1995, the government announced plans for the privatization of disability insurance (WAO), shifting contributions from employees to employers. Such a policy should have a tremendous impact on government finances. Nevertheless, it is also likely to have a strong adverse effect on industrial competitiveness.

The prospect of privatizing Dutch social welfare raises the final consideration of maintaining export competitiveness. If government financial reforms are likely to raise non-wage labor costs for businesses, then either government or industry will have to obtain some influence over wage costs in order to sustain price competitiveness. Analytically, the challenge of maintaining cost competitiveness should be addressed on two levels, which is to say both in terms of a monetary union encompassing relatively few members and, more generally, in terms of the development of real effective exchange rates.

The Dutch export position in international markets is relatively unchanged from the late 1980s. In goods trade, the Dutch currently export 43 percent of the gross domestic production, with 30 percent going to European markets. More than one-half of Dutch exports fall in SITC categories 0 to 4 and 6, which cover food, raw materials, and basic manufactures. In aggregate terms, Bernard Ullmo (1989: 60) estimates that the Dutch price elasticity of demand for exports is 2.0, while the price elasticity of demand for imports in less than 1. Thus, for the foreseeable future, Dutch economic prosperity will continue to depend on the maintenance of cost competitiveness in spite of exchange rate fluctuations between the Netherlands and those countries not participating in EMU, and between the Netherlands and the rest of EMU.

In terms of a "multispeed" Europe, it is possible to examine the Dutch reaction to the Schäuble-Lammers paper of late autumn 1994. The Foreign Ministry's reaction to the paper was very lukewarm, but not exactly negative—indicating that the paper contained some interesting ideas that deserve further discussion. These sentiments were shared by the (then) opposition Christian Democrats as well. A joint letter from the Belgian and Dutch Christian Democrats described the paper as "an interesting thought exercise" but then went on to argue that a Europe of variable geometry might be "a dangerous way to proceed" (*De Standaard*, 22 September 1994: 9). Such ambivalence is surprising insofar as the previous government had gone on record in opposition to "multispeed" Europe, and the Dutch had long argued in favor of a unitary organization.

A possible explanation for Dutch ambivalence has to do with the diminished importance of the British in managing the joint hegemony of France and Germany within Europe. The Dutch are loath to see a Union without the United Kingdom, but they are also more confident that the institutions of the Union can protect their interests against large-country domination. Thus, even if the United Kingdom chooses not to join EMU, the Dutch are less concerned about the prospects for a Franco-German condominium that they were, for example, in the 1960s. Dutch commentators from across the political spectrum have been open in their acknowledgment that "monetary" Europe will begin with a hard core and (it is hoped) spread outward. The situation today is thus similar to that immediately after 1983, and there is a broad consensus in the Netherlands that exchange rate stability with Germany is better than the alternative of higher long-term interest rates.

What has changed is the ability of Dutch labor organizations to enforce wage restraint. Given the decline in trade union membership and the growing diversification of the workforce, trade union leaders have little ability to set binding wage targets. Nevertheless, wage policy remains an essential tool for managing the macroeconomy. The difficulty is how to use it. To illustrate this dependence, a German economist, Alfred Kleinknecht, suggested (ironically) that Dutch wage costs should be encouraged to rise in order to stimulate the creative-destruction process and thereby promote productive investment. His proposal sparked a storm of protest from labor, industry, and political elites—many of whom clearly misunderstood Professor Kleinknecht's irony. Labor contended that while wage restraint not was the cure to all economic ills, wage growth would lead to massive unemployment and undermine government accounts. Industry argued that productivity growth should lead real wage rises and not vice versa. Politicians concurred with industry and noted that the rate of firm bankruptcy was already "sufficiently high" in the Netherlands (*De Volkskrant,* 1 October 1994: 43).

Conclusion

The Dutch will certainly be among the first and most enthusiastic members of a monetary union in Europe. However, that does not mean they will have an easy time of it. This chapter has argued that Dutch adaptation to de facto monetary integration was part of a larger program for economic adjustment and fiscal consolidation. In the end, economic adjustment was possible because the government was willing to accept a moderation of fiscal austerity in exchange for price-wage restraint. In turn, price-wage restraint was necessary to shift the distribution of value added from labor to industry while maintaining price competitiveness under a hard currency regime. In effect, successive center-right cabinets purchased the structural adjustment of the Dutch economy with a structural weakening of Dutch government accounts.

Now it is the fiscal situation that requires adjustment. Demographic statistics reveal that Dutch social welfare outlays would have to be reformed even if there were no EMU. Under such circumstances, it is not surprising that the convergence criteria are not debated in the Netherlands. Nevertheless, the prospect of fiscal consolidation raises the question of how the government will be able to maintain support for price-wage restraint in the future. The erosion of trade union discipline and the weakening of traditional corporatist policy frameworks give this question added importance. If the government is faced with adverse labor costs developments, how will it effect a redistribution of value added, and how will it maintain the price competitiveness of exports?

The prospect of economic and monetary union forms a backdrop for concerns about the future of Dutch macroeconomic policy. Certainly the more inclusive the monetary union, and therefore the more export competitors subject to the trade-price stability of a single monetary regime and to the discipline of a hard currency in external markets, the less the Dutch will need to resort to relative real wage restraint. However, if the monetary union encompasses only a few countries and leaves open the prospect of a nominal appreciation between the Dutch and some of their larger export competitors, the importance of controlling real wage developments in the Netherlands will grow even as the capability to do so has diminished. Under such conditions, as during the 1980s, something will have to give way. In view of the constraints on fiscal policy imposed by demographics and indeed by the Maastricht Treaty, it is not clear what that something may be. What is clear, however, is that staying at the top of the class for monetary integration will continue to be a challenge for the Netherlands.

Notes

1. Both the 1961 decision to revalue with the Deutschemark and the 1969 decision to stay behind involved important trade-offs. The 1961 revaluation did check inflation but only to set the stage for important real wage "explosions" in 1963. And the 1969 decision maintained growth but sparked important capital inflows that further fueled domestic inflation. See Abert (1969: 158–172); Den Dunnen (1973: 322–323); Van Doorn, et al. (1976: 81–90).

2. In his reflections on the role of central bank independence in the Delors plan for monetary union, one-time Dutch finance minister Pieter Lieftinck, the man responsible for the nationalization of the Dutch central bank in 1948, explained that his decision to provide for ministerial oversight was precisely to avoid having the central bank give priority to domestic price stability over

the economic objectives of the government. See Bakker and van Lent (1989: 160–168).

3. Before the mid-1980s, a rule-of-thumb definition of the liquidity ratio was the ratio of M2 to net national income.

4. Den Hartog and Tjan's analysis sparked a major controversy among Dutch economists about the relative size of the structural component in national unemployment. For a broad overview of this debate, see Driehuis and van der Zwaan (1978).

5. Wellinck (1987) explains this internal conflict between the central bank and the government as deriving from confusion over whether the problems in the Dutch economy were structural or cyclical.

6. Here it may be useful to note that wage moderation did not have the same effect on the sheltered sector of the economy, which reacted to the decline in the relative cost of labor with capital broadening rather than capital deepening (OECD, 1994c: 75).

7. The decreasing dependence on German markets is somewhat difficult to document solidly. Nevertheless, the available statistical information is supportive of this assertion. The German share of Dutch exports declined from 38 percent in 1979 to only 32 percent in 1988. Meanwhile, the composition of Dutch exports became more similar to those originating in Germany. The correlation coefficient between Dutch and German export composition measured at two-digit SITC categories was only 0.16 in 1982, while already in 1987 that coefficient was 0.37. Taken together, these data suggest that the Netherlands became less dependent on German markets as Dutch exports began to compete more directly with those from Germany.

8. The relative decline of service sector wages compared to manufacturing wages can take place either as a result of wage drift in manufacturing under statutory wage restraints or as a result of accelerated wage increases in manufacturing once the wage restraints are lifted.

9. Data are from the April 1994 Eurobarometer survey.

10. The same point can be made in terms of economic integration more generally, given that 64 percent of the Dutch were "rather hopeful" as a result of the completion of Europe's internal market, compared to a European average of only 46 percent, and 60 percent of the Dutch thought European integration should proceed more quickly (Eurobarometer, 1994: A29, A32).

CHAPTER EIGHT

Portugal toward EMU: A Political Economy Perspective

Francisco Torres

The aim of a successful political and economic integration has shaped Portugal's economic policy since it joined the European Community (EC) in 1986. Portugal has benefited significantly from European integration. Structural and cohesion funds have undeniably made an important contribution to the Portuguese process of catching up with the rest of Europe and to the expression of social cohesion at the European level. Moreover, the challenges posed by the European Single Market and economic and monetary union (EMU)—both broadly corresponding to the model of economic and social development supported by the two main political parties, the moderate trade unions, and part of industry—have prompted necessary reforms. The pressure and promise of European integration made it possible for ruling politicians to agree to change the economic constitution in 1989 and to pursue structural reforms and the liberalization of the economy.

Initially, the case for a European single currency was not perceived as a central question for Portugal. The idea of a monetary union in Europe was well received by the public in general as a long-term European goal, although Portugal's capacity to participate from the outset was regarded with some skepticism. But Portuguese attitudes toward EMU evolved with the European discussion around the ratification of the Maastricht Treaty. The exchange rate crisis, the European recession, and the adoption of a convergence program designed to allow Portugal to participate in EMU together brought the issue of membership to the forefront of the public debate. General attitudes toward a European currency under European control have since changed with external economic conditions. Still, even today there is a strong (and loud) ideological opposition to EMU (and European integration) in spite of a clear political majority in favor.

Maintaining the objective of participation in EMU during the recession of 1993–94 and throughout the electoral year of 1995 was possible only because of the steps taken in 1992—that is, joining the European exchange rate mechanism (ERM) and liberalizing all administrative controls on capital flows. In October 1995, the new Socialist-led minority government adopted the convergence program of the previous executive, initially with some "political reservations" in order to gather support from the right-wing anti-Maastricht party, the Democratic and Social Center-Popular Party (CDS-PP), and later, by May 1996, as a government commitment with the opposition. In October 1996, it became clear that both the government and the main opposition party, the Social Democratic Party (PSD), fully subscribed to satisfying as quickly as possible the macroeconomic convergence criteria in order to participate in EMU from the start. This opens the way to fulfill all the convergence criteria by 1997.

The purpose of this chapter is to discuss the political economy of Portugal's participation in EMU. The discussion is divided into six sections. The first of these presents the political background of macroeconomic convergence, with an emphasis on the change of macroeconomic regime (to exchange rate convertibility and ERM participation) and political consensus building. It also discusses the adoption of a new policy stance on European integration, the institutional conflict between the treasury and the central bank, and the effects of the exchange rate crisis and recession on exchange rate policy and the convergence program. The second looks at how the characteristics of the Portuguese economy fit the optimum currency area criteria. The third section examines different institutional features of the Portuguese economy: the flexibility of the labor market and the unemployment problem; the issue of structural versus coinsurance funds in a monetary union; privatization and competition policy. This section also touches on the institutional role of the central bank. The fourth section looks at attitudes toward EMU and at the evolution of the policy debate on monetary integration. The fifth section assesses the prospects for fiscal consolidation. Some concluding remarks are presented in the sixth and final section.

The Political Background
of Macroeconomic Convergence

Between 1980 and 1982, while Europe was stagnating, Portugal grew at an average annual rate of 3 percent. The terms of trade deteriorated 3 percent a year. At the same time, there was a political impasse due to tensions within the center-right government coalition between PSD and CDS, between the poles of the executive (the government and President Ramalho Eanes), and over proposed changes to the constitution between the two main political parties, the PSD and the Socialist Party (PS). It was not until the 1982 amendment to the constitution that the blocking Revolutionary Council chaired by the president was abolished. But, despite its first amendment in 1982, the constitution remained socialist in character until its second revision in 1989.

In 1983, Prime Minister Mário Soares headed an emergency cabinet—a PS-led coalition with PSD, known as "bloco central"—whose major tasks were to restore the external balance, through an adjustment program with the International Monetary Fund (IMF), and to complete negotiations with the European Community concerning the accession of Portugal. By 1985, after a rather severe adjustment program, inflation was reduced ten percentage points to 19.3 percent and the current account was again in surplus. However, public sector imbalances were not tackled: The public debt kept rising until 1988 (to a peak of almost three-quarters of gross domestic product [GDP]). Domestic recession improved the external accounts but failed to curb the public sector deficit and its inflationary consequences. The acute economic crisis had not triggered economic reform.

Fiscal Adjustment and Structural Reform

After the IMF adjustment program, new elections, and entry in the EC, the successive governments of the PSD, headed by Prime Minister Cavaco Silva, pursued a strategy of gradual convergence toward Community standards. Formally, the strategy comprised a sequence of adjustment programs. The character of each of those programs and the extent to which they were implemented (from 1985 to 1995) reflect the evolution of factors such as the amendment to the constitution, external economic conditions, integration with the European Community, the model of integration adopted by the government, and the electoral cycle.

The first adjustment program, prepared by the PSD minority government elected in October 1985 and approved shortly before the party won a Parliamentary majority in 1987, was dubbed PCEDED. Its successor, P2, featured added fiscal adjustment and privatization of state-owned enterprises to stabilize the ratio of public debt to GDP. This was possible only because of the second constitutional amendment of 1989. The Government then decided at the finance minister's suggestion to use 80 percent of privatization revenues to stabilize public debt. This option was reversed in 1993 (to a minimum of 40 percent) but reintroduced in 1996. Meanwhile, public debt as a percentage of GDP not only stabilized but declined significantly from 1989 through 1992 and decreased marginally in 1996. The programs were aimed at redressing major macroeconomic imbalances but did not modify the exchange rate regime, officially still a crawling peg.

In 1986 and 1987, the Portuguese economy was characterized by relatively high economic growth and substantial progress in reducing inflation (from 19.3 percent in 1985 to 9.4 percent in 1987), which was due mainly to the decline of both the dollar and the price of oil and to world economic growth. Entry into the European Community at the end of the period of Euro-sclerosis and the beginning of EC-1992 optimism was also an important factor in promoting economic growth and moderating inflation. Due to its increased openness, the Portuguese economy benefited substantially from that effect. Between 1985 and 1988, Portugal's terms of trade improved by almost 6 percent a year. This in turn allowed for the pursuit of an expansionary policy without a major adverse impact on inflation, in spite of the introduction of an extra tax on oil products and, especially, of the value added tax (VAT) in 1986, which is estimated to have had a negative impact of 2 to 3 percent on the consumer price index (CPI).

At the same time, domestic fiscal transparency, meaning both greater fiscal discipline and especially a more open reporting of fiscal decisions, was increased significantly and curbing inflation with specific annual targets became a clearly stated policy objective. Fiscal reform included, besides the introduction of VAT, reform of direct taxation in 1989, which raised total revenue as a percentage of GDP.

The Lack of an Exchange Rate Strategy

By 1988, the anti-inflation effort came to a standstill, due partly to the combination of full employment with high economic growth, a clearer perception by the private sector of the inflationary effects of a high public debt and the lack of a clear-cut strategy for disinflation in the face of slowing global growth. The deemphasis on fighting inflation was underscored by a stated shift in policy objectives: from the priority of fighting inflation to the need not to slow down the catching-up process with the rest of the European Community. Less control of domestic capital markets; large capital inflows; a postponed transition to a system of indirect credit control that reflected the fears of the monetary authorities to liberalize, coupled with the lack of a clear strategy for the exchange rate policy; and the slowdown of the pace of fiscal adjustment further weakened the authorities' anti-inflation credibility.[1]

In 1985, the crawling peg regime was suspended for four months; it was resumed thereafter at a decreasing rate. The crawling peg regime, coupled with capital controls, credit ceilings, and administratively set interest rates, had allowed the government to collect implicit revenues from the productive sector. However, the crawling peg was no longer effective in altering relative prices or compensating for inflation differentials with Portugal's main trading partners. At a time of greater financial openness and closer monetary integration, this exchange rate limbo was incompatible with a strong commitment to fiscal adjustment. In 1989, the inflation rate turned out to be almost 8 percent above the initial (successively revised) target.

The ambiguous Portuguese response to the need for institutional reform and European integration was mirrored by complete discretion regarding the future course of exchange rate policy and the timing of monetary reform. Nevertheless, capital controls, credit ceilings, and administratively set interest rates (by then only partly dismantled) gave the monetary authorities the illusion that monetary autonomy could last forever.

For many years (well into the 1990s), the Portuguese government, although firmly committed to European integration, sided with the United Kingdom, its traditional Atlantic ally, in its skeptical attitude toward rapid institutional reform, namely monetary reform, in the European Community. The minister of finance responsible for the PCEDED and P2, now a prominent anti-EMU voice, felt very uneasy about a swift European monetary integration because of its perceived potential costs in terms of economic and social cohesion and loss of national sovereignty. (See Cadilhe, 1990.) In fact, he was never an enthusiast of central bank independence and shared the government's initial skeptical view on rapid European monetary reform. Conversely, the monetary authorities, unlike their European counterparts, initially favored an exchange rate rule based on external competitiveness (the crawling peg) and later on a national (protectionist) solution for increased central bank independence (power), that is, capital controls rather than EMS discipline.

The National Adjustment Framework for the Transition to Economic and Monetary Union, dubbed QUANTUM, was approved in June 1990. In the beginning of that year, a new minister of finance, formerly a central bank board member, not only continued to emphasize the package of fiscal consolidation but also announced the preparation for membership in the ERM as a step toward EMU and reestablished disinflation as a priority. Soon it became clear, however, that he would follow the central bank, postponing the liberalization of capital controls and EMS entry. A sweeping adjustment of the public sector wage scale increased substantially the government's wage bill. Public sector wage increases also influenced wage bargains in the private sector. As a result, fiscal adjustment did not materialize in the period 1990 to 1991. The fact that elections took place in October 1991 made it appear as part of the political business cycle.[2]

Toward European Monetary Integration

The new government that came out of the general elections of 1991 announced full participation in EMU as a clear policy objective. The adjustment program designed for the period between 1992 and 1995, named Q2, marked a clear change in regime: from discretion to rules and from capital controls to free capital mobility.[3]

The new program embodied a global approach to economic reform and to the process of European integration. The objective of the Q2 convergence program was to bring inflation under control by 1995 and thus to lay the groundwork for sustained economic growth and for the third phase of EMU (Ministry of Finance, 1992): Its aim, in other words, was to eliminate the inflation differential vis-à-vis the Community average, while maintaining the positive differential in regard to rates of economic growth.

The budgetary process rested on the principle of nonaccommodation. The principal targets of the convergence program for 1992 to 1995 were to be decided along with the respective annual budgets. The program laid down the projected macroeconomic framework under which convergence requirements for full EMU participation could be met. The first measure to be adopted in 1992 was the harmonization of the VAT rate structure in line with the EC. This adjustment is estimated to have increased consumer price inflation 2.4 percentage points in 1992.[4]

The escudo joined the ERM on 6 April 1992 as part of the convergence program and at a time when Portugal held the presidency of the European Council.[5] A few months later, the turmoil in the European exchange rate markets began and the momentum for EMU was lost amid the recession. Meanwhile, in 1992 the fiscal deficit fell from 6.7 to 3.6 percent of GDP, and public debt fell from 71.1 to 63.3 percent of GDP. The Portuguese public debt-to-GDP ratio as a percentage of the average EU public debt-to-GDP ratio fell from 1.28 to 1.05.

Conflict over Liberalization

The policy of capital controls had resulted in artificially high interest rates that were, in turn, responsible for a higher debt service of the treasury, significant losses by the central bank, and substantial distortions in the functioning of the economy. Moreover, they implied an unwarranted transfer of resources from the productive sector to the sheltered financial sector. This transfer angered the social partners, meaning representatives of industry and labor. It also fueled the opposition, which sided with the central bank in blaming ERM participation and government "obstinacy" (regarding nominal convergence) for the recession.

The political consensus needed for reforms was nearly broken, since the blame for high interest rates was placed on exchange rate policy and on the convergence program (responsible, according to that view, for the lower rate of growth of the economy). (As a result of the exchange rate policy, constant calls for a devaluation of the escudo grew with the recession in the Portuguese traditional export markets, such as textiles and clothing.)[6]. As in other such reform efforts, antireform interests tried to blame liberalization for the economic recession and advocated increased protectionism. Such interests were manifest within the banking system, which did not face external competition, and also the traditional export sectors. Protectionism promised to deliver specific rents to such groups (such as higher interest rates in the case of the banking system) and to enhance their political power within the government, the PSD and the central bank.[7]

Soft Landing on the ERM

The period of exchange rate turbulence in the EMS, in spite of its negative effects, provided clear relief to the Portuguese economy.[8] During the same period, inflation came down from 9.8 percent in May 1992 to 5.6 percent in June 1993 (see Figure 8.1) and interest payments on the stock of outstanding debt, while rising in most EU countries, fell significantly in Portugal.[9] During the crisis, Portugal was also the only country in the European Union (the last country had been Ireland in 1989) whose foreign debt was upgraded from A+ to AA–.

The early 1990s proved to be an inestimable learning period for policy makers, social partners, and economic agents in general. (See Torres, 1996b.) It was possible for the private sector to learn more about the policy rule and eventually understand it, while the various realignments were seen as an escape clause, beyond government control, to be triggered in exceptional circumstances, such as the German unification shock (a textbook example of an asymmetric shock).

Those circumstances granted some breathing space to the real sector of the Portuguese economy while accomplishing the change in regime. It was the first time for many years (since 1891, when the Portuguese currency left the gold standard, except for less than three months in 1931, when it returned to gold convertibility) that Portugal was living in a regime of full currency convertibility. While it had been impossible to pursue structural reforms without the liberalization of the economy, having a clear economic and political strategy for achieving macroeconomic convergence before the European recession of 1992 to 1993 and especially before the outbreak of the ERM crisis proved decisive. (See Torres, 1995.) The escudo managed to survive the deepest postwar recession in

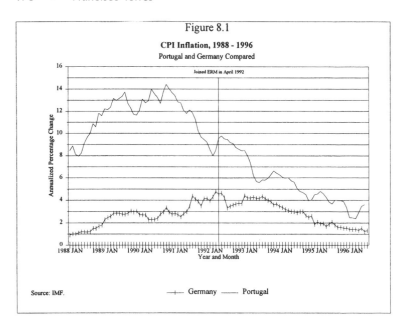

Figure 8.1

CPI Inflation, 1988 - 1996
Portugal and Germany Compared

Source: IMF.

—+— Germany ——— Portugal

Europe without leaving the ERM and without resorting to capital controls at any time.

Still, the escudo was forced to devalue several times after the beginning of the ERM crisis: In November 1992, following the second realignment in the EMS and the devaluation of the Spanish peseta; in May 1993, following only partially the third devaluation of the Spanish peseta; and in March 1995, "following the decision to change the central rate of the peseta [by 7 percent], the Ministers and central bank Governors also agreed on a downward adjustment of the central rate of the Portuguese escudo by 3.5 percent in line with the market rate prevailing since August 1993" (European Monetary Institute [EMI], 1996: 31). After this latter adjustment the escudo recovered to levels close to those prevailing at the end of 1994. Because the financial markets had been associating the escudo with the peseta, the authorities followed, since the beginning of the period of turmoil, an intentional policy of decoupling the two currencies. This policy has been relatively successful (as can be seen by the reduction of daily exchange rate volatility and of the need for official intervention in the foreign exchange markets). (See Figures 8.2 and 8.3.) Interest rates on ten-year government bonds fell 300 basis points in the following 12 months.

In nominal effective terms, the escudo behaved in a rather stable way since it joined the ERM in April 1992. (See Figure 8.2 and Table 8.1.) During the

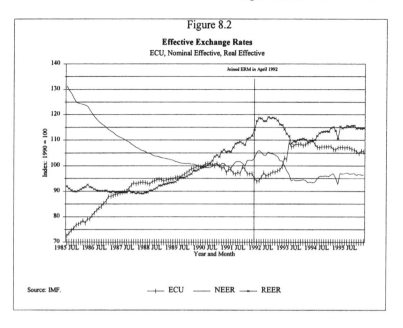

Figure 8.2
Effective Exchange Rates
ECU, Nominal Effective, Real Effective

Source: IMF. — ECU — NEER — REER

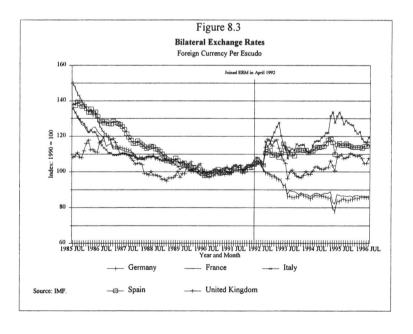

Figure 8.3
Bilateral Exchange Rates
Foreign Currency Per Escudo

Source: IMF. — Germany — France — Italy — Spain — United Kingdom

Table 8.1: Key Macroeconomic Indicators

Indicators	1991	1992	1993	1994	1995	1996
General Economy						
Real GDP growth[a]	2.3	1.1	1.2	0.8	2.3	2.5
Short-term interest rates[a]	18.4	16.7	13.4	11.1	9.9	7.6
Unemployment (percent labor force)	4.1	4.1	5.5	6.8	7.2	7.2
Convergence Criteria						
CPI inflation[a]	11.3	8.9	6.5	5.2	4.1	3.1
Reference value[a]	4.4	3.8	3.1	3.1	2.7	2.6
Long-term interest rates[a]	14.5	13.8	11.2	10.5	11.5	9.4
Reference value[a]	10.7	10.7	9.3	10.0	9.7	8.7
General government deficit[b]	6.7	3.6	6.9	5.8	5.1	4.0
Gross public debt[b]	71.1	63.3	68.2	69.6	71.7	71.1
Exchange-rate Performance Indicators (Index 1990=100)						
Deutschemark exchange rate	87.1	86.5	97.2	102.3	104.7	102.8
Nominal effective exchange rate	100.7	104.2	97.8	93.8	95.7	95.2
Real effective exchange rate	107.1	115.9	112.2	110.2	113.8	114.1
Exchange-rate volatility[c]	0.27	0.42	0.43	0.23	0.23	0.11
Other Factors						
Unit labor costs[a]	15.1	12.9	6.5	3.9	1.7	3.6
Current account balance[b]	-0.9	-0.1	0.4	-1.7	-0.3	-0.8
Net foreign assets[b]	n/a	n/a	15.6	10.2	4.1	1.0
Exports[b]	33.5	35.1	33.7	37.1	40.3	42.4

Notes: [a]Annual percentage change. [b]Percent GDP. [c]Standard deviation on day-to-day log changes. In 1994, the share of intra-EU exports in total national exports was 80 percent compared to an EU average of 62 percent.
Sources: European Commission; European Monetary Institute.

two years ending in September 1996, the behavior of the escudo against a basket comprising the currencies of 26 industrialized countries was the most stable of all EU currencies (Bank for International Settlements [BIS] data). In real effective terms (using the consumer price index [CPI] as a deflator), the Portuguese escudo was by far the most stable currency in the EU, from joining the ERM until September 1996: Its real effective exchange rate (REER) appreciated by only 0.5 percent. Since 1987, it appreciated 27.2 percent, more than any other EU currency. This is because from 1989 to 1991 there was a substantial rise in relative unit labor costs.in any case, exchange rate stability should reduce the cost of capital, which in turn will contribute to economic recovery.

The Consequences of the Recession

It is obvious that the European recession should have had a strong impact on the Portuguese economy and on the program of convergence. While state expenditure remained on target in 1992 and 1993, tax revenue fell much below its predicted value and social security expenditure exceeded its target in 1993, inducing a slippage in the process of fiscal consolidation. The fiscal deficit and public debt ratios to GDP jumped to previous levels, 6.9 and 68.2, respectively, thus discontinuing the process of fiscal convergence.[10]

This interruption was due mainly to the recession. Negative growth generates lower tax revenues—total revenue fell from 34.1 to 31.7 percent of GDP (OECD, 1996b)—and increasing unemployment induces higher social security transfers. (See Figure 8.4.) However, the slowdown in fiscal consolidation also derives from the virtual collapse of the tax administration. In 1992, the tax authorities had to adapt to the new rules of the internal market and to the adjustment of the VAT rate structure. At the same time, many

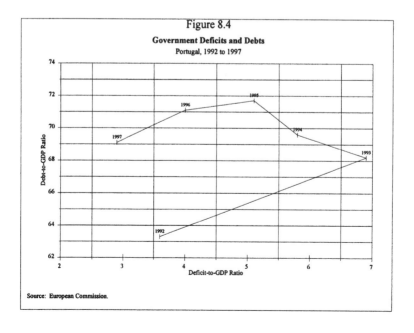

Figure 8.4

Government Deficits and Debts
Portugal, 1992 to 1997

Source: European Commission.

firms resorted to the old practice of ignoring their tax and social security obligations during a recession. As a result, the scale of revenue slippage was totally unexpected and provoked a general feeling of failure. Although the inflation differential vis-à-vis the Community average had been reduced significantly, the differential in regard to rates of economic growth became negative. Opposition to the strategy of macroeconomic convergence for participation in EMU focused the debate on the costs and benefits of EMU and specifically on the issue of real divergence. However, the news was not entirely bad for the government. From 1993 to 1996, Portuguese public debt-to-GDP as a percentage of the average EU debt-to-GDP ratio kept falling until it became less than 1.

Building a New Consensus

The prime minister made it clear that the government remained committed to exchange rate stability and free mobility of capital, and that the convergence program would be respected. Nevertheless, the mid-1990s was a difficult period in political terms: the Government lost the regional elections in 1993 and faced European elections in June 1994, parliamentary elections in October 1995, and presidential elections in January 1996. Although the Socialist Party had sided with the PSD government in support of the broader aims of European integration, namely the ratification of the Maastricht Treaty, it attacked what it called a fundamentalist obsession with the nominal convergence criteria and early ERM entry.

As the elections approached, however, the Socialist Party gradually came to adopt Portugal's participation in EMU as its own objective. And, after achieving power through the 1995 elections, the new Socialist-led minority government adopted the convergence program of the previous cabinet. Initially the Socialists acted with some "national reservations" in order to ensure support from the right-wing anti-Maastricht CDS-PP but, by May 1996, EMU membership became a government commitment with the main opposition party, the PSD (DAR nº 75—I Série, 25/5/96: Question time: answer of the Minister of Finance to the author). In October 1996 it became evident that both the government and the PSD were clearly in support of satisfying the macroeconomic convergence criteria as quickly as possible in order to participate from the beginning in EMU.[11]

The budget for 1997 aimed at satisfying all the necessary requirements established in Maastricht.[12] The two anti-EMU parties indicated early on that they would vote against a budget geared toward Portugal's participation in EMU. Nevertheless, the budget was approved in parliament because the PSD abstained. The PSD had many reservations about the 1997 budget, but did not vote against it in order to avoid a serious political impasse that could damage Portugal's chances to participate in EMU.

Specific Features of the Portuguese Economy

According to the theory of optimum currency areas, the condition for a country to surrender its monetary autonomy and join a monetary union is that the microeconomic efficiency gains outweigh the macroeconomic costs of participation. The balance between cost and benefit depends on the characteristics of the country wishing to join a monetary union: similarity of its economic structures (in the sense that the growth rates of output and employment do not tend to diverge with respect to the other partner countries when asymmetric shocks occur); flexibility of its labor market (real wage flexibility and labor mobility); and the availability of fiscal funds that would go together with monetary integration. Countries satisfying some conditions of similarity and flexibility could benefit from the elimination of foreign exchange transaction costs and the reduction of exchange rate uncertainty.

At the same time, these countries would aim at minimizing the output losses resulting from the need to give up exchange rate policy as a means to offset asymmetric shocks. In the sense that countries face different supply or demand disturbances that require different responses, they might wish to keep control of a policy tool such as the exchange rate. Through changes in the exchange rate, governments can spread the negative impact of an asymmetric shock that hits a particular sector or industry of the economy over the entire population, which has to put up with a deterioration of the country's terms of trade. In any case, however, exchange rate flexibility can have only a transitory impact and hence does not eliminate the need for a long-run real adjustment of the economy.

Nominal exchange rate devaluations are totally ineffective, however, if they cannot affect the relative price of domestic and foreign goods (the real exchange rate, a relative price). In Europe, wages respond quite rapidly to price movements (there is little nominal inertia), although less so to unemployment.[13] In Portugal, wages are highly elastic with respect both to inflation and unemployment: The wage response (the semielasticity) to unemployment is one of the largest among European countries, smaller only than Japan and Sweden in absolute value. (See Figure 8.5.) Therefore, forgoing exchange rate autonomy seems not to be very costly.[14]

In terms of flexibility, what is then important for the smooth functioning of a European monetary union is the capacity of real wages to adjust to asymmetric shocks. Labor mobility in Europe is low but, since one can expect that prices move faster than production factors (see Bean, 1992), that

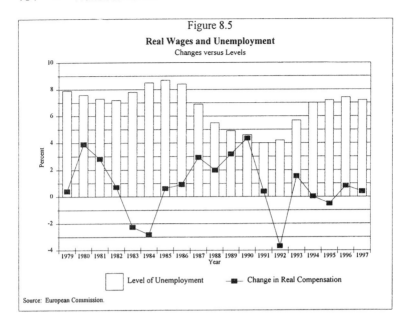

Figure 8.5

Real Wages and Unemployment
Changes versus Levels

Level of Unemployment   ▬■▬ Change in Real Compensation

Source: European Commission.

fact seems not to be crucial for the decision on whether Portugal should participate in EMU.[15] This is true even if one rejects money neutrality and takes the view that discretionary exchange rate policy can affect output: Real wage flexibility would provide for the necessary alternative adjustment mechanism. Without any change in the nominal exchange rate, unit labor costs would adjust to the new terms of trade. For the same level of economic integration and regardless of the view on the efficacy of exchange rate adjustments (neoclassical or Keynesian), a higher degree of real wage flexibility, as is clearly the Portuguese case when compared with most of its European partners, implies lower costs of participation in EMU and, as will be discussed later in this chapter, less urgency for other type of mechanisms (such as a federal budget or emigration) to help smooth country-specific shocks.

Trade Integration with the European Union

A small open economy tends to lose less (gain more) than a larger closed economy by giving up its monetary autonomy and joining in a monetary union with its trading partners. This is even truer if one does not believe in the efficacy of discretionary monetary policy. Foreign exchange transaction costs and exchange rate uncertainty tend to affect mainly small open economies, because a relatively important fraction of their trade is done with other countries and therefore they face large (and potentially unstable) foreign exchange markets. As the degree of openness increases, the benefits of adopting a common currency increase and the cost of relinquishing control over an autonomous exchange rate policy diminishes, because a devaluation has a much stronger impact on the price level of a relatively open economy such as Portugal than on the price level of a relatively closed economy such as Spain.

Portugal's trade integration with the European Union is well above the EU average (80 percent of total exports and 74 percent of total imports in 1995). With respect to Portuguese imports, Spain has been the most important supplier since 1991 (with a share of about 28 percent of total imports from the EU), followed by Germany (21 percent). Regarding the most important markets for Portuguese exports, the situation is inverted: Germany leads (with a share of about 28 percent of Portuguese exports to the EU) and Spain follows (17 percent, a lower level than in 1991). France is Portugal's third most important trading partner (15 percent and 18 percent, respectively) followed by the Benelux, Italy, and the United Kingdom.[16] (See Figure 8.6.) This high degree of Portuguese trade integration with the European Union points to high benefits and low costs of participation in EMU.

With respect to the likelihood of asymmetric shocks affecting the future European monetary union, it is important to know how similar are the trade

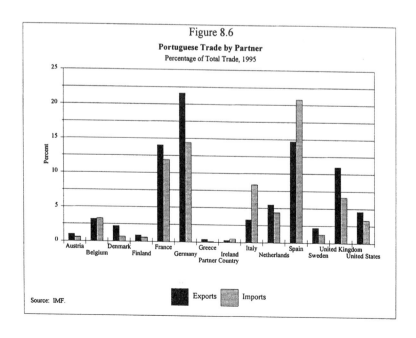

Figure 8.6

Portuguese Trade by Partner
Percentage of Total Trade, 1995

Source: IMF.

Exports   Imports

and industrial structures of Portugal and the EU. According to 1992 data on the correlation between the average structure of intra-EU exports and exports of each EU member to other EU members, the trade structures of Ireland, Denmark, and Portugal deviate moderately, but not as much as the trade structures of Finland and Greece, from the EU average (Gros and Vandille, 1995).

EC membership and hence better access to the internal market in 1986 generated an initial rapid expansion of the traditional Portuguese manufacturing sectors (textile, clothing, and shoe production) and an increased specialization of the economy. But increased worldwide competition, fragmentation, poor marketing, higher interest rates (due to the policy of capital controls followed in 1990 and 1991), and the modernization of the economy have since modified that trend toward more similar structures.

Exports from Auto Europa, a joint venture by Ford and Volkswagen with investment outlays equal to 2.9 percent of GDP that began production of multipurpose minivans at its new car plant in Palmela (greater Lisbon area) by mid-1995, was projected to reach 9 percent of total merchandise exports in 1996. This investment has compensated for the fall in employment in textile, clothing, and shoe-producing sectors (mostly based in the north of the country), areas that have accounted for almost the entire employment reduction in 1995. This trend is likely to continue with the phasing out of the international multi-fibre agreement (MFA).

Table 8.2: Merchandise Exports by Product Type (percentage share of total exports)

	1993	1994	1995
Food	6.7	7.3	7.4
Energy	2.8	4.1	3.3
Chemicals	5.6	6.3	6.2
Wood, cork and paper	11.0[a]	10.8	11.1
Hides, leather and textiles	n/a	8.4	7.7
Clothing	29.8[b]	18.2	15.9
Footwear and clothing accessories	8.6[c]	9.5	7.9
Mineral and metal	5.9	6.1	5.9
Machinery	14.6	15.8	18.0
Transport equipment	7.5	6.0	9.4
Miscellaneous finished goods	7.3	7.6	7.3

Notes: [a] Wood, cork, paper, and hides. [b] Clothing and footwear. [c] Textiles, clothing, and footwear.
Source: National Institute of Statistics; Bank of Portugal; Directorate-General for Commerce.

Besides a precarious agricultural and traditional specialization in manufacturing sectors such as textile and clothing, the Portuguese industrial structure has been highly fragmented. (Firms with fewer than 500 people account for 79 percent of total employment.) Such a structure is good for competition (and for the flexibility of the economy) but bad from a resource allocation point of view. For instance, in 1992, half of the industry research and development still was concentrated in five large firms in the electronics, telecommunications, and paper sectors (OECD, 1996b) and more than half geographically concentrated in Lisbon and the Tagus Valley. This concentration of domestic resources prevents a faster real convergence with the EU. At the same time, most of the foreign direct investment that took place between 1989 and 1992—after liberalization and before the opening up of the Central and Eastern European countries—went to the tertiary sector (banking, insurance, and business services), which experienced a substantial increase in productivity.

In short, the structure of the Portuguese economy is still quite different from the EU average. While it seems that it is becoming more similar to the European average, differences in the Portuguese industrial structure will persist for some time to come, and with them the possibility of asymmetric shocks relative to other EU countries. In any case, exchange rate considerations seem irrelevant to the long-term structural differences between Portugal and Europe both because of the high Portuguese wage flexibility and the permanent nature of the foreseen shocks. What is important is to look at the institutional features that will constrain the economy's ability to modernize within the context of deeper European and worldwide integration.

Other Institutional Features

Labor Market Institutions and Unemployment

The labor market in the EU is characterized by high and persistent unemployment. The economic recovery of the mid- to late 1990s has sparked only a marginal decrease in unemployment rates from their peak in 1994, and does not seem likely to return them to 1990 levels. Moreover, this phenomenon is not limited to Portugal. The recent evolution of EU unemployment appears to confirm the view that the natural unemployment rate remains at a higher level after each economic cycle. By the same token, the average length of unemployment today is significantly higher than in the 1970s. Cyclical unemployment is becoming structural, for a variety of reasons related to labor market institutions. In the EU, collective wage negotiations (emphasizing job security), legal provisions and generous unemployment benefits have led to wage rigidity (prices could not respond to demand changes) and higher unemployment, in particular of the young and less qualified (CEC, 1995).[17]

In Portugal, the number of workers covered by collective bargaining is around 70 percent. There are two unions: one Socialist (the UGT) and the other Communist (the CGTP). The level of bargaining is predominantly sectoral, and there is limited coordination between bargaining units. Firm-level bargaining is still very rare while national agreements are attempted each year. Benefit entitlements before tax as a percentage of previous earnings before tax (the so-called gross unemployment benefit replacement rates) are rather high for Portugal: They stand at 65 percent during the first year and 39 to 43 (if there is a dependent spouse) percent during the second and third years. (Data refer to 1995; see Martin, 1996.) Eligibility for unemployment benefits is strict: It requires applicants to have worked 1.5 years out of the last two. There is a minimum wage (54,000 escudos in 1996).

Within this institutional setting and against that background of high persisting unemployment rates in the EU even during economic growth phases (a problem especially manifest in the 1980s), it is noteworthy that the Portuguese experience contrasts with that of Spain. In 1995, the Portuguese yearly average unemployment rate was 7.2 percent, a 0.4 percent rise from the previous year. This rate compares favorably with the other EU member states, in that only Luxembourg (2.8 percent) and Austria (4.8 percent) reported lower rates in 1995. While Portugal and Spain had a comparable level of unemployment at the end of the 1970s (higher than the EC average), in 1995, Spain reported an unemployment rate of 22.9 percent.

Both Portugal and Spain have experienced high budget deficits. Indeed, that fact has contributed, through high interest rates, to the rise of structural unemployment; the same holds, to a lesser extent, for several other factors, such as unemployment benefits, the way unions work, and the terms of trade. But in contrast to all other countries, specific effects (unobserved components) are responsible for 40 to 50 percent of unemployment rates—negatively in the case of Portugal and positively in the case of Spain. (See Scarpetta, 1996.)

The large size of the state sector in Portugal first ensured low unemployment in the 1980s, albeit at the risk of high inflation. Low unemployment compensation benefits (practically nonexistent until 1977) also increased the cost of being out of work.[18] That model, as opposed to Spain's, led to both the lowest wages and the lowest strike rates in the EU.

A possible explanation for the fact that Portuguese unemployment did not persist at ever higher levels after the 1980s despite structural adjustment but actually fell could be what Nancy Bermeo (1994) called trading wage increases for job security, given that it was impossible to liberalize firing practices in Portugal. Still today, according to the Organization for

Economic Cooperation and Development (OECD, 1994d), Portugal has the highest index of employment protection. (It is followed very closely by Spain but is much further ahead of other countries.) The fact that Portugal had low unemployment benefits and, in practice, a rather loose employment protection legislation also may have led to a higher response of wages to unemployment.[19] In turn, disinflation may have a less adverse effect on unemployment and on unemployment persistence—an argument put forward by Olivier Blanchard and Juan Jimeno (1995).

Disinflation and structural adjustment in Spain took place three years before the country's accession to the European Community, just after the oil price increase and while the labor share still reflected the wage explosion of the 1970s. It was of a labor-compensating nature: high wages with high unemployment. Portugal delayed its restructuring until there was an upswing: The price of oil was falling, the labor share was already much smaller, privatization and liberalization were becoming effective, and transfers and investment associated with EC membership were gaining momentum, in turn opening up the hope for employment possibilities.[20]

The timing for stabilization and structural adjustment also may reflect the fact that there always has been a consensus among political parties and social partners on pursuing an active employment policy to ensure social cohesion (although a large part of these programs has been financed by the Community support frameworks). Two episodes during the recessions of 1983 to 1984 and 1993 to 1994 illustrate well this idea: In the face of a serious and widespread unemployment threat, the unions immediately accepted lower wage increases. From 1983 to 1984, many workers agreed to work without being paid for several months in order to avoid being on the dole. This de facto flexibility of the labor market, in spite of its rigid regulation, shows that the Portuguese economy has some capacity to adjust to uneven shocks in a monetary union.

As a note of caution, and although it seems that there is no hysteresis in the Portuguese unemployment rate, one should not ignore labor mismatch problems (see OECD, 1996b, for a description), which indicate that the economy may have entered a more difficult period of labor market adjustment. The Regional Development Program of 1993 recognized the need to undertake structural reform measures but has not been implemented as yet. In any case, the need for such structural reforms lends weight to the contention—stressed by Gros (1996a)—that past unemployment problems have little to do with external shocks or exchange rates.

Variations in the Portuguese unemployment rate correlate with the cyclical fluctuations of economic activity (Okun's law). With higher unemployment in 1995 than in 1994, nominal wage growth in the Portuguese economy as a whole fell slightly (although less sharply than in the previous years). In 1995, the flexibility of wages to labor market conditions was expressed in average wage rises of 4.4 percent (based on the collective wage bargaining regulation), while real wages per worker are estimated to have risen by 1.4 percent that year. As this rise was lower than productivity gains, labor unit costs fell while firms' profit margins rose from 1994 to 1995.

Fiscal Transfers

The implementation of the European Single Market directives has contributed greatly to accelerating the pace of other reforms, as diverse as environmental quality and consumer protection. In 1994 and 1995, the total amount of EC transfers reached 3.5 and 4.6 percent of GDP, respectively. Of these, the structural funds exerted particular pressure for internal reform. Because they had to be matched by national public expenditure, they required a definite establishment of long-term priorities in Portugal. Net transfers from the EU are of course much lower and, with the exception of 1995 (when they overtook private transfers—see Figure 8.7), they are expected to fall, although Portugal will remain a net receiver until at least 1999.[21]

Estimates of the impact of the first Community Support Framework (CSF) of 1989 to 1993, based on a general equilibrium model, point to an

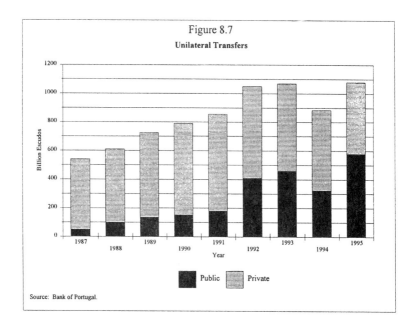

Figure 8.7

Unilateral Transfers

Source: Bank of Portugal.

additional GDP growth of 0.4 percentage points in the short run and 0.5 percentage points in the long run. The official estimated impact of the second CSF, 1994 to 1999, based on an input-output model, is also a 0.5 percentage point increase in the rate of growth. (See Gaspar and Pereira (1995) for the general equilibrium model and Ministry of Planning (1993) for the input-output model.)

The CSF for 1994 to 1999 aims at reducing the main weaknesses of the Portuguese economy: education, economic infrastructures, the productive structure (characterized by an excessive weight of low-productivity industrial sectors and a very low-productivity agricultural sector), social security, disadvantaged social groups, the environment and regional imbalances.

Structural versus Coinsurance Funds

In Portugal, there has been a consensus among the major political forces and trade and business groups about the goals of active participation in the process of European integration and increased economic and social cohesion.[22] This consensus translates into an active employment and social policy, in order to avoid what may be called "dependent federalism" (as in the Italian Mezzogiorno or, within the country, with respect to any particular sector of the economy or social group that comes to depend on fiscal transfers), and into participation in the major institutional reforms of the European Community, as a means of securing political and macroeconomic stability while preserving Portugal's "universal vocation."

The objectives of inflation reduction and improved efficiency of labor, product, and financial markets feature prominently in the adjustment effort, in line with the understanding that the most useful structural policy measures are those which reinforce the role of market mechanisms in resource allocation. While this understanding is stressed in several government documents—namely in the Portuguese contribution to the White Paper on Growth, Competitiveness and Employment (Ministry of Finance, 1993) and in the Strategic Options of the Government for 1997 (Ministry of Planning, 1996)—the political debate tends to take longer to internalize it.

That is why there were constant calls from party circles and later from within the government for automatic transfers (a safety net for EMU). When it became clear that it would be possible to fulfill the convergence criteria and that such claims would affect the very credibility of the government's commitment to EMU, the idea was suddenly abandoned.[23] Because transitory transfers are wrongly mixed up with the regional or cohesion funds of the EU and/or with fiscal integration, which raise issues of redistribution, they are regarded as inappropriate without an important leap forward in the process of European political integration, which is not foreseen in the near future. The government seems now to have understood that this confusion would only exacerbate the displeasure of those northern countries with cohesion and structural funds and/or would imply the shifting of resources from cohesion countries with relatively low unemployment, such as Portugal, to countries with high unemployment. Rather than hope for a federal coinsurance fund, Portugal should aim at reducing the main weaknesses of its economy and making good use of the available structural funds.

Privatization and Competition Policy

Portugal is among the largest "privatizers" of the OECD (OECD, 1996b): From 1989 to 1995, more than 30 state-owned firms were privatized, yielding revenue of 11 percent of GDP. The biggest chunk of sales (about two-thirds of total revenues) were in the banking and industry sectors that had been nationalized in 1975; partial privatization of public utilities (telecommunications and electricity) has just begun. While regulatory reform in the financial sector already took place, it is still being implemented in the utilities sector. Public transport companies, television, steel, and chemicals have not been restructured. TAP—Air Portugal, the national carrier—features among the most heavily subsidized airlines in the EU, along with Air France and Olympic Airways from Greece.

In 1995, efforts to improve product market competition included the transcription of EU directives concerning public procurement policies, financial control over public enterprises by the audit court, the simplification of notification procedures for foreign direct investments, and more consumer-friendly credit regulations. In 1996, further measures were taken in order to increase public utilities' responsiveness to consumers. But, as stressed by Barros and Mata (1996), while the legal provisions appear satisfactory, there seems to be a generalized bias regarding the interpretation of the principles (concerns with domestic firms' competitiveness and other businesses rights dominate concerns with the consumers' surplus and social welfare), and decisions are left to sectoral supervisory bodies and to a competition authority that does not rank clearly above these sectoral organizations.[24]

Monetary Institutions

While monetary policy faced some additional difficulties stemming from external liberalization in the late 1980s, the anti-inflation reputation of the monetary authorities took time to build, despite the significant steps taken since the beginning of 1990 to increase the independence of the Bank of Portugal.[25] In 1990, it became clear, however, that no commitment would be taken with respect to EMS membership and even less to the liberalization of capital mobility. The monetary authorities, which had never been enthusiastic about subjecting their intermediate targets to EMS membership, were not willing to transfer their newly acquired monetary autonomy (political power) to the ERM. The central bank opted for monetary discretion (keeping the escudo inside an undisclosed band), ignoring the QUANTUM in regard to the exchange rate regime. One of the stated aims of not revealing the band was indeed to create enough uncertainty concerning escudo fluctuation as to reduce the amount of capital inflows (especially those of a speculative nature) that, if not fully sterilized, would torpedo the effects of a tight monetary policy.

Portugal experienced a sudden inflow of capital much as did Spain and Italy. A positive nominal interest rate differential together with a relatively credible (in the financial markets) nonaccommodating exchange rate policy generated substantial capital inflows. Following the examples of Italy and Spain with some time lag, Portugal introduced controls on capital inflows in response to a phase of strong speculation in favor of the escudo. But as with controls on outflows since mid-1986, controls on inflows proved to be ineffective: Capital inflows amounted to $10 billion between 1989 and 1992.

Paradoxically, it was already during the period of turbulence and recession in the summer of 1992 that the government forced monetary authorities to dismantle the controls on capital inflows, giving nonresidents full access to the Portuguese money market. (Outflows had been completely liberalized in June 1992.) This liberalization of capital inflows was completed in December 1992, before the beginning of the European single market, just before the derogation granted to Ireland and Spain, and well before the derogation granted to Portugal and Greece until 1996. This more open attitude of the government, followed a change in the general attitude toward the process of European integration during the government's preparations to assume the presidency of the European Council. Capital market liberalization marked a turning point in the Portuguese strategy toward EMU and the beginning of a new exchange rate regime: full convertibility cum ERM membership.

By 1994, after the (first time ever) dismissal of the governor and the two vice governors of the Banco de Portugal—to which the markets reacted positively, given that there was no disagreement over the conduct of monetary policy but just the need to clarify what had been an ambiguous role on matters of banking supervision during bank privatization's—the conflict between the treasury and the central bank had been surmounted.[26] The conflict had started with central bank resistance to the dismantling of capital controls, whose financial costs (higher debt interest payments and loss of central bank provisions) were larger than the structural funds received during the same period. Nevertheless, the conflict soon spilled over into the issue of banking supervision and the Bank Reform Act of 1993.

By 1995, the statutes of the central bank were amended by Decree-Law 235/95 prepared by the PSD government and brought to ratification in parliament by the PS. The ensuing Law 3/96 of 5 February 1996 established that the primary objective of the central bank is to maintain price stability, taking into account the government's general economic policy. The bank became solely responsible for the conduct of monetary policy, having the obligation of cooperating with the Government in the definition and implementation of the exchange rate policy. In the new law, and as in most European countries, the central bank retains responsibilities for banking supervision; the governor is also obliged to inform the parliament about monetary policy matters following the publication of the bank's annual report. As in other ERM countries, there are still some legal inconsistencies with the Treaty on European Union (TEU) and some central bank statute requirements that must be adapted if Portugal is to participate in EMU (CEC, 1996; EMI, 1996).

Public Opinion and the Policy Debate on EMU

The discussion about Portugal's participation in EMU has evolved significantly since the objective was put forward in the Delors plan. Initially, the idea of a monetary union in Europe was well received by the public in general as a long-term European goal, although it was regarded with some skepticism with respect to Portugal's capacity to participate. The case for a European single currency was not perceived to be a central question for Portugal. The Government, opposition, and social partners viewed Portugal as a catching-up and peripheral country that still would need a long transition period for monetary and financial liberalization and had to concentrate on coping with the more immediate challenge of the Internal Market. Portuguese public opinion became used to what was until then the norm, namely that Portugal was granted a transitional period.

Against this background of relative indifference and the stubbornness of the authorities in not discussing the matter, the parliament was at the forefront of the discussion: In 1990 it organized an open debate on Portugal and EMU that prompted political debate and forced the authorities to take a position on the matter, although political commitment to EMU was not on the agenda until 1992. Contrary to most other EU countries (not to mention the special case of Finland described in Chapter 4), the Portuguese central bank was never an enthusiast of ERM participation, free capital movements, or European monetary integration; when reforms were accomplished or decisions taken, sometimes against its preferences, it followed the new rules.

But Portuguese attitudes toward EMU evolved with the European discussion around the ratification of the Maastricht Treaty. One renewed political party, the CDS-PP, adopted as its main political strategy an anti-Maastricht (anti-EMU) campaign. The issues was at the forefront of public debate with the exchange rate crisis, the European recession, and the adoption of a convergence program designed to allow Portugal to participate in EMU. Having said that, 46 percent of the population supports monetary union compared with an EU average of 47 percent, and 21 percent opposes monetary union compared with an EU average of 33 percent. However, polls taken in December 1995 indicate that 92 percent of all Portuguese thought they had insufficient information about the future European currency compared to 79 percent for the EU as a whole (Eurobarometer, 1996).[27]

The Policy Debate

As stressed by the modern political economy literature, joining a monetary union that is based on institutions that deliver price stability is probably the best way to implement a solid strategy of sustained economic development. This is because this alternative also precludes many of the transition costs (the output losses of a disinflation strategy) of such a regime change. Fixed exchange rates, unlike other policy targets, are easily observable by the private sector and easily implemented by the authorities. (See Torres, 1987.) Also, making the costs of government activity more transparent to the public gives elected officials better incentives to focus on improving the productivity of the private sector instead of playing redistribution games.

With such an exchange rate regime, the authorities raise the political costs of inflation because their anti-inflation commitment is monitored constantly by the private sector and any different behavior would imply a loss of competitiveness for the tradable sectors. Accordingly, one could argue that, as a tendency, high-inflation countries tend to gain more than low-inflation countries by sharing their monetary autonomy in a common monetary institution.

This argument has been understood in academic circles in Portugal, but its importance has been disputed if not contested by most outspoken (Keynesian) economists. They claim that the exchange rate is still a very important adjustment mechanism, not only in the case of asymmetric shocks but also in face of permanent shocks such as world trade liberalization and EU enlargement to Central European countries.

This is in fact the most popular argument discussed among political economists, "economic gurus," and political commentators with no specific economic background.[28] It is argued that regions characterized by persistent differences in productivity growth or even by any other type of persistent differences as well as economies with different structural characteristics (non-wage labor costs, saving ratios, or demographic structures) should not form a monetary union.

Although these are problems that have nothing to do with the exchange rate regime—as Buiter (1996) puts it, real convergence or divergence is irrelevant for EMU—the entire "economic" discussion around the question of Portugal's participation in EMU has been centered on these very issues.

Of course, economists at the central bank and at the Ministry of Finance and academics with international experience, and also the two main political parties and a small part of the business community, tend to defend the fact that, given the current macroeconomic disequilibria in Portugal, the criteria are important and instrumental, independent of the Maastricht Treaty, to achieve sustained economic growth. Part of the business community, such as the Confederation of Industry (CIP) and the Portuguese banking association (traditionally more skeptical than its associates), the left-wing trade unions, the right-wing PP and the left-wing PCP, the technocrat (Keynesian) and "liberal" wings of the PSD, the president's economic adviser, and many independents close to the PS and/or influential in the media tend to see the Maastricht criteria as a problem for real convergence.

Even the sectors more favorable to Portugal's participation in EMU, such as the center-left UGT and the Portuguese Industrial Association (AIP), caution against the negative effects of EMU on unemployment and growth. But besides the already mentioned argument of persistent differences in productivity, no explanation is put forward to justify that presumption. It seems, however, that although people cannot explain why and how EMU may be a problem for Portugal and understand that exchange rate autonomy does not serve to resolve the structural problems that affect Portugal and Europe (on the contrary, it could only aggravate them), there is a generalized concern that Portugal is not up to the job, that somehow things will go wrong. Many do not believe that the Portuguese economy can ever compete at any level within the Internal Market, especially with the forthcoming enlargement of the EU to Central European countries and liberalization of world trade. The pessimists warn against the social and political unrest that will spread, from countries such as France, to the whole of Europe.[29] In any case, real versus nominal convergence promises to remain the central issue in the Portuguese public debate about EMU.

At the same time, however (mind the contradiction), most social partners (with the exception of CGTP), political economists (with the exception of some economic commentators who are anti-EMU for ideological reasons), and public opinion at large also caution against the possibility of being left out of EMU and the weakening of Portugal's position in the European Union as a whole. They realize that there is no alternative and that it is better to be inside than "out in the cold." This is, in fact, the reasoning that the government used to overcome ideological reservations (Keynesian or others) to EMU within the PS.

The banking sector (through the Portuguese banking association) is almost alone in the country in expressing concern with replacing all national currencies by one single European currency, given the importance of currency exchange trading in their activities and the financial setup costs involved. In spite of a growing awareness, public debate has not yet turned to these questions.

Variable Geometry EMU

The Portuguese parliament adopted the notion of variable geometry in a resolution on the principles for the revision of the Treaty on European Union. (See Torres, 1996c.) As in other domains of European integration, Portugal would accept that if it is unable to participate from the beginning in EMU, other countries should go ahead. It is feared, however, that, in practice, the first group of countries to take part in the executive board of the European Central Bank would move forward in all other domains of political cooperation, leaving the others effectively out of the political core. At the same time, it is also feared that convergence will be more difficult for outsiders. That is why both the government and the main opposition party now argue that Portugal should participate in EMU irrespective of any automatic transfers and of what happens to other southern countries, including Spain.

If Portugal was to participate from the start in EMU while Spain was not, there should not be any significant costs even in the short run. Unlike Ireland (see Chapter 6), Portugal is much less dependent on its bigger neighbor: Germany is by far the biggest client for Portuguese exports (in 1996, even France ranks above Spain), although Spain has become the biggest supplier of Portuguese imports and competes directly with Portugal in third markets. Besides, Spanish attitudes toward EMU are rather different from the United Kingdom's: If Spain did not participate from the start in EMU, it would most likely pursue a policy of exchange rate stability in order to join one or two years later. Some (such as the former Prime Minister, Aníbal Cavaco Silva) argue that, politically, it will prove very difficult to separate the two countries if Portugal happens to perform only marginally better in terms of the convergence criteria.

Conditions for Fiscal Consolidation

Contrary to most EU countries, Portugal is taking no special measures (on the expenditure side) to reduce the budget deficit to 2.9 percent of GDP. In fact, government current spending depends basically on the public sector wage bill that in 1997 will grow more than in most other EU countries. As in 1995 and 1996, fiscal consolidation will come largely through mounting tax pressure in the form of both stronger economic growth and tougher tax enforcement, after the negative effects of the 1992 to 1993 recession on the general government deficit and debt. (See Figure 8.4.) The government intends to tax both firms and the self-employed on their imputed earnings before implementing a more comprehensive fiscal reform. The danger of slippage comes in the short run from the possibility of deficient expenditure control, namely in regard to health.

Although the level of public debt continued to be excessive in 1996, it was already converging to the reference level and it is expected to fall to 69 percent of GDP by the end of 1997. Portugal is not making a big effort to reduce the deficit and debt: The general government primary balance after a record level of 4.2 percent of GDP in 1992 remained slightly above zero until 1996, when it reached only 0.9 percent of GDP; only in Portugal have noninterest expenditures grown from 1993 to 1996. On the other hand, no other country in the EU has experienced such a dramatic fall in the implicit interest rate on public debt—and, indeed, a reduction in interest payments—from 1991 to 1996.

Nevertheless, concerning the sustainability of public debt, given the growth-adjusted effective interest rate and not taking into account any stock-flow adjustments, Portugal is in a situation similar to the Netherlands and Denmark and clearly better than the European average, with a falling debt ratio and a positive primary gap. The latter is the difference between the actual primary balance and the debt-stabilizing primary balance. It means that there is no need for additional measures to stabilize the debt ratio. Whether that is sufficient not only to stabilize the debt ratio but to comply with the convergence criteria, namely "sufficiently diminishing and approaching the reference value at a satisfactory pace," depends on the distance to the reference level and, especially, on the size of the actual primary surplus in relation to the debt-stabilizing primary surplus. The fulfillment of this criterion hinges then on the capacity for increasing the primary surplus for 1997. Cutting public current spending would increase confidence and reduce the growth-adjusted effective interest rate, but pressure on tax increases tends to have the opposite effect.

In addition, the speed of debt reduction also will be determined by the receipts from privatization and pension expenditures. In the longer run, fiscal sustainability depends on the capacity of restructuring the social security system whose deficit (2.6 percent in 1994) will reach 8.5 percent of GDP in 2035 if no measures are taken, according to OECD simulations (OECD, 1996b).

Conclusion

In economic terms, Portugal should benefit from participation in EMU because its trade is highly integrated with the rest of the European Union. To be sure, Portugal's industrial structure differs from other European countries. However, the appropriate reaction is not to stay out of EMU but instead to focus on those institutional features of the Portuguese economy that constrain its adjustment and modernization. The country's (de facto) flexible labor markets offer one potential adjustment mechanism. Wages in Portugal are highly elastic with respect both to inflation and unemployment, so foregoing exchange rate autonomy should be less costly than EMU skeptics fear. The challenge, therefore, is to use available structural funds wisely to support reforms targeted to eliminate remaining rigidities in the marketplace.

Considering the political conditions for European monetary integration, even the sectors more favorable to Portugal's participation in EMU caution against the negative effects of EMU on unemployment and growth. Nevertheless, aside from the argument of persistent differences in productivity, no explanation is put forward to justify that presumption. It seems that although people (without ideological reservations) cannot explain why and how EMU may be a problem for Portugal and do understand that exchange rate autonomy does not serve to resolve the structural problems that affect Portugal and Europe, there is a generalized concern that Portugal is not up to the job, that somehow things will go wrong. Many do not believe that the Portuguese economy can ever compete at any level within the Internal Market, especially with the forthcoming enlargement of the EU to Central European countries and increasing liberalization of world trade. Such pessimists warn against the social and political unrest that will spread all over Europe.

What such arguments lack is a reasonable alternative to EMU membership—particularly in political terms. If Portugal fails to join EMU, this would weaken the country's position in the European Union as a whole. In fact, both the government and the main opposition party, the PSD, believe that those countries that form EMU also will move forward in other areas. Meanwhile, those countries that choose to remain outside EMU will be left behind and even may find it more difficult to "converge" on the monetary union. That is why both the government and the PSD agree that Portugal should participate in EMU even if other southern countries, such as Spain, do not. The 1997 budget aims at satisfying all the convergence criteria, and was approved in parliament with the abstention of the main opposition party, in order to create the conditions for Portugal's participation in EMU.

As in most other EU countries, in Portugal, EMU has worked as a mechanism for economic stabilization and, therefore, as a precondition for structural reform and long-term development. It has created the necessary consensus to overcome specific interests in the pursuit of social and economic welfare. The political consensus took long to build—much longer than in countries such as Ireland or Spain—and it still faces a strong opposition—a time-lagged mimic of France's—but seems to be mature with respect not only to EMU but also to the wider goals of European integration.

Notes

1. The reform of both personal and corporate taxes was implemented in 1989. Because taxes on income of both 1988 and 1989 were collected in 1989, the budget deficit was significantly reduced.
2. The government deficit increased from 2.5 percent in 1989 to 5.6 in 1990 and 6.6 in 1991.
3. The Q2 was subsequently revised in October 1993, taking into account both common time horizons (1996) and the same macroeconomic underlying assumptions for all EC members.
4. Estimates are based on the assumption of a full pass-through of changes in indirect taxes to consumers (European Monetary Institute, 1996).
5. The country's first presidency of the European Council constituted a landmark in the Portuguese government's attitude toward the European integration process: The initial skeptical view was abandoned and from siding with the United Kingdom Portugal turned toward the Franco-German axis.
6. Textile and clothing (with productivity levels at two-thirds and one-half of the Portuguese manufacturing average in 1989) experienced an initial rapid expansion with free access to the EC market, but worldwide competition, fragmentation, no marketing, and higher interest rates (due to the policy of capital controls followed in 1990 and 1991) accelerated those calls.
7. This fact is recognized even by the then prime minister, Aníbal Cavaco Silva, who stated that some segments of the administration had difficulties in digesting the new monetary regime (Silva, 1994: 512).
8. A monetary policy of capital controls designed to keep domestic interest rates stable at very high levels was substituted for a monetary policy of capital mobility and exchange rate stability (the escudo in the ERM) designed to keep domestic interest rates at the (much lower) international levels al-

though more volatile (in the very short-term) in the wake of speculative attacks against the escudo.

9. Interest payments on the debt fell from 8.6 percent in 1991 to 7.8 percent in 1992, 6.8 percent in 1993 and 4.9 percent in 1996. Meanwhile, the official inflation target, met in 1992 and 1993, was then met in the three subsequent years.

10. The fiscal deficit-to-GDP ratio fell subsequently without interruption until 1996, while the debt-to-GDP ratio kept rising until 1995. (See Table 8.1 and Figure 8.4.)

11. After the prime minister made several statements reaffirming his commitment to that objective, the consensus on the goal of Portugal's participation in the core group of countries moving ahead to the third phase of EMU was established in parliament during the first debate of 1996–97 on the single currency. In October, a special congress of the PSD confirmed its support for that objective. In both the PS and the PSD, and especially outside party circles, some sectors remained unsatisfied with such a convergence of views.

12. The deficit- and debt-to-GDP ratios were set to fall to 2.9 and 69, respectively, while inflation and long-term interest rates are expected to converge to the reference values satisfying the convergence requirements. These projections were confirmed by the European Commission in November 1996.

13. These nominal rigidities (nominal wage rigidities) are more important in the United States than in Europe. But even in the United States they are, of course, transitory.

14. See, among others, Luz and Pinheiro (1994) and OECD (1992b). Increasing wage bill differentials also suggest high nominal and real wage flexibility (OECD, 1996b). On the other hand, the rate of structural unemployment has almost not changed since the beginning of the 1980s.

15. For a number of reasons that have to do with the existence of different languages, cultures, and other barriers to people's mobility, such as imperfect housing markets within and between the European countries, labor mobility is not expected to increase even with economic integration. One should note, however, that international labor movements (mainly from third countries) in the EU are of comparable order of magnitude as interregional migration within member countries. (See Gros, 1996a.)

16. Data refer to the first six months of 1996, Instituto Nacional de Estatística, June 1996.

17. This situation contrasts with that of the United States, where flows in and out of unemployment have been faster; the same is true for job creation by the private sector. (In the EU, public sector job creation has been very important.) In the absence of collective wage negotiations, larger wage flexibility meant that the fall in demand for less qualified work due to technical change in production technology translated in lower real wages rather than higher unemployment.

18. The average replacement ratio of the OECD was 34 percent in 1995, 25 percent in the period from 1987 to 1991, 7 percent in the period from 1979

to 1985, and 1 percent in the period from 1973 to 1977 (Blanchard and Jimeno, 1995).

19. Small firms tend to circumvent regulations by not paying social security contributions and relying on short-term contracts. Also, a significant number of
workers with permanent contracts were laid off during the recession of 1993
to 1994, suggesting that there is a de facto flexibility in the labor market
(OECD, 1996b).

20. Sacrifice ratios (the number of percentage points between real production
and equilibrium production for each point less in the inflation rate) con-
firms that view for the period from 1980 to 1994: Italy and Portugal have
ratios of 0.65 and 0.66, respectively, while Ireland and Spain have ratios of
1.0 and 1.47, respectively. See Barbosa and Machado (1996).

21. This is because the bulk of EU expenditures is related to the Common Agricultural Policy. Given its structure, in the agricultural sector Portugal is a net
contributor to the EU.

22. PCP and the CDS-PP have remained opposed to any external liberalization
of the economy and to European integration.

23. At the same time, early participation in EMU has been attacked on the
grounds that Portugal should participate in a EMS II, a kind of "olive belt"
monetary arrangement, with the other southern European countries. This
position changed dramatically well before Italian Prime Minister Romano
Prodi had asked for a slower pace in the transition to EMU.

24. The first competition law dates from 1983 and was revised in 1993 (Decree-
Law 371/93).

25. The new statutes of Banco de Portugal, approved only in October 1990, although the new law had been ready for approval in December 1989, gave
the central bank a high degree of economic independence while maintaining an average degree of political independence (increased to the U.S. level
in 1995), as compared with other OECD countries. See Torres (1996a) for
a discussion on Portugal and Grilli, Masciandaro, and Tabellini (1991) for
the criteria of political and economic independence.

26. During bank privatizations, the central bank had to compete with both the
privatization's committee and the stock market regulatory agency. See
Macedo (1996).

27. Of those 92 percent, 44 percent are not very well informed about EMU and
48 percent are "not informed at all" about the European currency.

28. Willem Buiter's refreshing article (Buiter, 1996) gives some examples for the
British case. Very similar ones can be found in Portugal. Many just behave
opportunistically: Not being familiar with the issue, they find it politically
interesting to oppose what they call the gray technocracy and monetary fun-
damentalism. On the other hand, few defend EMU as a desirable political
reform instead of an external constraint. In fact, many politicians and especially bureaucrats just see it as unavoidable.

29. Some commentators have been busy, since 1995, announcing the end of the
entire EMU project on the occasion of any European truck drivers' strike,
social security reform, report on European unemployment, and so on.

CHAPTER NINE

Sweden and EMU

Jonathon W. Moses[1]

Sweden's track record with regard to the costs and benefits of economic and monetary union (EMU), like the record of the other recent members of the European Union (EU), is rather short and uncertain. Most discussion about monetary union has been couched in more general terms concerning membership in the political union. As a result, this chapter provides somewhat of a different angle in evaluating Sweden's EMU membership. In particular, the first section offers a historical backdrop against which we can better understand Sweden's rather unique path to EMU membership. This historical section aims both to outline Sweden's previous monetary history and to describe its political path to EU membership more generally.

Each of the following sections pertains to the different types of factors that will influence Sweden's approach to EMU. The second section, on the economic criteria, addresses the potential costs and benefits according to the Maastricht convergence criteria and to more general optimal currency area criteria. This long section attempts to quantify the economic costs associated with a potential monetary union. The third section takes up the distributional and institutional issues associated with EMU. Sweden's unique institutional characteristics facilitate discussion about the distributional consequences of EMU. This section maps out the institutional and distributional fault lines. The final section, on linkage issues, describes how EMU is coupled to other issues in order to make it more politically palatable to a hesitant constituency. EMU in itself is not a main Swedish objective; it is attractive only insofar as it can be used as a scapegoat for the difficult discussions needed to rectify the current economic crisis. The chapter concludes with an evaluation of the various perspectives, speculating that Sweden might eventually pursue membership despite its historical record and the potential distributional costs. Whether it does rests on the ability of Sweden's political and economic elites to convince a skeptical public.

Swedish Conditions

This section introduces relevant history of Sweden in order better to understand the context in which Swedes will evaluate their potential membership in EMU. This history unfolds in two parts. The first asks: To what extent has Sweden employed active exchange rate policies in the past? An answer to this question sheds light on the degree of autonomy that Sweden will jeopardize should it join EMU. The second part of this section provides an overview of the political struggle for membership in the EU.

Exchange Rate History

Swedish monetary history can easily be read from two different perspectives. (See Moses, 1995b.) Generally, supporters of fixed exchange rates can find comfort in Sweden's long-standing commitment to such regimes. Although it joined late (1951), Sweden benefited from the relatively fixed exchange rates of the Bretton Woods system; it participated actively as a member in the Group of Ten to secure a similar environment at the Smithsonian Meetings (1971); and Sweden has been publicly committed to fixed exchange rates since the early–1980s. The Swedish krona was fixed after the "Big Bang" (16 percent) devaluation of 1982 until the 1992 crisis in the European exchange rate mechanism (ERM).

Proponents of flexible exchange rates, however, also can draw on much of Swedish history. In the theoretical realm, economists associated with the Stockholm school have long pursued an interest in real and nominal price mechanisms; the concept of purchasing power parity (PPP) in its modern variant is a legacy of this school (Jonung, 1991). In the real world as well, Swedes have used exchange rate changes effectively to defend their full employment objectives throughout most of the 1970s. Indeed, Sweden left the "snake" in 1977 to avoid what it felt was a too restrictive German monetary policy. After 1977, Sweden tried to distance itself from the price stability goal—building and actively employing a trade-weighted basket for the krona in the period from 1977 to 1991. Only in 1991 did the Swedish government decide to link the krona to an ECU basket rather than a trade-weighted one.

Throughout most of the 1980s, there was growing support for fixed exchange rates in Sweden. Before the market-forced float in the fall of 1992, there was a general consensus among the political parties—as well as among most economists—that fixed rates of exchange with the rest of

Europe were both a political and an economic necessity. But economic fads are often fickle. Fears of inflation in the wake of the substantial depreciation of November 1992 have proven unjustified. The consumer price index has remained relatively stable in recent years—2.3 percent (1992), 4.7 percent (1993), and 3.2 percent (1994)—and the competitiveness gains from the devaluation helped to spark much reinvestment in Sweden. While there is a general recognition of the enormous gains accrued by the 1992 devaluation, this has (quite peculiarly) had little impact on the nature of the debate in Sweden on EMU membership. Indeed, this mirrors the confused advice of the influential Lindbeck commission: Sweden should apply flexible exchange rates until its economic house is once again in order (Lindbeck, Molander, Persson, Petersson, Sandmo, Svedenborg, and Thygesen, 1994: 33).[2]

Support for Membership in the European Union

The path to membership in the EU parallels the journey just discussed above. Indeed, ECU linkage can be seen as part of a larger strategy on the part of political elites to gain Sweden back-door entry into the EU (Moses, 1997). The Swedish decision to apply for EU membership came as a shock and surprise to many; it was the result of a cataclysmic change in Swedish politics. In two years, from 1989 to 1991, most of the major political parties had completely reversed their positions on EU membership (see Sandholtz, 1995); by the 1994 referendum, all of the major political parties in Sweden came to support membership.[3] The electorate followed suit on 13 November 1994, when a majority of Swedes decided to support EU membership in the national referendum. (See Moses and Jenssen, 1998.) The reason for the turnaround can be explained mostly by developments on the foreign policy front. Economic arguments played a more important role only later.[4] Sweden's European ambitions had become less problematic in that membership could be sold in terms of the country's security concerns and the solutions contained in international cooperative arrangements.

While neutrality and cooperation issues still dominated much of the debate about EU membership as Sweden approached its November referendum, skepticism had increased. One reason for this is that the Swedish economic picture had changed radically. Alongside the figures on Swedish unemployment, rank-and-file skepticism to EU membership had skyrocketed. Interest had shifted away from the positive effects of membership to its potential negative effects. Security issues were replaced by issues regarding the potential loss of sovereignty, the effect on the domestic welfare state, the threat of bureaucratic meddling from Brussels, and so forth.

An example of this anti-EU emphasis on social policy can be seen in polling figures that indicate a high degree of resistance among Swedish women to the European Union. Like their Norwegian counterparts, Swedish women are concerned that EU membership will undermine their well-developed social welfare network. In a poll taken prior to the referendum, 44 percent of Swedish women opposed, while only 33 percent supported, EU membership. (The corresponding figures for Swedish men were: 42 percent yes, 38 percent no. See *Berlinske Tidende,* 22 September 1994: 4.)

One important impetus for this change was the Danish rejection of the Maastricht agreement. In Sweden, as in the other Nordic countries, support for EU membership dropped significantly in the wake of the 1992 Danish referendum. Political and economic sovereignty issues took center stage, and public support for the EU began to fall. As Table 9.1 suggests, public opinion changed dramatically in a three-month period surrounding the Danish decision.

During the early to mid-1990s, Swedes generally were skeptical about the ability of either the EU or national politicians to deliver on issues of high political saliency. The September 1994 election can be read as a protest vote against further liberalization, but it did not provide much instruction to the newly elected (Social Democratic) minority government as to how to go about solving the most important issues. Until unemployment is again under control, larger geopolitical issues probably will remain secondary concerns, and the role of the EU will be delegated to a second-class policy issue: a hopeful means of spurring economic recovery.

In short, Sweden's historical record does not provide much ground for supporting its membership in EMU. Sweden has a long history of maintaining an

Table 9.1: Party Support for EC/EU Membership Before and After the Danish Veto (percent)

Vote	Left	Social Democrat	Liberal	Agricultural	Christian Democrat	Conservative	New Democrat	Total
Before the Danish Veto (May 1992)								
For	8	33	63	19	37	71	42	44
Against	67	47	23	58	36	14	45	36
Other	25	21	13	23	27	15	14	19
After the Danish Veto (June 1992)								
For	9	20	46	13	17	66	25	32
Against	88	56	32	67	58	18	57	47
Other	2	24	22	21	26	16	18	21

Source: Lindström (1992), pp. 24-5.

autonomous monetary policy, it has actively employed flexible exchange rates in the past to help secure its internal balance, and the 1992 devaluation was very beneficial (both politically and economically). As a result there is general support for maintaining flexible rates into the foreseeable future. In addition, support for the European Union is based less on the economic promise of an EMU and more on the potential of cooperating in international solutions. A potential monetary union was not a major selling point in the negotiations over Swedish EU membership.

Economic Criteria

This section presents the structure and makeup of Sweden's economy with an eye toward evaluating the potential economic costs and benefits of the country participating in an EMU. The first part looks at Sweden's standing with respect to Europe's so-called convergence criteria. The second looks at some particular structural elements of the Swedish economy to see the extent to which Sweden might be susceptible to asymmetric shocks given EMU.

Convergence Criteria

Sweden's record high unemployment figures are cause for the greatest concern. Unemployment continues to grow, from 5.3 percent in 1992 to around 8.0 percent for the years following. In January 1996, the figure remained at 8.1 percent.[5] Any attempt to better Sweden's record on the formal convergence criteria is likely to influence (negatively) this politically charged variable. Thus, unemployment remains a significant background variable for evaluating Sweden's record on the convergence criteria.

If we consider only the formal convergence criteria, Sweden's budget deficits are the most worrisome element. Currently, the budget deficit is at nearly 10.4 percent of gross domestic product (GDP), leagues away from the 3 percent required by the criterion. (See Table 9.2.) Much of the deficit is set; it consists of remnants from the old Swedish model, overburdened with enormous demands by a growing army of Sweden's unemployed. So long as unemployment continues at such high levels, reducing these deficits will be difficult and costly. In addition, however, the budget deficit includes some expensive bailout programs. In particular, several Swedish banks lost money between 1990 and 1993 (to the amount of, roughly, 234 billion kronor). The state was forced to intervene and "socialize" two of the largest banks (Nordbanken and Securum), at the cost of about 36 billion kronor. These bailouts were a significant element of the deficit in the years straddling the referendum but became only marginal in the following years.

Sweden managed to meet just one of the convergence criteria in 1995: the inflation level criterion. However, the country's governments do not seem concerned about eventually reaching the other criteria; instead, the relevant question has been *when* Sweden can meet them. For example, a 1994 government report evaluated Sweden's position with regard to the convergence criteria and found it inconceivable that the country would manage to satisfy all of the convergence criteria before 1996 (Assarsson and Olsson, 1993). Besides fixed exchange rates (Sweden has only begun to participate in the European Monetary System), the main problem was seen to be Sweden's public finances. In 1993, the Finance Department (Finansdepartementet, 1993) figured that the government should be able to wrestle out a budget deficit in 1996 that is about 9 percent of GDP. After that period, the department expects the situation to improve radically. In its *kompletteringspropositionen* (completion proposition), the government presented a savings plan that is expected to shrink the deficit to 3.6 percent in 1998.

Annual budget deficits add up to debt. In 1993, Sweden—for the first time—exceeded the 60 percent of GDP ceiling laid out in the Maastricht criteria. How the debt situation will continue to develop, however, is uncertain. The report just mentioned did not address the debt issue according to the convergence criteria. This is interesting in that the EU apparently considers different types of public sector debt, such that parts of the debt that answer to changes in some other part of the public sector are not taken into consideration (Assarsson and Olsson, 1993:15). In the Swedish context, this means that the universal pension, or "AP" funds (that is, AP funds that are holding state obligations) are not added into the government's gross debt.[6] Still, the European Commission's figure for the Swedish debt in 1994 was 79.9 percent of GDP.

Although the Swedish economy is suffering its worse depression since the interwar period, its government promises a stringent budgetary diet.[7] The potential distributional costs of this fiscal fasting are discussed in the third section of the chapter. For now, it is enough to show that, in 1995, the government presented detailed plans for eliminating the deficit problem by 1998. While debt probably will remain well above the specified levels, Sweden's government hopes that the EU will forgive its debt, Irish fashion, if it sees movement in the direction of its alleviation.

In conclusion, Sweden can—and apparently intends to—effectively meet three of the four convergence criteria by 1998. The public debt problem will remain. The real question, as we shall see, is about the political sustainability of the plan. The current government, already burdened with large unemployment figures, can hardly afford to lose more jobs through fiscal consolidation in an effort to satisfy an already unpopular European objective.

General Economic Structure

This section evaluates Sweden's production and export structure with an eye toward measuring its susceptibility to asymmetric shocks. This evaluation relies on data at three different levels: export structure, general trade structure, and production composition. The underlying assumption here is that the more integrated the Swedish economy is with the other economies in the Union, the less likely that it will suffer asymmetric shocks resulting from a future EMU.[8]

Sweden's integration with the rest of Europe can be measured in several ways, the first of which is in general export terms. Fifty-three percent of Sweden's exports in 1993 went to member states of the EU; and 55 percent of its imports come from the same countries.[9] But two of Sweden's five most important export markets, the United States (which accounts for 10 percent of Sweden's exports) and Norway (8 percent), are not EU members. Of the three main export markets that remain, Germany purchases 14 percent of Sweden's exports, while trailing after are the United Kingdom (8 percent) and Denmark (7 percent).

Of the Swedish goods being exported, road vehicles and paper products are the most important. Table 9.2 lists the five most important export items at the two-digit SITC level. As with Finland's export structure (see Chapter 4), the prominent role of Sweden's paper products' industry is troublesome from an optimal currency area perspective. Otherwise, the composition of Sweden's main exports is fairly well suited to that of the rest of the Union, if a bit concentrated. Five product groups account for 41 percent of all Swedish exports.

Another way to capture the degree of export dependence is to measure how much manufacturing production relies on foreign markets. Although suitably comparative figures are difficult to obtain, Table 9.3 attempts to gauge the share of production that is exported in some of Sweden's most significant industries.[10] Like Table 9.2, Table 9.3 begins by listing the five most important export industries at the two-digit SITC level. It then lists the nearest production equivalent, in ISIC terms. In some of the most significant export sectors, over 60 percent of production is being exported: 63.1 percent of road vehicles, 71.8 percent of machinery, and 77.4 percent of Sweden's iron and steel production. In employment terms, machinery production in Sweden is very significant. At the two-digit ISIC level, 46.4 percent of industrial employment works in the manufacturing of fabricated metal products, machinery, and the like (*Yearbook of Nordic Statistics,* 1994). Thus, Sweden's production and employment base is heavily reliant on export markets.

Previous authors have tried to capture Sweden's degree of economic integration by measuring its reliance on intraindustrial trade (that is, the degree

Table 9.2: Five Most Important Swedish Export Items, 1993

SITC Product Group	Description	Export Share (percent)
78	Road Vehicles	12
64	Paper and paper products	10
74	General industrial machinery	7
76	Telecommunications equipment	6
67	Iron and steel	6
Total export share of all five products		41

Source: Yearbook of Nordic Statistics (1995).

Table 9.3: Top Five Export Industries and Export Composition of Manufacturing, 1992

Export Industry		Share in Total Exports (percent)	Nearest Product Equivalent		Export Share in Production (percent)
SITC Code	Description		ISIC Code	Description	
78	Road vehicles	13.1	384	Transport manufacturing	63.1
64	Paper, paper products	11.0	34	Paper, paper products	44.8
74	General machinery	7.3	382	Machinery	71.8
72	Specialized machinery	5.1			
67	Iron and steel	5.7	371	Iron-steel, basic industry	77.4

Source: Yearbook of Nordic Statistics (1994, 1995).

to which a country imports and exports goods that are identical or nearly identical). In particular, Assarsson and Olsson (1993: 49) have employed a Grubel-Lloyds (GL) index for measuring Sweden's reliance on intraindustrial trade.[11] This index represents the share of intraindustrial to total trade worldwide (Greenaway and Milner, 1986: 59–70). Assarsson and Olsson found the Swedish export economy to rely fairly heavily on intraindustrial trade, compared to other EU-economies (with Britain scoring highest, and Greece the lowest). At the interindustrial level, Sweden's record is equally middle of the road. This interindustrial figure reflects both a country's openness and its reliance on intraindustrial trade. (See Assarsson and Olsson, 1993.) The larger the figure, the more exposed an economy is to price changes in the world market. In other words, Sweden's average performance suggests that it is not particularly susceptible to price shocks, compared to other EU member states.

The final step is to quantify the susceptibility of Sweden's economy to stochastic shocks. Previous studies have employed vector-auto-regression models that try to quantify the risks of a country's participation in a monetary union, measured in terms of correlation between shocks (both type and size) in various countries. (See, for example, Bayoumi and Eichengreen, 1992a and 1992b.) A country is assumed to benefit from joining a monetary union if its shocks are strongly and positively correlated with shocks in the other countries. Assarsson and Olson (1993) have applied such an analysis to Sweden and found that shocks to the Swedish economy are correlated only very weakly with corresponding shocks in other EU countries. Indeed, which other countries were considered made little difference to their results. But they also found that domestic shocks were not dominant in the Swedish economy; this was especially true for domestic supply shocks (the effects of which were found to be relatively small in comparison with the effects that arose from either demand shocks and/or foreign supply shocks). Thus Assarsson and Olsson (1993) conclude that the risks of Swedish membership in EMU, in terms of the costs of asymmetric shocks, should be limited.

The most significant difference between Sweden and the EU, in terms of production structure and vulnerability to shocks, is that Sweden is a net exporter of forest industry products (which totaled 3.6 percent of GDP in 1991). All of the EU countries, except Finland and Portugal, are net importers of forest products. Swedish exports of some types of workshop industries are also significantly larger than the Union's net exports, while its net imports of textile goods are large compared to those of the EU. It is in these sectors that there is the greatest likelihood for asymmetric shocks.

In general, then, the Swedish economy—when compared to the other EU economies—does not seem particularly ill-suited to participating in EMU. Sweden can, with some strain, meet most of the convergence criteria and might even be forgiven its debts. In terms of its production and export structure, the picture is not particularly convincing one way or the other. Sweden is, like many other member states, fairly well integrated with the other member state markets. Its production structure is not particularly vulnerable to stochastic shocks, with the possible exception of the timber and some workshop industries. The relevant question, as it is with so many other member states, depends on the government's willingness to swallow the bitter pill: Will it accept higher unemployment figures in exchange for being a member of the inner circle? It is to this question that the next section turns.

Institutional Cleavages and Distributional Consequences

This section combines two distinctive categories, distributional and institutional consequences, into one section, as they overlap so frequently on many issues. Institutions in the Swedish context largely reflect distributional interests. Institutional cleavages arise primarily along three frontiers: labor market, party political, and bureaucratic. On the other hand, the distributional consequences reflect class, sectoral, and regional interests. We turn first to the institutional cleavages.

Institutional Cleavages

One of the most relevant institutional features of the Swedish economy is the highly organized nature of its industrial relations. In terms of both bargaining coverage (83 percent) and union density (83 percent) rates, Sweden scores among the world's highest (Traxler, 1994: 173). Whereas other countries may have higher bargaining coverage rates (for example, Austria and Finland), Swedish union density levels are the highest in the world. Sweden is also one of the few countries in the world in which union density rates continue to increase over recent decades. While there is great controversy as to whether or not centralized labor unions and bargaining arrangements contribute to greater nominal wage increases (see Calmfors and Driffill, 1988; and Holmlund, 1993), Lindbeck et al. (1994: 36) argue that multi-level negotiations contribute to total larger wage increases than do single-level negotiations. In this respect, Sweden is less concentrated than other nations.[12] Indeed, Traxler (1994: 175) characterizes Sweden's capacity for economy-wide coordination as "limited."

What are the consequences of this institutional structure for facilitating (or exacerbating) the effects of shocks? Of primary importance is the degree to which unions can contain wage demands in the aftermath of devaluation or adjust wages efficiently in the event of an asymmetric shock in the context of a currency union. As Froats (1995) has argued, the structure of industrial relations has much to say about the effectiveness of potential currency unions.

Swedish industrial relations are currently in a state of flux. As a result, it is difficult to say much about the effects of these institutions in an EMU context. In the past, the highly centralized nature of industrial organization has facilitated the use of devaluations—as wage guarantees could be secured in private before devaluation. (See, for example, Bergström, 1987: 198.) Such coordination could be equally useful in a currency union. Whether these guarantees and coordination can continue in today's more fragmented context, however, remains to be seen.

Coordination is difficult, as much of the collective bargaining framework has broken down. Traditionally, labor markets in Sweden have been understood in terms of an institutional arrangement characterized by cooperation between two centralized peak bargaining organizations representing capital (the Swedish employers' federation, SAF) and labor (the trade union confederation, LO). In practice, several smaller bargaining organizations were also represented. Until recently, private sector negotiations were regularly conducted between the SAF, the LO and the "white collar" workers federation (PTK) at the national level. In the public sector, negotiations are between the government's own bargaining representatives (SAV), the public sector "white collar" union (TCO) and the other principal public sector union (SACO). As the LO covers about 90 percent of all blue-collar workers in Sweden, and the TCO covers about 70 percent of all white collar workers, collective agreements between the government, the SAF, and the two main labor organizations were able to guarantee a fairly stable investment environment, thereby ensuring even growth.[13] In 1983, however, exposed sector unions and employers broke out of the collective bargaining arrangement. Since then, there have been several, largely unsuccessful, attempts to return to the security of the previous collaborative negotiations' structure. The result has been a move toward a more fragmented bargaining process, at the expense of the general price trend and structure as well as the investment environment.

Although there may be ideological reasons for blaming labor market institutions for the current sluggish economy, the data do not support the position wholeheartedly. Price rigidities and wage inflation do not appear to be the cause of the current problems. In Sweden, product real wage growth was significantly larger than productivity growth rates in the years from 1973 to 1977. Since 1978, however, Swedish product real wages grew at considerably restrained rates and fell below productivity growth rates. Although these figures are somewhat outdated, one can assume that the institutional framework in Sweden has relaxed only in the period since 1987 and that wage rigidities cannot be held responsible for the current unemployment levels. The *Nordic Economic Outlook* (14 November 1994) reports that Swedish wage increases between 1993 and 1995 (predicted) underscored productivity increases; the reason was that wage demands were very modest and that there were cuts in social payroll charges of about 3 percent. Thus Swedish industrial organization does not appear to hinder the possibilities for the efficient wage adjustment necessary in a single-currency context.

Sweden's institutional setting offers another unique aspect to the EMU debate; as a result of these institutions, the debate about EMU membership in Sweden is probably the most developed in the Nordic region. The main reason for this is the relative autonomy of the LO's economic policy unit.

Whereas the Social Democratic Party has strongly (if sometimes quietly) supported Swedish membership in EMU, the labor unions in general have been skeptical about the costs to labor of prioritizing price stability at the (possible) expense of full employment.

Whereas the peak labor organizations in both Norway and Finland have more or less towed the Labor (Social Democratic) line, the LO in Sweden has aggressively attacked the Social Democratic line on monetary policy priorities in the editorial pages of Sweden's largest newspaper: *Dagens Nyheter*. On 24 June 1990, the chief economist of the LO, P.-O. Edin, and Dan Andersson (another leading LO economist), criticized Allan Larsson (then finance minister) and the rest of the Social Democratic economic group for sacrificing the full employment objective on the altar of price stability. Allan Larsson returned the joust with an editorial two days later entitled "LO Economists Capitulate."[14] Although one might expect sectoral divisions within each group that would oppose either position, the LO's position represents a general concern that the government's EU ambitions were placed ahead of all other policy options, including full employment.

The peak bargaining organization for capital interests (SAF), on the other hand, has voiced no such hesitancy in its support of EMU membership for Sweden. Despite sectoral (and size) divisions within the membership, the SAF is a strong (and wealthy) ally of the pro-EU movement (including EMU membership). Though economists at the SAF realize that the decision to support EMU membership for Sweden may provoke some sectoral strains within the organization, they argue that the economic benefits (not only in terms of reduced transaction costs, but also in terms of investment dynamics) make the position attractive to the SAF.

The second potential institutional divide is among Sweden's political parties. One might expect that some social groups prefer inflation (or monetary policy autonomy) more than others—and would influence party positions accordingly. Yet—like Finland, and as was discussed in the historical section—all of Sweden's major parties support membership in the European Union; and they have not exerted great effort to clarify their position with regard to future EMU. Instead, the parties all seem to agree about the basic type of economic measures that are required, but they are afraid to be caught taking the costly measures. For example, Carl Bildt's Moderate (read: Conservative) government prescribed neoclassical medicine for Sweden's economic woes. His government introduced a series of measures, including limits on interest-rate deductions, new pension-saving measures, less regulation of stockholders, and weaker social-insurance measures. But eventually this government was removed from office in large part because of its ambitious restructuring and deficit-cutting goals. Fiscal conservatism is not seen as necessary on its own (in political terms); but the size of the deficit clearly makes it necessary in economic terms.

To the extent that parties reflect different sectoral interests, they might be expected to have different positions with respect to Sweden's participation in EMU. The agricultural (center) parties in the rest of the Nordic region are examples of such differentiation. But farmers (and foresters) are less politically influential in Sweden than in Norway or Finland. As much of the farming lobby is dominated by larger, export-oriented concerns in the south of Sweden, the Center Party and the farmer's lobby have been less adamant (than their counterparts in, say, Norway) about keeping Sweden out of the European Union and EMU. Thus, party cleavages do not appear along a number of anticipated (sectoral) fault lines.

One final institutional divide is between the government and the central bank, Sveriges Riksbank. This is not an uncommon cleavage, but it has been exacerbated of late by increased calls for greater central bank autonomy in Sweden (as elsewhere). Actually, Sweden is the first of the Nordic countries to come out with a formal parliamentary report on the status of the Riksbank with respect to the proposed changes in EMU's third stage of transition, and to provide for some appraisal of the consequences for Sweden (Statens Offentliga Utredningar, 1993: 20). Although politically contentious, the report made several recommendations about the primary objectives of central bank policy including a series of institutional changes to ensure greater autonomy for the central bank and a firm institutional and legal commitment to price stability as the primary objective of the Riksbank.

This independence has shown itself most recently in a fairly open split between the government and the Riksbank over the degree of enthusiasm shown for the third stage of monetary union. In mid-June 1995, for the first time, the Riksbank announced that Sweden should join EMU, saying that if offered "overriding advantages" for the economy (Carnegy, 1995a). This strong and open support for membership is quite at odds with the government's restrained position. Although the then government, in particular Ingvar Carlsson (the prime minister) and Göran Persson (the finance minister), indicated support for Sweden joining the final stage of EMU, it was very careful to stress that the decision will ultimately be taken by parliament—where there is certain to be much opposition. This careful strategy on the part of the government probably will continue as long as opinion in Sweden is skeptical of membership.

Distributional Consequences

From these institutional cleavages we can expect several potential distributional consequences. The most important distributional divide has to do with the employment costs associated with meeting the initial criteria for joining a monetary union, and the possibilities of painful asymmetric shocks once Sweden is in such EMU. These divisions might be expected along class, sectoral, and regional lines.

In 1994, Sweden's unemployment rate soared to 14 percent (including those on training schemes) from below 5 percent just three years earlier. The unemployment problem is worse in the mid-1990s than it has been in the past 60 years. As the convergence criteria section documented, this has led to enormous budget problems.

Estimating the potential costs of meeting the convergence criteria is no easy matter, and there can be much disagreement over the particulars of each study. On average, however, the government predictions, unsurprisingly, are much lower than outside estimates. Three external studies, however, are not very encouraging. First, *Veckans Affärer,* a business paper, estimated that tying the krona to an ECU basket cost Sweden a decline in productive potential valued at between 120 and 150 billion kronor, which corresponds to about 5 percent additional unemployment. Later another business paper, *Månadens Affärer,* estimated that the employment costs of meeting the Maastricht criteria (according to the government's current strategy) ranges between 300,000 and 400,000 jobs.[15] Finally, in a study carried out by the National Institute for Economic and Social Research (London) for the European Parliament, it has been estimated that the Swedish economy will sacrifice 250,000 jobs in its fiscal entrenchment (Barrell, Morgan, and Pain, 1995).

Generally, we can expect two types of distributional consequences to result from both the convergence stage and the currency union phase of EMU. Meeting the convergence criteria will have distributional consequences on two constituencies: public policy patrons and public sector employees. Balancing the budget and paying off the debt burden will have significant distributional and employment consequences (Moses, 1995a). Not only will social spending need to be pruned radically, but the economy itself will experience disinflationary pressures. These consequences are only exacerbated by the fact that the reforms are being forced under the EMU's time constraint. Resistance can be expected from all who benefit from social spending as well as from the growing number of unemployed.

Providing more specific predictions about the distributional fallout of these policies, especially in the private sector, is more difficult. After EMU is established, however, two major divisions affecting employment may emerge. First, the tradable and nontradable sectors may divide over the distribution of adjustment costs (Frieden, 1991). Regions that are heavily dependent on sheltered industry incomes might be expected to lose relative to other regions, because of the loss of an autonomous monetary policy. Alternatively, those regions that rely heavily on forest industry products may be less able to cope with a monetary policy aimed at different (that is, pan-European) business cycles from those that influence the forest industry. Measuring the regional effects of these changes is not easy. Swedish fiscal policy is not designed along regional terms, as it is in some of the larger countries. There are few regional aid packages, and they are not listed as such in the government's budget. Instead, regional business cycles are handled within the general, national framework of a large network of job-matching facilities and resources. Thus regional transfers are not a significant, detailed budget item. Instead, the costs of regional economic downturns (either structural or cyclical) are listed (fiscally) under the larger social welfare and labor rubrics of the budget.

Nevertheless, it is possible to examine the regional contributions to the gross domestic product and provide some rough estimate of which regions will be hardest hit in all three of the above scenarios. Tables 9.4 and 9.5 can help us in this endeavor. Table 9.4 reveals that the costs of cutting public sector employment will be spread fairly evenly across all of Sweden, with Stockholm and the smaller regions being hurt the least, in part because they rely less on public sector contributions. Public concerns represent over 20 percent of the regional product in most of the remaining regions provided for in the Finance Department's reports (Finansdepartementet, 1994). The employment effects can be expected to be (roughly) the same.

In evaluating the potential costs that might result from asymmetric shocks to different regions after the establishment of EMU, the northern and most sparsely populated regions are likely to be hurt the most because they are more heavily reliant on forest industry production. In addition, however, Table 9.5 suggests that the "regional centers" and Stockholm will be hit hard by their proportionally heavier reliance on sheltered industry incomes.

Whereas the economic costs are difficult to quantify, the political costs might be more clear-cut. After the 1994 referendum, the EU became very unpopular in Sweden. On 15 June 1995, Sweden's Central Statistics Bureau published a poll of 74,000 voters (an unusually large sample) in which 61.9 percent of them said that they would reject joining the EU if a new referendum were held. Only 28.6 percent voiced support (Carnegy, 1995a). If government officials are not able to convince their voting publics that Sweden's current economic hardships are not the result of an attempt at EMU, or if the public begins to see the convergence criteria (and not full employment) as the government's primary economic objective, the government's popularity will go the way of the European Union's.

To sum up, Sweden's institutional framework is currently in flux, so it is difficult to predict how useful this framework will prove in the context of

Table 9.4: Sectoral Contributions to Regional Production in Sweden, 1991

Region	Regional Product	Agriculture	Industry	Services	State	Local	Private	Public
			Sectoral Subdivisions				**Aggregates**	
Stockholm	353,000	0.7	19.1	60.7	5.4	12.5	80.4	18.0
Göteborg	137,300	0.8	24.1	54.6	3.7	15.8	79.5	19.5
Malmö	94,300	2.3	25.7	49.5	4.6	16.9	77.5	21.5
Large Southern Centers	229,600	3.0	31.1	42.3	4.8	17.8	76.4	22.6
Regional Centers	338,400	3.8	29.8	41.8	5.1	18.3	75.4	23.5
Local Centers	205,900	3.7	40.3	35.2	2.8	17.1	79.2	19.9
Smaller Regions	52,400	8.6	35.5	33.2	3.3	18.5	77.3	21.8
Small Regions	36,400	5.4	43.3	33.5	2.3	14.4	82.2	16.7
National	1,447,000	2.7	28.6	46.7	4.5	16.2	78.1	20.7

Note: For more detailed descriptions of the 8 regions, see Finansdepartementet (1994: 20). The determining factor is the number of inhabitants in a commune. The cut-off numbers for each of the 8 regions are as follows: >1,000,000; >750,000; >500,000; >150,000; >75,000; >25,000; >12,500; <12,500.
Source: Finansdepartementet (1994), p. 32.

a future EMU. In the past, centralized bargaining structures have enabled the Swedish economy to adjust efficiently to large asymmetric shocks. Distributional fallout can be expected to result from the fiscal constraints imposed on potential EMU members as well as the possible asymmetric effects arising from Sweden's relative dependence on forest industry exports. Employees in the public sector, current beneficiaries of public policy, and the timber industry generally can be expected to be affected negatively and disproportionately.

Linkages

EMU membership often is linked to other issues. Meeting the convergence criteria is bitter medicine, but it is medicine that the finance minister would prescribe, regardless of the ailment. In other words, the convergence criteria have become the scapegoats for difficult decisions. In particular, two types of linkages reflect these largely negative concerns: fear of capital flight and the need for fiscal rectitude. Obviously, the two issues themselves are linked.

Table 9.5: Regional Industrial Production Shares by Sector (average percent 1990 and 1991)

Region	Regional Product	Manu-facturing Industry	Sheltered Industry	Industry intensive in:			
				Labor	Capital	Knowledge	R&D
Stockholm	24.4	15.4	20.6	4.7	6.3	10.0	44.0
Göteborg	9.5	9.0	7.5	6.3	13.3	12.5	2.5
Malmö	6.5	5.9	8.3	7.6	3.3	5.4	4.7
Large Southern Centers	15.9	17.8	18.6	18.5	12.1	18.4	23.7
Regional Centers	23.4	25.0	21.1	28.4	31.0	26.4	14.7
Local Centers	14.2	20.0	17.7	24.0	25.5	20.7	8.8
Smaller Regions	3.6	4.1	4.3	5.6	5.0	4.3	0.3
Small Regions	2.5	2.8	2.0	4.9	3.5	2.4	1.2
National	100	100	100	100	100	100	100

Note: For more detailed descriptions of the 8 regions, see Finansdepartementet (1994:20). The determining factor is the number of inhabitants in a commune. The cut-off numbers for each of the 8 regions are as follows: >1,000,000; >750,000; >500,000; >150,000; >75,000; >25,000; >12,500; <12,500.
Source: Finansdepartementet (1994), p. 48.

Of all the Nordic countries, Sweden's economy is the most industrialized and the most susceptible to the threat of outward flows of investment capital. Swedish industry and investment traditionally has been linked to a handful of large concerns, whose interests in Europe have played an enormous role in the debate about European membership and Sweden's interest in an eventual monetary union. An example of this influence can be seen in the run-up to the 1994 parliamentary elections. The chiefs of Sweden's four top exporting companies threatened to withdraw their domestic investments (totaling about 50 billion kronor per year) in Sweden if income tax levels in the country were changed after the election.[16] This was little more than an open threat to the Social Democrats that, in the wake of their almost certain electoral victory, they must continue to pursue the economic policies established under Moderate Party rule. Although the executives' concern was aimed mostly at proposed changes in Swedish tax levels, similar pressure can be seen on the monetary/exchange-rate front.

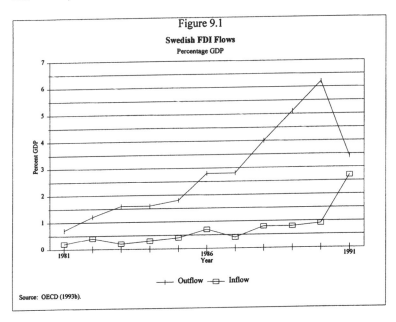

Figure 9.1

Swedish FDI Flows
Percentage GDP

Source: OECD (1993b).

With the lifting of foreign exchange controls, Swedish capital is no longer constrained to the collective bargaining table and has fled to Europe in search of higher yields. This flight had an enormously stifling effect on domestic investment in Sweden until the 1992 devaluation. Over the past four years, industrial investments have declined rapidly and the capital stock in industries actually has been declining. The volume index (1985=100) for gross fixed capital formation in Sweden dropped off dramatically from 1990 to 1993: 129.8, 118.9, 106, and 87.3, respectively (*Yearbook of Nordic Statistics*, 1995: 288). Since the devaluation, some Swedish capital has returned, and the domestic investment outlook seems hopeful. Nevertheless, a cloud still hovers over the Swedish investment environment. As capital's fear of devaluation, inflation, and transaction costs are lessened by movement in the direction of EMU, government officials can explain the potential benefits of EMU in terms of satisfying capital's demands.

The second linkage issue is the one associated with fiscal rectitude. Several officials in the central bank and in government have alluded to the fact that the convergence criteria are difficult but necessary in order to help put Sweden's economic house back in order. For example, the Riksbank, in its first formal announcement of support for Sweden's joining EMU, explained its decision in the following terms: "The economic policy which enables Sweden to participate in EMU is essentially the same as the policy that is needed for a lasting recovery in the Swedish economy after the decline in recent years" (Carnegy, 1995a: 3). In short, balanced public finances, controlled public debt, lower inflation, lower interest rates, and currency stability are the instruments chosen by the government and bank to try to rebuild the Swedish economy—regardless of EMU membership. This was, for example, the advice of the Lindbeck report (Lindbeck et al., 1994).

These two linkage issues suggest that EMU-participation in its own right is not desirable. That is, I believe, true. Sweden recognizes the need to participate for fear of potential investment flight; it also understands the need to get its fiscal house in order. But Sweden does not argue for EMU in its own right—EMU has become a means to other ends. In this respect, the discussion about EMU parallels those outlined in the historical section: Support for the EU is made on much broader grounds than its potential economic effects. But public support for EMU, and the EU in general, remains weak.

Swedish discussions on peace, defense, and social policy often are framed in pan-European terms. Sweden desires to participate in a cooperative European venture to secure objectives that are no longer (if ever) obtainable at the national level. This concern for Europe, however, does not carry over to discussions about monetary policy. The discussion about joining EMU (or not) is not framed in terms of the potential or economic benefit to Europe as a whole.

Conclusion

This chapter has attempted to gauge the support (and its price) of Swedish membership in EMU. To do so, it has considered a variety of historical, economic, and political vantage points. Unfortunately, these manifold perspectives do not provide a common or focused vision of Sweden's potential for membership. Still, in summary, we might offer a cautious conclusion.

The historical perspective is critical of Sweden's ability to participate in EMU. In the past, Sweden has relied on exchange rate flexibility and has been most willing to prioritize full employment over price stability. To the extent that these historical norms are embedded in current Swedish preferences, support for Swedish membership in EMU should be small. But there is pressure to change this historical consensus.

Sweden's standing with respect to the economic criteria offers more ambiguous lessons. The government and the central bank intend to meet the Maastricht criteria, and likely will do so (with the exception of the debt criterion). Should Sweden enter the final stage of EMU, its economic structure is probably broad enough to sustain the assaults of asymmetric blows. The Swedish economy is integrated as much as those of the other core member states. Its economy (unlike that of Finland, Greece, and Portugal, for example) does not distinguish itself remarkably in its makeup and/or size. In other words, the costs of Swedish participation in EMU will be similar to those for countries on the continent.

The strongest support for Sweden's membership in EMU comes from the more political perspective. Fear of capital flight, a newfound enthusiasm for fiscal conservatism, and the potential benefits of full membership in the other realms of the EU argue strongly for meeting the Maastricht criteria. In contrast to Sweden's historical preferences for monetary policy autonomy, and despite the potential costs of losing that autonomy, Sweden's elites strongly support membership in EMU. But public support for EU membership, including participation in EMU, is weak. As a result, Sweden's political elites are unwilling to commit themselves to EMU. In the end, Swedish membership in EMU will depend more on the ability of elites to convince a skeptical public than on any of the sundry economic costs and criteria involved.

Notes

1. I would like to thank Jeffry Frieden and Erik Jones, along with all of the other members of the EPG, for their comments and suggestions over the many drafts of this chapter. Of course, I alone remain responsible.

2. The Lindbeck commission's advice was confused in the sense that it held, on the one hand, that Sweden maintain a floating exchange rate for quite some time; on the other hand, the commission offered support for EMU membership in principle, "at least from a narrow monetary perspective" (Lindbeck et al., 1994: 42).

3. The Liberal Party, since 1989, has been at the forefront of the Swedish EU movement. It is strongly assisted in this measure by the New Democracy Party. These two parties are the strongest and oldest supporters of EU membership. In addition, a sizable wing of the Moderate Party has long advocated Swedish EC membership. Its party chairman (later prime minister), Carl Bildt, was enthusiastic about the European Economic Area (EEA), but worried that Swedish membership in the EU might delegate it to a "peripheral state" in Europe. By June of 1990, however, Bildt—and the reluctant wing of the Moderate Party—became confirmed as new believers to the European project. The Christian Democrats have been more cautious supporters. The Social Democratic leadership has long supported EC membership, but the party did not officially support the project until the fall of 1990. The Center Party traditionally has been skeptical of the membership movement and often was grouped together with the Greens and the Left Party as active opponents to EC membership. Their position over time, however, has weakened somewhat. Both the Green and Left parties have been, and remain, vehement opponents to Swedish EU membership.

4. One reason for this apparent lacuna was the (contemporary) Swedish decision to agree to participate in the European Economic Area (EEA). Throughout the latter part of the 1980s, Sweden had joined the other EFTA countries in bargaining for increased access to the European market. A large majority in the Swedish Riksdag had supported the EEA agreement, which came into place on 1 January 1994.

5. If those workers on government training schemes are also included in the figures, then the unemployment levels are 5.7 percent (1992), 8.9 percent (1993), and 14 percent (1994).

6. AP funds are a huge public pension fund system established in the 1960s. At their peak, in the early 1970s, these funds accounted for 35 percent of the total supply of Swedish credit (Pontusson, 1992: 12).

7. In June 1995, the government came out with an updated report on the costs associated with meeting the criteria. To accomplish this, the government proposed large cuts in the budget, totaling 18 billion kronor in both 1998 and 1999. These cuts, in addition to increased tax incomes, were designed to better the budget by 117 billion kronor. In addition, the government proposed to sell off about 70 billion kronor worth of assets (publicly owned facilities and firms). This, combined with hopes of a 3 percent growth rate over 1996–97, was intended to eliminate the budget deficit by 1998.

8. I assume that the reader is generally familiar with the optimal currency area (OCA) literature. If not, I recommend the introductions provided by De Grauwe (1994), De Grauwe and Vanhaverbeke (1991), Ishiyama (1975), and Masson and Taylor (1992).

9. All of the figures in this paragraph come from the *Yearbook of Nordic Statistics* (1995).

10. The most recent year for which we could obtain comparative statistics was 1992. In that year, Sweden's export structure was different from that in 1993: Specialized machinery was replaced by telecommunications equipment in the ranking. Contrast Table 9.3 with Table 9.2.

11. While these figures rely on two-digit SITC data, Hansson (1989) has shown the difference in Sweden at other digit levels (up to six) to be negligible.

12. For a comparative description of different bargaining levels and co-ordination, see Golden and Wallerstein (1995) and Table 5.1 in Traxler (1994: 175).

13. For reference, it may be useful to note that the community, social and personal service industries (SITC 9) represent 40 percent of Swedish employment. This is followed by manufacturing (18 percent) and wholesale and retail trade (14 percent). See *Yearbook of Nordic Statistics* (1995). Thus, the non-LO peak organizations that represent white-collar service sector workers control a significant share of Swedish employees.

14. This debate eventually found its way to an LO-Social Democratic Party (peace-offering) seminar, the contents of which (and the original *Dagens Nyheter* editorials) have been printed as Carlsson (1991).

15. This would be the equivalent of doubling the number of registered unemployed. In 1994, there were 340,000 registered unemployed in Sweden.

16. The four were Sören Gyll, chief executive of Volvo; Lars Ramqvist, chief executive of Ericsson; Bert-Olof Svanholm, chief executive of Swedish ABB; and Bo Berggren, chairman of Stora. Their threat came by way of an open editorial in the *Dagens Nyheter* (12 September 1994).

CONCLUSION

The Political Economy of EMU: A Small Country Perspective

Erik Jones, Jeffry Frieden, and Francisco Torres

For the smaller countries studied in this volume, context is what matters in debates about economic and monetary union (EMU): How does monetary integration fit into their larger political and economic objectives? What are the keys to preparation for EMU, and what are the pitfalls? Finally, does economic and monetary union hold implications beyond what is expected or even desired?

The answers to such questions tell a lot about the political economy of EMU, even if they do not reflect the structural position of smaller countries. What is at issue is "best practice" and not strictly costs and benefits—although doing what is best is sure to influence the net result of integration. Therefore, this chapter draws together what we believe to be the lessons from the small-country perspective.

The chapter has five sections. The first examines the link between EMU and broader economic strategies, such as liberalization, modernization, and diversification. Building on that analysis, the second section asks whether credibility is more important than real convergence—whether EMU truly can serve a broader economic strategy, or if the broad strategy must be completed before monetary integration can be attempted. The third section examines how different political and economic arrangements can facilitate or hinder the process of adjustment to monetary union, and the fourth suggests that there may be disadvantages to placing monetary questions outside the realm of political accountability or as the focal point for domestic debate. The fifth section forms a conclusion.

Modernization, Diversification, Liberalization

EMU is a European objective, but it is also a national policy instrument. For each of the smaller countries, monetary integration is only one instrument among several used in attaining larger political and economic objectives. This seems evident with respect to the Maastricht plan for EMU, but also with its institutional forerunner, the European monetary system (EMS), and arguably with any exchange rate regime (Argy and De Grauwe, 1990). The choice of exchange rate policy is not motivated solely—or principally—by the desire to take part in Europe's monetary club. Instead, it reflects the advantages membership has to offer in the broader context of a political and economic strategy such as modernization, diversification, or liberalization.

Examples of countries relying on monetary integration to facilitate the modernization of their economies might include Ireland, Finland, Greece, and Portugal. For Ireland and Portugal, participation in the EMS supported the development of an export manufacturing base. Chapter 6 provides evidence for the change in Irish production structures since 1979, and Chapter 8 documents the shift in Portuguese exports from light manufacturing, such as textiles, to more sophisticated items, such as automotive parts. In both cases, the choice of exchange rate regime was influenced by the desire to attract foreign direct investment as well as to change the pattern of domestic investment. The same combination of factors also can be found in Finland, where political authorities are perhaps even more concerned with the excessive concentration of domestic investment in wood and paper industries than with the attraction of capital from outside the country.

Examples of diversification include Ireland and Finland. As Chapter 6 claims, the history of Irish European policy is bound up with a desire to break with the country's deep dependence on British export markets. And the results have been startlingly successful. From 1979 to 1994, Irish exporters have shifted almost 16 percent of their trade from the United Kingdom to continental markets. Finnish motives for joining the exchange rate mechanism (ERM) have similar origins, although with a more restricted range of possible choices. Given the dramatic collapse of trade with the Soviet Union, Finnish exporters had little choice but to look to expand to new markets. From this perspective, the Finnish government supported a changeover in export orientation from East to West first by pegging the markka to the Deutschemark and then by joining the EMS.

The case for liberalization is the most widely spread of the three strategies. The claim here is that monetary integration facilitates the pursuit liberalization as an economic strategy—whether in the context of the single European marketplace or more specifically with respect to the integration of European financial markets. Evidence for this contention is abundant, and can be traced through the exchange rate histories of virtually all the countries discussed in this volume. The point to note, however, is that liberalization—and not monetary integration per se—is the principal objective.

By extension, the success of monetary integration depends on the success of whatever larger strategy in which it is embedded. For example, should Finland fail to diversify its export bundle, its prospects for participation in EMU will surely diminish. The same point can be made with respect to Greek and Portuguese privatization programs. And perhaps most strongly, the evidence can be seen in Ireland's reluctant devaluation. Although the country had made substantial progress in mitigating its dependence on UK markets, the results were insufficient to convince financial markets. Once the British pound left the ERM, market makers reasoned it was only a matter of time before Ireland would devalue as well. Speculation against the Irish pound made such perceptions a reality.

A similar point applies to the hard-currency countries such as Belgium and the Netherlands. Although both countries have fared well in the EMS and in the run-up to EMU, their success depends on the larger objective of maintaining and promoting export competitiveness. This explains the most interesting feature of Belgian and Dutch economic strategies during the 1980s, which is not the exchange rate policy per se but rather the draconian wage policies and myriad government expenditure programs used to shift value added from labor to industry. As the data for short-term exchange rate variability reveal, exchange rate targeting was relatively consistent for both Belgium and the Netherlands across the 1970s and 1980s. The decisive change was in the government imposition of competitiveness measures. And it is the success of such measures that explains both countries' successful participation in the EMS.

Credibility versus Real Convergence

The notion that monetary integration is enlisted in the service of broader economic development strategies begs the question of how monetary integration is related to economic structure: Are there structural prerequisites for participation in EMU, or is something else more important? Put another way, was the Irish pound condemned to follow sterling in the 1992 devaluation, or could it have held onto its peg within the ERM? Is the Portuguese escudo inextricably bound to the Spanish peseta, or can the Portuguese government chart its own fate in European currency markets?

The answer to such questions lies in the notion of credibility suggested by Handler and Hochreiter in Chapter 1. Credibility in this sense refers to three elements: the internal consistency of the broader political and economic strategy for modernization, diversification, or liberalization; the importance of monetary integration to that strategy; and the domestic political support for the strategy. "Credibility" exists (or is perceived) when the strategy is internally consistent, when monetary integration is central to its success, and when it benefits from broad political support. In other words, Austrian hard currency policy is credible "in the markets" because the broader strategy for consensual macroeconomic policy making is internally consistent; because the hard currency plays an important role in Austrian price stability, wage bargaining, and export pricing; and because the consensual basis for Austrian macroeconomic policy enjoys widespread support (Katzenstein, 1984).

Market credibility in this framework is a more complicated notion than what might be called the pure political determination to support a hard-currency regime. Yet at the same time, this more complicated understanding fits better with the observation that market credibility is hard to obtain and easy to lose—to borrow from Handler and Hochreiter, credibility has to be earned. At each step along the way, market makers will test different aspects of credibility, looking for inconsistencies in the broader strategy, a willingness to sacrifice exchange rate policy for other instruments, or a wavering in political support.

Seen this way, the speculative attack on the Irish pound was only a test of credibility, not a decisive defeat. The authors of Chapter 6 claim that the Irish government's determination to remain in the ERM signaled the importance of exchange rate policy to the country's broader economic objectives. Ultimately, the strength of the markets prevailed and the Irish currency was forced to devalue. Irish credibility in the markets increased nevertheless.

Built into this notion of market credibility is an idiosyncratic notion of the economic costs and benefits of a particular currency regime, rather than a notion of costs and benefits derived purely from economic structures. In this way, national estimations of the net benefits to be had from monetary integration are more important than general structural analyses. And this seems to be a better approximation of reality. Consider, for example, the Danish and Austrian cases. As Handler and Hochreiter have demonstrated, Austria has suffered from a number of asymmetric shocks. In Chapter 3, Iversen and Thygesen suggest that Denmark also has experienced significant asymmetries. Nevertheless, both countries remain credibly fixed within the ERM.

The same claim can be made even more strongly with respect to Portugal. As Chapter 8 explains, that country joined the ERM just before the exchange rate crises of 1992 and 1993, and the economy moved into recession. The decision to join the ERM was part of a larger strategy for liberalization and structural reform. The combination of exchange rate turmoil and European recession almost upset the consensus in favor of reform. Instead, however, participation in the ERM provided an important learning opportunity for Portuguese policy makers, and one that confirmed their original objectives. Rather than abandoning monetary integration, they reinforced their efforts for liberalization and reform from within the context of the hard-currency regime. And while the escudo ultimately followed the peseta in its devaluations within the ERM, the determination of Portuguese monetary authorities to support their government's modernization and liberalization strategies has increased Portuguese exchange rate credibility in the marketplace.

Adjustment: Flexibility, Consensus, Distributional Coalitions

The third element of credibility, domestic political support, perhaps deserves special treatment. The reason for this is that political support depends on the balance between winners and losers from the broader strategy as well as on the institutional framework within which distributional concerns are structured. This is true in general terms but is perhaps most evident with respect to economic adjustment. Any economic shock requires an economic adjustment. And the manipulation of exchange rate policy is only one instrument for facilitating such an adjustment. The pertinent question to ask is not whether the exchange rate should be retained as an instrument for adjustment, but rather how it should best be used as part of an adjustment strategy. Should the exchange rate be used as a lever to force economic change, or should it be relied on as a benchmark against which changes in other instruments are measured?

The dichotomy between "benchmark" and "lever" is central to discussions of exchange-rate policy as well as to German notions of *ordnungspolitik* (rule-based politics) embedded in the EMU project. Put another way, can a government achieve better results by fixing the exchange rate and other monetary variables as a "rule" while creating the conditions for markets to adjust within the constraints imposed by the exchange rate or monetary rule? Or is a government better advised to use monetary variables to move markets? The Portuguese experience during the early 1990s suggests that exchange rate policy offers a better benchmark than lever. The case studies of other countries support this view.

In the recent experiences of Austria, the Netherlands, and Belgium, there is repeated evidence that the exchange rate works best as a reference point for making adjustments or as a rule around which markets adjust. Indeed, this point is explicit in the Dutch decision to switch from a fixed but adjustable exchange rate within the ERM to a firm peg on the Deutschemark in the early 1980s. However, relying on the exchange rate as a benchmark leaves open the question of how economic adjustments are to be made.

The key to economic adjustment lies in labor market institutions and patterns for political decision making. As our case studies suggest, adjustment comes from flexibility, consensus, or at the dictates of a particular distributional coalition. For example, Chapter 8 argues that the Portuguese adjustment of the early 1990s was made through market changes in the wage rate. In other words, wage pressure decreased with the rise in unemployment, cushioning the fall in corporate profits and providing space for investment. The contrast can be seen in Austria of the early 1980s. When that country threatened to fall into recession, adjustment was made through consensual macroeconomic policy making, using centralized wage bargaining to induce real wage flexibility even before unemployment could make a substantial rise.

These two examples mark the extreme forms of labor market adjustment suggested by Calmfors and Driffil (1988), whose analysis focuses on the relationship between centralization in wage bargaining and unemployment. They claim that the relationship is bell-shaped, with the best employment outcomes coming from either very decentralized or very centralized wage bargaining. In this context, Portugal represents real wage flexibility in response to market forces, and Austria represents real wage flexibility as a result of a broader macroeconomic consensus. The area in between these two extremes is contested ground—neither wholly market driven nor purely consensual. Calmfors and Driffil suggest that such intermediate institutions offer poor opportunities for labor market adjustment.

Nevertheless, it is precisely in this middle ground that the distributional coalitions emphasized in Chapter 3 become important. Such coalitions not only bring forward broad economic strategies, they also determine how adjustment will be handled within those strategies. In the Danish case, the collapse of social partnership in the 1970s sparked a distributional conflict between labor and capital, sheltered and exposed sectors, low-skilled workers and the highly skilled. The conflict ended with a victory of the center-right, representing capital, traded-goods manufacturing, and highly skilled labor. As a result, the decision to harden the Danish krone within the EMS was embedded in a larger strategy for adjustment, redistributing income from left to right.

The Belgian and Dutch stories parallel closely the distributional conflicts witnessed in Denmark. There too, center-right coalitions came to power in the early 1980s and forcibly shifted the distribution of value added from labor to capital, and the distribution of investment resources from non-traded to traded-goods sectors. What is difficult to explain is why the left-of-center opposition gave up without enormous struggle. According to

Calmfors and Driffil (1988), such open conflict should have been the outcome given the structure of Belgian and Dutch wage bargaining and labor markets. Nevertheless, even in the contested area between market competition and centralized wage bargaining, there appears to be some mechanism for adjustment.

That mechanism for adjustment has been suggested by R.E. Rowthorn (1992) as "a spirit of cooperation"—a willingness to accept the adjustment of resources dictated by the ruling coalition. For our purposes, this "spirit of cooperation" might be thought of as political credibility—a popular belief that the broader strategy implemented by the distributional coalition is likely to work. Such political credibility would explain how the center-right Danish cabinet could be returned twice to power and also why the center-right in Belgium and the Netherlands held office throughout much of the 1980s. The success of such political credibility in effecting adjustment within a rules-based macroeconomic framework also explains why countries are eager to adopt the *ordnungspolitk* embedded in EMU.

The "Disadvantages" of Tying One's Hands

At this point, we should be clear about the distinction between credibility and what has come to be known in the literature on monetary integration as the "advantages of tying one's hands." During the disinflation of the 1980s, one argument in support of participation in the EMS was that the discipline of the ERM constrained the choices available to policy makers. In the domestic context, this meant that politicians could deny accountability for certain aspects of their disinflation strategies by claiming that such measures were necessary for successful participation in the exchange rate regime.

In their preparations for EMU, policy makers appear to be suffering from the side effects of such "hand-tying." Electorates in countries such as Denmark, Finland and Sweden, for example, express concern that participation in EMU will spill over into other policy areas, forcing the government to make choices against the interests of large groups of society and in a manner that the affected groups cannot influence. Specific examples from the Nordic countries include women and public sector workers. However, the same logic might apply to all the cases reviewed here, and a list of affected groups would include everyone from Greek farmers to Portuguese textile workers.

The argument here is that while governments may have succeeded in escaping accountability for specific policy choices by claiming their hands were tied by European integration, the history of such claims makes it difficult for policy makers to sell European integration as an objective today. To illustrate this, it is perhaps easiest to focus on the Danish example. A large percentage of Danish elites backed the Maastricht Treaty, and a large share of the population backed the ruling coalition, but still a popular majority rejected Europe in the referendum. Danish elites were unable to convince voters about the merits of European integration because groups inside the ruling coalition feared the implications of monetary union for their own vested interests.

The Danish experience has not stopped politicians from hiding behind Europe or from overselling the virtues of integration. The example of Austrian accession discussed earlier is one instance. Another can be found in Belgium. There the Catholic-Socialist coalition has focused attention on EMU in order to diminish the importance of debates about decentralization and social welfare reform. The difference is that the Belgian government does not describe EMU as tying its hands but rather as an important objective in its own right. Such a strategy raises obvious questions about what will happen once membership is achieved or, even worse, if EMU does not take place.

Joining Europe's Monetary Club

The conclusion to our analysis is that EMU continues as a result of the congruence of national interests—not only as a European objective, but also as the means to fulfill national objectives. This does not rule out the possibility that national objectives ultimately may coincide. However, it does suggest that having the same vision of monetary union is not necessarily a prerequisite for viable integration. Although Europe may have internal political differences, these need not spill over into economic integration.

The point can be extended to economic interest as well as political interest. Monetary integration does not need to be the same thing to all countries in order to succeed. Rather, it just has to be the best thing for a given country's particular needs. Moreover, in most—if not all—of the countries we have surveyed, this appears to be the case. Virtually all of our contributors agree that monetary integration represents the best assignment of the exchange rate instrument in the context of larger strategies for modernization, liberalization, and diversification. In other words, there seems to be a consensus that EMU would make a valuable contribution to national economic strategies, albeit perhaps in different ways depending on the country.

The challenge will be to ensure that the other instruments used in the strategy are consistent with each other and with monetary union. This is the real question of convergence, and not the nominal convergence outlined in the Maastricht Treaty or the "real" convergence of economic structures from one country to the next. Moreover, part of this challenge will be to ensure that there is an adequate (and political acceptable) means of adjusting to economic shocks. All countries do not have to adjust in the same manner, but they all must have some means for adjusting.

The final challenge will be selling monetary integration to the electorate. This is perhaps the most difficult of all. What we might suggest is moderation. EMU is neither the source of all evil, nor the fount of all goodness. Monetary integration is a tool at least as much as it is an objective. And that means EMU is only as good as the politicians who use it.

A Note on Data
Sources and References

In order to provide up-to-date, comparable data for each of the national case studies, we have relied on four principal data sources. The Eurostat CD (Eurostat), the AMECO database of the European Commission (European Commission), the historical statistics of the OECD Economic Outlook (OECD), and the International Finance Statistics CD of the International Monetary Fund (IMF). In addition, we have asked our contributors to supplement these data sets with national sources where necessary. In each case, we have chosen to cite only the institution responsible for the raw data.

Maintaining an up-to-date list of references for a collection such as this is a daunting challenge as well. With respect to books and journal articles, we have taken an ecumenical approach and listed materials in any one of ten different languages. However, with respect to national newspapers we chose to exercise greater selectivity. Rather than cite foreign-language newspaper articles in the list of references, we have only mentioned them either in the text or in the notes.

References

Aaltonen, Ari, Esko Aurikko and Jarmo Kontulainen (1994). *Monetary Policy in Finland.* Helsinki: Bank of Finland.

Abert, James G. (1969). *Economic Policy and Planning in the Netherlands: 1950–1960.* New Haven: Yale University Press.

Akkermans, T., and P. W. M. Nobelen, eds. (1983). *Corporatisme en verzorgingsstaat.* Antwerp: Stenfert Kreuse.

Alesina, Alberto, and Roberto Perotti (1995). "The Political Economy of Budget Deficits." *IMF Staff Papers* 42:1 (March), pp. 1–31.

Alogoskoufis, George S. (1992). "Monetary Accommodation, Exchange Rate Regimes and Inflation Persistence." *Economic Journal* 102 (May), pp. 461–480.

Alogoskoufis, George S., and Apostolis Philippopoulos (1992). "Inflationary Expectations, Political Parties and the Exchange Rate Regime: Greece 1958–89." *European Journal of Political Economy* 8 (June), pp. 375–399.

Andersson, Jan-Otto, Pekka Kosonen, and Juhana Vartiainen (1993). "The Finnish Model of Economic and Social Policy—From Emulation to Crash." *Working Paper* (Ser. A:401) Helsinki: Nationalekonomiska Institutionen, Åbo Akademi.

Argy, Victor, and Paul De Grauwe, eds. (1990). *Choosing an Exchange Rate Regime: The Challenge for Smaller Industrial Countries.* Washington, D.C.: International Monetary Fund.

Arndt, Sven, ed. (1982). *The Political Economy of Austria.* Washington, D.C.: American Enterprise Institute.

Arpa, Markus (1995). "The Credibility of the EMS and Speculative Attacks." Mimeo.

Assarsson, Bengt, and Clas Olsson (1993). "Makroekonomiska chocker och ekonomisk struktur." *EG-konsekvensutredningen, Samhällsekonomi.* Stockholm: Statens Offentliga Utredningar.

Baker, Terry (1993). "Manufacturing Output and Employment by Market Area." *Economic and Social Research Institute, Quarterly Economic Commentary* (Spring), pp. 32–56.

Baker, Terry, David Duffy, and Delma Duggan (1996). "The Manufacturing Sector" in Baker, Fitzgerald, and Honohan (1996), pp. 174–221.

Baker, Terry, John Fitzgerald, and Patrick Honohan, eds. (1996). *Economic Implications for Ireland of EMU.* Dublin: ESRI.

Bakker, A., and M. M. P. van Lent (1989). *Pieter Lieftinck 1902–1989: Een leven in vogelvlucht.* Utrecht: Veen uitgevers.

Bannon, Seamus (1996). "EMU and Ireland's Sterling Trade." Paper presented to the Statistical and Social Inquiry Society of Ireland (28th March).

Barber, Lionel (1995). "1997 Is Dead—but EMU Is Far from Buried." *Financial Times* (21 June), p. 2.

Barbosa, António P., and José A. Machado (1996). "O Custo da Desinflação Portuguesa: uma Nota." *Boletim Económico Trimestral do Banco de Portugal* 46 (September), pp. 47–50.

Barrell, Ray, ed. (1992). *Economic Convergence and Monetary Union in Europe.* London: Sage Publications.

Barrell, R., J. Morgan, and N. Pain (1995). "The Employment Effects of the Maastricht Fiscal Criteria." *Discussion Paper No. 81.* London: National Institute for Economic and Social Research.

Barros, Pedro P., and José Mata (1996). "Competition Policy in Portugal." *Working Paper 15/96.* Lisbon: Banco de Portugal (September).

Barry, Franc, and Michael Devereux (1995). "The 'Expansionary Fiscal Contraction' Hypothesis: A Neo-Keynesian Analysis." *Oxford Economic Papers* 47:2 (April), pp. 249–264.

Bayoumi, Tamim, and Barry Eichengreen (1992a). "Is There a Conflict between EC Enlargement and European Monetary Unification?" *Working Paper No. 3950.* Cambridge: National Bureau for Economic Research.

Bayoumi, Tamim and Barry Eichengreen (1992b). "Shocking Aspects of European Monetary Unification." *Discussion Paper No. 643.* London: Centre for Economic Policy Research.

Bean, Charles (1992). "Economic and Monetary Union in Europe." *Journal of Economic Perspectives* 6:4, pp. 31–52.

Belgian National Bank (1989). *Report 1989.* Brussels: BNB.

Belgian National Bank (1990). *Report 1990.* Brussels: BNB.

Bergström, Hans (1987). *Rivstart? Om övergangen från opposition till regering.* Stockholm: Tiden.

Berk, J. M. and C. C. A. Winder (1994). "Price Movements in the Netherlands and Germany and the Guilder D-mark Peg." *De Economist* 142:1, pp. 63–74.

Bermeo, Nancy (1994). "Comments on Francisco Torres and Guillermo de la Dehesa," in John Williamson, ed., *The Political Economy of Policy Reform.* Washington, D.C.: Institute for International Economics, pp. 197–206.

Bertola, Giuseppe, and Allan Drazen (1993). "Trigger Points and Budget Cuts: Explaining the Role of Fiscal Austerity." *American Economic Review* 83:1 (March), pp. 11–26.

Blanchard, Olivier J. (1990). "Comment on Giavazzi and Pagano." *NBER Macroeconomic Annual 5.* Cambridge: National Bureau for Economic Research, pp. 111–116

Blanchard, Olivier J., and Juan F. Jimeno (1995). "Structural Unemployment: Spain versus Portugal." *American Economic Review, Papers and Proceedings* 85:2, pp. 212–18.

Blanchard, Olivier J. and Lawrence F. Katz (1992). "Regional Evolutions." *Brookings Papers on Economic Activity* 1, pp. 1–75.

Bohets, Jan (1995). "Nationale Bank bijt van zich af." *De Standaard* (17 August), p. 1.

Böhm, Bernhard, and Lionello F. Punzo, eds. (1994). *Economic Performance—A Look at Austria and Italy.* Heidelberg: Physica-Verlag.

Bordes, Christian (1993). "The Finnish Economy: The Boom, the Debt, the Crisis and the Prospects," in Bordes et al. (1993), pp. 9–94.

Bordes, Christian, David Currie, and Hans Tson Söderström (1993). *Three Assessments of Finland's Economic Crisis and Economic Policy.* Helsinki: Bank of Finland.

Bosman, Hans J. (1984). "Monetary Policy in the Netherlands in the Post-Smithsonian Era." *Occasional Papers No. 43a.* Tilburg: Société Universitaire Européenne de Recherches Financières.

Bradley, John (1977). "Lags in the Transmission of Inflation." *Economic and Social Review* 8:2 (January), pp. 149–154.

Bradley, John, and Karl Whelan (1992). "Irish Experience of Monetary Linkages with the UK and Developments Since Joining the EMS" in Barrell (1992), pp. 121–143.

Brakman, S., J. de Haan, and C. J. Jepma (1991). "Is de gulden hard genog?" *Economische Statistisch Berichten* (2 June), pp. 16–20.

Brandner, Peter, and Alfred Jaeger (1992). "Zinsniveau und Zinsstruktur in Österreich." Mimeo. Vienna: WIFO (September).

Breuss, Fritz, Alois Guger, and Gerhard Lehner (1995). "Das Konsolidierungsvorhaben der Bundesregierung—gesamtwirtschaftliche Wirkungen." *WIFO-Monatsberichte* 68:1 (January), pp. 24–30.

Breuss, Fritz, Heinz Handler, and Jan Stankovsky, eds. (1988). *Österreichische Optionen einer EG-Annäherung und ihre Folgen.* Wien: WIFO.

Breuss, Fritz, and Fritz Schebeck (1995). "Budgetkonsolidierung in kurz- und mittelfristiger Sicht." *WIFO-Monatsberichte* 68:4 (April), pp. 270–274.

Browne, Franc, and Donal McGettigan (1993). "Another Look at the Causes of Irish Unemployment." *Technical Paper 1/RT/93.* Dublin: Central Bank of Ireland.

Buiter, Willem H. (1996). "Two Cheers for EMU." *European Economic Perspectives 9.* London: Center for Economic Policy Research (July), pp. 5–7.

Buiter, Willem, Giancarlo Corsetti, and Nouriel Roubini (1993). "Excessive Deficits: Sense and Nonsense in the Treaty of Maastricht." *Economic Policy* 16 (April), pp. 57–100.

Bundesministerium für Finanzen (1996). "Österreichisches Konvergenzprogramm." Mimeo. Vienna: Bundesministerium für Finanzen, (21 May).

Busch, Georg M. (1995). "Budgetkonsolidierung—Fast alles bleibt noch zu tun." *Wirtschaftspolitische Blätter* 2, pp. 86–91.

Cabie, I. (1994). "L'économie néerlandaise: forces et faiblesses." *Notes économiques (de Banque Paribas)* 4 (June).

Cadilhe, Miguel (1990). "Luzes e Sombras da UEM." *Revista da Banca* 16, pp. 199–214.

Callan, Tim, and John Fitzgerald (1989). "Price Determination in Ireland: Effects of Changes in Exchange Rates and Exchange Rate Regimes." *Economic and Social Review* 20:2 (January), pp. 165–188.

Calmfors, Lars (1990a). "Wage Formation and Macroeconomic Policy in the Nordic Countries: A Summary," in Calmfors (1990b), pp. 11–62.

Calmfors, Lars (1990b). *Wage Formation and Macroeconomic Policy in the Nordic Countries.* Oxford: Oxford University Press.

Calmfors, Lars, and John Driffill (1988). "Centralization of Wage Bargaining." *Economic Policy: A European Forum* 6, pp. 13–47.

Cantillon, Sara, John Curtis, and John Fitzgerald, eds. (1994). *Economic Perspectives for the Medium Term.* Dublin: ESRI.

Carlsson, Stig, ed. (1991). *Arbetarrörelsen och den ekonomiska politiken.* Stockholm: Tiden.

Carnegy, Hugh (1995a). "Central Bank of Sweden Backs Emu." *Financial Times* (16 June), p. 3.

Carnegy, Hugh (1995b). "Nordic States March to Different EU Tunes." *Financial Times* (5 July), p. 3.

Cavaglia, S. M. F. G., K. G. Koedijk and P. J. G. Vlaar (1994). "Exchange Rate Risk Premia in the European Monetary System." *Open Economies Review* 5, pp. 347–360.

Central Bank of Ireland (1986). *Central Bank of Ireland Quarterly Report* 3 (Autumn).

Central Bank of Ireland (1987). *Central Bank of Ireland Annual Report.* Dublin: Central Bank of Ireland Publications.

Central Bank of Ireland (1992). *Central Bank of Ireland Quarterly Report* 4 (Winter).

Central Bank of Ireland (1994). *Central Bank of Ireland Annual Report.* Dublin: Central Bank of Ireland Publications.

Central Statistics Office (1980). *Statistical Abstract of Ireland.* Dublin: Government Stationary Office (GSO).

Central Statistics Office (1987). *Statistical Abstract of Ireland.* Dublin: GSO.

Central Statistics Office (1994a). *The Census of Industrial Production.* Dublin: GSO.

Central Statistics Office (1994b). *National Income and Expenditure Accounts.* Dublin: GSO.

Central Statistics Office (1995a). *Statistical Abstract of Ireland.* Dublin: GSO.

Central Statistics Office (1995b). *Trade Statistics of Ireland.* Dublin: GSO.

Chambers of Commerce of Ireland (1995). *Economic and Monetary Union: The Business Survey.* Dublin: Chambers of Commerce of Ireland.

Chouraqui, Jean-Claude, Robert Hagermann, and Nicola Sartor (1990). "Indicators of Fiscal Policy: A Reassessment." *Working Paper No. 78.* Paris: OECD.

Commission of the European Communities (1992). *Economic Studies No. 8: Netherlands* Brussels: Commission of the European Communities.

Commission of the European Communities (1993). "Growth Competitiveness, Employment: The Challenges and Ways Forward into the 21st Century." *White Paper.* Volume C. Luxembourg: European Communities.

Commission of the European Communities (1995). *European Economy* 60 (July).

Commission of the European Communities (1996). "Report on Convergence in the European Union." Brussels: Commission of the European Communities (November).

Compston, Hugh (1994). "Union Participation in Economic Policy-making in Austria, Switzerland, the Netherlands, Belgium, and Ireland: 1970–1992." *West European Politics* 17:1 (January), pp. 123–145.

Considine, John (1996). "Deficit Based Measures of Irish Fiscal Policy." Mimeo. University College Cork.

Crotty, Raymond (1987). *Ireland in Crisis: A Study on Capitalist Colonial Under-development.* Second Edition. Cork: Brandon Press.

Currie, David (1993). "The Finnish Economic Crisis: Analysis and Prescription," in Bordes et al. (1993), pp. 95–134.

Curtis, John, and John Fitzgerald (1994). "Convergence in an Open Labor Market." *Working Paper No. 45.* Dublin: ESRI.

De Cecco, Marcello (1983). *International Economic Adjustment—Small Countries and the European Monetary System.* Oxford: Basil Blackwell.

de Clerq, Willy (1978). "Le franc belge, monnaie forte." Speech given before the Belgo-German association (19 April).

De Fontenay, Patrick, Giorgio Gomel, and Eduard Hochreiter, eds. (1995). *Western Europe in Transition: The Impact of the Opening Up of Eastern Europe and the Former Soviet Union—Selected Case Studies.* Rome: Banca d'Italia.

De Grauwe, Paul (1992). *The Economics of Monetary Integration.* Oxford: Oxford University Press.

De Grauwe, Paul (1994). *The Economics of Monetary Integration.* Second edition. Oxford: Oxford University Press.

De Grauwe, Paul, and Wim Vanhaverbeke (1991). "Is Europe an Optimum Currency Area? Evidence from Regional Data." *Discussion Paper No. 555.* London: Centre for Economic Policy Research.

Dehaene, Jean-Luc (1995). *Sleutels voor morgen.* Hasselt: Esopus.

Demekas, D. and Z. Kontolemis (1996) "Unemployment in Greece: A Survey of the Issues" *IMF Working Paper* 96/91 (August).

den Dunnen, Emile (1973). "Monetary Policy in the Netherlands," in K. Holbik, ed. *Monetary Policy in Twelve Industrial Countries.* Boston: Federal Reserve Bank of Boston, pp. 282–328.

den Dunnen, Emile (1979). "Postwar Monetary Policy." *De Economist* 127:1, pp. 21–57.

den Hartog, H., and H. S. Tjan (1976). "Investments, Wages, Prices and the Demand for Labour: A Clay-Clay Vintage Model for the Netherlands." *De Economist* 124:1/2, pp. 32–54.

Despiegelaere, Guido (1995). "De staat van de welvaart." *Knack* 25:17 (26 April–2 May) pp. 14–20.

de Wolff, P., and W. Driehuis (1980). "A Description of Post War Economic Developments and Economic Policy in the Netherlands," in Richard T. Griffiths, ed. *The Economy and Politics of the Netherlands since 1945.* The Hague: Martinus Nijhoff, pp. 13–60.

Dillén, Mats, Klas-Göran Larsson and Jens Matthiessen (1994). "Den offentliga skulden." *Långtidsutredningen 1995.* Stockholm: Finansdepartementet.

Dornbusch, Rudiger (1989). "Credibility, Debt and Unemployment: Ireland's Failed Stabilization." *Economic Policy* 8 (April), pp. 173–209.

Dowling, Brendan (1989). "Issues in Debt Policy." *Irish Banking Review* (Winter), pp. 3–16.

Doyle, Maurice (1992). "From EMS to EMU: The Case of Ireland." *Central Bank of Ireland Quarterly Report* 4 (Winter), pp. 43–53.

Doyle, Maurice (1994). "Monetary Policy after the Narrow Band." *Central Bank of Ireland Annual Report* 1 (Spring), pp. 47–52.

Driehuis, W., and A. van der Zwan, eds. (1978). *De voorbereiding van het economische beleid kritisch bezien.* Leiden: H. E. Stenfert Kroese.

Due, Jesper, and Jørgen Steen Madsen (1988). *Når der slås søm i: Overenskomstforhandlinger* og organisationsstruktur. Copenhagen: Jurist og Økonomforbundets Forlag.

Due, Jesper, Jørgen Steen Madsen, Carsten Strøby Jensen, and Lars Kjerulf Petersen (1994). *The Survival of the Danish Model. A Historical Sociological Analysis of the Danish System of Collective Bargaining.* Copenhagen: DJØF.

Duggan, Delma, John Fitzgerald, Justin Johnson, and Jane Kelly (1996). "The Macroeconomy in Stable Conditions," in Baker, Fitzgerald, and Honohan (1996), pp. 50–104.

Eizenga, Wietze (1983). "The Independence of the Federal Reserve System and of the Netherlands Bank: A Comparative Analysis." *SUERF Series No. 41a.* Tilburg: Société Universitaire Européenne de Recherches Financières.

Emerson, Michael, et al. (1992). *One Market, One Money: An Evaluation of the Potential Benefits and Costs of Forming an Economic and Monetary Union.* Oxford: Oxford University Press.

Eurobarometer (1994). *Public Opinion in the European Union* 41 (July).

Eurobarometer (1996). *Public Opinion in the European Union* 44 (Spring).

European Monetary Institute (1996). "Progress Towards Convergence: 1996." Francfürt: European Monetary Institute (November).

Eyskens, Gaston (1993). *De Memoires.* Collected and edited by Jozef Smits. Tielt: Lannoo.

Farnleitner, Johann (1994). "Die Rolle der Wirtschaftskammer—Organisation nach einem EU Beitritt." *Wirtschaftspolitische Blätter* 1, pp. 25–30.

Fase, M. M. G. (1987). "Dutch Monetarism in Retrospect." *Reprint No. 228.* Amsterdam: De Nederlandsche Bank.

Fase, M. M. G. (1992). "A Century of Monetary Thought in the Netherlands." *Reprint No. 321.* Amsterdam: De Nederlandsche Bank.

Fase, M. M. G., and G. J. de Bondt (1994). "Duitsland als spil van economische activiteit." *Economisch Statistische Berichten* 79:3978 (28 September), pp. 864–868.

Feinstein, Charles, ed. (1993). *Banking, Currency and Finance in Europe between the Wars.* Oxford: Oxford University Press.

Fessel + GFK—Institut für Marktforschung (1995). "EU-Einstellung 1 Jahr nach der Volksabstimmung." Wien: Bundesministeriums für wirtschaftliche Angelegenheiten.

Finansdepartementet (1994). "Sveriges ekonomiska geografi." *Långtidsutredningen 1995.* Stockholm: Finansdepartementet.

Finansdepartementet (1993). "Reviderad nationalbudget." *Regeringens proposition 1992/93: 150.* Stockholm: Finansdepartementet.

Fischer, Stanley (1982). "Seigniorage and the Case for a National Money." *Journal of Political Economy* 90:2 (April), pp. 295–313.

Forsman, P., P. Haaparanta and T. Heinonen (1993). "Kelluva kiwi ja uppoava emu—kokemuksia kelluvasta valuuttakurssista." *Kansantaloudellinen aikakauskirja* 2, pp. 183–191.

Frieden, Jeffry (1991). "Invested Interests: The Politics of National Economic Policies in a World of Global Finance." *International Organization* 45:4 (Autumn), pp. 425–451.

Frieden, Jeffry, Daniel Gros and Erik Jones Erik, eds. (forthcoming). *The New Political Economy of EMU.* Boulder: Rowman and Littlefield, forthcoming.

Frisch, Helmut (1983). "Stabilization Policy in Austria 1970–80," in De Cecco (1983), pp. 117–140.

Froats, Daniel K. (1995). "Sozialpartnerschaft und Hartwährungspolitik: Political Prerequisites and Effects of the Austrian Hard Currency Policy, and Implications for Post-Maastricht Monetary Union in Europe," in Hochreiter (1995), pp. 5–26.

Gallagher, Michael, and Dermot McAleese (1994). "Ireland's Trade Dependency on the UK." *Irish Banking Review* (Spring), pp. 16–28.

Gaspar, Vítor, and Alfredo M. Pereira (1995). "The Impact of Financial Integration and Unilateral Public Transfers on Investment and Growth in EC Capital Importing Countries." *Journal of Development Economics* 48, pp. 43–66.

Geary, Patrick (1976). "Irish Prices and the Inflationary Process in a Small Open Economy—The Case of Ireland." *Economic and Social Review* 7:4 (July), pp. 391–400.

Geary, Patrick, and Patrick Honohan (1995). "Can Better Contracts Help Solve Ireland's Sterling Dependence." Paper presented to the Dublin Economic Workshop (14th October).

Genser, Bernd, and Robert Holzmann (1995). "Die österreichische Finanzpolitik vor dem EU-Beitritt." *Forschungsbericht 9501.* Wien: Ludwig Bolzmann Institut (February).

Giavazzi, Francesco, and Marco Pagano (1990). "Can Severe Fiscal Contractions be Expansionary? Tales of Two Small European Economies." *NBER Macroeconomics Annual 5.* Cambridge: National Bureau for Economic Research, pp. 75–116.

Gibson, Norman, and John Spencer, eds. (1977). *Economic Activity in Ireland, A Study of Two Open Economies.* Dublin: Gill and Macmillan.

Giovannini, Alberto (1990). "European Monetary Reform: Progress and Prospects." *Brookings Papers on Economic Activity* 2, pp. 217–91.

Gladdish, Ken (1991). *Governing from the Center: Politics and Policy-making in the Netherlands.* DeKalb: Northern Illinois University Press.

Gnan, Ernest (1995). "Austria's Hard Currency Policy and European Monetary Integration." *De Pecunia* 6:3, pp. 28–72.

Golden, Miriam, and Michael Wallerstein (1995). "Unions, Employers, and Collective Bargaining: A Report on Data for 16 Countries from 1950 to 1990." Paper presented at the 1995 annual meeting of the Midwest Political Science Association. Chicago, (6–8 April).

Goosens, Paul (1995). "Het begint met vuurwerk." *Knack* 25:17 (26 April–2 May), pp. 22–26.

Goul-Andersen, Jørgen (1989). "Social Klasse og Parti," in Jørgen Elklit and Ole Tonsgaard, eds., *To Folketingsvalg.* Aarhus: Politica.

Goul-Andersen, Jørgen (1992). "The Decline of Class Voting Revisited," in Peter Gundelach and Karen Siune, eds., *From Voters to Participants.* Copenhagen: Politica, pp. 91–107.

Graafland, J.J. (1992). "Insiders and Outsiders in Wage Formation: The Dutch Case." *Empirical Economics* 17:4, pp. 583–602.

Greenaway, D., and C. R. Milner (1986). *The Economics of Intra-Industry Trade.* Oxford: Basil Blackwell.

Grilli, Vittorio, Donato Masciandaro, and Guido Tabellini (1991). "Political and Monetary Institutions and Public Financial Policies in the Industrialized Countries." *Economic Policy* 13 (October), pp. 341–392.

Gros, Daniel (1996a). "A Reconsideration of the Cost of EMU: The Importance of External Shocks and Labor Mobility." Mimeo. Brussels: Centre for European Policy Studies.

Gros, Daniel (1996b). "Towards Economic and Monetary Union: Problems and Prospects." *CEPS Paper No. 65.* Brussels: Centre for European Policy Studies.

Gros, Daniel and Niels Thygesen (1992). *European Monetary Integration: From the European Monetary System to European Monetary Union.* London: Longmans.

Gros, Daniel and Guy Vandille (1995). "The European Trade Structure." Manuscript. Brussels: Centre for Economic Policy Research.

Gugler, Klaus, Heinz Handler, and Manfred Schekulin (1995). "Central European as an Economic Area? Prospects for Further Economic Integration." *Working Paper No. 81.* Wien: WIFO.

Gylfason, Thorvaldur (1990). "Exchange Rate Policy, Inflation, and Unemployment: The Nordic EFTA Countries," in Victor Argy and Paul De Grauwe, eds., *Choosing an Exchange Rate Regime: The Challenge for Smaller Industrial Countries.* Washington D.C.: International Monetary Fund, pp. 163–192.

Haaparanta, P., and T. Heinonen (1991). "Finland and EMS: Some Evidence on Symmetries and Asymmetries." *Working Paper No. F269.* Helsinki: Helsinki School of Economics.

Haavisto, T. and L. Jonung (1993). "Off Gold and Back Again: Finnish and Swedish Monetary Experiences in 1914–25," in Feinstein (1993).

Handler, Heinz (1989). *Grundlagen der österreichischen Hartwährungspolitik: Geldstabilisierung, Philipskurve, Unsicherheit.* Wien: Manz.

Handler, Heinz ed. (1996). *Wirtschaftsstandort Österreich: Wettbewerbsstrategien für das 21. Jahrhundert.* Wien: Bundesministerium für wirtschaftliche Angelegenheiten, Sektion Wirtschaftspolitik (February).

Handler, Heinz, and Eduard Hochreiter (1996). "The Austrian Economy in the Wake of Joining the EU." *Working Document No. 103.* Brussels: Centre for European Policy Studies (June).

Handler, Heinz, Gustav Stifter, and Klaus Wiedner (1995). "Market Power of Food Retailers in Austria: General Legal and Economic Conditions." Paper presented to the European Competition Forum, Brussels (April).

Hansson, P. (1989). "Intra-Industry Trade: Measures, Determinants and Growth." *Economic Studies No. 205.* Umeå: University of Umeå.

Hibbs, Douglas and Håkan Locking (1991). "Løneutjamning och loneokningstakt under den solidariske lonepolitiken." *Ekonomisk Debatt* 8, pp. 653–64.

Hilbers, P., and G. Wolswijk (1994). "Den Haag en Maastricht." *Economisch Statistische Berichten* 79:3981 (19 October), pp. 947–949.

Hochreiter, Eduard (1994a). "Austria's Role as a Bridge Between Eastern and Western Europe," in OECD (1994b), pp. 63–71.

Hochreiter, Eduard (1994b). "Reflections on Central Bank Independence and Monetary Policy, the Case of Austria," in Böhm and Punzo (1994), pp. 198–207.

Hochreiter, Eduard, ed. (1995). "Austrian Exchange Rate Policy and European Monetary Integration." *Working Paper No. 19.* Wien: Oesterreichische Nationalbank.

Hochreiter, Eduard, and Adalbert Knöbl (1991). "Austria's and Finland's Exchange Rate Policy—Two Examples of a Peg." *De Pecunia* 2, pp. 33–61.

Hochreiter, Eduard, and Aurel Schubert (1990). "The Management of Economic Power in Selected OECD Countries—Austria, Canada, and Sweden," in Salvatore (1990) pp. 133–168.

Hochreiter, Eduard, and Georg Winckler (1995a). "The Advantages of Tying Austria's Hands: The Success of the Hard Currency Strategy." *European Journal of Political Economy* 11, pp. 83–111.

Hochreiter, Eduard, and Georg Winckler (1995b). "Signaling a Hard Currency Strategy: The Case of Austria." *Kredit und Kapital* 13, pp. 163–184.

Holmlund, B. (1993). "Arbetslösheten—konjunkturfenomen eller systemfel?" Expert Report No.12 to the Economic Commission. Stockholm: Allmänna Förlaget.

Honohan, Patrick (1989). "Comment on Dornbusch (1989)." *Economic Policy* 8 (April), pp. 174–209.

Honohan, Patrick (1992). "Fiscal Adjustment in Ireland in the 1980s." *Economic and Social Review* 23:3 (April), pp. 285–314.

Honohan Patrick (1993). "An Examination of Irish Currency Policy." *Policy Research Series Paper No. 18.* Dublin: ESRI.

Honohan, Patrick (1994). "Costing the Delay in Devaluing 1992–3." *Irish Banking Review* (Spring), pp. 3–16.

Honohan, Patrick (1996). "Adapting to Regime Change," in Baker, Fitzgerald, and Honohan (1996), pp. 10–36.

Honohan, Patrick, and Charles Conroy (1994). "Irish Interest Rate Fluctuations in the European Monetary System." *General Research Series Paper No. 165.* Dublin: ESRI Banking Research Center.

Hutchinson, Robert (1996). "The Financial Services Sector," in Baker, Fitzgerald, and Honohan (1996), pp. 222–268.

International Monetary Fund (1979). *International Financial Statistics Yearbook.* Washington, D.C.: IMF.

International Monetary Fund (1994). *International Financial Statistics Yearbook.* Washington, D.C.: IMF.

Ireland (1992). *White Paper: Treaty on European Union.* Dublin: GSO.

Ireland (1985–1994). *Budget Books.* Dublin: GSO.

Irish Business and Employers Confederation (1995). *Changeover Scenario to the Single Currency, the position of Irish Business, An Interim Report.* Dublin: IBEC.

Ishiyama, Yoshihide (1975). "The Theory of Optimal Currency Areas: A Survey." *IMF Staff Papers* 22, pp. 344–383.

Italianer, Alexander (1993). "Mastering Maastricht: EMU Issues and How They Were Settled," in K. Gretschmann, ed., *Economic and Monetary Union: Implications for National Policy Makers*. Maastricht: European Institute for Public Administration, pp. 51–113.

Iversen, Torben (1996). "Power, Flexibility and the Breakdown of Centralized Wage Bargaining: The Cases of Denmark and Sweden in Comparative Perspective." *Comparative Politics*, 28:4 (July), pp. 399–436.

Johansen, Hans Christian (1987). *The Danish Economy in the Twentieth Century*. London: Croom Helm, 1987.

Jones, Erik (1995). "The Transformation of the Belgian State" in Patrick McCarthy and Erik Jones, eds., *Disintegration or Transformation: The Crisis of the State in Advanced Industrial Societies*. New York: St. Martin's, pp. 153–177.

Jonung, Lars ed. (1991). *The Stockholm School of Economics Revisited*. Cambridge: Cambridge University Press.

Joustra, Arend, and Erik van Venetië (1991). *Ruud Lubbers: Manager in de politiek*. Baarn: Sesam.

Karamouzis, N. (1995). "The Management of Pension Fund Assets." *Kathimerini* (21 May—in Greek).

Katzenstein, Peter (1984). *Corporatism and Change: Austria, Switzerland, and the Politics of Industry*. Ithaca: Cornell University Press.

Katzenstein, Peter (1985). *Small States in World Markets: Industrial Policy in Europe*. Ithaca: Cornell University Press.

Kavanagh, Ella (1997). "Irish Macroeconomic Performance Under Different Exchange Rate Regimes." *Journal of Economic Studies* 24:1/2, pp. 10–42.

Knöbl, Adalbert (1990). "EC-EFTA: Why Does Unemployment Differ?" *Working Paper No. 38*. Wien: WIFO.

Kollyntzas, T. (1995). "The Inertia of the Status Quo." *Epiloghi* (January—in Greek).

Korkman, Sixten (1978). "The Devaluation Cycle." *Oxford Economic Papers* 3 (November), pp. 357–366.

Korkman, Sixten (1980). "Exchange Rate Policy, Employment and External Balance." *Bank of Finland Series B:33*. Helsinki: Bank of Finland.

Korkman, Sixten (1992). "Exchange Rate Policy and Employment in Small Open Economies," in Pekkarinen, Pohjola, and Rowthorn (1992), pp. 298–337.

Kramer, Helmut (1993). "The Impact of the Opening-up of the East on the Austrian Economy." *Working Paper No. 11*. Wien: Oesterreichische Nationalbank, pp. 4–17.

Kristiansen, Michael, Thomas Larsen, and Michael Ulveman (1992). *Poul Schlüter, En Biografi*. Copenhagen: Spektrum.

Kuipers, S. K. and G. H. Kuper (1990). "De ontwikkeling van de Nederlandse economie in de eerste helft van de jaren negentig." *Maandschrift Economie* 54, pp. 425–38.

Kurzer, Paulette (1988). "The Politics of Central Banks: Austerity and Unemployment in Europe." *Journal of Public Policy* 8:1 (January-March), pp. 21–48.

Kurzer, Paulette (1993). *Business and Banking: Political Change and Economic Integration in Western Europe*. Ithaca: Cornell University Press.

Layard, Richard, Stephen Nickell, and Richard Jackman (1991). *Unemployment: Macroeconomic Performance and the Labor Market.* Oxford: Oxford University Press.

Leddin, Anthony (1991). "An Analysis of the Irish Unemployment Problem in the Context of EMS Membership." Mimeo. Limerick: University of Limerick.

Leddin, Anthony, and Jim O'Leary (1995). "Fiscal, Monetary and Exchange Rate Policy," in O'Hagan (1995), pp. 159–194.

Leddin, Anthony, and Brendan Walsh (1995). *The Macroeconomy of Ireland.* Third Edition. Dublin: Gill and Macmillan.

Lehner, Gerhard (1995). "Steuerreform und EU-Beitritt prägen den Bundeshaushalt 1994 und 1995." *WIFO-Monatsbericht* 68:4 (April), pp. 275–288.

Lester, Richard A. (1970 [1939]). *Monetary Experiments: Early American and Recent Scandinavian.* Princeton: Princeton University Press/David and Charles Reprints.

Lijphart, Arend (1969). "Consociational Democracy." *World Politics* 21:2, pp. 207–225.

Lijphart, Arend (1975). *The Politics of Accommodation: Pluralism and Democracy in the Netherlands.* Second Edition, Revised. Berkeley: University of California Press.

Lindbeck, Assar, Per Molander, Torsten Persson, Olof Petersson, Agnar Sandmo, Birgitta Svedenborg, and Niels Thygesen (1994). *Turning Sweden Around.* Cambridge: MIT Press.

Lindström, Ulf (1992). *Euro-Consent, Euro-Contract, or Euro-Coercion? Scandinavian Social Democracy, the European Impasse, and the Abolition of Things Political.* Oslo: Scandinavian University Press.

Ludlow, Peter (1982). *The Making of the European Monetary System: A Case Study of the Politics of the European Community.* London: Butterworths Scientific.

Ludlow, Peter (1994). "Public Opinion in the Nordic Candidate Countries: An Overview." *CEPS Paper No. 56.* Brussels: Centre for European Policy Studies.

Luz, Silvia, and Maximiano Pinheiro (1994). "Wage Rigidity and Job Mismatch in Europe." *Working Paper 2/94.* Lisbon: Banco de Portugal.

Macedo, Jorge Braga (1996). "Selling Stability at Home, Earning Credibility Abroad," in Francisco Torres, ed., *Monetary Reform in Europe. An Analysis of the Issues and Proposals for the Intergovernmental Conference.* Lisbon: Catholic University Press, pp. 23–58.

Mallekoote, P. M. and R. Th. L. Moonen (1994). "The Effect of Changes in Interest Rates on the Dutch Economy." *National Differences in Interest Rate Transmission.* Basle: Bank for International Settlements, pp. 179–196.

Martin, John (1996). "Measures of Replacement Rates for the Purpose of International Comparisons: A Note." *OECD Economic Studies* 26, pp. 99–115.

Masson, P. R. and M. P. Taylor (1992). "Common Currency Areas and Currency Unions: An Analysis of the Issues." *Discussion Paper No. 617.* London: Centre for Economic Policy Research.

McAleese, Dermot (1977). "The Foreign Sector," in Gibson and Spencer (1977), pp. 115–148.

McArdle, Pat (1994). "How Many Currencies does Europe Need?" Paper presented at the Kenmare Economic Policy Conference (14 October).

McKinnon, Ronald (1963). "Optimal Currency Areas." *American Economic Review* 53:4 (September), pp. 717–725.

McNamara, Kathleen (1993). "Systems Effects and the European Community," in Robert Jervis and Jack Snyder, eds., *Coping with Complexity in the International System.* Boulder: Westview Press, pp. 303–327.

Mielke, Seigfried, Peter Rütters, and Kurt P. Tudyka (1994). "Trade Union Organization and Employee Representation," in Wolfgang Lecher, ed. *Trade Unions in the European Union: A Handbook.* London: Lawrence and Wishart, pp. 129–233.

Milward, Alan S. (1992). *The European Rescue of the Nation-State.* London: Routledge.

Ministry of Finance (1992). "Portugal from P1 to Q2: A Strategy of Sustained Regime Change 1986–1995," abridged version in Francisco Torres and Francesco Giavazzi, eds. *A Single Currency for Europe: Monetary and Real Impacts.* London: CEPR Report (March).

Ministry of Finance (1993). "Contribuíção Portuguesa para o Livro Branco sobre o Crescimento, Competitividade e Emprego." Lisbon: Ministério das Finanças (October).

Ministry of Planning (1993). *Plano de Desenvolvimento Regional.* Lisbon: Secretaria de Estado do Planeamento e Desenvolvimento Regional (July).

Ministry of Planning (1996). *Grandes Opções do Plano para 1997.* Lisbon: Ministério do Equipamento, do Planeamento e da Administração do Território (October).

Mjøset, Lars (1986). *Norden Dagen Derpå.* Oslo: Universitetsforlaget.

Moses, Jonathon W. (1995a). "Bonded Polity: The Distributional Consequences of Relying More Heavily on Bond-Financed Social Policies." Paper presented at the 1995 Annual Meeting of the American Political Science Association (31 August–3 September).

Moses, Jonathon W. (1995b). "Devalued Priorities: The Politics of Nordic Exchange Rate Regimes Compared." Ph.D. dissertation. Los Angeles: University of California, Los Angeles.

Moses, Jonathon W. (1997). "Trojan Horses: Putnam, ECU Linkage, and the EU Ambitions of Nordic Elites." *Review of International Political Economy* 4:2 (Summer) pp. 382–415.

Moses, Jonathon W. and Anders Todal Jenssen (1998). "Nordic Accession: An Analysis of the EU Referendums," in Barry Eichengreen and Jeffry Frieden, eds. *Forging an Integrated Europe.* Ann Arbor: University of Michigan Press, pp. 211–246.

Mundell, Robert (1961). "A Theory of Optimum Currency Areas." *American Economic Review,* 51:4 (September), pp. 657–665.

Murray, Charles (1979a). "The European Monetary System: Implications for Ireland." *Central Bank of Ireland Annual Report* 1 (Spring), pp. 96–108.

Murray, Charles (1979b). "Living with the EMS." *Central Bank of Ireland Quarterly Bulletin* 4 (Winter) 62–70.

Nannestad, Peter (1991). *Danish Design or British Decease? Danish Economic Crisis Policy 1974 in Comparative Perspective.* Århus: Aarhus University Press.

National Economic and Social Council (1991). *The Economic and Social Implications of Emigration.* Dublin: National Economic and Social Council.

National Economic and Social Council (1992). *The Relationship between Employment and Growth in Ireland.* Dublin: National Economic and Social Council.

National Economic and Social Council (1993). *A Strategy for Competitiveness, Growth and Employment.* Dublin: National Economic and Social Council.

Nypels, Frans, and Kees Tamboer (1985). *Wim Kok: Vijftien jaar vakbeweging.* Raamgracht: Stichting FNV Pers.

O'Connell, Maurice (1995). "Presentation by Maurice O'Connell, Governor Central Bank of Ireland to the Monetary Sub-Committee of the European Parliament on 30 October, 1995." *Central Bank of Ireland Quarterly Report* 4 (Winter), pp. 53–58.

O'Connell, Philip, and J. J. Sexton (1994). "Labor Market Developments in Ireland, 1971–1993," in Cantillon, Curtis, and Fitzgerald (1994), pp. 3–41.

O'Hagan, John, ed. (1995). *The Economy of Ireland.* Dublin: Gill and Macmillan.

O'Leary, Eoin (1997). "The Convergence Performance of Ireland among EU Countries: 1960–1990." *Journal of Economic Studies* 24:1/2, pp. 43–58.

O'Leary, Jim (1993). "The Currency Crisis and its Aftermath: Prospects for Irish Interest Rates and the Irish Pound." Paper presented to the Institute of Chartered Accountants in Ireland, First Annual Conference (23rd April).

Olson, Mancur (1971). *The Logic of Collective Action: Public Goods and the Theory of Groups.* Cambridge: Harvard University Press.

Organization for Economic Cooperation and Development (1983). *Historical Statistics 1960–1981.* Paris: OECD.

Organization for Economic Cooperation and Development (1990). *Economic Survey: Netherlands.* Paris: OECD.

Organization for Economic Cooperation and Development (1991). *Historical Statistics 1960–1989.* Paris: OECD.

Organization for Economic Cooperation and Development (1992a). *Economic Outlook: Historical Statistics.* Paris: OECD.

Organization for Economic Cooperation and Development (1992b). *Economic Survey: Portugal.* Paris: OECD.

Organization for Economic Cooperation and Development (1993a). *Economic Outlook* 53 (June). Paris: OECD.

Organization for Economic Cooperation and Development (1993b). *OECD Reviews on Foreign Direct Investment: Sweden.* Paris: OECD.

Organization for Economic Cooperation and Development (1994a). *Economic Survey: Austria, 1993–1994.* Paris: OECD.

Organization for Economic Cooperation and Development (1994b). *New Economic Partners: Dynamic Asian Economies and Central and Eastern European Countries.* Paris: OECD.

Organization for Economic Cooperation and Development (1994c). *Economic Surveys: Netherlands.* Paris: OECD.

Organization for Economic Cooperation and Development (1994d). *The OECD Jobs Study.* Paris: OECD.

Organization for Economic Cooperation and Development (1995). *OECD Economic Survey: Ireland.* Paris: OECD.

Organization for Economic Cooperation and Development (1996a). *Economic Outlook*. Paris: OECD (December).

Organization for Economic Cooperation and Development (1996b). *Economic Survey: Portugal*. Paris: OECD.

Organization for Economic Cooperation and Development (1997). *Economic Outlook*. Paris: OECD (June).

O'Sullivan, Mary (1995). "Manufacturing and Global Competition" in O'Hagan (1995), pp. 363–396.

Pauer, Franz (1996). "Will Asymmetric Shocks Pose a Serious Problem in EMU?" *Working Paper No. 23*. Wien: Oesterreichische Nationalbank.

Pekkarinen, Jukka, Matti Pohjola, and Bob Rowthorn eds. (1992). *Social Corporatism: A Superior Economic System?* Oxford: Clarendon Press.

Plasser, Fritz, and Peter A. Ulram (1994). "Meinungstrends, Mobilisierung und Motivlagen bei der Volksabstimmung über den EU-Beitritt," in Anton Pelinka, ed. *EU-Referendum: Zur Praxis direkter Demokratie in Österreich*. Wein: Zentrum für angewandte Politikforschung, pp. 87–119.

Plavsak, Kristina (1995). "Why Did the Austrians Decide to Join the European Union? The Formation of Public Opinion Before the Austrian Referendum on EU Membership, 12 June 1994." Mimeo. Budapest: Central European University, Department of International Relations and European Studies (21 June).

Pollan, Wolfgang (1995). "Zur Entwicklung der Verbrauchpreise seit dem EU-Beitritt." *WIFO-Monatsberichte* 68:5 (May), pp. 329–332.

Pontusson, Jonas (1992). *The Limits of Social Democracy*. Ithaca: Cornell University Press.

Pontusson, Jonas, and Peter Swenson (1996). "Markets, Production, Institutions, and Politics: Why Swedish Employers have Abandoned the Swedish Model." *Comparative Political Studies* 29, pp. 223–50.

Quinn, Ruairi (1995). "Opening Address." *Proceedings of the Tenth Annual Conference of the Foundation for Fiscal Studies Dublin*. Dublin: Foundation for Fiscal Studies (6th October), pp. 1–3.

Riksgäldskontoret (1994). *Statistisk Årsbok*. Stockholm: Riksgäldskontoret.

Rowthorn, R. E. (1992). "Centralization, Employment, and Wage Dispersion." *Economic Journal* 102:412 (May), pp. 506–523.

Ruane, Frances, and Francis O'Toole (1995). "Taxation Measures and Policy," in O'Hagan (1995), pp. 127–158.

Salvatore, Dominic, ed. (1990). *Comparative Handbook of National Economic Policies*. New York: Greenwood Press.

Sandholtz, Wayne (1995). "Sweden's EU Accession: Domestic Dilemmas and Political Leadership." Manuscript. Department of Politics and Society, University of California Irvine.

Scarpetta, Stefano (1996). "Assessing the Role of Labor Market Policies and Institutional Settings on Unemployment: A Cross Country Study." *OECD Economic Studies* 26, pp. 43–98.

Scharpf, Fritz (1991). *Crisis and Choice in European Social Democracy*. Ithaca: Cornell University Press.

Schebeck, Fritz (1996). "Budgetkonsolidierung im Vorfeld der Verwicklung der Währungsunion: Mittelfristige Prognose der österreichischen Wirtschaft bis 2000." Manuscript. Vienna: WIFO (April).

Schebesch, Helene, and Andreas Wörgötter (1995). "Impact of Opening Up of Eastern Europe on Austria," in de Fontenay, Gomel, and Hochreiter (1995) pp. 58–107.

Schneider, Matthias (1995). "Bilanz der ersten Erfahrungen mit dem Gemeinsamen Agrarmarkt." *WIFO-Monatsberichte* 68:5 (May), pp. 333–339.

Scholten, Ilja (1987). "Corporatism and Neo-conservative Backlash in the Netherlands," in Ilja Scholten, ed. *Political Stability and Neo-corporatism: Corporatist Integration and Societal Cleavages in Western Europe.* London: Sage, pp. 120–152.

Schuberth, Helene, and Gert Wehinger (1997). "Costs of Monetary Union: Evidence of Monetary and Fiscal Effectiveness." Mimeo, Oesterreichische Nationalbank (24 July).

Seidel, Hans (1993). *Der Beirat für Wirtschafts- und Sozialfragen.* Stuttgart: Gustav Fischer Verlag for the Oesterreichisches Institut für Wirtschaftsforschung.

Silva, Aníbal A. Cavaco (1994). "Combinação de Políticas de Estabilização num Quadro de Integração: a Experiência Portuguesa." *Brotéria* 138: 5/6, pp. 493–515.

Siune, Karen (1993). "The Danes Said NO to the Maastricht Treaty: The Danish EC Referendum of June 1992." *Scandinavian Political Studies,* 16:1, pp. 93–103.

Siune, Karen, Palle Svensson, and Ole Tonsgaard (1994). "The European Union: The Danes Said 'No' in 1992 but 'Yes' in 1993: How and Why." *Electoral Studies* 13:2 (June), pp. 107–16.

Söderström, Hans Tson (1986). "Exchange Rate Strategies and Real Adjustment After 1970: The Experience of Smaller European Economies." *SNS Occasional Paper.* Stockholm: Center for Business and Policy Studies (February).

Söderström, Hans Tson (1993). "Finland's Economic Crisis: Causes, Present Nature, and Policy Option," in Bordes, Currier, and Söderström (1993), pp. 135–222.

Statens Offentliga Utredningar (1993). *Riksbanken och prisstabiliteten.* Stockholm: Statens Offentliga Utredningar.

Szász, A. (1993). "A Dutch Perspective," in P. Temperton, ed. *The European Currency Crisis: What Chance Now for a Single European Currency?* Cambridge: Cambridge University Press, pp. 199–205.

Tarkka, J. and J. Åkerholm (1992). "Fiscal Federalism and European Monetary Integration." *Bank of Finland Discussion Paper. No. 2.* Helsinki: Bank of Finland.

Tatom, John A. (1996). "Swiss Exchange Rate Appreciation and Domestic Economic Activity." Mimeo, Union Bank of Switzerland (March).

Thom, Rodney (1993). "The Influence of Sterling on Irish Interest Rates." *Working Paper No. 94/24.* Dublin: Center for Economic Research, University College Dublin.

Thom, Rodney (1995). "Irish Exchange Rate Policy Under Wide ERM Bands." *Working Paper No. 95/15.* Dublin: Center for Economic Research, University College Dublin.

Thygesen, Niels (1979). "Exchange Rate Experiences and Policies of Small Countries: Some European Examples of the 1970s." *Essays in International Finance No. 136.* Princeton: Princeton University (December).

Tiilikainen, Teija, and Ib Damgaard Petersen, eds. (1993). *The Nordic Countries and the EC.* Copenhagen: Copenhagen Political Studies Press.

Toirkins, S. J. (1989). "De Minister van Financiën: In het spanningsveld van financiële wensen en mogelijkheden," in R. B. Andeweg, ed., *Ministers en Ministerraad.* s'Gravenhage: Velotekst, pp. 127–145.

Torres, Francisco (1990). "Portugal, the EMS and 1992: Stabilization and Liberalization," in Paul De Grauwe and Lucas Papademos, eds., *The EMS in the 1990's.* London: Longman, pp. 225–246.

Torres, Francisco (1987). "Policy-Making in Small Open Economies." *Working Paper 10/87.* Lisbon: Faculdade de Economia e Ciências Empresariais, Universidade Católica Portuguesa.

Torres, Francisco (1994). "The European Periphery: Portugal," in John Williamson, ed., *The Political Economy of Policy Reform.* Washington, D.C.: Institute for International Economics, pp. 141–152.

Torres, Francisco (1995). "Portugal and the EMS: The Politics of Monetary Integration," in João Loureiro, ed., *Portugal e a Integração Monetária Europeia.* Porto: Universidade do Porto Editora, pp. 81–91.

Torres, Francisco (1996a). *Da Ambiguidade e Conflito à Moeda Única. As Razões de uma Batalha Política.* Lisbon.

Torres, Francisco (1996b). "Modeling Credibility in the Transition to a Monetary Union: Discretion, Secrecy and Rules with Escape Clauses." Manuscript. Lisbon: Universidade Católica Portuguesa.

Torres, Francisco (1996c). "The Political Economy of Monetary Reform in Europe," in Francisco Torres, ed., *Monetary Reform in Europe. An Analysis of the Issues and Proposals for the Intergovernmental Conference.* Lisbon: Catholic University Press, pp. 61–82.

Torres, Francisco, and Francesco Giavazzi, eds. (1993). *Adjustment and Growth in the European Monetary Union.* Cambridge: Cambridge University Press.

Traxler, Franc (1994). "Collective Bargaining: Levels and Coverage." *OECD Economic Outlook* (July), pp. 167–194.

Ullmo, Bernard (1989). "Le taux de change et l'emploi: Une critique des modèles macroéconomiques." *Revue d'économie politique* 99:1.

van Doorn, Kees, et al. (1976). *De beheerste vakbeweging: Het NVV tussen loonpolitik en loonstrijd, 1959–1973.* Amsterdam: Van Gennep.

Vanthemsche, Guy (1994). *De beginjaren van de sociale zekerheid in België: 1944–1963.* Brussels: VUB Press.

Väyrynen, Raimo (1993). "Finland on the Way to the European Community," in Tiilikainen and Petersen (1993), pp. 64–78.

Viñals, Jose and Jimeno, Juan (1997). "European Unemployment and EMU." *CEPS Paper No. 68.* Brussels: Centre for European Policy Studies.

Voormeulen, C. (1994). "The EMS Seen From Amsterdam." *Economic and Financial Review* 1:1 (Spring), pp. 65–71.

Walsh, Brendan (1993). "The Irish Pound and the ERM: Lessons from the September Crisis and its Aftermath." *Working Paper No. 93/14.* Dublin: Center for Economic Research, University College Dublin.

Waris, Klaus (1979). "In search of an exchange rate policy." *Unitas—Jubilee Issue for the Union Bank of Finland: 50 Years of Unitas* 51: 2, pp. 11–28.

Wellinck, A. H. E. M. (1987). "De ontwikkelingen in de jaren zeventig en tachtig en enkele daaruit te trekken lessen." *Reprint 201.* Amsterdam: De Nederlandische Bank, pp. 333–365.

Wellinck, A. H. E. M. (1989). "Dutch Monetary Policy in an Integrating Europe," in Bub Norbert, Dieter Duwendag and Rudolf Richter, eds. *Geldwertsicherung und Wirtschaftsstabilität.* Frankfurt am Main, pp. 391–410.

Wester, Robert (1992). "The Netherlands," in Finn Laursen and Sophie Vanhoonacker, eds., *The Intergovernmental Conference on Political Union: Institutional Reforms, New Policies and International Identity of the European Community.* Maastricht: European Institute of Public Administration, pp. 177–88.

WIFO (1994). "Oesterreich in der Europäischen Union: Anforderungen und Chancen für die Wirtschaft." *WIFO-Monatsberichte 67*: Special Issue.

Wolinetz, Steven B. (1989). "Socio-economic Bargaining in the Netherlands: Redefining the Postwar Policy Coalition." *West European Politics* 12 (January), pp. 79–98.

Xafa, Miranda (1991). "EMU and Greece: Issues and Prospects for Membership." *Rivista di Politica Economia* 81:5 (May), pp. 587–616.

Yearbook of Nordic Statistics 1994 (1994). Stockholm: Nordic Council of Ministers.

Yearbook of Nordic Statistics 1995 (1995). Stockholm: Nordic Council of Ministers.

Zijlstra, Jelle (1979). "Monetary Theory and Monetary Policy: A Central Banker's View." *De Economist* 127: 1, pp. 3–20.

Index

Introduction into the Social Security Law of the Member States of the European Community

Second edition

prof. dr. Danny Pieters

in cooperation with
Mr. Gabriel Amitsis
Prof. dr. Eberhardt Eichenhofer
Mr. Claude Ewen
dr. Bent Greve
dr. Francis Kessler
Prof. Ilídio das Neves
Mrs. Maria B.C. Pacheco Turnes
Mr. John Schell
Prof. Adrian Sinfield
Mrs. Josée van Rooij
dr. Gijsbert Vonk
Prof. Gerry Whyte
Mr. Nick Wikeley

MAKLU Uitgevers
Antwerpen - Apeldoorn

BRUYLANT
Brussel

Prof. Dr. Danny Pieters - Introduction into the Social Security Law of the Member States
of the European Communities

©**1993 MAKLU Uitgevers**
       Antwerpen - Apeldoorn

ISBN 90 6215 361 5
D/1992/1997/44
NUGI 691/695

Preface to the first edition

In each Member State of the European Communities, politicians and people responsible for the administration of social security are paying more and more attention to the social security systems of other Member States. Various explanations can be suggested for this increase in attention. Since the latter half of the seventies, Due to the economic crisis, the national social security systems of nearly all the Member States have been under severe pressure; indeed, the systems, which have often been in existence for decades, to many people seem no longer in line with newly arisen circumstances. This leads to research into ways of reorganising and, as far as possible, qualitatively improving social protection; and since the grass is always greener on the other side...

Furthermore, since the so called operation "1992" was launched by the European Community, the interest in foreign social security systems has gained momentum. Within the perspective of this operation the question has arisen whether it is possible, desirable and practical to harmonise the national social security systems. Also an improvement of the coordination regulations, which are designed to protect the rights of intra community migrants, has been called for. However, before methods of greater harmonisation and means of improving the instruments for coordination can be contemplated, some insight is needed into the charac-teristics of the systems which are to be harmonised or coordinated. Apart from that, the operation "1992" has also increased the already existing interests in foreign social security systems regarding the internal use: do we not often hear or read in the media (of all the Member States!) how much a country's own system contrasts badly with that of it's partners within the European Community. Figures are often supplied which can support such views and propositions: "arithmétique hollandaise" on a European scale!

In view of the great deal of interest in the social security systems existing within the European Community, we were surprised and disturbed to find out that no clearly structured key to these systems was available. There were only the "Comparative Tables of the Social Security Schemes in the Member States of the European Communities. General schemes (employees in industry and commerce)." are published approximately every two years by the Commission of the European Community [1]. As the name suggests, these contain tables in which it is attempted to place similar (sometimes small) aspects of the social security schemes of the twelve Member States alongside each other. Without throwing doubt upon the value of the tables, it must be aggreed that they are not suitable for deriving a general insight into the infrastructure of the social security systems. Then there are of course

---

[1] *Comparative Tables of the Social Security Schemes in the Member States of the European Communities. General scheme (employees in industry and commerce)*, 15th edition (1st July 1988), Official Publication Office of the European Communities, Luxembourg, 1989.

numerous works about comparative social security law, as well as publications on specific themes. In introductory chapters these sometimes give a brief, general overview of the systems in the light of the specific theme of the comparison; but generally, these too are not suitable for providing an overview of the social security systems compared.

In short, we believed that it was necessary to embark upon an introduction to the social security systems of all the Member States of the European Community, written in a simple language and within the "unreasonably" brief space of a few hundred pages. This Introduction will offer the social security expert with some comparative experience the opportunity to place his knowledge of (aspects of) foreign social security systems within the broad national context of these systems; for others, this Introduction will simplify first ventures into the field of comparative social security law. The Introduction is thus a true introduction and does not presume to provide an exhaustive description of all aspects of social security within each of the Member States. Thus, on the basis of the Introduction, the reader can decide for himself which foreign social security systems deserve attention for his/her area of comparison, whithout necessarily being confined to a study of the larger and/or linguistically accessible states. The reader will not be able to rely upon this work for the purpose of a true comparison of specific themes, e.g. the role of the means-test in social security; nevertheless, he can use it as a guide which tells him from where he could best start his further research.

Although the fundamental aim was to offer a brief overview of the national social security systems of the twelve, we also wanted to facilitate the broad comparison of these systems. As a matter of fact, even for the purpose of obtaining a good understanding of the social security system in a single country, it often makes sense to structure that system in the same way as the systems of the other countries that are studied. For this reason, our description of the social security systems of each of the twelve Member States is based upon a uniform structure, i.e.:

1. Concept and sources of social security law;
2. Administrative organisation;
3. Personal scope of application;
4. Risks and benefits;
5. Financing;
6. Judicial review.

For each country we have also given a brief enumeration of the most important normative texts and the leading text books and journals in the field of social security law.
Below, the above elements of description will be dealt with consecutively. However, first of all this remark: the authors are all social security lawyers and thus their main intention was to offer a legal introduction into the social security systems of the twelve as presently being used. Information with regard to the demographic situation in which the social security system of a

country operates, with regard to the economics of social security, or with regard to sociological questions, will be searched for in vain. This book describes the normative state of social security. Only if the legal norms blatantly conflict with the social security reality within a Member State, are the above subjects dealt with.

Now more about the various components which served as a basis for the description of each Member State.

The description of social security law within each Community country starts each time with an introductory chapter devoted to the concept of national social security and to the national sources of social security law.

An introduction to social security law in a particular country must include a clear description of what is understood by social security within that country, for there is no such thing as an international or community definition of social security; in international or community instruments with regard to social security, the material scope of application is determined differently for each instrument and thus, (implicitely or explicitely) the concept of social security which is used is described, but there is no uniformity. Nevertheless, the enumeration of risks as laid down in I.L.O. Convention no. 102 containing minimum standards of social security, exercises considerable influence: medical care, sickness, unemployment, old age, employment injury, family, maternity, invalidity and death. The material scope of application of the important regulation (EEC) no. 1408/71 concurs with this. It is now of interest to find out whether the concept of social security in a specific national context includes exlusively all benefits schemes for the coverage of one or more of the risks listed above and whether it excludes the schemes for the coverage of other risks. Of course, to a large extent, the national social security concept will conform with the concept of the above international instruments, but there are exceptions. Sometimes, a specific branch of social security, e.g. unemployment benefit, is not considered to be a part of social security, whereas it may equally be the case that the coverage of a non-social risk branche, e.g. study costs, is included within the concept of social security. Sometimes social assistance and (other) schemes providing minimum means of subsistence are included within the social security concept and sometimes they are not. From his own experience the reader will know that even within his own system there is no general consensus of opinion with regard to the social security concept. However, we do not concern ourselves too much with problems of definition. Our starting point is the concept of social security which has gained the highest degree of national consensus. For the purpose of the subsequent description of national social security law we then depart from the national social security concept, supplemented by the schemes which, although not considered to be within the national concept, cover one of the social risks as enumerated in the above international instruments. As a rule, social assistance (covering the risk of need) is also included. If a particular scheme only falls within the social security concept of one country, it is not discussed.

The sources of national social security law are dealt with in the next section of the first chapter. Special attention is paid to constitutional provisions which are relevant for social security, especially clauses concerning fundamental rights, provisions with regard to the organisation of social security and the possible division of powers between central government and federal states. Furthermore, it is discussed which source must be considered to be most important for the main body of social security rules; formal statutes, administrative regulations, self-administration of social security institutions, or collective agreements? Social security schemes, which derive their source from collective labour agreements, or contracts under private law are mentioned, but generally are not taken into consideration in the subsequent chapters.

Finally, it must be mentioned that in line with the objective of this study, international law which applies for or within the Member States is not taken into consideration, even if this grants directly enforceable rights to citizens in particular Member States.

Before we continue with the description of the contents of the various chapters, first a remark of a more general nature.

Within the national borders of the Community countries there are various social security schemes. It was not always possible to map out all of them.

Due to the limited scope of this work, attention could only be paid to the most important schemes; and so the "general schemes" have been discussed, as well as the schemes which apply for employees in general. To the extent that this coincided with the national social security traditions. Also have the non-professional schemes for self-employed persons been discussed, or at least mentioned. Due to the large distance which exists in the Member States between on the one hand schemes for civil servants and on the other hand schemes for those who carry out other occupational activities, and regarding the fact that the social coverage of civil servants is often closely connected with administrative law, it was decided not to discuss the social security schemes which apply for this category of people.

The administrative structure is highlighted in the second chapter of the country reports. It is perhaps surprising that we concentrated first upon the administrative structure of social security and only after that upon it's actual contents (e.g. benefits, financing). However, it is often the case that the understanding of the organisation of administration, management and supervision is necessary in order to gain access into the material aspects of social security law. As mentioned above there is no country within the Community which only has one social security scheme; there are always a number, sometimes even more than a hundred social security schemes co-exist within the borders of a single country. Often there appears to be as many social security schemes as there are corresponding administrative bodies, rather than perhaps more logically, the opposite. In any case, the experience of drafting the brief descriptions of social security for each country gradually taught the authors that is was preferential to start with the administrative organisation. Thereby attention has been paid to, among other things, the competent ministers, the (other) bodies charged with supervision, advice and/or policy development and the institutions charged with the actual administration of the social security schemes.

The personal scope of application is discussed in the third chapter of the reports. For each scheme it is considered which people are potentially eligible for benefit. Here attention has been paid to the usual distinctions, such as between general insurance schemes and employee insurance schemes, or between obligatory and voluntary insurance. Furthermore, attention has been paid to the question of whether entitlement to benefits exists upon an individual basis or upon a family basis. Also in this chapter the effect of international and community law upon social security, in this case upon the delimination of the personal scope of application of the national schemes, are disregarded.

The fourth chapter of the reports deals with the social risks which are covered and the benefits payable upon the materialization of these risks. First of all, when this was considered to be useful, some general remarks were made which are relevant for a number of, or for all the risks and/or benefits within a country. Subsequently the following risks are dealt with consecutively: old age, death, incapacity for work (short term and long term), unemployment, medical care, family and need. In principle, the coverage of professional risks is discussed under the heading of the risk which is actually covered (irregardless of the professional origins), i.e. incapacity for work, death or medical care. Benefit levels are not included, but attention has been paid to the question of whether or not there exists a mechanism for the adjustment of the benefit levels to increases in prices and/or to increases in the general wage level.

In this chapter we were sometimes confronted with the problem of classifying certain rather hermaphroditic benefit schemes under a particular risk, e.g. the difficulty of classifying specific benefits either as unemployment benefits or as old age benefits. Where such a problem arose, we dealt with the scheme in question within the framework of the most appropriate risk, taking into account national traditions of classification.
Obviously, the entitlement conditions of the various benefit schemes could only be roughly described. Specific regulations which are designed to prevent overlapping of benefits, were generally not discussed.

The legal framework for the financing of social security is dealt with in each fifth chapter. As lawyers, the authors have not taken the risk of describing the financing of social security as such, but have limited themselves to mapping out the most important legal provisions which exist in this area.

Judicial review is the subject of the sixth and final chapter. It is not sufficient to grant rights to citizens (or to specific groups); there must also be certain ways for the citizens to realize these rights. Here, attention is paid to legal procedures, as well as to some "extra legal" procedures which are of importance in a country. In view of the legal nature of this study, no attention is paid to possible factual obstacles which prevent the citizen from obtaining access to justice.

The annex includes a brief enumeration of the most important acts and other normative texts and of the leading text books and journals in the field of social security law in each of the countries. These offer the reader the opportunity to look more closely at certain (parts of the) national social security systems.

In editing this work, the reports were not only uniformly divided into chapters, but also the description of each national system within the seperate chapters was based upon the utmost uniformity. Yet, the individuality of each system sometimes required special attention yielding some of the uniformity within each chapter.

As far as possible, names of systems, benefit schemes and institutions are referred to in the (or a) language of the country studied. A personal, rather literal translation is given whenever a name is mentioned for the first time.

In principle, this description of the national social security systems was concluded on 31st December 1989. In full accordance with the aims of this Introduction as described above, an overview is given of the law as it applied at that time. Thus, as a rule, attention is neither paid to historical developments, nor to future expectations with regard to the systems studied. On the same grounds, temporary transitionary schemes are not discussed.

This Introduction to social security law within the countries of the European Community is affiliated to the research programme "Comparative constitutional and administrative law" of the Catholic University of Brabant. The Introduction in it's present form was commissioned by the (Dutch) Ministry of Social Affairs and Employment.

The first versions of the country reports in this Introduction have been written by lecturers in social security law at Tilburg University. Mrs. J.W.P.M. van Rooij was responsible for the contribution with regard to France, G.J. Vonk drafted the text on British social security law, J.L.M. Schell was the author of the contributions with regard to the Federal Republic of Germany and Ireland and the undersigned was in the first instance responsible for the texts on Belgium, Denmark, Greece, Luxemburg, the Netherlands, Italy, Portugal and Spain. In collaboration with J.L.M. Schell and S.M.E. Vansteenkiste the undersigned was also responsible for the drafting and the editing of the report in it's final form.

However, this introductory book was much more team work than the work of a number of individuals. Thus the above authors sometimes contributed to a large extent to the realization of texts, the final editing of which was done by another team member. Each country report, with the exception of Greece, was realized on the basis of original material from the relevant country; in drafting the introduction, no use was made of existing legal comparative studies, nor of studies with regard to a national system which were not written by a national author of that country. This serves to offer the purest possible picture of the systems, without the interference from implicit comparisons of a scheme with others schemes which are common within the author's country.

This method of working was not possible for Greece, due to the fact that none of the authors has command of New Greek.

It was consciously decided that each country report should be drafted by authors from the same team; the frequently employed method of entrusting the editing of a national report to an author from the relevant country was rejected in order to secure the uniformity of the descriptions. But this does not detract from the fact that the authors would not have been able to draft their country reports if they had not been able to rely upon active support from a number of advisers from each member state. These people have collected material for us or helped us by gathering the necessary information about the social security systems within their countries. They have dealt with some specific problems, have read our texts and have often offered us all possible assistance. For this we extend our grateful thanks to them; in a real sense they participate in the authorship of this book. For Belgium, these persons were prof. dr. J. van Langendonck and F. Robben, both attached to the Institute for Social Law of the Catholic University of Leuven; for Denmark, a number of staff of the Ministery of Social Affairs and of the Socialforskningsinstitut, notably Mr. T. Fridberg and Ms. I. Koch-Nielsen, as well as G. Varmer; for the Federal Republic of Germany, dr. B. Schulte of the Max-Planck-Institut für ausländisches und internationales Sozialrecht and Prof. Dr. E. Eichenhofer of the University of Osnabrück; for France, dr. F. Kessler of the University of Nancy; for Greece, prof. dr. K. Kremalis and Mr. G. Amitsis of the University of Athens and Ms. M. Vosiki, as well as the Greek participants in the 1989 and 1990 session of the ERASMUS-programme "Social security in the European Community"; for the Republic of Ireland, G. Whyte of Trinity College, Dublin; for Italy, prof. avv. G.C. Perone of the Libera Università Internazionale di Studi Sociali in Rome, as well as Mr. P. Keysers; for Luxembourg, Mr. Y. Béchet; for Portugal, Mr. V. Vieira Dias and staff of the CRSS Leiria and Mr. S. M. da Nobrega Pinto Pizarro; for Spain, Mr. F. Ferreras Alonso; and for the United Kingdom, Mr. A. Wilton of the University of Newcastle upon Tyne.

Furthermore, we would like to give our thanks to the student assistants who helped us in this work, to Mr. H. Dhaeyer and Mr. W. Palm. We also give our thanks to those who have assured the practical realization of this work, which was not always an easy thing to do, and to Drs. Vonk and Mrs. Cunningham who were responsable for the translation in English.

It was not always easy to include sufficient and correct information within the space of twenty pages per country. Generalisation and simplification should of course not result in incorrect statements. Sometimes collecting relevant material was a problem. If readers consider that any of the country reports contains unexpected mistakes or flaws, the authors will be pleased to hear about this. However, in our view, the above way in which each report was drafted and the exceptional care that the authors have given to the realization of this introduction guarantee the quality of the information contained. Nonetheless, comments which we may receive could further improve this quality.

This book is to be situated within the framework of the European and International orientation of the juridical branch of the Department of Social Security Science of the Catholic University of Brabant. Our ambition for the future is to proceed along the undertaken path, to delve deeper into European social security law and systems of the twelve. We intend to make legal comparative studies of further specific aspects of social security law and broaden our knowledge about European social security law and foreign social security systems, always with the same objectives before us: a unified, free and social Europe.

On behalf of the authors,
prof. dr. Danny PIETERS.
Leuven/Tilburg, July 11, 1990.

Preface to the second edition

The second edition of this Introduction to the Social Security Law of the Member States of the European Community offers an update of the first edition, published some three years ago. No fundamental changes have been introduced; the choices made when redacting the first edition have not been altered. We only decided not to incorporate the annexes, giving the most important acts and literature, as this information appeared to be less usefull, quickly outdated and easily incomplete.

The national social security law systems of the Member States are discribed as they were on January 1st, 1992.

In order to realize this update, the text of the first edition was sent to colleagues in the countries concerned. They were found ready to make the update for their own country. As such this second edition can be considered the product of the efforts of dr. Bent Greve (Denmark), prof. dr. Eberhard Eichenhofer (Germany), dr. Francis Kessler (France), prof. Adrian Sinfield and Mr. Nick Wikeley (United Kingdom), Mr. Claude Ewen (Luxembourg), Mr. Gabriel Amitsis (Greece), dr. Edoardo Ales (Italy), prof. Gerry Whyte (Ireland), prof. dr. Ilidio das Neves (Portugal) and Mrs. Maria B.C. Pachero Turnes (Spain). I have been responsible for the updating of the Belgian and Dutch country reports, as well as for the final redaction of the entire second edition.

Very valuable remarks have been reached us concerning the structure and contents of the first edition of this Introduction. We are gratefull to all those who by giving us their views have contributed to the improvement of the Introduction text in this second edition. One category of critical readers of the first edition deserves a special mention here: a special word of thanks to three generations of students of the ERASMUS and TEMPUS Programme Social Security in Europe who have used this Introduction to penetrate the jungle of Europe's social security systems.

prof. dr. Danny PIETERS,
Leuven, November 1992.

SUMMARY

Chapter 4: France

Chapter 5: Grand Duchy of Luxembourg

Chapter 6: Great Britain

Chapter 7: Greece

Chapter 8: Ireland

Chapter 9: Italy

Chapter 10: The Netherlands

Chapter 11: Portugal

Chapter 12: Spain

Chapter 1: Belgium

1. Introduction: concept and sources of social security law.

There are two different kinds of schemes in Belgian social security law, i.e. social insurance and social assistance. The social insurance system is of a professional character, that is to say there exist different schemes for various professional groups. In particular, there are separate insurance schemes for employees and for self-employed people. Although a certain tendency towards a harmonisation of social insurance benefits exists (especially in the field of the employee's schemes), in principle one still holds on to the mentioned division.

The social insurance schemes include benefits supplementing income, which cover costs associated with children and with medical care. They also include income maintenance benefits in respect of incapacity for work due to illness, invalidity and industrial injuries or occupational diseases, as well as unemployment, old age and the death of a person who guaranteed the livelihood of his other partner or child. The above benefits supplementing income exist for employees as well as for self-employed people and are not related to income or wage; yet the personal scope of application of these benefits may differ. Wage-related income maintenance benefits exist for all employees in respect of all contingencies mentioned above. Self-employed people only obtain income maintenance benefits in cases of sickness and invalidity (flat-rate) and upon the attainment of pensionable age (mixed, partly wage-related, partly flat-rate).

Assistance schemes ensure that child benefits are payable in respect of children for whom there is no right to child benefit within the professional scheme, (guaranteed family allowance)(*gewaarborgde gezinsbijslag*). A minimum income is guaranteed to the handicapped (*tegemoetkoming aan mindervaliden*), to the elderly (*gewaarborgd inkomen voor bejaarden*) and finally, to all citizens (subsistence level) (*bestaansminimum*). Furthermore, handicapped people who are determined as being incapable of self-help, or whose capacity for self-help is reduced, are eligible for an integration allowance. Apart from these minimum income schemes, the possibility to apply for material and non material social welfare services from the municipal public centre for social welfare is also provided (individualized assistance).

So far we only have dealt with social security which is based upon the statute (or decree). Now we will refer to the extra legal social security benefits. These mainly take the shape of additional sickness costs insurance schemes (of special importance for self-employed people) and social security funds which, on grounds of collective labour agreements, provide extra benefits for workers in specific sectors (building, docking, diamonds) on top of the benefits on grounds of the social insurance schemes for employees. Furthermore, there are industrial and occupational pension funds, as well as group insurance schemes to guarantee additional (extra-legal) pensions. Materially, these are not regulated (except where it concerns solvency guarantees and fiscal treatment) and are, in comparison with other countries, only relatively successful.

The Belgian constitution does not contain any fundamental rights or declarations in relation to social security. However, there does exist a law of 29th June 1981, containing general principles on social security for employees, in which *inter alia*, a number of fundamental principles concerning social security rights are enumerated. As yet, the provisions concerning these general principles have not entered into force and possibly, due to among other things the pressure of legal doctrine, they will never do so.

On grounds of the Belgian constitution some powers in the area of vocational training, health care and social assistance to people and families were attributed to the Communities (Flemish, French and German speaking), while other powers, in areas like housing or employment policy, were attributed to the Regions (Flanders, Walonia, Brussels).
However, these powers are not concerned with the social security benefit schemes as described above, but rather with various sorts of provisions and services. Therefore the Belgian social security applies to the whole of Belgium. This unitary character of Belgian social security is nowadays increasingly challenged; the Flemish make claims for splitting up the system, especially the health care scheme.

The professional social insurance schemes, as well as the social assistance schemes, all find their basis in the statute, albeit that sometimes the statutory provisions may be very minimal (for example, with regard to unemployment benefits, there is only one article from a (decree) statute of 1 944!).

Here we also have to note that important parts of the existing social security schemes are not the work of parliament but of the government ("The King"), who for that purpose was temporarily attributed with "special powers" by the formal statute to take decisions, which in their legal effect are principally equal to those of the formal statute. In this way delicate interventions in the area of social security could be realized and executed without subsequent parliamentary approval. Decrees with statutory force, taken by virtue of the attribution of special powers, can be recognized by the fact that only these royal decrees are numbered.

In principle, the formal statute offers the framework of social security schemes; the statutes must therefore be read together with the administrative Royal and Ministerial decrees. Sometimes, if a statute is frequently modified and supplemented, the statutory texts are coordinated by Royal Decree. This is done for reasons of clarity.

Social security is one of the very few areas of the Belgium law where national, independent governmental bodies have been granted powers to enact binding regulations. With regard to social security, such powers were attributed to the managerial committee of the National Institute for Employment Services (*de Rijksdienst voorArbeidsvoorzieningen, (R. V.A.)*) and to that of the Benefits Service of the National Institute for Sickness and Invalidity Insurance (*Rijksinstituut voor ziekte- en invaliditeitsverzekering, R.I.Z.I.V.*). Until now, the independent governmental bodies have made limited use of these regulating powers of which the constitutional status is uncertain.

2. Administrative organisation.

We will discuss succesively the administrative organisation of the insurance schemes for employees, the insurance schemes for self-employed people and the social assistance schemes.

The social security schemes for employees come under the authority of the Minister of Social Affairs and, in respect of unemployment benefits, the Minister of Labour and Employment. The corresponding ministers determine the policy and exercise administrative control over the social security institutions, as described below.

Other aspects of the administration of social security for employees, except that of the industrial injuries insurance scheme, is entrusted to 'parastatal' organisations, public institutions of social security which may be assisted by various co-operating institutions under private law. The administration of the industrial injuries insurance scheme is entrusted to private insurance companies and communal insurance funds; all employers are affiliated to one of these bodies. The Fund for Industrial Injuries (*Fonds voor Arbeidsongevallen, F.A.O.*) controls these insurers, compensates for the disadvantages which are typical of private insurance, and takes responsibility, whenever necessary, for the affiliation ex officio of non- compliant employers.

For all other employee insurance schemes the National Institute for Social Security (*Rijksdienst voor Sociale Zekerheid, R.S.Z.*) is encharged with the collection of contributions, as well as the distribution of contributions over the various branches of social security for employees. The payment of benefits on grounds of these insurance schemes is entrusted to other public social security institutions, i.e. the National Institute for Sickness and Invalidity Insurance (*Rijksinstituut voor ziekte en invaliditeitsverzekering, R.I.Z.I.V.*), the National Institute for Employment Services (*Rijksdienst voor arbeidsvoorziening, R.V.A.*), the National Institute for Pensions (*Rijksdienst voor pensioenen, R.V.P.*), the National Institute for Child Allowances for Employees (*Rijksdienst voor kinderbijslag voor werknemers, R.KW.*) and the fund for occupational diseases (*fonds voor de beroepsziekten, F.B.Z.*).

These public institutions are set up by the government, are legal persons and enjoy administrative autonomy. Nevertheless, they are subject to the

21

administrative control of a competent minister. The latter is represented in the 'parastatal' bodies by a governmental commissioner whose aim is to exercise permanent control over the decisions and the action of these bodies. The management of the institutions is entrusted to a managerial committee, which is composed of an equal number of representatives from the respective employer - and employee organisation under an independent chairman, who, like the other members, is appointed by the King. Within the managerial bodies of the National Institute for Sickness and Invalidity Insurance (*R.I.Z.I.V.*), representatives of the sickness funds and of health care providers also have seats and within the management of the National Institute for Child Allowances for Employees (*R.K.W.*) there are also representatives of family organisations.

In the field of the administration of the employee insurance schemes some tasks are often attributed to certain co-operating bodies under private law; these are often the successors of the first free social insurance associations. They are mostly responsable for the direct contact with the beneficiary. Thus, within the sector of sickness and invalidity, approved sickness funds and their (national) unions often co-operate in the administration; the insured persons who do not wish to be affiliated to an (ideologically tinted) sickness fund, can join a public institution: the auxiliary fund for sickness and invalidity insurance, coming under the *R.I.V.I.Z.* There is also the possibility of co-operation from unemployment funds set up by three trade unions which are empowered for that purpose, with as "last resort" the auxiliary fund for unemployment benefits of the *R.V.A.* In its activities the *R.K W.* not only enjoys co-operation from the public compensation funds, but also from the recognized free child allowance funds. The government lays down rules, which the co-operating bodies must satisfy, and exercises control, usually through the above mentioned parastatal bodies.

The National Labour Council (*Nationale Arbeidsraad*) carries out an important advisory function. It is composed of an equal number of representatives of the most representative employee's and employer's organisations.

The social status of the self-employed falls under the political responsibility of the Minister of Small Trade, except where the sickness and invalidity insurance scheme is concerned. The latter is the responsibility of the Minister of Social Affairs.

The sickness and invalidity insurance scheme of the self-employed is entirely structured as an extension of the scope of insured people under the sickness and invalidity insurance scheme for employees. Hence, it has the same administrative structure as described above, with the exception of the collection and distribution of contributions which, as is the case for all other social insurance schemes for self-employed persons, is encharged to the National Institute for Social Insurance of the Self-Employed (*Rijksinstituut voor de Sociale Verzekeringen der zelfstandigen, R.S.V.Z.*). This public institution is a legal person and is subject to the control of the Minister of

Small Trade. The *R.S.V. Z.* is also encharged with granting benefits from the pensions branch and child allowances branch for the self-employed. The *R.S.V.Z.* is governed by a board of directors, within which a management committee is formed; the members of the board of directors are appointed by the King on the recommendation of the various representative organisations for self-employed persons. The *R.S.V.Z.* orders the *R.V.P.* to pay retirement and widow(er)'s pensions. The latter also carries out this task in the area of the employee insurance schemes.

For the collection and distribution of contributions, the payment of a so called unconditional pension and child allowances, the *R.S.V.Z.* makes use of the co-operation of the free social insurance funds for self-employed persons. Self-employed persons who do not wish to join such a fund may join the National Auxiliary Fund for Social Insurance of the Self-Employed (of the *R.S.V.Z.*) (*Nationale Hulpkas voor de sociale verzekeringen der zelfstandigen*).

The High Council for small trade, in which the organisations of the self-employed are represented, advises the competent ministers.

The (financial) allowances for the handicapped are administered and managed directly by a special service of the Ministery of Social Affairs.

The guaranteed family allowances and the guaranteed income for the elderly are administered by the respective administrative bodies of the scheme for employees, i.e. the *R.K W.* and the *R.V.P.*

The Public Centres for Social Welfare are encharged with the administration of the minimum subsistence legislation, as well as the granting of social services directly on grounds of the *O.C.M.W.* Act. Each municipality has a Public Centre for Social Welfare (*O.C.M.W.*). This is an autonomous institution under public law, governed by a (politically composed) council for social welfare, appointed by the municipal council. The Minister of National Health is politically responsible in respect of the minimum subsistence legislation.

In order to simplify the social security administration and to facilitate the informatisation of social security with full guarantees for the respect of privacy, the "Crossroads Bank of Social Security" has been created (*Kruispuntbank der Sociale Zekerheid*). This databank does not centralize all information necessary for the execution of the various social security schemes, but links the various social security institutions, each of them keeping (exclusively) that data wich are most relevant for them.

Finally, we mention that some benefits (for example pensions, allowances for handicapped persons) must be claimed from the municipal government. The municipality and its government, which as such cannot be labelled as administrative social security bodies, pass the claim on to the competent institutions.

3. Personal scope of application

The division in professional social security schemes is based upon the differences between the potential beneficiaries. Therefore, we will firstly discuss the two professional schemes.

Employees, within the meaning of the employee insurance schemes, are those who are bound to their employers by a contract of employment, as well as certain categories of people who are treated as such. *Ratione loci*, in principle, a double link with Belgian territory is required; i.e. the place of labour and the location of the employer's business must be in Belgium. Nevertheless, there are exceptions to this rule; in respect of workers who work abroad for a Belgian undertaking, in respect of mariners, in respect of the child allowance legislation, and on grounds of public international law. A contract of employment is a contract whereby an employee agrees to perform work under the authority of an employer in return for a wage. Subjection to the authority of the employer is sufficient proof of the existence of a contract of employment, regardless of the special nature of the work which is performed (e.g. professional football trainers, hostesses).

Next to the employees in the classical sense of labour law, other categories of people are explicitly included within the personal scope of applicaton, in respect of all or some of the insurance schemes for employees. Thus, the coverage for all employee insurance schemes is extended to, amongst others, apprentices, handicapped persons in occupational retraining, working students, domestic workers, paid musicians and actors, paid governors and the mandatories of non-profit making organisations.

Some groups of employees are only submitted to a limited number of employee insurance schemes, for example, professional sportsmen (only health care, pensions, industrial accidents and child allowance; for professional cyclists also unemployment and incapacity to work benefits).

On the other hand, some employees are excluded, such as e.g. domestic servants who work less than four hours a day and 24 hours a week for one or more employers.

Certain specific groups of employees are totally excluded from the employee insurance schemes in order to be submitted to an own professional social security system. This is the case for the schemes of mineworkers and merchant seamen. There is also the possibility for those working abroad, who find insufficient social security coverage there, to join the "overseas social security", which includes retirement and widow(er)'s pensions, an industrial injuries insurance scheme, a scheme for health care and benefits in respect of severe illness or injury.

The scope of insured people under the family allowance scheme for employees is extended considerably (for example to retired employees, the orphans of an employee, students younger than twenty five years of age, etc.).

Those who are unemployed and have stopped their studies and who are, in principle, younger than thirty years of age, may be eligible for unemployment benefit as 'young graduates", provided they are the head of a family. If not, they may be eligible for a flat-rate waiting benefit.

Every natural person who carries out an occupational activity within Belgium, on the basis of which he is neither bound by a contract of employment nor by the status of a civil servant is self-employed within the meaning of the scheme for the self-employed. The concrete meaning of this is that the social security provisions for the self-employed constitute the residual scheme of the professional social sequrity system and as such it covers the very heterogeneous group of people (industrialists and traders, free professions, farmers) who are engaged in employment other than as employee or civil servant. Affiliation takes place on grounds of a professional activity, regardless of whether or not an income is obtained from this activity. Not only the self-employed person, who carries out a certain occupational activity, is affiliated, but also his helper, the latter being the person who assists or replaces the self-employed person in his work, without being bound by a contract of employment.

The following are excluded from the insurance scheme for the self-employed:
- writers (for example journalists) who have another main profession;
- spouse/helpers, unmarried helpers under twenty years of age and occasional helpers (that is to say those who occasionaly act as helpers during a period of not more than ninety days per year).

The sickness and invalidity insurance schemes, notably the medical care branch, not only provide benefits for the beneficiary himself (the employee or self-employed person), but also for benefits in respect of the persons who are dependent upon him (her). The main category of dependent persons consists of spouses and children. Also treated as such are ascendents of the beneficiary or of his (her) spouse, provided they are older than fifty five years of age or incapable of work, have an annual income from labour or from social security which does not exceed a certain amount, and have been registered as a family member of the beneficiary for at least six months. In principle, children remain dependent as long as they continue to give rise to entitlement to family allowance, or as long as they are younger than twenty five years of age and are living at home.

We will now deal with the personal scope of application of the assistance schemes.

Income maintenance is payable to handicapped persons who are of age but younger than 65, in respect of whom it is determined that their physical or mental state has reduced their earning capacity by one third or less of that which a healthy person can earn through an occupation in the general labour market. Integration allowances are payable to handicapped persons if damage to, or a reduction of, their independence is established.

Every resident who is either of age, or married, or unmarried with at least one dependent child, may be eligible for minimum subsistence.

All men of sixty five years or older and all woman of sixty years or older, may be eligible for the guaranteed income for the elderly.

Give right to guaranteed family allowances the dependent children, actually residing in Belgium, of residents provided that family allowance is not payable on grounds of any other scheme.

All above mentioned assistance schemes are open to Belgians, citizens of other EC-countries, stateless people and political refugees. They all require the claiments to be really residing in Belgium. People of other nationalities will have to fullfill additional conditions in order to qualify for these assistance benefits.

As stated, all assistance schemes are payable on the condition that a persons's income falls below subsistence level.
Finally we should mention that in principle everyone can apply for the social services offered by the Public Centers of Social Welfare.

4. Risks and benefits.

Here we must preliminary mention that the level of social security benefits is linked to the index of consumer prices, in other words to price increases. Furthermore, many social security acts provide for a supplementary adjustment of the benefits to the standard of living. However, in practice this adjustment is no longer made.

4.1. Old age.

Under the social insurance schemes for employees as well as for self-employed people a retirement pension is payable to insured persons who have attained a certain age and stopped working. The pensionable age for employees has been flexibilized, both for men and women: they can take up their pension between the age of 60 and 65. The pensionable age is still sixty years for self-employed women and sixty five for their male colleagues. Under certain conditions, and subject to the application of proportional decreases, self-employed women take early retirement from sixty years of age Those claiming retirement pension must cease their professional activities and may only perform a limited amount of permitted work.

The retirement pension of the employee amounts to 75% or 60% of the average wage (fictitious or real) over the period between twenty years of age and the age of 65 (men) and 60 (women), depending upon whether the insured person is married and provided that his partner has neither income from work nor income maintenance ("family pension") or does not belong to this group ("single person's pensions").

Pensions for self-employed people are determined in a double way. Since 1984 one year of a career as a self-employed gives rise to the same retirement pension as for employees, albeit that instead of the earned wages, about half of the business income of the self-employed person is taken into account. For the years prior to 1984, pensions are based upon a low, flat-rate business income per year. Furthermore, in respect of limited and partial periods of self-employment, this part of the pension may be subject to a means test.

In case of a full professional career (45 years for men, 40 years for women) employees and self-employed persons are entitled to a minimum pension. The industrial and occupational pension funds, the group insurance schemes for employees and the supplementary pensions for self-employed persons guarantee a supplementary pension of their members.

4.2. Death.

The spouse of a deceased, insured employee or self-employed person is entitled to widow(er)'s pension at the level of 80% of the (effective or fictitiously calculated) retirement pension of the deceased insured person, subject to the condition that the widow(er) is over 45 years of age or has a dependent child, or is 66% incapable of work. Entitlement ends upon remarriage.

If the conditions for widow(er)'s pension are no longer satisfied, the pension continues to be paid for one year; if the surviving spouse is less than forty five years of age, ceases to have dependent children or to be incapable of work, the period until the attainment of forty five years of age is bridged by payments on a minimum level. As for permitted labour, the same rules apply as those in respect of retirement pension.

No survivor's pension- is payable to the pseudo widow. However, in the scheme for employees and self-employed persons the divorced spouse is granted a personal and individual right to a pension for the years during which he or she was married to an employee or self-employed person. The divorced spouse is then treated as if he or she has carried out an activity as an employee or self-employed person during the period of the marriage. The level of pension is based upon a wage which is equal to 62.5% of the wage which would be used as a basis of calculation for the ex-spouse's pension; however this wage is only used as a point of departure if it is higher than the wage which the claimant himself earned during this period. The retirement pension of the ex-spouse is not dependent upon the claim to pension of the other spouse. It is fully independent and payable when the claimant attains the age of 65 (men) or 60 (women).

No orphan's pension is payable, but the orphan does receive an increased child allowance, subject to the condition that the deceased parent has not remarried nor formed a household with a partner.

On the death of an employee due to an industrial injury or an occupational disease, benefits are provided on grounds of the employees insurance scheme to the surviving members of the family. These are calculated as a percentage of the basic wage of the person concerned: 30% for the widowed spouse and 15% for each orphan (with a maximum of 45%; increased to 20%, *c.q.* 60% when both parents are deceased). Also parents, grandparents, grandchildren, brothers and sisters can be entitled to such benefits (usually at a level of 15%) under certain conditions, notably if they can prove that they have been dependent upon the wage of the deceased person.

4.3. Incapacity for work.

The sickness and invalidity insurance schemes guarantee benefits to the employee who is incapable of work and who has not attained the age of 65 (men) or 60 (women) on the condition that he ceased all activities due to a disease or an injury which is recognized by a specially appointed doctor. Furthermore, benefit is subject to the condition that the incapacity for work was directly followed by a decrease in the earning capacity of at least 66% of that which a comparable person could earn. For the first six months this condition is gauged upon the occupation of the claimant. Thereafter, (or earlier if no cure can be expected), it is gauged upon his entire occupational category or against any occupation which the person involved could have carried out in view of his education. There is a presumption of incapability of work when there is entry into hospital. During the first period of one year (primary incapacity for work) benefit normally consists of 60% of the wage which gives rise to contribution liability. From the second year of incapacity for work (period of invalidity) people who are at the head of a household obtain 65%. Otherwise, this percentage is 45 or 40% of the previously earned wages (depending upon whether or not the lost income was their only income). Benefit is subject to minimum and maximum amounts. As these do not always lie very far apart, the benefits assume a quasi flat-rate character.

On a benefit level, the sickness and invalidity insurance scheme for the self-employed is substantially different from that for employees. The self-employed person (who has not attaind pensionable age) is incapable of work if, due to an illness or an injury, he has to cease his self-employed activities. The first three months of incapacity for work are not compensated, but the following months are. The self-employed person who is incapable of work receives (low) flat-rate benefits, the level of which rises slightly after one year of incapacity for work and is higher for people who are at the head of a household than for single people. The amounts hover around the minimum subsistence.

If the incapacity for work of an employee is due to an industrial injury or an occupational disease, the former will receive a percentage of his wage from the previous year that is equal to his degree of incapacity for work. However, if this percentage amounts to less than 10%, benefit is calculated on the basis of a lower percentage; if the claimant needs the constant attendance of another person, the benefit is increased.

4.4. Unemployment.

Only the scheme for employees provides an insurance scheme in respect of unemployment. In order to be entitled to benefit the employee must be younger than 60 (women) or 65 (men), and must either have worked as an employee for a number of days during the period of reference relevant for his age (the required number of days and the period of reference increase with the age of the beneficiary; those younger than 18 years of age must have worked at least 75 days during the preceding 10 months, those who are older than 50 years of age must have worked for at least 600 days during the preceding 36 months), or have stopped his studies, not being thirty years of age, and be registered as looking for work (or have performed work) during a number of days (77 to 300) depending on his age. The mentionned young graduates, however, are only eligible for benefit if they are at the head of a household; if this is not the case they merely entitled to the less favourable waiting benefits.

Unemployment benefit is subject to a number of entitlement conditions, i.e. one must be unemployed without a wage, be involuntarily unemployed, be registered as looking for work, be willing to accept suitable employment, be capable of work, and subject oneself to periodical control.

Benefits on grounds of the insurance scheme for employees are divided into unemployment benefits (*werkloosheidsuitkering*), waiting benefits (*wachtgeld*) and bridging benefits (*overbruggingsuitkeringen*), early retirement pensions (*brugpensioenen*) and interruption benefits (*onderbrekingsuitkeringen*).

The level of unemployment benefit is expressed as a percentage of the (limited) wage previously earned: i.e. 35% plus:
- an allowance of 5% for the loss of income, payable to the single unemployed person and to the unemployed person who cohabitates with his spouse and one or more children from inside or outside the marriage, who do not enjoy income from employment or income maintenance;
- an adjustment allowance of 20% during the first year of unemployment:
- an extra allowance in respect of dependent family members, equal to 20% after the first year of unemployment, subject to the condition that the beneficiary is the head of a household;
- an additional allowance of 2% for the loss of sale income, paid to single unemployed persons after the first year of unemployment.

Wage-related benefits are subject to a minimum as well as to a maximum limit. Unemployed people who are not eligible for the 5% allowance for the loss of income, lose their wage-related benefit after a specific period of time and receive a flat-rate benefit. The unemployed person who has worked for twenty years, or who is at least 33% incapable of work, unlimitedly continues to enjoy a wage-related benefit.

Young graduates who are not at the head of a household receive a low flat-rate waiting benefit (in respect of unemployed people who are obliged tc follow part-time education this is referred to as "bridging benefit"). If the young graduate is at the head of a household the minimum wage is used as a basis of calculation for unemployment benefit.

At the present time, early retirement pension refers to benefits enjoyed by employees who were discharged after their sixtieth (sometimes their fiftieth) year and who receive from their employer a supplement on top of their unemployment benefit at a level of half the difference between unemployment benefit and their net wage. The unemployment benefit upon which the supplement is payable is not reduced after one year of unemployment.

Finally we mention the possibility for employees to interrupt their employment for at least six months and for a maximum of one year, or to change a full time job into part-time work for a maximum period of five years. The interruption benefit is low and flat-rate.
The same benefit is payable to the unemployed who decides to step out of the labour market because of social or family reasons; the benefit can then last up to 5 years.

4.5. Medical care.

Insured employees and people dependent upon them enjoy financial compensation for the costs of medical care, borne by the health care branch of the sickness and invalidity insurance scheme.

The insured person pays for medical services himself and obtains a certificate stating the help that was given. After that he receives re-imbursment from his sickness fund, minus a personal contribution for costs (*remgeld*), equal to the amount which may be charged according to the of ficial scale of tariffs for such medical practices (the real amont paid may be higher than the official amount). In a certain number of situations, such as hospitalisation, the "third payer" rule is applied: in that case the provider of care will send his bill directly to the sickness fund and the patient only pays the personal contribution.

The mentioned personal contributions in the costs are meant to restrict, medical consumption, the amount is calculated as a certain percentage (for example 25% for normal medical care; 50% for kinetic therapy; 0, 25, 50 or 100% for specialist treatment) or as a flat-rate payment (for example for visits of the doctor, preventive dental care under twelve years of age, medicine prepared by the pharmacist, stays in hospital). For widow(er)'s, invalids, less able-bodied persons, retired persons and orphans with a modest income (*WIGW's*), the conditions are considerably more favourable (no or very low personal contributions).

For self-employed people the sickness and invalidity insurance scheme is limited to the so called major risks, such as admission into hospital, major surgery, delivery and specialist care. These are covered like for employees, as described above. Minor risks, for example normal doctor`s visits, dental care and medicine do not fall under the compulsory insurance for self-employed persons. However, many self-employed people take out an additional sickness insurance against minor risks on a voluntary basis.

If medical care is necessary for employees due to an industrial injury or occupational disease, the relevant insurance schemes will ensure that the victim does not have to pay any personal contributions. Furthermore, the Fund for Occupational Diseases sometimes will compensate preventive care. If the private employer of the victim of an industrial injury has a recognized medical service, the employee concerned must be cared for by this medical service (cost free).

4.6. Family.

Female employees enjoying their 15 weeks maternity leave, are granted a maternity allowance. The benefit is similar to the sickness benefit, except that the maternity allowance for employed women amounts to 82% of the (unlimited) wage during the first 30 days of the maternity leave. Afterwards the benefit amounts to 75% of the (limited) wage.

For self-employed women the maternity insurance is less generous: it provides a lump sum payment, composed to cover the three weeks after confirment.

Family allowance is payable in respect of the claimant's own children, children of their spouse or ex-spouse or their unmarried partner, grandchildren belonging to their family or brothers and sisters (if the latter are not entitled to family allowances in any other way) and families with children under state care.

Normally family allowance is payable over the years in which school is obligatory (up to sixteen years of age), albeit that this period is extended to twenty one or twenty five years of age in respect of various students. Under certain conditions child allowance is also payable up to twenty five years of age for a child who helps in the household. Handicapped children or children incapable of work give rise to the entitlement to child allowance up to the age of twenty five years, if they are 66% incapable of work. If they are fully incapable of carrying out any kind of occupation or work in a sheltered work shop, they give rise to a lifelong right to benefit. Unemployed young graduates who have no benefits on grounds of unemployment insurance enjoy continued entitlement to child allowance.
Family allowances include the following benefits:
- flat-rate maternity pay (per birth);
- normal child allowance, in respect of which the amount for the second

child is almost double that for the first, the amount for the third and following children almost threefold that of the amount for the first child.
Children of a less able-bodied claimant give rise to a slightly higher allowance. Orphans give rise to entitlement to a higher allowance providing that the surviving parent does not start a new family.

For less able-bodied children, in addition to the usual child allowance, a considerable supplement is paid up to the age of twenty five.
Furthermore, there is an age allowance for all children (groups between six and twelve, twelve and sixteen and from sixteen years; the allowance increases per age group).

The professional family allowance schemes are almost identical. The main deviation in the scheme for self-employed people is the significantly lower amount of child allowance for the first child (not one third of that for children of employees). Also the amount for the second child differs slightly. The age allowances are almost the same.

The guaranteed family allowances almost entirely coincide with those of the scheme for employees, although of course the right to this guaranteed family allowance only exists when the subsistence means of the person concerned do not rise above a certain level.

4.7. Need.

The income maintenance allowances for handicapped people guarantee the handicapped person a benefit amounting to at least the minimum subsistence level which is relevant for him. The (flat-rate) integration allowances are payable to handicapped people for whom damage to or a reduction of their capacity for self-help is determined. The amount of both allowances is reduced by the amount of income in excess of certain limits of the handicapped person, his/her spouse or the person with whom he/she forms a household. These limits may vary for both allowances, they may be depending upon whether there are people who are dependent upon the beneficiary, whether the beneficiary is single or cohabiting and upon whether or not the beneficiary enjoys a pension.

Every Belgian or person treated as such, who is of age, with a real place of residence in Belgium, who has inadequate means of subsistence (means test), and who cannot earn such means through own efforts or in some other manner, is entitled to minimum subsistence. The level of minimum subsistence varies for cohabiting spouses, single people (about 3/4 of the amount for the former) or someone living with one or more than one person (1/2 the amount for spouses).

Here we recall that on grounds of the legislation on the Public Centers for Social Welfare every person has the right to social services which are necessary for him to lead a life that is worthy of a human being. The social service may take the shape of cash benefits. The administrative bodies have rather a wide margin of policy discretion with respect to the suitable form of assistance (cash or other), as well as in respect of the amount and the conditions for the granting of municipal services in cash.

5. Financing.

The financing of social security for employees consists of contributions from employees and/or employers, state subsidies and other resources.

The basis of calculation for contributions is the gross wage of the employees. The contribution percentages are fixed by law. In some cases special rules apply, for example in the form of a reduced contribution rate for specific types of employers or by fixing special contributions for all kinds of non-employees to whom the insurance schemes for employees have been extended.

The employer deposits his own contribution as well as the contributions from the wages of his employees with the *R.S.Z.* The contributions, after deductions for administrative fees according to the budget, are divided between the *R.I.Z.I.V.* (both branches) the *R.K W.* the *R.V.P.*, the *R.V.A.*, the *F.A.O.* and the *F.B.Z.* This division takes place according to a ratio corresponding to the division of the contribution rates over the various branches. The contributions are therefore not distributed according to the financial needs of the branches of social insurance. Recently the large financial autonomy of each of the branches has been slightly restricted.

Whereas before contributions were only paid on the wage, now contributions are also paid on some social security benefits i.e. on industrial injuries and occupational diseases benefits, (the same percentages as on wage), on the invalidity benefits and early retirement pensions (which is 3.5% to the extent that benefits exceed a certain amount; contributions for the, insurance scheme in respect of retirement and survivor's pensions), on all pensions, including occupational pensions and group insurance schemes (1. 8% to the extent that the pension exceeds a certain amount), and on some child allowances (fixed amount).

State subsidies automatically cover the differences between income from contributions and the expenditure (benefits) of the unemployment insurance scheme (also of invalidity pensions for miners). In respect of the other branches of social security for employees the statute defines the way in which the state subsidies are fixed, that is to say at:
- 20% of the expenditure for retirement and survivors's pensions
- 80% of the expenditure for sickness and invalidity insurance, branch medical care, in so far as this payment is made for *WIGW's* (Widows, invalids, pensioners and orphans);
- 50%, 75% or 95% respectively of the expenditure for the sickness and invalidity insurance scheme, benefit branches, applicable from the

second, third or fourth year of invalidity; funeral costs are fully subsidized by the state;
- 100% of the expenditure for the so called "war risks" in the industrial injuries insurance scheme; and
- 60% of all the expenditure for miner's lung disease in the branch of occupational diseases.
In principle there are no state subsidies in the area of family allowances.

The employee insurance schemes are also financed from other (para-fiscal) sources, such as:
- a special lump sum contribution to be paid by the pharmaceutical industry per product they commercialise as well as 2% of their turnover to be paid by the same (benefits the *R.I.Z.I.V.*);
- a part of the indirect tabacco taxes (these "health taxes" are collected by the normal tax service and supposed to be passed on to the *R.I.Z.I.V.*); and
- a supplementary premium of 10% of the usual insurance schemes premium for vehicle taxes (also for the *R.I.Z.I.V.*).

The last two taxes not only help to cover the costs of the *R.I.Z.I.V.* for the scheme of employees but also the costs for the other schemes.

The financing of social security for the self-employed person consists of contributions from self-employed people and of state subsidies.
The social security contributions of the self-employed are calculated on the business income i.e. on the basis of their income declaration for tax purposes. There are various contribution rates for people whose main activities are in self-employment people with a self-employed secundary occupation and self-employed people who have attained pensionable age, yet who continue to work (for the two latter groups there are lower contribution rates than for people who are self-employed in their main profession). There are three income levels in the contributions scheme; if the business income falls below the minimum level, then a minimum contribution is still levied on the amount of this minimum level (also when no real income or even a loss was entered); if the business income falls above the middle level then a lower percentage applies than that which is applicable for an income below this middle level; all income above the maximum level is free from contribution charges. Thus the system of contributions in this case is degressive.

For both sickness and invalidity insurance state subsidies are determined in the same manner as in the employees scheme. In the annual budget low state supplements are set for pensions and family allowances

The social security system for self-employed is also financed by a low flat-rate contribution paid by every entreprise.

The guaranteed income for the eldery, the guaranteed child allowance and allowances for handicapped people are financed entirely out of general taxation. In contrast, the minimum subsistence is financed for one half by the local Public Centers for Social Welfare and for the other half by the central government. The Publis Centers for Social Welfare also bear the costs for their social welfare services. The State bears the full costs of assistance to political refugees.

6. Judicial review.

Disputes between insured employees or self-employed people and the administrative organisations are referred to the authority of the labour courts (*arbeidsrechtbanken*) (in first instance) and that of the higher labour courts (*arbeidshoven*) (in further appeal). This is also the case for disputes concerning the assistance schemes. Cassation is possible on points of law to the Court of Cassation (*Hof van Cassatie*).

The labour courts are fully autonomous legal institutions integrated within the judiciary. Besides social security cases they also deal with labour law cases. They are composed of one professional magistrate who is appointed for life and of two laymen. Unless otherwise provided, one of the laymen is appointed on the nomination of the most representative unions, the other one on the nomination of the most representative employer's organisations. In disputes concerning less able-bodied allowances one of the laymen is appointed on the nomination of one of the professional organisations, the other on the nomination of the unions. In respect of disputes concerning the self-employed there are two professional magistrates and one layman appointed on the nomination of the professional organisations for the self-employed.

The application of law by the labour courts is almost similar to that of ordinary courts; mostly the principles of the civil procedure are applied, albeit in a simplified wy and tempered by the principles of inquisitorial procedure, inter alia as a result of the actions of the labour auditorium (a specific public ministery in social affairs). Like the civil court, the labour court can call upon medical and other expertise (for example in order to give evidence of incapacity for work).

The decisions of the labour courts are in principle subject to appeal to the higher labour courts. In appeal the application of law is similar to the one in first instance (full appeal).
The Court of Cassation receives appeals of all judicial decisions taken at last instance, also of those of the labour courts, against which there is an alleged infringement of the law (or a violation of substantial procedural requirement). The Court does not decide on points of fact.

Only some of the matters dealing with social security fall outside the jurisdiction of the labour courts, i.e.
- The normal (criminal) jurisdiction: the application of penal provisions of social security acts (the labour courts are competent to deal with administrative sanction);

- The juvenile court (*Jeugdrechtbank*) or the justice of the peace (*Vrederechter*): some disputes concerning the determination of the person who is allowed to receive the benefit payments;
- The "Council of State" (*Raad van State*): only purely administrative disputes concerning administrative and co-operative bodies; ,"
- The Civil Courts: disputes concerning the damages of insured people or those entitled to social assistance as a result of maladministration e.g. wrong information.

In the social security litigation the costs of the administration of justice are not necessarily borne by the loser of the court case: these must always be carried by the government or the institution charged with the application of the laws upon which the insured person bases his appeal.

Chapter 2: Denmark

1. Introduction: concept and sources of social security law.

The concept of social security does not refer to a clearly defined body of social benefits and services. Yet there is a clear-cut distinction between social insurance and social assistance, each resorting under different managements of the Ministry of Social Affairs.

Thus the social insurance schemes comprise: social and part-time pensions, daily benefits in respect of sickness, maternity and child benefits; furthermore (in a broader sense of the word): the benefits on grounds of occupational damage insurance (industrial injuries and occupational diseases), additional labour market pensions, unemployment insurance, as well as health care services.

Next to that, in various forms, exists social assistance.

Until 1970 there were no family benefits in Denmark. When they were introduced, they were considered to be part of the domain of social security and adminstered as such. Since 1.7.1987 benefits for children in general, i.e. child benefits (thus excluding specific child allowances) have been removed from the competence of the administrative bodies for social security (Ministry of Social Affairs) and attributed to the national taxation service. As from that moment these benefits are no longer dealt with in social security literature. However, below we will discuss all family benefits governed by public law.

In the seventies, Danish social security law was subject to a major simplification as a result of the introduction of a number of acts replacing numerous previous statutes, i.e.

- the act concerning social administration (*lov om styrelse af sociale og visse sundhedsmaessige anliggender*);
- the act concerning public health insurance (*lov om offentligsygesikring*);
- the daily benefits act (*lov om dagpenge ved sygdom eller fødsel*);
- the act concerning social administrative adjudication (*lov om den sociale ankestyrelse*)
- the social assistance act (*lov om social bistand*).

The reform was based upon the principle that for his social security and assistance the citizen should have optimal access to one service, closely situated to his place of residence. The realisation of this principle implied a major harmonisation of the numerous acts previously in existence, as well as a decentralisation of the administration to local communities (*kommune*).

Section 75 of the Danish constitution (latest version: 1953) deals with social security (lato sensu). Section 75(1) lays down the principle that in the interests of general welfare, each able bodied citizen should have the opportunity to perform work of his own choice which enables him to provide in his own subsistence. Section 75(2) gives the right to assistance from the state to each person who cannot provide his own subsistence or that of his dependants, and in respect of whom no person carries a maintenance liability. On grounds of the latter provision, the beneficiary of state assistance may be restricted in the enjoyment of civil and political rights. Indeed, in the last century such restrictions were linked to the granting of the poor relief. However, at the present time they have entirely disappeared from Danish social security law.

Section 7 5 constitution has not had any impact upon the creation of Danish social law. It was almost entirely ignored both in legal doctrine and in case law. At the most the following principles may be derived from Section 75(2):

- there must be a system of social assistance under public law which guarantees to every person a certain subsistence level;
- social assistance is a right, not a charity; those who satisfy the legal requirements are entitled to it;
- the primary duty to grant subsistence does not rest (necessarily) upon the state but upon other individuals. The government is constitutionally entitled to recover the granted aid from those who are liable to maintenance.

Social benefits and services all rest upon a formal statutory basis. Sometimes parliament empowers the Minister or an administrative body to enact further rules which are binding to administrative bodies and citizens; the *Bekendtørelser* which are issued on the basis of such authorisations are published in the same way as statutes. For social security law they are not unimportant.
Neither unimportant, yet not binding to the citizen, are guidelines, etc. which are issued by the competent ministers and administrative organisations. Depending on the case, the administrative guidelines are or are not legally binding to administrative bodies. These texts, as well as the leading judgements of the higher adminstrative judiciary may be consulted in the *Sociale Meddelelser*, an important source of information for the legal practitioner.

For questions of interpretation one can often successfully consult the parliamentary preparation of acts (the *Betaenkning* which are formulated in respect of new material legislation) and even political policy guidelines concerning (social security) problem areas (the *Redegørelser*).

Unemployment funds have their own regulations. By collective labour agreement a supplementary pension has been introduced for more than half of the employees.

In accordance with the general scheme of this work, we will not deal with social security law of the Faroes and Greenland.

2. Administrative organisation.

The administration of almost all social security schemes is strongly decentralised. As was said before, the system is based upon the principle that each citizen should have access to social security in his local community or, as the case may be in larger communities, in parts thereof (there are 275 *Kommuner*).

Within each local community council (periodically elected by the inhabitants of the *Kommune*) a commission is encharged with the administration of social security schemes (*det sociale udvalg*). The actual administration of social security takes place under the supervision of the *sociale udvalg* by an unique local community social service to which a person has access, for among others, his (daily) benefits in respect of incapacity for work, social and part-time pensions, family benefits, rent rebates, social assistance (in cash or in kind), as well as a number of other social services. There exist national associations of *Kommuner (KLF)* and of *sociale udvalg (Sammenslutning af sociale udvalg)*.

Danish territory is subdivided into 14 districts, the so called *amtskommuner*. Each *kommune* is part of a *amtskommune*. However, this is not the case for København and the neighbouring Frederiksberg. In fact, for these places the *kommune* and the *amtskommune* are joined together, a circumstance which gives rise to special administrative regulations which we will not consider here. The *amtskommune* is governed by an elected council which also appoints a social commission (*social og-sundhedsudvalg*). The council leaves the routine administration of the social security and health schemes to the social and health administration (including the social centre) of the *amtskommune*. Most of the secondary health services are offered on this district level; also the formation of hospital policy and specific medical and social services (among other rehabilitation centres) can be situated on this level. If they are confronted with specific complex questions, the *sociale udvalg* of the local communities may rely upon the expert aid of the social centre of the *amtskommune*.

Some local communities and districts got the status of *frikommune* or *friamt*. This administration is more flexibel; there is e.g. no need for a specific commission dealing with social security.

On a district level, the *sociale brugerraad* gives advice with regard to social policy affairs. This council of clients consists of seven members and a chairman; three people represent the Association of organisations of the handicapped, two represent the parents of children in day care institutions and boarding establishments and one person the inhabitants of institutions of the *amtskommune*; furthermore, one more representative of other client groups of the district may be added.

On a national level most social security affairs resort under the authority of the *Socialministerium*. However, sometimes the health minister or the Ministry of Labour is competent. The *Socialministerium* consists of politically independent civil servants; only the Minister himself bears political responsibility. The personnel of the *Socialministerium* operates as the secretariat of the Minister and deals mainly with policy questions and the preparation of statutes.

Furthermore, on a central level there is also a *Centrale handicapraad*, which advises on matters of policy with regard to the handicapped. The council consists of 11 members, five of whom represent the *samvirkende Invalideorganisationer*; the other members represent various levels of the administration.

There are a number of important exceptions to the decentralised system of administration as described above.
For example, as from 1987, child benefit for children younger than 18 years of age is awarded by the national taxation service; in case of problems, a person may still contact the *sociale udvalg* which, however, merely operates as an intermediary between citizens and the competent tax services.
Furthermore, the unemployment insurance scheme, which is still optional, is traditionally administered by the unemployment funds (*Arbejds-løshedskasser*) set up by the trade unions, as organised on an industrial branch level (or with respect to two funds, linked to the main organisations for the self employed). From the point of view of book-keeping and administration, unemployment funds are independent from the related trade unions; union membership is not a prerequisite for membership to a fund; however, such a link is often established in the reverse case. In order to be able to operate as an administrative body of the unemployment insurance scheme, the funds must receive recognition by the competent minister; for such recognition a minimum number of members (5000) is required; the minister can withhold recognition if there already exists a fund for the industrial branch concerned. Most of the funds have local of fices which can be contacted by the insured persons. The Direktorat for *Arbejds-løshesforsikringen* of the Ministry of Labour supervises the unemployment funds. The funds are mutually associated in the *Arbejdløshedskassernes Samvirke*.
A central body, which is governed by the employer and employee organi-sations on a parity basis, administers the additional labour market pensions *(Arbejdsmarkedets Tillaegspension/ATP)*.

The industrial damage insurance scheme (industrial injuries and occupational diseases insurance) is set up by the employers with private insurance companies. The Arbejdsskadestyvelsen are empowered to award benefits; furthermore, they control the insurance companies.

3. Personal scope of application.

Every person living in Denmark is entitled to social assistance. The entitlement to assistance in cash which is expected to have a long term character, in the terms of the present administrative practice: an expected duration of more than one year, is restricted to Danish citizens, political refugees and citizens of states with which Denmark has concluded a reciprocal arrangement relating to this matter. Those who are not entitled to such social assistance benefits, but who are nevertheless in need of them, may be expelled from Danish territory. Danish citizens who are abroad may under certain circumstances claim a right to subsistence. This is, for example, the case for Danish citizens who stay abroad for a longer period due to illness and who cannot be expected to return home.

Every person living in Demark is equally entitled to medical care.

In order to be eligible for a social pension, it is required that one:
- has Danish nationality; or
- has had permanent and legal residence in Denmark for a period of at least 10 years between the ages of 15 and 67; furthermore, of these 10 years at least 5 must immediately precede the moment that entitlement to pension arises; or
- is a political refugee.

Furthermore, it is required that when the pension is claimed, one lives or has lived in Denmark during a period of at least 30 years between the ages of 15 and 67. In order to actually become entitled to benefit, all people, i.e both Danish and non-Danish must have lived three years in Denmark between the ages of 15 and 67.
Once entitlement to a social pension is recognized, a person may continue to receive benefit if he emigrates to another country; he should then satisfy the condition that he has had his permanent residence in Denmark for at least 30 years after the age of 15, as well as immediately preceding the moment that entitlement to benefit arises. Temporary residence abroad does not affect entitlement to a pension, at least when the pensioner maintains his real and actual residence in Denmark.

Already in this stage it should be noted that for the right to the full amount of social old age pension a period of 40 years of residence in Denmark (between the age limits mentioned above) is required; if this condition is not satisfied, the amount of old age pension is reduced pro rata temporis. With regard to the other social pensions, the right to the full amount of pension is made dependent upon the condition that a person must have lived in Denmark during a period of at least 4/5 of the years between the age of 15 and the moment that entitlement to a pension arises.

Only those who are employed in Denmark (including civil servants) for at least 10 hours a week or 43 1/3 hours a month (between the ages of 16 and

66) are compulsorily affiliated to the additional labour market pension insurance (*A.T.P.*).

In order to be eligible for a part-time pension (*delpension*), it is required that one:

- is an employee or self-employed person in Denmark;
- has a permanent residence in Denmark;
- is between the age of 60 and 67; and
- if he is employee, has paid *A. T.P.* contributions during the last 20 years for a total equivalent to 10 years full time contribution.

All employees are compulsorily insured for income maintenance in respect of sickness and maternity. Self-employed entrepreneurs and their spouses who are engaged in the same activity are equally insured, but only for the income maintenance as from the fourth week of incapacity for work; however, they can insure themselves on a voluntary basis in respect of the first three weeks. Voluntary insurance also exists for those who carry out domestic activities at home for at least one person other than himself. In principle all these people must be subject to income tax liability in Denmark.

Employees (as well as self-employed fishermen, people who act in order to prevent accidents or to save human lives, people who are remanded in custody and some other categories) enjoy a special protection on grounds of the industrial injuries and occupational diseases accidents insurance scheme.

Child allowances and child benefits are only granted on the condition that the child or one of his parents is a Danish citizen; that the child is permanently resident in Denmark; is not maintained outside the family nor by public funds; and is not yet married. In legislation it is specifically provided that the child allowance is a right of the child.

Every person who lives in Denmark, who is between 16 and 65 years of age, and has the status of an employee or a self employed person (or as a person doing his military service) can become a member of an unemployment fund available to him. Pensioners only have limited rights and those who become 67 years of age lose their membership altogether. About 80% of the employees and 1/3 of the self-employed are members of a fund for (optional) unemployment insurance.

In order to be eligible for *efterløn* one has to satisfy the additional requirement that one lives in Denmark; one has been a member of an unemployment fund for at least 20 years in the rast 25 years and is older than 60 years of age but has not yet attained the age of 67. Between 1992 and 1995 long-term unemployed can already receive *efterlon* from the age of 55.

4. Risks and benefits.

By the first of July of each year the amounts of the social benefits are increased in accordance with the evolution of the yearly income of the workers in the private sector during the preceeding calendar year.

4.1. Old age.

There are various schemes in Danish social security law which insure income maintenance for the elderly. Thus, we can make a distinction between: the social old age pension (*folkepension*), the additional labour market (old age) pension (*ATP*) and the part-time pension (*delpension*). Furthermore, many employees and civil servants have joined pensionfunds, which often take the shape of a collective life or pension insurance.

The social old age pension is payable to those who belong to the group of people insured for social pension and who have reached the age of 67. The full amount of pension is payable to those who have lived in Denmark for 40 years between the ages of 15 and 67.

The social old age pension consists of a basic amount and a pension supplement. In addition there may be a whole range of special supplements. The basic amount is flat-rate; it is paid to insured persons who are 70 years of age or older. The basic amount of old age pension for the pensioner between 67 and 70 years of age is reduced by 60% of the income arising from employment (subject to a certain upper earnings limit).

The pension supplement is means tested; both the income of the person himself and that of his spouse are taken into account. Of the further supplements which are payable on grounds of the legislation concerning the social pension, the personal supplement is the most important. This supplement is subject to a means test and payable to pensioners who find themselves in particularly difficult economic circumstances; a supplement is then granted as a payment towards the costs of heating, although the pensioner himself is liable to pay a certain contribution for the heating costs. Furthermore, as an exception, a personal supplement may be granted to meet certain other costs (e.g. for the coverage of medical expenses), yet only if the person finds himself in particularly difficult economic circumstances. *The kommune* has a general budget for the financing of personal supplements.

Special rules apply for those who remain in institutions.

The part-time pension creates the possibility for those between 60 and 67 years of age to retire gradually from the labour market by reducing their work without fully ceasing it. For employees and the self employed the entitlement conditions for part-time pensions differ.

The employee who is elegible for a part-time pension must reduce his weekly hours of work by either 1/4, or 7 hours per week (based upon a 37 hours maximum working week, as a starting point for the method of calculation). After the reduction of the regular working hours the employee must continue to work for at least 20 days in three months, and minimum 15 hours and maximum 30 hours in one week. The part-time pension is calculated by multiplying a uniform rate by the average number of reduced weekly working hours. Thus the amount of benefit payable corresponds to the maximum amount of daily sickness benefit which would have been payable over the same period. Finally, it must be mentioned that legislation does not grant the employee a right to change to part-time employment with his employer, although arrangements to this effect are often adopted in collective labour agreements. Also those who receive *efterløn* are covered by the part-time pension scheme.

For employees it is required that within the last 20 years they should have contributed to the scheme an amount which is equivalent to 10 years of full contributions payments in respect of a full-time job.

The self-employed who are covered by the part-time pension scheme must have enjoyed an income of at least half the above mentioned maximum in the year preceding partial retirement. A self-employed person must reduce his professional activities by at least 18 1/2 hours a week, leaving a working week of 18 1/2 hours. Thus for the self-employed there is only one possible amount of part-time pension, i.e. 18 1/2 times the uniform rate. The scheme is not means-tested but the part-time pension may not exceed 90 % of the difference of income from labour before and after the moment of partial retirement.

For the self-employed it is required that they have been self-employed in Denmark for a period of at least 4 of the last 5 years; that he has been occupied full-time for a period of at least 5 years preceding the moment that entitlement to a part-time pension arises; and that in the last year he has had an income from self-employment which is higher than half the maximum amount of daily benefits in respect of sickness. Furthermore there are conditions with regard to a reduction of the professional working hours.

After 2 1/2 year of partial retirement (+ possibly the period of enjoyment of (*efterløn*), the part-time pension amounts are reduced to 80% of the previous amount. Again two years later the beneficiary only receives 70 % of the orginal part-time pension.

Entitlement to *A. T.P.*-old age pensions exists from the age of 67. It is built up with reference to each year of employment between the ages of 16 and 66 . Those who started to participate in the *A TP*-scheme after the moment of its introduction (1.4.1965) are granted a set amount for each pensionable year of service. For those who partipate in the *A. T.P.* scheme from the moment of its introduction, there are age-related flat-rate amounts in respect of the preceding years.

The amount differs for people employed in the public and these employed in the private sector.

The pension is depending upon the number of years one has paid contributions. The additional labour market pension, however, provides higher amounts, as these are augmented with a bonus (the bonus may not exceed 50% of the amount of the original pension). This bonus follows from the profits made by the scheme, that is to say: from the difference between the income on the one hand, and the legally prescribed expenditures and benefits on the other. Indeed, the legislative provisions concerning the A. T.P. pensions are determined in such a way as to guarantee a profit of 4, 5% of the contributions; if the interest rate appears to be generally higher, a surplus arises which then flows back to the beneficiaries in the form of a bonus.

4.2. Death

As such there exists no survival pension any longer in the Danish social security law. The function of these pensions has been taken over, but only to a very small extent, by the early social pension (see section 4.3).

The beneficiary of a social old age pension, continues to receive this pension for a period of three more months after the death of the spouse.

The additional labour market pension for survivors (A.T.P.-survivor pension) is payable to the surviving spouse of an A. T.P. insured person from the age of 62 on. The deceased must have worked for a period corresponding to at least 10 pensionable years and also the marriage must have lasted at least 10 years. The A TP-survivor's pension provides 50% of the A TP-old age pension plus a bonus which the deceased received or would have received at the age of 67 on grounds of the number of years that he worked under the A TP-scheme. If the surviving spouse satisfies the entitlement conditions for an ATP-old age pension himself, he receives the highest of both A TP-pension amounts. Entitlement to ATP-survivor pension ends with a new marriage, but may revive at its termination.

Under the insurance scheme for occupational damage a lump sum is payable in respect of the costs which arise from the death of a victim of a professional risk. Normally, this sum is paid to the surviving spouse or partner. Also the surviving spouse or partner may be compensated for the death of the breadwinner, taking into account the possibility open to the survivor for providing his own subsistence, considering his age, health, education, activities, etc. Compensation is payable for a maximum period of 10 years and the annual amount consists of 30% of the yearly wage (subject to a ceiling similar to the one which applies in respect of the compensation for a loss of earning capacity (see below)); as an exception, this period may be extended, albeit maximally, to the age of 67. Sometimes the benefit is capitalized. The benefit does not end in case of a new marriage, but it does end if a person reaches his 67th year of age. In that case the beneficiary receives a lump sum, the amount of which corresponds to two years of benefit.

For each child of the victim younger than 18 years of age (or, in case of education, 21) 10% of the yearly wage (subject to an upper wage limit), or 20% in respect of a child without any parents, is payable. Maximally, the total of all these benefits to children may add up to 40% of the yearly wage mentioned above (or 50% if only the deceased was responsible for the children).

If the total amount of benefits to the spouse and to the children does not exceed 70% of the yearly wage, a lump sum or an annuity may be granted to another survivor. For all the persons mentioned above it is required that they were maintained by the deceased or that their financial position deteriorated as a result of his death.

On grounds of the health care insurance scheme there is a right to a funeral benefit (*begravelseshjaelp*). Additional benefits in respect of death or a funeral are also often granted by, among others, the providers of collective pensions schemes and trade unions.

4.3. Incapacity for work.

A person who does not work as a result of sickness, injury, birth or adoption of a child and thus has lost his income from labour, is entitled to an income maintenance benefit (daily benefit) for as long as he can be expected to return to work. If the incapacity for work is no longer to be considered as temporary, but permanent, the entitlement to daily benefit ends and it may be considered whether the person is elegible for a social pension.

For daily benefits in respect of incapacity for work as a result of injury or sickness (*sygedagpenge*) a distinction must be made between two periods of compensation: the period during which daily benefit is payable by the employer and the period during which the daily benefit is payable by the *sociale udvalg*. The duration of the employer's period is two weeks for a private employee and unlimited for a public employee; the other period lasts as long as the duration of the temporary incapacity for work, yet not longer than 52 weeks.
In order to be entitled to daily benefit from the employer, it is required that the insured employee has been employed for at least 120 hours in the last 13 weeks and that he is not entitled to a continuation of wage payments. The daily benefit is calculated on the basis of the average weekly income during the last four weeks preceding the illness.
The amount of daily benefit is equal to the lost income from labour and in any case not more than a legally set upper level. Together with other possible compensation payments in respect of illness, the amount of daily benefit may never exceed the normal income from labour. If daily benefit amounts to less than 10% of the maximum amount of daily benefit, benefit is not payable by the *sociale udvalg*, except when daily benefit is due on grounds of voluntary insurance. In cases of partial incapacity for work, daily benefits are paid according to special rules.

Self-employed can get sickness benefit from their first day after a three weeks waiting period. It is possible to insure oneself for the first three weeks. It is further a condition that the activity as self-employed has been significant (at least half of the income of an employed person in the specific sector) in at least 6 months before sickness. The amount payable is calculated in the same way as for employed people.

During the last four weeks of pregnancy, employees, self-employed entrepreneurs and their spouses, who are engaged in the same activity, may receive daily benefit from the *sociale udvalg*. After a birth (or adoption) daily benefit continues to be payable during a period of 24 weeks, the last ten of which may be claimed by the father of the child. The father is also entitled to two weeks of daily benefit immediately at the birth of the child or at the moment that the newly born child returns home. It is required for entitlement to these daily benefits that professional activities are ceased during the relevant period. Daily benefit can only be received by one of the spouses during the same period.

We will now discuss the benefits in respect of permanent incapacity for work. These constitute a part of the scheme for early social pensions (*førtidspensioner*). Although early social pensions do not consist exclusively of benefits in respect of invalidity, for the sake of clarity we have chosen to give an unique systematic overview of all the social pensions concerned.

The act concerning social pensions distinguishes between high, middle, increased general and general early pensions. These benefits will be briefly discussed, each time with reference to the person who is eligible as well as the different parts which consitute the benefits. All benefits are flat-rate, generally a distinction being made between whether one is married to another social pensioner or not.

The highest early pension may be awarded to those between 18 and 59 years of age, who, due to health reasons, have entirely or almost entirely lost their working capacity. The highest early pension consists of a basic amount, a pension supplement, an invalidity amount and an earning incapacity amount; both of these last mentioned amounts are free of tax liability. The pension is paid till the beneficiary is 67 years of age. From that moment on an old age pension will be paid.

The middle early pension is awarded to those who:
- are between 60 and 66 years old and satisfy the entitlement conditions for the highest early pension or
- are between 18 and 59 years old, and whose working capacity has for reasons of health not been reduced entirely, but by 2/3.

The middle early pension consists of a basic amount, a pension supplement and early invalidity amounts (not subject to tax liability), depending on the question of whether one belongs to the first or the second group of people eligible for a middle early pension.

The increased general early pension is payable to those who:
- are between 18 and 59 years of age, and whose earning capacity has been reduced by reasons of health by at least 50%;
- are between 18 and 59 years of age, and whose working capacity has been reduced as a result of medical and social reasons by at least 50%;
- are between 50 and 59 years of age, and in respect of whom the granting of a pension is justified on grounds of social or health reasons; in the latter case a reduction of working capacity is not required.

The increased general early pension consists of a basic amount, a pension supplement and an early payment which is free of tax liability.

The general early pension is payable to those who:
- are between, 60 and 66 years of age, and whose working capacity has been reduced for reasons of health by at least 50%;
- between 60 and 66 years of age, and in respect of whom the granting of a pension is justified on grounds of social and health reasons or only social reasons; a reduction of the earning capacity is not required.

The general early pension consists of a basic amount and a pension supplement. The pensions for social reasons are not awarded if the income exceeds the maximum unemployment benefit for a couple or 2/3 of this benefit for a single person.

Under certain circumstances widowhood with dependent children, of a person who has never had any ties with the labour market, is accepted as a purely social reason for granting an early pension; thus the early social pension granted on grounds of purely social criteria offers some compensation (in cases of severe hardship) for the abolition of the social survivor pension.

Finally, we mention that there is a possibility of granting a personal, an assistance or a treatment supplement. The personal supplement has already been dealt with in the discussion of the social old age pension. An assistance supplement is payable to an invalid who regularly requires the aid of another person, as well as to the severly visually handicapped. If a person requires continuous care and attendance, he is entitled to a care supplement. Neither are liable to taxation; the supplements cannot cumulate.

A person for whom a plan has been established as to how to be able to man age his own life, is entitled to a rehabilitation benefit instead of a pension. The plan shall include educational measures and vocational training in order to bring the concerned person back to the labour market. The rehabilitation benefit can be received up to 5 years; its amount equals that of the unemployment benefit, except for people younger than 23 years of age for whom it equals half the amount of the unemployment benefit.

If the insured person is the victim of an occupational risk, entitlement to benefit can arise on grounds of the insurance scheme for occupational damage.
Those whose earning capacity has been affected by more than 15% as a result of an occupational risk are, in case of full incapacity for work, entitled

to an annuity of 4/5 of their yearly wage, subject to an upper wage limit. For the determination of the percentage of incapacity for work, both social and economic and labour market factors are taken into account; however purely medical facts are not taken into consideration. In cases of partial incapacity for work, a percentage of the full annuity is paid; this percentage corresponds to the degree of incapacity for work. The annuity is payable until a person reaches his 67th year; at that time he will receive a lump sum equal to the amount of two years annuity payments. Incapacity for work of less than 50% does not result in entitlement to an annuity, but to the payment of a lump sum.

Finally, compensation is payable in respect of permanent purely medical damage. In accordance with medical scales percentages have been determined which express the discomforts experienced as a result of health damage. Thus, the amount of benefit can be determined, related to a flat-rate basis of calculation. Normally the amount is paid as a lump sum on the basis of the life expection of a person and his age, but with medical damage of 50% or more payment of a periodical monthly benefit is also a possibilty.

4.4. Unemployment.

A person who has been a member of an unemployment fund for at least one year and who has worked in insured employment for at least 26 weeks within the last three years is entitled to unemployment benefit (*arbejdsløshedsdagpenge*). Normally the entitlement lasts maximally two and a half years. However, it should be added that each person looking for employment, in respect of which the entitlement is about to expire, is entitled to be offered suitable employment or vocational training. Employers obtain a premium in order to make extra jobs available; those who cannot be offered a job in the private sector must be given employment in the public sector.

The unemployment must be involuntary. The unemployed beneficiary is under a duty to register with the labour exchanges and to acccept suitable employment.

The level of unemployment benefit in relation to previously earned wages is determined by each of the unemployment funds; benefit may not exceed 90% of previously earned wages, subject to an upper wage limit. Those who have been allowed membership of an unemployment fund without having had any previous work experience (people carrying out their obligatory military service or having taken an education of at least 18 months) receive a flat-rate weekly amount. If the unemployed person has fully exhausted offers of employment and training, which normally will take 6 to 7 years, then the person will be eligible for social assistance.

The unemployment fund cannot pay benefit when unemployment is due to a strike or a lock-out.

The *efterløn* scheme constitutes an important addition to the unemployment insurance. Members of an unemployment fund who are at least 60 years of age and who have been members of the fund for a period of at least 20 years within the last 25 years may make use of this scheme. Furthermore, they must be capable for work. During the first five weeks of *efterløn* all employment is prohibited; subsequently 200 hours of employment per year is allowed (subject to an upper earnings limit). The beneficiary may not receive a social pension.

During the first 2 1/2 years (to be determined from the moment that employment ceased, thus possibly from the start of the unemployment), *efterløn* is equal to unemployment benefit; in the subsequent years it is 80% of this amount. *Efterløn* is payable up to the age of 67.

4.5. Medical care

All residents are compulsorily insured; the insured population may make a choice between two classes of insurance. The greatest majority chose class l; less than 5% have opted fo class 2 insurance.

Those who are ensured in class 1 enjoy free care by a medical practitioner, yet they may only change their (personal) practitioner once a year; specialist care in hospitals is also free, albeit on the condition of a reference by their personal practitioner.

Those who insured in class 2 are completely free in the choice of their personal pactitioner, but they are only reimbursed the amount which corresponds with the tariffs for class I which have been negotiated between the practitioners, organisations and the state.

The income of the medical practioners is dependent upon the number of medical operations carried out (one refund for each medical operation). Specialists are also fully paid on the basis of their medical achievements. Dental treatment, as specified in a list, is in principle 55% financed by the (class 1) patient himself; the rest is covered by social insurance; class 2 patients are reimbursed an amount which is equivalent to the part of the costs of the same dental treatment which is not borne by the class I patients themselves.

Regardless of the class, hospital care (in principle in a hospital of one's own *amtskommune*) and obstetric care are free of charge (except for extra services, for example, a private room). With the consent of the *amtskommune*, it is possible to receive treatment in a private hospital; the costs of such treatment are reimbursed to the patient.

Under certain conditions ambulance services are (partly or wholly) free of charge. If required, free interpreter services may also be provided. However, the treatment of a chiropractor is subject to a personal contribution. On prescription a patient may receive free care by a nurse at home.

The insured person must pay a personal contribution towards medicine equal to a certain percentage of the cost price, depending upon whether the purchased medicine is registered in list A or list B. Medicine, which has not been registered in either of these lists, must be paid in full, unless in an individual case it is decided that a remission should particularly be granted. Ear and eye prothesis are subject to a partial reimbursement.

A pregnant woman is entitled to five free preventive check-ups by a medical practitioner. Also birth assistance is free of charge. Abortion and sterilisation costs are also free of charge.

In cases of illness or industrial injury due to an occupational risk, the cost of medical care provided by a practitioner or dentist, of hospital care, and of medical aids and rehabilitation services are borne by the occupational damage insurance scheme.

People who are financially incapable of paying their own charges for medical care, medicine, etc. may apply for assistance on grounds of social assistance legislation. There is also the opportunity of taking out private insurance for (a part of the costs) of the personal charges.

4.6. Family.

On I July 1987 family benefits were fundamentally changed. The means tested general child benefit scheme and the youth benefit scheme which were previously in existence, have been abolished. There now exists:
- a flat-rate family child benefit for each child per year (*børne-familieydelse*). The benefit is higher for children until 6 years of age than for children above 6 years and younger than 18 years old. This benefit scheme is free from tax liability and administered by the taxation services. It is regulated in the new act concerning personal income taxation and, contrary to its forerunner, the general child benefit scheme is no longer considered to be part of the domain of social security;
- the normal child allowance (*børnetilskud*), previously "increased child benefits", is payable if the beneficiary is alone responsible for a child younger than 18 years of age or if both parents receive a social old age or invalidity pension;
- the extra child allowance, payable, regardless of the number of children, to recipients of the normal child benefit who are lone breadwinners.
- the special child allowance, payable if both parents of the child have died, if there is only one parent, or if one of the parents receives a social pension. In the latter two cases benefit consists of only 50% of the amount which is payable in the former case;
- the extra benefit for families with twins, triplets or more.

Finally, it must be mentioned that the legislation which governs family benefits also contains provisions concerning the granting of advance payments by the state of alimony for children in cases when the liable person is not fulfilling his obligations in time. The advance payment may not exceed the amount of the special child allowance.

4.7. Need.

On grounds of the act concerning social assistance the state is under a duty to provide assistance to any person who is present in Denmark and who, in view of his personal and family circumstances, needs council, financial or practical help, support in the recovery of his earning capacity, care, special treatment or educational support. From this provision it emerges that the scope of the assistance scheme is very wide; it contains a plethora of benefits. The assistance act is therefore governed by the principle that only one office, i.e. the service of the *kommune*, should deal with all questions of social assistance. Another principle is that care should be provided regardless of the cause of the need for help and the professional category to which the beneficiary belongs.

In view of the wide scope of the social assistance scheme, we will only deal with assistance in cash; thus, the services which are provided on the basis of the assistance act to the handicapped, home and child care facilities, as well as the juvenile protection measures, are not taken into consideration.

Assistance in cash may be divided into assistance for subsistence (*hjealp til underhold*) and assistance for special costs (*hjaelp i saerlige tilfaelde*).

The assistance for subsistence is payable to those whose life circumstances have altered to such an extent that they can not longer provide for the subsistence of themselves and their families. Assistance for subsistence consists of a basic benefit, a housing supplement and a child supplement. Basic benefit for single persons consists of half the amount payable to a couple. After 9 months, the amount of basic benefit is reduced, unless it can be proved that in the near future the person in question will be able to take care of himself again. A single young person up to 23 years of age receives benefit at a reduced rate, here a distinction is made between juveniles living at home and juveniles who live on there own. The housing supplement is intended to cover the costs of rent or the costs of home ownership, after deduction of other housing subsidies. Furthermore, the housing supplement covers the costs of water, gas electricity, heating and other costs connected with housing; all real costs are covered, unless these are considered to be excessive.

Assistance in cash is subject to an income and capital test. Furthermore, both spouses must have exhausted all possibilities of finding employment. At the latest after three months of payment of assistance in cash, the *sociale udvalg* will consider whether there is reason to change over to other forms of assistance payments, for example budget advising. The total amount of assistance for subsistence may not exceed the maximum amount of daily benefit on grounds of the unemployment insurance scheme (after tax deduction).

Special rules apply for those who do their obligatory (non-military) service in the civil sector or in a developing country, as well as for people who stay in a penal institution.

Assistance in cash for special costs is payable to people regardless of whether they receive assistance for subsistence. Assistance for coverage of justifiable isolated expenses is payable, if the payment of these expenses by the beneficiary himself would constitute a real threat to future possibilities of providing for his own livelihood. Assistance may be provided for the coverage of the costs of medical treatment, medicine, dental care, etc., as far as these are not already covered by other schemes. Furthermore, assistance may be given for expenses resulting from the exercise of parental care duties, as well as for the coverage of removal costs to a place with better housing- and earning circumstances. Severely handicapped people living on their own, as well as people who care at home for a physically or mentally handicapped person, younger than 18 years of age, are entitled to compensation for the extra costs resulting from their attendance.

5. Financing.

Social assistance and a number of social insurance benefits are wholly financed out of general taxation. The state and the *kommuner* and *amtskommuner* together bear the largest share of the total social security expenditure. The employers and the insured people only contribute to a small part of this.

Social assistance in cash is 50% financed by the state and 50% by the *kommune*. Advice given on grounds of the assistance act, as well as the general administration, is financed wholly by the *kommune*; this also applies to the social assistance services for people older than 67 years of age. The assistance services which are offered to people younger than 67 years of age are mostly 50% financed by the *kommune* and 50% by the *amtskommune*.

The daily benefits in respect of sickness and maternity are 25% financed out of the budget of the *kommune*; the remaining 75% is borne by a fund which is administered by the Ministry for Social Affairs. This fund is fed by:
- voluntary insurance contributions, determined in such a way as to cover a total of 3/8 of the benefit costs on grounds of voluntary insurance;
- contributions from (smaller) employers who have bought off the obligation to pay the daily benefits during the initial period of incapacity for work; the rates of these contributions are set so as to fully cover the expenditure which thus arises for the *kommune*;
- and for the major share by state subsidy.
The daily benefits which are paid by the employer are financed fully by the employers themselves.

Pensions to people over 60 years of age are fully financed by the state; pensions to younger people are paid for 50% by the State and for 50% by the *kommune*.

The social and part-time pensions are fully refunded by the state to the *kommuner*. Only the personal pension supplements which are granted by the *kommune* on a discretionary basis are merely refunded for 75%.

The additional labour market pensions are financed fully from contributions. These are borne for 1/3 by the employees and for 2/3 by the employers.

Family benefits are financed entirely by the state.

The costs of medical care are borne by the *amtskommuner* and the state.

Employers who bear contribution liability pay 12 times the amount of maximum daily (unemployment) benefit as an annual contribution toward the unemployment insurance scheme; the members of unemployment funds pay 8 times this amount. The remaining means which are necessary for the financing of unemployment benefits are financed by the state (subsidy on the basis of the expenditure of the fund in the previous year; also here the state subsidy constitutes the major financing share). Furthermore, the members of the unemployment funds are liable to pay contributions for the costs of administration; the rates of the administration contributions are set by each fund. Employers bear no contribution liability in respect of their first employee. Further, unemployed members are liable to pay contributions; recipients of *efterløn* pay contributions at a 50% rate.

The *eftertløn* scheme is mainly financed out of general taxation. The employers and employees also contribute through an increase of the contribution rate for the unemployment insurance scheme.

In respect of the insurance scheme for occupational damage, the employers pay a contribution corresponding with the risk to their private insurance company. The private insurers pay back the benefits granted to the administrative body. The state itself fully finances the benefits due to a result of an attempt to save human lives.

The system underlying the additional financing of the labour market pension and the income maintenance benefits on grounds of the scheme for occupational damage bears characteristics of both the pay as you go principle and the capitalization principle.

6. Judicial review.

If a citizen wants to challenge an unfavourable decision by an administrative body, he is not dependent upon the ordinary Danish judiciary, but upon a number of judicial bodies, which constitute part of the administration, yet operate independently. These administrative judicial bodies are subject to the supervision of the ordinary courts and are controlled by the ombudsman. Each of the different acts determines which judicial body is competent to deal with particular disputes. The term for appeal is usually four weeks, counting from the moment that the litigious decision is made known to the claimant.

Previously there was a double appeal possibility; however, currently the adjudication system is based upon the principle that a decision of the administration can only be challenged before one judicial body, albeit that a system has been introduced which allows the administrative body to reconsider its contentious decision.

Thus, a person who wants to challenge a decision of the *sociale udvalg* or of an administrative body operating on a district level must first notify this to the administrative body. This body then subjects its decision to a reconsideration. Only if this does not result in a fresh decision which fully satisfies the claimant, then the *Social ankenøvn* will take up the case.

As a rule, decisions of the *social udvalg* of the local community are open to appeal to the *Social ankenøvn*. This body is linked to the *amtskommune* of the district. The *Social ankenøvn* consists of the head of the district (the *amtsmand*) and six other members appointed by the Minister of Social Affairs after recommendation of the local and district councils and of the Association of organisations of the handicapped.

The *social ankenøvn* is competent to deal with complaints about decisions taken at the local or district level as well as in cases dealing with early pensions. In urgent cases the chairman may give immediate judgement; he alone is also competent to give judgement in first instance in simple and straightforward cases. The *Social ankenøvn* is bound by the case law of the *Sociale ankestyreslse*, however, not by the administrative instructions of the *kommune*, district or ministry.

The *Sociale ankestyrelse* is the highest appeal authority in matters of social affairs. Although this body is linked to the *Socialministerium*, it operates fully independently; thus it is not bound by the instructions which are issued by the ministry or by lower administrative bodies.

The appeals are dealt with by a chairman-civil servant and further two members, who are nominated by the central employer organisations and trade unions, the councils of København and Frederiksberg, the national association of *kommuner*, the association of district councils, the associations for the handicapped and the beneficiaries of a social pension.
As from 1983 the *Sociale anstyrelse* only hears further appeals against decisions of the *Social ankenøvn* to the extent that these involve points of principle, in particular with regard to the interpretation of the law.
Furthermore, the *sociale ankestyrelse* decide some cases in first instance, i.e. appeals against the decisions of the *sociale udvalg* in København and Frederiksberg (as said, these *kommuner* do not constitute a part of an *amtskommune*), appeals against the decisions which are taken on a district level, and appeals against some decisions concerning occupational damage insurance taken by the *Arbejdsskadestyrelsen*.

Appeal against decisions concerning family child benefits must be made to the *sociale udvalg*. Such appeals are passed through to the taxation inspection service which itself sends them to the national taxation directory, accompanied by a recommendation concerning the decision. The final decision is not subject to further appeal.

Appeals against decisions of the unemployment funds may be made to the *Direktorat for arbejdsløshedsforsikringen*; their decisions are subject to further appeal to the *Arbejdsløshedsforsikringens Ankenaevn*. The latter consists of five members, one of whom is nominated by the employers' organisations and one by the trade unions.
The *A. T.P. 's Ankenaevn* hear appeals against decisions of the *A. T.P.* concerning additional labour market pensions.

It should be mentioned that the decisions of all administrative organisations may be challenged before the ordinary courts. However, there are some restrictions with regard to the power of these courts to judge decisions which are made on a discretionary basis. In matters of social security law, appeal to the ordinary courts is very rare.

The ombudsman plays a much more important role in the settlement of social security disputes. The ombudsman hears complaints against decisions or against the conduct of public authorities, however not against acts and judicial decisions. His duty is to make sure that acts and other legal norms are not violated by the administration. Possibilities of administrative appeal must first be exhausted before a complaint can successfully be lodged with the ombudsman; however, if the dispute involves the treatment of a case by the administration, it is possible to address the ombudsman immediately. After investigation the ombudsman informs the plaintiff about his findings and actions; if necessary, he will also confront the administrative body with criticism or recommendations. The ombudsman can neither cancel the contentious decision or conduct, nor act as a substitute for the administrative body.

Chapter 3: Germany

1. Introduction: concept and origins of social security law.

After the unification of East and West Germany took place on october 3rd, 1990, the social security system of East Germany has been replaced by the social security system of West Germany. The process of transformation started on July 1st, 1990, when the currency union between the former two German states had been shaped. The transitional period will end in 1996, when the last traditional provisions of East German law will be terminated. The social security system of Germany is based on the laws, enacted by the former West Germany.

In Germany we can distinguish three branches of social security, namely social insurance, social compensation and assistance.

Traditionally the system has been based upon the principle of social insurance (*Sozialversicherung*); in addition to a health insurance scheme, an industrial injuries insurance scheme and an invalidity and old age insurance scheme, (together referred to as classic social insurance schemes), there is also an unemployment insurance scheme.

As a consequence of the first world war a new branch of social security was created for war veterans, called *soziale Entschädigung*. The State took the responsibility upon itself of compensation for damage to health suffered by persons as a result of service offered to the State. By this way of thinking, the *Bundesversorgungsgezetz* aimed to compensate war victims. Later this branch of social security was extended to cover, inter alia, victims of vaccination or crime.

The third and, at the same time, the oldest branch of social security is assistance (*Sozialhilfe*).

In addition to these traditional branches of social security, a number of more recent brances may be distinguished, which belong to the social security scheme, but which are difficult to place within the three given sections. Here we mention the system of study grants (*Ausbildungsförderung*), family benefits (*Kindergeld, Erziehungsgeld, Unterhaltsvorschuß*) and housing benefits (*Wohngeld*). This branch of law is referred to as *soziale Förderung* (social promotion).

The German constitution hardly includes any provisions which are of direct importance for social security law. Social security is only expressly mentioned in respect to the rule concerning legislative competence; the Federation is appointed to be the competent body. Of indirect, but great importance, is the *Sozialstaatsprinzip*, drived from case law and legal doctrine from articles 20 and 28 of the constitution. It reckons and justifies legislative activities on the various fields of social policy. A comparison with social rights, yet to be discussed, is called for here; many people characterize social rights as a realization of the *Sozialstaatsprinzip*. Finally, albeit very indirectly, some fundamental rights, are of importance for social security, for example the principle of equality (art. 3), the right of free personal developement (art. 2), the special protection for marriage and the family (art. 6) and the protection of property (art. 14). In addition to the national constitution, attention should also be paid to the constitutions of the single states. Within these we often encounter fundamental social rights which are described in detail but from which no subjective rights can be derived.

In 1970 it was officially resolved to codify social security law within one Code, called *Sozialgesetzbuch*. The aim of this codification was to simplify, to unify and to clarify social security law, which is haphazardly regulated by numerous separate acts, by shaping all social security laws into one comprehensive system of law in order to promote citizens' understanding of the law and thereby their trust in the constitutional welfare state, to simplify application of the law and to guarantee legal certainty.

In the meantime a general part has been realised, which includes introductory material as well as formal legal provisions which, but for specific provisions cover the entire ambit of the *Sozialgesetzbuch*; a chapter concerning common provisions for social insurance and a chapter regulating the benefit payment procedure, data protection, and the cooperation between the administrative bodies and their relation to third parties. From 1984 to 1986 a further section of the *Sozialgesetzbuch* had been enacted; it contains the main provisions on administrative procedures. In 1989 health insurance, 1991 social assistance for children and young adults (*Jugendhilfe*) and 1992 old age, invalidity and survivors pensions have been integrated into the *Sozialgesetzbuch*. On grounds of article 1 of the transitional and final provisions, until they are actually adopted within the *Sozialgesetzbuch*, a whole series of acts are considered to be special parts thereof (for the most important acts, see Annex I). The exhaustive enumeration of the specific acts also provides us with a possible delimitation of the concept of social security; one often understands by this all law that is regulated in the *Sozialgesetzbuch*.

Within articles 3-10 of the general part of the *Sozialgesetzbuch* there are a number of so called social rights (*soziale Rechte*) with reference to the branches of social security mentioned above. No entitlement to benefits can be derived on the ground of these provisions. For this the articles refer to the relevant provisions of the special acts. The law requires that social rights must be taken into consideration in interpreting the remaining provisions of the statute book and in applying discretion. In this, care must be taken that the social rights are extensively realised.

From the above it can be deduced that the act is the most prominent source of social security law. Legislative norms are regularly supplemented by changing the Code itself or by subordinate legislation. Jurisprudence also forms an important source of law, both for the interpretation of legislative concepts and for the review of decisions taken by social security institutions. For the purposes of this chapter two schemes will not be considered, although they do fall under the formal social security concept. The schemes in question are the system of study grants and the system of housing benefits.

2. Administrative organisation.

In respect of the administration of the social security schemes, a fundamental distinction must be made between the social insurance schemes on the one hand and the remaining schemes on the other.

The administration of the three classic insurance schemes is encharged to corporations under public law. The common provisions for social insurance schemes within the *Sozialgesetzbuch* contain elaborate rules explaining the existence and the structure of these corporations. The principle of *Selbstverwaltung*, self-government, is applied to the social insurance schemes. This is apparent from the composition of the various bodies of those corporations. Firstly we distinguish the general assembly which is composed, on equal shares, of representatives of the insured people and by the employers for a period of six years, on the ground of lists of preference, submitted respectively by organisations of employers and employees (*Sozialwahlen*). Usually the relevant organisations are able to agree on the composition of the preference lists, and a vote is not necessary. The general assembly subsequently choses the members of the governing board. With regard to the mutual divisions of tasks, the general assembly takes decisions of a general nature, for example the determination of internal regulations, the fixing of the contributions and the issuing of administrative directives; the managerial activities are divided between both other bodies. The general secretary, f.i. is responsible for current affairs, for which he represents the legal person to the outside world.

In the light of detailed legislation one wonders whether one should speak of indirect state government rather than self-government. In this respect the state supervision of administrative bodies is of importance. This too is regulated by the general provisions for the social insurance schemes within the *Sozialgesetzbuch*. According to these provisions, supervision is aimed at examining the lawfulness of the acts of administration; in addition, the management and book keeping of the administrative body is controlled. On a Federal level supervision is carried out by the *Bundesversicherungsamt* and on a state level by the *Arbeits- und Sozialminister*.

The three separate insurance schemes have the following administrative bodies. The *Krankenkassen* are responsible for the administration of the health insurance scheme. Among others, we distinguish *Orts-, Betriebs and Innungskrankenkassen*, as well as the so called *Ersatzkassen*. The latter have a special position due to the fact that internal regulations indicate who may become a member. As a result the members are exempted from membership of another fund. The general assembly of such a fund is entirely composed of representatives of the insured persons. It enacts the contributions autonomously.

The injury insurance scheme is administered by so called *Berufsgenossenschaften* on the one hand, and on the other by the so called *Eigenunfallversicherungstrager*. The *Berufsgenossenschaften* are divided into industrial bodies, agricultural bodies and bodies for mariners. For special categories of insured persons, either the federation, the states, the municipalities, or the *Bundesanstallt fur Arbeit* (see below) may act as the *Eigenunfallversicherungstrager*. In these cases administration is carried out by civil servants of one of those bodies. Administration of the invalidity and old age insurance scheme for workers is the responsibility of the *Landesversicherungsanstalten*; administration of the insurance scheme for *Angestellte* is the responsibility of the *Bundesversicherungsanstalt für Angestellte*. The *Bundesknappschaft* administers the invalidity and old age insurance scheme for mine workers and the *landwirtschaftliche Alterskassen* administes the latter insurance scheme for farmers.

To strengthen their position nearly all categories of administrative bodies have federations on a national level: these constitute corporations under public law. Another example is the *Verband deutscher Rentenversicherungsträger*, a corporation under private law. Administration of the unemployment insurance scheme is organised, in a slightly different way, under the specific provisions of the *Arbeitsförderungsgesetz*. Administration is in the hands of the *Bundesanstalt für Arbeit*, a corporation under public law; it is subdivided into a headquarter (the *Bundesanstalt*), the *Landesarbeitsämtern*, and the *Arbeitsämtern*. The *Bundesanstalt für Arbeit* has a *Verwaltungsrat* and a *Vorstand*, the *Landesarbeitsämter* and *Arbeitsämter* have administrative commissions. These bodies are composed of representatives of the employees, employers and public bodies (Federal, federal state and municipal). However, the representatives are not elected but appointed, albeit on the recommendation of the organisations of employers and employees.

All social security schemes, with the exception of social insurance schemes, are directly administered by the State on a decentralised level. Thus the states are responsible for the administration of the *Bundesversorgungsgesetz*, a task which is carried out via the *Versorgungsämter* and the *Landesversorgungsämter*. Firstly the *kreisfreie Städte* and the *Landkreise*, and in adition the *Länder* are responsible for the administration of the *Bundessozialhilfegesetz* and *Jugendhilfe*.

The *Bundesanstalt* für Arbeit takes a somewhat special place as administrator of the *Bundeskindergeldgesetz*. In this capacity the *Bundesanstalt für Arbeit* carries the title of *Kindergeldkasse*. It is further subj ect to the administrative directives of the minister. Decisions in individual cases are taken by the competent *Arbeitsamt*. The states may appoint the *Bundesanstalt für Arbeit* as the administrative body for the *Bundeserziehungsgeldgesetz*.

3. Personal scope of application.

The four social insurance schemes do not have the same scope of personal coverage; there are differences which vary according to the aim of the scheme. Nevertheless, in view of the existence of large similarities, the following overview is focused upon categories of people and not upon separate insurance schemes

An important distinction exists between compulsorily insured people and voluntarily insured people. People in gainful employment are obligatorily insured. The legislation uses the term *beschäftigt sein* and takes the *Beschäftigungsverhältnis* as a point of departure for the insurance obligation. Those employed in gainful employment must be distinguished from self-employed workers. According to jurisprudence, the main characterisic of the *Beschäftigungsverhältnis* is the personal dependence of the employee on the employer. This dependence is notably assumed when there is a duty to follow various instructions in respect of work or behaviour during work.

Arbeiter and *Angestellte* are insured according to the criteria mentioned above. *"Arbeiter"* means an employee who executes predominantely manual work; *"Angestellte"* means an employee who executes predominantely intellectual work. In a postindustrial society this distinction becomes old-fashioned; however it still exists. This distinction is important for determining the competent administrative body in old age invalidity and survivors insurance: For *"Arbeiter"* the *Landesversicherungsanstalten* and for *"Angestellte"* the *Bundesversicherungsanstalt für Angestellte* is the competent administrative body to cover an employee.

The compulsory insurance exists only in respect of activities which are carried out for a wage. All income from work carried out is included within this concept, regardless of the name or form under which it is paid, whether there exists a right to it or whether it is gained in cash, goods or services services. These rules are further elaborated in regulations, in respect of which one has aimed at the greatest possible harmony with the concept of wage known in taxation law.

Equally compulsory insured are those in vocational training. The,wage requirement is not applicable in respect of these people.
Furthermore, some smaller groups of self-employed people, whose economic position in comparable with that of people in a position of a dependent labour relationship and who are consequently considered to be in need of protection, are obligatory insured. To be mentioned here are home workers, midwives, artisans, manual workers, artists and writers. Those who execute so called "liberal professions" (e.g. physicins, dentists, lawyers, architects, notaries, etc.) as self-employed are mandatorily integrated into a

pension scheme, framed for the various professions and regulated by various state laws. The insurance obligation of these self-employed people does not extend to the unemployment insurance scheme. Sometimes special rules are applicable for them, for example in respect of farmers.

In addition to the self-employed people mentioned, there are other people included within the obligatory insurance scheme who are considered in need of protection by the legislator. To be mentioned here are cooperating family members in the agricultural sector, students, apprentices and handicapped people who are active in a work place for the handicapped. Generally, the compulsory insurance only covers the sickness (costs), invalidity and old age insurance schemes.

A final category of compulsory insured people consits of people who interrupt a dependent labour relationship or terminate it without losing the need for protection, for example those executing military service and those in receipt of an unemployment benefit or pension.

All civil servants are excluded from the compulsory insurance; while they are protected under a special scheme. Also excluded, are those who carry out minor activities. The legislation gives further instructions as to when such *geringfügige Beschäftigung* exists.

Apart from these statutory exclusions, in some cases the opportunity of applying for exemption from the insurance obligation exists. In respect of these cases the legislator has attempted to build in some control with regard to the existence of other adequate forms of protection.

All the insurance schemes, except for the unemployment insurance scheme, offer the opportunity of voluntary insurance. The old age and invalidity insurance scheme offers this opportunity to all Germans and EC-citizens and to everyone who lives or whose usual place of residence is within the Federal Republic; those who make use of this possibility are, for example, people who carry out domestic activities.

To the extent that they presuppose the existence of a labour relationship or a self-employed activity, the provisions with regard to compulsory and voluntary insurance only apply when the activity is carried out within the Federal Republic. The place of residence of the employee or self-employed person is not the deciding factor, but the place in which the activity is performed (*Beschäftigungsort*). There are two exceptions to this rule. Persons insured in Germany who are temporarily sent abroad in the course of their activities remain insured (*Ausstrahlung*). In contrast to that, people insured under a foreign system who are only temporarily active in the Federal Republic do not fall under compulsory insurance (*Einstrahlung*). The so called principle of territoriality (*Territorialitätsprinzip*) is applicable to the remaining social security schemes. This principle, as laid down within the general part of the *Sozialgesetzbuch*, declares the law of the *Sozialgesetzbuch* to be applicable to all people whose ordinary or habitual place of residence is within Germany, irrespective of his nationality. The term ordinary residence (*Wohnsitz*) refers to the place where a person has a house under circumstances which indicate that the house is kept up and used, also on a long term basis. The term habitual residence (*gewöhnlicher Aufenthalt*) refers to the place where a person stays with a certain regularity and for a certain time.

The principle of territoriality or residence, must yield to derogating rules within the specific parts of the *Sozialgesetzbuch*. Here it is already shown that the social insurance schemes depart from the principle of residence by focusing upon the place where the activity is carried out. We also encounter modifications in the other social insurance schemes. Thus in the field of the *soziale Entschädigung*, the principle of residence has been extensively modified by the principle of nationality (*Personalitätsprinzip*). Therefore benefits are awarded only to Germans, even if they live abroad, but then subjected to certain conditions. Also within the *Bundessozialhilfegesetz* the principle of residence has been moderated by the principle of nationality, albeit to a lesser extent.

4. Risks and benefits.

4.1. Old age.

When the insured person attains a certain age he is no longer expected to provide for his own livelihood. The usual limit, as laid down by the legislator, is 65 years of age. When this age is attained one is entitled to old age pension (*Altersruhegeld*) even though the activity carried out until this time may not actually have been abandoned. Furthermore, the old age insurance scheme operates with a flexible pensionable age which enables the insured person to apply for a person who is partially incapable of work 60 years of age. Here there is the further condition that the claimant must carry out no, or very minor, activities. The early (*vorgezogenen*) pensionable age of 60 years must be distinguished from the flexible pensionable age, the former is intended for specific situations, laid down in the legislation. Use of this can be made by people who are handicapped or unemployed at 60 years of age and who have been unemployed for 52 weeks of the preceding one and a half years. Equally, there is an opportunity for insured women who, in the 20 years preceding the attainment of 60 years of age, were predominantly employed in activities giving rise to obligatory insurance. Here too, in respect of both groups of beneficiaries, there is the further condition that no, or only very minor, activities may be carried out. The system of the pensionable age will be changed in the following years. The political intention behind this change is to make it more attractive to the insured person to apply for benefits at a later age. For this purpose deductions of increasing percentages are made in case of earlier retirement and supplementary benefits are paid to those applying for a pension after reaching pensionable age. The political aim is to regain 65 as the regular pensionable age. However, early retirement will be possible.

With respect to entitlement to old age pension, the actual or ficticious completion of a waiting period of sixty months is required; when making use of the flexible or early pensionable age, the contribution period is equal to 180 months and an insurance period of 35 years. Periods of payment of contributions are recognized as periods of completion of the waiting periods (*Beitragszeiten*). Furthermore, subject to certain conditions, periods are taken into account during which no contributions were paid, due to specific reasons, e.g. military service or raising children (*Ersatzzeiten*).

The amount of the pension is dependent upon four factors, i.e. the general basis of calculation, the special basis of calculation, the number of insurance years and a multiplication factor, which for this scheme is 1,5%. The general basis of calculation is an amount determined by regulation, derived from the average annual income of all insured people. It is adjusted annually to increases in gross wages (*Dynamisierung*). The special basis of calculation reflects the relationship between the individual income of the insured person during his insured career and the average income of all insured persons. Finally, the number of insurance years to be taken into account constitute, on the one hand, the sum of periods to be counted for the completion of the waiting period (see above) and, on the other, the so called *Anrechnungszeiten* and *Zurechnungszeiten* are periods in which the insured person was prevented from carrying out obligatorily insured work, due to circumstances beyond his control, for example periods of incapacity for work or unemployment. *Zurechnungszeiten* play a role in situations of early invalidity (see section 4.3.). *Anrechnungszeiten* as well as *Zurechnungszeiten* are only taken into account when a certain number of contributions have been paid.

Benefits from the statutory old age insurance scheme are often supplemented by occupational schemes set up on a collective agreement between employer and employees or an individual basis.

4.2. Death.

Death of an insured person gives the right to benefits for the survivors. The widow or widower is entitled to *Witwen-* or *Witwerrente* if the deceased was entitled to a pension, or had satisfied, actually of ficticiously, a waiting period of 60 months. The widow/widower is the person who was married to the insured person at the time of his/her death. The survivor pension is derived from the pension rights of the deceased person and amounts to respectivly 60% of the pension on account of *Berufsunfähigkeit* (small survival pension). The latter is only granted to survivors who ware 45 years of age or older or are incapable of work, or are raising at least one child. For the first three months the survivors pension amounts to 100% of the insured person's pension. The survivor's pension is income-tested: apart from a disregard determined by legislation, all earnings of the beneficiary are dedecuted from the pension. These benefits are income-tested.

In case of divorced widows or widowers pension is paid if the insured had to maintain his/her former spouse before death and the divorce was enacted before July 1st 1977. For divorces after this date a credit splitting is provided, designed to split credits equally earned by the married couple during the period of mariage.

Children are entitled to orphan's pension (*Waisenrente*) until the age of 18 or 25 if they are following vocational training. The amount of the orphan's pension is also related to the pension of the insured person. If the death of the insured person was due to an industrial injury or an occupational disease, the widow(er) or the orphan are entitled to *Hinterbliebenenrente* on the basis of the injuries insurance scheme. Following the same cirteria as above, a distinction is made between a small and a large pension. The amount is respectively three tenths and two fifths of the basis of calculation for the *Verletzenrente*, and two thirds of this for the first quarter following the death of the insured person. The survivor's pension is subject to an income test. On the grounds of the injuries insurance scheme benefits are also payable to ex-spouses and orphans.

Within the framework of the *soziale Entschädigung* the survivors are entitled to benefit on the death of the victim. If death was due to a cause covered by the *soziale Entschädigung* (see section 4.3.), there is a right to *Hinterbliebenenrente*, otherwise there is a right to *Beihilfen*. The pension for the surviving spouse is made up of different components. Firstly there is the flat-rate *Grundrente*. The supplementary *Ausgleichsrente* is also flat-rate, but is only granted to the spouse who, due to certain circumstances, is expected to be unable to earn any income; it is means-tested. If the spouse earns an income amounting to less than half the amount which would have been earned by the deceased person, there is a right to *Berufsschadensausgleich*. Within certain limits the compensation amounts to four tenths of the difference between both incomes.

Subject to further conditions, the above benefits are also granted to the exspouse of the deceased person.

Orphans receive a flat-rate *Grundrente* and possibly a means-tested *Ausgleichsrente*.

Subject to further conditions, the parents or grand parents of the deceased are entitled to a means-tested *Aszendentenrente*.
Beihilfen are granted with a view to the fact that the deceased person, due to damage suffered to his health, has not been able to build up sufficient rights for his spouse and children during his lifetime. As a rule they are smaller than the *Hinterblienenrente* and, within a certain limit, are subject to a means-test.
All cash benefits are annually adjusted by law as in the old age insurance scheme.

4.3. Incapacity for work.

The health insurance scheme is a social insurance scheme which offers coverage against the risks of sickness-related loss of income, maternity and medical care (see section 4.5.). By sickness (*Krankheit*) the *Bundessozialgericht* understands an upset of the physical or mental condition which requires medical treatment by physicians and/or results in incapacity for work. The cause of the upset is not important nor is the duration of it. The system operates on the principle of 'all or nothing': one is either fully incapable or fully capable of work.

The risk of maternity (*Schwangerschaft/Mutterschaft*) is understood as being limited to the condition of pregnancy, the birth and the period of confinement.

The most prominent benefit in cash of the health insurance scheme is sick leave payment (*Krankengeld*). In order to be eligible for sick pay, a person must be incapable of work due to sickness. Sick leave payment constitutes an income maintenance benefit: thus it is not granted to (insured) students and apprentices. Benefit amounts to 80% of the so called *Refellohn*, i.e. the wage or income which also formed the basis for the calculation of contributions. In respect of one and the same disease, sick leave payment is to be paid for a maximum period of 78 weeks within three years.

In respect of maternity, the woman is entitled to *Mutterschaftsgeld*, the amount of which is equal to the net wages, subject to a rather low flat-rate maximum. If the real wages are higher than this limit, the employer is obliged to give a supplement on the grounds of the *Mutterschutzgesetz*. Benefit is granted for six weeks preceding the birth and for eight to twelve weeks thereafter.

Two types of incapacity for work are distinguished under the invalidity insurance scheme, the *Berufsunfähigkeit* and the *Erwerbsunfähigkeit*. According to the legislative definition, a person is considered to be *berufsunfähig* when his capacity for work, as a result of sickness or disablement, is considered to be less than half that of a healthy person with a comparable education and with equivalent knowledge and ability. The determination of the remaining capacity of a person depends upon an assessment of the extent to which he is still able to carry out an occupation that reflects his strength and ability and with which, taking into account his previous occupation, he can reasonably be encharged. Then there is an assessment of the extent to which the remaining capacity to work can be realised on the labour market (*konkrete Betrachtungsweise*). The risk of *Erwerbsunfähigkeit* is also further defined within the legislation. According to the definition a person is considered to be *erwerbsunfähig* when, as a result of sickness or disablement, he cannot, for an unforeseeable time, regularly carry out an occupation, or earn more than only a minor income in such an occupation.

The insured can be compared with any occupation that is compatible with his strength and ability; his education or previous activities are not taken into consideration, which constitutes a major difference with the concept of *Berufsunfähigkeit*.

Similarly to the determination of the *Berufsunfähigkeit*, it should further be assessed to what extent the remaining capacity for work can be realised on the labour market.

The existence of *Berufs-* or *Erwerbsunfähigkeit* is not in itself sufficient to give rise to entitlement to benefit. There are two more conditions. The first condition is that in the five years preceding the moment of incapacity, work should have been carried out on the grounds of which contributions must have been paid over at least 36 months. Furthermore, a waiting period of sixty months must have been completed, similar to the one which applies in respect of entitlement to old age pension. Here too, account is taken of contributory periods (*Beitragszeiten*) and non-contributory periods (*Anrechnungs-* und *Ersatzzeiten*). If the risk realizes as a result of a circumstance for which society must take responsibility, the waiting period is always considered to be completed. This is for instance the case for industrial injuries. The completion of the waiting period is also fictitious if the risk occurs before the waiting period possibly could have been completed. This covers the situation whereby a person has only worked for a short period because he had previously followed vocational training. In principle, the waiting period must be completed prior to the moment that the risk materialized. However, there is a special rule concerning the early handicapped. They may claim invalidity pension if they have been insured for 240 months, irrespective of the fact that the incapacity for work existed at the onset of the insurance.

In certain cases the invalidity insurance scheme provides rehabilitation benefits. There is no right to such benefits; the granting of them is at the discretion of the administrative body. The law distinguishes medical benefits, supplementary benefits, and benefits which are designed to improve the chances of carrying out an occupation.

The most important cash benefit is invalidity pension. This benefit is calculated in the same way as the old age pension (see section 4.1.). A multiplying factor of 1% is applicable to the *Berufsunfähigkeitsrente* and 1,5% to the *Erwerbsunfähigkeitsrente*. The difference arises from the presumption that the person who is *berufsunfähig* is still supposed to realize his remaining earning capacity. The *Zurechtnungszeiten* play a special role here. These are the periods between the occurance of *Erwerbs-* or *Berufsunfähigkeit* and the attainment of 56 years of age. They are intended to ensue that persons who become invalid at an early stage of their career receive an adequate pension.

In principle, invalidity pensions are payable till the benificiary reaches pensionable age, then the pension is transferred into an old age pension. If there are well founded expectations that the incapacity will terminate within the foreseeable future, the pension is granted only after 26 weeks, and at the most for three years. A period of three years is considered as foreseeable.

There are special rules within the injuries insurance scheme regarding cases of incapacity for work as the result of an industrial injury or an occupational disease.

Firtsly, the injuries insurance scheme provides benefits in kind. These include medical and surgical help, home care or care within an institution and help within the occupational sphere aimed at future rehabilitation into working life. Secondly, benefits in cash consist of *Verletztengeld* and *Verletztenrente*. The former is payable to a person who is incapable within the meaning of the injury insurance scheme. It amounts to 80% of the gross annual income. If, after thirteen weeks, there is still a reduced incapacity as a result of the injury and if this is at least 20%, a person is entitled to *Verletztenrente*. There is a distinction between a permanent (*Verletztenrente*) and a provisional pension (*Verletztengeld*). The latter is granted for a maximum period of two years after the injury, if the condition is not yet stable enough to fix the pension on a permanent basis. In cases of full incapacity, pension amounts to two thirds of the gross earnings of the previous year, and in cases of partial incapacity to a percentage of these earnings.

Entitlement to benefit in the field of the *soziale Entschädigung*, as regulated in the *Bundesversorgungsgesetz*, exists for those who have sustained a service injury as the result of military service during the time of national socialism, or who has suffered health damage as the result of actions which were characteristic of this service (*Wehrdienstbeschädigung*). A number of other possible causes of damage to health are treated as those under military service activities, for example the direct effects of war (in respect of civilian victims) and war imprisonment. Other acts within the field of the *soziale Entschädigung* are set up along the lines of the *Bundesversorgungsgesetz*. The issue continually concerns the occurance of damage to health as a result of particular causes. For example, within the *Soldatenversorgungsgesetz*, this is the service activities of soldiers in the present *Bundeswehr*. In the *Opferentschädigungsgesetz* it is the premeditated, unlawful assault on a person. In the *Bundesseuchengesetz* it is forced or recommended vaccination.

There is entitlement to benefits in kin, as well as to cash benefits. The package of benefits in kind largely coincides with medical and surgical help from the sickness insurance scheme. If damage results in the incapacity for work of the claimant, then he may be entitled to *Übergangsgeld*, which is calculated in the same way as the *Krankengeld*.

If the incapacity is permanent a person has the right to a pension. This pension (*Rente*) consists of a number of components. Firstly, there is an non means-tested *Grundrente*, payable to those who are at least 30% incapable of work. Depending upon the degree of incapacity for work, the *Grundrente* is determined as a fixed amount. Subject to further conditions, those who are 50% incapable, or more, may also be entitled to an *Ausgleichsrente*. This also consists of fixed amounts corresponding to the degree of incapacity for work, although, except for certain disregards, it is means-tested. Finally, every beneficiary of a *Rente* is entitled to the so called *Berufs-schadensausgleich*. This benefit covers the loss of income due to the reduced incapacity; within certain limits, it is payable at a rate of four tenths of the loss of income.

Legislative fixed supplements are payable in respect of the spouse and/or the children of the victim.

4.4. Unemployment.

The unemployment insurance scheme is determined to avoid, to combat and to replace income in case of unemployment (*Arbeitslosigkeit*). Employees who are available for work, but who are temporarily without employment, or whose employment is only 18 hours or less per week, are considered to be unemployed. According to the *law*, an employee is any person who at the time of the claim and during the consecutive period is considered to belong to the category of persons who normally carry out a dependent activity, other than of a minoor character. The employee must be available for the labour market. This is the case if the person is capable (able), as well as willing, to carry out suitable employment, or to comply with suitable measures within the framework of education or rehabilitation.

Another risk covered by the unemployment insurance scheme is the temporary reduction of working hours (*Kurzarbeit*). The cause must lie in economic circumstances (e.g. decline in trade) or in unavoidable events (natural disasters), it must not be caused by something within the power of the employer. The reduction of working hours must be unavoidable and must have a certain dimension. It must also result in a reduction of wages for the employee. Apart from that, there is a separate benefit for workers in the construction industry in case of reduction of working hours due to bad weather (*Schlechtwettergeld*).

Finally, the unemployment insurance scheme also covers the risk of the employer's insolvency in respect of overdue wage claims of the employees, albeit limited to the last three months prior to the bankruptcy of the employer (*Konkursausfallversicherung*).

An important benefit in kind for the unemployed is the labour exchange. Other important benefits in kind are vocational training and retraining. The most important cash benefit is *Arbeitslosengeld*. Entitlement depends upon the registration of the unemployment with the *Arbeitsamt* and the completion of the so-called *Anwartschaftszeit*. The latter is comparable to the waiting period within the old age insurance scheme. It is considered to be completed if, in the three years preceding the unemployment, the unemployed has carried out 360 days compulsory insured work for which he received wages. Again, certain *Ersatzzeiten* may be credited, e.g. periods of executing military service.

The level of unemployment benefit for unemployed persons with at least one child amounts to 6% and for all others to 63% of the average net income from work enjoyed during the period of reference. The duration of the benefit is limited and varies, depending on the employment record, from 17 to 52 weeks. For older unemployed persons an extension to 104 weeks is possible.If the *Arbeitslosengeld* is exhausted, the unemployed may be entitled to *Arbeitslosenhilfe*. This benefit is means-tested. Nevertheless, the level of the benefit is related to net income from work; for the unemployed persons with at least one child, it amounts to 58% and for all others to 56% of this income. In principle, the duration of entitlement to *Arbeitslosenhilfe* is unlimited.

Benefits on the same differentiated level as the unemployment benefit are payable in cases of reduction in working hours, but for a maximum of six months (*Kurzarbeitergeld*). The same applies with respect to loss of work due to bad weather (*Schlechtwettergeld*).

In cases of insolvency of the employer, employees receive a benefit equal to their net labour wage, as already stated, for the income loss of a maximum period of three months (*Konkursausfallgeld*). In addition to the payments made for income losses, social security contributions are paid to the social security institutions.

4.5. Medical care.

The medical care branch of the health insurance scheme provides for a whole series of diverse benefits. There are benefits of a preventive character, for example the annual check-ups for certain categories of insured for certain diseases (cancer) and the granting of artificial aids and help in respect of a threatening handicap. Benefits with a curative function are to be found within the package for medical and surgical help, to be distinguished between help to out-patients and clinical help (*Kranken- und Krankenhauspflege*). The out-patient's help encompasses treatment by a doctor or a dentist, the granting of medicine and wound dressings, as well as occupational therapy. The granting of these curative benefits is subject to further legislative conditions and limitations, e.g. the help must be truly sufficient and appropiate, yet may not exceed what is necessary. Entry into, and nursing in, a hospital is indicated when this is necessary for diagnosis, treatment or cure of the disease. Instead of this, or to prevent it, nursing at home is also possible. Furthermore, the administrative body is authorised to grant treatment in a health resort (*Kurort*).

Medical and surgical help is granted through a system of benefits in kind (*Sachleistungen*) and, only by way of exception, through reimbursement of costs ensued by the insured person. The administrative body does not provide the benefits itself, but this is done by third parties, such as dentists, doctors, hospitals and pharmacists. The relationship between the *Krankenkassen* as the administrators of the insurance scheme and respectively the dentists, doctors and hospitals is regulated in leglislation. It gives competence to regulate the system by contracts (collective agreements). The concerned parties are united in organisations on federal state and on state level, and on these levels they negotiate. Such negotiations should result in agreements governed by public law; if not, a court of arbitration determines similar agreements. Individual dentists, doctors and hospitals may only become involved in treatment with the permission of the administrative authorities of the sickness (costs) insurance scheme. If permission is refused by the competent authorities, appeal is possible to the *Sozialgerichte*. The insured person has freedom of choice of doctor, dentist and hospital.

Insured persons are not only entitled to benefits for themselves, but also to benefits for their spouses and their dependent children, albeit with the exception of sick leave payment. There is a condition that the family members of the insured person can not have any income in excess of a certain level. Entitlement to this? *Familienhilfe* has no effect upon the contributions to be paid by the insured person.

4.6. Family.

German social security law contains a number of diverse benefits in respect of family economic burden.

Thus, *Kindergeld* is payable to everyone who maintains a child, irrespective of marital status, for own or adopted children, provided that the children belong to their household or get alimony in cash. When more than one person is entitled to benefit, the actual maintenance of the child is decisive. Benefit is only payable until the moment that the child becomes 16 years old. Subject to further conditions (especially concerning stury or occupational training) the limit is extended to 27 years of age, or even more.

Kindergeld forms a legislatively fixed supplement to the family's income. *Erziehungsgeld* is payable to parents with a child less than one year old, born after 31 December 1985, living within the household. The parents must be alone in the upbringing of the child and, as a consequence, carry out no or little work (i.e., less than 19 hours per week). *Erziehungsgeld* is especially aimed at encouraging the working parent to devote time to the raising of the child. For parents in similar circumstances, under labour law one may be entitled to *Erziehungsurlaub*, which is complementary to *Erziehungsgeld*. However, *Erziehungsgeld* is equally granted to the parent with no labour record.

The benefit is flat-rate. Only for the first six months it is non means-tested, but income-tested. For children born before 1 January 1988, the right to benefit expires after ten months, for children born thereafter, after twelve months; from 1993 onwards, it is paid for three years.

Finally, the *Unterhaltsvorschuß* is a benefit payable to children less than six years of age who live in a single parent family and who do not receive any regular maintenance from the other parent, despite the fact that this maintenance is due and has been frequently demanded. The *Unterhalts-ausfallleistung* is a comparable benefit, granted to children below the age of six years whose 'other' parent is deceased or the abode of whom is not known.

Both benefits are payable for a maximum period of three years. The income and capital of the parent with whom the child lives has no influence upon the (scope of) entitlement to benefit. The maintenance liability in respect of the child is subrogated to the administrative authorities.

4.7. Need.

The *Bundessozialhilfegesetz* offers coverage for the risk of an existing emergency situation in the form of requirements which cannot be met by the individual himself, and thus is coupled with need. In certain circumstances the danger of the(re) occurance of an emergency situation may also give rise to entitlement to benefit. Benefits are in principle not payable in respect of the past. The cause of the need is of no importance. A distinction is made between need in respect of living costs (general need) and special needs; the special needs are defined with reference to specific situations, such as sickness, blindness or pregnancy. With regard to benefits for general needs there is a right to benefit. Benefits for special needs are granted, subject to the discretion of the competent administrative bodies.

The benefits in respect of special needs are nearly all benefits in kind. On the contrary, general needs gives rise to entitlement to cash benefits, the *Hilfe zum Lebensunterhalt*. The level of this benefit is determined according to a mechanism set up by legislation on a federal state level; acoording to the *Bundessozialhilfegesetz* the amount of benefit payable must be below the wage level of the lowest paid wage groups. The characteristic of this scheme is its subsidiary nature. This implies that the granting of a benefit is subject to an unlimited income and asset test of the claimant and of the people within his household.

5. Financing.

Two thirds of social security expenditures are financed out of contribution. The level of contributions is dependent upon two factors, the basis of calcu-lation of the contributions and the contribution rate. The basis of contri-bution is respectively made up of the wage or the income from employment. In delegated legislation these concepts are to a large extent harmonised with the relevant concepts under taxation law. There is a statutorily fixed wage ceiling for contribution liability (*Beitragsbemessungsgrenze*). In the health insurance scheme this limit is 75% below that of the remaining insurance schemes and at the same time it forms the *Versicherungspflichtgrenze*. This means, employees earning more than this wage ceiling are dispensated from coverage in health insurance.. Within the health insurance scheme the contribution rate is determined by the *Krankenkassen*; for the other insurance schemes it is determined by statute. The contribution level must be sufficient. This means that the income from contributions together with other income (for example from capital), is sufficient to cover the expenditure of a given year. Thus, apart from a compulsory reserve, the system operates upon the 'pay as you go principle'.

In respect of those who carry out wage labour, the employer and employee each pay half the contributions for the insurance schemes, except for the injuries insurance schemes. However only the former must actually pay contributions; the employer may deduct the contributions payable by the employees from their wages. For people with a small income, i.e. less than 10% of the *Beitragsbemessungsgrenze*, the employer must make all contribution payments on his own expense. Equally, the employers are responsible for all the contributions regarding the injuries insurance scheme, the *Konkursausfallversicherung* and the *Winterbauförderung*. This arises from the special character of these insurance schemes (covering employers risks). For all these schemes there is a special basis of calculation of the premiums. Sometimes it is the insured person himself who is liable to pay all contributions. This is the case for self-employed persons and for voluntarily insured persons. Finally, in some cases contributions are paid by a third party, not being the employer. For example, the administrative bodies which are responsible for the payment of income maintenance benefits may operate as such.

The contributions for all the insurance schemes are collected by the *Krankenkassen* as so called *Gesamtversicherungsbeitrag*. These *Krankenkassen* decide in cases concerning contribution liability. Besides income from contributions, State subsidies (*Zuschüsse*) also play an important role within the old age and invalidity insurance and the unemployment insurance scheme.

The State also finances all the social security benefits outside the sphere of the insurance schemes; the source of this financing is general taxation. The Federation is responsible for all the costs arising from the *Bundesversorgungsgesetz*, *Arbeitslosenhilfe*, *Kindergeld*,,and *Erziehungsgeld*. The Federation and the states ach bear half the costs of the *Unterhaltsvorschüsse*; the costs of the *Opferentschädigung* are met in a relation of 40% - 60%. The states are wholly responsible for the expenditure arising from the *Bundesseuchengesetz*. Finally, the expenditure of the *Sozialhilfe* is met respectively by the *kreisfreie Städte*, the *Kreise* and, to a small extent, by the states.

6. Judicial review.

In 1953 the *Sozialgerichtsgesetz* introduced a special branch in the judicial system for the settlement of social security disputes, which is separate from the genaral administrative system for the settlement of disputes. However, judicial review via the *Sozialgerichtsgesetz* does not extend to all social security law. It is limited to disputes within the framework of the social insurance scheme, the remaining tasks of the *Bundesanstalt für Arbeit*, the *soziale Entschädigung* and the relations physician - health insurance (*Kassenartzrecht*). Other social security disputes are subject to the jurisdiction of the administrative courts.

The *Sozialgerichtsgesetz* firstly regulates the existence and the composition of three different judicial authorities, i.e. the *Sozialgericht*, the *Landessozialgericht* and the *Bundessozialgericht*. The *Sozialgericht* consists of a professional judge and two lay judges. In the other tribunals are three professionnal judges and two lay judges. The lay judges are appointed by the state on the recommendation of the organisations for employers, employees, doctors, handicapped people and victims of war.

The procedure is set in process by the lodging of a complaint with the competent *Sozialgericht*. In some cases the lodging of a complaint entails a preliminary procedure. This *Vorverfahren* does not belong to the actual judicial procedure and gives the administrative body the opportunity to reconsider the legality and the suitability of its decision.

The procedure according to the *Sozialgerichtsgesetz* is characterized by a number of procedural principles. Thus there is the so called principle of easy access to court (*Klagefreundlichkeit*). This results for example, in a large extent of freedom of form, the absence of obligatory representation in the first two instances and in the fact that the procedure is costless. Another important principle is that of *Amtsermittelungsgrundsatz*, which obliges the judge to search independently for the truth; he does not play a passive role. The final procedural principle is the right to be heared; according to this principle an oral hearing forms the heart of the process. The tribunals make their decisions on the basis of the oral hearing.
In principle, the decision of a judge is expressed in a judgement. However, if a judge regards the appeal as not admissible, or without grounds, he can settle it by reasoned decision. Nevertheless, parties still have the opportunity of enforcing an oral hearing of their case.

In principle, decisions of the *Sozialgerichte* are subject to further appeal with the *Landessozialgerichte*. The *Sozialgerichtsgesetz* contains a limitative list of cases, in respect of which further appeal is excluded. Among others, such cases concern disputes relating to lump sum benefits or reciprocal benefits with a duration of less than three months. In principle there is no appeal against a decision of the *Landessozialgericht*. However, in certain cases the *Landessozialgericht* or the *Bundessozialgericht* may give leave to a plaintiff for a revision of the decision by the *Bundessozialgericht*. The disputes must then either involve points of law of fundamental significance, a judgement which deviates from a decision of the *Bundessozialgericht*, or certain procedural irregularities. The revision serves in the first place legal certainty and the development of the law. For this purpose a separate chamber has been established within the *Bundessozialgericht*, the so called *großer Senat*. This chamber decides on cases in which a chamber of the *Bundessozialgericht* intends to deviate from a decision of another chamber, as well as in cases of fundamental significance.

To the extent that judicial review is not encharged to the *Sozialgerichte*, it is encharged to the administrative courts. The procedure regulated in the *Verwaltungsgerichtsordnung* largely corresponds that of the *Sozial-gerichtsgesetz* and is characterized by the same principles. Here too, judicial review is carried out by three judicial bodies, i.e. the *Verwaltungs- gerichte*, the *Oberverwaltungsgerichte* and the *Bundesverwaltungsgericht*. Equally there exists a preliminary procedure before the actual process begins (*Wider-spruchsverfahren*).

Chapter 4: France

1. Introduction: concept and sources of social security law.

French social security is characterized by the simultaneous existence of separate schemes for the diverse occupational groups. We distinguish in succession:

(1) the general scheme (*le régime général*). This is the most important scheme. To the extent that no special scheme is applicable to them employees engaged in trade and industry as well as categories of people who are considered as such, are insured for the risks of sickness, maternity, incapacity for work, industrial injuries and occupational diseases, old age and death. The scheme also covers family benefits for these employees, as well as for the self-employed (with the exception of agricultural workers) and for non-active persons;

(2) the agricultural scheme (*le régime agricole*). People working within the agricultural sector other than in a self-employed capacity enjoy a comparable protection as people who are covered by the general scheme. The self-employed are insured for the risks of sickness, maternity, old age and family charges;

(3) the special schemes (*les régimes spéciaux*) for certain groups of employees (railway workers, miners, civil servants, etc.). The protection varies from scheme to scheme. If a certain risk is covered, the relevant benefits must be of at least the same level as the benefits within the general scheme;

(4) the multiple schemes for self-employed persons with the exception of those working within the agricultural sector (*les régimes autonomes des professions non salariés non agricoles*). These offer protection against the risks of sickness, maternity and old age.

There is a certain of coordination and harmonisation between the general scheme and the other schemes. Most importantly, for all or part of the schemes uniform legal rules exist with respect to, for example, administration, financing and judicial review.

The above described schemes together form what one generally refers to as "statutory social security" (*les régimes légaux*). In addition there exist a number of schemes which are embodied within the concept of supplementary social security. As such we distinguish:

(1) the supplementary pension schemes, first established on the basis of collective agreements and since 1972 made obligatory by law for all employees from the general scheme and from the agricultural scheme;

(2) the supplementary sickness benefits. A whole series of collective schemes guarantee that statutory benefits in respect of sickness are fully or partially supplemented;

(3) benefits in respect of unemployment. The risk of unemployment is not only covered by statutory social security in the above sense of the word,

but also by statutory labour law. At present, for all people who are active on the basis of a contract of employment there exists a compulsory scheme which is a synthesis of two previously existing schemes, namely one of public assistance and an insurance scheme on the basis of collective agreement;

(4) assistance. Like the unemployment scheme, assistance does not belong to statutory social security in the narrow sense of the word. Instead it carries out a residual function in relation to this system.

Throughout the course of this chapter, in principle our discussion will be limited to the general scheme (*le régime général*), completed with the schemes in respect of unemployment and assistance.

The constitution of the fifth French republic (of 1958) maintained the preamble of the constitution of 1946, in which a number of social principles are proclaimed to be "of special necessity in our time". Thus the nation must ensure the conditions for the individual and their families, which are necessary for their development. (al. 10) and guarantee to everyone, especially to the child, to the mother and to elderly employees, protection of health, material means of subsistence and rest and leisure time. Furthermore, al. 11 states that each person who, due to his age, physical or mental state, or due to the economic situation, is unable to work, is entitled to suitable means of subsistence from the community.

Until now, neither these principles of social fundamental rights nor the qualification of France in article 2 of the constitution, as a social republic would appear to have produced legal consequences for positive social security law.

In order to determine the fundamental principles of social security law, article 34 Constitution requires the intermediation of an act adopted by parliament. Where these fundamental principles are not involved, according to the French constitutional system, legislative powers lie with the government (which acts by decrees); parliament can authorize the government, for a certain period and with a specific goal, to legislate in an area belonging to the competence of parliament (the government then makes ordinances, *ordonnances*).

The most important act in the field of the general scheme of social security is the *Code de la Sécurité Sociale*. The realization of this act in 1956 brought about a codification of the legislation in respect of the general scheme of social security. The code was reviewed in 1985.

The statutory framework as laid down in de *Code du Travail* (articles L. 351-1 e.v.) is of importance within the field of unemployment law. This framework is further implemented by a collective agreement between employers and employees.

The *Code de la Famille et de l 'Aide Sociale* is of importance with regard to assistance law.

Within the legislation we distinguish three levels of regulations i.e. acts (*lois*), decrees (*décrets*) which must be submitted to the *Conseil d'Etat* and decrees (*décrets*) in respect of which this requirement is not applied. The letters preceding the different provisions from the *Code de la Sécurité Sociale*, "L", "R" and "D", indicate the respective levels of regulation.

Although in principle Alsace-Moselle falls within the scope of French social security law, there are still some derogating rules applicable in this region, e.g. in the area of contributions and benefits and in the organisation of medical care. In the course of this chapter these special rules will not be dealt with.

2. Administrative organisation.

We will discuss consecutively the administrative organisation of the general system, the scheme for unemployment and the assistance scheme.

In order to describe the administrative organisation of the general scheme we must introduce a further differentiation.
The *Caisse nationale de l'assurance maladie des travailleurs salariés (C.N.A.T.S.)* is responsible for the administration of the insurance schemes in respect of sickness, pregnancy, incapacity for work, death and industrial injuries and occupational diseases on a national level. Among others this body has the tasks of guaranteeing the financing of the above insurance schemes, organising medical control, advising about the introduction of proposed acts or administrative decisions and the negociations with the medical profession with regard to conditions of cooperation.
On a regional level there are the *Caisses régionales d'assurance maladie (C.R.A.M.)*, which are responsible for the administration of tasks which are of importance for all departmental bodies within the region. For example the development and coordination of the prevention of industrial injuries and occupational diseases.
Finally the *Caisses primaires d'assurance maladie* operate on a departmental level. They are concerned with the registration of the insured people and with the granting of benefits. Possibly, these tasks may be transferred to so called *sections locales* or to representatives of certain enterprises.

On a national level the administration of the schemes in respect of family benefits is in the hands of the *Caisse nationale des allocations familiales (C.N.A.F)*. Among others this body is responsible for ensuring the financing of the above schemes, the financial supervision of the lower bodies and advising the government about the financial position of this branch of social security.
Besides the national umbrella organisation, there are the *Caisses d'allocations familiales* on a departmental level. This is encharged with the granting of benefits.

In principle only one central body is responsible for the administration of the old age insurance scheme, the *Caisse nationale d'assurance vieillesse des travailleurs salariés (C.N.A.V.T.S.)*. Besides the financial management of this insurance scheme this body is also responsible for the granting of benefits. In practice, for the time being, the *Caisse* finds it necessary to appeal regularly for help from the *Caisses régionales d'assurance maladie*.

The national administrative bodies are united in the *Union des caisses nationales (U.C.A.N.S.S.)*. This body is involved with cases of equal concern for all the bodies, such as the conditions of employment of the personnel of the bodies.

The above bodies are managed by a board of governors. This board consists of 25 to 28 members, 15 of whom are representatives of the employees, chosen by the employees on the recommendation of representative employee organisations, and 6 representatives of the employers, appointed by representative employer organisations. Furthermore, the board consists of representatives of certain interest groups and external specialists; sometimes these people merely have an advisory function.

The above concerns the distributive function of the general scheme. Now attention will be paid to the administration of the collective function. With regard to this there exist the *Unions pour le recouvrement des cotisations de sécurité sociale et d'allocations familiales (U.R.S.S.A.F.)* on a departmental level, which is encharged with the collection of the various contributions, except the unemployment contributions. The board of governors of these bodies consists of employees' representatives on the one hand (3/5) and on the other hand representatives of self employed persons (2/5), again appointed by the relevant representative organisations.
On a national level the *Agence centrale des organismes de sécurité sociale (A.C.O.S.S.)* directs and controls the departmental bodies.

The supervision of the administrative organisation is carried out on a national level by the competent ministers, namely the minister responsible for social security as well as the Minister of Finance. Furthermore, there exist regional boards for social security, as well as a board on the level of the department.
The government is further represented via a *préfet* within all the administrative bodies operating on a national level. Such representation is possible in view of the public law character of the bodies.
To conclude it should be mentioned that all the administrative bodies come under the financial control of the *Cour de comptes*.

Two organisations are involved with the administration of the scheme for unemployment, the *Associations pour l'emploi dans l'industrie et le commerce (A.S.S.E.D.I.C.)* and the *Union nationale interprofessionnelle pour l 'emploi dans l 'industrie et le commerce (U.N.E.D.I.C.)*, governed by boards composed on an equal basis of representatives of employees and of employers. Among others the *A.S.S.E.D.I.C.* are responsible for the association of the enterprises, the collection of contributions and the granting of benefits. The *U.N.E.D.I.C.* governs a national compensation fund and controls the operation of the *A.S.S.E.D.I.C.*

The minister responsible for social security and the Minister of Finance carry out a certain degree of supervision. Furthermore, essential matters such as the entitlement conditions and the level and scope of the benefits are determined by the government, or by law. Also the granting of individual benefits within the framework of the *régime de solidarité*, as well as the granting of the *allocation spécifique* (see section 4.4), is encharged to the state. As a matter of fact, the latter benefit is actually paid out by the employer, the benefits of de *régime de solidarité* are paid out by the *A.S.S.E.D.I.C.*

Since the administrative decentralisation of 1984, assistance has been organised on a departmental level. The department can make arrangements with municipalities for certain competences to be carried out directly by the latter. A so called *Centre communal d 'action sociale (C.C.A.S.)* functions on a municipal level. It collects the dossiers of claimants and recipients of assistance and sends them through, accompanied by advice, to the *Direction départementale des affaires sanitaires et sociales*. This department examines the dossiers and advises the competent *Commission d'admission à l 'aide sociale*, the body which, except for some specific procedures, takes the final decision. The commission, which operates on an (inter) canton level, is chaired by a judge and is further composed of civil servants from the central government and/or the departmental authorities, depending on who bears the responsibility for the cost of the benefit in question.

3. Personal scope of application.

When determining the personal scope of application of the general scheme, a distinction must be made between the social insurance schemes in a narrow sense (*assurances sociales*), the insurance scheme in respect of industrial injuries and occupational diseases and the scheme in respect of family benefits.

People who carry out work in return for a wage, under the authority of an employer of the private sector, are compulsory insured within the framework of the *assurances sociales*; these concern employees in trade and in industry. The insurance obligation is extended to certain categories of workers, such as people working at home, travelling salesmen, journalists etc. Furthermore, other categories of people are included within the scope of the insurance schemes, such as students, single parents, invalids, war widows and unemployed persons. However, as a rule, the coverage of these people is limited to a number of specific risks, especially those of medical care and old age.

To be eligible for benefits, a person must register with the administrative body to which he is assigned by the act (*l'immatriculation*).

Besides compulsory insurance voluntary insurance exists and so called personal insurance (*assurance personnelle*). Voluntary insurance in respect of the risks of invalidity, old age and death is open to people who were previously compulsory insured. The *assurance personnelle* covers benefits in kind under the sickness and maternity insurance scheme and is available for all people who do not fall under an compulsory insurance scheme. In principle, affiliation to an insurance scheme is final.

The personal scope of application of the insurance scheme in respect of industrial injuries and occupational diseases is rather similar to that of the *assurances sociales*. It includes some extensions to e.g. students in workshops and apprentices.

The various family benefits are open to employees and those considered as such, as well as to self-employed people who are not active in the agricultural sector and to all non-active people. The benefits are granted to people living in France who actually and permanently maintain one or more children. Except when the contrary is explicitly expressed, the beneficiary is the female partner of a couple; in case of divorce or termination of cohabitation, the person in whose household the child lives is entitled to benefit.

In some cases statutory protection extends not only to the insured person himself, but also to his dependent family members. For example this is the case where, within the insurance scheme in respect of sickness and pregnancy, benefits in kind are concerned, as for the insurance schemes in respect of invalidity and death also. The concept of family member includes the spouse of the insured person in so far as he/she is not insured him/herself, as well as under further conditions, the children. In respect of the sickness insurance scheme the concept of family members also includes ascendants, descendants, kins(wo)men and relatives through marriage who live within the same household as the insured person and who are exclusively concerned with the care of the household and with the raising of at least two children under the age of 14 years.

With respect to the sickness and maternity insurance scheme the concubine of an insured person is treated in the same way as a spouse, provided she is actually, completely and permanently maintained by the insured person. In the insurance scheme with regard to industrial injuries and occupational diseases, the spouse, dependent children and ascendants are entitled to a pension on the death of the insured person.

In respect of the loss of an insured status or dependency status, entitlement to benefits continues for another twelve months in the framework of the sickness, maternity, invalidity and old age insurance schemes.

The unemployment insurance scheme extends to all those who are active on the basis of a contract of employment. The unemployment assistance scheme covers young claimants in their first position as well as other categories of persons who are excluded from the insurance scheme.

Assistance is payable to every person who is resident in France.

4. Risks and benefits.

4.1. Old age.

We must distinguish between the contributory and non-contributory benefits of the general scheme, and assistance to the elderly. The insured person who has paid contributions over 150 quarters, is entitled to a *pension de retraite* on the attainment of 60 years of age, at the level of 50% of the average salary (up to a certain maximum) over the 10 most favourable years in which work was carried out. If there was an involuntary interruption in the payment of contributions, for example during periods of enjoyment of sickness or unemployment benefit or periods of strike, a person is considered to have paid contributions over this period. A reduction takes place of 1.25% for each quarter one falls short of the desired 150. If it is more favourable for the claimant, the reduction is calculated with reference to the number of quarters remaining until 65 years of age is attained. This relates to the fact that at the moment of attainment of this age, one is entitled to a full pension even when one has not fully satisfied the contribution conditions. Furthermore, a full pension on the attainment of 60 years of age is payable to a number of specific categories of people, such as people who are incapable of work (an incapacity for work of 50% or more) and war veterans.

The pension is increased if the beneficiary has had at least three dependent children or a dependent spouse of a certain age who has no means of her own above a certain level, or who needs the permanent help of a third person. The pension is subject to an upper and a lower limit, similar to those of the non-contributory pensions. Entitlement to pension is subject to the condition that the beneficiary must have terminated his work with his present employer.

An occupational pension scheme on the basis of collective agreements exists for all employees of the general and the agricultural scheme, which has been made compulsory by statute since 1972.

Non-contributory benefits are payable to people older than 65 years of age (or 60 in case of incapacity for work), who are of French nationality (except for agreements with other countries), who are resident in France (possibly during a certain period), and who do not have means in excess of a certain upper limit. There are the *allocations de base* and the *allocation supplémentaire du fonds national de solidarité (F.N.S.)*. Nowadays, the former are only of little practical importance. That is not the case with the *F.N.S.* This scheme is set up in order to guarantee that the services for old age, i.e. pensions on a contributory basis as well as the allocations de base, reach a certain minimum level (the *minimum vieillesse*). The benefit consists of a flat-rate amount which varies depending upon the claimant's family circumstances.

People from the age of 65 years (or 60 in case of incapacity for work) with insufficient means, are entitled to *aide à domicile* or to placement with private people or in an institution. The *aide à domicile* may be in cash as well as in kind (help in the household). Due to the fact that a *minimum vieillesse* is guaranteed within the framework of the old age insurance scheme, the assistance in cash within this field is of little practical importance.

4.2. Death.

The a*ssurance décès* insures to dependants of the deceased person an amount equal to 90 times his average daily wage over the three months preceding the death. The amount is subject to an upper and a lower limit. There are minimum conditions concerning the past employment record, as well as the contribution record. People entitled are those who, on the day of the death of the insured person, were actually, completely and permanently dependent upon the deceased. If no priorities can be determined on the basis of this starting point, the entitled person is the spouse who was neither divorced nor separated; if there is no such spouse, the descendants or, failing them, the ascendants are entitled.

The spouse of a person who was insured for old age, or who was entitled to an *allocation aux adultes handicapés*, or to benefits in kind from the sickness insurance scheme for three months preceding his death, is entitled to *allocation de veuvage*. There are conditions in respect of age (younger than 55), dependent children (the claimant must be raising at least one child or have raised a child during at least 9 years preceding the child's 16th birthday), the place of residence (in France) and personal means. The benefit is temporary (maximum three years); however, beneficiaries who have attained 50 years of age on the death of their spouse, remain entitled until they attain 55 years of age. The benefit is flat-rate and degressive (decreases yearly). Entitlement ends upon remarriage or cohabitation.

The spouse of the deceased person who (in due course) was (or would have been) entitled to a *pension de retraite*, is entitled to the *pension de réversion*. There are conditions with regard to the means of the spouse, the age of the spouse (minimum 55) and the duration of the marriage (minimal two years, unless there are children from the marriage). The divorced spouse of the deceased person who has never remarried is equally entitled to the pension. In some cases there is a pro rata division of the pension between the surviving spouse and the divorced ex-spouse(s) who has/have not remarried, depending upon the duration of the respective marriages. The scope of the pension amounts to 52% of the *pension de retraite* to which the deceased was or would have been entitled upon his death, if he was insured for a minimum of 15 years. In cases of a shorter period of insurance there is a pro rata reduction. If the beneficiary has been responsible for the raising of at least three children, the pension will be increased.

The spouse of an insured person who (in due course) was (or would have been) entitled to a *pension de retraite* or a *pension d 'invalidité*, is entitled to a *pension de veuf ou veuve*, provided he is younger than 55 and is himself incapable of work to such a degree that, if he had been insured, he would have been entitled to an invalidity pension. The pension amounts to 52% of the pension to which the deceased person was or would have been entitled. The benefit is subject to a lower limit and will be increased in cases where the claimant has been responsible for the raising of at least three children. Entitlement terminates upon the remarriage of the beneficiary. Upon reaching 55 years of age the pension is automatically changed into a *pension de réversion.*

If death was due to an injury or an occupational disease the dependent spouse and children up to a certain age are entitled to a *rente viagère*. With regard to the spouse there is a condition that the marriage must have taken place prior to the injury or two years preceding the death, unless there are one or more children from the marriage. The divorced spouse is only entitled to a pension if he enjoyed an alimony from the ex-partner. In case of remarriage entitlement to a pension is suspended, but a lump sum is paid. Entitlement can be revived in case of divorce or renewed widow(er)hood. To the extent that the deceased person had neither a spouse nor children, the ascendants of the deceased person are entitled to a pension if they can demonstrate that they would have been entitled to maintenance from the deceased person; if the deceased person had a spouse and/or children, the ascendants are entitled to pension, if they were dependent upon the deceased person.

The pension for the spouse amounts to 30% of the wage of the deceased person or to 50%, if the spouse is older than 55 years of age, or is incapable of work (50% or more). The divorced spouse is entitled to 20% of the wage. The pension for the first two semi-orphans amounts to 15% of the wage and 10% for each subsequent semi-orphan with a maximum of 30% for all the ascendants in total. The total pensions may not exceed 85% of the wage of the deceased person.

In addition to pension there is entitlement to a reimbursement of the funeral costs, borne by the administrative authority.

In case of death during the receipt of an unemployment benefit under the insurance regime, an amount is paid to the spouse equal to 120 times the daily benefit of the deceased person, increased by 45 times the daily benefit in respect of each dependent child.

4.3. Incapacity for work.

If the insured person is diagnosed by a doctor as being incapable of work, the sickness insurance scheme (*assurance maladie*) provides *indemnités journalières* (daily compensations). This is subject to minimum conditions concerning the employment and contribution record of the insured person.

For certain longterm disorders, benefit is payable, and this for a maximum period of three years, from the fourth day of incapacity. Otherwise, a person is entitled to benefit over a maximum of 360 days during a term of three years. The level of benefit amounts to half the average daily wage during the three months preceding the incapacity. There is both an upper and a lower limit. After 31 days, benefit is increased to 2/3 of the daily wage, provided that the beneficiary has at least three dependent children.

The conditions with respect to entitlement to cash benefits (*indemnites journalières de répos*) within the *assurance maternité* are the same as those which apply in the *assurance maladie*. However, in addition, a woman is obliged to undergo four examinations prior to the birth. The benefit is granted for a minimum period of 16 weeks (6 weeks before and 10 weeks after the birth). Providing the birth increases the total number of children to three, the duration of the benefit is 26 weeks (8 weeks before and 18 weeks after the birth). Regarding a multiple birth, the duration is extended by two weeks. The level of the benefit amounts to 84% of the average daily wage during the last three months of work. Here also there is an upper and a lower limit.
The man or woman who adopts a child also belongs to the scope of entitled people, as well as the father on the mother's death due to the birth.

Occupational schemes generally provide additions on top of sickness benefit, up to the level of the wage.

Beneficiaries of the *aide médicale* (benefits from which are subject to a means test; see section 4.5), who have received this benefit for at least three months, who are 15 years of age or older and, due to their sickness, are not capable of carrying out any occupational activity, are entitled to a monthly cash benefit, the *allocation d'aide médicale*. Nor the *aide médicale*, nor the *allocation* are of much importance in practice.

Under the invalidity insurance scheme (*assurance invalidité*) the insured person, younger than 60 years of age, whose work or earning capacity is reduced by at least 2/3, is entitled to *pension d'invalidité*. The beneficiary must not be capable of earning a wage from any occupation that amounts to more than 1/3 of the normal wage for employees within the same region and active in the same occupational category as the claimant himself. In assessing the incapacity for work not only the remaining capacity is taken into account, but also the general state of the claimant, his age, his physical and mental capacity, as well as his education and past employment record.
Entitlement to benefit depends upon the claimant having registered himself as an insured person for at least twelve months, as well as upon his past employment record.
In determining the level of benefit those incapable of work are sub-divided into three categories:
- people who are capable of carrying out a certain activity;
- people who are not capable of doing this;
- people who are not capable of doing this and who, furthermore, need the, help of a third person regarding the daily necessities of life.

With respect to the first category benefit amounts to 30% of the average salary during the ten most favourable working years, with respect to the second category the rate is 50% and for the third 90%. There are upper and lower limits. Possibly, in combination with the means tested *allocation supplémentaire F.N.S.* a minimum invalidité is attained, equal to the *minimum vieillesse*.

The beneficiary may undergo rehabilitation training; during the training the pension is fully or partially maintained.

With respect to temporary or permanent incapacity due to an industrial injury or an occupational disease there may be entitlement to benefit under the insurance scheme for industrial injuries and occupational diseases (in kind, as well as in cash).

The benefits in kind encompass *inter alia* compensation for the costs of medical treatment, medicine, artificial aids and the costs of rehabilitation. The costs are paid directly to the people or institutions in question; the claimant pays nothing.

In case of temporary incapacity a person is entitled to an *indemnité journalière* (daily benefit). Entitlement exists from the second day of the incapacity for work (the first day is payable by the employer) until full recovery, the consolidation of the injury or the death of the claimant. Consequently, the duration of benefit is unlimited. Initially the level of the benefit amounts to half, and from the 29th day 2/3 of the average daily wage during the last period of payment. The benefit is subject to an upper and a lower limit, both of which are more favourable than those applied in the other social security schemes.

In case of permanent incapacity, that is to say the consolidation of the physical state, the claimant is entitled to a pension. This is calculated on the basis of, on the one hand the wage during the twelve months preceding the incapacity (here also there is a relatively favourable lower and upper limit), and on the other the degree of incapacity for work. The latter is determined by comparing the nature of the injury, the general state of the claimant, his age, his physical and mental capacity, as well as his education and work experience, taking into account a list drawn up for this purpose.

In determining the level of the benefit only half account is taken of incapacity for work of up to 50%; full account is taken of incapacity for work if this incapacity is above 50%. If the claimant requires the permanent help of a third person, pension is increased by 40%.

Entitlement to pension exists only if the incapacity for work is estimated to be at least 10%. If not, a person is entitled to a lump sum payment (*indemnité en capital*) which is flat-rate and dependent upon the percentage of incapacity for work.

A special compensation is granted to the employee who, due to a certain occupational disease, has to change his job in order to prevent the worsening of his condition, yet who does not satisfy the conditions for pension. This compensation, the *indemnité de changement d'emploi*, is equal to 60 days wages for each year in which a person has been exposed to the risk, with a maximum of 300 days wages.

Special rules apply if the industrial injury is due to the deliberate or grave misconduct of the victim or the employer (or the latters representative). The application of these rules can lead to the loss (deliberate action of the victim), reduction (grave misconduct of the victim) or increase (grave misconduct of the employer) of the benefits to the victim or to the survivors. There exist benefits for physically or mentally handicapped persons who are not entitled to a benefit in respect of incapacity for work, within the framework of the invalidity insurance scheme.

The person with a dependent, handicapped child younger than 20 years of age, is entitled to the *allocation d'éducation spéciale*, provided the degree of incapacity of the child is at least 80%. The benefit amounts to 32% of the basis applied for the family benefits (see section 4.6). There is entitlement to an increase of benefit if there are extremely high costs associated with the handicap or if the help of a third person is required. The increase varies in accordance with the costs and the need of help (24% or 72% of the basis).

The benefits can also be granted in respect of a child with a degree of incapacity of between 50 and 80%, if the child attends a special school or the condition of the child makes educational help necessary at home.

The *allocation aux adultes handicapés* is payable to handicapped persons of French nationality who are older than 16 years of age and are no longer entitled to the *allocations familiales* and whose degree of incapacity amounts to at least 80%, or who, due to their handicap, are not in the condition to procure a field of activity for themselves. A further condition is that the claimant may not be entitled to an invalidity or old age pension on the same level as the allocation. The benefit is equal to the *minimum d'invalidité* and is subject to a means test.

The same conditions with respect to age and incapacity apply for the *aide sociale aux personnes hanicapées* as for the *allocation aux adultes handicapés* described above. There does exist entitlement to a cash benefit: the *allocation compensatrice*. Furthermore there are specific possibilities of placement, for example in sheltered workshops. The benefits are subject to a means test.

4.4. Unemployment.

In order to be entitled to a benefit within the framework of the unemployment insurance scheme (*assurance chômage*) the unemployed person must have lost his job involuntarily; furthermore, he must be capable of work, registered with the *Agence Nationale Pour l'Emploi (A.N.P.E.)*, actively looking for employment and younger than 60 years of age (or younger than 65 years of age if he cannot be entitled to a full old age pension, due to his employment record). Finally, he must have been insured for a certain period during the reference period.

Three benefits can be distinguished, the *allocation de base normale*, the *allocation de base minorée* and the *allocation de fin de droits*.

The *allocation de base normale* is payable to those who have been insured either for 6 months during the 12 months preceding the unemployment, or for 12 months during the preceding 24 months, or for 182 days during the preceding 12 months under the condition of at least 10 years membership of the scheme. The benefit consists of a flat-rate and a proportional part, the latter at the level of 40.4% of the average gross wage during the previous twelve months (subject to an upper and a lower limit). The total benefit may not fall below 57.4% and may not exceed 75% of the wage. There is also an absolute minimum amount. The duration of the benefit varies from 3 to 27 months, depending upon the duration of the insurance. On an individual basis, an extension by 3 to a maximum of 18 months is possible, though in this case the benefit for those younger than 55 years old is reduced. Those who on the attainment of 57 1/2 years of age have not enjoyed benefit for more than one year and who have a employment record of at least ten years, maintain their benefit until the moment that they may be entitled to a full old age pension.

Entitlement to the *allocation de base minorée* exists if one has been insured for less than 6 months, yet for at least 3 months during the 12 months preceding the unemployment. This benefit is also composed of a flat-rate and a proportional part, the latter being at the rate of 30.3% of the average gross daily wage during the previous 12 months. There is a flat rate minimum and benefit may not exceed an amount equal to 56.25% of the basis. The benefit is granted for 3 months; an extension is not possible.

The *allocation de fin de droits*, which is intended for unemployed people who have exhausted their entitlement to the *allocation de base*, is flat-rate, to be increased for unemployed persons who are older than 55 years of age and who *inter alia*, have an employment record of at least 20 years. The duration varies from 6 to 18 months depending upon the duration of insurance and the age of the claimant. Here also, an extension of nine months is possible in individual cases. But, then it must be taken into account that the granting of the *allocation de base* and the *allocation de fin de droits* together are subject to a maximum duration. Also for the latter cash benefit there are special rules for beneficiaries of 57.2 years or older.

An *allocation de formation reclassement* can be paid for a longer period. Its amount equels that of the *allocation de base* or the *allocation de fin de droits*. This allowance benefits people participating in special professional training programmes.

Unemployment assistance (*régime de solidarité*) includes two benefits, the *allocation de solidarité spécifique* and the *allocation d'insertion*.
The *allocation de solidarité spécifique* is granted to long term unemployed people after their period of entitlement to contributory benefits. Entitlement is subject to the same conditions with respect to age, capacity for work, registration with the A.N.P.E. and applying for jobs, as those which apply in the unemployment insurance scheme. Furthermore, the claimants must have carried out paid work for 5 years during the 10 years preceding the unemployment; when a person is raising a child the latter requirement is moderated. Entitlement to the allocation is subject to a means test.
The allocation is flat-rate and it provides certain increases for people older

than 55 years of age, depending upon their labour record. It is granted each time for a period of 6 months, until the moment when there is entitlement to an old age pension.

The *allocation d'insertion* is payable to a limited number of categories of people who have not yet worked or who have not worked enough to eligible to the contributory benefits. Subject to further conditions, it is payable to widows, divorced women who have one dependent child, ex convicts, refugees, and some other categories. The condition that one must register as seeking employment and be active to this end applies for all categories of people. The benefit is flat-rate and different for the young persons, the women and the other categories of persons. It is subject to a means test. The duration is one year, with a waiting period of 1 to 6 months with respect to young persons.

If the unemployment is due to a temporary closure of the place of work or to a reduction of the working time to less than 37 hours per week, caused by, for example, the economic conjecture, problems regarding the supply of raw materials or energy, disaster, extreme weather conditions or a reorganisation, there may be entitlement to a so called *allocation spécifique*. For all beneficiaries the level of benefit is equal to 65% of the minimum hourly wage and is payable for a maximum period of 500 hours per year. Furthermore, on the basis of collective agreements there may be entitlement to an *indemnité conventionelle complémentaire*, equal to 50% of the gross wage per hour, taking into account the *allocation spécifique* that is payable. Employees who have not carried out any work for more than four consecutive weeks are considered as normal unemployed people and excluded from this scheme.

The employee who is active for a minimum of 39 hours per week (the statutory working time), is entitled to a monthly minimum wage. If there is a reduction in the number of working hours, for example due to sickness, maternity or a strike, entitlement to the minimum wage is maintained. Consequently, if the sum of the salary and the unemployment benefit is equal to less than the minimum wage there exists entitlement to an *allocation complémentaire* equal to the amount of the difference.

4.5. Medical care.

Among others, the sickness insurance scheme covers the costs of the general practioner, surgeon, dentist, pharmacist, entry into hospital, entry into a nursing home, rehabilitation, transport costs and housing for the handicapped. Not only the costs of the insured person himself, but also those of other people are covered. These other people are the spouse of the insured person, a cohabitant who is actually, completely and permanently dependent upon the insured person, dependent children and the ascendants, descendants and relatives to the third degree, who live with the insured person in the same house to the extent that they are exclusively responsible for the care for the household and the raising of at least two children who are dependent upon the insured person.

Entitlement to compensation of costs depends upon specific employment and contribution conditions.

In the first instance, the insured person must pay the costs himself. They are retrospectively compensated for by the administrative authorities. There is never a full compensation. For each activity regulations determine a personal contribution for the insured person (*ticket modérateur*). However, in practice the system of the personal contributions does not apply; often, such contributions are no longer applicable. For example, this is the case for very expensive operations; if the contributions which have previously been paid by the insured people are in excess of a certain amount; or for certain categories of people such as those in receipt of an invalidity pension. Furthermore, it must be pointed out that when the personal contribution is still due, it will often reimbursed by a *mutualité*, an insurance fund to which most insured persons are affiliated voluntarily or by collective agreement.

The doctor's fees, medicine and entry into hospital, regarding pregnancy or birth, and other related costs are covered by the maternity insurance scheme. Entitlement exists for women who are insured on their own title as well as dependent spouses, concubines and daughters of insured people. The conditions with respect to the employment and contribution record are the same as those which apply in the sickness insurance scheme. An extra requirement is that the insured person must have been insured during at least 10 months preceding the birth. The costs of medicine are only compensated for up to a flat-rate amount the remaining benefits are free of charge.

Assistance (*aide médicale*) provides benefits in kind, comparable to those of the sickness and maternity insurance schemes. Also the sickness costs which remain payable by the claimant may be reimbursed. Entitlement to benefit exists when the costs payable by the claimant bear no relation to his means. In view of the extensions of personal scope of application of the sickness costs insurance scheme, the *aide médicale* is only of small significance.

4.6. Family.

We distinguish family benefits in the framework of the general statutory scheme and assistance to families.

There are a large number of family benefits within the general statutory scheme, to be divided into three groups:
- *prestations générales d'entretien*;
- *prestations liées à la naissance*;
- *prestations à affection spéciale*.
Subject to certain exceptions concerning specific family benefits, there are general rules with regard to the personal scope of application (see section 3), the scope of the children giving rise to entitlement and the basis of calculation of the benefits.
Every child living in France (exceptions are possible) gives rise to entitle-

ment until the age when compulsory education ceases (16). Beyond this age, entitlement to benefit also exists in respect of the child who is younger than 17, with no income from work above a certain limit. Finally, entitlement exists for children until they reach 20 years of age, if they are engaged in education or an apprenticeship, or if they are incapable of work, again only to the extent that any possible income from labour is not in excess of an upper limit. The daughter, sister or spouse, who lives with the claimant in the same household and who is exclusively responsible for the care of the household and the raising of the children dependent upon the claimant, is treated the same as the child following education. The latter is subject to the condition that the mother necessary within the household must either be carrying out paid labour, have died, have abandoned the household, is physically incapable of being active within the household or raising children. A legal relationship between the child and the potential beneficiary is not required.

The level of the family benefits depends upon the so called *base mensuelle de calcul*. By decree this basis is adjusted twice per year, corresponding at least to price increases.

There exist four *prestations générales d'entretien*; these are payable on a monthly basis.

The *allocations familiales* represent approximately 52% of the total family benefits. They are payable as from the second dependent child. The benefit amounts to 32% of the basis for the first two children and 41% for the third and subsequent children, to be increased for children of 10 years of age and older (9% as from the 10th year of age and 16% as from the age of 15); the increase is also applicable in respect of the first child, provided that the total number of dependent children is at least three.

The *complément familial* is payable to a family or to the person whose means do not exceed a certain limit and which/who has at least three dependent children older than three years of age. The level amounts to 41.56% of the basis.

The *allocation de soutien familial* is payable in respect of the full or semi-orphan, the child whose descent from one or both parents is unknown, and the child whose parents, or one of whose parents, are not willing or capable of maintaining the child. Benefit is payable to the father, the mother or a third person who actually and permanently takes on the maintenance of the child. The father or mother who remarries or who cohabitates loses entitlement to benefit. The level of benefit amounts to 30% of the basis for full orphans and comparable children and 22,5% for semi-orphans and comparable children.

The *allocation de parent isolé* is payable to the single parent who is exclusively responsible for the maintenance of at least one child. As 'single parent are considered: the surviving, divorced, separated, abandoned and unmarried parent, as well as the single pregnant woman, provided that they do not cohabit. The allocation amounts to 150% of the basis for the single parent increased with 50% for each child, and is subject to a means test. Benefit is payable for a period of twelve months and possibly for a longer period until the moment that the youngest child has reached the age of three years.

We distinguish three *prestations liées à la naissance.*

The *allocation au jeune enfant* is payable from the fourth month of the pregnancy until the end of the month in which the child has reached three months. One can also be entitled to benefit after this time, albeit subject to a means test and maximally until the moment that the child reaches three years of age. The benefit amounts to 45.95% of the basis.

If a birth or an adoption brings the total number of children to three, and the person on whom the child is dependent no longer carries out any paid employment, there is a right to an *allocation parentale d'éducation,* until the moment that the youngest child reaches the age of three years. The claimant must have been employed for at least 2 years during the 10 years preceding the birth or adoption. The benefit amounts to 142.57% of the basis (the *allocation au jeune enfant* is included within this amount). Those who during the child's third year resume at maximum, half time paid employment or paid training, remain entitled to benefit, albeit at a 50% level. There are important anti-cumulation provisions which are intended to prevent the *allocation* (which in view of it's level threatens to take on an income maintenance character) from coinciding with, for example, a wage or an income maintenance benefit in case of maternity.

The *allocation de garde d'enfant à domicile* is payable to the family which or the person who has appointed one or more people to care for the children at home, due to the fact that the parents or the single parent carry out an occupational activity of a certain scope. The level of the allocation is equal to the social security contributions which are payable by third person(s), subject to an upper limit. The benefit has had only a very limited degree of success.

Of the *allocations à affections spéciales* we will only deal with the *allocation de rentrée scolaire* (see section 4.3 for the *allocation d'education spéciale* which also belongs to this category). This benefit is payable to families who are also entitled to another family benefit for children attending school between the ages of 6 and 16. The benefit amounts to 20% of the basis for each child and is paid at the beginning of the school year. It is subject to a means test.

The head of a family with at least two dependent children and without sufficient means to raise the children is entitled to the *aide sociale aux familles.* This benefit is subject to an extensive means test. However, due to the extention of the scope of application of the family benefits from the general scheme, this assistance scheme is of little practical significance.

4.7. Need.

We have already observed that in French social security law there is a whole series of specific assistance benefits, which are designed for specific categories of persons or for the coverage of specific needs. Recently a more general assistance scheme has been established, the *revenu minimum d'insertion.*

Entitlement to benefit depends upon a person residing in France. Nationality requirements are not imposed, although for non-EEC nationals there are requirements regarding the duration of residence; for this category entitlement to benefit only exists after a minimum period of residence in France of three years.

The claimant must be older than 25 years of age; if he is younger he must have one or more dependent children. Students and apprentices are excluded from entitlement.

There are various benefit rates depending upon the composition of the households. The basis amount for the single parent is increased by 50% for the spouse or the partner; for each child, in respect of which there is entitlement to family benefits, there is another 30% increase; the latter also applies for each person younger than 25 years old who belongs to the household and is dependent upon the claimant. The level of benefit is determined by deducting all the means within the household from the applicable rate. The means include all income with the exception of a limited number of specific benefits; they also include rights to maintenance. The means of all persons belonging to the household are taken into account.

The claimant must agree to participate in activities aimed at integration. The *revenu* is at first granted for a period of three months. During this period a "contract" is proposed by the state, which includes a plan for integration. The integration should not necessarily be aimed at paid employment; training or an apprenticeship are equally valid objectives; the act even allows for the drawing up of a more social integration programme, for example aimed at alfabetizing or the combat against alcoholism. After the conclusion of the contract benefit is granted for a period of 3 to 12 months; when this period has expired, benefit may be renewed, each time for an equal period. If the claimant does not fulfil his obligations under the contract, benefit will be terminated.

5. Financing.

The general statutory scheme is almost entirely financed by contributions from the insured persons and the employers. The state is only involved in the financing on an incidental basis, especially in making contribution payments for certain categories of persons. There is no statutory obligation for the state to supplement possible shortages. A source of financing of a supplementary nature is further obtained through the taxing of alcohol, pharmaceutical advertising and the possession of a car. The financing of the general scheme is based upon the pay as you go principle.

Contributions are levied on the wages or the occupational income of the insured people, subject to an upper earnings limit. Furthermore, some social security benefits are also subject to contribution liability.

Generally, contributions have a proportional character. The rates differ from scheme to scheme. For certain categories of people, such as domestic

personnel, hotel personnel and taxi drivers the contributions are flat - rate.
Contributions are generally jointly paid by the employers and the employees, according to a certain ratio of distribution. As a departure from this starting point, the contributions for the insurance schemes in respect of industrial injuries and occupational diseases, as well as for family benefits, are completely borne by the employer. In contrast, the employees are fully responsible for the payment of contributions in the framework of the *assurance veuvage*.
The employer deposits all the contributions, including those of the employee with the fund of the *U.R.S.S.A.F./ A.C.O.S.S.* These divide the contributions between the three national funds, which in their turn take care of the distribution between the regional and primary funds.

A contribution on all income, the *contribution sociale généralisée (C.S.G.)* has recently been introduced. It constitutes the first step towards the financing by taxes of social security. The actual law percentage of the *C.S.G.* (1.1 %) will increase along with the financial needs of social security. Now the *C.S.G.* is only used for financing the family allowances.

The financing of the different sections of the unemployment scheme is regulated in various ways. The insurance scheme of the *chômage total* is financed from contributions, borne jointly by the employees and the employers. The *régime de solidarité* is borne almost completely by the state. There is also a so called solidarity contribution levied upon certain categories of persons active within the public sector. The state also finances the *allocation spécifique* within the framework of the *chômage partiel*. The *indemnité conventionelle complémentaire* is in principle borne by the employers, although the state can also bear a part of it. Finally, the *allocation complémentaire* is borne half by the employees and half by the employers. The contributions are paid to the *A.S.S.E.D.I.C.*

Except for a limited number of benefits which are financed by the government, the expenses of the categorical benefits within the framework of *aide sociale* are borne by the departments. However, part of the financial obligations are transferred to the municipalities.
The expenditure of the *revenu minimum d 'insertion* is entirely borne by the central government.

6. Judicial review.

Judicial review in the area of social security is subject to a special procedure for the settlement of disputes. The procedures are simple, fast and inexpensive. In special cases, the regular courts are competent, e.g. in disputes concerning the recovery of benefits from third parties, in disputes concerning the election of governing boards of the administrative bodies, in disputes concerning the application of penal sanctions and in respect of disputes concerning the occupational pension scheme and the unemployment scheme.

The special procedure for the settlement of disputes is subdivided into the *contentieux général* and a number of *contentieux spéciaux*.

The *contentieux générale de la sécurité sociale* governs all disputes in the field of statutory social security, which, due to their nature, do not fall under another procedure for judicial review. It mainly covers all disputes concerning insurance obligation, contribution liability and the granting of benefits.

Competent in first instance is the *tribunal des affaires de sécurité sociale* which is chaired by a judge and assisted by a representative of the employees and the employers. Before the claimant can turn to this tribunal, he must adress a *commission de recours amiable* within two months after the litigious decision. This commission, which constitutes a part of the administrative body in question, takes a fresh reasoned decision. If after one month the claimant has not received a decision, or if he wishes to challenge the decision, appeal to the *tribunal* within a period of two months is open. The parties can appear personally before the *tribunal*, but they may also be represented or accompanied by certain people (a spouse, direct ascendants and descendants, a lawyer, a colleague or a representative of a union). The *tribunal* may order a further inquiry to be carried out, summon advisory experts, in short, collect all necessary information. If the case concerns a dispute of a medical nature, the *tribunal* is obliged to apply a special procedure (see below).

If the case subject to the judges decision, does not amount to a certain level, determined by legislation, then the decision of the *tribunal* constitutes a final judgement which is not subject to further appeal. Otherwise, appeal is possible within one month to the *Cour d'appel, chambre social*. The decision taken by this court can be disputed within two months in the *Cour de cassation, chambre sociale*.

With respect to disputes of a medical nature, there is a separate procedure of the *expertise médicale*. This procedure must be started within one month after the litigious decision. A physician or a board of physicians, appointed by the attendant doctor and the doctor from the administrative body, give their opinion. Subject to further conditions, that opinion is binding on the claimant, the administrative body and the judge.

Apart from the *contentieux général* there are two special procedures for judicial review.

The *contentieux du contrôle technique* is a procedure which must be followed in cases of error, misuse, fraud and facts concerning the performance of the medical profession, in the framework of medical care provided to insured persons.

The *contentieux technique de la sécurité sociale* is the judicial procedure applicable with respect to disputes concerning the degree of invalidity within the meaning of the social insurance schemes, the incapacity for work in the old age insurance scheme and the state of permanent incapacity in the scheme regarding industrial injuries and occupational diseases. In first instance the disputes are dealt with by the *Commissions régionales*, consisting, among others, of physicians. Appeal is possible to the *Commission nationale technique* and in the last instance to the *Cour de cassation*.

Objections against decisions taken by the *Commissions d'admission d'aide sociale* can be made with the so called *Commission départementale*, a commission which, in composition, is similar to the *Commission d'admission*. The claimant is heard at his request. The *Commission centrale d'aide sociale* hears appeals; it is chaired by a member of the *Conseil d 'Etat* and further composed of members of the *Conseil d'Etat*, judges and members appointed by the competent minister, e.g. on grounds of their specific expertise in the assistance field. If required, the commission is supplemented by advisory physicians. In view of the administrative character of this judicial procedure, further appeal can be made with the *Conseil d'Etat*.

Chapter 5: Grand Duchy of Luxembourg

1. Introduction: concept and sources of social security law.

Although it is difficult to describe the concept of social security in a way which is endorsed by everybody, there does exist some unanimity regarding the scope of this concept. Thus social security (*sécurité sociale*) encompasses:

- social insurance schemes (*assurances sociales*), within which a distinction is made between sickness and maternity insurance schemes (*assurance maladie-maternité*), a pension insurance scheme (*assurance pension*) and an injuries insurance scheme (*assurance accidents*). The ickness and maternity insurance schemes include benefits in kind (medical care), invalidity benefits and funeral grants. The pension insurance scheme covers old age, invalidity and survival pensions. The injuries insurance scheme includes medical care, grants in cash and pensions; it covers industrial injuries as well as occupational diseases and some other risks (e.g. injuries sustained at school and injuries sustained when going to or coming from the work place or when carrying out rescue operations);
- family allowances (*prestations familiales*) composed of a maternity supplement (*allocation de maternité*), a birth supplement (*allocation de naissance*) and monthly family benefits (*allocations familiales mensuelles*);
- unemployment benefits (*prestations de chômage*).

Within the broader concept of social security the following benefits are included as well:

- the guaranteed minimum income and
- social assistance (*assistance sociale*).

From it's beginning, social security in The Grand Duchy was influenced by German law; therefore, the Luxembourg social insurance schemes are still mainly set up along professional lines. Nowadays, family benefits have virtually lost their professional character. Unemployment benefits, as well as the guaranteed minimum income and assistance, do not in principle distinguish between the various occupational groups. An enumeration of the most important professional groups with their own social security status includes: blue collar workers, white collar workers in the private sector, civil servants and white collar workers in the public sector, municipal white collar workers and civil servants, artisans, traders and industrialists, self-employed intellectual occupations and agricultural occupations. Furthermore, for employees of specific employers there are separate social security schemes, e.g. for blue collar workers of Arbed, for white collar workers of Arbed and for employees of the National Railway Company.

There is a certain tendency towards harmonisation of the various statutes. Below, we will direct our attention specifically towards the schemes for blue collar workers, white collar workers in the private sector, artisans and self-employed intellectual occupations.

It must be noted that apart from the social security schemes referred to above, occupational insurance schemes also exist, concluded with *mutuelles* or on the level of enterprises.

As such, occupational social insurance schemes offered by enterprises are not regulated by specific regulation, legislative rules merely provide a favourable regime for the taxation of these schemes. Next to that the general rules of collective labour law and insurance law must be applied. The occupational insurance schemes offered by the enterprises are primarily aimed at providing additional old age and survivor's pensions and additional invalidity pensions.

The activities of the mutual assistance societies (*sociétés de secours mutuel/ mutuelles*) are regulated by legislation and a High Council for the mutual societies esists (*Conseil supérieur de la mutualité*). The numerous assistance societies grant their members benefits in respect of risks such as death as well as, for example, additional benefits for injuries other than industrial injuries. In addition, compensation to members of the mutual assistance societies may also be payable in respect of any medical costs which are not covered by (statutory) social security. The mutual guarantee funds enjoy support from the State as well as a favourable taxation regime.

In 1948 the constitution of Luxembourg laid down a number of provisions which are of importance to us:
- article 11.4 Constitution: "The statute guarantees the right to work and ensures the realization of this right for every citizen";
- article 11.5 Constitution: "The statute organises social security, the protection of health and leisure for active people and guarantees syndical freedom".

Although these constitutional provisions may be regarded as the legal basis for all social security legislation, the real significance of the provisions for positive law remains minimal. Perhaps the constitutional clauses have no role other than to require the intermediation of a formal statute for the development of social security rules (that is to say, to offer a statutory framework for such rules); specially subject to this requirement, are, for example, rules with regard to granting compensation for not being able to exercise the right to work, i.e. unemployment benefits.

Each branch of social security is based upon at least one formal act; these are usually further elaborated by decree. It must be noted that the social insurance act (*Code des assurances sociales*), which was introduced in 1925 and subsequently frequently modified, no longer contains a codification of social insurance law: in the last decade a large number of newly introduced social insurance acts and important decrees were not integrated in the act.

2. Administrative organisation.

The Minister for Social Security is competent in respect of social security and in respect of all social security institutions, the mutual assistance societies, the *Conseil supérieur* and the *Conseil arbitral des assurances sociales*. The Minister for Family and Solidarity is, among other things, competent in respect of family benefits, the guaranteed minimum income and social assistance. The Minister for Labour is competent for unemployment benefits as well as for employment policy and labour exchanges.

A supervisory body, i.e. the *Inspection générale de la sécurité sociale*, was established within the Ministry of Social Security and under the authority of the Minister. It carries out policy and supervisory functions in respect of social security as a whole. There is also a separate board, le *Contrôle médical de la sécurité sociale*, which is encharged with tasks within the framework of invalidity schemes, e.g. the determination and revaluation of incapacity for work.

The Common Social Security Centre is encharged with the compilation and the processing of computerized data, the registration of insured people and the receipt and collection of contributions.

The sickness and maternity insurance scheme is administered by the sickness funds (*caisses de maladie*), which all come together within he *Union des caisses de maladie*, a legal person under public law.
In addition the sickness funds themselves are legal people under public law. Separate sickness funds exist for blue collar workers, blue collar workers of Arbed, public civil servants and white collar workers, municipal civil servants and white collar workers, railway personnel, white collar workers in the private sector and intellectual free professions, white collar workers of Arbed, self-employed occupations and agriculturists. The institutions of the sickness funds for wage earners (except for those funds which belong to only one enterprise) are composed on a parity basis of representatives of the employers and representatives of the insured people. The position of chairman rotates. All members of the enterprise's sickness funds, except for the chairman-manager (or his deputy), are elected representatives of the insured people. The institutions of the sickness funds for self-employed people and for agricultural occupations are composed only of representatives of the insured people.

The pension insurance scheme, which was made uniform in 1987, continues to be administered by bodies, the powers of which are determined by the professional category of the insured person, i.e.:
- the Pension Fund for white collar workers in the Private Sector (*Caisse de pension des employés prives*) which is competent in respect of all insured people, white collar workers as well as self-employed people who are primarily engaged in an intellectual activity;
- the Pension Fund for Artisans, Traders and Industrialists (*Caisse de pension des artisans, des commerçants et industriels*) which, more speci-

fically, , is competent in respect of these categories of self-employed people;
- the Agricultural Pension Fund (*Caisse de pension agricole*) which is competent in respect of people active within the agricultural sector;
- the Insurance Institution for Old Age and Invalidity (*Etablissement d 'assurance contre la vieillsse et l'invalidité*), competent in respect of the remaining insured people (e.g. blue collar workers).

The management of each pension fund is encharged to a board of directors. This board is chaired by a chairman-civil servant appointed by the Grand Duke. The remaining members are appointed by the commission of the Pension Fund. The board of directors is responsible for taking decisions regarding affiliation, contributions, administrative fines and the concerned statutory benefits. The commission of the Pension Fund operates as a representative body: it drafts the internal regulations of the Pension Fund as well as the annual budget and accounts. The chairman of the board of directors also chairs the commission and has the right to vote.

In both the commission and the board of directors of the Pension Fund for Employees of the Public Sector and in that of the Insurance Institution for Old Age and Invalidity, there is parity between representatives of the employers and of the insured people. Elsewhere, these bodies are composed entirely of representatives of the insured people. All representatives are directly elected respectively by the insured people and the employers for a period of five years. In order to be eligible, the same conditions as for the local elections apply.

Meetings of the board of directors and the commission are attended by a governmental commissioner, who, just as the chairman of the board of directors, is competent to suspend decisions taken by these bodies which are in his opinion contrary to the relevant statute; the competent minister then decides the case, after a recommendation of the inspectorate.

Enterprises which are subject to the injuries insurance scheme have associated themselves within a mutuality, i.e. the Injuries Insurance Scheme Association. The management of this association is entrusted to a management committee, the chairman of which is appointed by the government. Some affairs must be dealt with by the general assembly of the association. The association is composed of two sections; the industrial section and the agricultural and forestry section. The supervision of both sections rests with separate general associations and management committees, but takes place according to the same principles.

The National Fund for Family Benefits (*Caisse nationale de prestations familiales*) is responsible for the administration of the family benefits.

All in all there are more than twenty administrative bodies involved with the administration of the social insurance schemes. It is true that a certain degree of administrative concentration was ensured by the services of the two sections of the Injuries Insurance Scheme Association and the Insurance Institute for Old Age and Invalidity, united to form the Social Insurance Service (*Office des assurances Sociales, O.A.S.*). The following

institutions have also amalgamated their administrations:
- the Sickness Fund for Self-Employed Occupations and the Pension Fund for Artisans, Traders and Industrialists, i.e. under the name *Administration commune des caisses de sécurité sociale des classes moyennes;*
- the Agricultural Sickness Fund and the Agricultural Pension Fund, i.e. under the name *Administration commune des caisses de sécurité sociale de la profession agricole;*
- the National Fund for Family Benefits and the Pension Fund for white collar workers in the Private Sector.

The National Solidarity Fund (*Fonds National de Solidarité, F.N.S.*) is a legal person, under public law, with financial autonomy. The *F.N.S.* is encharged with the administration of the guaranteed minimum income. The *F.N.S.* is managed by a board of directors, the members of which are appointed by the government.

In each municipality there is a benevolence office (*bureau de bienfaisance*), composed of five members, voted for in secret elections by the municipal council. One member is annualy renewed. The office is responsible for the supervision of goods intended for helping the poor, and with tasks of social assistance. The office is supervised by the Court of Mayor and Aldermen.

3. Personal scope of application.

Above we have seen that the personal scope of application of the social insurance schemes is still very much determined upon a professional basis. Below, this will be most clear when we deal with the personal scope of application of the sickness and maternity insurance scheme.

Compulsory insured within the scheme for sickness and maternity are,
(1) in the scheme for blue collar workers:
- blue collar workers, journeymen, students and domestic personnel whose main occupational activity is in gainful employment;
- people who, in their quality as being active in the above sense, receive old age, survivor's or invalidity pension or who receive a pension on grounds of the compulsory industrial injuries insurance scheme or on grounds of legislation for victims of war (on the condition that this pension is payable in respect of an incapacity for work of at least 50%);
(2) in the scheme for civil servants and white collar workers:
- all people who work for the State, magistrates included;
- members of the teaching profession and ministers of the church;
- municipal white collar workers;
- white collar workers of the railway;
- white collar workers of employers in the private sector;
- people who in the quality of carrying out one of the above activities, receive unemployment pay, old age or survivor's pension;
- free intellectual occupations and people who receive a pension in respect of carrying out such an occupation;

(3) in the scheme for self-employed occupations:
- all those regularly carrying out a legal activity on their own account who fall under the Chamber of Occupations or the Chamber of Commerce;
- Associates of trade companies who actively and effectively participate in management and who are excluded from compulsory affiliation to a sickness fund for wage earners;
- helpers of the above, spouses excluded;
- people who, in respect of the above activities receive a pension; '
(4) in the agricultural scheme:
- those who regularly carry out an agricultural occupational activity on their own account;
- helpers of the above, spouses excluded; and
- people receiving a pension in respect of the above activities.

The spouse and all direct descendants of the insured person are jointly insured, subject to the condition that they are dependent upon the insured person and are themselves not covered against the same risks on grounds of the legislation regarding the *F.N.S.*. Adopted or foster children are treated as descendents. Also insured are close relatives who, in the absence of a spouse care for the household of the insured person.
All people older than eighteen years of age, who loose the quality of insured or jointly insured person may continue the affiliation with their sickness fund within three weeks (continued insurance). All people resident in the Grand Duchy, who are not otherwise insured against sickness, can voluntarily affiliate themselves to the sickness insurance scheme. This results in the sickness and maternity insurance schemes covering virtually all residents, although they are still strongly established upon a professional basis.

Nowadays there is a uniform pension insurance scheme. All people in the Grand Duchy who are gainfully employed, be it for another person or on their own account, or who can demonstrate periods which are treated as periods of professional activity are compulsory insured under the old age, invalidity and survivor's pension insurance scheme. Periods treated as periods of professional activity, include the following: periods of enjoyment of income maintenance benefits which gave rise to pension insurance contribution liability, periods during which a person has been a helper for a self-employed person, periods of employment in relief work and periods of military service. On the request of one of the parents of a child, (made within twenty four months of the birth or adoption of the child), a period of twenty four months (the so called baby year) may count as a period of professional activity, subject to the condition that the claimant was insured for a pension for at least twelve months during the three years preceding the birth or adoption and that this period does not fall under one of the above periods (e.g. continuation of wages or the enjoyment of income maintenance).

Apart from compulsory pension insurance there exists the possibility of 'optional continued insurance'. The latter possibility is open to those who were insured for a pension for at least twelve months preceding the loss of status as an insured person. A request for continued insurance must be made within six months. Periods of continued insurance are counted as periods of compulsory insurance.

Not insured on grounds of the pension insurance scheme are civil servants and white collar workers of the government and of the railway; for these categories there exist private pension schemes, which we will not discuss here

People who have attained the age of sixty five are no longer admitted to the pension insurance scheme.

The members of the Injuries Insurance Scheme Association are the enterprises. Benefits from the injuries insurance scheme are payable to all employees, domestic personnel and self-employed master artisans, as well as the dependent family members of the latter. The heads of the enterprises who are subject to the injuries insurance scheme can take out voluntary insurance for themselves and for other people who are not compulsory insured. Furthermore, the injuries insurance scheme covers people working for a governmental body or the army, as well as free intellectual occupations. Also pre-schooling, schooling (including universities) and after schooling of those following education in the Grand Duchy is covered, as well as all help and rescue operations for the benefit of a third person in danger and the theoretical and practical activities of people who take part in volunteer corps involved with help and rescue.

Below, we will not discuss the particular features of the injuries insurance scheme for government personnel, members of the military service, students and rescuers-helpers Equally, we will not discuss the special injuries insurance scheme for people employed in the agricultural and forestry sector (called a*ssurance accidents agricols et forestiers*).

All pregnant women and women who have just given birth, whose legal place of residence at that time is in the Grand Duchy and has been so for one year before they became entitled, belong to the scope of people who are eli- gible for maternity allowance and prenatal birth allowance. The residence requirement is also considered to be satisfied if the spouse was legally resi- dent within the Grand Duchy for at least three years immediately preceding the birth. In order to be entitled to the actual birth allowance, one of the partners must have been resident in the Grand Duchy in the year immedi- ately preceding the birth and, in principle, the child must be born in Luxem- bourg.

All children brought up in the Grand Duchy are eligible for the post natal birth allowances.

Each child that has regularly been brought up in the Grand Duchy and who has his legal place of residence there, is entitled to the monthly family allowances from his birth until he attains eighteen years of age. The claimant is eligible until the age of twenty five if he follows higher education and for an unlimited time if he is incapable of providing for his own needs due to a chronic illness or disability.

Eligible for benefit as full time unemployed people are employees, as well as young people whose training is finished (subject to a 'waiting period'), and self-employed people who had to cease their activities due to sectorial or general economic problems.

In order to be able to claim services from the authority for the placing and professional retraining of handicapped employees, the claimant must have Luxembourg nationality (or of another EEC Member State) and be registered with an employment board.

In order to be able to enjoy the guaranteed minimum income, the claimant must be resident in the Grand Duchy; he must also have resided in the Grand Duchy for at least ten of the last twenty years. With respect to the allowances for handicapped persons, it is also required that a claimant's legal place of residence is in the Grand Duchy and he must have resided in the Grand Duchy for at least ten years. In order to be able to receive an advance on the payment of alimony from the *F.N.S.*, the claimant must have his legal place of residence in the Grand Duchy and must have resided there for at least five years.

4. Risks and benefits.

4.1. Old age

Every person insured for a pension, who can demonstrate that he has been insured for at least 120 months, is entitled to old age pension (*pension de vieillesse*) from the age of 65 on. Every insured person who can demonstrate that he has been insured for 480 months is entitled to early retirement pension from 60 years of age on (*pension de vieillesse anticipée*). In order to satisfy the latter requirement, not only the actual periods of insurance are taken into account, but also periods during which an invalidity pension was received, periods of study as well as waiting time for school leavers in the scheme for unemployment compensation and periods during which a parent has raised one or more children under the age of six in the Grand Duchy. The latter periods may not amount to less than eight years on the birth of the second child, nor to less than ten years on the birth of the third child. If the child is physically or mentally handicapped and is not brought up in a specialized institution, the above maximum age limit is eighteen.
The injured person can enjoy an early retirement pension even from 57 years of age on the condition that he has effectively been insured for 480 months (i.e. without taking into account the above mentioned assimilated periods).
A person who is enjoying an early retirement pension must forgo all significant or non-incidental occupational activities.

Old age pension consists of two elements, the proportional increases and the flat-rate increases. The amount of the proportional increases is mainly a function of income from work on which contributions are payable throughout the whole career. The proportional increase are 1.78% per annum of the total, revalued income from work, which is taken into account for the payment of contributions. The amount of the flat-rate increases is exclusively dependent upon the duration of the period of insurance. For each yaer of insurance a flat-rate amount is payable, up to a maximum of 40 years. The old age pension which is based upon at least 40 years of insurance and periods treated as such, is subject to a minimum limit; if the claimant can demonstrate at least 20 years, but not 40 years, the amount of the minimum pension is reduced by as many fortieths as there are years less than 40. Old age pension is subject to a maximum limit.

A person who is insured for a pension and who, at the end of his 65th year does not satisfy the minimum conditions with regard to the duration of insurance, is entitled to repayment of all contributions which he has paid himself and which his employer has paid on his behalf; these contributions are indexed when they are repaid. Repayment excludes any entitlement to benefit.

The above conditions with regard to old age pension also apply mutatis mutandis to the invalidity and survivor's pensions described below.

4.2. Death.

The surviving spouse of the beneficiary of an old age or invalidity pension, as well as the surviving spouse of a person insured for a pension for at least twelve months during the three years preceding his death, is eligible for a survivor's pension (*pension de survie*). If the death of the insured person was due to an injury or to a recognized occupational disease, the above minimum insurance requirements are not relevant.

The ex-spouse of the deceased insured person, who has not remarried, is also entitled to a survivor's pension. If there is no surviving spouse, subject to further conditions, parents and relatives in the ascending line and relatives twice removed in the side line, are entitled to a survivor's pension.

If several people satisfy the conditions, the survivor's pension is divided equally between them. In cases where there is also an ex-spouse who is eligible, the survivor's pension is divided pro rata temporis between the ex-spouse and the remaining eligible persons.

The widow(er)'s survivor's pension terminates upon remarriage. If the beneficiary is younger than 50 years of age at the time of his remarriage, he receives five times the amount of pension of the preceding year as a lump sum. If remarriage takes place after the age of 50, the beneficiary is only entitled to three times the above amount of pension.

Children of the insured person are entitled to a survivor's pension, subject to the same requirements regarding the employment record, as for the spouse's survivor's pension. This survivor's pension is payable until the child attains 18 years of age or 27 years of age if he is studying. The survivor's pension of an orphan is terminated upon marriage, unless he is studying.

Widow(er)'s and orphan's survivor's pensions are related to the old age or invalidity pension which the deceased insured person received or would have received. The surviving spouse receives two thirds of the proportional increases and, in specific cases, of the special proportional increases, plus all the flat-rate increases and, in specific cases, the special flat-rate increases. An orphan receives one fifth of the proportional increases and, in specific cases, of the special proportional increases, plus one third of the flat-rate increases and in specific cases, of the special flat-rate increases. When special flat-rate or proportional increases are payable, they are determined in an analogous way as for the invalidity pensions (see above).

To the extent necessary, a supplement is payable to the survivor's pension of the widow(er) and the orphan of an insured person or pensioner, provided that the latter satisfied the conditions regarding insurance and periods treated as such with respect to a minimum pension; the supplement is two thirds in respect of the widow(er) and one fifth in respect of the orphan.

The maximum survivor's pension is determined in the same way as the maximum old age pension.

A funeral grant (*indemnité funéraire*) is payable on grounds of the sickness and maternity insurance scheme, on the death of the insured person or of one of his family members. The grant is payable to the person who is responsible for the funeral. The grant is reduced respectively to half or one fifth of the standard amount, if the deceased was younger than six years old or was dead at birth. However, in the voluntary scheme there is a waiting period of three months before a person is entitled to a funeral grant.

If death was due to an injury covered by the injuries insurance scheme, a funeral grant equal to one fifteenth of the annual income from work is payable together with a pension to the relatives of the deceased person. The surviving spouse receives a pension equal to 42.8% of the annual income; if she is at least 53.5% incapable of work and has been so for more than three months, she receives 50% thereof. Upon remarriage, the survivor loses his right to pension. If, upon remarriage, he is younger than 50 years, he receives 60 times the monthly pension as a lump sum; if he is 50 years old or more, he receives 36 times this amount.

The widow of a person who was at least 50% incapable of work due to an insured professional risk, but whose death was not caused by this risk, receives a lump sum of 40% of the annual income from work as a roughly estimated compensation.

To the extent that it gives rise to entitlement to family allowance, a dependent child of the deceased person receives a pension equal to 21.4% of the annual income from work of the deceased person. The ascendants of the victim, who shared the same household as the victim, and whose maintenance was largely dependent upon the victim, receive a pension equal to 32.1% of the annual income from work of the victim (however, the amount as well as the duration of this pension may be reduced in accordance with the real damage suffered). The same pension is payable to the father or mother, father-in-law or mother-in-law, step-father or step-mother of the victim, as well as to his brother or sister or unmarried son or daughter, who at the time of death were at least 45 years of age, subject to the condition that they cared for the household of the victim for the five years preceding death. The pension is terminated upon the marriage or remarriage of these people. The total survivor's pensions may not exceed 85.6% of the annual income from work of the deceased person.

4.3. Incapacity for work.

Benefits in cash on grounds of the sickness and maternity insurance scheme in case of maternity are only payable if the claimant was affiliated with the sickness fund for at least six months immediatly preceding the birth.

The schemes for wage earners include benefits in cash in case of illness and benefits in cash in case of maternity. These compensations always amount to the equivalent of what the insured person would have earned by continuing his work, although benefits payable under the scheme for white collar workers in the private sector may not exceed the maximum limit. Benefits in cash in case of illness are payable from the first day of incapacity for work for a maximum duration of 52 weeks. Benefits in cash in case of maternity are payable during at least eight weeks before and eight weeks after the birth. However, cash benefits are not payable if the claimant's wages continue to be paid on grounds of legislation or agreement (e.g. this is determined in the act for white collar workers in the private sector: they are entitled to a continuation of their wage during the course of the month and the following three months).

People insured under the scheme for self-employed occupations receive cash benefits only from the fourth month of incapacity for work due to illness; this cash benefit equals the income the self-employed declared and on which contributions were leved.

On grounds of the pension insurance scheme, each insured person younger than sixty five years old, who can demonstrate that he has been insured for a pension for twelve months during the three years preceding the determination of invalidity by the controlling physician or after the expiry of sickness compensation in cash, is entitled to an invalidity pension (*pension d'invalidité*). The required minimum period of insurance is not applied if the invalidity was due to an occupational disease or injury, which arose during a period of insurance.
Treated as invalid is the insured person whose capacity for work has, as a result of a long duration of illness, a defect or old age, reduced to such a degree that he can no longer carry out his former occupational activity nor any other profession which reflects his strength and ability. The recipient of an invalidity pension may not carry out any paid work; the pension is suspended if the occupational activity of the claimant is carried out by another person on his account. Until the age of fifty, the insured person must attend all rehabilitation and retraining projects which are offered to him.

Invalidity pension consists of proportional increases and flat-rate increases (as in the old age pension), increased by special proportional increases or special flat-rate increases. The special proportional increases supplement the proportional increases until 55 years of age; they equal a yearly amount of the total income from work for which contributions were paid between the age of 25 and the time when invalidity occured, divided by the number of civilian years in this period. The special flat-rate increases supplement the flat-rate increases by an identical amount until 65 years of age. If the insurance record of the claimant between the age of 25 and the time when invalidity occured is interrupted, the increase is only payable in relation to the number of effectively covered years as a proportion of the total number of civilian years that this period includes.

There is a minimum invalidity pension which is calculated in the same way as the minimum old age pension, albeit that the years between the moment of entitlement to pension and the 65th year are treated as insurance years. However, if invalidity occurs after the age of 25, the above years are only counted as a proportion of the claimant's length of insurance to the number of years between his 25th birthday and the occurance of the risk.

The maximum invalidity pension is determined in the same way as the maximum old age pension.

A person insured on grounds of the injuries insurance scheme is entitled to a pension from the thirteenth week of incapacity for work and for as long as the complete or partial incapacity for work lasts. The pension in respect of complete incapacity for work amounts to 85.6% of the average income from work over the previous year, or a part thereof in respect of partial incapacity for work. The basis of calculation is subject to a maximum limit in the same way as the basis of calculation for the payment of contributions.

If the person who is partially incapable for work due to an injury is involuntarily without employment, pension is increased up to the amount of the pension in respect of full incapacity for work, but for no longer than three months while possible unemployment benefits are deducted.

If the victim of an insured injury is not only completely incapable of work, but his capacity is reduced to such an extent that he needs the continuous help of another person, pension is increased in proportion to the degree of incapacity with a maximum limit equal to the annual income from work.

For as long as the insured person receives a pension for incapacity for work of at least 50%, he is granted an allowance of 10% for each dependent child for whom he receives child allowance. The pension and pension allowance may not exceed the annual income from work.

The degree of incapacity for work can only be reviewed within three years after the determination of the pension, except in respect of a worsening of the incapacity for work by at least 10%.

On grounds of the injuries insurance scheme, pension payable in respect of incapacity for work of less than 10% is, after a period of at least three years, payable as a lump sum; the pensions can be paid off on the request of the claimant, if his incapacity for work due to an injury is higher than 10% but not higher than 40%.

4.4. Unemployment.

People belonging to the scope of application of the unemployment scheme are entitled to unemployment benefit (*indemnité de chômage*) subject to the condition:
- that they are between sixteen and sixty four years of age;
- that the waiting period is completed (if they are school leavers);
- that they are capable of work and living in the Grand Duchy;
- that they are registered as seeking employment and submit a claim for unemployment benefit;
- that they are involuntarily unemployed, i.e. the employee has not become unemployed as a result of unjustifiably leaving work or as a result of a dismissal for urgent cause which follows from an act or error of the employee;
- that all suitable work is accepted.

The beneficiary must sign on at the registration office or during a control on the appointed days and hours. He must participate in the occupational training or general training programmes to which he is invited by the competent administrative authority. The granting of benefit can be made dependent upon carrying out work which is declared by the government to serve the public interest. Unemployment benefit is payable for a maximum duration of 365 days within a two year period; however, the director of the employment authority can, on request, decide to include a further period of 182 days. For this it is required that the unemployed person appears to have little chance on the labour market due to his age, physical or mental afflictions, or any other serious circumstances. The benefit will also be payable for a longer period if the unemployed is at least 50 years old and satisfies a certain number of insurance years. The right to benefit is terminated at an earlier stage if the entitlement conditions are no longer satisfied, e.g. by unjustifiably refusing an offer of employment.

Unemployment benefit amounts to 80% of the average gross wage of the three months preceding the occurance of unemployment, without the amount thus calculated exceeding two and a half times the social minimum wage or exceeding two times the social minimum wage if the unemployment has already lasted for longer than 182 days during a period of twelve consecutive months. In case the unemployment benefit is paid for more than 365 days, the amount of the benefit should not exceed one and a half time the social minimum wage.

The percentage of the gross wage is raised to 85% when the unemployed has children at charge; it is reduced when he is living together with a partner earning more than two and a half times the social minimum wage.

Unemployment benefit for younger school leavers amounts to 70% of the social minimum wage in respect of an uneducated blue collar worker of the same age. However, young people of 16 or 17 years of age who cannot produce a certificate of completion of school age or of termination of technical training, only receive 40% of the social minimum wage. Elderly self-employed people receive 80% of the social minimum wage that would be payable to them as skilled workers.

4.5. Medical care.

The sickness and maternity insurance scheme covers the costs of medical care due to illness or maternity. These benefits in kind are payable from the time of affiliation with a sickness fund (exception: the voluntary insurance scheme includes a waiting period of three months). They are payable as from the time of occurance of the illness and for the entire duration of the illness, provided that the claimant remains affiliated with his sickness fund. In case of termination of affiliation, the benefits are continued for a further 26 weeks in respect of ill persons who are undergoing treatment. Benefits in kind notably cover medical and dental care, travel and ambulance costs of the ill person, pharmaceutical costs, costs of curative aids and aids (artificial aids etc.), radiological examinations, hospital costs and birth costs.

Medical care may be provided by any of the physicians who are recognized by the State. The physician's fees are determined by collective agreement or, failing this, by arbitration via the *Commission de conciliation et d'arbitrage*. In the latter case, the solution agreed upon requires ministerial approval. Tariffs are annually adjusted. Hospital tariffs are determined on grounds of an agreement with the *Entente des hôpitaux*.
The insured person has freedom of choice in respect of his doctor and hospital and, with the approval of his sickness fund, may be treated abroad. The fees are reimbursed by the sickness fund. The insured person pays a personal contribution towards the costs of 20% for the first normal visit to a doctor in a period of 28 days; for the next or other than normal visits he pays 5% of the costs. In case of hospitalization no personal contribution is required; a contribution is merely payable towards the 'hotel costs' of stay in a hospital. Refunds of the costs of dental care are made in accordance with collective agreements. A personal contribution of 5% is charged for dental consultations; for artificial dental prothesis, the personal contribution may not exceed 20%. Other artificial aids are, after the approval of the sickness fund, compensated according to the tariffs determined by an agreement. Medicine is divided into three categories: non-refundable medicine; priority medicine, the costs of which are fully refunded; and normal medicine, the costs of which are refunded for 80% (except in cases of hospitalization when a refund of 100% is payable).

The costs of hospitalization are payable directly by the sickness fund; the patient only pays the part of the cost for which he is liable. This also applies for medicine in respect of persons affiliated with the sickness fund for blue collar workers. Medical care costs ensued by the victim of an injury within the meaning of the injuries insurance scheme are borne directly by the association of the injuries insurance scheme. Victims of an insured injury pay no personal charges; personal contributions which would have been payable irregardless of the occurance of such injuries are borne by the association of the injuries insurance scheme.

4.6. Family

Entitlement to maternity allowance arises from the eighth week before the estimated date of delivery with a maximum duration of 16 weeks. Similar provision applies in respect of an adoption. Maternity allowance is reduced by the amount of maternity or sickness benefit in cash payable under the social insurance schemes, by the wage that the claimant continues to enjoy, and by the amount of unemployment benefit of the claimant.

In order to be entitled to birth allowance in the period preceding the birth, the mother must undergo five medical examinations and a dental examination. In order to be entitled to the actual birth allowance, the mother must undergo a post-natal examination within ten weeks of the birth. For post natal-birth allowances, the child must be subject to two pre-natal examinations and it must have at least four medical examinations before the age of two years.

The amount of the monthly family allowance (*allocation familiale*) varies according to whether it concerns the first, the second or the third child; for each subsequent child the same amount is payable. The allowances are increased when the child has attained the age of respectively 6 and 12 years. Handicapped children under the age of 18 are entitled to an additional, special allowance. This allowance is continued, without an age limit, for people who are not capable of providing for their needs due to a defect or chronic illness, at least to the extent that the claimants receive no benefit from the *F.N.S.* or any other social security organisation.

The education allowance (*allocation d 'éducation*) is paid to the parent residing in the Grand Duchy who cares at home for one or more of his children younger than two years of age. The beneficiary does not exercise a professional activity or, if he does, his income and that of his spouse do not exceed a certain maximum.

4.7. Need.

The guaranteed minimum income is due to:
- people of at least 30 years of age and ready to accept all suitable work;
- adults incapable of work due to illness or handicap;
- persons raising a child younger than 15 years old for which they are entit-

led'to family allowance;
- adults taking care of an old or very ill person, needing constant help;
- people over 60 years of age.

The personal income and capital of the beneficiary and of the members of his household are deducted from the guaranteed minimum income. If these exceed the latter, no guaranteed minimum income is due.

Once a year the *F.N.S.* also pays out a heating allowance. The amoun of this allowance is determined each year with reference to the number of people concerned. In order to be eligible, the claimant may have no income in excess of a certain limit (the relation of the annual heating allowance to the income limit equals two to five).

Furthermore, the *F.N.S.* affiliates beneficiaries of a solidarity pension who are not already affiliated with a sickness fund, with the *Caisse nationale d'assurance maladie des ouvriers.*
For the sake of completeness we mention that the *F.N.S.* is also empowered to grant advances on alimony payments.

The municipal welfare offices are responsible for the municipal duty of providing social assistance. This duty consists of providing the necessary means for assistance to the needy. Assistance may be paid in cash, but can also involve measures in order to allow poor people to carry out useful work or to help them find paid work.

5. Financing.

The sickness and maternity insurance scheme is mainly financed from contributions and direct and indirect subsidies from the government. The system of financing is based upon the pay as you go principle.

In the schemes for employees, insured people who are gainfully employed pay half of the contributions, their employers the other half. In the schemes for self-employed occupations, agriculturists and intellectual free professions, as well as in the voluntary insurance scheme, the contributions are entirely borne by the insured people themselves. Half the contributions of beneficiaries of pensions are payable by the beneficiaries and the other half by the body responsible for paying the pension. If the wage or pension falls below the lower contribution limit, the insured person is merely liable to pay contributions over the actual amount of his wage or pension; the remainder is the responsibility of the employer or pension institution.

There is a uniform contribution rate in respect of the sickness and maternity insurance scheme, other than benefits in cash for sickness and maternity, except for the agricultural sickness fund. The contribution rate is increased to cover the above cash benefits for those funds which include such benefits. Contributions are expressed as a percentage of the income from work or of the pension, subject to a lower earnings limit equal to the social minimum wage and a maximum limit equal to five times the social minimum wage. The minimum earnings limit is increased by 30% for pensioners.

The contribution rate is determined annually by decree. The State bears the contributions of certain categories of people, e.g. trainees and students. The State also finances benefits in respect of maternity and benefits due to traffic injuries, if such benefits are not the responsibility of a third party. Furthermore, through the intermediation of the Serious risk fund, the State bears the costs of inter alia, hospitalization and medical care in a hospital for the treatment of mental illnesses, tuberculosis, cancer and polio, as long as the benefits last longer than six months. The State compensates the sickness funds for the benefits to retired people and pensioners, as long as the benefits are not covered by the receipt of contributions from this category of insured people. The State intervenes in the agricultural scheme through the Agricultural Orientation Fund, which bears half the costs of benefits to active people.

The Sickness funds (except for the agricultural fund) collectively constitute a 'risk community', in which the excesses or shortages are annualy compensated.

The pension insurance scheme is financed by contributions amounting to 24% of the gross income from work; one third of these is borne by the insured person himself, one third by his employer or the institution which pays his income maintenance, and one third by the State. Here, the State does not act as subsidiser, but as contributor. Insured people who are active on their own account pay a personal contribution of 16% and the State pays 8% this is also the case in the voluntary insurance scheme.

Income from work which is used as a basis for calculation of contribution liability is determined at minimally the social minimum wage for an unskilled employee of at least eighteen years of age and maximally four times this amount. In the continued insurance scheme, contributions are flat-rate (determined by decree) and not calculated as a percentage of the income from work of the insured person. Some periods of insurance, for example the so called baby year (see above), are financed fully by the government.

The income giving rise to contribution liability for the schemes in respect of old age, invalidity and survivor's pensions is indexed; it is also annually adjusted to increases in the standard of living. Pensions are not only regularly price indexed, but also adjusted to increases in wages. The latter takes place by a special act; at least every five years there is a government enquiry into whether or not it should take the initiative for such an adjustment.

The costs of the injuries insurance scheme are entirely borne by the heads of enterprises. Their contributions are determined in relation to the degree of risk of the particular type of enterprise and the total sum of wages which are payable. The administration costs of the association of the injuries insurance scheme are paid half by the association itself, and half by the State.

Benefits which are payable on grounds of the injuries insurance scheme are not only price indexed, but also adjusted to the level of wages (at least every five years; standard of living increases). The State assumes the responsibility for one third of the costs of adjustment to the standard of living of pensions, as well as the indexing of pensions.

The monthly family allowance is half financed by contributions, and half by the State. Contributions are payable by the employees (as a rule, at a rate of 1.7% of the wages, subject to an upper limit) and by all tax paying residents who are not employees, not older than sixty five years of age and who do not enjoy retirement, invalidity or orphan's pension. The latter category is again divided into various professional categories, for which there are different contribution rates.

Maternity allowance and birth allowance, as well as the costs of administration of the family benefits, are borne entirely by the State.

Unemployment benefits are payable by the Employment Fund.
Deposited in this fund are:
- solidarity taxes, levied in the form of increases in the income tax of natural people and from the taxation of the income of collectivities; and
- a contribution borne by the municipalities (divided among the municipalities in according to the gains from taxation of trade).

Furthermore, a special contribution can be charged from employees in the private sector over the sum of the wages which give rise to contribution liability for the pension insurance scheme.

If the unemployment fund remains without sufficient means, the money is advanced by the State; however, the fund must pay this money back.

The *F.N.S.* derives it's means from an annual government subsidy, a contribution from the municipality equal to 10% of benefits payable by the *F.N.S.*, part of the lottery and lotto proceeds and from gifts and personal income.

The means of the municipal welfare offices are derived from the income from property belonging to these offices, gifts, fund raising, lotteries, taxation on theatre performances,... and, to the extent necessary, from State subsidies.

6. Judicial review.

In first instance, disputes between insured people and the administrative bodies of the social insurance schemes are dealt with by the *Conseil arbitral* and in case of a higher appeal by the *Conseil supérieur des assurances sociales*. In cases of violation of the law or of violation of substantial procedural requirements, judgements in last instance of the *Conseil arbitral*, as well as judgements of the *Conseil supérieur des assurances sociales* are open to cassation to the *Cour supérieur de justice*, operating as a *Cour de cassation*.

The *Conseil arbitral* sits with a chairman and two delegated assessors (*délégués assesseurs*); the *conseil* can be assisted by one or more doctors who appear as experts during the oral proceedings of the case. The chairman and deputy chairman of the *Conseil arbitral* are lawyers and are appointed by the Grand Duke; they have the status of civil servants. The delegated assessors and their substitutes are referred to respectively as delegated employer and delegated insured person.

The *Conseil supérieur des assurances sociales* consists of a chairman and two assessors, to be chosen from among the magistrates, one delegated employer and one delegated employee. The chairmen, the assessors and their substitutes are appointed by the Grand Duke for ,a period of three months. The appointment of the delegated person and his substitute takes place in the same way as is the case for the delegated assessors in the *Conseil arbitral*.

Appeal is possible within forty days of the publication of the contested decision; this period is considered to be respected when the appeal or higher appeal was instituted by another (not competent) Luxembourg state authority or social security institution.

Appeal is not open to decisions concerning disputes between an insured person and a sickness fund in respect of the sickness and maternity insurance scheme, if such appeal is not accompanied by a formal statement of the *Inspection générale de la sécurité sociale*, in which it is established that the Inspectorate was previously consulted in order to avoid an administrative dispute (this does not apply for the agricultural sickness fund).

Disputes concerning the sickness and maternity insurance scheme are dealt with in a written procedure by the chairman of the *Conseil arbitral*; the parties involved can appeal against the decision within fifteen days. The appeal is dealt with by the *Conseil arbitral*; the decision of the *Conseil arbitral* is final. The *Conseil arbitral* also takes decisions in last instance in cases which involve only a minor sum of money (below a certain limit).

Disputes with regard to family benefits and the guaranteed minimum income are dealt with in first instance by the chairman of the *conseil arbitral*, in higher appeal by the *Conseil supérieur des assurances sociales*, consisting of a chairman and two magistrates.

Decisions of the board of employment concerning unemployment benefit are subject to appeal with the *Commission nationale de l'emploi*, a body established on a tripartide basis; the *Conseil arbitral* decides in last instance.

All costs concerning social security disputes are borne by the State, but the administrative bodies which instigate and subsequently lose a case must pay a certain amount. The procedure is free for insured people.

Chapter 6: Great Britain

1. Introduction: concept and sources of social security law.

The institutional concept of social security law covers benefit schemes which provide cash benefits under the competence of the Department of Social Security.
The social security benefits may be divided into three categories:
1) *contributory benefits*. These are insurance benefits which exist for the risks of unemployment, sickness, pregnancy, invalidity, industrial injuries, old age and death.
2) *non-contributory benefits*. These are benefits financed out of general taxation for the risks of invalidity, old age and death, intended for specific categories of people who are not covered by the insurance system. This category also includes child benefits.
3) *means tested benefits*. These benefits too are financed out of general taxation, albeit that they are subject to a means test. In addition to *income support* we distinguish *family credit*.

Within this concept, medical care as provided by the *National Health Service* is excluded from the ambit of social security. However, in line with the starting point chosen for this work, we will nevertheless pay some attention to this service. The same applies for *statutory benefits*, which are payable by the employers.

The most important source of social security law is the statute. Nonetheless, the statutes merely offer a general framework of legislation. The main body of material law is contained in a range of *statutory instruments* (commonly referred to as 'regulations'). The regulations are enacted by the Secretary of State in pursuance of specific delegation powers laid down in the statutes.
A third source of social security law is case law. Among others this plays a role in clarifying vague legal concepts and in assessing the validity of 'delegated' legislation.

In social security legislation provisions mostly refer to "Great Britain" as a geographical unit. Thus, the general legislation applies to England, Wales and Scotland. Other parts of the British Isles, such as the Channel Islands, the Isle of Man and Northern Ireland fall outside the territorial scope of British social security law. However, legislation applicable to Northern Ireland is often similar to legislation in Great Britain.

2. Administrative organisation

The administration of social security in Great Britain lies almost exclusively in the hands of the *Department of Social Security (D.S.S.)* under the authority of a *Secretary of State*. The *D.S.S.* is the competent department concerning the administration of all social security schemes which provide cash benefits. The scheme for unemployment benefit (the unemployment insurance scheme) is in fact administered by the *Department of Employment* but subject to *D.S.S.* policy directions. Similarly, housing benefit is paid through local government housing departments.

Since April 1991 most operational tasks within the Department have been undertaken by separate executive bodies, known as '*Next Steps Agencies*', in which the great majority of the Department's staff work. By far the largest is the *Benefits Agency* which is responsible for the delivery of benifits through some 500 local offices in some 160 districts in 3 territories. They usually deal with routine administration of the social security schemes. The Benefit Directorate in Newcastle deals among others with the administration of contribution records, while another in North Fylde concerns itself with claims for war pensions, *constant attendance allowance*, (section 4.3) and *income support* (section 4.7). The departmental headquarters remain responsible for policy development and central research allocation Decisions concerning individual cases are taken by *adjudication officers.* These are active in the local offices of the Benefit Agency and in the *unemployment benefit offices*. The *adjudication officers* act independently of the department, but are subject to the directives and guidance of the *chief adjudication officer*. The latter is required to report annually to the Secretary of State on the standards of adjudication.

The *Department of Health* is responsible for the administration of the *National Health Service (N.H.S.).*
At the operational level three divisions are distinguished: the personal practitioner services (doctors, dentists, etc.), which conclude agreements with the competent authorities, hospitals, managed by the *N.H.S.* (each district has a general district hospital and one or more specialised hospitals) and the *community health services,* e.g. home help and family planning.

The *District Health Authorities* are responsible for the hospitals and the *community health services.* These bodies consist of up to eleven members, the chairman of which is appointed by the Secretary of State. Most of the other members are representatives of the medical profession or officers of the District Health Authorities. The *District Health Authorities* are advised by *District Management Teams*, most of its members are medical specialists.
On a higher organisational level there exist *Regional Health Authorities* appointed by the minister to carry out supervisory and administrative tasks. The rninister himself, as head of the Department of Health, is responsible for the overall strategic control of the *N.H.S.*

It appears from the administrative structure of the British social security system that the authority of the State in the running of the social security schemes is virtually omnipotent. The recent trend towards privatisation, which puts greater emphasis on the role of new 'statutory' benefits administered by the employers, does little to change this. In fact only the routine application and administration of these benefits is dealt with by the employers; the detailed provisions of the statutes leave the employers little room for discretion.

The administrative structure does not make provision for the insured population to be directly involved in the administration. They can only voice their opinions via advisory bodies such as the *Social Security Advisory Committee*. Within the sphere of the *N.H.S.*, the *Community Health Councils* watch over the interests of the patients.

3. Personal scope of application.

Both employees and self-employed people belong to the group of compulsorily insured people for *contributory benefits*, although the insurance scheme for the latter does not extend to unemployment benefits. Thus it is important to distinguish between these two categories.

An employee is a person who is gainfully employed on the basis of an apprenticeship or a contract of employment.
This rule is futher elaborated in case law, which recognizes a number of relevant factors, the relative importance of which vary from case to case. Important factors to be considered are, among others, the question of who bears the financial risk of the professional activity, whether there is supervision of work, whether there exists a possibility of substituting an employee or whether there is discretion on hours of work, etc. In regulations issued by the Secretary of State certain activities are specifically classified as employed activities, e.g. cleaning and agency work. Special rules to this effect apply to the insurance scheme for industrial injuries and occupational diseases; here for example probationers and firemen are considered as employees. Self-employed people are not covered by this insurance scheme.

Apart from compulsorily insured people there are also voluntarily insured people. Voluntary insurance is available to all employees and self-employed people who satisfy the relevant contribution conditions, to self- employed people who are not covered by the compulsory insurance scheme, for example because of low income and to certain categories of non-active people.

The types of contributions payable are divided into five classes (see section 5). Employees pay class 1 contributions, the self-employed class 2 and 4 contributions and the voluntarily insured class 3 contributions. Employers only pay class 1A contributions in respect of their employe's private use of company cars. The scope of coverage and the contribution rates are different for each class. Employees paying class 1 contributions are insured against all risks. The self-employed paying class 2 contributions are excluded from entitlement to unemployment benefit. Class 3 contributions are only made for the purpose of insurance against death and old age. Class

1 A and 4 contributions are pure taxes, giving rise to no benefit entitlement. Both compulsory and voluntary insurance are subject to age limits, i.e. from 16 years up to pensionable age.

The personal scope of application of the *non-contributory benefits, means tested benefits*. and *child benefit* is delimited on the basis of territorial criteria. In respect of some benefits the 'residence test' is fairly simple and straightforward. Thus, for example, in respect of *income support* it is merely required that a person is present in Great Britain on the day of the claim. Other benefits, however, impose much more stringent residence conditions. Thus, with regard to *severe disablement allowance*, the basic conditions are that the claimant must have been:

1) present in Great Britain on the day that the allowance is claimed;
2) ordinarily resident in Great Britain at the time of the claim;
3) present in Great Britain at the time preceding the date of the claim.

Applicants to *constant attendance allowance* or *invalid care allowance* must have resided in Great Britain for at least 26 weeks in the year preceding the claim. For certain categories of people there are less stringent conditions.

Apart from residence conditions, each sceme imposes certain other qualifying conditions which result in a further delimitation of the personal scope of application. For example, war pensions are only payable to former members of the armed forces.

The essential feature of the *National Health Service* is that it covers all people who are in need of medical care in Great Britain. Nonetheless, the applicable legislation allows the Secretary of State to enact regulations providing for the recovery of charges from people who are not ordinarily resident in Great Britain.

4. Risks and benefits.

Before embarking upon a discussion of the various risks and benefits, attention must be paid to two general points which are relevant for all the insurance schemes, i.e. the contribution conditions and the benefit structure.

Except for benefits in respect of industrial injuries and occupational diseases, entitlement to all contributory benefits depends upon the fulfilment of contribution conditions. These conditions are not the same for all benefits.

For the right to *unemployment benefit* and *sickness benefit* the insured person must:
- have paid contributions in one of the last two years preceding the year in which the benefit is claimed (*unemployment benefit*) or in any year before the benefit is claimed (*sickness benefit*), on an income corresponding to at least 25 times the lower contributions limit in that year;
- have paid or been credited contributions in each of the last two years pre-

ceding the claim, over an income corresponding to at least 50 times the lower contributions limit in that year.

In order to be entitled to *maternity allowance* only one contribution condition is imposed: within the 52 weeks preceding the 14th week of the expected date of birth, the insured person must have paid at least 26 weekly contributions.

Also for the *widow's payment* there is only one condition: that the late husband of the widow has paid contributions during any one year on an income corresponding to at least 25 times the lower contributions limit.

The right to *widowed mother's allowance, widow's pension* and *retirement pension* is again dependent upon the fulfilment of a double contribution condition. The insured person must:
- have paid contributions during any one year on an income that corresponds to least 52 times the lower contributions limit in that year;
- have paid or been credited contributions for not less than 90% of his working life on an income again corresponding to 52 times the lower contributions limit.

If a person only satisfies part of the latter condition, benefit is paid at a reduced rate (subject to a minimum contribution condition).

Certain categories of people who are clearly established within the contributory scheme (this must be apparent through the people having paid a certain number of contributions), but who have failed to make the requisite number of contributions for making up entitlement to benefit, are credited with contributions. Credit facilities are open to, among others, unemployed people and people incapable of work, those caring full time for invalids and new entrants to the contributory scheme.

If the entitlement conditions of the contributory benefits are satisfied, the claimant has the right to a basic benefit. Furthermore, subject to the satisfaction of further conditions, there may be a right to additions for an adult dependant, usually the spouse of the claimant, and/or for any children.

In principle, the right to additions for children exists only in respect of long-term benefits; in respect of short term benefits only those above pensionable age are entitled to such additions. Entitlement to an addition exists when the following conditions are satisfied:
- the claimant concerned must be entitled to *child benefit* in respect of the child;
- the child must live with the claimant or be maintained by him/her;
- when a person is married or cohabitating, the partner's income may not exceed a certain level.

The right to an adult dependant addition exists first of all for the spouse of the person entitled to the basic benefit. The latter must live together with his/her spouse or maintain him/her. Furthermore, the income of the spouse may not exceed a certain level.

The right to an adult dependant addition also exists for an adult who is caring for the children of the entitled person (a child carer). Here, too, the right to the addition is subject to the conditions that the entitled person lives with the dependant or maintains him and that the income of the dependant does not exceed a certain level.

Basic contributory benefit, as well as the dependency additions, are flat-rate. Furthermore, in the area of invalidity, widow's and retirement pensions, there may be a right to certain earnings related supplements under the *State Earnings-Related Pension Scheme (S.E.R.P.S.)*. These supplements are calculated on the basis of payment of contributions on the income that is 52 times the lower earnings limit. Over a maximum period of 20 years a person will build up pension rights up to a maximum of 25% of the upper minimum income level.
The contribution liability constitutes a certain percentage of the weekly earnings above the lower earnings limit. In the period of 20 years a person will build up pension rights up to a maximum of 25% of his extra-minimal earnings. For each year that a person contributes less than 20 years, the pension rate will be reduced by 1%. As the system was first introduced in 1978, no full supplements will be payable until the end of this century. However changes in the Social Security Law mean that, for people retiring after 1998, the maximum amount of *S.E.R.P.S.* payable will be only 20% of a person's extra earnings over the whole working career. However, this change will not become fully effective until the year 2010.

The Secretary of State is legally bound to review annually most of the social security benefits. The increase in benefits has usually been based on the impact of inflation in a twelve month period before the uprating.

4.1. Old age.

The right to *contributory retirement pension* exists for all people who have attained pensionable age (60 for women, 65 for men) and who satisfy the contribution conditions.
Claimant's earnings do not affect pension, although addition may not be payable for adult dependant if latter earns.
A person may defer drawing his pension and carry on working for a maximum period of five years, i.e. up to the age of 65 (women) or 70 (men). The deferred pension is increased by 7.5% for every year (up to five years) that the retirement is postponed.

People who were entitled to *invalidity allowance* (see section 4.3) before they attained pensionable age, receive an *invalidity addition* on top of their pension, the level of which is the same as the allowance. The possible income from *S.E.R.P.S* is deducted from this amount.

Approximately half the working population enjoys some additional protection of occupational pension schemes, established on a collective or individual basis. If their occupational pensions are considered to offer sufficient protection, these people are offered the opportunity to opt out of *S.E.R.P.S.*

For two special categories of people there exist *non-contributory retirement pensions*. Here contribution conditions are replaced by residence conditions. The level of these benefits is markedly lower than that of the contributory retirement pensions.

All pensioners over 80 years receive on top of their pension a very small weekly *age-addition*.

4.2. Death.

Subject to the fulfilment of contribution conditions, a widow is entitled to a number of benefits. When the death of the spouse is due to an industrial injury or an occupational disease, no contribution conditions are applicable. On the death of her spouse a widow is in the first place entitled to a *widow's payment*, a flat rate benefit payable in a lump sum.
Furthermore, there are two periodic benefits, i.e. the *widowed mother's allowance* and the *widow's pension*. The former benefit is intended for the widow who is expecting a child of her deceased spouse or who already has a child in respect of whom she receives child benefit.

A widow, who at the time of death of her spouse or at the time of the termination of the *widowed mother's allowance* has attained the age of 45, has the right to a *widow's pension*. If the widow has attained the age of 55 or older at these times, she receives the maximum pension. For every year that she is younger than 55 there is a reduction of 7% in the pension. For the further duration of the benefit this reduction is not reversed.
The right to benefits terminates if the widow remarries. If the widow cohabits with a man, the right to benefit is suspended for the duration of the cohabitation.

Those who have an orphan living with them or who maintain an orphan who gives rise to entitlement to *child benefit*, are entitled to a *guardian 's allowance*. Entitlement to this allowance depends upon the fulfilment of residence conditions.

4.3. Incapacity for work.

A person who is physically or mentally incapable for work, and who satisfies the relevant contribution conditions, is entitled to contributory sickness benefit. The first three days of incapacity count as waiting days; the maximum duration of benefit is 28 weeks.

In practice for most employees the importance of *sickness benefit* is very minor. For the first 28 weeks of their incapacity they are entitled to *statutory sick pay*, payable by the employer. The entitlement conditions for this benefit are very similar to those for *sickness benefit*, albeit that in calculating the level of the benefit, less account is taken of the composition of the household. There are two flat rate amounts; the higher amount is intended for employees whose weekly income exceeds a certain level. Trough individual or collective labour agreements many employees are guaranteed extra protection.

A person may be disqualified from receiving sickness benefit or statutory sick pay during a period of up to six weeks, if he became incapable of work through his own misconduct or if he fails without good cause to attend for or submit himself to medical or other treatment.

A woman who satisfies the relevant contribution conditions is entitled to *contributory maternity allowance*, starting from between 11 to 6 weeks preceding the expected date of birth; the maximum duration of entitlement is 18 weeks. A woman may be disqualified from receiving benefit if she fails to attend a medical examination or if she is engaged in any employment. In view of the existence of a *statutory maternity pay* scheme (payable by the employers), the *contributory maternity allowance* has little practical importance; the statutory scheme is available to all female employees who have worked for the same employer for at least 26 weeks and in addition have average earnings in excess of the lower earnings limit. Benefit covers the same period as the *contributory maternity allowance*. During the first 6 weeks the benefit amounts to 90% of the normal weekly income, providing that the claimant has worked for the same employer for 16 hours per week for two consecutive years (or 8 hours per week for five consecutive years). If the claimant does not satisfy all the necessary conditions, as for the period after the expiry of the first 6 weeks, she is only entitled to a flat rate benefit.

Various benefits exist for long term incapacity. Below we will distinguish between *contributory invalidity benefits*, benefits for industrial injuries and occupational diseases, benefits for invalidity as a result of military service and *non-contributory benefits* in respect of special groups of handicapped people.

If incapacity for work continues at the end of the maximum period of duration of the sickness benefit or statutory sick pay, there is a right to *invalidity pension*. This incapacity must not only exclude the person from his own work but also from other suitable employment. Besides the pension, there is a right to a small increase in the form of an *invalidity allowance*. The rate of the allowance varies according to the age of the beneficiaries; younger people receive a higher allowance than older claimants. The allowance serves as compensation for the fact that the invalid can only make unsatisfactory or no provision with a view to retirement. Possible pension rights under *S.E.R.P.S.* are deducted from the allowance. In principle *invalidity pension* and *invalidity allowance* are received up to the point that a retirement pension is drawn.

When, as a result of an industrial injury or an occupational disease, there is a loss of physical or mental capacity, there exists a right to *disablement benefit*. There does not have to be a loss of earning capacity. No contribution conditions are applied. *Disablement benefit* is payable from the fifteenth week after the accident, and may continue until the death of the beneficiary. The amount of the benefit depends upon the extent of the disability. This is judged by comparing the disabled claimant with a person of the same age and the same sex whose physical and mental state is normal. There are a number of special supplements which may be payable on top of disablement benefit. These allowances are designed to defray some of the expenses which result from the physical or mental state of the severely disabled. In this respect mention may be made of the *constant attendance allowance* and the *exceptionally severe disablement allowance*.

The scheme for *war disablement pensions* largely resembles that for industrial accidents and occupational diseases. The pension is payable in respect of disablement which is attributable to service in the British forces. Here too the amount of the pensions depends upon the extent of the disablement, and extra supplements and allowances are payable on top of the basic pension.

The following *non-contributory* benefits are payable in respet of invalidity:
1. *disability living allowance*, payable to severely disabled people under the age of 66 who need help with personal care and/or getting about;
2. *attendance allowance*, payable to severely disabled people over the age of 65 who require attention or continuous supervision by another person;
3. *disability workingallowance*, payable after a means test to people whose earning capacity is affected by illness or disability;
4. *severe disablenent allowance*, payable to long term severely handicapped people who normally do not qualify for benefits under the war pensions or contributory benefit schemes;
5. *invalid care allowance*, payable to a person who is providing regular and sunstantial care for someone in receipt of specific disability benefits, and who, as a result, is not available for employment, or for full-time education.

4.4. Unemployment.

Contributory unemployment benefit is payable to an insured person who satisfies the contribution conditions and who is unemployed. A person is not eligible for benefit during the first three days of unemployment. Benefit is payable for a maximum period of one year in respect of one and the same period of unemployment. Periods of unemployment are added together if they are interrupted by periods of employment shorter than eight weeks. If the maximum period of unemployment benefit has expired, new entitlement to benefit may arise if a person has been employed for at least 13 weeks in the last 26 weeks for at least 16 hours per week.

The unemployed person must be available for work, i.e. able and willing to accept suitable employment. The unemployment must be involuntary. This requirement is not fulfilled if the person has lost his employment through his own misconduct, or has voluntarily left his employment without just cause. In such cases the claimant is disqualified from receiving benefit for a maximum period of 26 weeks. The same is possible if the unemployed person refuses to accept or fails to apply for employment without good cause. Also disqualified from benefit are people who are unemployed by reason of a stoppage of work, due to a trade dispute at his place of work. However, this disqualification rule does not apply for those who are not directly interested in the trade dispute, or who otherwise do not withdraw their labour in pursuance of it.

The unemployed person is obliged to sign on at the unemployment benefit office usually every two weeks, and to be actively seeking employment.

There are special rules with regard to the position of certain groups of unemployed people such as fishermen and seasonal workers. The same applies for part-time workers and those whose contract of employment is suspended until more work is available.

4.5. Medical care.

The *National Health Service (N.H.S.)* is open to all British residents. Among other things, it provides care from general practitioners; the general practitioners have a contract with the local *N.H.S.* branch. Equally covered is the entry into and care by an N.H.S. hospital. The beneficiary is not required to pay any personal contributions for either of these two services. This is not the case for dental care; the beneficiary is liable for 75% of the costs, albeit up to a certain maximum level. Certain people are excluded from the payment of personal charges such as, for example, pregnant women and women who have recently given birth, juveniles up to depending upon the circumstances, 16, 18 or 19 years of age and people on low income. There is also a flat-rate, personal contribution for all prescribed medicine, but here too different categories of people are excluded from payment such as, for example, children younger than 16 years of age, people who have attained pensionable age and persons on low income.

4.6. Family.

Above we have seen that there are dependency additions payable on top of social security benefits in respect of the children of the beneficiary. Besides this, the *child benefit* scheme aims at helping to meet the costs of bringing up children. Entitlement to *child benefit* exists for every child up to the age of 16 or up to the age of 19 if the child is still in full-time non-advanced education. It may also be paid for a short 'extension' period if seeking employment and receiving no other income immediately after leaving school. The child must live with the beneficiary or be maintained by him. Residence conditions apply in respect of both the child and the beneficiary. If a person lives alone with one or more children, he is entitled to an *in-*

creased child benefit. This *one parent benefit* is only payable in respect of one child. People who already receive an increase due to e.g. the right to *widow's benefit* or *retirement pension* are not entitled to one parent benefit.

The *family credit* scheme is intended for low paid workers with children. Those who claim benefit (or whose partner claims benefit) must be carrying out paid work for a minimum time of 16 hours per week, be it as an employee or as a self-employed person. Besides this, there must be at least one child of 16 years of age or younger, or between the ages of 16 and 19 years of age, who follows full-time education. Again residence conditions apply.
The right to maximum *family credit* exists when the income of the family lies below a legally fixed threshold. If the family income lies above this threshold, the maximum credit is reduced by a percentage of the amount by which the income exceeds the threshold.
The maximum *credit* consists of an adult credit and child credits for each child. The former is the same for a beneficiary with a partner and for one without a partner. There are four different *credits* for children depending upon their age.
A characteristic feature of this benefit is that it is payable for a period of 26 weeks, during which no account is taken of a change in circumstances.

From April 1993 the *Child Support Agency* will take the responsibility for the means-tested support of people for whom child maintenance is an issue and may assist in the collection of any maintenance due from absent parents.

4.7. Need.

The *income support* scheme acts as a safety net under the social security system. In order to be entitled to benefit, the means of the claimant must lie below a legally applicable level. Besides this, there are a number of supplementary conditions. Thus, in principle, one must be 18 years of age or older (or between 16 and 18 and belonging to a specific category of persons), be present in Britain, not in full-time employment (normally, 16 or more hours per week) and available for work. This last condition does not apply for everbody; excluded are those above a certain age, those caring for children or ill family members and those incapable for work.

The so called *'applicable amount'* constitutes the starting point for the calculation of *income support*. This amount is made-up of three separate parts, i.e. the *personal allowance*, any *premiums* and the *housing costs*. The personal *allowance* constitutes the basis of *income support*. Standard amounts exist for married couples, single parents, single persons and children. Within these categories various amounts apply which are dependent upon the age of the claimant.
Fixed *premiums* are paid on top of the basic amounts in respect of family responsibility, age and state of health. Also the increases are standardized. There is no possibility of obtaining income support payments for exceptional costs.

Housing costs constitute the final part of *income support*. These consist of payments covering the expenses mainly of the owner occupiers. People in rented accommodation are covered by the *housing benefit* scheme.

Special rules apply for different categories of people, such as, for example, those who have been admitted into residential accommodation or a hospital.

After the applicable amount for the claimant has been determined, the next step is to determine his means which include those of any partner and a contribution from adult non-dependents. A limited amount of income and capital may be disregarded. The difference between these two amounts constitute the amount of *income support* payable.

Income support for families is not granted individually but on a household basis, i.e. in respect of the claimant, the claimant's partner an any children. Married people and cohabitants are treated the same.

Apart from the *income support* scheme some attention should be given to the *social fund*. This fund provides benefits for special needs. Some benefits are granted on a discretionary basis, others not.

The latter applies especially for the *maternity expenses payment* and the *funeral expenses payment*. The *maternity expenses payment* is a flat-rate benefit which is intended to defray some of the costs of giving birth. The *funeral expenses payment* compensates for certain costs arising from a funeral. Both benefits are means tested. A small fixed amount known as a 'cold weather payment' is automatically allocated to many categories of *income support* recipient for each period of seven days of exceptionally cold weather.

Besides the above benefits, three more benefits are payable out of the *social fund* on a discretionary basis, i.e, *budgeting loans, crisis loans* and *community care grants*. Each of these benefits is means tested. The first two benefits are payable in a loan, subject to a maximum limit. The *budgeting loans* are meant to cover sudden expenses for which a person has no reserves. Certain costs are excluded from indemnification, others are given priority. *Crisis loans* are intended for emergencies, in which there are not enough personal means to meet certain unavoidable costs. Some people are excluded from receiving *crisis loans*; furthermore, certain expenses are excluded from *crisis loan* coverage. Guidelines determine in which situation *crisis loans* should be granted.

Among other things, the *community care grants* help people in their return to, or maintenance in the community. Here too certain expenses are not covered by the grant. Guidelines determine in which situations a grant should be awarded.

In the awarding of discretionary payments account should be taken of the fact that there is only a limited budget available which is set annually for each local office. There is no right of appeal against decisions concerning the granting of benefits, but merely an internal review procedure.

5. Financing.

The costs of the *contributory benefits* are covered by the contributions paid by the insured people and the employers. The contributions are deposited in the *National Insurance Fund*.

Five contribution classes are distinguished. Employees and employers pay class 1 contributions. Contributions from employees are paid on all earnings up to an upper earnings limit being over seven times the amount of the lower earnings limit. For employers earnings are divided into four bands; for each band there is a specific contribution rate which increases when one reaches a higher band. The upper earnings limit does not apply for the employer; four further income bands and corresponding contribution rates are distinguished in respect of the employer.

Class 1 A for private use of company cars, paid only by employers.

Class 2 contributions payable by self-employed people are flat-rate and are to be paid when earnings exceed a certain level. Self-employed people are simultaneously liable to pay class 4 contributions. These are income-related and consist of a percentage of the income of a person between certain lower and upper limits.
Finally, voluntary class 3 contributions are flat-rate.

Statutory sick pay and *statutory maternity pay* are largely financed from contributions. The employers are able to reclaim most of the payments by deducting 80% of the cost from their contribution liability, with limited extra relief for small employers.

Expenses within the framework of the *non-contributory benefits, means tested benefits* and the *child benefit* scheme are fully financed from general taxation.

The *National Health Service* is also almost entirely financed by the government. Furthermore, a small amount is born by the *National Insurance Fund*.

6. Judicial review.

There exists a more or less uniform machinary for the adjudication of benefits, which operates independently of the ordinary British courts and the D.S.S.
As we have seen above, the *adjudication officers* decide in the first instance upon almost all questions concerning social security.

Appeal against the decision of the *adjudication officer* may be made within three months to the *Social Security Appeal Tribunal*. Each *Tribunal* consists of three members: a legally-qualified chairman and two lay members. The *Tribunals* can, if they do not confirm the decision in issue, substitute the decision of the *adjudication officer* with a fresh one. The decision may be taken with a majority vote.

The claimant as well as the *adjudication officer* can appeal against the decisions of the *Tribunal* to a *Social Security Commissioner*. Appeals must be made with the leave of either the chairman of a *Tribunal* or a *Commissioner*. Appeal may only be made on points of law and not on points of fact. The *Commissioner* usually decides a case himself, although he can refer it back to a *Tribunal*. Apart from the *Chief Social Security Commissioner*, there are thirteen *Commissioners*.

In principle the decision of the *Commissioner* is final, albeit that further appeals on points of law may be made to the *Court of Appeal* and even to the *House of Lords*. For this, leave is required from either the *Commissioner* or the *Court of Appeal*.

The procedure applied in *Social Security Appeal Tribunals* and before *Social Security Commissioners* is partly determined by legislative rules. These relate to matters such as the right to representation, the right to call and to cross-examine witnesses and the presence of medical assessors. The fairness of the procedure is guaranteed through the application of *rules of natural justice*.

In addition to the usual machinary for adjudication, there are a number of special provisions.

Thus only the Secretary of State is competent to take decisions in questions concerning insurance obligations or contribution conditions. He also takes decisions relating to the granting of a number of special benefits, such as, for example, *constant attendance allowance*. Only some decisions of the Secretary of State are subject to appeal to the *High Court*.

Certain medical questions, which are relevant for entitlement to *disablement benefit*, are determined by special medical adjudicating authorities: the *Adjudication Medical Practitioners* and the *Medical Appeal Tribunals*. The latter is composed of three members, one of whom is a legally qualified chairman, two of whom are medical practitioners. On points of law decisions of the *Tribunals* are open to appeal to the *Social Security Commissioners*.

There is also a special adjudication procedure with regard to the entitlement to *attendance allowance* (the *Attendance Allowance Board*) and for the entitlement to war pension (*Pension Appeal Tribunals*). The *Dis- ability Appeal Tribunals* hears appeals on *disability living allowances* and on *disability working allowances*.

Individuals who feel unjustly treated by an administrative body can complain to the *Parliamentary Commissioner for Administration*. Although the ombudsman is in fact not a part of the system for the settlement of disputes, due to his practical importance, he must still be mentioned. The ombudsman cannot alter or rescind decisions, but he can make a report on his investigations which may have some influence.

Chapter 7: Greece

1. Introduction: concept and sources of social security law.

The Greek social security system can be divided into social insurance social assistance and a national health scheme. The term social security is not commonly used in Greece. Instead one speaks of social insurance systems (*systima koinonikis asphalisseos*). Indeed a characteristic aspect of Greek social security is the relatively minor importance of social assistance, together with the existence of five major and a total number of over 300 social insurance schemes, the scope of protection of which may vary considerably.

The pluriformity of the social insurance schemes makes it impossible to link the concept of social insurance systematically to clearly defined social risks. This applies even more, since the schemes also cover atypical risks, for example the loss of income as a result of a call-up for military training (below referred to as reservists benefit) within the scheme of most employees and benefit in respect of the destruction of agricultural production within the scheme for farmers.

Social assistance is not very developed. Until recently most forms of assistance were aimed at the coverage of emergency situations, for example care for hundreds of thousands of refugees, for victims of the civil war or for victims of earthquakes. There is no general social assistance scheme. Instead there are a number of schemes for specific categories of people, for example the elderly and the handicapped with insufficient means. Presently a total revision of the assistance system is being prepared; the introduction of a general assistance scheme is under consideration.

The rather minor importance of the existing assistance schemes is also related to the existence of "mixed social security benefits". The term "mixed benefits" refers to certain social insurance schemes which do not grant a subjective right for benefit (for example the housing benefit scheme as discussed below), as well as to benefits with an assistance character which are granted by the administrative bodies of social insurance schemes (for example a pension for each Greek citizen who is older than 68 years of age, living in Greece, not entitled to any social insurance benefit and whose income is below a certain income level).

The large number of social insurance schemes and the absence of a guaranteed minimum income are responsible for the fact that social security law has been laid down in hundreds of legislative texts. A degree of harmonisation is urgently required and indeed efforts to this effect are currently being undertaken. Already at this stage the legislative framework of the social insurance schemes of the *I.KA.* (to be discussed below) serves as a model for the other social insurance schemes. All employees who are not affiliated to another social insurance scheme are affiliated to *I.KA.*, and the minimum benefit level under the *I.KA.* scheme is also applicable for other social security schemes. Hence it is obvious that we will pay attention mainly to the employee insurance schemes as administered by the *I.KA*.

An important step towards harmonisation was made with the introduction of the national health system (*ethniko systima ygeias*) in 1983. This system is designed to offer all medical benefits in kind and is currently being gradually phased in. As yet, medical benefits in kind are still provided by the various social insurance bodies which are also encharged with the payment of cash benefits in respect of sickness and invalidity. So the Greek health care system finds itself in a transitionary stage, which makes a description of it even more difficult. In view of the fact that the transition will still take quite a number of years, we have opted to discuss both the system of medical care for employees, as governed by the *I.KA* scheme, and the main features of the national health system.

The common basis of all social security schemes is embodied in the constitution, although the constitution itself does not mention the concept "social security". Two provisions of the constitution are particularly relevant in the area of social security, i.e.
- Section 21 (1) constitution: "The family, as the basis for the preservation and progress of the nation, as well as marriage, mother and childhood are under the protection of the State.
(2) Large families, war invalids and invalids of peace time, victims of war, war widows and orphans, as well as the incurable physically and mentally sick, are entitled to special State care.
(3) The State will care for the health of citizens and will adopt special measures for the protection of young people, the elderly, invalids, as well as for assistance to the needy.
(4) For those without any or with insufficient accommodation, housing is subject to special State care".
- Section 22(1) Constitution: "Employment is a right and is placed under the protection of the State which watches over the creation of conditions for full-time employment for all citizens, as well as over the moral and material progress of the active, agricultural and urban population.
All people in employment are entitled to equal remuneration for equivalent work, without distinction on grounds of sex or any other grounds."
(5) "The State will care for the social insurance of the working people, as specified by law".

Social assistance and the national health system find their legal basis in Section 21(3) Constitution; the social insurance schemes, in Section 22(4). It is not possible to determine the legal effect of these social fundamental rights in a general manner. Both in legal doctrine and in case law the legislator is given a wide discretion with regard to the concrete implementation of social rights. It should also be pointed out that in Greek law no legal remedy by which the legislator can be forced to act exists.

There can be no doubt that the statute constitutes the main source of social security law. Special statutes regulate the social insurance and social assistance schemes, sometimes in their entirety, sometimes in respect of certain parts thereof. Also the setting up of social security institutions, as well as their main principles and procedures, are regulated in the statute.

In the Greek context, the term statute must be understood as referring to acts which stem from the plenum of the Parliament or departments thereof, as well as the legislative texts issued by the government or, under certain conditions, by the President of the Republic.

The legislator has delegated certain legislative powers to the executive, which may be encharged to give further rules concerning specific parts of social security law. Such delegated legislation may take the shape of a decision of the President, a ministerial decision or a decision of the social insurance administration. In the case of delegation to an administrative body, the previous approval of the competent Minister or of a supervisor body is often required. Delegation is often used as a technique. The pluriformity of the social security schemes obliges the legislator to delegate extended powers to administrative bodies for the direct regulation of detailed subjects.

The Greek legal system recognises general principles of law, considered as unwritten fundamental rules, justified by rational thinking and deduced from the meaning or the scope of the existing written law. In the field of social security law, principles such as the principle of social solidarity and the principle of the favour to the insured, are regarded as autonomous sources. As such principles we can also regard the general principles of, among others, proper administration, of equal treatment, of legal security and of trust.

Jurisprudence does not constitute a source of social security law. Nevertheless case law may play an important role in practice. For instance, if the highest judiciary overrules a precedent in a concrete case, the relevant social insurance institution will have to reexamen every case that has a strong connection with the change of the jurisprudence.

A statutory provision explicitly prohibits the inclusion of social insurance provisions concerning pension schemes in collective labour agreements. Through this prohibition the legislator aims to realise a uniform social policy in this important sector. However, some collective labour agreements still contain rules concerning occupational social insurance schemes.

2. Administrative organisation.

Social insurance benefits are provided for by several independent institutions of public and private law, aiming to protect the individuals of a certain categorie against certain risks. These institutions, according to the structure of the insurance branches, are divided into institutions of main insurance, auxiliary insurance and sickness insurance. There are also institutions which provide lump sum benefits and institutions which provide complementary protection.

In 1988 there were as many as 325 social insurance institutions, each of them being more or less different from the others. More specifically there were 28 institutions of main insurance which have their own legal personality as legal bodies of public law. They fall under the competence of the ministry of Health, Welfare and Social Insurance. There were 54 institutions of auxiliary insurance, 18 of sickness insurance, 60 institutions which form Assistance Funds and 59 mutual aid societies which provide complementary benefits to their members. There are also institutions that belong to the competence of other ministries (Agriculture, Labour, Justice and Marine). The State itself provides main insurance and sickness insurance for the civil servants and the military forces. The majority of the insurance institutions, however, belong to the competence of the ministry of Health, Welfare and Social Insurance.

According to the professional status of the insured, these institutions can be divided into the following categories:
a) institutions of employees and workers under private law,
b) of employees in the banking sector,
c) of public servants
d) of self-employed people,
e) of people employed in the press,
f) of farmers,
g) of clergy,
h) and institutions for auxiliary insurance of public servants.
Almost the totality of the Greek population is covered by one of these insurance organisations.

As a rule, the social insurance institutions have their own legal personality and exercise public authority in the form of legal bodies under public law. In principle, each institution has its own administrative structure with its own administrative bodies. However, there are certain institutions which have been created by private initiative or have been qualified by the legislator as belonging to the private sphere of law. The common legislator has, however, tried to limit the operation of private social insurance. Since 1970 it seems to be impossible to establish new private mutual aid societies. Now, employers have only the possibility to open special accounts or to provide bonus payments to employees. The private group insurance slowly starts to play a significant role.

Where the social insurance schemes are administered by many different legal persons it could be expected that these institutions enjoy a certain degree of self government. Yet autonomy is very restricted.
The powers of the administrative bodies concern, in principle:
- the determination of the budget of the social insurance institution;
- the proposal of internal administrative rules;
- the decision with regard to affiliation, contribution liability and benefit entitlement;
- taking all sorts of other decisions.
However, autonomy is in reality very limited, as a result of a number of

powers which have been attributed to the State. Thus the State (the competent minister) has substantive supervisory powers which, for example, result in the power to withhold approval of the budgets of the social insurance institutions and to check their accounts and book-keeping. Furthermore, for each important administrative decision the social security institutions require the approval of the competent minister. Thus the administrative bodies must first receive ministerial approval before they can introduce qualitative or quantitative improvements of social insurance benefits. Moreover, the administrative bodies are not free in the way they spend their reserve assests; these are blocked by the Greek National Bank at a relatively low interest rate.

As early as 1946 it was determined that the boards of management of the administrative institutions must be comprised of representatives of the State, of the insured population, of pensioners, and of employers. The members of the boards of managers, as nominated by the representative organisations, are appointed by the competent minister. In the past the Council of State has provided that the nominations by representative organisations are not binding to the competent minister but merely have an advisory character. However, since 1985 this situation seems to have been changed; an act of that year provides that the majority of members of the board of managers must consist of representatives of the insured population and of pensioners. As a result of the application of this new act, the competent minister is obliged to appoint the representatives, who have been chosen by the trade unions which represent both the insured population and pensioners.

By far the most important social insurance scheme is that of the majority of the employees. For the purposes of sickness and maternity benefits (benefits and medical care) and pensions, the management and administration of this scheme is encharged to the Institute for Social Insurance (*I.KA.*). Family allowances, unemployment benefits and reservists benefit are administered for the *I.K.A.* insured persons by the *O.A.E.D.*, the Organisation for the Employment of Workers. The *I.KA.* is encharged with the levying of contributions in respect of all benefits mentioned above.
It has been mentioned that there is a certain tendency of the *I.KA.* to incorporate smaller social insurance schemes, resulting in a gradual extension of the scope of the scheme, as administered by the *I.KA.*; hence the *I.KA.* may develop as the single social insurance institution for all employees and possibly in future even for the self-employed.
On a local level there are a number of *I.KA.* offices. In largertowns there are *O.A.E.D* offices as well, but in other places this institution makes use of the offices of the *I.KA.*.
The competent minister for the scheme administered by the *I.KA.* is the Minister of Health, Welfare and Social Security; for the *O.A.E.D* this is the Minister of Labour.

For the sake of completeness some attention must be paid to other important administrative bodies of the larger insurance schemes. The *T.A.E.*, the fund for trade insurance, is encharged with insuring the risks of sickness and maternity, invalidity, old age and death in respect of the self-employed. The same risks in respect of farmers are insured by the *O.G.A.*, the Organisation for Agricultural Insurance. The *O.G.A.* is also encharged with the administration of the assistance scheme for people older that 68 years of age. Mostly, the state itself administers the schemes for civil servants. Here the Minister of Finance acts as the competent minister. The *E.E.*, the fund for worker's homes, is there to support the social and cultural activities of the workers and their families (for example, free leisure activities, special care for children, marital benefits for female employees, education and library facilities, etc.). Also the activities of the trade unions are financed by the *E.E.*

The social assistance schemes are administered on a local level under the supervision of the Minister of Welfare, Health and Social Security. In each prefecture there is a social welfare department which bears responsibility for the assistance schemes in the region; furthermore, some powers in the area of social assistance have been delegated to local communities. In some cases the administration of social assistance schemes is encharged to separate legal people under public law, which are specifically set up for this purpose.

3. Personal scope of application.

Of the large number of social insurance schemes each has its own affiliation conditions. A common general characteristic is that, in order to be affiliated to a scheme, a person must be engaged in employment. It depends upon the character of the specific employment (sometimes also upon the region) to which social insurance institution a person belongs. Not only people who are actually in employment are insured, but sometimes also the spouse, the children, the brothers or sisters, or even the grandchildren. The actual scope of the group of insured people varies from scheme to scheme.

With regard to the main categorial schemes, the personal scope of application of the various social insurance schemes may roughly be desribed as follows:

Most employees are affiliated to the *I.KA.* The affilation conditions for the *I.KA.* apply for the whole nation; if a person satisfies the affiliation conditions, he is insured with the *I.KA.* wherever he works in Greece (or sometimes even outside the country). A worker is affiliated to the *I.KA.* scheme unless he is covered by another insurance scheme for employees. Such special social insurance schemes exist, for example, for employees in the banking sector and for employees of state companies. The main condition for affiliation to the *I.KA.* is that one carries out professional employment in a subordinate relationship. Thus it is essential that employment is carried out professionally, that it constitutes the main profession of the person concerned and that wages are being paid. Apart from employees stricto sensu, there are also a number of categories of people who are treated as such, i.e.:

- people who do not carry out employment as reognized under labour law, for example state accountants;

- people whose employment is not really subordinate, such as those without a regular employer or persons without a fixed place of employment; such as newspaper sellers and writers.
- unpaid workers, for example apprentices.
- people whose employment is not a main profession (e.g. members of administrative boards).
- people encharged with management duties.

Not covered under *I.K.A.* while fulfilling the conditions are some limited categories, such as extraordinary civil servants, prefects, and persons with a foreign nationality who carry out only temporary employment. Hence, *I.KA.* covers all workers and employees not covered by another specific social insurance institution.

With regard to the medical care branch of the *I.KA.* health insurance covers not only the active insured population but also retired pensioners, insured unemployed, and their dependants. Benefits in kind in respect of maternity are also payable to the non-dependent spouse.

The most important of the specific institutions for employed people are the following: The *O.A.E.D.* (manpower employment organisation) provides family allowances, unemployment benefits and reservists benefits. It also provides vocational training to the unemployed. The *E.E.* (labour home) supports social and cultural activities of the workers and their families (e.g. special care for children). The *O.E.K* (Workers Housing Organisation) provides appartments and housing loan benefits.

Farmers are affiliated to the *O.G.A.* (Organisation of Farmers Social Insurance) which now insures more or less two million active and retired people and thus constitutes a major social insurance institution. It is considered to be one of the main institutions in Greece.

The term farmer is understood to refer to each person who personally carries out an agricultural activity as his main profession. Agricultural activity means an activity in ploughland farming, cattle raising or forestry. Also here the scheme is extended to some additional groups of persons, i.e.:
- self-employed people and craftsmen working in villages of less than 2.000 inhabitants;
- employees of all categories living in areas or communities with a population of up to 5,000 persons on the condition that these are not affiliated to any other social insurance institution;
- fishermen;
- Greek priests and nuns working in the agricultural sector.
- persons over 68 years of age who have not been affiliated to any other social insurance institution.

In respect of the free professions, there is a large number of social insurance schemes. Here the term free profession refers to intellectual professions, traders and craftsmen.

For each intellectual profession there is a separate administrative body and social insurance scheme. Thus, there are separate insurance schemes for practising lawyers, doctors and engineers. The effective legal exercise of the profession constitutes the main affiliation condition.

Also traders and craftsmen have their own insurance scheme. The statute determines which trade activities must be carried out in order to qualify as a trader. Engaging trade is not sufficient for affiliation to the categorial social insurance scheme; it is also required that a person is more than 18 years of age and is registered with the Chamber of Commerce, the Chamber of Industry or the Chamber of Crafts. Finally we mention that the absence of a statutory definition of "craftsman" causes many difficulties with regard to the delimitation of the scope of application of the social insurance scheme concerned.

The national health system (*E.S.Y.*), covers the entire Greek population, without any special entitlement condition, regardless of professional category or region.

There is no universal social assistance scheme in Greece, but there are several social assistance organisations. In order to become entitled to social assistance benefits it is normally required that a person has Greek nationality or Greek citizenship. However, there is a special assistance scheme for refuges.

Finally, we must mention the different types of social insurance periods as they are distinguished in Greece. The most usual form of a permanent legal relation, referring to social insurance, is the compulsory social insurance period. Only the state or legal persons under public law can be institutions of compulsory insurance. Other forms of social insurance are the formal insurance and the voluntary insurance. The former refers to the period in which a person contributes to a social insurance scheme, for a reasonable time and in good faith, without actually fulfilling all the legal conditions to affiliate to the concerned institution. Although the legal conditions were not met, the social insurance institution which accepted the contributions under those circumstances must accept the contributor as a member. Within the voluntary insurance three forms must be distinguished. In the strict sense of the word, voluntary insurance is mainly created for Greek nationals living abroad. A second form is the voluntary continuation of an interrupted compulsory insurance, the third form is the additional voluntary insurance for which a special branch has been established within the *I.KA*.

4. Risks and benefits.

Social insurance benefits are linked to wages of civil servants; thus social insurance benefits follow increases in these wages. The basis for calculation of pensions is also periodically adjusted, they are automatically adjusted: each year the estimated daily incomes associated with the earning classes are adjusted to the consumer price index.

4.1. Old age.

In a recent judgement of the Greek Constitutional Court the existing difference in pensionable age for men and women was declared as being incompatible with the Constitution. However, regulations of the various social insurance schemes which discriminate on grounds of sex are currently being modified; as yet, social insurance institutions normally still apply the previous distinction in pensionable ages (mostly 65 years for men and 60 years for women).

The pensionable age for those who are affiliated to the *O.G.A.* is, in principle, 65 years for both men and women. In principle, the pensionable age for the compulsory retirement of civil servants is 56 years, if they have worked for 35 years. Civil servants, especially women, are furthermore offered a lot of possibilities concerning early retirement. Further our discussion will be restricted to the *I.KA.* old age pension scheme.

There is a right to an *I.KA.* pension for insured people who have established a contribution record of at least 4,050 working days (approximately 13 1/2 years). Per year after 1991 the required record of working days is increased with 150 days per year (so e.g. 4,200 in 1992). Termination of employment is not required but if the monthly income exceeds 35 times the statutory minimum daily wage for unskilled workers, payment of pension is suspended.

Subject to various conditions, there are several opportunities for early retirement:

a) People who have carried out heavy and unhealthy work can retire at the age of 60 (men) or 55 (women) if they have established a contribution record that corresponds with four fifths of at least 4.050 working days (plus 150 each next year after 1991). From these working days at least 1.000 must be included within the 10 former years before the claim for pension.

b) People who have a contribution record of 10.500 working days (approximately 35 years) can retire at the age of 58 (both for men and women). For those who are insured after 1.1.1983: at the age of 60.

c) People who have a contribution record of at least 10.000 working days can retire at the age of 62 (men) and 57 (women). We must notice that there is no reduction in the amount of pension as far as the three afore mentioned possibilities for early retirement are concerned.

d) There is also the opportunity to retire at the age of 60 (men) or 55 (women) when a person has a contribution record of 4.050 working days (plus 150 x n) of which at least 100 days must have been worked in each of the five calendar years preceding early retirement. However, the amount of benefit is reduced by 1/200 of the basic amount for each month till 65 or 60 year of age.

e) The person who has established a contribution record of 10.000 working days, of which at least 100 days must have been worked in each of the five calendar years preceding early retirement, can retire at the age of 60 (men) or 55 (women).

f) Finally, if a person has established a contribution record of 10.500 working days, it is possible to retire at the age of 56. The reduction is then also 1/200 for each month till 65 or 60 year of age.

Married women and widows with unmarried children under 18, are entitled to a complete old age pension from the age of 55 on, on condition they have contributed during at least 5.500 days and have no entitlement to another pension. They can enjoy early retirement at the age of 50; in that case the pension benefit will be reduced with 1/200 for each month of early retirement, however, the level of benefit may not fall below the minimum amount of pension. For the blind, the above mentioned contribution conditions are halved.

The pension amount consists of a basic amount (the so called "basic pension") plus different supplements. The calculation of the basic amount depends on the insurance record of the pensioner and his estimated daily income which is linked to real previous earnings of the employee. There are now 28 classes of real earnings, each of which corresponds to a set amount of estimated daily income. The basic amount of old age pension is calculated as a percentage (usually 70% till 30%) of the estimated daily income within the particular earnings class. The pension rates decrease as the pensioners move from a low earnings class to a higher: thus, the rate is 70% for the 1st class and 30% for 26th, 27th and 28th classes.
The basic amount of old age pension may be augmented by a supplement. The amount of the supplement is connected with the specific number of working days. For each 300 working days on top of 2.999, the basic amount of old age pension is augmented by 1% up to 2,5% of the estimated daily income within the earnings class. If a person has established a contribution record between 2.999 and 7.799 working days, the increase of the basic amount is 1% for each of the earnings classes. On a contribution record of 7.800 working days and more, the increase is 2,1% for the 5th class, 2,2% for the 6th class, 2,3% for the 7th till 11th classes and finally 2,5% for the 12th till 28th classes.
It is important also to notice that the basic amount of the pension is augmented by a flat-rate supplement (its percentage corresponds with one and a half times the minimum daily wage of an unskilled worker) if the spouse of the pensioner does not work and she does not receive a pension from any Greek social insurance organisation. In practice it is also accepted that this supplement can be provided in case of a needy and handicapped wife or husband.
Another supplement (20% of the basic pension) is payable in respect of the first unmarried dependent child younger than 18 years of age or 24 years of age if the child is still in full-time education and does not work. If the child is not able to work due to an important disease or sickness, the supplement is payable without age limit. This supplement is 15% in respect of the second child and 10% for the third, but is not provided if any of the children receives a lump-sum benefit due to incapacity for work. The supplements are calculated on the basic of the basic pension corresponding to the estimated daily income of the 10th class.

142

Since 1991 the total amount of the pensions may not exceed fifty times the specific estimated income of the 20th earnings class. The minimum pension level is not associated with the daily wage of an unskilled worker but is statutory defined. It is also important to notice that from 1991 the indexation of the basic minimum pensions is linked with the increase of the civil servants wage and not with the consumer price index.

A special fund has been established for the protection of people without a suffisiant social insurance record. This special fund is administered by OGA and provides certain benefits a minimum pension to every Greek citizen living permanently in Greece, who is older than 68 years of age, does not receive social benefits from other sources and whose income falls below the OGA pension.

4.2. Death.

Normally, the death of an insured person gives rise to benefit for the survivors. As a to illustrate this we will discuss the *I.KA.* pension scheme for survivors.

In order to be entitled to widows pension the deceased must either
- have a contribution record of 1,500 working days, 300 of which, during the last five years preceding death;
- have a contribution record corresponding to the number of days required for entitlement to an invalidity pension; or
- have been entitled to old age pension.
The former two conditions do not apply if death resulted from industrial injury or an occupational disease. In case of death as a result of a normal injury the conditions are halved.
An additional entitlement condition is that the marriage must have lasted at least six months, unless the death resulted from an injury, there is a dependent child, or the child has been conceived before the moment of death.
Widows pension is not payable if on the day of marriage the employee enjoyed an invalidity pension or old age pension and the marriage had yet lasted two full years, again unless the death resulted from an injury, there is a dependent child, or the child has been conceived before the moment of death.
The widower is entitled to the same survivor pension as the widow, however only on the condition that he is incapable of work and formerly dependent upon the deceased wife or insured person.
The pension constitutes 70% of the old age pension to which the deceased would have been entitled. There is a minimum monthly level of 18 times the statutory minimum daily wage for the unskilled worker. Entitlement to widows pension comes to an end in case of remarriage.
Mutatis mutandis, the entitlement conditions and modalities in respect of orphans pension are the same as those for widows pension. Orphans pension is payable to each unmarried child older than 18 years of age (or 24 if the child is in full-time education; there is no age limit in respect of inca-

pacitated children). The pension amount is 20% of the old age pension which the deceased enjoyed or would have enjoyed. If both parents have died the child receives 60%.

Widows pension and orphans pension together may not exceed the amount of old age pension to which the deceased has been (or would have been) entitled. If a widows pension is not payable, the total amount of orphans pension may not exceed the amount of old age pension which the deceased enjoyed (or would have enjoyed). The minimum amount of orphans pension is equal to the minimum widows pension.

The health care insurance scheme of the *I.KA*. also provides a death allowance of at least eight times the estimated income of the lowest earnings class.

4.3. Incapacity for work.

In respect of social insurance schemes we normally make a distinction between sickness insurance and invalidity insurance. The sickness insurance schemes cover medical care and the loss of income as a result of sickness and maternity. Invalidity insurance schemes cover permanent incapacity for work; the benefits which are payable under these schemes often bear strong similarities to old age pensions. Again we will discuss the *I.KA*. scheme to illustrate this.

The insured person who is not able to exercise his "job" due to illness, is entitled to sickness benefit.

In order to be intitled to a sickness allowance a person must satisfy the following conditions: he must be incapable for work; he must abstain from work; he must have established a contribution record of at least 100 working days in the year before the sickness or in the previous 15 months; he must wait for 3 days after the announcement of the sickness and he must not be a pensioner. In respect of incapacity for work due to industrial accident or occupational disease there are no-contribution conditions.

In principle, sickness benefit provides 70% of the estimated income of the insurance class to which the claimant belonged the last 30 days of the previous year. A sickness benefit is payable from the fourth day of incapacity (3 waiting days) over a period of maximally 6 months. However, if the claimant has established a contribution record of 300 working days in the two last years preceeding the sickness, the maximum duration is 1 year. It must also be noted that during the first month of sickness the employer is obliged to additional payments, as a supplement on top of sickness benefit; so the last wage level remains intact.

Sickness benefit is also payable in respect of maternity; in order to qualify for such cash benefit, a woman must have worked 200 days in the two years preceeding the excepted day of birth. The period of entitlement is 105 days; 52 days before the expected day of birth and 53 days after this event. The woman must also not work during this period.

There are also additional benefits payable by the OAED. The main supplement is calculated over the same period (105 days) and covers the difference between the IKA maternity allowance and the previous monthly earnings of the beneficiary.

The IKA provides lump-sum benefits in case of maternity, in order to replace hospital and medical care. Those payments consist of 30 times the minimum wage for an unskilled worker.

All the women who are not entitled to any of these allowances and are not affiliated to another social insurance institution, can claim for a social assistance benefit. This benefit is a lump-sum payment and is granted by the Minister of Health, Welfare and Social Insurance for a period of 84 days.

Invalidity benefit is payable after the right to sickness benefit has expired. The degree of incapacity for work which gives rise to benefit varies from scheme to scheme. Most social insurance schemes provide full invalidity pensions if the degree of incapacity for work is more than 67%.

Under the *I.KA.* scheme there is a right to invalidity pension for those who have established a contribution record:
- of 1.500 working days, 600 of which were in the last five years preceeding incapacity for work; or
- of 300 working days during the last five years, if he is under 21 years of age, or
- of 4.050 working days (4.200 after 1992), 300 of which were in the last five years preceding incapacity for work.

In respect of incapacity for work as a result of an industrial injury or an occupational disease there are no contribution conditions; in respect of a normal injury the requirements are halved.

In order to become entitled to invalidity benefit, a person's earning capacity must have been reduced by at least one third. For those under 55 years of age and at least 33% incapable of work, the sickness insurance scheme covers the first two years; after this period has expired a right to invalidity pension may arise if people are at least two thirds incapable for work. An entitlement on a partial invalidity pension arises for those more than 50% incapable for work.

For those who are at least two thirds incapable for work, the amount of invalidity pension equals the amount of old age pension to which the person concerned would have been entitled. If a person is between 50% and 66,66% incapable for work, he receives 75% of this amount. If constant care is required, the level of invalidity pension is increased by 50%. Those who are 55 years or older and at least 33% incapable for work but not more than 50% receive 50% of the afore mentioned amount.

The minimum levels of invalidity pension are the same as those for old age pension; also the method of calculation is the same as for old age pension (mutatis mutandis).

As has been mentioned, there are no contribution requirements with regard to industrial injuries and occupational diseases. The normal invalidity pension is payable, albeit that the minimum benefit level is 60% of the esti-

mated income in the relevant earnings class. In cases of temporary incapacity for work due to an industrial injury or an occupational disease, sickness benefit is payable during a period of six months.

4.4. Unemployment.

In order to become entitled to unemployment benefit a person must be
capable for work, involuntarily unemployed and registered with the labour
exchange. Furthermore it is required that a person has established a contribution record of 125 working days during a period of 14 months preceding
the two months prior to the commencement of unemployment. In cases of
first claims, proof must be given of at least 80 working days in each of the
three years prior to the commencement of unemployment. Those who are
older than 65 years of age are not entitled to unemployment benefit.
Benefit is paid after a waiting period of six days. The duration of the benefit
is two months. This period may be extended by one month, if the person
concerned has worked during at least 150 days within the previously mentioned period of 14 months, or by three months if 180 working days within
this period can be established. Employees of 49 years of age and older may
be entitled to eight months of unemployment benefit; the condition here is
that the person concerned must have established at least 210 working days
within the period of reference.

After the expiration of various periods of unemployment benefit, a person
may receive benefit at a reduced rate for a period of another three months on
grounds of the *O.A.E.D.* scheme.
Young people between the ages of 20 and 29 years, who have recently entered the labour market and have been unemployed for more than one year,
are entitled to unemployment benefit during a period of maximally five
months.
For manual workers the rate of unemployment benefit is 40% of the estimated income within the relevant earnings classes; for other employees this
percentage is 50%. Furthermore, there are dependency additions of 10% in
respect of each dependant (subject to a maximum of 70% of the basis of calculation). The minimum level of unemployment benefit is equal to two
thirds of the statutory minimum daily wage for unskilled workers. The level
of reduced benefit payable after expiration of the initial benefit period is
50% of the benefit previously enjoyed.

Those who are not eligible for unemployment may in certain extraordinary
circumstances, nevertheless, receive benefit for a period of maximally 45
days. Examples of such circumstances are catastrophes, violent stoppages of
work and long-term unemployment within certain professions. The decision to award benefit is taken by the Minister of Labour. Equally, during
Christmas or Easter special forms of assistance may be granted to the unemployed who are not entitled to unemployment benefit.

Two typical Greek schemes which are related to the coverage of the unemployment risk (yet to be discussed separately) are the reservists benefit scheme for employees and the insurance scheme for the loss of agricultural produce for farmers.

Reservists benefit is payable by the *O.A.E.D.* to employees who remain in military service for a longer period than their regular service term, or to employees who are called up for military training for the second or subsequent time. On a loss of income as a result of military service a person may receive benefit at a rate of 50% up to 100% of the lost income.

If the agricultural production of an *O.G.A.* insured person is destroyed by hail, frost, flooding, or a storm, benefit may be payable on grounds of the insurance scheme for the loss of agricultural production. However, it should be mentioned that the loss of agricultural production as a result of a drought or heat wave is not covered (more than 50% of the anual loss of agricultural production is due to these causes).

4.5. Medical care.

As a result of the introduction of the national health system in 1983, the present situation with regard to the coverage of the costs for medical care (practitioner, hospital and medicine) has become rather complicated. On the one hand there is the national health system (not linked to any social insurance scheme) which is currently gradually being phased in, on the other hand there are a number of categorical social insurance schemes which still provide medical care (for example the medical care branch of sickness insurance under *I.KA.*). The statute provides that the branches of medical care of the national insurance schemes shall be incorporated within the national health system; also their capital should be transferred to this system. However, this transference has not yet been realised. Consequently, both systems still lead a parallel existence, the whole system is therefore in a transitory period. Below, we will first look into the national health system and then into the insurance scheme for the costs of medical care, as set up by the *I.KA.*

The national health system is intended to cover the costs of medical care for the entire Greek population on the basis of equality. It operates upon a decentralised level. In order to become eligible for medical care under the national health system a person should only satisfy one condition: he should be in need of medical care. Since the system is entirely financed by the State, there are no contribution requirements.

Under the social insurance scheme, as managed by the *I.KA.*, there is a right to medical care for those who have worked 50 days in the preceding year; also the dependants of such persons are entitled to care. Days of sickness benefit, unemlloyment benefit or pension are treated as working days. The working day requirements are waived in case of an occupational disease or industrial injury. In cases of injury not related to a person's work, the requirements are halved. Medical care is permanently covered by the *I.KA.* from the first day of the disease. The insured people are entitled to free, consultations from a local *I.KA.* practitioner (both general practitioners and specialists). The *I.KA.* practitioners work for and are paid by the *I.KA.*. The insured person can also receive treatment in public *I.KA.* hospitals, as well as in private hospitals recognized and designated by the *I.KA.*. Furthermore, the costs of medicine on prescription of an *I.KA.*-doctor, are covered by the *I.KA.*, subject to a personal charge of 20% of the costs of the product. A personal charge is not demanded if the patient is being treated in a recognized hospital, in cases of pregnancy or in cases when medicine is prescribed in respect of an occupational disease or industrial injury. Tuberculosis patients only pay a personal contribution of 10% of the costs. For prothesis a personal contribution of 25% is required.

In order to become entitled to treatment in a sanitarium, tuberculosis patients need to have worked at least 350 days in the preceding four years.

Employees in higher earnings classes and their dependants may have a right to treatment in hospital accomodation of a higher grade than the one to which persons from lower earnings classes may be entitled. However, such a right is subject to extra working days requirements. The higher category of hospital accommodation does not apply for the medical treatment but only for the "hotel function" of the hospital (rooms for four, two or only one person). Better hospital accommodation can only be enjoyed for a period of maximally six months and the employee has to pay 10% of the extra costs during the first month of hospitalisation. However, the 10% charge is not required from victims of industrial injuries and occupational diseases. Under certain conditions, the *I.KA.* also covers the travelling expenses of the sick who live in remote parts of the country.

4.6. Family.

In Greece there is no uniform family benefits scheme. There are no family benefits in respect of the children of persons who carry out an intellectual profession, of traders, of craftsmen or of farmers. Sometimes family benefit is granted by different social insurance institutions in respect of the same child, which results in an overlap. Here we only discuss the family benefits as payable by the *O.A.E.D.* to the majority of employees.

Each employee with children under the age of 18 years (22 years in cases of full-time education and without an age limit in respect of incapacitated children) is entitled to family benefits. The contribution requirement is that a record of at least 50 working days must have been established during the previous calendar year.

Family benefit consists of a flat-rate amount corresponding to four recognized earnings classes. Within each earnings class this amount differs depending on whether there are one, two, three, four or more children. If one of the parents is handicapped or has died and the widow is not entitled to invalidity or widows pension or when the spouse is doing his military service, the amount of family benefit is doubled, if there are one or two children and increased by 50% if there are more children.

The family benefits are paid annually in a lump sum between April and June; large families receive the benefit first.

Apart from family benefits, there is a system of dependency additions within the pension schemes.

Furthermore, the *O.A.E.D.* pays a lump sum benefit at the end of the period of pregnancy and maternity leave. The amount of this benefit is equal to the difference between the *I.KA.* benefit and the real lost wages during the 84 days of pregnancy and maternity leave. Lastly, certain lump sum birth premiums are payable by the *I.KA.*

4.7. Need.

Instead of setting up a general social assistance scheme, Greece preferred to build assistance elements within the social insurance schemes. Presently, a general revision of the assistance legislation is being prepared.

There is no general guaranteed minimum income scheme in Greece, but the introduction of such a scheme is under consideration. Greek social assistance consists of a number of specific programmes for certain groups of the needy, e.g. families with children, handicapped people, victims of catastrophes and the elderly. The assistance schemes are comprised of both preventive benefits in kind (e.g. medical care, family care) and curative benefits, both in kind and in cash. The benefits in cash are regulated in detail in statutory provisions, thus leaving the administrative bodies with little room for discretion. As a rule, only people who are not eligible for any social insurance benefit are entitled to assistance. The levels of assistance benefits vary considerably from scheme to scheme, but are generally very low. Usually the benefits are subject to a means test.

Assistance may also be provided in kind. Benefits in kind may consist of help from social councillors, rehabilitation services for the handicapped, child care facilities, etc. With regard to benefits in kind the administrative bodies have much wider discretionary powers. Usually there are more claimants than means, so that a selection must take place. Not all benefits are means tested; some benefits in kind are not available upon the free market (e.g. rehabilitation centres for the handicapped), and also those who are better off may be dependent upon them.

Finally, it should be recalled that there are also a number of "mixed benefit" schemes. As has been mentioned, the *O.G.A.* pension is payable to Greeks living in Greece, who are older than 68 years of age, who do not enjoy other benefits and whose income falls below a certain level.

Apart from these public programmes, social welfare services are also provided by a number of public organisations on a national level. Moreover, welfare services are provided through national networks by departments of various ministries. Welfare services are also provided at a local level by local public authorities, the Church and private organisations. The municipalities have the following competences for the granting of welfare services: they can provide cheap housing, services for the elderly, public land for cultivation at low prices and finally they can provide food, clothing and small sums of money in case of extra-ordinary circumstances such as earthquakes or heat waves.

5. Financing.

The various social insurance schemes are financed in a different way by contributions from employers and/or employees (or other insured people) from "social financing sources" (these are designated indirect taxes), from general or extraordinary state subsidies out of general taxation and from the proceeds of the exploitation of the capital owned by the social insurance institutions. Normally, the financing system is based upon the pay as you go principle.

The situation with regard to the methods of financing of each of the social insurance schemes is somewhat confused, which results in a strong diversification of the financing structures within the various schemes. The contribution rates vary, depending, among others, upon the type of enterprise, region and industrial branch. Contributions are levied upon the (real and fictitious) earnings from employment. The division between the contribution shares of the employers and the employees shows a diverse picture, even where the groups of insured persons bear a strong resemblance to each other. In the area of pensions the contribution rates for the employees are usually half as high as the rates which apply for employers. However, there are also schemes where the contribution shares of the employers and the employees are the same, or schemes where the employers contribute six times as much as the employees. A same lack of uniformity applies in the area of sickness insurance (medical care and sickness benefit); sometimes the insured people pay more than the employer, sometimes they pay the same or less. The same applies with regard to the contributions for the supplementary social insurance funds.

As from 1982 the employers who employ (unemployed) young workers, women or handicapped persons fall under a more favourable contribution system.

In respect of the schemes for the self-employed, contribution liability obviously rests only upon the insured people themselves. There is a great degree of inequality between the various groups of the self-employed with

regard to the contribution/benefits relationship. The contribution rates within the schemes for civil servants and farmers are very minor. Contrary to
the situation for employees, the failure by self-employed people to pay their
contributions does affect their entitlement to benefit.
The "social financing sources`' constitute another source of financing. So-
metimes these constitute a highly important source of financing. As an
example we mention the social insurance fund for lawyers: the resources of
this fund from social financing sources constitute 270% of the contributions
paid by those involved. As an example of a social financing source we can
mention the sum which each person must pay to the car owners fund when
he wants to acquire a driving licence; another example: a 1% tax on tobacco
and lottery profits payable to the fund for assistance to accommodation of
employees.

The State itself also contributes towards the financing of the social insurance schemes by means of periodical (mostly annual) subsidies to the social insurance institutions. Thus the shortages of the *I.KA.* are annually
made up out of general taxation. In the last years the state subsidies have
gradually increased. The State finances most of the expenditure of the social
insurance schemes for civil servants and farmers. The national health system which is currently being set up is financed entirely by the State. The public social assistance schemes and sometimes also the private assistance
schemes are also financed out of general state means.

6. Judicial review.

A person who wants to challenge a decision of a social insurance institution
needs to bring foreward proof of illegality of such a decision; if not, the possible deficiencies in the decision are covered by the presumption of legality
of legal actions under public law.
A decision of a social insurance institution can only be challenged before a
court, if all possibilities of internal administrative appeal have been exhausted.

All social insurance institutions have internal regulations which should enable the insured people to invite the administrative body to reconsider their
case. Such reconsideration of the litigious decision may take place by a bod
which is higher in hierarchy than the body which has taken the decision, by
the same body that took the litigious decision, or can be dealt with by a
body within the same institution which is specifically set up for this
purpose. The former two possibilities constitute hierarchal appeal, the latter
constitutes a request for redress.
Special bodies for dealing with requests for redress are very rare. However,
they do exists within the *I.KA.* and the *O.G.A.* In most cases the requests for
redress are dealt with by the Board of Management of the institutions concerned.

Internal administrative appeal mostly deals with an investigation into the facts upon which the decision was based, but sometimes also points of law are considered. It is possible that also opportunity arguments are dealt with. The procedures and principles of internal administrative appeal are laid down in internal regulations of the social insurance institutions. After the internal appeal procedure is finished, the old decision is substituted by a fresh one in which the litigious decision may be reaffirmed, nullified or modified.

If the insured person still has objections against the decision, he may appeal to the administrative courts. These courts consist of three judges. The administrative courts hear appeals, in first and in last instance, in disputes concerning contribution liability and benefits. Also the failure to act by an administrative body is subject to appeal. The administrative courts may confirm, nullify or modify the litigious decision. The judgement of the administrative courts is final, although appeal cassation may be made to the Council of State, on points of law which merely judges the legality of the litigious judgement.

The citizen can also base legal protection against illegal acts of administration on a claim for damages against the administrative body concerned. The administrative courts are competent to deal with such claims. Judgements of the administrative courts in damages proceedings are subject to further appeal to the Administrative Court of Appeal. Cassation to the Council of State is also possible.

Chapter 8: Ireland

1. Introduction: concept and sources of social security.

In Ireland, instead of the term *social security*, the term *social welfare* is used. This concept includes all income maintenance schemes. We distinguish three categories of schemes, i.e. social insurance schemes, social assistance schemes and also a residual category.

Social insurance schemes exist for the risks of old age, sickness and invalidity (with a special insurance scheme for industrial injuries and occupational diseases), maternity, survivorship, unemployment and something which is peculiar to the Irish system, namely, the risk of loss of maintenance following desertion by one spouse of the other.

In respect of all these risks (with the exception of the risk of industrial injuries and occupational diseases) there are also special assistance schemes. Special assistance schemes also exist for lone parents and others. As a safety net under these categories, there is a general assistance scheme (*supplementary welfare allowance*).

Besides the social insurance and assistance schemes, there is a residual category of income maintenance schemes. These are the *child benefit schemes*, a scheme for supplements to families on low income from employment (*family income supplement*) and a number of schemes providing benefits in kind, such as free travelling and free energy services.

The scheme for medical care falls outside the Irish concept of social welfare. However, in line with the starting point chosen for this work, we will, nevertheless, pay some attention to this scheme.

The Irish Constitution contains hardly any clauses of direct importance to social security. An exception to this could be made in relation to Section 41 of the Constitution, which includes fundamental rights clauses in connection with the family. According to the Irish Courts, the state duty to protect marriage (as laid down in Section 41(3)(1) Constitution), prohibits unfavourable treatment of married beneficiaries who do not live apart vis-avis beneficiaries who are either cohabiting, or who are married, yet living apart.

The main source of Irish social security law is the Social Welfare (Consolidation) Act, 1981. This act contains all social security acts (except one) which existed at the moment of the introduction of the Act. However, it has not brought about a fundamental simplification or reform. This explains why the act was explicitly referred to as a Consolidation Act.

The Social Welfare Act of 1981 is modified at least once a year. This follows from the fact that the rates of benefits are contained in the Act and that modification of these rates has not been delegated to the authority of the lower legislature. As a rule the new benefit rates are accompanied by some material changes in the Act. The Acts of modification are referred to by the year in which they were implemented, for example the Social Welfare Act, 1988.

The modification acts are integrated within the Social Welfare (Consolidation) Act, 1981, yet are in practice also individually quoted. Materially, there is really only one act, which is virtually all-inclusive, that is to say, it includes all formal statutes. Besides this Act, only three paragraphs in the Health Act of 1970 are of importance to social security law (stricto sensu). These embody the assistance schemes for the risks of sickness and invalidity. Furthermore, the Health Act offers a framework for the medical care system.

Thus the applicable legislation is almost completely consolidated in one act. However, this does not imply that it contains the entire body of social security law. This follows from the fact that the *Minister for Social Welfare* and the *Minister for Health* have issued a large number of *statutory instruments (regulations)* which provide further details concerning the Act. The legal basis for the regulations are contained in the Act itself. In some cases the prior approval of parliament is required. In other cases parliament can retrospectively nullify the regulations (within a certain period of time). Also the Minister of Finance must sometimes give his approval to delegated legislation. Apart from *regulations*, internal guidelines may also play a role in the daily application of social security law. Mostly, these remain concealed from the citizen.

2. Administrative organisation.

The administration of social security is fully state-controlled. Almost all social security schemes are administered on a central level. The competent department for the *income maintenance* schemes is the *Department of Social Welfare*, with, at its head, the *Minister for Social Welfare*. The latter is encharged with the general supervision of the administration. The *Department of Health*, under the authority of the *Minister for Health*, is reponsible for the medical care system.

Various civil servants from the department are involved in the routine administration of the *income maintenance* schemes. For example, *deciding officers* are in charge of taking decisions in individual cases. In the preparatory phase, *investigating inspectors* and *social welfare officers* collect the necessary information. For this they are equipped with far-ranging legal powers.

The residual social assistance scheme (*supplementary welfare allowance*), as well as the assistance schemes in respect of sickness and invalidity, are administered on a regional level by the *Health Boards*. These are the state bodies normally involved in the administration of the Health Act. They are composed of eight elected members of local institutions (representing the medical profession), as well as three members appointed by the *Minister for Health*. The fact that *Health Boards* are also encharged with the task of administrating the income maintenance assistance schemes is rather the result of a historical development than of a well considered decision. A recent report concerning the future development of Irish social security law has recommended that this task should be transferred to the *Department of Social Welfare*. As a matter of fact, this *Department* supervises the administration by the *Health Boards* of the *supplementary welfare allowances*. The administration of the other schemes takes place under the supervision of the *Department of Health*.

The unemployment schemes are administered on a local level by the *employment exchanges*, which constitute a part of the *Department of Social Welfare*. The means test is administered by the *Department* itself.
The schemes for (school) meals and energy services are administered on a local level.

The above is concerned with the so called distributive function of social security. Some attention will now be paid to the collective function. This consists mainly of the collection of contributions from the insured people and employers. The contributions are collected by the taxation service, in particular the so called *Revenue Commissioners* and are lodged in the *Social Insurance Fund*.

3. Personal scope of application.

In describing the personal scope of application we make a distinction between social insurance, social assistance schemes and other schemes.
Insurance can be both compulsory and voluntary. In principle, every person between the ages of 16 and 66 years, who is 'employed', as specified in the Act, is compulsory insured. From the further statutory provisions, it appears that 'employment' must be paid and carried out on the basis of an apprenticeship or contract of employment, within the Irish territory. Employment on an aeroplane or a vessel which is registered in the Republic of Ireland (or the owner of which is resident, or has its main place of business in the Republic), equally gives rise to insurance.
The basic principles are subject to a number of extensions. On grounds of these extensions certain explicitly mentioned categories of people are compulsory insured. Here we mention civil servants, military personnel, police officers, domestic workers, midwives and trainee nurses.

On the other hand, the basic principles are subject to a number of restrictions. Thus employment carried out for a spouse or for certain other family members does not give rise to insurance. Another important restriction concerns secondary activities and activities of insignificant importance. In regulations it is further defined which activities are to be considered as secondary activities and consequently not as a primary source of living. According to yet other regulations, activities of insignificant importance are those where the employee earns less than 25 £ per week.

Recently the self-employed were made compulsory insured. For them also there are age limits of 16 and 66 years. Furthermore, there is a minimum earnings limit, under which there is no compulsory insurance.

In respect of insurance for industrial injuries and occupational diseases there are special rules, on grounds of which there are limitations as well as extensions in relation to the description of the group of insured people.

Compulsory insured people are not equally insured for all social risks. With regard to certain categories the Act provides a *modified insurance* scheme. This is regulated in delegated legislation, on grounds of which there, are thirteen insurance classes. The majority of compulsory insured people are insured for all risks. Where coverage is limited to certain risks, this can be explained by the fact that, for example, there is no need for more extensive coverage. Thus civil servants are already protected against unemployment and incapacity for work on the basis of their employment relationship. In principle, the self-employed, who have only recently become compulsory insured, are only insured for the risks of old age and death.

The Act also provides for the possibility of voluntary insurance. This possibility is open to those who have ceased to be compulsory insured on reaching pensionable age, and who have paid contributions over a minimum period of 156 weeks. The people concerned must make an application for voluntary insurance within 12 months after the year in which their compulsory insurance ended. Voluntary insurance offers coverage against only a limited number of risks, especially old age and/or death (optional). The benefits which are paid when these risks materialize are highly dependent upon the number of paid or credited contributions (see below Section 4). These constitute the justification for the existence of voluntary insurance.

Almost all the assistance schemes in the Irish system are of a categorical character. Thus for example there is a potential right to *unemployment assistance* for every person between 18 and 66 years of age who lives in the Republic of Ireland and who is capable and willing to carry out suitable employment. A special scheme, *preretivement allowance*, is available to long term unemployed over the age of 58 . Blind people of 18 years or older have the right to a *blind pension* on the condition that they live in the Republic of Ireland. Those of 66 years or older are in principle entitled to *old age, (noncontributory) pension*, provided they live within the Republic. Lone parents are entitled to *lone parents allowance*, while persons looking after a welfare pensioner may claim *carer's allowance*.

There are other assistance schemes directed towards certain groups of women. Thus there is a *deserted wife's allowance* for the woman who is deserted by her spouse and who is younger than 40 years of age with at least one dependent child. The *prisoner's wife allowance* provides assistance to the woman whose spouse is sentenced to prison for at least six months, provided she is younger than 40 years of age with at least one dependent child. For all these schemes there are no residence or nationality requirements in respect of the women.

In order to be entitled to a *widow's (non-contributory) pension*, one must be a widow and live within the Republic of Ireland. The latter also applies to the guardian of an orphan who has a right to an *orphans (non-contributory) pension*. Also certain other people specified by the minister, are entitled to this orphans pension.

Besides the categorical assistance schemes, there exists a general scheme: the *supplementary welfare allowance*. In principle, there is a right to this allowance for every person with insufficient means of subsistence, who lives in the Republic of Ireland. However, the Act contains a number of restrictions: people who follow full time daily education, people in full-time employment, or those who are involved in a trade dispute, are excluded from this right.

Beneficiaries to *child benefit* must live in the Republic of Ireland. The same also applies to the child for whom the right exists.

Obviously, in order to be entitled to the benefits in kind, one must also live within the Republic of Ireland. However, this requirement is not explicitly laid down in statutory provisions.

In order to be entitled to *family income supplement* one must be a member of a family (not a child) in full-time, paid employment. If two members of the same family satisfy the employment conditions, then the one with the highest income is considered to be the entitled person.

4. Risks and benefits.

Before we proceed with the description of the various risks and benefits, we will make two remarks of a general nature. These concern, firstly, the requirement for all benefits of a satisfactory *contribution record* and, secondly, the general uniform structure of the various social security benefits.

All social insurance schemes, with the exception of the insurance against industrial injuries or occupational diseases, link the right to a benefit to *contribution conditions*. A person has the right to benefit on grounds of the following conditions:

a) he must have paid a certain number of weekly contributions (39 for short term benefits and 156 for long term benefits) in the period falling between the commencement of the insurance and the day before benefit is claimed; and b1) in respect of *disability, maternity allowance* and *unemployment benefit* he must have paid or been credited with at least 39 contributions in the year before benefit is claimed (at least 13 of which, in the case of disability benefit, are paid contributions); while in respect of invalidity pension, 48 paid or credited contributions in the relevant year are necessary in order to qualify for the maximum pension; or

b2) in respect of *old age (contributory) pension, retirement pension, widow's (contributory) pension* and *deserted wife's benefit* he must have paid or been credited with an average yearly number of contributions over a fixed period, ranging from 20 or 24 to 48, with the amount of the basic benefit varying slightly in accordance with the claimant's insurance record.

As can be seen, in the contribution conditions under b, not only contributions actually paid, but also those credited, are taken into account. The latter are meant for those who are (or have been) insured and yet, for reasons beyond their control, are not in a position to pay sufficient contributions in order to satisfy the contribution conditions. Thus there are, for example, *pre-entry credits*, granted to those who are insured for the first time. Equally important are credits given during periods of unemployment or incapacity for work. ,,
A record of all insured people (*contribution record*) is kept by the *Department of Social Welfare*.

The insurance schemes, as well as the assistance schemes, operate with a system of basic benefits and additions, both being flat-rate.
The basic benefits are granted to those who satisfy the relevant entitlement conditions. These are not the same for all schemes.
Additions to basic benefit are given for various reasons and in diverse situations. Thus, for example, there is an addition for adult dependants. Usually an adult dependant will be the spouse of the insured person. This person may only have limited means.
There are also additions for children younger than 18 years who usually live with the entitled person. When the child is following full time daily education, the age limit is extended to 21 years in the case of certain payments. The additions to assistance benefits are subject to the applicable general means test. However, in principle, additions to insurance benefits are not dependent upon the income or financial position of the beneficiary(ies). Recently, however the rule has been introduced that only one half of the additions is payable if the spouse of the entitled person is not considered to be an adult dependant. The reduction does not apply to married people who live apart.
In addition to these two general additions, as described above, we can distinguish a number of additions intended for special situations. Thus there is, under certain conditions, a right to an addition for the entitled person who is older than 66 years and living alone. An equally modest increase of basic benefit is granted to the entitled person who attains the age of 80 years (*old age allowance*).

All the additions vary in level, dependent upon the basic benefit to which they are attached.

Besides additions in cash, there is also a right to benefits in kind attached to certain social security benefits. These concern matters such as free travel, free energy and fuel supplies, free telephone connection and other such things. These benefits are granted mainly to people of 66 years or older.

The Irish social security system operates not only with *flat-rate benefits,* but also with *pay-related benefits.* However, the latter are merely of subsidiary importance. The right to pay-related supplements, to flat-rate basic benefit only exists in respect of unemployment benefits. There is an upper as well as a lower limit. Thus the supplement is 12% of the weekly wages 75 and 220 pounds; the total of flat-rate benefit and pay-related benefit may not amount to more than 85% of these incomes.

Pay-related benefit is payable from the 19th to the 393rd day of unemployment.

There exist no legal requirements with regard to the periodic adjustments of social security benefits. Nevertheless, such adjustments are usually made annually in respect of both the basic benefits and the additions. The inflation figures are taken as a point of reference. There seems to be an increasing tendency to give priority to the adjustment of long-term benefits over the adjustment of short-term benefits.

4.1. Old Age.

When a person reaches the age of 66 years, he may be entitled to an old age pension, either on the basis of insurance or on the basis of assistance.

Entitlement to an insurance pension (*old age contributory pension*) exists when the contribution conditions are satisfied and the insurance commenced before the person involved reached the age of 56 years.

When these conditions are not satisfied, an assistance pension (*old age non-contributory pension*) may be payable. This pension is subject to a means test.

At the age of 65 years, insured people are entitled to pension covering a one year period, preceding the entitlement to old age pension (*retirement pension*). For this pension similar contribution conditions apply, as for the (*contributory*) *old age pension,* albeit that the person's insurance must have commenced before the age of 55 years. Another condition is that a person of 65 years must have stopped his work. However, to this rule there are some important exceptions.

Of recent date is the so called *pre-retirement allowance.* This is an assistance benefit payable to long-term unemployed people of 55 years of age and older who have not yet reached pensionable age. The level of benefit is equal to that of *unemployment assistance.*

4.2. Death.

The Irish social security system provides an extended list of benefits in respect of death. For widows there is an assistance pension as well as an insurance pension. The right to an insurance pension (*widow's contributory pension*) exists when the contribution conditions are satisfied. The basis for this can be either the insurance record of the deceased spouse or of the widow herself.

When the insurance conditions cannot be satisfied, the widow can claim an assistance pension (*widow's non-contributory pension*). This pension is subject to a means test. Both schemes entail a definite loss of the right to a pension, if the widow remarries. Benefit is suspended during a period of cohabitation.

In Irish social security law there is no general pension scheme for widowers. Yet there is a special scheme for the spouse of a deceased women who was entitled to *old age (contributory) pension* or *retirement pension* and who received an *adult dependant addition* for her spouse. Such a spouse is entitled to a *survivors benefit,* the level of which is equal to the widow's pension, including possible additions for children. Entitlement is subject to the condition that the spouse cannot provide a living for himself due to his mental or physical state. The right to survivors benefit is lost on the remarriage of the entitled person; benefit is suspended during a period of cohabitation.

As is the case for widows, there is also a distinction between an insurance and an assistance pension for orphans. For the one contribution conditions apply (which must be satisfied by the parent or the stepparent of the orphan), for the other a means test is applied.
In principle the right to orphans pension exists until the orphan is 18 years of age. However, this limit is extended to 21 years when the orphan follows full-time day education.

Special rules apply in respect of a death resulting from an industrial injury or occupational disease. The widow is entitled to a substiantally higher pension and there are no contribution conditions. However, here too remarriage or cohabitation of the widow results in the loss, c.q. suspension of the pension.

When death was due to an industrial injury or occupational disease the widower is also entitled to a pension, albeit that this entitlement is subject to restrictive conditions. In particular the widower must have been completely or largely dependent upon his deceased spouse. Furthermore, a periodic pension is only payable, if and for as long as the widower cannot support himself, due to physical or mental reasons. If he can support himself, he is merely entitled to a lump sum flat-rate benefit.

Orphans, like widows have better pension rights, not subject to any contribution conditions.

Besides the widow(er) and orphan, the parent of the deceased is also a potential beneficiary. The parent must have been fully or partly maintained by the deceased person.

Finally, on the grounds of these special rules, there is a right to a flat-rate payment for the coverage of funeral costs.

The *death grant* also covers funeral costs. This grant is payable on the death of an insured person, the spouse of an insured person, the widow(er) of an insured person or the child of an insured person. Again, contribution conditions apply. The death grant consists of a lump sum, flat-rate benefit which varies according to whether the deceased was a child of younger than 5 years, a child between 5 and 18 years or an adult.

To conclude it must be mentioned that most periodic social security benefits are payable to an adult dependant for another six weeks after the death of the beneficiary. During this period none of the death benefits, as described above, are payable.

4.3. Incapacity for work.

In the area of social insurance a distinction is made between *disability benefit* and *invalidity pension*. The former benefit is for those who are incapable of suitable work and who satisfy the contribution conditions. During the first three days of incapacity there is no right to a benefit.

When someone is continuously incapable of working for one year, and the incapacity is permanent, there is a right to an *invalidity pension*. This benefit is more favourable than the *disability benefit*, and there are stricter contribution conditions.

When the incapacity to work is the result of an industrial accident or an occupational disease, the applicable rules are different from those mentioned above. In such a situation, there is the right to *injury benefit* during the first 26 weeks. Here too, there is a waiting period of three days. However, if the incapacity lasts longer than 4 days, benefit is payable from the first day. There are no contribution conditions.

The latter also applies for *disablement benefit*; this benefit is payable after the initial period of 26 weeks has expired, provided that at that time the right to injury benefit still existed. There must be an incapacitity of at least 1% as a result of a loss of physical or mental capacity due to an industrial injury. The calculation of the degree of incapacity is carried out on a strictly medical basis; whether or not there is a loss of earning capacity remains outside consideration.

The percentage of incapacity is rounded up to the nearest ten. If this percentage amounts to less than 20, *disablement benefit* is paid as a flat-rate gratuity (*disablement gratuity*). However, when the incapacity is expected to last more than 7 years, the beneficiary may opt for a pension instead of a gratuity. In case of incapacity of more than 20%, *disablement benefit* is paid periodically at a rate related to the percentage of incapacity. In the latter case the beneficiary may also be entitled to two supplements. The first, an *unemployability supplement*, is payable to the beneficiary who, as a result of a loss of physical and mental faculty, is permanently incapable for work. The supplement can be granted for a limited period and may be withdrawn at any time. The latter applies equally to the so called *constant attendance allowance*, a supplement intended for beneficiaries of a pension who are 100% incapable of work and who, as a result, are in need of constant care.

The benefits in respect of incapacity due to an industrial accident or an occupational disease are much more favourable than the benefits in respect of normal" incapacity. The difference can sometimes reach 40%. Note though that in 1992 injury benefit was reduced to the same rate as disability benefit.

Within the area of assistance, the *disabled person's allowance* provides a benefit for those who are incapable of work and who are not entitled to an insurance benefit. The incapacity must be substantial and likely to last for at least one year. It is measured against employment which, with regard to age, experience and training, is considered to be suitable. The allowance is means tested.

There is a separate scheme for blind people. Someone who is blind to such a degree that he is either unable to perform work for which sight is essential, or unable to continue his activities, is entitled to a pension for the blind. This pension is subject to the same means test as the one which applies for old age pension assistance.

There are also separate schemes for two other categories of persons. Thus there is an *infectious diseases maintenance allowance* for those who are not capable of working due to the fact that they are undergoing treatment for an infectious disease. The *rehabilitation maintenance allowance* is payable to people who are substantially incapable of suitable employment and are undergoing rehabilitation treatment in an approved institution. For both the benefits the same means test applies, as for the *disabled person's maintenance allowance*.

There is a separate insurance scheme in respect of maternity. A woman who satisfies the contribution conditions and who can produce a statement of the date at which her baby is due (issued by a recognized practitioner) is entitled to *maternity allowance*. This allowance is payable for a period of 14 weeks, beginning not later than 4 weeks before the expected date of birth and ending not earlier than 4 weeks after the birth has taken place. This benefit amounts to 70% of the average weekly wage of the woman.

4.4. Unemployment.

A person who is unemployed and who satisfies the contribution conditions is entitled to *unemployment benefit*, provided that he is able to and available for work. Among other things, the availability must follow from the fact that a person looks for employment which, in view of age, sex, physical state, training, useful work activities, place of residence and family, is considered to be suitable.

Those unemployed due to a strike are disqualified from entitlement to *unemployment benefit*, unless the person concerned is not directly involved in the strike.

Equally disqualified from benefit are those who are unemployed due to their own fault, those who have turned down an offer of a job, those who have not taken enough initiative in finding suitable employment and those, under the age of 55, who have been made redundant and have reclined redundancy pay in excess of a prescribed limit. In the latter case the disqualification lasts for a maximum period of 9 weeks.

There are three waiting days for the right to *unemployment benefit*. The duration of benefit is dependent upon the age of the persons concerned. In respect of those younger than 18 years, benefit covers a maximum period of 26 weeks. For those between the ages of 18 and 65 the maximum duration is 65 weeks. If one attains the age of 65 years during this period, benefit is continued for one year, provided that a minimum of 156 contributions have been paid.

After the first half year, benefit is payable at a lower rate. Two catogories are exempted from this rule, i.e. those above 65 years of age who have paid at least 156 weekly contributions and those below 65 years of age who, in the year in which they were unemployed and in the 7 preceding years, have paid 280 weekly contributions.

In the assistance unemployment scheme, unemployment benefit is payable in the form of *unemployment assistance*. Instead of contribution conditions a means test is applicable. Furthermore, there is also a condition that the unemployed person is capable and available to accept any suitable employment. The same disqualification rules apply, albeit that the maximum period of disqualification is three months and that there is a minimum period of one week.

The duration of *unemployment assistance* is unlimited. After 65 weeks the level of the benefit is slightly increased.

All the unemployed have a regular duty to register with the *employment exchange*. The frequency of the registration duty varies from once a day to twice in two weeks. Benefit is often paid in cash on these occasions. Also there is an opportunity to check whether a person has made sufficient job applications, or whether there are offers of employment.

4.5. Medical care.

The statutory provisions concerning medical care provide two packages of benefits in kind.

The widest range of benefits are payable to those who cannot be expected to pay medical care out of their own pockets because this would cause severe hardship.

An income limit determines which people fall within this category; thereby the situation of the entire family is taken into consideration. An increased income limit applies for those who are more than 66 years of age. The beneficiaries receive a so called *medical card*. The package of benefits for this group comprises practitioner's treatment, specialist's treatment, medicine, dental care and hospital care in a state hospital. A personal charge is only required for each day that a person stays at a hospital. The personal charges are subject to an annual maximum. Only those who have a contagious disease are exempted.

If a person (and possibly his spouse) has an income which exceeds the income limit, practitioner's treatment must be paid entirely out of his own pocket. If a person's income exceeds a second (higher) income limit, also specialist's treatment must be paid. Hospital care is granted under the same conditions as those which apply for the above mentioned category. Dental care for children younger than 6 years of age and school children is free; also certain dental treatment to adults is free of charge, provided that certain contribution conditions are satisfied. Medicine is free to the extent that the costs thereof exceed a certain monthly level; for those who suffer certain listed diseases (long duration), all medicine is free of charge.

The scheme for medical care may be supplemented by voluntary insurance, which may offer varying benefit packages. Voluntary health insurance is administered by the *Voluntary Health Insurance Board*, set up by the competent minister.

Care is provided by self-employed practitioners on the basis of an agreement concluded between the national organisation of general practitioners and the competent department. The *Health Boards* employ dentists. The state hospitals also fall under the authority of the *Health Boards*; there are private hospitals too.

4.6. Family.

In the Irish social security system there are various forms of child support. Firstly, there is a general *child benefit* scheme, providing uniform benefits to all residents. In addition, the benefit structure of the income maintenance schemes provides child additions on top of the basic benefits (see below). Finally, there is a *family income supplement* scheme as a sort of equivalent foh employees on low income.

Only people who actually live with the child are entitled to *child benefit* When the child is staying in an institution, maintenance of that child is required. Entitlement only exists in relation to children below the age of 16. This age is increased to 18 in cases where the child is in full-time day education or when the child is not able to sustain itself due to a physical or mental defect. *Child benefit* consists of a monthly amount, which varies, depending on whether it concerns the first 3 or subsequent children.

Family income supplements provide weekly payments to support families on low income. Thus, a *family income supplement* is payable to those with a full-time job who have at least one child for whom there is a right to *child benefit*, and whose income lies below a legally defined level. The benefit consists of 60% of the difference between the legally defined level and the family income, subject to a maximum. Under the condition that a person remains in work, the supplement is payable for a period of 52 weeks. During this period a change in the family income does not affect the level of benefit.

4.7. Need.

Irish assistance is predominantly set up on categorical lines. Nevertheless there does exist an assistance scheme, which operates as a general safety net: the *supplementary welfare allowance*. This allowance is intended for those who have insuffucient means to support themselves and their families. Those excluded are people following full-time day education, those who are in full time employment and those involved in a strike. A person should be registered as looking for employment.
The subsidiary character of the scheme follows from the fact that the beneficiary must do every thing possible to obtain other benefits.
The right to (possibly supplementary) benefit is subject to a means test. Alongside this benefit or as a supplement to an insufficient income, the administrative body can provide a supplement to cover extra costs. It is also competent to provide a lump sum benefit intended to cover exceptional expenses. Apart from this, the administrative body may, as an exception, provide benefits in kind. A lone parent's allowance is payable to unmarried single parents, separated parents and parents whose spouses are dead or imprisoned.

Two special assistance schemes are payable to women who it is presumed cannot provide for themselves.
Women who have been deserted by their spouse are entitled to a *deserted wife's allowance*, provided they are more than 40 years of age. The latter requirement also applies for the right to *prisoner's wife's allowance*, a benefit for women whose spouse is sentenced to prison for at least 6 months.
All these benefits are means tested. The level of the benefits is equal to that of the (non-contributory) *widow's pension*.

The *deserted wife's allowance* has an insurance equivalent, i.e. the *deserted wife's benefit*. Instead of a means test there are contribution conditions. The woman can choose whether to rely upon the contribution record of her husband or that of herself. From 1992, however, this benefit will not be paid to claimants whose income is in excess of a prescribed limit.

In respect of all these benefits there is a so called *cohabitation rule*. On grounds of this rule benefit is suspended when a claimant lives together with another person as if husband and wife.

Finally, a carer's allowance is payable to a person providing full-time care and attention to certain categories of welfare claimants.

5. Financing.

The social insurance expenditure, except for insurance against industrial accidents and occupational diseases, is financed from four sources. Apart from contribution payments from employers, self-employed and employees, there is an annual state supplement, which covers the shortage of the *Social Insurance Fund.*
There are varying contribution rates for compulsory and voluntarily insured people. Also within these categories the rates vary considerably, depending on the scope of coverage. The basis for contribution liability are the earnings from employment in the current year (compulsory insured people), or the past year (voluntarily insured people) There is an upper earnings limit.
The employer is liable to pay contributions in respect of compulsory insured people. He can deduct the amount of employees' contributions from their wages.

The expenditure for industrial accidents and occupational diseases insurance is financed entirely by the employers. There is a uniform contribution rate. Here also the basis for contribution liability is the earnings from employment, subject to the same earnings limit as the one applying for the other insurance schemes.

The assistance expenditure is borne entirely by the state. The same applies in respect of *child benefits* and *family income supplement.* The costs of (school) meals are borne together by the central and local government.

The state also finances most of the medical care expenditure. The remaining costs are met by contributions.

6. Judicial review.

With the exception of *supplementary welfare allowance,* all decisions in relation to insurance and contribution liability and the entitlement to benefit within the framework of the different social security schemes are taken by the so-called *deciding officers.* These are appointed by the Minister out of his own civil servants.
Within 21 days the *deciding officer's* decision is subject to appeal before an *appeals officer.* The latter is also appointed by the Minister from his civil servants in the *Department of Social Welfare.* One of the appeals officers is appointed *chief appeals officer.*

The *appeals officer* has a range of semi-judicial powers; for example, he can call upon witnesses, under threat of penal sanctions, and hear these under oath. He can follow a purely written procedure, which in fact happens in 60% of the cases. In certain cases the *appeals officer* can be assisted by laymen experts, for example a medical practitioner; the experts have no voice in the final decision.

The appellant is entitled to be accompanied by a member of his family. With the approval of the *appeals officer*, he can also bring another (third) person, such as a lawyer. Thus there exists no obligatory legal representation, let alone a legal assistance scheme.

Further aspects of the procedure are fully in the hands of the *appeals officer*. This constitutes one of the main points of critisism against the appeals-system. However, the jurisprudence of the *High court* and the *Supreme Court* (see below) increasingly recognizes certain procedural guarantees.

The *appeals officers* judge the contested decision to its full extent, i.e. both on points of fact and points of law. There is no obligation for the *appeals officers* to motivate their decisions, nor are the decisions published.

In principle, further appeal is only open in disputes concerning contribution liability and disputes concerning the question of whether an accident resulted from the performance of an employment giving rise to insurance. This appeal is open to the *High Court*, an independant judicial body. The *High Court* only decides on points of law.

Perhaps due to the very limited possibility of further appeal, increasing use is being made of *judicial review*. This general remedy (that is to say not restricted to a certain legal area) is available against decisions which, according to the appellant, are either contrary to the Constitution, or taken unauthorized, or contrary to procedural requirements, or which are utterly unreasonable. The competent judicial bodies are the *High Court* and the *Supreme Court*.

The decisions of the administrative officers and tribunals, dealing with welfare schemes, are not made available to the general public. The small, but steadely growing number of High and Supreme Court cases dealing with welfare law are published.

There is a separate appeal procedure in respect of *supplementary welfare allowances*. This is solely a matter for the *Health Boards*. The procedure is even more unclear than the ordinary appeal procedure. Although the Act offers the opportunity to enact regulations on this matter, so far this has never happened.

A special appeal procedure exists for those who are refused *unemployment benefit* or *assistance* because of a strike. Further appeal against the decision of the *appeals officer* is possible to a judicial body which has been created especially for this purpose, the *Social Welfare Tribunal*. This body consists of five members, appointed by the Minister, two of whom are representatives of the employers and the employees. The decision of the *Tribunal* is open to appeal to the *High Court* on points of law. Furthermore, on the request of an interested party, the *Tribunal* can review its decision in the light of new facts and circumstances.

Chapter 9: Italy

1. Introduction: concept and sources of social security.

In the past, in Italy the distinction between social assistance (*assistenza sociale*) and social insurance (*previdenza sociale*) was considered to be fundamental for social security. Social assistance was generally characterized as general protection fore people in need, within the limits of the financial ability of the social security institutions; within this dichotomy, the protection of employees against specific social risks was the responsibility of social insurance. Only people who were covered by the social insurance scheme enjoyed subjective rights to benefit; people receiving assistance merely enjoyed a 'legitimate interest' (*interesse legittimo*). The Italian constitution of 1948 has blurred this distinction. With regard to subsistence and the opportunity to exercise effectively civil and political rights, the citizen now has full subjective rights to benefits. At the same time social insurance became a public service, an instrument able to cover situations of need, regardless of any professional activities. To the extent that it has been maintained, the distinction between social assistance and social insurance is no longer fundamental, even though differences in the scope of application and in the intensity of social protection partly arise from a different estimation of the different needs of the citizens.

We will no longer deal with the complex problems of defining the concept of social security, but suffice with a description of the most important branches of social security which together constitute the general scheme of social security. First of all there are social insurance schemes which cover a loss of income from work as a result of sickness, maternity and tuberculosis, as well as involuntary unemployment. Furthermore, there are pensions: invalidity benefits and pensions for incapacity for work, survivor's pensions and old age pensions. A special scheme provides 'social retirement pensions' (pensions for persons older than sixty five years of age who are living under difficult economic circumstances), and there are the benefits paid by the *Cassa integrazione guadagni*. There is also a national health service. Industrial injuries and occupational diseases are the subject of a separate insurance scheme.

In addition to the general scheme of social security (which covers people working for private employees), a number of special schemes also exists, the administration of which is often also entrusted to the *I.N.P.S.* (see section 2), albeit sometimes in the form of special funds. Due to the complexity of all these special schemes, unless specifically mentioned, we will only concern ourselves with the general scheme. Here, we merely point out that, although subject to special insurance schemes, the following categories are integrated within the *I.N.P.S.*: airline personnel, public transport personnel, personnel from the electricity company, the self-employed, and some other groups of people. However, there are also adminstrative bodies which are independent from the *I.N.P.S.* for example for managers, performing actors, journalists and practising lawyers.

The principle of social security (which is understood to mean that every individual, being freed from need, may fully enjoy civil and political rights in the interest of the whole nation) is based upon article 3 Constitution: "It is the Republic's task to remove all economic and social obstacles, which limit the freedom and equality of the citizens and which stand in the way of the development of the people and of the effective participation of all active people in the political, economic and social organisation of the country'

Article 32 Constitution regards health protection as "a fundamental right and of importance to the whole community", while article 38 Constitution gives further substance to the principle of solidarity, "Every citizen who is not capable of work and who has insufficient means of subsistence is entitled to maintenance and social assistance. Economically active people are entitled to the provision and insurance of means adjusted to their daily needs in case of injury, sickness, invalidity, old age and involuntary unemployment. People incapable of work and handicapped people are entitled to employment and vocational training. Bodies and institutions set up or integrated by the State will be responsible for carrying out the tasks determined within this article. Private assistance is free". Article 38(4) Constitution is of special importance: the State not only regulates the relations between and the constitution of the social security institutions, but also provides for their integration, as the social protection of the people concerned reflects a public interest.
It is the legislator who, by an evaluation of the necessities of life on the one hand and of the existing financial means on the other, determines how and on which level the benefits provided for in article 38 Constitution should be granted and adjusted to any change in circumstances. Yet the *Corte costituzionale* has reserved the right to ensure the minimum level of the constutionally guaranteed benefits.
One of the results of article 36 Constitution, which recognizes the right of workers to earnings which are "sufficient to insure for themselves and their families a free and worthy existence", is that social insurance benefits must be sufficient not only for the necessities of life of the claimant himself, but also of his family.

On grounds of the jurisprudence of the *Corte costituzionale* the social constitutional provisions of the Italian constitution should be considered as enforceable legal norms. The legal effect of these provisions varies from the granting of subjective rights to legally binding guidlines of interpretation. It follows that statutes, decrees and administrative decisions which are directly contrary to the social constitutional provisions can be nullified. Many social constitutional provisions do require the intermediation of the legislator to grant subjective rights to the legal subjects concerned. Whether or not article 38 Constitution requires such intermediation is debatable, but article 36 Constitution is considered to be a directly applicable norm containing subjective rights.

170

The constitutional social security principles have been implemented by the legislator, albeit neither in a uniform nor a consistent manner. Nevertheless, if one considers the Italian social security system in the light of its constitutional principles, this system can be considered to be unitary. As a matter of fact, with the introduction of the constitution (1948), some general tendencies within social security law have been initiated, e.g. the blurring of the distinction between social assistance and social insurance, the weakening of the equivalence between contributions and benefits, and the extension of the scope of application.

For the sake of completeness it should be mentioned that the Statutes of the regions contain provisions concerning regional action for removing economic and social obstacles which hinder the free development of a person and the fundamental equality of citizens, as well as for the effective realisation of fundamental rights with regard to the family, social security, health, education and to labour. Although such provisions are moulded in various forms, it appears from their very wording that they are of a programmatic nature. Furthermore, as the provisions are situated on the same level as the provisions of statutes, the latter may be left out of consideration. Obviously, we can also not deal with measures in the field of social protection, especially of social and medical assistance, which have been taken by the different regions, municipalities and provinces.

The occupational (pension) schemes which supplement social insurance benefits are not the object of social security legislation, but are governed by private and labour law. They may take the shape of earmarked capital within the enterprise or of special funds. Below, the occupational (pension) schemes will no longer be dealt with.

2. Administrative organisation.

The Minister for Labour and Social Security is competent in the area of social security. The Minister of Health is responsible for health care.
The competent minister carries out control over the administrative institutions as described below.

The National Social Security Institute (*Istituto nazionale della previdenza sociale, I.N.P.S.*) is competent in the area of benefits in cash for sickness and maternity, as well as for insuring the risks of old age, death, invalidity, family allowance and unemployment. It is also encharged with the collection of contributions. The *I.N.P.S.* has regional inspectorates, provincial, town and district services (also empowered to collect contributions) and local services and information centres.
Within the *I.N.P.S.*, the Management of social assistence interventions and of the support to the social insurance schemes (*Gestione degli interventi assistenziali e di sostegno alle gestioni previdenziali*) the state intervention in social security is concentrated. The Management guarantees the payment of pensions for people older than sixty five years of age who find them-

selves in difficult economic circumstances, of the ordinary invalidity benefit, of the pensions to agricultural workers retired before 1989 etc. Within the *I.N.P.S.* operate also the Ordinary and Extraordinary Loss of Earnings Compensation Funds (*Casse Integrative Guadagni Ordinaria e Straordinaria*).

On grounds of the law, employees should be in the majority on the board of government of the *I.N.P.S.*; the same majority is required for the provincial commissions of the *I.N.P.S.*, which decides in first instance on appeals in respect of social security benefits. Furthermore, the employers and the personnel of the *I.N.P.S.*, of the competent departments, and of some other administrative bodies are represented on the board of government.

In addition to the general social security scheme governed by the *I.N.P.S.*, there exist other special regimes, which either have or have not been integrated. The *I.N.P.S.* is not the only administrative body for these special schemes. Other administrative bodies exist, smaller social security institutions which are responsible for the social protection of some special categories. Yet within the *I.N.P.S.* are also boards which are competent for certain special schemes, which were integrated within the general scheme (such as self-employed farmers, craftsmen and traders).

Health protection is entrusted to the National Health Service (*Servizio sanitario nazionale*), which operates via the local health units (*Unità sanitarie locali*). These health units are not legal persons. Each unit is responsible for the realisation of health protection for all citizens within a certain area. The local health unit is composed of a council, a president, a general manager and a Board of Directors.
The responsabilities of each body is defined by administrative decree of the responsible minister.
The organisation, administration and operation of the local health units are regulated in regional statutes which, for example, provide for the establishment of specific bodies of a technical nature within which the representatives of those providing medical care and other co-operative persons also take part. The State has the task of determining the objectives of health care within the framework of the general economic policy. The level of benefits which are offered to citizens are also determined by national legislation.

Social protection in case of industrial injuries or occupational diseases is entrusted to the National Institute for the Insurance against Industrial Injuries (*Istituto nazionale per l'assicurazione contro gli infortuni sul lavoro, I.N.A.I.L.*). The *I.N.A.I.L.* is also encharged with the granting of benefits and the collection of contributions. The *I.N.A.I.L.* operates via central bodies, as well as via bodies organized on a regional or provincial level. Where medical care is involved, the administration of social protection lies with the local health units; tasks concerned with cash benefits, such as the determination of incapacity to work, lie with the *I.N.A.I.L.* With regard to some categories of workers, the protection against professional risks has been removed from the *I.N.A.I.L.* and entrusted to other specific bodies (e.g. the *Casse marittime* in respect of mariners and fishermen). Employees of the post office and the railway are insured for professional risks by their employers.

3. Personal scope of application.

We have already referred to the existence of special schemes for social security, in addition to the general scheme (which was initially developed for employees). These can be distinguished from the general scheme by their personal scope of application (self-employed, agricultural workers, employees of specific employers etc). Here we will only deal with those insured within the general scheme.

Blue collar workers and those treated as such are covered by sickness and maternity insurance under the general scheme. White collar workers are not entitled to sickness benefit, but are entitled to continued wage payments from their employers for a period of at least three months. In case of tuberculosis also all family members of the insured person are covered by the sickness insurance scheme. The scope of the invalidity benefit scheme, the pension scheme for incapacity for work, the invalidity pension scheme and the old age pension scheme encompasses all employees. Invalidity and old age pensions as well as survivor's pensions, are subject to contribution conditions and thus to the previous employment record. In contrast, the pension for persons older than sixty five years of age, who find themselves in difficult economic circumstances, is merely subject to residence conditions. The employment insurance scheme applies to all employees; the benefits of the *Cassa integrazione quada* and the mobility benefits only cover certain categories of employees. People with no previous employment record are not eligible for unemployment benefit.

All citizens are equally covered by the national health service. National health service insurance is compulsory, as is the payment of an annual contribution. Each person making use of the national health service receives a health card, which enables him to make use of the services of the national health service.
The industrial injuries insurance scheme covers those who carry out paid manual subordinate labour; the majority of white collar workers are as a consequence excluded from the industrial injuries insurance scheme.

Subject to certain conditions, those not compulsory insured, who do not or no longer carry out any professional activities, are given the opportunity of voluntary insurance (continuation of compulsory insurance) with the I.N.P.S. Also housewives are offered the possibility to insure themselves; in practice the latter possibility is of no great significance.

4. Risks and benefits.

As there is no national guaranteed minimum of subsistence, and competence in matters of social and medical assistance lies mainly with the regions, so this chapter lacks a paragraph concerning need.

With regard to the up-rating of social security benefits, it may be observed that pensions are adjusted every six months according to the official inflation rate published by the Central Statistic Institute. Pensions above the minimum are only partly adjusted:
- for a pension with a maximum amount equal to twice the minimum pension, by 100%;
- for pensions amounting to between twice and three times the minimum pension, by 90%; and
- for those pensions amounting to more than three times the minimum pension, by 75%.

The annuities due on ground of the insurance scheme for industrial injuries and occupational diseases are annualy automatically adjusted to the evolution of wages within industry.

4.1. Old age.

In order to be entitled to old age pension (*pensione di vecchiaia*) it is required that contributions have been paid for at least fifteen years. Pensionable age is set at 60 years for men and 55 for women; however, in view of legislation with regard to equal treatment of men and women in the area of employment, women may continue to work until their sixtieth year. The employee is permitted to continue his professional activities after having attained pensionable age, so that, by paying more contributions, he can build up a contribution record of 40 years, albeit this is only possible maximally until 65 years of age.

Retirement pension amounts to as many times 2% of the average annual income from work over the last five years, as there are contribution years (with a maximum of 40). There is a maximum limit for the yearly wage which is taken into account, and there is a minimum old age pension. 1992 important changes to the old age pension scheme were decided: the pensionable age will be raised to 65 for men and 60 for women and this by one year every two years (e.g. 61 for men in 1994); the retirement pension amount will also be calculated in the future over the average income over the last 10 years, and this by biennal increases juste like for the pensionable age (e.g. 6 lost years in 1994).

Employees of enterprises in difficult economic circumstances are, five years before their normal pensionable age, entitled to a normal retirement pension; the remaining years until pensionable age, are considered to be covered by contributions.

The seniority pension constitutes a special form of old age pension (*pensione di anzianità*). Entitlement to this pension exists, irrespective of the age of the claimant, after 35 years of professional activity, which results in 35 years of contribution payments. Entitlement is subject to the condition that the beneficiary has fully ceased his professional activities.

The pension for elderly people in difficult economic circumstances (*pensione agli anziani in disagiate condizione economiche*) is not subject to conditions concerning previous professional activites. The pension is awarded to all citizens older than 65 years of age, who are resident in Italy and who have an income below a certain (indexed) minimum. The pension is flat-rate, the level being below the minimum benefit applicable within the general social scheme.

4.2. Death.

Entitlement to survivor's pension (*pensione ai superstiti*) exists upon the death of a retired person or of a person satisfying the entitlement conditions for invalidity or old age pension. The level of the survivor's pension is expressed as a percentage of the pension of the deceased person, subject to the same minimum and maximum levels. The surviving spouse receives 60% of the pension and each child 20% (40% where there is no surviving widow or widower). In order to be eligible the child must be younger than 18 years, incapable of work or a student.

Survivor's pension is payable on the condition that the deceased person has paid contributions for a period of at least five years, at least two of which must fall within the period of the last five years. Privileged survivor's pension (this is a pension, due to a death while performing work in respect of which no pension is payable under the industrial injuries insurance scheme) is not subject to contribution conditions.

Survivor's pension is payable to the surviving widower as well as to the surviving widow. In cases of divorce the judge may decide that the ex-spouse, who formerly received alimony, should receive all or part of the widow's pension.

The right to survivor's pension ends upon remarriage, but the claimant receives a lump sum of twice the annual amount of the survivor's pension.

The total of all survivor's benefits may never amount to more than 100%. If this should appear to be the case, widow(er)'s pension is paid in full with the remaining amount being divided among the surviving orphans.

If there are no surviving widow(er) or orphans, the parents, brothers and sisters of the deceased person receive 15% of the pension to which the deceased person was entitled; here too the benefits may not exceed 100% of the deceased persons pension.

If the deceased insured person did not enjoy a pension, the survivors are awarded a lump sum amounting to 45 times the total number of contributions paid, subject to a minimum and a maximum level. This lump sum is payable, in order of priority, to the surviving spouse, the surviving children or the surviving parents.

If the deceased was a victim of an industrial injury or an occupational disease, survivor's pension is payable to the survivors. The level of this pension is expressed as a percentage of the benefit for permanent incapacity for work which the victim obtained or would have obtained, i.e. 50% thereof for the surviving spouse, 20% for each semi orphan and 40% for each orphan; should none of these exist 20% is payable to each parent, grand parent, grand child, brother or sister. Again the total sum of the survivor's benefits may not exceed 100% of the annuity. In respect of a person liable for alimony after a divorce, who is deceased as a result of an industrial injury or an occupational disease, a court may grant the survivor's benefit fully or partly to the ex-spouse. Also a lump sum is payable on the death of a victim of an industrial injury or occupational disease.

For the sake of completeness we mention that a death benefit is included within the sickness insurance scheme.

4.3. Incapacity for work.

In order to be entitled to sickness benefit, the employee must be incapable of work. There is a waiting period of three days. The total duration of the benefit is six months per year. Benefit amounts to 50% of the lost wage; from the 21 st day of sickness the benefit rate amounts to 66% of the wage. However, if the person who is incapable of work is hospitalized, benefit for a person with no dependants is reduced to two fifths of the wage.

The tuberculosis insurance, which is integrated within the sickness insurance scheme is subject to derogating provisions.

In case of pregnancy/maternity, maternity benefit is payable to the insured women, possibly also to the fathers, for two months preceding the estimated date of birth and for three months thereafter. Benefit amounts to 80% of the lost wage. Where the wage continues to be paid by the employer no benefit is payable. The mother, or the father if the mother makes no request or if the father is solely responsible for the child, may subsequently claim benefit for a further six months. During the optional period benefit amounts to 30% of the lost wage.

In Italian law there is a distinction between an invalid and a person incapable of work. A person, whose capacity to work is reduced to less than one third, is considered as an invalid; people who are completely and permanently incapable of carrying out any work, are considered to be incapable of work.

If the reduction of the working capacity is due to sickness or to a physical or mental handicap, the invalid is, from the age of 18 years, entitled to a monthly benefit. In contrast, a person who is incapable of work is entitled to a normal benefit in respect of incapacity for work, which excludes him from any other rehabilitation services or income maintenance benefits. Neither the invalidity benefit (*assegno di invalidità*) nor the normal pension in respect of incapacity for work (*pensione di inabilità*) are granted for life; an affirmation of benefit entitlement must be requested every three years. Yet after the third consecutive affirmation benefit is automatically extended.

In order to be entitled to benefit for invalidity or incapacity for work, the person incapable of work must have paid contributions for at least five years, two of which must have been in the last five years. However, if the invalidity or incapacity for work is due to circumstances at work other than those covered by the industrial injuries insurance scheme, the contribution conditions do not apply (professional incapacity for work). Invalidity benefit amounts to as many times 2% of the average annual income from work over the preceding five years (with income from the first four years indexed) as there are insurance years (with a maximum of fifty). Where the annual taxable income of the claimant amounts to less than twice the social old age pension for persons above 65 years of age who are in difficult economic circumstances, invalidity benefit calculated in this way is increased up to the level of the social pension. The pension in respect of incapacity for work is calculated in the same way, albeit that not only the actual insurance years are taken into account, but also the years between the granting of a pension and the attainment of pensionable age. The average annual income which is taken into account is subject to a maximum limit.

Those who are fully incapable of work and who need help in order to move or who need permanent assistance in carrying out tasks necessary for daily life, are entitled to an extra monthly flat-rate benefit; a supplement of 5% is payable in respect of a spouse and of each dependent child.

Special rules apply if incapacity for work is due to an industrial injury or an occupational disease.

Temporary benefits in respect of professional risks are only payable from the fourth day after the industrial injury; for the day on which the injury occured the claimant receives 100% of his wage paid by the employer, for the three following days 60% of his wage. Benefit continues until the damage to health is cured or consolidated. For the first ninety days temporary benefit in respect of a professional risk amounts to 60%, thereafter 75% of the average wage during the fifteen days preceding the occurance of the professional risk.

The degree of incapacity for work is determined according to a table of permanent percentages of incapacity for work concerning industrial injuries. In respect of occupational diseases, the degree of incapacity for work is determined on grounds of an estimation by the advisory doctor to the *I.N.A.I.L.* The degree of incapacity for work may be annualy reviewed, over a period of four years after the first diagnosis; afterwards revision is only possible every three years. After ten years further review is not possible. Incapacity for work of 10% or less does not give rise to entitlement to any benefits.

Benefit for permanent incapacity for work due to an industrial injury or occupational disease is calculated on the basis of the average wage during the year preceding the termination of work, albeit that the amount of this average is reduced according to a scale of percentages. There exists a minimum and a maximum basis of calculation. The basis of calculation determined in this way is then multiplied by the degree of incapacity for work.

In case the help of a third person is necessary, a supplement will be granted as it is for the people totally incapable of work.

In respect of some cases, special provisions allow for a conversion of pension into a flat-rate amount.

If the industrial injury or the occupational disease results in total permanent incapacity for work, an extra flat-rate benefit is payable to the claimant.

4.4. Unemployment.

A distinction must be made between the real unemployment insurance scheme and the special unemployment supplement. The latter is only payable to employees who do not fulfil the conditions under the unemployment insurance scheme.

Entitlement to benefit on grounds of the unemployment insurance scheme is subject to the condition that the claimant has been insured for at least two years and has paid contributions for at least 52 weeks during the preceding two years. Entitlement to unemployment supplement is subject to the condition that the claimant has been insured for at least five weeks (or one month before 1949 or during the preceding two years). People who have never worked (school leavers) are therefore neither entitled to insurance benefit nor to the supplement.

Under both unemployment schemes the unemployed person is required to register as looking for employment with the labour exchange.

A waiting period of seven days applies in respect of the unemployment insurance scheme; in respect of unemployment supplement there is a waiting period of one day. Benefit on grounds of the unemployment insurance scheme is payable for 120, 180 or 360 days, according to the sector. Unemployment supplement is payable for 90 days per year (with a possible extension to 180 days). The benefits amounts to only a quarter of the previously earned wage.

If unemployment is the result of dismissal due to the closure of an enterprise or a reduction in staff, a special unemployment benefit is granted. This benefit amounts to two thirds of the previously earned wage; it is payable over a period of 180 days. The minimum contribution condition is reduced to thirteen weeks.

If an employee of the industrial, building or agricultural sector is temporarily unemployed due to a reduction in the number of working hours as a result of temporary problems which are outside the employer's responsibility, or by virtue of temporary market problems, he can claim a supplement to his wage, payable by the *Cassa integratizione guadagni ordinaria*. This supplement amounts to 80% of the wage which would have been earned in the hours in which work is not performed.

A benefit of the same amount will be paid for maximum 6 months by the *Cassa integrazione guadagni straordinaire* in case of temporary unemployment due to the restructurary, reorganisation or reconversion of the enterprise (or due to certain other reasons such as e.g. the destruction of the enterprise by a natural disaster). The exceptional situation may not last for longer than three years.

The payment of the benefits by the *Cassa ordinaria* or the *Cassa straordinaria* is only possible after a procedure in which the resources of the considered economic problems are verified and in which the trade unions and the *I.N.P.S.* play an important role.

In case an enterprise not falling under the scope of application of the *Cassa* and employing at least 15 employees, is facing non reversible major economic problems, it may decide a collective dismissal.
The employees victims of such a collective dismissal will receive a mobility benefit for a period up to 24 months (or 36 months for persons of at least 60 years of age).
They will also be put on a mobility lost, controlled by the regional employment board, which has the duty to take all possible inchalves to find a new job to the dismissed employees. Employees who have previously proceeded to collective dismissal are obliged in case of new recritments to have workers from the mobility list.

4.5. Medical care.

The national health service constitutes the realisation of the principle as laid down in article 32 Constitution. The improvement, maintenance and recovery of the physical and mental health of the whole population is entrusted to the national health service. The national health service provides prevention, diagnosis, recovery, as well as rehabilitation. Furthermore, it is responsible for the determination and the removal of the health risks which exists in the living and working environment. The objective of the national health service is the health of the entire state community.

All residents (including all foreigners, at their request), are insured by the national health service. Medical care is provided for an unlimited duration from the beginning of sickness. The national health service operates with doctors who have a contract with the region, the public and recognized private hospitals and other cooperating bodies.
The general practitioners receive a fixed monthly payment for each patient. This amount is determined in accordance with a scale which is laid down in an agreement between the Minister of Health, the regions and the practitioner's organisations. The fixed amount per patient is dependent upon the age of the patient as well as upon the experience of the doctor. . Each general practitioner may register a maximum of 1,500 persons.
Hospital physicians receive a fixed monthly wage. Individual agreemens are concluded with specialists who are not bound to a hospital; such agreements provide compensation on the basis of a fixed amount per hour of consultation.
Public hospitals, as well as recognized private hospitals, are managed on a regional basis.

Patients enjoy freedom of choice with regard to general practitioner, recognized specialist or (recognized) hospital. A personal contribution is charged

for clinical tests and laboratory tests, i.e. at the level of 25% of the official tariff (subject to a minimum and a maximum; in case of multiple tests the maximum is doubled). A personal contribution is also required for pharmaceutical products: here the contribution amounts to 25% of the costs plus a fixed amount per prescription (with a maximum of three products per prescription). A maximum personal contribution is applicable per prescription. No personal contributions are required from families on low income, families with many children, the severely handicapped, the seriously ill and the people with a low old age pension, nor for benefits in kind in respect of maternity.
Pregnant women are eligible for the services of a midwife; their hospital stay and medicine are free of charge.

The cost of artificial aids are refunded by the national health service, provided that the purchase of these aids was previously approved; the payment of the refund takes place in accordance with an official scale.

Under the threat of loss of benefit, the victims of an industrial injury or an occupational disease must make use of the services of physicians appointed by the *I.N.A.I.L.* and act in accordance with their instructions and also, where applicable, their possible recommendation for surgical intervention. The benefits are paid by the *I.N.A.I.L.*, which also pays all personal contributions which would have been due for medical care.

4.6. Family.

Family allowances must ensure that in accordance with article 36 Constitution the income of the employee is sufficient not only for himself but also for his family. The family allowances (*assegno per il nucleo familiare*) are borne by the *I.N.P.S.*

The payment of the *assegno per il nucleo familiare* depends upon the number of members of the family unit and the income of the family unit. Are considered to be members of the family: man and wife, the children younger than 18 years of age, the invalid brothers and sisters of one of the spouses untill the age of 18 and without age limit in case of total incapacity to work.
Every family unit registered with the local authorities is eligible for the *assegno*, even if the unit consist of only one person, on condition that the income of the unit does not exceed a fixed amount.

5. Financing.

The basic principle with respect to the financing of social security is based upon national solidarity. This solidarity has been realised and coordinated by the State by means of the imposition of contribution liability (the contributions have a parafiscal nature) and direct financial support (via the social fund). The financing of Italian social security is based upon the "pay as you go" system. However, in the area of industrial injuries and occupational diseases the system of financing is mixed; here certain mathematical reserves are construed which express the actual value of pensions.

Contributions constitute a certain percentage of earned wages, in principle not subject to any wage limits. Employees pay contributions in respect of the risks of maternity and sickness, invalidity, old age and death, as well as a special solidarity contribution. The solidarity contribution is levied upon wages between a lower and an upper wage limit.
Employers pay contributions in respect of the risks of maternity and sickness, invalidity, old age and death, unemployment and family allowances. Furthermore, the employers pay a part of the solidarity contribution.
The employer's contributions vary in accordance to whether the employer is involved in industry or trade. The contributions from employees are the same in both sectors.

For people who are voluntarily affiliated to the national health servic there are special contribution rates. Some categories of employers pay lower contributions for the branches of family allowances and old age, for example certain mining enterprises, exporters and certain enterprises providing services (such as transport or tourism).

In respect of the insurance scheme for professional risks, employers pay contributions, the level of which is dependent upon the degree of risk within their branch of industry. This percentage varies between 3 and 5% (with an average of 3.9%). Furthermore, the employers are liable to pay an additional contribution, which is equal to 20% of the total sum of (other) social security contributions.

The National Health Service fund acquires it's capital from a contribution from the sickness insurance fund, from the surplus of the tuberculosis insurance scheme and from contributions from the regions, the provinces, the municipalities and other legal persons under public law. The social fund is completely financed by public means 'Annual subsidies are granted for the unemployment insurance scheme and the family allowance scheme. The industrial injuries and the occupational diseases scheme is not subsidized. The State guarantees the benefits from the *I.N.P.S.* The actions and benefits of the *Gestione degli interventi assistenziali e di sostegno alle gestioni previdenziali* are entirely financed by the State; benefits from the *Cassa integratizione guadagni* are financed for a major part by the State.

6. Judicial review.

Judicial review in respect of social security is divided into two phases, i.e. an administrative phase and a judicial phase.

In the administrative phase the claimant must inform the administrative body of his complaint concerning a decision made by that body. This body has ninety days in which to respond to this complaint. If the body remains silent this is considered as a rejection of the complaint (silence as a negative decision). Once the administrative phase is completed (without result), the claimant may turn to a court, in first instance the *pretore del lavoro* (judicial phase). Employees may be represented and assisted by "institutions of patronage and assistance" which are financed by the State and the labour unions.

Chapter 10: The Netherlands

1. Introduction: concept and sources of social security law.

The financial memorandum concerning social security, which the Ministry of Social Affairs and Employment presents annually to parliament, makes a distinction between four main categories of social security schemes, i.e. social insurance schemes, complementary social services, schemes for civil servants and occupational pension insurance schemes.

The social insurance schemes are divided into general insurance schemes and employee insurance schemes. This division is based upon the personal scope of application. There are employee insurance schemes with respect to the risks of unemployment, temporary and permanent incapacity for work and medical care. The general insurance schemes cover the risks of old age, death, permanent incapacity for work (hereafter: invalidity), family expenses and medical care (serious medical risks).

The complementary social services are distinguished from the social insurance schemes by virtue of the fact that they are entirely financed by general taxation. The most important complementary social service is social assistance. Furthermore, a number of other services exist, the purpose of which is to supplement social insurace benefits (up to the relevant social minimum), or to offer coverage to people whose right to benefit has expired (or, as may be the case, were never insured at all).

Civil servants and people treated as such generally fall outside the scope of the employee insurance schemes and the general insurance scheme against incapacity for work. They are covered by separate schemes. Some schemes for civil servants have a general character, others cover special groups of civil servants (e.g. military personnel, railway personnel).

In addition to the general pension schemes which are contained within the general insurance schemes, there is an opportunity to build up an occupational pension with industrial and enterprise pension funds, or by collective agreement with life insurance companies. These private pension schemes are not, obligatory by law. However, on the request of a sufficiently large group of people the Minister of Social Affairs and Employment may make participation in such a pension scheme obligatory for all branches of industry c.q. occupation. The majority of employees and self-employed people are guaranteed an occupational pension, usually linked to their previous income.

For the sake of completeness, we will refer to a number of other occupational schemes. These schemes are the result of negotiations between employers and employees and are usually embodied in collective labour agreements. Thus there are 'extra legal benefits', in addition to benefits on grounds of the employee insurance schemes. Some employees in the private and public sector may enjoy an early retirement benefit (*VUT*), whereby the beneficiary is offered the opportunity to withdraw from his professional life before he attains pensionable age. Until he attains pensionable age the employee receives a wage-related benefit.

Throughout the course of this chapter our attention is mainly devoted to the social insurance schemes and the complementary social services. The remaining schemes will receive only marginal attention.

Article 20 (chapter 1 "fundamental rights") of the Dutch constitution provides:
"1. The security of existence of the population and the distribution of prosperity are subject to the care of the government.
2. The statute provides rules concerning social security rights.
3. Dutch nationals in the Netherlands, who cannot provide for their own existence, are entitled to assistance provided by the State and regulated by the statute."

The legal importance of the social fundamental rights to benefits is disputed. Most of the arguments put forward to Parliament in favour of the adoption of such rights were of an ideological or political nature. Their legal importance, i.e. the duty of the government to protect social legislation against possible revocation, seems irrelevant in practice. In this respect it must be borne in mind that according to article 120 of the Constitution, the judiciary is not allowed to judge the contents of formal statutes on their compatability with the constitution. In other words, although the constitution is the highest source of social security law, in practice it has very little to offer.

The formal social security acts either contain the contents of the social security schemes, or are restricted to a framework for the creation of schemes which are not primarily entrusted to the Government. In almost all social security acts some material legislative powers have been delegated, albeit not always to the same extent or to the same subordinate legislator (Crown, Secretary of State, administrative body). Some regulations issued in pursuance of delegated powers to the crown are important and voluminous. By or on grounds of the formal statute, powers are also often delegated to the Minister and to the Social Insurance Council (*Sociale verzekeringsraad*). When powers are delegated to an administrative body, the exercise of such powers is often subject to prior approval of the Minister or that of a supervisory body. For example, this is the case when the industrial councils (*bedrijfsverenigingen*) want to make use of their power in order to provide benefits at a higher level than that prescribed under the employee insurance schemes (as a consequence of collective labour agreements relating to extra legal benefits).

Sometimes legislative powers are not delegated to an administrative body, but rather a certain degree of discretionary powers with respect to the application of the social security acts. As the exercise of discretion may not result in arbitrary decisions, the administrative body must make it's own rules with regard to the use of such powers. To this end, internal directives,

circulars etc. are framed and possibly issued to the public. Such directives do not have any legal basis in the constitution, nor in delegated powers in formal statutes. Hence, they do not constitute material legislation, but 'pseudo legislation'.
The judiciary is not directly bound by it. However, if an administrative body deviates from pseudo legislation, it must do so for particular reasons. When these do not exist, the administrative body may violate the so called 'general principles of proper administration', such as the principle of equality, the prohibition of arbitrary decision making and the principle of trust. These principles are important guidelines for the judiciary, in respect of which it can judge the validity of acts of administration. The importance of pseudo legislation in the area of social security law must not be underestimated.

In many areas of social security law an important (factual) source is case law. This is not only due to the complexity of social security law, but also to the fact that the legislator has sometimes deliberately adopted 'open' concepts, the application of which is, as it were, delegated to the judiciary.

2. Administrative organisation.

The employee insurance scheme is, as far as the collection of contributions and the granting of benefits are concerned, (with the exception of benefits granted in the framework of the insurance scheme for medical care), administered by the industrial councils. For this purpose, the Minister of Social Affairs and Employment has categorized professional activities in one or more branches of industry or occupation (or parts thereof). Any association set up by one or more representative organisations of employers and employees may be recognized as an industrial council by the Minister. However, for each branch of industry or occupation there may be only one competent industrial council. Each employer is obligatorily affiliated to the industrial council which governs his particular (part of) industry or occupation. The recognized industrial council is a legal person; the boards of the industrial councils are composed on a bipartite basis by representatives of the specific industrial organisations for employers and employees.

Some industrial councils carry out their own administration. However 13 out of the 19 industrial councils have entrusted their administration to the Communal Administration Office (*Gemeenschappelijk Administratie-kantoor, GAK*), an association set up by the central organisations of employers and employees. The actual administration of the social security acts is then carried out by the regional *GAK offices*, supported by the head office. Nevertheless, the industrial councils remain responsible for their own policy and decisions.

Apart from the above employee insurance schemes, the industrial councils also administer, in view of the similarities with the corresponding employee insurance scheme, the general insurance scheme with respect to incapacity for work, as well as the Supplements Act (*Toeslagenwet, TW*); the allowances granted in the framework of this act supplement inadequate employee insurance benefits.

Where the granting of benefits is concerned, the general insurance schemes for the risks of old age, death and dependent children, are administered by the Social Insurance Bank (*Sociale Verzekeringsbank, SVB*). The *SVB* is a legal person under public law. It is composed on a tripartite basis: five members are appointed by the representative employer organisations, five by the representative employee organisations and five directly by the Minister for Social Affaires and Employment, two of whom are members of interest groups. The *SVB* operates with a system of district offices.
The collection of contributions for the general insurance schemes takes place via the Inland Revenue (*Rijksbelastingdienst*). Contributions are levied both through wage and income tax.

The granting of benefits within the framework of the sickness costs insurance schemes is encharged to the sickness funds (*Ziekenfondsen*), as well as, where it concerns the general insurance scheme against serious medical risks, private insurance companies and bodies which administer sickness costs schemes under public law.
The sickness funds are foundations or mutual societies which are recognized as such by the Minister. Their task is to ensure that insured people can succesfully claim medical benefits. For this purpose they conclude agreements with people or institutions which provide medical care. A reasonable degree of influence of the members over the boards of the Funds must be ensured.

The Communal Medical Service (*Gemeenschappelijke Medische Dienst GMD*) plays an important role in the administration of the invaldity insurance schemes. It is an advisory body for the industrial councils, and deals with matters of physical rehabilitation and determination of the degree of incapacity.

The complementary social services are financed out of general taxation. The distributive function for all the services, except for the *TW*, is encharged to the Courts of Mayor and Aldermen (*Colleges van Burgermeester en wethouders*) of the municipalities. In larger municipalities the administrative tasks have often been delegated to special commissions in which people other than members of the muncipal council may also sit. Decisions are prepared and implemented by a special civil servant or by the Municipal Social Service (*Gemeentelijke Sociale Dienst, GSD*).
The municipalities are controlled by the competent Ministers. It should also be mentioned that there are a number of advisory bodies both on a local or national level, some of which have been made obligatory by the statute.

186

A number of funds (of diverse importance) play a role in the governing of the finances of the various insurance schemes, for example the General Unemployment Fund for the unemployment insurance scheme.

Control over the administration of the insurance acts, except with regard to medical care, as well as over the administrative bodies concerned (including the funds and the *GMD*) is in the hands of the Social Insurance Council (*Sociale Verzekeringsraad, SVR*). The administrative bodies of the medical care insurance schemes are supervised by the Sickness Fund Council (*Ziekenfondsraad, ZFR*). The *SVR* consists of a chairman and an equal number of representatives of the government and the national employers- and employee organisations (tripartite composition). The *ZFR* is composed of five groups of seven members, appointed by the Minister and by the representative organisations of employers and employees, sickness funds and participants (medical practitioners etc.). Both are a legal person.

Apart from supervisory functions the *SVR* and the *ZFR* also carry out other administrative tasks. Thus the *SVR* can issue directives in the interest of a proper and coordinated administration. However, this power is seldomly used. Sometimes the *SVR* is entrusted with delegated legislative powers and sometimes it may act as a judicial body, especially in disputes concerning conscientious objections against social insurance and the affiliation of the employer to an industrial council. Also the *SVR* and *ZFR* carry out some advisory tasks. Sometimes the statute requires prior consultation with these bodies by the competent minister. These advisory activities mainly involve technical matters. Advice in policy matters is more the domain of the Social Economic Council (*Sociaal Economische Raad, SER*).
The *SVR* and the *ZFR* are responsible to the competent minister, who can issue guidelines regarding the performance of tasks.

The Minister for Social Affairs and Employment is competent both in the field of social insurance and in the field of complementary social services. The Minister for Welfare, Public Health and Culture is competent in the field of the medical care insurance schemes.

Finally, it must be pointed out that, apart from the administrative structure as determined in social security legislation (formal), there is also an organisational structure which is commonly referred to as informal. The informal structure includes certain associations within the administrative bodies e.g. the Federation of Industrial Councils (*Federatie van Bedrijfverenigingen, FBV*), the Association of Dutch Municipalities (*Vereniging van Nederlandse Gemeenten, VNG*), and the Association of Dutch Sickness Funds (*Vereniging van Nederlandse Ziekenfondsen, VNZ*). These are organisations under private law which have established themselves in practice. Their activities range from consultation and advise to the coordination of administrative policies. Notwithstanding their lack of power, they exercise considerable influence.

3. Personal scope of application.

As the personal scope of application constitutes the difference between the general insurance schemes and the employee insurance schemes, the two types of insurance will be dealt with separately.

People residing in the Netherlands, as well as people not resident in the Netherlands but who are subject to taxation with respect to work which is carried out within the Netherlands, are obligatorily insured for the general insurance schemes. This is the basic starting point.
Resident means every person who is living in the Netherlands. Whether or not a person lives in the Netherlands is a question of fact which is to be judged in the light of circumstances. The important question is whether someone has established a permanent link with the Netherlands, or whether this country constitutes the genuine centre of his personal activities.
Not resident but nevertheless insured for the general insurance schemes, are people who work in the Netherlands and for that reason are liable for wage and income tax.
Each general insurance act provides the possibility of derogation from the starting point by subordinate legislation. The extension and limitation of the personal scope of application of the general insurance schemes with regard to specific groups of people generally purports to draw a demarcation line between those, who, in view of their income, are subject to the Dutch general insurance schemes on the one hand, and to foreign schemes on the other.

The general insurance scheme with regard to the risks of old age, death and incapacity for work offers a limited possibility of voluntary insurance. Voluntarily insured people pay the same contributions and receive the same benefits as obligatorily insured people.

In discussing the personal scope of application of the employees insurance schemes we will pay separate attention to the insurance scheme for medical care. However, firstly we will discuss the sickness, invalidity and unemployment insurance schemes. The starting point is that each natural person, under the age of 65, who has a contract of service under public or private law, is obligatorily insured as an employee within the employee insurance scheme. People who carry out a contract of service abroad are not considered to be employees, unless they live in the Netherlands and their employers are likewise settled or resident in the Netherlands (or whose main seat of business or permanent representative is in this country).
A contract of service under private law is considered to be a relationship between the employee and the employer which exists on the grounds of a contract of employment within the meaning of the civil code. The courts which are competent in social security disputes will, more than the regular civil courts, disregard the legal status of a contract of service and judge the employment relationship in the light of the specific facts of the case. Three main criteria are considered essential, i.e. personal service, wage as a consideration for labour, and subordination to the authority of the employer.

188

Here too, there are exceptions to the fundamental starting point: the scope of application of all the statutes with respect to the employee insurance schemes is explicitly extended to a number of people who do not (or not easily) satisfy the fundamental criteria, for example travelling salesmen, apprentices and, subject to further conditions, home workers, musicians and artists. On the other hand, some people who do satisfy these criteria are excluded; here we mention especially civil servants.

According to the respective acts, those who are no longer employed under a contract of service are nevertheless treated as employees within the meaning of the employee insurance acts (e.g., those who receive sickness or unemployment benefit).

Subject to certain conditions relating to the minimum period of insurance, a person whose sickness or invalidity benefit has expired and who becomes incapable of work within a number of days (maximally one month) is nevertheless entitled to benefits on the basis of the employees insurance schemes (the so called aftereffect of insurance).

The three insurance acts also provide a (limited) opportunity for voluntary insurance.

In principle, the personal scope of application of the obligatory sickness costs insurance scheme for employees is the same as the one which applies for the sickness insurance scheme. The most important restriction is a corollary of the determination of the insurance wage limit: those, whose annual income arising out of one or more contract of employment exceeds a certain amount, are not obligatorily insured. Here also there are a number of extensions; thus, for example, railway personnel are also affiliated to the sickness fund.

The sickness costs insurance scheme provides an opportunity for joint insurance. Jointly insured are:
- the spouse of the insured person, if he or she belongs to the same household and the insured person is considered to be the breadwinner; subject to further conditions, the unmarried partner of the insured person is treated as a spouse;
- the natural and unmarried children and foster children of the insured person, for whom the insured person is the breadwinner, to the extent that children are younger than 16, 18, 21 or 27 years of age according to the case.

When a person is insured in the sickness costs scheme, he remains within it when retiring.

Insured people (both directly and jointly) belong to the personal scope of application of the sickness costs insurance scheme; however, if they want to make a claim on the basis of this scheme, they must be registered with a recognized sickness fund; this requirement is of a purely administrative nature.

The Netherlands is the only country in the European Community whose law contains provisions for people who have conscientious objections against insurance in general and consequently also against social insurance.

Those who have conscientous objections, of whatever nature, may be exempted from contribution liability for the general insurance schemes; however, they are liable to pay wage or income tax at the same rate as that applying for the general insurance contributions. If the risk covered by the general insurance scheme materializes, the conscientous objector is entitled to benefits; due to it's character only the old age insurance scheme knows a separate payment arrangement. There is a different arrangement for conscientous objections in the employee insurance schemes. Those with objections may be exempted from contribution liability. If the risk materializes, the insured person (and the jointly insured person) is not entitled to benefit.

In describing the personal scope of application of the complementary social services, we will only make some general remarks.
The coverage of the General Assistance Act (*ABW*) is very wide: any Dutch person in the Netherlands who is in such circumstances (or may be so in the near future) that he cannot meet the necessary costs of subsistence, is granted assistance by the municipality in which he resides. Furthermore, subject to further conditions, it is possible to provide assistance to Dutch people living abroad. Social assistance is also provided to foreign nationals who remain legally in the Netherlands.
The *ABW* has a general scope of application ,but it is possible to set up group schemes for certain categories of people. These have a categorical character; for example, there is a scheme for unemployed employees (unemployed is considered to be: any unemployed person whose subsistence depends upon employment under a contract of service and in respect of whom conditions may be imposed as to the performance of work under a contract of service for at least half of the normal working week), unemployed school leavers included.

The personal scope of application of the Supplements Act (*TW*) and the income scheme for elderly and unemployed employees, who are partially incapable of work (*IOAW*), follows the insurance scheme on which these are grafted. The scope of application of the income maintenance scheme for the elderly and formerly self-employed persons, who are partially incapable of work (*IOAZ*), reflects the image of the scope of the *IOAW*, but is for people who were previously self-employed.

4. Risks and benefits.

Before we deal with the various risks and benefits, we will first discuss a subject of a more general nature, namely, the level of income maintenance benefits. In the employees insurance scheme these are wage-related, in the general insurance schemes and in the complementary social services they are based upon the relevant social minimum, which is expressed as a percentage of the minimum wage.
The level of employee insurance benefits is expressed as a percentage of the daily wage of the insured person. Generally, the daily wage is the wage that

the person earned in the period immediately preceding the materialization of the risk. There are maximum daily wages; since the introduction of the *TW*, the minimum daily wages have been abolished.

In order to answer the question of how the daily wages are determined in practice, we need to consult the daily wage regulations, as implemented by the *SVR*. The system of the various daily wage regulations is largely identical. The wages which give rise to contribution liability (the contribution wages) constitute the basis for the calculation of daily wages. There are special rules for certain groups of employees, such as musicians, artists and seasonal workers.

The level of benefits from the general insurance schemes and complementary services are based upon the relevant social minimum. Except for some disregards, this implies that the beneficiary will be guaranteed a (net) income equal to:
- 100% of the net minimum wage for the beneficiary and his or her spouse (or 50% thereof for each of them);
- 90% of the net minimum wage for the beneficiary with a child younger than 18 years of age, who gives rise to entitlement to child benefit (single parent family);
- 70% of the net minimum wage for the unmarried beneficiary (single person).

In the *ABW* there is a special, lower social minimum at a level of 60% of the net minimum wage which is payable to the so called 'house sharers'. Generally speaking (exceptions disregarded), these are the beneficiaries who live in a house with one or more persons, not being the spouse of this person.

Every half year social benefits, the minimum wage and pensions must in principle be adjusted to wage developments within the market sector (indexing). The contribution wage limit is also linked to the index of wages.

In Dutch social security law (except for the widow pensions scheme) not married partners of the same or a different sex, constituting a stable common household, are in principle put on the same footing as married people.

4.1. Old age.

Every Dutch resident who attains the age of 65 is entitled to an old age pension. When a person has been resident in the Netherlands for 50 years, he is entitled to the full amount of pension, i.e. a monthly amount of 50%, 70% or 90% of the net minimum wage, depending upon whether he is married, single or the head of a single parent family. For each year in which one has not been insured or has culpably failed to pay contributions, there is a prorata reduction in the pension.

Married people with a partner who is below 65 years of age, are, subject to further conditions, entitled to a supplement which brings the benefit up to 100% of the net minimum wage. In such a case the income of the partner may not be in excess of a certain limit.

According to various legal techniques, in addition to the statutory old age pension, there is an occupational pension scheme for the majority of civil servants, employees and people carrying out a self-employed occupation

Generally the amount of this pension is related to the previously earned income from work, as well as to the length of time that a person has been affiliated to the occupational pension insurance scheme. The full occupational pension and the full statutory old age pension together often reach 70% of the last earned wages.

Sometimes employees and civil servants are offered the opportunity to retire before they attain pensionable age (65), i.e. from the age of 60, or sometimes even earlier. Those who accept this possibility may receive a preretirement pension (*VUT*) until they attain 65 years of age, at a level of 80%, 90%, or sometimes even higher, of the previously earned salary.

4.2. Death.

The death of a person may deprive the survivors of their income. The death of the insured person thus gives rise to entitlement to survivor's pension for widows (not for widowers) and full orphans. All women of 40 years or older are entitled to a widow's pension on the death of the insured person; younger women are only entitled to this pension if they have unmarried children, or are incapable of work. Widows who do not meet these conditions are only entitled to benefit on a temporary basis. Also unmarried divorced widows (pseudo-widows) are eligible for benefit. Benefits to widows are terminated when they attain 65 years of age; when a widow remarries she receives a lump sum. The widow's pension and the temporary widow's benefit amount to 70% of the net minimum wage; if the widow has a child under the age of 18 this is 100%. The level of orphan's pension depends upon the age of the orphan and is also related to the minimum wage.

As a result of a judgement by the Central Court of Appeal (*Centrale Raad van Beroep*) in 1988, widowers, subject to the same conditions as widows, may now claim survivor's pension. At this moment a new general survivor's pension act (*algemene nabestaandenwet/ANW*) is in preparation.

The occupational pension schemes usually provide benefits to the widows (but rarely widowers) of the participants. The amount is deducted from the amount of occupational retirement pension which the deceased person enjoyed or would have enjoyed. Sometimes there are schemes for divorced couples and, increasingly, for cohabiting partners.

Under most social insurance schemes death benefit is payable to the relatives of the beneficiaries under these schemes. As a rule, the level of the death benefit is equal to the previous benefit-entitlement of the deceased person, and covers the remaining days of the month in which death occurred, as well as a period of two months thereafter.

4.3. Incapacity for work.

There is an important difference between, on the one hand, temporary incapacity for work and, on the other hand, permanent incapacity. With regard to temporary incapacity for work, there is no general insurance scheme, but only a scheme for employees; with regard to permanent incapacity there is both a general insurance scheme and an employee insurance scheme.

The insured employee, who is not capable of carrying out his work due to illness, is entitled to sickness benefit. The concept of illness includes physical defects, pregnancy and birth (from six weeks before the birth to six weeks after the birth when there is irrefutable evidence of incapacity for work).
Sickness benefit is payable from the third day of incapacity for work, over a maximum period of one year. The first two days are waiting days; on grounds of the special waiting days decrees of the industrial councils there is often a right to benefit covering these days. Sickness benefit amounts to 70% of the gross daily wages of the insured person (subject to an upper wage limit); incapacity due to real or expected pregnancy gives rise to a benefit at a level of 100%.
The scheme described above is complemented by provisions under civil law, on the grounds of which the employer is obliged to continue wage payments during relatively short periods in case of illness of the employee; the payments must cover a period of at least six weeks and must be equal to the level of the minimum wage. On the basis of collective labour agreements, for the majority of employees, sickness benefit is supplemented up to 100% of the wage previously enjoyed.

Those who are completely or partially incapable of work are, after a waiting period of one year, entitled to invalidity benefit on the grounds of a general insurance scheme. Furthermore, employees are entitled to an invalidity benefit on the grounds of an employees insurance scheme. This latter insurance scheme offers employees a wage-related supplement to the benefit from the general insurance scheme.
A person is considered incapable of work if he, as a result of illness or a physical defect, is not able to earn an income from work, which his "stan-

dard man" would (theoretically) be able to earn, in the place where he is, or has been employed, or in the environment of that place. The standard man is the person in the same physical state as the person concerned, before his illness or physical defect occurred and with comparable education and experience. Only the theoretical earning capacity of the person is relevant: whether a person can actually obtain suitable employment is not taken into consideration.

In order to be eligible for invalidity benefit on the grounds of the general insurance scheme, a person must have earned an income from work in industry or from an occupation in the year preceding the moment that he became an invalid, or be early handicapped.

The level of the benefit on grounds of the general insurance scheme and the employees insurance scheme amounts to, respectively, a certain percentage of the gross minimum wage, and a percentage of the previously earned wages up to an upper wage limit. With a degree of incapacity of 80% or more, this percentage equals 70%. When the degree of incapacity is less than 15%, invalidity benefit is not payable; with a degree of incapacity between 15% and 25% no benefit is payable on grounds of the general insurance scheme, but on grounds of the employees insurance scheme benefit is payable at a level of 14% of the last earned wage (subject to an upper limit). The person who's degree of incapacity is at least 80% and who finds himself in an at least temporarily permanent state of helplessness that requires regular attendance and care, can be provided with a benefit of 100% of the gross minimum wage or previously earned wages.

Recently several statutory measures have been taken to reduce the (high) number of people having a benefit for incapacity for work. These measures encourage employers to keep or to have invalids and penalize employers whose employees become invalid.

The general insurance scheme in respect of incapacity for work does not only provide invalidity cash benefits, but also a number of benefits in kind for persons who are incapable or who are likely to prove so. Examples of such benefits are aids to maintain or to cure the capacity, or for the improvement of living conditions, and medical services (training, mobility services, family help, etc.).

4.4. Unemployment.

The employee who becomes unemployed is entitled to unemployment benefit, if he has worked at least 26 weeks in a period of 12 months immediately preceding his unemployment. The employee who has lost at least 5 or at least half of his normal working hours per week, who is not entitled to a continuation of his wages and who is able and willing to accept employment, is considered to be unemployed.

All beneficiaries of unemployment benefit receive income maintenance benefit for a period of half a year (basic benefit); this period may be extended by one or more periods of three months, if the beneficiary satisfies certain requirements with regard to his past employment record, i.e. he must have worked for at least 3 years in employment of at least 8 hours per week during the last 5 years. Periods, during which the person was entitled to the full amount of invalidity benefit, are taken into account, as are periods in which the person has taken care of children under the age of 6 (these are counted for 50%, if the children are between the ages of 6 and 12).

In determining the employment record, the 'actual' employment record over the last five years and the 'fictitious' employment record (this is the period between the eighteenth birthday and the day five years before the occurrance of unemployment) are added together. With an employment record of 5 years, the duration of the basic benefit is extended by three months, with an employment record of 10 years, the basic benefit is extended by half a year, and for each further period of five years, by another half year. Those with an employment record of 40 years or more are eligible for the maximum extension of four and a half years, implying a total duration of income maintenance benefit of five years.

When the period of income maintenance benefit has expired, those who satisfy the requirements with regard to their past employment record receive a 'continued' benefit for one year.

The income maintenance benefit amounts to 70% of the last earned wages (subject to an upper wage limit); the 'continued' benefit is equal to 70% of the minimum wage.

Some groups of unemployed people who are no longer entitled to unemployment benefit can claim complementary social services which guarantee an income equal to the level of the social minimum which is relevant for them (see section 4.7).

Unemployed people between 16 and 20 years of age, as well as unemployed school leavers up to the age of 26, who have been unemployed during half a year, are from 1.1.1992 onwards entitled to a job offer by a municipal service created to that effect (the Jeugdwerkgarantie Organisatie / JWGO). The employment lasts 6 months with the possibility of prologation with 6 more months. These people is paid the relevant minimum wage.

4.5. Medical care.

Employees and people treated as such, who are obligatorily insured on grounds of the sickness costs insurance scheme, are entitled to medical benefits in kind, provided that such benefits are not already covered by the general insurance scheme for serious medical risks. People who are jointly insured (usually the spouse and children) are also entitled to benefits. The package of benefits includes medical, curative, maternal, dental help, nursing in a hospital, ambulance services, home care and psychiatric treatment. Sometimes, a personal contribution is required from the claimant.

All residents are covered for the most serious health risks on grounds of the general insurance scheme, created for this purpose. The package of benefits includes treatment and nursing in an institution for the handicapped from the first day (e.g. nursing homes) and in psychiatric hospitals from the 366th day. Vaccinations and wheel chairs are also compensated for by the general insurance scheme for the length of stay in an institution. As a rule, a personal contribution is required from the claimant, which is sometimes dependent upon the ability to pay. Recently the package of benefits of the general scheme has been broudened (and accordingly the employee insurance's package reduced) in order to include also pharmaceutical help and (artificial) aids.

As mentioned before, the sickness funds themselves do not provide any benefits. The granting of benefits takes place via competent practitioners, for example doctors and dentists, as well as via recognized institutions, for example hospitals and nursing homes; the procedure for recognition is laid down in the statute. Agreements are concluded between the sickness funds on the one hand and those providing care on the other, or between their respective representative interest organisations. The statute contains a number of rules which inter alia provide a system of model agreements, deviation from which is only possible with the approval of the Sickness Fund Council. The tariffs which are agreed by the parties must be approved by the Central Body for Health Care Tariffs (*Centrale Orgaan Tarieven Gezondheidszorg*), established by the government.

4.6. Family.

Every person who is resident in the Netherlands is entitled to child benefit for his own children, his children through marriage and foster children for whom he cares or who are maintained by him, provided that they are under the age of 18.
A child younger than 18 years of age, not taking part in the household of the insured person, but financially depending upon him, counts for two children. Children of 18 years and older do in principle not open any right to child benefit, as they qualify themselves for study subvention, social assistance etc.
The amount of child benefit increases for each child within the family and with the age of the child. The former factor determines the basic amount of child benefit. Subsequently, 70% of the applicable basic amount is payable, if the child is under the age of 6; if the child is between the ages of 6 and 12 years 100% of the basic amount is payable; for children between the ages of 12 and 18 years the rate is 130%.

Entitlement to child benefit is determined quarterly.

4.7. Need.

Here we discuss a number of social security schemes which are designed to provide minimum subsistence to persons without sufficient means. These

196

schemes have in common the fact that the award of benefit is subject to a means test.

Every person who is in such circumstances (or may be so in the near future) that he cannot meet the necessary costs of subsistence, is awarded assistance. The level of the necessary costs of living (for those who do not stay in an institution) are laid down in statutory instruments and consist of a percentage of the net minimum wage. Here, it should be born in mind that benefit is payable on a family basis to married couples (with or without minor children) and to one parent families with minor children. Depending on whether benefit is awarded to married couples, one parent families, single persons, or a single person sharing a house, the level of benefit is 100% (or two times 50%), 90%, 70% or 60% of the net minimum wage. Derogation from these benefit levels is possible in special cases, now that social assistance should take into account the personal circumstances and the capacities of the beneficiaries. Special rules apply to those who reside in mental or physical institutions.

The municipalities managing social assistance are now obliged to claim back the costs of the granted assistance from the person, his partner or from persons liable for his maintenance, whenever this is possible according the law.

The beneficiary who is unemployed, and whose subsistence depends on labour under a contract of employment, receives assistance under the special scheme which has been set up for this purpose. The benefit levels correspond with those of the general assistance scheme, but the beneficiary's duties differ. School leavers under 21 years of age must satisfy a waiting period of half a year after they have finished their studies. No right to assistance exists for those who have not yet reached 18 years of age.
Special rules apply to the self-employed who have a business or carry out a profession and who are in need of assistance.
Apart from assistance for the 'general necessary costs of subsistence', subject to certain conditions, assistance may also be payable for 'special necessary costs of subsistence'. The benefit for the general necessary costs of subsistance should basicly cover all costs, including special expenses. Benefit is not necessarily in the form of free periodical or incidental payments, but can also take the shape of a loan or a security.

The legislator thought it desirable that some groups of people should be guaranteed a miminum of subsistence without having to rely upon the general assistance legislation and the extensive means test which is a characteristic of the *ABW*. At the present time, there are a number of special benefit schemes which offer a minimum income to certain groups whose income has fallen below the relevant social minimum, i.e.:
- beneficiaries under the employee insurance schemes and under the general invalidity insurance scheme;
- elderly and partially incapable unemployed employees; and
- elderly and partially incapable formerly self-employed people.

By virtue of the Supplements Act (*TW*) sickness benefit, unemployment benefit and invalidity benefit are, if necessary, supplemented up to the relevant social mimimum (corresponding to the levels applying to the general assistance scheme: 100%, 90% or 70% of the minimum wage, albeit that those under the age of 21 who are unmarried and living with their parents, are not entitled to any supplement. Benefit is subject to a means test.

The income scheme for elderly and partially incapable unemployed employees (*IOAW*) guarantees benefits on the level of the relevant social minimum (twice 50%, 90% or 70% of the net minimum wage) to:
- unemployed people under the age of 65 who became unemployed between the ages of 50 and 57.5 and whose right to continued unemployment benefit has expired;
- unemployed people, under the age of 65, who became unemployed after the age of 57.5 and who received income maintenance benefit but not a continued unemployment benefit;
- unemployed people, who became unemployed after their 50th birthday and whose right to unemployment benefit has fully expired, while they remained entitled to an invalidity benefit, calculated on the basis of a degree of incapacity of less than 80%;
- early-handicapped beneficiaries of invalidity benefit, calculated on the basis of a degree of incapacity of less than 80%.
  Benefit is subject to a means test.

The income scheme for elderly and partially incapable formerly self-employed people (*IOAZ*) contains an analogous arrangement for people under the age of 65 and their cooperating spouses, who were formerly dependent upon their own business or profession, subject to the condition that they either stopped their gainful activity before the age of 55, or stopped their activities as a result of incapacity for work on grounds of which there is entitlement to invalidity benefit, calculated on the basis of a degree of incapacity of less than 80%.

5. Financing.

At the present time, social insurance benefits are financed almost entirely out of contributions. The central government guarantees the payment of the benefits, in case it should appear that the funds do not possess sufficient means of financing.

The basis for charging contributions is the income (general insurance schemes) or the wage (employee insurance schemes) of the insured person, subject to upper limits. Nowadays employee insurance benefits and extra legal benefits also give rise to employee insurance contribution liability. In the sickness costs insurance scheme, employees pay next to a wage-related contribution a nominal contribution to the sickness fund they are affiliated to.

The contribution rates are set periodically by the competent Minister or by the administrative body, sometimes subject to the approval of the former. The rates normally apply for the whole country. However, for sickness and umemployment insurance they differ per branch of industry, depending on the "weight" of the risk. The contribution rates are set annually in respect of the expected expenditure in the next year (pay as you go); with regard to some schemes the creation of a reserve is required, but in fact the funds of other schemes equally maintain reserves.

The employers pay their own contributions, as well as those of their employees (both for the employee- and the general insurance scheme), to the competent administrative body. For this purpose they deduct the amount due by the employees from the wage of the latter. The division of contributions between employers and employees is obligatory prescribed by law. Employers contributions only exist for the employee social insurance schemes. As previously employers also had to pay part of the general insurance contribution of their employees, they now pay their employees a "transfert allocation" (*overhevelingstoeslag*) in order to compensate for the increased contributory burden supported by the employees. The employer bears the financial risk of a wrong judgment as to the insurance obligation of the employee.

The self-employed and other insured people pay all general insurance contributions themselves, provided their income exceeds the minimum limit.
As a result of recent changes, the state nowadays pays the contributions in respect of the child benefit scheme.
The contributions which are collected are normally transferred to the funds created by the various social security schemes.

The complementary social services are financed entirely out of general means, which are brought under the yearly budgets of the central and local governments. Most complementary social services are financed by the central government; this is 100% the case for the *TW*, while the costs of the *ABW*, the *IOAW* and the *IOAZ* are born for 10% by the municipalities.

6. Judicial review.

Those who want to contest decisions in the area of the employee insurance schemes and the *TW*, or in the area of the general insurance schemes, must appeal to the Appeal Court (*Raad van Beroep, RvB*), and further to the Central Appeal Court (*Centrale Raad van Beroep, CRvB*) (administrative jurisdiction).
The *RvB* consists of three members, one of whom is a lawyer appointed for life by the Crown and the other two laymen appointed for six years on the nomination of employer and employee organisations. There are 10 Appeal Courts, each of which is competent in a certain region. The *CRvB* consists exclusively of three lawyers, who are appointed for life.

199

However, from July 1st, 1992 the *RvB* are abolished and replaced by the Section Administrative Law of the arrondissemental tribunals ('*Sector Administratief Recht' van de arrondissementsrechtbank*).

This means social security cases will be heard by a single, professional judge; provisionally the appeals procedure has remained uncharged. The *CRvB* has been maintained.

In order to contest a decision before the *RvB* (the arrondissemental tribunal), such decision must have the status of 'subject to appeal' (*voor beroep vatbaar*). In order to appeal against a refusal to grant benefits in kind or a compensation on grounds of the insurance schemes for medical care, prior application for a non-binding recommendation of the Sickness Fund Council is required, 30 days after a 'decision subject to appeal has been received.

The judges of the administrative jurisdiction have to judge whether or not the contested decision is compatible with the law. The procedure is almost entirely free from procedural requirements and there is no obligatory representation. In this way it is attempted to promote access to justice.

The so-called 'permanent-expert procedure' is a special procedure which should be followed in a number of statutorily determined disputes of a medical nature. Here, the judge relies heavily upon the opinion of the permanent expert, who is a general practitioner. The procedure normally ends with a reasoned decision of the chairman, which, in principle, is not subject to appeal.

Disputes concerning contribution liability for the general insurance schemes are subject to the judicial procedure for income taxes, respectively wage taxes. This procedure will not be discussed.

No specialised machinery exists for the settlement of disputes concerning the complementary social services (except for the *TW*). There is merely a general administrative review procedure. This implies that the case is referred to a higher (political) administrative body, i.e. the excecutives of the provinces (*Gedeputeerde Staten, GS*), with a possibility of further appeal to the Crown.

Crown appeals are dealt with by the Department for Administrative Disputes of the Council of State (*Afdeling Geschillen van Bestuur*). However, the role of this body has been altered. In order to comply with the requirements formulated by the European Court of Human Rights, the *Afdeling Geschillen van Bestuur* has changed from an advisory body into a judicial body; the grounds on which the validity of decisions are judged are the same as those which apply for the regular administrative courts.

Disputes concerning industrial councils to which an employer is affiliated, as well as disputes concerning the recognition of conscientious objections against social insurance are dealt with by the *SVR*.

In case a beneficiary has grievances not so much about the contents of a decision, but about the attitude (activities or lack of any activity) of an administrative body, he can lodge a complaint with the complaint commission of the *SVR* or of the *ZFR*, depending on the case.

The civil court, more specifically the president of the high court in immediate judgment, may play a role in cases in which there is no jurisdiction for the administrative courts. For example, the civil court is competent if an administrative body does not implement a judgment of the appeal court. The civil court can use means of coercion to force parties to comply with a judgement.

Judgments of the *CRvB*, as well as judgments of the Court of Appeal in matters of contribution liability for the general insurance schemes, are open to cassation to the Supreme Court, but only in so far as the disputes concern the interpretation of concepts like 'wage', resident'..etc. Here the legislator has aimed to establish a uniform interpretation throughout the entire body of social security and tax law.

Chapter 11: Portugal

1. Introduction: concept and sources of social security law.

Social security (*segurança social*) is a relatively new concept in Portugal. The use of the term social security constitutes an expression of the transition from the dichotomy 'social assistance/social insurance', connected with the corporative state, to social security as a leading principle of the social constitutional state. Thus, the starting point for our treatise on social security in Portugal can only, be article 63 Constitution, which provides in it's first paragraph: "All people are entitled to social security" and which specifies in it's fourth paragraph: "The social security system must protect citizens in case of sickness, old age, invalidity, widowhood, orphanage, unemployment and in all other cases of a loss or reduction of the means of subsistence or of the ability to work".
Within this meaning, the term social security refers to contributory and non-contributory schemes which provide cash benefits, together often referred to as social security in the narrow sense, and the forms of social protection organised by benefits and schemes for children and young persons, as well as for the elderly and the handicapped. These benefits are often collectively described by the term social action. The benefits from social security in the narrow sense, provide subjective rights to beneficiaries; subjective rights to (certain forms of) social action are not recognized.

The contributory schemes provide:
- family benefits. The following family benefits exist: family allowances, birth benefit, nursing benefit, benefit for the care of sick minors, marriage benefit, maternity benefit (also for fathers), adoption benefit and the pension addition for the dependent spouse;
- benefits in respect of a temporary loss of income due to sickness or unemployment, i.e. sickness benefit, tuberculosis benefit, two unemployment benefits (an insurance benefit and a social benefit) and compensation in respect of occupational diseases;
- benefits in respect of old age or invalidity, i.e. old age pension, invalidity pension, pension additions in respect of severe invalidity and pension for occupational diseases;
- benefits for specific needs of handicapped people i.e the supplementary allowance for young handicapped people, special education benefit, monthly annuity benefit, invalidity pension, the pension allowance for severe invalidity and a benefit for the assistance needed from a third person;
- benefits in respect of death, i.e. funeral benefit, death benefit and the survivor's pension.

There are non-contributory schemes which guarantee a minimum protection to each person who finds himself in a social-economic position of need and who has not paid any or insufficient contributions. These are:

- social invalidity and old age pensions;
- pension additions for severe invalidity;
- family allowances and other family benefits;
- an integration benefit for youngsters between the ages of 18 and 25 in search of a first employment;
- widower's/widow's pension; and
- orphan's pension.

As mentioned, the Portuguese concept of social security, in its broad sense, also encompasses organised forms of social action to the advantage of young people, elderly and handicapped persons. These include child care facilities, leisure centres and protected housing for elderly.

The right to health care is autonomous from the right to social security and does not depend upon the link to the social security system. The National Health Service is universal and general, covering all residents.
Also the work injuries are not yet included in the social security system. The protection belongs to the employers who may transfer their responsability to the insurance companies.
However, the main act concerning social security of 1984 provides for the future integration of work injuries into the general social security scheme.

The Portuguese constitution of 1976 which is based upon the revolution of the 25th of April 1974 and reviewed in 1982 and in 1989, lays down the framework within which social security within Portugal was to develop. Apart from article 63 (concerning social security as such) and 64 (concerning health care), also articles 67 to 72 Constitution are relevant here; the latter provisions are dedicated respectively to the family, maternity, children, young persons, handicapped persons and retirement persons.
The most important sources of Portuguese social security law are the formal statute (adopted by parliament) and the decree (originating from the government); both sources have equal legal value. According to article 168, (n° 1, sub f) Constitution the determination of the principles of the social security system and the national health care service belong to the relative legislative competence of parliament; in other words this subject matter falls under the domain of the statute, unless parliament empowers the government to enact legislation in this area.

The main act concerning statutory social security announces special provisions concerning supplementary schemes of statutory social security, which would be introduced in order to provide a better coverage of the social risks which are already covered by social security or in order to provide social protection of risks which are not yet covered by social security.
In the past there has already been a lot of support for a codification of the various legislative measures in one social security statute. The main statute regarding social security (act number 28/84 of 1984) constitutes a first step in this direction.

2. Administrative organisation.

The administrative organisation of social security is laid down in the second and third paragraphs of art. 63 Constitution:
"2. It is the responsibility of the government to organise, co-ordinate and subsidize a unified and decentralised social security system, with the participation of the unions, the other organisations representing employees and the representative associations of the beneficiaries themselves.
3. There is a right to establish non-profit private institutions of social solidarity which pursue the objectives of social security (expressly mentioned with reference to the relevant articles of the constitution), which are allowed and which are regulated by the statute and are subject to the control of the State".
It appears that the organisation of social security is characterized by: unity of the system, decentralisation and participation.

The intended organic unification of social security and the integration of the various existing social security systems in the general system have still to be completed.

The administrative organisation of social security is decentralised. There are three levels of organisation: the central bodies, the regional bodies and the local bodies.
On the central level there are the general directories under the responsibility of the Minister for Employment and for Social Security, through the Secretary of State for Social Security, unemployment schemes, fall under the domain of the department for employment and vocational training of the Secretary of State for Employment of the same Ministry.

Apart from these services which are integrated in the central administration, there are also on a central level:
- the department for international relations and social security conventions (*Departemento de relaçoes internacionais e convençoes de segurança social*);
- the Institute for the financial Administration of Social Security (*Instituto de gestão financeira da segurança social*);
- the National Pension Centre (*Centro nacional de pensoes*), which is not only concerned with pensions but also with the data banks of social security; and
- The National Centre for Protection against Professional Risks.
  (this body does not function yet, its tasks are still carried out by the National Insurance Fund for occupationnal diseases).

These four bodies have a legal person status and enjoy administrative and financial autonomy.

The actual administration of social security is entrusted to the regional social security centres (*Centros regionais de segurança social, C.R.S.S.*), which are legal people under public law and autonomous from the central government. The latter retains administrative control; the *C.R.S.S.* are obliged to follow the orientations and general guidelines of the central administration.

All or almost all contact between social security and the citizen, takes place via the *C.R.S.S.* within the district of the citizen. The *C.R.S.S.* are governed by a board of directors, set up by the state department for social security. These directors ask advise about the matters which are of importance for the administration of the *C.R.S.S.* of their Regional Social Security Council (*Conselho regional de segurança social*), consisting of representatives of the local authorities, the unions, the employers and the governing boards of private social security institutions. Within each *C.R.S.S.* there is a commission for the verification of cases of permanent incapacity for work, as well as an appeals commission. The system of control over permanent incapacity for work (*S.V.I.P.*) serves both the contributory and the non-contributory invalidity scheme, the allowance scheme for severe invalidity and in certain cases also the pension scheme for survivors.

The *C.R.S.S.* have local points of contact to which insured people can turn within their immediate environment.

On a regional level, although separate from the *C.R.S.S.*, there are regional employment centres, which, together with the *C.R.S.S.* are responsible for the administration of the two schemes for unemployment.

A whole range of non-profitmaking private institutions of social solidarity, work together with the *C.R.S.S.* in the field of social action. The *C.R.S.S.* cooperate with and supervise these institutions.

The administrative organisation of social security is characterized by participation. The right to participation is recognized for (organisations of) employers, employees and beneficiaries. This consultative participation of the employers and employees takes place both on a national level, within the National Council of Social Security and on a regional level within the *C.R.S.S.*

The public organisation of health care, which, as already mentioned, is strictly speaking not part of the social security system, is entrusted to the National Health Service (*Serviço Nacional de Saúde*) under the Ministry for Health.

The evaluation of medical criteria throughout the different schemes has been coordinated between the Ministry for Health and the Ministry for Social Security.

The work injuries insurance scheme is administrated by private insurance companies and is supervised by the Minister of Finance.

3. Personal scope of application.

We have seen above that article 63 of the Portuguese constitution proclaims the universality of social security. However this does not alter the fact that the compulsory contributory schemes of social security only cover people and their families who carry out, or who have carried out, paid work. Traditionally, contributory social security encompassed a general scheme and various special schemes.

Nowadays, and according to the main act, Portugese social security consists of the general social security system (the contributory scheme) and the non contributory system.
The general social security system covers, compulsorily, the employed and self-employed people in agriculture, trade, industry and services of the private sector of activity. The general system also includes the voluntary social insurance, open to people who exercice an activity not covered by the compulsory system nor by another system of social protection.
Special systems exist covering the civil servants and the military.

Unless it is otherwise stated, we will deal only with the compulsory general scheme here after.

The non-contributory social security scheme protects all persons who do not fall under a contributory scheme; but not all risks are covered.

If we were to try to give an overview of the personal scope of application of the various schemes, we would arrive at the following summary. Each person carrying out work on account of another person as well as the selfemployed, are covered by the schemes for sickness, maternity, paternity and adoption benefits, by the old age and invalidity pensions and by the dependent spouse addition; these people also give rise to entitlement to death benefit and survivor's benefit for the surviving relatives.
Only people carrying out work on account of another person are covered by the schemes of occupational diseases benefits, by the benefit scheme for assistance to sick minors, by the unemployment benefit scheme and by the social unemployment benefits.
Self-employed people may be covered by the scheme of occupational diseases benefits if they want so.

Family benefits are granted to two large groups of beneficiaries, i.e.:
a) people who are active, retired or unemployed for less than twelve months, as well as their spouses; and
b) people not covered by any social security scheme, and whose monthly income does not exceed 40% of the national minimum wage or whose family income per capita' does not exceed 30% of this national minimum wage.

Both categories are equally covered by the supplementary allowance scheme for young handicapped persons, by the nursing benefit scheme and by the special education benefit scheme.
Only people mentioned under a) are insured for birth, marriage, funeral and monthly annuity benefits. Only people mentioned under b) receive orphan's benefit.

The social pension covers all Portuguese citizens (and people treated as such) who are resident in Portugal, do not fall under another contributory social security scheme, or who, although affiliated to a scheme, do not fully satisfy the relevant contribution requirements for entitlement to a contributory pension and whose monthly income does not exceed 30% of the national minimum wage if alone, or 50% of the same wage for a couple. People in receipt of an invalidity, old age or survivor's pension from the contributory scheme, may also receive a (supplementary) social pension, if the amount of the contributory pension is lower than that of the social pension.

The pension allowance in respect of severe invalidity may be granted to any beneficiary of an invalidity, old age or survivor's pension, the beneficiaries of social pensions included.

All residents are covered by the national health service.

Each person working on account of another person is covered by the industrial injuries insurance scheme of his employer.

4. Risks and benefits.

Old age-, survivors- and invalidity pensions under the non-contributory as well as the contributory scheme, are, as a rule, revalued once a year by decree. The mechanism of adjustment of benefit rate applies also for the other benefits which are flat-rate, and for family benefits. The permanent compensations for professional risks are also adjusted by government decree.

4.1. Old age.

There are two old age pension schemes, i.e old age pension under the contributory scheme and the social old age pension.

Contributory old age pension (*pensâo de velhice*) is payable to people who have paid contributions during at least 120 months and who have attained 62 years of age in respect of women and 65 years of age in respect of men. The amount of old age pension is equal to as many times 2.2% of the average wage over the five most favourable years during the preceding ten active years as there are years of contributions. There is a minimum pension. Old age pension may be accumulated with a salary; this salary gives rise to contribution payments and the pension is increased by 2% per extra year of activity.

The beneficiary of an old age pension with a spouse, whose income is lower than a statutory limit, is entitled to an dependent spouse addition. The possible income of the spouse is deducted from the allowance.

Social old age pension (*pensão social*) is only payable to people with a monthly income not in excess of 30% of the national minimum wage or not in excess of 50% thereof in cases where the pension is granted to a (head of a) family. Social old age pension is only payable from the age of 65.

4.2. Death.

Death benefits within the broad meaning of the word may be divided into funeral benefit, death benefit and the survivor's benefit as well as, within the non-contributory schemes, widower's pension and orphan's pension. Furthermore special benefits exist for death which was due to a work injury or an occupational disease.

Funeral benefit (*subsidio de funeral*) is payable on the death of the worker or retired person, his spouse or his descendant who gave rise to entitlement to family allowance, or the ascendant of the insured person or of his spouse, provided that they were dependent upon the insured person or upon his/her spouse. All these benefits are flat-rate and payable to those who have supported the funeral charges.

Death benefit (*subsidio por morte*) is in principle due to the same people as those qualifying for a survivor's pension (see hereafter); however, the death benefit is payable without the requirement of a minimum qualifying period. Death benefit consists of a lump sum payment equal to a half year's average wage of the two most favourable years during the preceding five insured years of the deceased person. The surviving spouse receives at least 50% of this amount when benefit is also payable to descendants. A supplement is paid to severely disabled people who are permanently incapacitated for work and require constant attendance from a third person.

Survivor's pension (*pensão de sobrevivência*) is payable, on the condition that the deceased person has paid contributions for at least 36 months to:

- the surviving spouse and, under certain conditions, the surviving ex-spouse;
- the descendants or people treated as such who are less than 18 years of age, or who give rise to entitlement to family allowance; and
- other relatives and people treated as such who were dependent upon the deceased person.

The above people receive a percentage of the pension that the deceased person would have received if he had been an invalid at the moment of his death. The percentage varies according to the category to which the surviving beneficiary belongs (60% for the spouse, 20% for one child, 30% for two children and 40% for three or more children).
If the survivor is a widow she is entitled to survivor's pension on the condition that she:

- was married to the deceased person for at least one year, unless there are children from the marriage or unless the death was due to an injury; and
- is at least 35 years old; if she is younger the duration of the pension is limited to five years, unless the widow has dependent children or suffers permanent incapacity for work.

The widow loses her survivor's pension if she remarries.

If the survivor is a widower, he is only entitled to survivor's pension if he is at least 65 years old or suffers permanent incapacity for work. Divorced and separated spouses who fulfil the above conditions are entitled to survivor's pension if, as rarely happens, she received alimony from the deceased person.

The rate of calculation of survivor's pension for orphans of the father/mother varies, depending upon whether the pension is granted to one, two or more children who are not older than 18 years (increased to 21 or 24 in case of secondary or higher education); there is no age limit with respect to permanent and complete incapacity for work. The amount of pension is doubled if the insured person does not leave behind a spouse or ex spouse.

Together, the total amount of the survivor's pensions may not exceed 100% of the amount of reference.

Widow(er)'s pension (*pensão de viuvez*) is granted to the surviving spouse of the person who received a social pension. The beneficiary of the widow(er)'s pension may not be entitled to another pension and must satisfy the means test for a social pension. The widow(er)'s pension amounts to 60% of the social pension.

The orphan's pension (*pensão de orfandade*) is a non-contributory pension which, subject to a means test, is payable to orphans until they come of age (18 years old or earlier if the child is no longer dependent upon a guardian). The amount of pension is calculated on the basis of the same percentages as those for the survivor's pension for descendants, but as the basis of calculation it takes into account the social pension rate.

There are derogating rules if death was due to an industrial injury or an occupational disease. In these cases survivor's benefit is payable to:
- the widow of the deceased person, at a level of 30% of the basis of calculation. This benefit is only payable until the widow attains the age of 65; after that it is only payable in case of physical or mental sickness of the widow;
- the widower of the deceased person, at the same level as above, but subject to the condition that the marriage took place prior to the injury and that the beneficiary suffers from a physical or mental sickness which reduces his capacity for work, or that the beneficiary is older than 65 years of age at the moment of death;
- the ex-spouse of the insured person, subject to the condition that he was entitled to an alimony pension and that he satisfies the same conditions as

the spouse; if so, the same amount is payable as that to a widow or widower, although the amount is never higher than the amount of the alimony pension;
- the orphan of the mother or father, i.e. respectively 20, 40 or 50% of the basis of calculation for one, two or more children until they attain the age of 18 years of age (21 or 24 in case of secondary or higher education; there is no age limit in cases where the child is permanently fully incapacitated);
- the orphan of the father or mother, i.e. respectively 40, 80 or 100% of the basis of calculation for one, two or more children under the same conditions as for the orphan of the father or mother, but subject to a total amount of 70% of the previous salary of the victim;
- the dependent parents or ascendants of the insured person, i.e. 15% of the basis of calculation for each ascendant younger than 65 years of age for a man or 62 years of age for a woman and 20% of the basis of calculation for these ages on, or if they suffer a physical or mental sickness which makes them incapable of work. If there is a spouse or orphan who is equally entitled to a pension, each ascendant receives 10% of the basis of calculation.

It is provided that the total benefits paid to beneficiaries may never exceed 80% of the basis of calculation.

There is also a benefit for funeral costs, amounting to thirty days wages; the amount of this benefit is doubled with respect to possible transportation of the deceased person.

4.3. Incapacity for work.

The insured person, who suffers temporary incapacity for work, is entitled to sickness benefit (*subsidio por doença*), subject to the condition that he:
- can demonstrate that he carried out paid work during at least six months, as well as during at least twelve days, in the four months preceding the determination of the incapacity; or
- if he is self-employed, can demonstrate that he has paid contributions over a period of six months.

Sickness benefit amounts (in general) to 65% of the average daily wage during the first six months prior to the second month preceding the beginning of the incapacity, and to 70% of this reference salary after a continuous period of 365 days of incapacity for work.

The first three days of incapacity for work of paid workers and the first sixty days of incapacity for work of the self-employed are waiting days and thus do not give rise to entitlement to benefit.

This benefit is payable during a maximum period of 1095 days.

If incapacity for work is due to tuberculosis the duration of benefit is unlimited and benefit amounts to 80 or 100% of the reference wage, depending upon the individual case.

Maternity benefit (*subsidio de maternidade*) is payable to female employees who are temporarily prevented from working due to a birth or an abortion. The conditions of benefit are similar to those with respect to sickness benefit. Maternity benefit amounts to 100% of the average income from work that would be considered when calculating sickness benefit. Maternity benefit is payable for 90 days, at least 60 of which being after the birth; in case of abortion or a stillbirth maternity benefit is payable for a maximum of 30 days; in case of the death of a child who was born alive, benefit is payable for at least 30 days, to be counted from the date of the birth.

To insured self-employed men and male wage corners, paternity allowance (*subsidio de paternidade*) may be granted during 30 or 60 days, not immediately after child-birth, in case of physical or mental incapacity of the mother.

If the mother dies within the period of 90 days, the father is entitled to the allowance for the period the mother would still have been entitled to it. This period cannot be inferior to 10 days.

Paternity benefit amount, to the reference salary of the first 6 months preceding the second one, prior to the risk.

There is a minimum amount of 5% of the minimum salary valid for the worker's sector of activity.

With respect to the risk of permanent incapacity for work there is a distinction between invalidity pension and the allowance for severe invalidity. The social invalidity pension belongs to the domain of the non-contributory social security system.

Invalidity pension (*pensão de invalidez*) is payable to an insured person who has paid contributions for at least 60 months and, for reasons of health (which are not the result of a work injury or an occupational disease), finds himself permanently incapable of carrying out his occupation. The employee who can no longer earn one third of his normal income from work, and who has not attained pensionable age, is (immediately) considered to be invalid. Also those who, after three years of incapacity, can no longer earn 50% of the normal income are considered to be permanently incapable of work. The incapacity for work must be determined by the *S.V.I.P.* of the *C.R.S.S.* The amount of invalidity pension and minimum invalidity pension is calculated in the same way as old age pension. Here too there is the possibility of entitlement to a dependent spouse addition. Invalidity pension is converted into an old-age pension after the pensioner has reached the retirement age. It should be mentioned that there is no scale of degrees of incapacity; a person is either invalid or not invalid.

Social pension is only payable to people with a monthly income which does not exceed 30% of the national minimum wage, or 50% thereof with respect to a head of a household. Social invalidity pension is payable to those who are at least 18 years of age and are recognized to be unfit for full-time work and who are not covered by a contributory scheme. Social pension is flat-rate.

The pension allowance for severe invalidity (*suplemento de pensão de grande inválido*) is granted to the beneficiary of an invalidity, old age, survivor's or social pension, in respect of whom the medical advisors are of the opinion that he is incapable of carrying out any work and is in need of the constant assistance of a third person. The allowance is paid in addition to the pension. The allowance varies according to whether it is payable as an addition to invalidity or old age pension, on a survivor's pension or on a social pension.

A number of social secrity benefits are concerned with the specific needs of handicapped people, i.e the supplementary allowance for young handicapped people, special education benefit, the lifetime monthly benefit, the, invalidity pension and the allowance for severe invalidity. The latter two benefits have already been dealt with.

The supplementary allowance for young handicapped people (*abono complementar a crianças e jovens deficientes*) is payable to people below the age of 24, who satisfy the entitlement conditions under the non-contributory scheme or who are dependent upon a person insured under the contributory scheme, on the condition that the child cannot maintain himself, that he attends a special education institution and that he needs individual therapeutic treatment.
The level of supplementary allowance for young handicapped people varies according to whether the person is less than fourteen years of age, between fourteen and seventeen years of age or between eighteen and twenty four years of age. The allowance may not overlap with the special education benefit.

Special education benefit (*subsidio de educacão especial*) is payable to handicapped people below 25 years of age who fulfil the entitlement conditions under the non-contributory scheme and to the descendants of persons who are treated as insured workers, who follow forms of specialized education. The benefit covers the costs of special education, subject to a personal contribution of the family of the handicapped person. This personal contribution is determined in relation to the costs of the special education and the financial position of the family. The special education benefit may not overlap with the supplementary allowance for young handicapped people nor with the monthly annuity benefit.

A lifetime monthly benefit (*subsidio mensal vitalicio*) is payable to descendants and people insured under the contributory scheme and person treated as such, on the condition that the descendants are at least 24 years of age and satisfy one of the conditions mentioned for the supplementary allowance for young handicapped people; the beneficiaries may not be entitled to an invalidity pension or to a social pension.

If the incapacity for work is due to a work injury or an occupational disease, different provisions apply. A benefit for total temporary incapacity is paid provided that the victim is undergoing medical treatment or rehabilitation therapy. The benefit is calculated on the basis of 80% of the lost wages which exceed the national minimum for the applicable branch of industry (= basis of calculation). The victim receives two thirds of the basis of calculation. However, the victim only receives one third of this amount in the first three days following the injury, when he is admitted into hospital or when the medical costs and maintenance are borne by the responsible institution, again except if there are people dependent upon the claimant.

In case of work injury, the degree of permanent incapacity is determined by the labour courts and in case of occupational disease by either the labour courts or by the national fund of the occupational diseases insurance scheme. The degree of incapacity can be reviewed on the initiative of the competent institution or of the victim himself.

The basis of calculation for the pensions is determined in the same way as for temporary incapacity; however, if the incapacity is less than 50%, the basis of calculation is reduced to 70% of the lost wages which exceed the national minimum wage for the person's branch of industry.

In case of permanent incapacity for all work, an annuity pension is payable at the level of 80% of the basis of calculation. In case of permanent incapacity for the usual work, the annuity pension varies between one half and two thirds of the basis of calculation, according to the degree of the remaining capacity to carry out another suitable occupation. In case of permanent partial incapacity, the annuity pension amounts to two thirds of the basis of calculation.

If the victim requires the assistance of a third person, the amount of pension is increased by 25% (subject to an upper limit). If the victim is completely permanently incapable of carrying out any work, his annuity pension is increased by 10% of the basis of calculation (subject to an upper limit) for each dependent family member.

There are special provisions which allow a person to pay off certain pensions on the request of the pensioner or the competent institution. Paying off is compulsory if the degree of invalidity is equal to or lower than 10% and if the amount of benefit does not exceed a certain percentage of the national minimum wage.

A pension for permanent incapacity may be enjoyed together with a new salary.

4.4. Unemployment

On grounds of the contributory scheme, full or part-time employees are entitled to unemployment benfit (*subsidio de desemprego*) if they satisfy the following conditions. They must
- be involuntarily unemployed;
- be fit for work;
- be available and willing to work;
- be registered as a candidate for work with the Employment Center of his area;
- have been employed for 540 days within a period of 24 months immediately prior to the date of unemployment.

The amount of the unemployment benefit is equal to that of sickness benefit; however there is a lower and an upper limit. Unemployment benefit may not exceed three times the national minimum wage of the insured person's branch of industry.

Unemployment benefit is payable for 10 to 30 months, depending upon the age of the claimant (minimum for those under 25 years of age; maximum for those over 55 years of age).

Full-time employees are entitled to social unemployment benefit (*subsidio social de desemprego*) if they fulfil the following conditions. They must
- have worked and paid contributions for the general contributory scheme of social security for at least 180 in the lost 12 months;
- be involuntarily unemployed;
- find themselves in a situation of economic need; and
- have reached the end of the period in which the unemployment benefit was granted and have remained unemployed.

Thus all employees who have exhausted their right to contributory unemployment benefit or do not fulfil the relevant conditions with respect to previous periods of work and contributions are entitled to social unemployment benefit.

Social unemployment benefit amounts to a certain percentage of the national minimum wage for the employee's branch of industry, i.e.
- 100% for employees with six or more dependent persons;
- 90% for employees with three, four or five dependent persons;
- 80% for employees with no to three dependent persons; and
- 70% for employees with no dependent persons.

However, the amount of social unemployment benefit may never exceed the average wage of the employee, as it is calculated for sickness benefit. The amount of social unemployment benefit is reduced by 20% for the last 90 days in which the beneficiary is entitled to benefit.

The daily amount of this benefit is calculated in function of the highest minimum salary and calculated as follows:
- 100% for employees with at least four or more dependant people;
- 90% for employees with one to three dependant people;
- 70% for employees with no dependant people.

The benefit is due for the same period of time as the unemployment benefits, except when it is following the paiment of such an unemployment benefit. In the latter case the period of payment of the social unemployment benefit equals half the period of payment of the unemployment benefit.

4.5. Medical care.

There is a national health service in Portugal. No fees need to be paid for medical services. There is freedom of choice of physician between the general practitioners and specialists of the health centres and the recognized physicians. The government has introduced a variable personal contribution. Beneficiaries of invalidity pension, old age pension, survivors pension or those entitled to benefit on the grounds of the occupational diseases insurance scheme (for permanent incapacity of at least 50%), as well as their spouses and minor children, are not required to pay any personal contribution regarding consultations with a physician, treatment in a public hospital or a health centre, or treatment by a recognized physician. A similar exemption applies for pregnant women and their babies below one year of age, for persons with certain young dependent handicapped persons, and for certain categories of socially and economically vulnerable persons.

Physicians working for the national health service are either civil servants of the regional health boards, or civil servants of the hospitals. The physicians may also have remained self-employed, but recognized on the grounds of an agreement between the order of physicians and the Ministery of Health. The latter doctors may be consulted by people who cannot reach an official health centre within a specific time for reasons of distance. The physicians-civil servants receive a salary, the amount of which is determined by the government and which varies according to the occupational category of the physician. The recognized physicians receive a flat-rate sum per consultation.

Entry into public hospitals as well as into health institutions approved by the Minister of Health, is also free of charge. No personal contributions towards the costs are required for care in a public ward, nor for care in a private room if this was prescribed by the physician. Entry into private hospitals and clinics is also free if the public hospitals cannot offer the required health care within three months.

Both dental and medical care are provided within health centres. If a private, approved dentist is consulted, the fee may be reimbursed according to a tariff determined by the government.

Depending upon the type of the disease the claimant must pay between 20% and 50% of the costs of medicine which appears on an official health service list. No personal contribution is required from the beneficiary if he suffers from a certain disease. A personal contribution of 20% is required for artificial aids which appear on the official list. For optical and dental aids prescribed by a health centre, a personal contribution of 25% is required. If the optical and dental aids are prescribed by a recognized private specialist, the beneficiary must pay the full price and the health service will offer a refund of 75%.

Transport costs of are only reimbursed to sick people who live in a remote district and even then only under certain conditions.

Health care with respect to victims of an industrial injury or an occupational disease is financed in the former case by a private insurance company and in the latter by the national health service. No personal contributions are required from the victim.

It seems necessary to mention that the system of health care, as described above, presupposes an ideal situation more than it reflects the current practice. In practice, admittance to free health care is very difficult; this state of affairs can, among others things, be explained with reference to the fact that the physicians working for the national health service also maintain at the same time a private practice, which provides them with a much more attractive income.

4.6. Family

Family allowance (*abono de familia*) is granted subject to the following conditions:
- the child may not carry out any paid activity;
- from the age of compulsory school, the child must be enrolled in a school of the following level:
  - until the age of 18 year basic or equivalent education;
  - between the age of 18 and 22, in secondary or equivalent education;
- for the age of 23 until the age of 25, in university or equivalent education. However there is no age limit with respect to handicapped people who are entitled neither to lifetime monthly benefit nor to a social pension;
-the child must, in principle, reside in Portugal.
Family allowance consists of a monthly flat-rate amount per month for each descendent or people treated as such; from the third descendant an increased amount is applicable, subject to the condition that the monthly income of the family lies below 150% of the highest legal minimum wage.

On it's birth the child of an insured employee gives rise to entitlement to a lump sum birth benefit.

There is a monthly nursing benefit (*subsidio de aleitção*) for all the beneficiaries of family allowance during the first ten months of the child's life.

A marriage benefit (*subsidio de casamento*) is payable as a lump sum to each of the spouses.

An adoption benefit (*subsidio por adopção*) is payable to the insured worker who has adopted a child younger than three years old. The requirements with respect to the employment and contribution record are the same as those for sickness benefits. Adoption benefit is payable for 60 days, in order to support the arrival of the adopted child within the family. The amount of the adoption benefit equals that of the average income from work which serves as a basis for the calculation of sickness benefit.

Workers who carry out activities on account of another person, who stay away from their work in order to give necessary assistance to their children

who are under 10 years of age, who are ill or were the victim of an accident, may be eligible for a benefit for assistance to minor children, provided that:
- they fulfil the entitlement conditions for sickness benefit, except for the requirement regarding incapacity for work;
- the child is part of a single parent family;
- the family of the beneficiary does not have an income in excess of double the relevant minimum wage; and
- the entitled person does not enjoy a continuation of his wages.

The level of benefit may not exceed the level of sickness benefit which the beneficiary would have received should he become ill himself. The benefit for assistance to underaged children is payable for a maximum period of 30 days per year, except in case of the child entering hospital, when it is paid for the whole period of hospitalization.

The dependent spouse addition is payable to the beneficiary of an old age or an invalidity pension under the contributory scheme, who has a dependent spouse with an income which falls below the amount of the allowance. Any possible income of the spouse is deducted from the allowance.

5. Financing.

The contributory schemes of social security are almost entirely financed by their own resources. The government does not participate in the financing.

In the general scheme a flat-rate contribution for social security is levied upon wages; approximately one third of these contributions are borne by the employees, approximately two thirds by the employers. The flat-rate contribution as well as it's division between employees and employers is determined by the parliamentary discussion concerning the social security budget.
Employers of handicapped people (people with a capacity for work of at least 20% below the normal capacity of an employee carrying out the same activities) only pay half the employer's contribution in respect of the handicapped employees.

A special wage contribution is levied upon the employers in respect of the occupational diseases insurance scheme.

Under the special contributory schemes there are special contributions rates; however, these are never in excess of those of the general scheme and are often remarkably lower.

The *C.R.S.S.* collect the contributions for social security and deposits these with the Institution for the Financial Administration of Social Security. This institution provides the *C.R.S.S.* with the financial means necessary for the payment of the benefits.

In Portugal the collection of social contributions is an enormous problem. Despite special legislative measures to make possible a flexible collection of the debts which many enterprises have with respect to social security, the application of these legislative measures remains extremely difficult in a context of economic crisis. Many enterprises which are in debt to social security do not have enough financial means to make it possible for them to propose a plausible plan for the repayment of their social security debts. Recently, measures were taken in order to strengthen sanctions in respect of enterprises which are not prepared to present a plan for the regular repayments of their debts; thus, among other things, these enterprises will be excluded from every public contract, neither will they be able to register their stocks and shares with the exchange, nor can they pay any dividends. Furthermore, penal sanctions are provided.

The non-contributory social security scheme is totally financed by the State.

In respect of the work injury insurance scheme, the employers pay insurance contributions which vary depending on the risk. The financial system of the work injuries insurance scheme is mixed (both pay as you go and capitalization).

Social action is financed by State subsidies, as well as the yield from sanctions due to social fraud within the contributory scheme, and by the payable, but not yet paid social security benefits which are superannuated.

6. Judicial reiew.

People who have an interest in the granting of social security benefits (in the broad sense) and are of the opinion that their rights have been violated, can lodge a complaint or a petition with the administrative body which is empowered to grant these benefits. This is related to the constitutionally guaranteed right of petition, which enables people who have allegedly sustained damage as a result of maladministration to refer their case to the hierarchical higher, or supervisory bodies of the competent administrative institutions, as well as to the President of the Republic. Such people can also refer their case to the *provedor de justiça*. This ombudsman takes on complaints regarding improper acts or omissions of public authorities. He has no adjudication powers, but can direct necessary recommendations to the competent authorities, in order to induce them to prevent or repair the established injustices.

The act also provides a right of appeal to the administrative courts to people who are refused affiliation to the social security scheme or benefit. In practice claimants hardly ever make use of their right to judicial review in respect of social security.

Chapter 12: Spain

1. Introduction: concept and sources of social security law.

Chapter III, title I of the Constitution of the democratic kingdom of Spain, 27 December 1978, ("concerning fundamental rights and duties") is devoted to the "guiding principles of social and economic policy". In contrast to the provisions in the previous chapter, concerning classic rights and freedoms, the rights contained within chapter III cannot be directly invoked by the citizen in legal proceedings. The recognition, respect and protection of these guiding principles should be manifest within legislation, jurisprudence and the administration. They can only be invoked in court in so far as they are implemented in statutory provisions (cfr. article 53, section 3 Constitution).
Article 39 Constitution concerns the social, economic and legal protection of the family. Article 41 Constitution is explicitly devoted to social security, it states: "The government shall maintain a public system of social security for all citizens, which guarantees sufficient social benefits and assistance in case of need, especially in case of unemployment. The additional benefits and assistance are free". Article 43 Constitution recognizes the right to health care and attributes the organisation of this to the government. Article 49 Constitution is devoted to social services for the handicapped. Finally in article 50 Constitution it is provided that "the government (...) guarantees sufficient economic means to elderly citizens, by means of adequate and periodically adjusted pensions. Equally, the government promotes the welfare of the elderly, independent of their family duties, by means of a system of social services, which takes care of their special health, living, leisure and cultural problems".

It is rather difficult to delimitate the Spanish concept of "social security" (*seguridad social*) in terms of positive law. This difficulty springs, among others, from the pretention of the State to re-integrate a number of functions which were formerly part of social security, yet which, according to the State, still do not belong to this area, such as tasks concerning employment policy, education and social services, which belong more within the concept of public services than within the limited framework of social security benefits. This pretention of the State is seen by some constitutional lawyers as confirmed by the separate adoption in the constitution on the one hand of an article concerning social security (article 41 Constitution), and on the other hand articles concerning the family, health care, services for the handicapped and pensions.
So, strictly speaking, do the benefits in respect of unemployment, social services and health care belong to social security? From the above it would appear not. But, on the other hand, unemployment is the only social risk that is explicitly mentioned in the constitutional provision concerning social security, (article 41 Constitution) and the competence in the area of social services is distributed over the State, the autonomous communities and local

government. It can also be pointed out that the conditions and financing of the health care system are barely integrated. In the light of article 41 Constitution there is also some doubt as to whether the free occupational benefit schemes should be excluded from the concept of social security.

In the light of the rather dogmatic debate between experts in constitutional and social security law about the exact scope of the Spanish concept of social security, we will adopt a pragmatic approach, taking as a starting point the General act on social security (Decree 2065/74 containing the modified text). Article 2 of the General act defines the goals of social security; it guarantees an adequate protection in the events enumerated within the act, as well as a progressive improvement of the standard of living on a medical, economic, and cultural level to those who, due to their professional activities, fall under the scope of application of social security, as well as to their dependent family members and those considered as such. According to article 20 of the same act the protection offered by the social security system includes:

a. specialist care in respect of maternity, sickness or occupational disease, a normal injury or an industrial injury;
b. the return to working life after these events have occured;
c. benefits in respect of temporary incapacity for work, invalidity, retirement, unemployment, death and survival, as well as other special situations, specifically provided for;
d. family benefits in cash; and
e. social services.

To these can be added the social assistance benefits.

Thus all benefit schemes which cover the risks enumerated in the I.L.O. convention no. 102 are included albeit that no separate social insurance schemes exist which cover professionial risks or maternity. Social assistance and social services are also covered by the broad concept of social security. Within social assistance and the social services schemes which differ from the insurance schemes exist (although they largly cover the same risks), because the assistance schemes have been entrusted to institutions outside social security. In contrast to other social security schemes, including medical care, the right to assistance benefits is not fully subjective. The degree in which 'rights" to social assistance or to social services may be enforced, varies. Assistance benefits are also subsidiary to the other social security benefits. They are only granted when a person is not (or not any longer) entitled to social security benefits stricto sensu. In view of the decentralised powers which exist in this area (to be discussed below), social assistance and social services will not be dealt with in this chapter.

In Spain, since 1963, a general scheme exists which operates to some degree as a model (general scheme for employees borne by industry and services), as well as a series of special schemes. The scope of application of the special schemes depends upon the sector of activity (e.g. special schemes for agriculture, for coal mining or for people working at sea) or upon the sort of activity done (e.g. schemes for self-employed people, for civil servants, for domestic personnel, for students). In recent years there has been a certain degree of harmonisation of these schemes (e.g. in the area of financing and the determination of entitlement conditions for an old age pension).

A new range of non contributory level benefits has recently been introduced in Spain. They cover the risks of old age, invalidity, and family. They are available under certain conditions to those people who cannot profit from the contributory level. We will deal with these benefits later on in this chapter.

The three basic statutes which regulate Spanish social security are the General act on social security, substantially modified by the above mentioned Decree 2065/1974 of 31 May 1974, the Real Decreto-Ley 36/1978 of 16 November 1978 concerning the institutional administration of social security, health and employment and the Act 26/1985 of 31 July 1985 containing urgent measures for the rationalisation of the structure and protective effect of social security. Previously, unemployment was regulated in the General act for social security, but now it is made subject to the basic act in respect of employment policy 51/1980 of 8 October 1980, as modified by the act 31/ 1984 of 2 August 1984 concerning protection in case of un-employment. Here we note that, on a statutory level, the basic schemes date from before entry into force of the consitution (29 December 1978).
The present social security system is still based upon the basic act on social security 193/1963 of 28 December 1963. Even the act 26/1985 cannot be considered as an implementation of the constitutional provisions; it should rather be seen as an answer to the malfunctioning of the pre-constitutional system for social protection. Yet, in the preamble of this act, a series of measures is announced which purport to serve as an universal and unitary model for social protection in order to realise the goals of the constitution.

The legislative basis for social security was extended further by means of governmental decrees and ministerial orders; the majority of these do not have a general application, but cover specific parts of social security law, such as the scope of application of social security, contributions or pensions.

The general act on social security determines that the compulsory social protection for which it provides may be supplemented; supplementary schemes are most likely to be found within collective labour agreements. The supplementary (occupational) benefits are mostly intended to adjust income maintenance as much as possible to the lost real earnings.

The specific form of federalism, established in the constitution of 1978, has led to a very complicated division of powers between the central government and the autonomous communities. Schemes can vary according to the autonomous community, and the reality does not always fully coincide with the provisions concerning the division of powers as adopted within the constitution.

On the ground of article 149 Constitution, the Spanish State enjoys exclusive authority in respect of the economic regime of social security, as well as the basic legislation on social security, without this detracting from the possibility of entrusting the administration of social security to the autonomous communities (article 149(1)(17) Constitution). Basic legislation includes all legislation that is not concerned purely with administrative organisation. The economic regime of social security includes provisions concerning the resources of the social security system and the territorial and functional division of the means. Article 148 Constitution determines that the autonomous communities can be given powers in respect of social assistance, health and hygiene (article 148 (1)(20,21) Constitution). In line with this the regulations of the autonomous communities contain provisions concerning social security competences with regard to the statutory implementation of the basic legislation of the State, except for norms which concern the economic regime of social security, as well as to administration of the economic regime. For this purpose the autonomous communities are able to set up and administer all services which are considered necessary within their territory; they will also exercise the control on these institutions without neglecting the high supervision of the State.

The autonomous communities link the exercise of their powers in the field of social security and health to rules concerning the democratic participation of all people involved, as well as of the organisation of employers and employees. It thus appears that the extensive, albeit still embryonic, legislation of the autonomous communities gives further contents to the social security system. Nevertheless, below this legislation will not be dealt with.

2. Administrative organisation.

With regard to the institutional administration of social security, health and employment policy, there are the following specialized administrative bodies:
- the National Social Security Institute (*Instituto Nacional de la Seguridad Social, I.N.S.S.*), responsible for the administration of all social security schemes which provide benefits in cash, excluding the schemes for the unemployed and mariners;
- the National Health Institute (*Instituto Nacional de la Salud - INSALUD*), encharged with the administration of health care;
- the National Institute for Social Services (*Instituto Nacional de Servicios Sociales, INSERSO*), encharged with the administration of social services, in kind as well as in cash, in respect of the less able bodied, invalids and the elderly;
- the National Institute for Employment Policy (*Instituto Nacional de Empleo, INEM*), in which both the administration of the scheme for unemployment and the labour exchanges and employment policy are concentrated;
- the Social Institute for Mariners (*Instituto Social de la Marina - I.S.M.*), which is encharged with the benefit schemes for mariners; and
- the (General) Treasury of Social Security (*Tesoreria General de la Seguridad Social - T.G.S.S.*), encharged with the administration of the resources of social security, the collection of contributions and the payment of benefits, except unemployment benefit.

All these administrative bodies have a legal person status. They are functionally decentralised bodies of the central government and fall under the authority of the competent minister; this, depending upon the case, is the Minister of Labour and Social Security, the Minister of Health or the Minister of Social Affairs. The competent minister is head of the administrative bodies and carries out supervision.

As mentioned before, the constitution gives the autonomous communities certain administrative tasks in respect of social security. Some of these tasks, especially in the field of health care and social services, are already at this stage carried out by the autonomous communities. It is expected that in time all the autonomous communities will succeed in taking over the entire administration of social security (as is provided in the constitution), whereas the central government retains competence in the field of legislation and the fundamental principles of social security policy. Although in principle the administration of social security is attributed to the autonomous communities, the administration of the resources of social security remain with the general treasury of social security.

The administrative organisation of the insurance scheme for industrial injuries has some special features. Enterprises are free to insure industrial injuries either with the public social security institutions or with the industrial injury insurance mutual aid associations of the employers (*Mutuas de Accidentes de Trabajo y Enfermedades Profesionales*). The latter are non-profitmaking private institutions exclusively encharged to insure industrial injuries. However, the resources of these institutions constitute a part of the social security resources and not of the employer's industrial injuries scheme themselves.

Article 129 Constitution gives the claimants the right to participation within the administration of social security; this right is to be further implemented by the statute. The constitution does not state how intensive the participation should be, nor does it state which representatives will carry out the right to participation.
The participation of the claimant is chanelled via the employee and employer organisations as well as via the public administration itself. These three levels participate and are present on the general board of the *I.N.S.S.*, of the *INSALUD*, of the *INSERSO*, of the *INEM* and of the *I.S.M.* . The general boards consist of thirteen representatives from the administration, thirteen representatives from the most representative employers' organisations and thirteen representatives from the most representative employees' organisations.
The following competences are attributed to these participation bodies:
- participation in and control over the administration of the afore mentioned social security institutions;
- developement of internal regulations of these institutions;
- developement of a concept proposal for the budget of these institutions;
- approval of the annual report of these institutions.

However, the activities of the participation bodies get little response from the claimants. Indeed the great majority of employees are not aware of their existence; this is partly due to the fact that the unions send representatives to the boards without any intermediation from the employees. Moreover, none of the previously mentioned competences of the participation bodies have a real impact upon the social security institutions concerned; the competences do not consist of participation within the administration, but merely of the control thereof.

For the sake of completeness we repeat that some of the regulations of the autonomous communities also establish a right to participation for the claimant in the administration of social security.

3. Personal scope of application.

Since 1985 social security consists of a general scheme and special schemes, the latter being mainly for the self-employed, for the agricultural sector, for mariners, for mineworkers, for domestic servants and for students. The general scheme covers all dependent employees who are active on account of industry and services, except those who, in view of the enterprise for which they work, belong to a special scheme. The special schemes for the agricultural sector and for mariners cover both workers who are active on their own account and workers who are active on account of others.

People carrying out an occupational activity (employees or self-employed persons) are compulsory affiliated to a social security scheme. Yet there are still employees who do not belong to a social security scheme; for example, this is the case for a number of free professional groups, such as lawyers and self-employed doctors. These groups have their own independent schemes for social protection which operate within the margins of the public scheme. Some of the free professional groups have been previously integrated within the public system of social protection (for the self-employed). This took place as a result of a request from the professional board of the occupational group in question; once incorporated, affiliation to the legislative scheme (of the self-employed) becomes compulsory to all members of the profession. Among others, architects and pharmacists were incorporated in this way.

The Social Security non contributory level covers those people in need who have never contributed or who have not contributed enough time as to be entitled to benefits under the contributory level.

Civil servants and military personnel have their own special system, the benefits and financing of which are different from those for workers who are active on their own account or on account of others.

The separate social protection schemes for certain free occupational groups, as well as those for civil servants will not be considered further.

Finally, it should be mentioned that not only the employees who are active on the account of others, the diocesan clergy, pensioners and other people entitled to a periodic benefit from the general system, qualify for health care under the general scheme, but also people who enjoy unemployment benefit on assistance level, provided they are registered with the labour exchange and have an income below the minimum wage. Since 1989 the law also extended the right to health care to all Spaniards residing in Spain without sufficient financial means. Spaniards who have emigrated yet who have temporarily returned to Spain, also qualify for health care under the general scheme. The following people are also insured for health care provided they live together with, or are dependent upon a person insured under the general scheme: the spouse, descendants, underaged brothers and sisters, ascendants and their spouses and foster children. The joint insurance of the ex-spouse and the descendants is not terminated as a result of a divorce.

4. Risks and benefits.

4.1. Old age.

Entitlement to an old age pension (*pensión de jubilación*) under the general scheme of social security is subject to the condition that the claimant has paid contributions for a minimum period of 15 years, two years of which must have been during the eight years immediately preceding the termination of employment (or the claim for pension). Furthermore, he must be 65 years of age or older.
However, there are exceptions concerning both requirements. Thus, some transitionary schemes merely require a contribution record of 10 years, or a pensionable age of 60 years, and old age pensions are granted before the age of 65 to persons who have performed heavy or dangerous work, such as underground mining.

The amount of the old age pension is determined by two factors, i.e. the basis of calculation and the pension rate.
The basis of calculation is related to the income for work of the insured person during his active career, in respect of which he has paid contributions. The basis of calculation is equal to the quotient determined by a common denominator of 112 and the contribution bases during the 96 months immediately preceding the materialization of the insured risk. However, only the real contribution basis of the last 24 of these 96 months is actually taken into account; the above contribution bases are first actualized. This means that they are increased in accordance with the evolution of the index of consumption prices (between the contribution year and the two years preceding the entitlement to a pension). If, during some of these 96 months, the claimant has not paid any contributions, account is taken of the minimum contribution basis for adult employees, applicable for the corresponding period (possibly actualized).

The pension rate is related to the number of contribution years of a person. The statute contains a scale of contribution rates; this scale starts with a minimum period of contributions and recognizes an increase of 2% for each extra contribution year. Thus a maximum of 100% is attained upon a contribution record of 35 years. The maximum of 100% also applies to people over 65 years of age who continue to work and thus obtain an extra 2% per year. The final amount of the pension may in no case exceed the statutory upper limit, nor may it fall below the minimum pension. The minimum pension varies according to whether or not one has a dependent spouse; the amount is lower for those below 65 years of age.

.The statute provides the opportunity for people who paid contributions before 1 January 1967 to retire at the age of 60. For each year of early retirement the early retirement pension (*pensión de jubilación anlicipada*) is reduced by 8%. Employers have used this formula to discard their surplus employees or to reduce the age of their work force; they offer their employees a benefit from 60 years of age upon early retirement, which compensates for the loss of 8% per year of early retirement.

In principle, old age pension is incompatible with any employment of the pensioner, although activities which are not within the scope of any social security scheme are permitted. If the pensioner nevertheless wishes to carry out some other work, he must give notice of this to the social security institution and request a suspension of his pension.

Nearly all collective labour agreements provide supplements to the old age pension. Firstly, these provide for early retirement benefit, as described above. Furthermore, there are supplementary benefits which aim to bring the income of the retired person as far as possible in line with his income during his active life. As a rule the amount of the supplementary benefit is dependent upon the seniority of the claimant within the enterprise and upon his previous income.
There exist three further types of early retirement.

Early retirement pension from the age of 64 is possible while maintaining 100% of pension rights, if the provisions for this purpose are adopted within the collective or individual labour agreements. The claimant must fulfil all the conditions of the usual old age pension, except for the age requirement. Also, the job which is made available must be taken immediately by a younger employee or by a person enjoying unemployment benefit at the assistance level.
Benefits from the sectorial industrial reconversion are payable to people who are at least 55 years of age and when the enterprise has requested and obtained a statement from the government declaring a crisis situation. Between the age of 55 and 60 the claimant receives 80% of his average income during the six months preceding the crisis declaration. Between the age of 60 and 65 he receives 75% of his average wages during the 60 months preceding his early retirement. In some enterprises part-time retirement is possible from the age of 62. The level of the pension is calculated in the same way as for the normal old age pension. The old age pension is reduced in proportion to the number of hours which the retired person works.

This risk is also covered by the non contributory level. People entitled are those older than 65, who live in Spain, and who don't have enough resources for subsistance even if they have never paid contributions to Social Security or they have not paid enough times as to get a pension at the contributory level. These benefits are flat rate and they are not compatible with those of the Social Assistance Scheme.

4.2. Death.

In 1983 the Constitutional Court declared that the existing inequality for men and women with respect to the entitlement condition of survivor's pensions was incompatible with the constitution. Since this judgement the same conditions for the survivor's pensions apply for both widows and widowers. As a matter of convenience, we will only refer to widower's pensions' as indicating equally a widow's pension and a widower's pension.

Upon their death, employees who are affiliated to the social security system (or who are treated as such), give rise to entitlement to a survivor's pension or to other survivor's benefits. It is further required that the deceased must have paid contributions for at least 500 days during the five years preceding his death. The latter requirement does not apply if death was due to an accident, to a terrrorist action or if the deceased was retired. The surviving spouse must have normally lived with the deceased employee, albeit that widower's pension is also granted in case of divorce or separation, i.e. in ratio to the period of cohabitation.
The widower's pension (*pensión de viudedad*) amounts to 45% of the basis of calculation. The basis of calculation is determined in a similar way to the basis of calculation for old age pension. If the deceased already enjoyed a retirement or invalidity pension, the basis of calculation of such a pension is simply taken over, albeit after a revaluation. A minimum widower's pension, which varies, is payable depending on whether the survivor is younger or older than 60 years.
Entitlement to widower's pension terminates upon remarriage. If the remarriage takes place before he reaches 60 years of age, the widower receives a lump sum equal to 24 months of widower's pension.
Widower's pension is compatible with all the widower's income from work, just as with retirement or invalidity pension to which he would have been entitled.

Orphan's pension (*pensión de orfandad*) is payable to all children of the insured deceased person, who are under 18 years of age or who are handicapped. Where adopted children or children of the deceased spouse are concerned, there must be at least two years between the adoption or marriage on the one hand and the death on the other hand. In respect of the deceased the same conditions apply as the entitlement conditions for widower's pension. The level of the orphan's pension is also calculated in the same way as that of the widower's pension, albeit not at a rate of 40%, but at a rate of 20% of the basis of calculation. If there is no surviving spouse who is entitled to widower's pension, the orphan's pension is increased by an amount equal to the (fictitious) widower's pension, which is divided between the number of orphans who are eligible for benefit. The total amount of widower's pension and orphan's pension must in no case exceed the basis of calculation. Orphan's pension is compatible with income from work; a minimum orphan's pension is provided.

If death was due to an industrial injury or occupational disease, no contribution conditions apply for entitlement to benefit. Widower's pension and orphan's pension are payable at the same level as when death was due to another cause. However, in addition the widower is entitled to six times the amount of the monthly basis of calculation; for each orphan this additional payment amounts to one time this amount.

Also included within the concept of survivor's pensions are a number of pensions which are payable to family members of the deceased other than his spouse and children, notably his grand children, brothers or sisters, grand parents, as well as the children and brothers or sisters of the survivor entitled to pension, provided that they are older than 45 years of age. In order to be eligible for such a pension the survivors must have lived with and been dependent upon the deceased person. Furthermore, they must be without sufficient means for subsistence after the death of the insured person.

Survivor's pensions are often supplemented by collective labour agreements in which, just as with invalidity and old age pensions, certain supplementary benefits are provided. Frequently the collective labour agreements provide an obligation for the enterprise to conclude life insurance in favour of the family members of the employees who could become victims of an industrial injury.

Under some schemes which are part of the general scheme (such as survivor's pensions and invalidity pensions) a death benefit is payable. This benefit is flat-rate.

4.3. Incapacity for work.

Social protection in respect of incapacity for work consists of three parts:
- Insurance for temporary incapacity for work.
- Insurance for provisional invalidity.
- Insurance for permanent invalidity.
The risks covered by the insurance for temporary incapacity for work (incapacidad laboral transitoria) are:
- Common or professional disease.
- Industrial or non industrial injuries (i.e. accident both if it occurres at work or not).
- Periods of observation of professional diseases when interruption of work is necessary).
- Maternity, paternity and adoption.

The requirements for entitlement and the amount and duration of the benefit will depend upon the risk which is covered.

In case of common disease, the insured person must have paid contributions for at least 180 days in the five years immediately preceding the interruption of work. In case of maternity it's required that the claimant has been affiliated to the Social Security System during the nine months preceding the birth. Furthermore she must have paid contributions during at least 180 days in the year immediately preceding the termination of work as a result of pregnancy. In case of maternity apart from cash benefits, specialist care is provided to the woman concerned in the same way as to other people who are entitled to specialist care. Entitlement to benefits in case of professional disease or accident don't require period of contribution.

The amount of the benefits varies according to the basis of calculation and the cause of the incapacity. The basis of calculation is determined by the average income of the claimant during the period of reference preceding the incapacity for work. In case of common disease and no industrial injury, the benefit amounts to 60% of the basis of calculation, from the fourth to the twentieth day, thereafter at a rate of 75%. Duration of entitlement is also twelve months with the possibility of being extended to eighteen. Maternity benefits amount 75% of the basis of calculation for the entire duration of the benefit which is subjet to a maximum of sixteen weeks (eighteen in case of multiple birth).

Provisional invalidity (invalidez provisional) exists when at the end of the maximum duration period of temporary incapacity for work, the insured person needs further care and cannot return to his work, yet the invalidity is not excepted to be permanent. The benefit for provisional invalidity starts when the temporary incapacity for work ends and continues until work is resumed in view of recovery, the recognition of permanent invalidity, or entitlement to old age pension. In any case, the benefit ends after six years of incapacity for work. The amount of the benefit is 75% of the basis of calculation which is the same as for the temporary incapacity for work.

Benefits in respect of provisional invalidity are sometimes supplemented through collective agreements up to a certain percentage of the lost income. It is not unusual for this percentage to be 100%.

In order to be entitled to a pension in respect of permanent invalidity (pension de invalidez permanente), the insured person must have paid contributions during a specified period, except where the invalidity was due to an accident (both industrial or not) or a terrorist action in which case there are no contribution requirement.

If at the moment that invalidity occurs the claimant is registered with the social security system, the required minimum duration of contribution payments amounts to one fourth of the time between a person's twentieth birthday and the start of the invalidity, subject to a minimum contribution record of five years. Furthermore, it is required that at least one fifth of the minimum period of payment of contributions falls within the last ten years. If the claimant is not registered with social security at the moment that the injury occurs, the minimum contribution record amounts to 15 years. There are reduced contribution requirements for employees younger than twenty six years of age; for them the minimum period of contributions merely covers half of the time between their sixteenth birthday and the start of the invalidity.

Entitlement to permanent invalidity pension is further subject to the condition that the claimant has sustained a severe anatomical or functional health damage, which can be objectively determined and which is assumed to be definite. This health damage must notably diminish the capacity for work of the claimant, or bring it down to nothing. The statute recognizes various degrees of incapacity, each with corresponding benefits:

- with partial incapacity in respect of the usual occupation, there is a presumed reduction of the capacity for work of at least one third; this degree of incapacity does not give rise to entitlement to pension, but to a compensation of an amount equal to 24 months of the basis of calculation;

- total incapacity in respect of the usual occupation supposes that it is impossible for the employee to carry out all or the most important tasks within his usual occupation, without excluding the possibility that he could carry out another occupation. The corresponding monthly pension is equal to 55% of the basis of calculation. This percentage amounts to 75 if the insured parent is older than 55 and does not work. In view of the relatively low level of this pension and the employer's opportunity to dismiss a beneficiary of such a pension, the potential beneficiaries often choose not to claim any benefit and fully exploit their capacity for work in order to claim one of the subsequent benefits in a later stage.

- absolute and permanent incapacity for work, which supposes full incapacity to carry out any occupation or service. The corresponding benefit amounts to 100% of the basis of calculation; and

- severe invalidity. Severe invalidity is aknowledged in respect of those who should not only be recognized as being absolutely and permanently incapable of work, but, also need the help of another person in order to perform the most essential tasks of daily life, such as dressing, moving around and eating. The pension for severe invalidity amounts to 150% of the basis of calculation.

The basis of calculation for the invalidity pensions is calculated in the same way as that for the old age pension. Special rules exist in cases where the required contribution record amounts to less than 96 months.

If the permanent invalidity is the result of an industrial injury or occupational disease, the level of the benefit is calculated in a different way; the real income of the employee during the year preceding the industrial injury is taken as the basis of calculation. If the consequences of an industrial injury or occupational disease do not result in permanent invalidity, yet do cause permanent damage, such damage is compensated by a benefit, the level of which is determined by the degree of severity of the damage and the part of the body where the damage occurred.

Invalidity benefits are usually supplemented by employer's benefits. Such benefits are provided for in approximately 50% of the collective labour agreements. The supplementary benefits which are borne by the enterprise are usually determined by the recognized degree of incapacity for work and by the seniority of the employee within the enterprise. In case of absolute invalidity, the supplement usually pays up to 100% of the previously earned income; in case of total incapacity for the usual occupation, up to 75% of the previously earned income. Today the supplements often do not only consist of a monthly benefit, but also of a capital sum, the amount of which is determined by the previously earned income and the seniority within the enterprise.

Benefits in case of invalidity are also payable under the non contributory level. People entitled to these benefits are those older than 18 and younger than 65 who at present have legal residence in Spain and who have lived in this country for at least five years. The degree of incapacity has to be at least 65% and their income has to be below a certain (indexed) minimum. The amount of the benefit is flat rate.

4.4. Unemployment.

In respect of unemployment a distinction must be made between two levels of protection, a contributory level and an assistance level. The cash benefits on a contributory level are called *prestación por desempleo*, those on an assistance level *subsidio por desempleo*. On the contributory level the totally or partially unemployed person is granted an income maintenance benefit, related to the lost previously earned wages. The assistance scheme provides benefits which are complementary to those of the contributory scheme, in the sense that the duration of the benefit is extended rather than that the amount is supplemented; thus, the level of extended benefit is not related to the previous wages of the unemployed person.

Unemployment benefits are payable to people who are capable and willing to carry out employment but have lost their job or whose duration of employment has been reduced with at least one third.
In order to be entitled to contributory benefit the unemployed person must have paid contributions over a period of twelve months during at least the last six years prior to the unemployment.
Furthermore, he may not have reached his normal pensionable age (as a rule 65 years of age).

Entitlement to unemployment benefit can also exist after 65 years of age if the claimant has not paid sufficient contributions to be entitled to the full old age pension.

The duration of the "prestacion por desmpleo' is dependent upon the contribution record of the employee (within six years preceding the unemployment). Thus, for example, the person who has paid twelve months contributions during the six years preceding the unemployment is entitled to benefit for four months; the person who has paid contributions over a period of 36 months is entitled to benefit for twelve months; and the person who has paid contributions during the complete six years period (72 months) preceding unemployment has the right to a (maximum) benefit of 24 months. During the first six months of unemployment, unemployment benefit amounts to 70% of the average basis of contribution during the six months preceding unemployment. From the seventh month till the ceasement of payment the amount of the benefit is 60% of the basis of calculation. The amount of unemployment benefit may neither fall below the interprofessional minimum wage nor exceed 170% of this amount, except if the employee has dependent children in which case the maximum amount of unemployment benefit comes to 195% (with one dependent child) or 220% (with two or more dependent children).

Unemployment benefit on assistance level (subsidio por desmpleo) is payable to employees who have exhausted their unemployment benefit under the contributory system and have responsibility for a family; to employees older than 45 who have exhausted their unemployment benefit of at least twelve months and don't have responsibility for a family; workers who when cesation of employment occurres have not covered the minimum contributory period necessary for the contributory benefit; and workers considered as fully capable or partially invalid after a situation of severe invalidity, or total or absolute permanent invalidity in respect of the usual occupation; under certain conditions, returned immigrants and exprisoners may also receive these benefits. Unemployment benefit on assistance level is payable for a maximum period of six months. However, this term may be renewed twice, thus to a total of eighteen months. The "subsidio por desempleo" amounts to 75% of the inter-professional minimum income. Depending upon certain conditions, workers over 52 years of age who are unemployed and workers over 45 who have exausted the unemployment benefit at contributory level may also benefit. In both cases their income must not be higher than the interprofessional minimum income. For the former, the benefit will last until they have reached pensionable age; for the latter it will end after six months.

4.5. Medical care.

Benefits in respect of health care within the general system of social security are payable from the first to the last day of sickness.
Specialist care is provided free of charge by the doctors who, after a comparative examination, are appointed by the *I.N.S.S.* to the vacant places. The general practitioners and specialists who do not work in hospitals, obtain a fixed amount for each insured person registered with them. In general, hospital physicians are compensated as employees. People are free to choose their general practitioner, paediatrician and gynecologist provided that in the area of their residence there is more than one doctor.

Also medical care provided by the hospitals of the *I.N. S.S.*, as well as in the other public and private hospitals which have a contract with the *I.N.S.S.*, is free of charge. However, for non-surgical hospitalisation medical care is only provided free of charge, if the administrative authorities determine that hospitalisation is required in order to make a diagnosis, if a person has a contagious disease, or if the general state and behaviour of the patient require continuous care.

The insured people pay 40% of the price of medicine; however, medicine is free of charge for pensioners, provisory invalids and those who have been admitted into hospital.

The granting and renewal of prothesis, orthopedic aids and wheel chairs for the handicapped are also free of charge. Dental prothesis, as well as optical, auditive and other special prothesis may be granted in the form of assistance. On ground of the assistance schemes certain categories of persons (e.g. pensioners, invalids and the mentally handicapped) may also receive home care.

4.6. Family.

The children of people insured under the general scheme give rise to entitlement to family benefits (*prestaciónes familiares*), until they have reached the age of 18, except when the child is severely handicapped, in which case the duration of benefit is unlimited. Family benefit consists of a monthly, fixed amount per child, to be increased by a fixed amount per child, if the beneficiary is unemployed or retired with a pension, the level of which is below the minimum old age pension for the 65 years old. Family benefits are also increased in favour of families with more than two children (15% per each newborn child).

There is a special family allowance for handicapped children. Furthermore, there are a number of benefits for the needs of the less abled bodied. Finally, there is a special education allowance for families with more than three children, one of which is partly invalid.

There are also family benefits in the non contributory level. People entitled to these benefits are those having children younger than eighteen or handicapped in a degree superior to 65%. Orphans and abandonned children are also entitled. As requirement, parents must not be entitled to other family benefits, neither under any other public scheme nor under the contributory level of this benefit. Besides, their income cannot be superior to a fixed amount. The amount of the benefit is flat-rate although it varies depending upon the age or the degree of handicap of the child. The same amounts apply for family benefits at contributory level.

5. Financing.

Income maintenance benefits, the level of which are related to the previously earned income from employment, are financed mainly by contributions from the insured people and the enterprises. Recently, these sources of finance have been supplemented by increasingly important state subsidies.

Within the general scheme, the contributions are levied upon the wages of the insured people. One sixth of these contributions are paid by the employees and five sixths by the employers.

The contribution liability is subject to both upper and lower wage limits; below and above the limits contributions are levied upon the respective minimum and maximum wage. Special rules apply for part-time workers. Here the lower and the upper limit vary according to the professional category in which a person may be classified. The lower and the upper wage limits are annually adjusted to the development of the interprofessional minimum wage and to the increases of the wages in general.

The special scheme for miners, seamen and the self-employed apply the same contribution rate as is applicable for the general scheme; in respect of activities on account of others the ratio of distribution of contributions between employers and employees is equally the same. Here too there are lower and upper income limits, except for the self-employed, in respect of whom there is only a lower income limit; if they wish to do so, they are free to pay contributions over a much higher occupational income. For domestic personnel, as well as for the special scheme for agriculture, there are derogating rates and ratios of distribution.

Within the general scheme there is a special contribution for the unemployment insurance scheme on a contributory level. This contribution is levied mainly upon the employers. Furthermore, there is a separate contribution for the wage guarantee fund exclusively borne by the employers and a special contribution for occupational training mainly borne by the employers and only to some extent by the employees.

The enterprises also pay contributions for industrial injuries and occupational diseases; the level of this contribution depends upon the degree of danger of the activities within the enterprise. The contribution is calculated on the basis of the real wages of the employees.

There is a large number of rules which provide a decreased contribution liability in order to promote employment.

As mentioned before, the state subsidies also constitute an important source of social security financing. Within the last ten years the state subsidies have increased considerably.

The state bears all the costs of unemployment assistance.

The supplementary benefit schemes, as set up by collective labour agreements, are mostly financed by the employers; as a matter of exception, sometimes the employees also contribute to the financing. However, the latter is not very common and is usually only the case when the supplementary benefits constitute a collective or personal insurance (collective life insurance, hospital insurance, etc.) in respect of which the employee is free to join in or to opt out.

236

6. Judicial review.

The constitution provides a framework for judicial review which protects the citizen's rights, including matters of social security. Article 24 Constitution provides that the law shall assist all people in obtaining protection of their rights and lawfull interests from the judges and the courts. Art. 29 Constitution recognizes the right of individual petition for each Spaniard. Furthermore, the constitution provides for the existence of a "protector of the people" (*Defensor del Pueblo*), who is a sort of ombudsman to whom all people may resort with complaints and suggestions concerning the operation of the public administration.

The purest form of judicial review is the one which results in decisions of the administration being challenged before the courts, i.e. the so-called social courts (*Juzgados de lo Social, Sala de lo Social de los Tribunales Superiores de Justicia de las Comunidades Autonomas and the Sala de lo Social del Tribunal Supremo*). Every *Social Juzgado* (one or more for every province) is composed of a single judge. The Social Chamber of the *Tribunales Superiores de Justicia de las Comunidades Autónomas* (17 courts) and the Social Chamber of the *Tribunal Supremo* are composed of several judges each, according to the legal provisions.

Before a person can appeal to a court, he must first lodge a complaint with the social security institution which has made the contested decision. The contestant can do so within 30 days from the time that the decision has been received. Then the social security institution has 45 days in which it must take a decision on the complaint. If no decision is made, it is assumed that the original contested decision has been confirmed (negative administrative reticence). After this 45-days term, or after the moment that the social security institution has responded to the complaint, the contestant has 30 days to start a procedure before the courts.

The case is dealt with by the *Social Juzgado*. The decision of this court is subject to appeal with the competent *Tribunal Superior de Justicia (recurso de suplicación)*. The judgements of the *Tribunales Superiores de Justicia* are subject to a limited appeal in cassation.

If the contestant considers the statutory provision on which the litigious decision was based to be incompatible with the constitution, he may also appeal to the *Tribunal Constituciónal*.